The Internationalization of the Firm

Second Edition

The Internationalization of the Firm

Second Edition

Edited by

Peter J Buckley and Pervez N Ghauri

INTERNATIONAL THOMSON BUSINESS PRESS

I(T)P® An International Thomson Publishing Company

London • Bonn • Johannesburg • Madrid • Melbourne • Mexico City • New York • Paris
Singapore • Tokyo • Toronto • Albany, NY • Belmont, CA • Cincinnati, OH • Detroit, MI

The Internationalization of the Firm

Copyright © 1999 Peter J Buckley and Pervez N Ghauri

First published by International Thomson Business Press

I⟨T⟩P ® A division of International Thomson Publishing Inc.
The ITP logo is a trademark under licence

British Library Cataloguing-in-Publication Data
A catalogue record for this book is available from the British Library

First edition 1993
Second edition 1999

Typeset by LaserScript Limited, Mitcham, Surrey
Printed in the UK by Clays Ltd, Bungay, Suffolk

ISBN 1–86152–401–3

International Thomson Business Press
Berkshire House
168–173 High Holborn
London WC1V 7AA
UK

http://www.itbp.com

Contents

Introduction and Overview

Peter J. Buckley and Pervez N. Ghauri

The internationalization of the firm has been a key issue in international business research right from the outset. Internationalizing means changing state and thus implies dynamic change. The growth of the firm is the background to internationalization and to some degree the distinction between internationalization and growth is false. The crossing of national boundaries in the process of growth may be argued to be a meaningless threshold (Buckley, 1993). However, there are features which are unique to internationalization, or, at least, there are significant degrees of difference between growth at home and internationalization. This volume seeks to explore these differences.

The rate and direction of internationalization have been the subject of many studies, some of which are represented here. Moreover, this area has not been without controversy. Do firms internationalize by a gradual, incremental process going through a number of definite stages? Is this 'stages of internationalization' model valid for established multinational firms or only for naive, small firms with little international experience? How far can firms use their experience (learning) to miss out stages in this process and move directly to a deep form of involvement in the foreign market? On how many fronts can a firm pursue internationalization? Should it proceed step by step, going first to nearby countries in terms of physical and cultural distance? Do established multinational firms need to obey any such rules? These and other questions were in the minds of the researchers who undertook the studies which follow and their efforts have illuminated our understanding of the forces at work. Naturally, definitive conclusions have not always been reached.

The relationship between internationalization and forms of foreign market servicing is a close one. The conditions under which a firm will choose exporting, licensing or foreign investment interact with internationalization. The management and control of the activities and organization of the multinational firm are also a crucial part of the conceptualization of internationalization. The impact of cultural differences, too, is a critical issue in this process.

This collection then covers: key works (introducing the product cycle, internalization and stages of development models), studies of the internationalization process, methods of foreign market servicing, work on the organization of multinational firms and the impact of culture on internationalization.

1 KEY WORKS

The first part of this collection covers key articles introducing basic concepts which have had a fundamental effect on subsequent research and writing.

The first reading in this volume is an abridgement (by Peter Buckley) of Yair Aharoni's 1966 study of the foreign investment decision process. The foreign investment decision is analysed as a complex social process which is influenced by social relationships both within and outside the firm. Aharoni provides a rich description of individual and organizational behaviour over time and shows the crucial effect of perception and uncertainty in the course of this process. A holistic understanding of all the stages is necessary to comprehend the decision. Although Aharoni analyses the decision as a succession of stages, he is at pains to point out that in real life these stages are ill defined and messy. This piece emphasizes the importance of the initiating force and explains many elements which may wrongly be labelled 'irrational'. Aharoni's work laid a firm foundation for studies of decision processes in multinational firms.

The second chapter is a work which can justly claim the epithet 'seminal', Raymond Vernon's 1966 article 'International investment and international trade in the product cycle'. The argument of this paper is that firms are highly stimulated by their local environment and are more likely to innovate when their immediate surroundings are more conducive to the creation of (particular) new techniques or products. For internationalization to occur these innovations must be transferable to other economies. In adapting to its market, the firm moves through stages from innovation to standardization and maturity according to the developing forces of supply and demand for its product. This model of sequential decision making has had a great influence on internationalization theory. The model was originally developed to explain US investment in Europe and also in cheap labour countries. Its usefulness goes beyond Vernon's reappraisal of its efficacy under changed world conditions (1979) or the sting of its critics (e.g. Giddy, 1978). Its relevance arises from the fact that the dynamic of the model lies in the interaction of the evolving forces of demand (taste) patterns and production possibilities. In some ways, its powerful, yet simple, dynamic resting on the changing equilibria of demand and supply over time, has never been bettered. The twin rationales of cost imperatives and market pull are simply explained in Vernon's model. Its programmatic nature may have straight-jacketed later analyses into a unilinear inter-nationalization path. Although its validity for the explanation of the behaviour modern multinationals may be questioned, this article spawned much of the empirical literature on international marketing.

The third article has been the focus of ideas for many subsequent researchers. Johanson and Wiedersheim-Paul examine the internationalization of four Swedish firms. For this admittedly small sample they find a regular process of gradual incremental change. The firm progresses from no regular exports to export through independent representatives and the establishment of sales subsidiaries to the establishment of production facilities. Flows of information between the firm and the market are (as in Vernon's model) crucial in this process and the cultural distance between spatially separated units of the firm is termed psychic distance. The establishment profiles of the four firms are mapped across a number of countries in time and the gradualist pattern is confirmed. This path-breaking article gave rise to considerable controversy centred on the general applicability of the findings and the underlying theory. Suggestions have been made that experienced firms can 'jump' stages and transfer learning from one market to another without having to go through each stage in each separate foreign market. The knowledge collection and planning processes of large multinationals can, some authors feel, obviate the need for incremental learning. Some empirical findings suggest a less gradualist and one-directional expansion path. The theory has also been questioned in its classification of stage or stages of involvement ranked in order of 'depth'. Is a licensing deal a deeper form of involvement than a foreign agency agreement? Methodologically, looking back in time a successful firm eliminates firms which have failed at an earlier stage, i.e. it induces a bias towards longer routes of establishment (see Hedlund and Kverneland, 1983). More carefully designed experiments are required to establish the conditions under which stages approach is valid. Nevertheless, the article reprinted here is a classic piece of empirical research with wide implications for internationalization.

It was followed, in 1977, by the piece by Johanson and Vahlne, reproduced here as Chapter 4. This chapter examines the internationalization process by investigating the development of knowledge and the building of a commitment within the firm to foreign markets. The twin notions of increasing knowledge about foreign markets as a means of reducing uncertainty and the creation of a commitment to foreign ventures had been examined in a key study by Aharoni (1966) (see Chapter 1) and the authors here tie these notions to the framework of the behavioural theory of the firm. Internationalization is again envisaged as the product of a series of incremental decisions. Decisions taken at a point in time affect subsequent steps in the process. Psychic distance is invoked and is defined as 'the sum of the factors preventing the flow of information from and to the market'. The decision-making process is dependent on the firm's previous experience. Again, the empirical evidence is based on a very small number of companies. Four Swedish companies are examined from Chapter 2, a case study of the Swedish pharmaceutical firm Pharmacia is introduced and other industry studies are quoted (special steel, pulp and paper and nine further cases). Casual empirical evidence from other countries is also adduced (Hornell & Vahlne, 1986). The two notions of market commitment and market knowledge entered the literature as key elements of internationalization.

The dominant paradigm in research on the multinational firm is the internalization approach. Chapter 5 is an early summary of the theoretical work in this tradition by Buckley and Casson whose book the *Future of the Multinational Enterprise* (1976) was a basic contribution. This chapter attempts to explain the division of national markets (and therefore of the world market) between domestic firms and foreign multinationals. It does so by reference to two effects: the location effect and the ownership effect. The location effect determines where value adding activities take place and the ownership effect explains who owns and controls those activities. The concepts of least cost location and growth by internalization of markets are thus introduced to internationalization theory. Firms grow by replacing the (imperfect) external market and earn a return from so doing until the point at which the benefits of further internalization are outweighed by the costs. The types of benefit and cost of growth by internalization are listed and it is suggested that certain types of market are more likely to be internalized than others, given the configuration of the world economy. These ideas were expanded in Buckley and Casson (1985), Casson (1987) and Buckley (1988, 1989, 1990). Thus the direction of internationalization can be predicted by predicting changes in cost and market conditions. These factors are classified as industry specific, region specific, firm specific and nation specific.

John Dunning has produced a massive corpus of work in international business. From them, we have chosen a piece originally written in 1977 (Chapter 6), which presents the key elements of Dunning's 'eclectic paradigm'. This approach uses three sets of explanatory factors to analyse international business issues – locational factors, internalization factors and ownership factors. Essentially, firms transfer their ownership-specific assets to combine with the most favourable sets of traditionally fixed elements in the global economy, and they do this, where appropriate, internally, in order to retain control of the revenue generation. Later versions of the eclectic approach refined this position and extended its taxonomy and it has become familiar to many generations of researchers and students as a set of key organizing principles in international business.

2 THE INTERNATIONALIZATION PROCESS

We have already introduced a pioneering study of the internationalization process in 'antecedents' (Chapter 3). Over the period from the late 1950s there has been growing interest in the internationalization process of firms. This is exemplified by the readings in this volume where we can see the gradual development of research in this area. Starting from Dunning (1958), Vernon (Chapter 2), Servan-Schreiber (1969) and Horst (1972), through Chapters 3 and 4, and Luostarinen (1979) we have seen how the focus has shifted from the decision to export to a more longitudinal approach, namely, the internationalization process. Chapter 7 is a good example of this development. This chapter points out that although widely used, the term internationalization has not been clearly defined. It should, according to the reading, be broadened to include both the inward and outward aspects of the process. As well as the longitudinal character of the research, the study also draws our attention to other aspects such as the impact of individuals and the evolution of communication patterns. It seems that more research is necessary both on the process and the analysis of the decision and that these should be integrated. Chapter 7 by Welch and Luostarinen surveys this literature. It presents a strong defence of the concept of internationalization as a sequential process. It adduces evidence from Luostarinen's study of Finnish firms (1979) and alludes to studies of Japanese companies and those from business history (a source mostly neglected by the chapters in this volume) to support evidence of sequential development. It also suggests *contra* Hedlund and Kverneland (1983) that jumps in the stage pattern in *any one foreign market* may result from learning across the firm, i.e. from other foreign markets. Thus overall foreign knowledge may diffuse through the firm and allow more rapid penetration of foreign markets tackled at a later date. More recently, the internationalization of industrial firms has been explained through networks and relationships between firms. The network model has been largely developed at Uppsala (Hagg and Johanson, 1982; Johanson and Mattsson, 1988; Thorelli, 1986; Ghauri, 1989). According to this approach firms internationalize because other firms in their national network internationalize. The industrial system is composed of firms engaged in production, distribution and use of goods and services. The relationships between the firms are described as a network. The firms within the network are dependent on each other, and their activities therefore need to be coordinated. These networks are either stable or they are changing, but the transactions take place within the framework of these established relationships. In the process, however, some new relationships are developed and some old ones are disrupted because of the competitive activities of different actors.

Thus, although there are competitive relationships, interdependencies are stressed in the network approach. The firms have to develop and maintain relationships with other firms in the network. This process of developing and maintaining relationships is of a cumulative nature and the firms are striving to establish a prominent position in their networks. At each point the firm has a position in the network which explains its relationship to the other firms. Here one basic assumption is that the firm is dependent on external resources controlled by other firms. Therefore, it is dependent on its network in foreign markets while internationalizing. The firm thus has to work for international integration. The network approach also influences the internationalization of the market – for example, a production net can be more or less internationalized. A higher degree of internationalization means that there are strong relationships between different national networks. These relationships developed by the firm are thus considered as market investments. Moreover, the firms which are highly internationalized would prefer to have a number of activities performed externally by sub-contractors and can still have the desired control arising from these relationships.

Chapter 8 examines the direct investment behaviour by small and medium-sized enterprises. It gives the theoretical background to the analysis of such investment from a number of viewpoints, both theoretical and empirical. The special factors influencing foreign direct investment by smaller firms are drawn out and key constraints are found to be the relationship between firm and market, shortages of capital and management time and the role of uncertainty. In passing, the evolutionary approach to internationalization is discussed.

Chapter 9 by Coviello and Munro on network relationships and the internationalization process of small software firms takes the analyses of the problems of smaller firms further and examines the influence of networking on the internationalization of smaller firms. Using 'multi-site case research' it integrates the traditional incremental model of internationaliza-tion with the network perspective. Their findings are that in smaller software firms, perhaps due to the dynamic nature of the industry, the internationalization process is accelerated but is heavily influenced by the firms' formal and informal network of relationships. Drawing managerial implications, they advise smaller firms to build the impact of networking and its merits into their foreign market entry strategy.

The next reading by Benito and Gripsrud discusses again the incremental model and questions whether there is a general expansion pattern of FDIs across industries. They develop two hypotheses regarding the location of FDIs. After testing these hypotheses on Norwegian manufacturing firms, they conclude that there is no support for the assumption that FDI first takes place in culturally closer (psychic distance) countries and at a later stage are spread to more distant markets. Moreover, for a given company, an expansion into more distant countries is not found as the number of investments increases. Instead, their study reveals that location choices are discrete rational choices and not a cultural learning process. This does not preclude experience effects, but it is the nature of the business that defines the feasible location for each FDI.

The service sector is often neglected in studies of international business. It is either completely ignored, or treated as a footnote to special cases of analyses designed for manufacturing. Chapter 11 examines the key aspects of services as they impinge upon international business theory and operations. It focuses in particular on the foreign market servicing choices of service forms using an eclectic paradigm type of organizing framework in which ownership, location and internalization factors are analysed. Tradeability of the service and the degree of separation between the producer and consumer emerge as key elements in internationalization strategies and the piece also emphasizes the 'people' element in service provision.

Chapter 12 by Clark, Pugh and Mallory, examines empirically the process of internationalization in 25 UK based organizations. It pays particular attention to the knowledge requirements, sources and needs underlying the internationalization process (see also Buckley and Carter 1998). The flows of knowledge within the firm – both market-specific and generalized knowledge from operating internationally – influence the choices and shifts between modes of foreign market servicing (see also Calof and Beamish 1995). The article further emphasizes the importance of switches within modes and (in Figure 1, p. 168) presents a model of shifts in foreign market servicing which encompasses shifts between modes (including retrenchment) and shifts within modes. This piece leads logically to Part III on methods of foreign market servicing.

3 METHODS OF FOREIGN MARKET SERVICING

There are three generic methods by which a firm can penetrate a particular foreign market: exporting, licensing or direct investment. Each of these methods are, in practice, very important. The readings here are representative of a huge literature on each of exporting, licensing, joint ventures and foreign direct investment. For a review of this literature see Young *et al.* (1989). Chapter 13 by Anderson and Gatignon is a widely cited analysis of modes of foreign entry using transaction cost theory. This chapter shows that entry modes are best analysed by comparison with concrete alternatives and that the 'default' hypothesis – that, other things being equal, low resource commitment is preferable – gives a testable anchor to the analysis. The list of hypothesis advanced in this piece provide a useful checklist of key factors in the choice of entry mode.

Exporting may be regarded as the most straightforward way of selling in a foreign market, avoiding, as it does, most of the costs of doing business abroad. It is separated from the other two main forms of foreign market servicing by the location factor in that the bulk of the value adding activities take place in the home (not the foreign) market. Exporting may attract tax advantages and the associated risks are low because usually little capital is involved. However, the fixed costs of exporting (including making contact, negotiating prices, arranging shipping, adaptation of product and promotion) mean that a small volume of export sales can be uneconomic. Costs of product adaptation, tariff and non-tariff barriers and transport costs may dictate local operations rather than exporting. A number of studies investigate export behaviour of all types of firms. The second reading in this section by Cavusgil (Chapter 14) utilizes an alternative approach and attempts to delineate differences among exporting firms when firms are classified by their degree of internationalization. It identifies three types of exporter; experimental exporters, active exporters and committed exporters. These firms are then compared with each other in respect of measurable company characteristics. These characteristics include domestic environment, nature of international business involvement, marketing policy aspects, and export market research practices. The database for the investigation is a series of interviews with 70 systematically selected American firms. The study builds upon the sequential nature of internationalization (see Chapter 3) and associates this sequential exporting with the three stages of internationalization identified. The reading reveals significant differences among the three types of exporters and provides further insight into the export marketing behaviour of firms. It provides a useful background for designing a more comprehensive investigation of the issues and suggests that future investigations may also consider classifying firms by alternative criteria in addition to stages of internationalization.

International licensing appears to combine the best of both worlds – the advantage in technology and skills of the licensing multinational plus the local knowledge of the licensee. However, licensing accounts for only 7% of the total foreign sales of British companies (Buckley and Prescott, 1989) and approximately the same proportion in the other major trading nations. The reasons lie in the costs and difficulties of designing and maintaining contractual arrangements. These transaction costs centre on the identifiability of the advantage, policing costs (constraining the licensee from using the knowledge in 'ways which have not been paid for'), the danger of creating a competitor, problems in the market for licences (including the buyer uncertainty problem; that the buyer does not know what to pay for the knowledge he needs until he has it, but when he has it he has no need to pay for it!) and the search costs in bringing buyer and seller together (Buckley and Davies, 1981). In other instances, the market structure may militate in favour of licensing as a form of market entry – cross-licensing in oligopolistic industries may be preferable to head-to-head competition. Licensing may also be a second best choice when exporting or direct investment are ruled out by government policy, intra-firm scarcities or risk profiles. Licensing may also be useful to extend the life of an idea or technology, or to reach small or difficult foreign markets. In the theory of international business, the choice between licensing and direct investment is crucial in illustrating the choice between a market (external) solution – licensing, and an internal solution – direct investment (Buckley and Casson, 1976; 1985).

Chapter 15 by Welch is unusual in that it attempts to quantify the costs of licensing and therefore captures the importance and magnitude of transaction costs. This piece is important not only for its insights into the licensing process but also for its meticulous interrogation of some valuable primary data. These data are suggestive of a number of interesting hypotheses but the piece also provides one of the few extant attempts to measure cost magnitudes. The survey of literature provides a useful backdrop to the empirical issues related to the importance of patents, know-how and other forms of proprietary knowledge and the difficulties for firms in appropriating benefits from the international exploitation of technological advances. It also covers the search costs of finding a licensee and the negotiation costs, which it pulls together (in the important Table 8). Licensing is also compared and contrasted to foreign direct investment. It is shown to be a potentially important part of the international operations of companies.

The foreign investment decision is a crucial step in internationalization. In fact foreign direct investment is often treated as if it were synonymous with internationalization. Just as there are many forms of contractual arrangements for conducting international business, of which licensing is just one (Buckley, 1989) so there are many forms of foreign direct investment. The major motives for conducting foreign direct investment are market orientated, cost orientated and for the control of key inputs.

Joint ventures are an important form of foreign direct investment and are currently subject to a great deal of theoretical and empirical scrutiny (Contractor and Lorange, 1988; Beamish and Killing, 1997). They are an important means of entry into markets which are difficult for foreign firms to penetrate because of legal, regulatory or cultural barriers. Japan is a case in point. Buckley, Sparkes and Mirza (1985) examine joint ventures for a sample of European firms. This article also notes the strategic importance of penetrating certain large foreign markets. It enables learning to occur which can be transferred to all parts of the company (including home operations), it enables competition to be met head-on and it closes down an opportunity for competitors to have a free ride in one market (the home market in the case of Japanese firms). Thus foreign direct investment and joint ventures must be seen as part of a global competitive game.

Chapter 16 by Harrigan relates joint venture activity to global strategies and proposes a framework for predicting whether firms will cooperate in forming joint ventures or other forms of interfirm cooperation. It also suggests which factors/forces destabilize cooperative joint ventures and suggests that under certain conditions joint ventures are most appropriate for strategic needs. Joint ventures are considered to be a better way to internationalize and may be used as pre-emptive manoeuvres to ensure that access to distribution channels, suppliers and technology in promising industries are not foreclosed. They are also ways of ensuring that potential entrants do not team up with competitors.

The entry of China into the world economy in the mid to late 1990s has resulted in China becoming a major host country for foreign multinationals. Most of these foreign investments are joint ventures with Chinese capital. The management, ownership and control is of vital importance, not only for Chinese development, but also for the integration of China into the global economy. The conduct of these ventures has important lessons which can be generalized beyond China. Child, Yan and Lu (1997), examined international joint ventures in China. They found that to predict relative levels of foreign and Chinese parent company control in joint ventures, it is necessary to utilize a broader definition of ownership than the purely legal one and to include the provision of non-capital resources and inputs on a non-contractual basis (this includes inputs into product design, production technology, management systems and management resources). Thus, if foreign firms wish to enhance their control over their Chinese joint ventures, they should have a high equity share and provide continuing non-contractual support to the venture. Reliance on purely legal contracts may have a negative connotation. Respect for social and political norms is also a vital precondition for success in China.

Chapter 17 by Parkhe on strategic alliances argues that the emergence and maintainance of cooperation between international alliance partners is related to the diversity in the partners' characteristics. The chapter develops a multilevel typology of interfirm diversity and examines its impact on alliance longevity and effectiveness. As has been shown in a number of earlier studies (e.g. Harrigan 1988), interfirm diversity severely impedes the ability of companies to work jointly and effectively. Taking that as a starting point, this chapter examines the impact of diversity on alliance outcomes and illustrates that deliberate learning/adaptation actions by firms can deter alliance failures and promote longevity. The paper points out that there is a need for longitudinal studies focusing on the phases of alliance development. Further, it draws attention to the crucial aspect of learning among alliance partners. It proposes that the ability of a firm to diagnose important differences between partners and to design a productive partnership through novel solutions, accommodating these differences, is likely to become imperative in achieving alliance longevity.

4 ORGANIZING THE MULTINATIONAL FIRM

A number of studies are available on the organization and management of the multinational firm. Studies such as 'Strategic Management in Multinational Companies' (Doz, 1986), 'Managing the Multinational Subsidiary' (Hulbert and Brandt, 1980) and Hedlund and Aman (1984) are worth mentioning. In this section, however, we have selected a number of readings which have been particularly innovative. Prahalad and Doz (1981) deal with the problems of maintaining strategic control over subsidiaries in a multinational firm. The authors argue that the nature of control in this relationship changes over time (see also Ghauri, Chapter 20). As resources such as capital, technology and management are invested in the subsidiary, the head office, over time, cannot control these resources by influencing the subsidiary. The authors present a conceptual framework to define organizational context, and argue that it can be used as a means of control. They also classify multinational corporations in four categories: (1) fragmented, (2) dependent, (3) autonomous, and (4) integrated. However, the conclusion is that HQ's ability to control cannot be taken for granted.

In Chapter 18, Kogut and Kulatilaka present strategic (foreign) investments as real options. Although the analysis is not fully developed in the reading, this notion has great potential in international business – joint ventures, for instance, may be analysed as options on future, deeper involvement in volatile markets (Buckley and Casson 1997; 1998). Kogut and Kulatilaka also examine organizational capabilities and core competences as strategic investments with long-term payoffs. Platform investments are seen as real options with future flexibility designed and planned into the investment. The conclusion points to vicious and virtuous circles in the life cycle of companies and the authors note that 'flexibility is of no value in the absence of resources required for execution' (p. 293). Real options thinking requires a new targeted long-term strategic planning. The incorporation of uncertainty into models of mode choice is a challenging task which is likely to drive much future research on internationalization (see Chi and McGuire, 1996; Rivoli and Salorio, 1996).

The classical study by Bartlett and Ghoshal on 'Organising for Worldwide Effectiveness: The Transnational Solution', which led to their best seller book, *Managing Across Borders: The Transnational Solution* (1989), discusses the enormous success of newcomers, Japanese companies, and the way in which they have forced Western firms to rethink their organizational strategies. On the other hand, the managers in Japan have focused on the forces of localization. At the same time both Western and Japanese firms are worried about barriers of trade. The growing demand of host governments for local investments and changing manufacturing technologies are making small-scale production and tailored products more feasible. The authors claim that all these changes demand more than efficient central management and flexible operations. Given a number of examples from companies like Philips, Ericsson and Matsushita, they conclude that dynamic interdependence is the basis of a transnational company – one that can think globally and act locally. They suggest that to deal with these new challenges, what is needed is a gradual approach that both protects and builds on the company's administrative heritage plus flexible, central and local management capabilities.

The next contribution (by Ghauri) on the management of headquarters–subsidiary relationships questions the existing literature on FDIs which deals with global management using traditional approaches. It presents evolutionary phenomena where foreign operations become more influential and independent from the parent firm. The paper suggests that a foreign subsidiary has a three-dimensional relationship: with the head office, with local authorities and with the local network. Presenting empirical evidence from Swedish firms and their subsidiaries in South East Asia, it claims that a new relationship pattern is emerging, where the foreign subsidiaries become more influential than the parent firms. They make their own decisions in regard to the purchasing of raw material and components, products and product decisions and in relationship with other actors in their network. Moreover, the paper suggests an emergence of a 'centre-to-centre' relationship, where some regional subsidiaries communicate directly with others, without the consent of their head office.

Chapter 21 by Hood, Young and Lal explores the strategic intentions of Japanese firms, which have manufacturing subsidiaries in Europe. Their strategies and performance are reviewed and evaluated. Empirical evidence is provided from Japanese manufacturing plants working in the UK. The focus is on the relationship between the strategic intentions behind the establishment of manufacturing plants in Europe and the directions in which these plants have evolved. It is suggested that Japanese companies are moving towards more added value investments and are developing multiple SMEs as component suppliers. It is accepted that this may be driven by local 'local content' requirements, but in a more strategic sense it is an intrinsic part of the Japanese competitive style. The study thus concludes that the net outcome of Japanese companies entering the UK appears to be positive on all accounts which explains the increasing interest of local governments in attracting foreign direct investments.

5 THE IMPACT OF CULTURE ON INTERNATIONALIZATION

Chapter 22 by Hallén and Wiedersheim-Paul, deals with psychic distance and buyer–seller interaction. The authors claim that the gap between buyers and sellers is two-dimensional. First, the 'hard' dimension such as the physical distance and second, the soft dimension connected with differences in attitudes and perceptions caused for instance, by differences in cultural environments (in a wide sense) between buyers and sellers. Although the reading addresses buyers and sellers, the approach is wide-ranging and can be applied to comparative management and management in multinational firms. The 'soft' dimension of distance is of particular importance in international marketing and management. As inter-firm relationships (such as that between head office and subsidiary) develop, mutual understanding between the units reduces this psychic gap.

Chapter 23 by Kogut and Singh examines the influence of national culture on entry modes. It finds strong support for the idea that cultural distance (see Chapter 22) and attitudes towards uncertainty avoidance (see Chapter 24) influence the choice of entry mode. It therefore provides an excellent bridge between the readings collected in Part III of this volume and those in Part V.

Expanding the results of his fundamental study (Hofstede 1980), Hofstede emphasizes the importance of culture on international business in the next reading. He distinguishes national cultures from organizational cultures. Using a huge database from 50 different countries, he discusses the validity of management theories across borders. A special emphasis is given to East Asian cultures explaining the recent economic growth of these countries. The four dimensions – 1) power distance, 2) individualism, 3) masculinity versus femininity, and 4) uncertainty avoidance – are discussed at length. A fifth dimension, long-term versus short-term orientation, is introduced to explain East Asian cultures. The study concludes that existing management theories have a limited validity across cultures, not only because many companies operate in different countries, but also because they operate in different lines of businesses. The managers thus have to see the relativity of their own cultural framework with that of others. The paper calls for improved inter-cultural management skills focusing on *working* rather than on *living* in other countries.

The next study on psychic distance by O'Grady and Lane discusses its impact on the mode of entry chosen by firms. They question the validity of the incremental approach based on psychic distance. Providing evidence from 32 Canadian firms, they state that only 22% were functioning successfully in the most (psychically) closest country, USA. They suggest that the paradox is that the psychically close countries become difficult to manage precisely because of this closeness. The closeness prevents managers learning about critical differences. In giving the example of USA and Canada they suggest that closeness does not mean similarity in culture. They claim that they found significant differences in values and attitudes between the two countries, that on the surface appear to have few differences.

6 SUMMARY

The analysis of internationalization has been a vital driving force in international business research. Seemingly disparate pieces of research based on product cycle models (Vernon, Chapter 2), stages of internationalization (Johanson and Wiedersheim-Paul, Chapter 3, Johanson and Vahlne, Chapter 4), studies of small firm or first-time foreign investors (Buckley,

Newbould and Thurwell, 1988; Buckley, Berkova and Newbould, 1983, Chapter 6), network approaches to internationalization (Johanson and Mattsson, 1986), internalization theory (Buckley and Casson, 1976; 1985), the international marketing and purchasing approach (Paliwoda and Turnbull, 1986; Turnbull and Valla, 1989) and studies critical of stages theories are now being crystallized into a coherent view of internationalization. Such a view has evolutionary stages elements as part of its make up. But these stages are now much more circumscribed in context and flexible in nature than the extrapolation of early studies would suggest. They also require more attention to be paid to management knowledge by the firm. For naive, first-time investors or internationally inexperienced larger firms, a strategy of creeping incrementalism may still be valid. However, for larger, diversified multinationals, a global planning horizon is now much nearer as several readings above demonstrate. The choice of methods of doing business abroad is now much wider than even 20 years ago and choices can be tailored to the precise needs of internationalizing firms. This flexibility (often gained through experience) may well, in many cases, obviate the need for incremental learning and feedback through stages. We should not, however, underestimate the importance of gradual learning, even for the most experienced and internationally diversified firms.

REFERENCES

Aharoni, Y. (1966) *The Foreign Investment Decision Process*. Graduate School of Business Administration, Harvard University: Boston, Mass.

Beamish, P.W. and Killing, J.P. (eds) (1997) *Cooperative Strategies*. New Lexington Press: San Fransisco.

Bartlett, C.A. and Ghoshal, S. (1989) *Managing Across Borders: The Transnational Solution*. Boston: Hutchinson Business Books.

Buckley, P.J. (1988) 'The Limits of Explanation: Testing the Internationalization Theory of the Multinational Enterprise', *Journal of International Business Studies* **XIX**(2) 181–193.

Buckley, P.J. (1989) *The Multinational Enterprise: Theory and Applications*. Macmillan: London.

Buckley, P.J. (1990) 'Problems and Developments in the Core Theory of International Business', *Journal of International Business* **XXI**(4), 657–665.

Buckley, P.J. (1993) 'Barriers to Internationalization Process of Firms', in L. Zan, S. Zambon and A. Pettigrew (eds) *Perspectives on Strategic Change*. Kluwer: Boston, Mass.

Buckley, P.J., Berkova, Z. and Newbould, G.D. (1983) *Direct Investment in the UK by Smaller European Firms*. Macmillan: London.

Buckley, P.J. and Carter, M. (1998) 'Managing Cross Border Complementary Knowledge', *International Studies of Management and Organisation* (forthcoming).

Buckley, P.J. and Casson, M. (1976) *The Future of the Multinational Enterprise*. Macmillan: London.

Buckley, P.J. and Casson, M. (1985) *The Economic Theory of the Multinational Enterprise*. Macmillan: London.

Buckley, P.J. and Casson, M. (1988) 'A Theory of Cooperation in International Business', in F. Contractor and P. Lorange (eds) *Cooperative Strategies in International Business*. Lexington Books: Lexington, Mass.

Buckley, P.J. and Casson, M. (1996) 'An Economic Model of International Joint Ventures', *Journal of International Business Studies*, **27**(5), 849–876.

Buckley, P.J. and Casson, M. (1997) 'An Economic Model of International Joint Venture Strategy', *Journal of International Business Studies*, **27**(5), 849–876.

Buckley, P.J. and Casson, M. (1998) 'Analysing Foreign Market Entry Strategies: Extending the Internationalisation Approach', *Journal of International Business Studies* (forthcoming).

Buckley, P.J. and Davies, H. (1981) 'Foreign Licensing in Overseas Operations: Theory and Evidence from the UK', in R.G. Hawkins, and A.J. Prasad (eds) *Technology Transfer and Economic Development*. JAI Press: Greenwich, Conn.

Buckley, P.J., Newbould, G.D. and Thurwell, J. (1988) *Foreign Direct Investment by Smaller UK Firms*. Macmillan: London. (Previously published in 1978 as *Going International: The Experience of Smaller Firms Overseas*.)

Buckley, P.J. and Prescott, K. (1989) 'The Structure of British Industry's Sales in Foreign Markets', *Managerial and Decision Economics*, **10**(3), 189–208.

Buckley, P.J., Sparkes, J.R. and Mirza, H. (1985) 'Direct Investment in Japan as a Means of Market Entry: The Case of European Firms', *Journal of Marketing Management*, **2**(3), 241–258.

Calof, J.L. and Beamish, P.W. (1995) 'Adapting to Foreign Markets: Explaining Internationalisation', *International Business Review*, **4**(2), 115–131.

Casson, M. (1987) *The Firm and the Market*. Basil Blackwell: Oxford.

Chi, T. and McGuire, D.J. (1996) 'Collaborative Ventures and Value of Learning: Integrating the Transaction Cost and Strategic Option Perspectives on the Choice of Market Entry Modes', *Journal of International Business Studies*, **27**(2), 285–307.

Child, J., Yan, Y. and Lu, Y. (1997) 'Ownership and control in Sino-Foreign Joint Ventures', in P.W. Beamish and J.P. Killing (eds) *Cooperative Strategies: Asia Pacific Perspectives*, Lexington Press: San Francisco, pp. 181–225.

Contractor, F. and Lorange, P. (eds) (1988) *Cooperative Strategies in International Business*. Lexington Books D.C. Heath & Co.: Lexington, Mass.

Doz, Y. (1986) *Strategic Management in Multinational Companies*. Pergamon Press: Oxford.

Dunning, J.H. (1958) *American Investment in British Manufacturing Industry*. George Allen & Unwin: London.

Ghauri, P.N. (1989) 'Global Marketing Strategies: Swedish Firms in South-East Asia', in E. Kaynak and K.M. Lee (eds) *Global Business, Asia-Pacific Dimensions*. Routledge: London.

Giddy, I.H. (1978) 'The Demise of the Product Cycle Model in International Business Theory', *Columbia Journal of World Business*, **13**, 90–97.

Hagg, I. and Johanson, J. (1982) *Foretag i natverk, ny syn pa Konkurrenskraft*. SNS: Stockholm.

Harrigan, K.R. (1988) 'Joint Ventures and Competitive Strategy', *Strategic Management Journal*, **9**, 141–158.

Hedlund, G. and Kverneland, A. (1983) 'Are Establishments and Growth Strategies for Foreign Market Changing?' paper presented at the 9th European International Business Association Conference, Oslo, 18–20 December.

Hedlund, G. and Aman, P. (1984) *Managing Relationships with Foreign Subsidiaries*. Sveriges Mekan Forbund: Vastervik.

Hofstede, G. (1980) *Cultures' Consequences: International Differences in Work-Related Values*. Sage Publications: Beverly Hills.

Hornell, E. and Vahlne, J.-E. (1986) *Multinationals – The Swedish Case*. Croom Helm: London.

Horst, T.O. (1972) 'Firm and Industry Determinants of the Decision to Investment Abroad: An Empirical Study', *Review of Economics and Statistics*, **54**, 258–266.

Hulbert, J.M. and Brandt, W.K. (1980) *Managing the Multinational Subsidiary*. Holt Reinhart and Winston: New York.

Johanson, J. and Mattson, L.G. (1988) 'Internationalization in Industrial Systems – a network approach', in N. Hood and J.E. Vahlne (eds), *Strategies in Global Competition*, Croom Helm, New York, pp. 25–47.

Luostarinen, R. (1979) *The Internationalization of the Firm*. Acta Academia Oeconomica Helsingiensis: Helsinki.

Paliwoda, S.J. and Turnbull, P.W. (eds) (1986) *Research in International Marketing*. Croom Helm: London.

Prahalad, C.H. and Doz, Y.L. (1981) 'An Approach to Strategic Control in MNCs', *Sloan Management Review*, **22**(4), 5–13

Rivoli, P. and Salorio, E. (1996) 'Foreign Direct Investment and Investment Under Uncertainty', *Journal of International Business Studies*, **27**(2), 335–357.

Servan-Schreiber, J.J. (1969) *The American Challenge*. Pelican: Harmondsworth.

Swedenborg, B. (1979) *Multinational Operations of Swedish Firms*. Almquist & Wicksell: Stockholm.

Thorelli, H. (1986) 'Networks: Between Markets and Hierarchies', *Strategic Management Journal* **7**, 37–51.

Turnbull, P. and Valla, J.P. (eds) (1989) *Strategies for International Industrial Marketing*. Croom Helm: London.

Vernon, R. (1979) 'The Product Cycle Hypothesis in a New International Environment', *Oxford Bulletin of Economics and Statistics*, **41**, 255–267.

Young, S., Hamill, J., Wheeler, C. and Davies, J.R. (1989) *International Market Entry and Development: Strategies and Management*. Harvester Wheatsheaf: Hemel Hempstead.

Part I

Antecedents

CONTENTS

1

The Foreign Investment Decision Process

Yair Aharoni

ELEMENTS IN THE DECISION PROCESS

In any decision process the following elements can be delineated. First, any one choice made in the organization depends on the *social system* in which the process takes place; second, the process, although not each one of the decisions from which it is composed, takes a long *time*; third, decisions are made under *uncertainty*; fourth, organizations have *goals*; and finally, there are many *constraints* on the freedom of action of the decision makers to be reckoned with.

A system is a set of interrelated parts. Any organization is a system of individuals, grouped in subsystems according to their role definitions, mutually influencing each other through a continual process of interactions. However, every participant in the organization is not only an involved member of the organization. He is intimately connected with the wider variety of other systems of which he is a part, and which he cannot ignore. The organization as a whole is also part of superordinate systems: the industry, the community in which it operates, the cultural environment of which it is a part. All these influence the way problems are defined, alternatives are perceived, and selected, and opinions are formulated. 'In order to survive, an organization must achieve what is called "symbiosis" (i.e., the mutually beneficial living together of two dissimilar organizations) with a variety of external systems.'

The first element in the analysis of any decision process therefore is the ORGANIZA-TION AND ENVIRONMENT in which it takes place. The decision is made within an organization which has established strategy, procedures, and standard operating policies, which is composed of different individuals, each with his own goals and aspirations, and which is influenced by other, superordinate systems. The organization has devised an established 'way of doing things' according to agreed-upon goals and past experience; these rules and specifications influence the behavior of its members, the information gathered by them, and their adaptive reactions to the environment. Moreover, individuals within the organization have established relations among themselves and with others outside the organization. These relations will also influence any specific decision.

Those making the decision will have to continue acting for the same organization and interacting with various people in and outside it long after any specific decision is made or implemented. Consciously or unconsciously, they will weigh these future relations throughout the decision process. For example, one may choose a certain course of action because somebody else to whom one feels an obligation for a favour done in the *past* prefers it.

Reproduced with permission in abridged form from Yair Aharoni's *The Foreign Investment Decision Process*, (1966), Harvard University, Boston, Mass.
Copyright © Yair Aharoni

One may also take a course of action because one feels that another decision will harm *future* relations with someone else inside or outside the organization. These future relations are not necessarily important in terms of the specific decision being considered. They are relevant only if we look at any one specific decision as part of a whole spectrum – the whole stream of past, present, and future events in the organization. Interdependence is a well-known phenomenon in the theory of oligopoly: the decision making of any one entrepreneur depends on his evaluation of his competitors' activities in the past and a projection of his reactions in the future. The same phenomenon, however, is common in all walks of life – among friends and collaborators as well as among competitors. The rationality of behavior is seen only if we observe the whole system, instead of concentrating our attention on one isolated phase of it. For example, the officials of a bank decide to lend money to a company despite their disapproval of a specific deal, because they 'look at the total picture' of relations with this specific customer. The executives of a company decide to invest in a certain country against their own business judgement because they were asked to do so by the company's largest supplier. They feel that a refusal to go along might hamper their future relations with the supplier with regard to totally different business deals.

The manner of handling a problem depends strongly on the other activities of the organization. A problem may be considered important enough for immediate investigation during an inactive period, but its solution may be delayed indefinitely if many other activities are going on at the same time. An organization's executives might not explore a profitable opportunity for investment because they were busy with other affairs at the time the opportunity presented itself. The same executives would have vigorously investigated this opportunity at other, less hectic times. An individual chooses to focus his attention on a problem at one time and ignore it at another, depending on his frame of mind or other preoccupations. The priorities set on one's time become an important factor in the decision of what issues should get any attention.

Another important element in the decision process that should be explicitly emphasized is the TIME DIMENSION. One of the major arguments to be developed in this book is that this dimension plays a very important role in the way any one decision in a process is made. At this point it is enough to emphasize that there is no investment decision made at a specific point in time. Rather, there is a long *process*, spread over a considerable period of time and involving many people at different echelons of various organizations. Throughout this process, numerous 'subdecisions' have to be made. These 'subdecisions' usually reduce the degree of freedom of the decision-making unit and therefore influence the final outcome of the process. Throughout the process, the persons involved change their perception of different variables, numerous shifts in the environment occur, and many changes in other activities of the organization take place. The conclusion to invest or to reject an investment possibility is only one step in a long sequence of decisions made during the process, and not necessarily the final one. Any attempt to 'fold' this time element into a 'point decision' would create grave distortions in the understanding of the process.

A third element to be reckoned with is UNCERTAINTY. Businessmen are not endowed with the faculty of blissful prescience. They operate in a world of uncertainty. Uncertainty creates anxiety, and anxiety, we are told by psychologists, is a situation human beings try to avoid. It is not surprising, therefore, to find that businessmen try to avoid uncertainty as much as possible. 'They impose plans, standard operating procedures, industry tradition, and uncertainty absorption contracts on that environment. In short, they achieve a reasonable manageable decision situation by avoiding planning where plans depend on predictions of uncertain future events and by emphasizing planning where the plans can be made self-confirming through some control device.'

Businessmen not only shy away from uncertainty; they also are not willing to take more than a certain degree of risk. The risk taken depends on the organization and on role-definition, for executives are willing to assume only what they consider to be 'normal business risks'. From our point of view, the avoidance of risk and uncertainty is a very important factor. Certainty for a person or an organization unfamiliar with foreign investments the uncertainty involved is quite large. Therefore, it seems advisable to pause momentarily and examine the meaning of these terms.

The first attempt to distinguish between risk and uncertainty was made by Frank H. Knight in 1921 as part of his treatment of profits. 'Risk' for Knight is a situation in which the probabilities of alternative outcomes are known. For example, contingencies that can be insured constitute risk. Uncertainty, on the other hand, is unmeasurable.

This definition, however, begs the question: what exactly constitutes 'a quantity susceptible of measurement?' For example, is it legitimate to measure probabilities on subjective beliefs or should only objective phenomena be gauged? Does it make sense to talk about the probability of a unique event, or can probability be measured only when the experiment is repetitive? These and related questions have been debated for centuries by those dealing with probability, and they are still unsolved. Here, suffice it to say that it is often argued that objective probability is a pure mathematical concept that cannot be found in real life. Therefore, only subjective probabilities must be used. However, when subjective probabilities are used, the distinction between risk and uncertainty loses much of its sharpness. Indeed, the Bayesian statisticians have developed theories in which management is conceived as assigning subjective probabilities to uncertain events, changing these probabilities when additional information becomes available. Thus, the decision is transformed into one under risk.

For our purposes it seems useful to distinguish between a subjective probability and the degree of belief in it. We shall therefore define 'risk' as the proportion of cases in a subjective joint probability distribution that fall below a subjectively defined expected minimum. Uncertainty will be used to refer to the degree of confidence in the correctness of the estimated subjective probability distribution; the less the confidence, the higher the uncertainty.

Note that this definition of risk is not commensurate with the one generally used in economics. Economists define risk as an estimate of a dispersion of a probability distribution; the greater the dispersion, the greater the risk. Our definition is nearer to the day-to-day use of the word. Risk is the chance of injury, damage, or loss, compared with some previous standard. Uncertainty, on the other hand, is a feeling of doubt and unreliability.

When businessmen talk about risk, they use this word to include both the subjective probability of loss, either in absolute terms or in relation to some expectations, and the amount the company may lose. The loss referred to may be a monetary one, or the waste of management time, or the inability to achieve a specific objective of the company other than profits (e.g., risk of losing control). Thus, when a businessman says that 'the political risks abroad are high', he may be referring to the possibility of losing his freedom of decision making because of a high degree of government regulation. Political risks may mean to him a high subjective probability of total or partial loss of the investment itself because of expropriation, nationalization, or war; they may mean that the unsettled conditions put the very basis of planning in question and make the work of management more difficult; or they may be any combination of all these factors.

The subjective evaluation of risk stems from uncertainty. Uncertainty is affected mainly by two factors: ignorance and perceived changes. Ignorance may prevail either because of lack of information (i.e., the information is not available at any cost), or because of lack of knowledge (i.e., the information in fact exists but the decision maker does not avail himself of it, either because he does not know of its existence, or because he does not want or is not able to spend the resources needed to get it). Perceived changes are conditions where there is a high subjective probability of unsettled or insecure conditions, which would question the very basis of consistent information.

Uncertainty exists not only in regard to the consequences of alternatives: there is also uncertainty about the alternatives themselves. Indeed, some authorities on economic development feel that lack of knowledge about opportunities abroad is a major obstacle to such investments. Moreover, the responses of others in the organization and of competitors, governments, and other outsiders are also unknown. Still, there is always *some* information on similar events that the decision maker considers similar. Using this information, decision makers reach some judgement about the future state of affairs and their effects. Therefore, one should learn how people behave in face of uncertainty, how judgements are formulated when knowledge is inadequate, and when a decision maker will acquire more information. Obviously, information on every possible opportunity is not available, and even if it were, one would have to be interested in such information in order to focus one's attention on it and to spend such scarce resources as time and energy to digest it. This brings us back to the question of priorities, already discussed above.

In any given business situation, few of the variables are known with precision. There are always many factors which are not subject to mathematical analysis. Many others can be analyzed mathematically only on the basis of subjectively arrived at figures. Because of uncertainty, we deal with perceptions and subjective estimates. No quantitative prediction can be made in an exact, objective manner. To predict a rate of return, one has to estimate investment costs, production costs, sales volume and prices, advertising costs, and so forth. All these are unknown, and many of them can be only subjectively estimated. Subjective estimates vary by their very nature. They also change because of changing expectations about the kind of pay off associated with various possible errors. Thus, if an executive feels that the punishment for an error resulting in a loss will be much greater than a reward for success, he will tend to bias his estimates on the pessimistic side. On the other hand, if he feels that the rewards for success will be much greater than the penalty for failure, he will have a bias on the optimistic side.

One reacts to facts as one perceives them and to what one infers from this perception. Two businessmen with the same motives and the same information may infer different things and reach different conclusions. The following two quotations from the interviews with two businessmen manufacturing the same product will suffice to illustrate this point:

> I know we shall have competition in India. However, you must realize that India is a fast growing market and one of the largest markets in the world.

> Sure, India has a large population, but they are all starving. It will take them another ten years before they will need another plant.

Needless to say, India is the same country, with the same number of inhabitants and the same size of gross national product in both cases. It is the perceptions of the two businessmen about the size of the market in India and the way they evaluate the factual data that are different.

Not only do subjective estimates and perceptions vary. They are also modified with time. Pay off expectations and subjective estimates of facts are changed during investigation and to a large extent because of it. Here again, the time dimension becomes a crucial factor in the decision process.

Additional information can be purchased before a conclusion is reached. Getting additional information may change perception and subjective estimates, but it costs money and time. Therefore, it will be bought only if the cost of obtaining it is deemed justified by some crude test. Decisions to buy more information are of necessity based on 'hunches' and intuition. The intuition is based on beliefs held and on information already available. Because of this fact, the *sequence* of steps in the investigation is a very crucial variable in the decision process. For example, businessmen evaluate risk at a very early stage of the investigation. They have a 'threshold' for risk and abandon any further consideration of a project that is deemed to be 'too risky'. They do not compensate for risk by higher profits for the simple reason that they evaluate risk at an early stage, when even cursory and precarious calculations of rate of return are still unavailable.

A fourth important element is GOALS. Any normative analysis must presuppose some model of behavior, based on certain assumptions about the goals to be achieved by the decision makers. However, our approach in this book is descriptive rather than normative. We do not intend to enlogize or condemn any behavior, or to label it as rational or irrational. Our aim is to show how businessmen actually behave in order to predict their behavior rather than to prescribe how they should behave. Because of this, we do not think it is necessary for us to probe into the question of goals and motivations. We should add that we do not feel it possible to explain our data on the basis of one narrow, rigid, or inimutable motivating force. In fact, our field research revealed clearly the existence of a multitude of objectives. The interaction of the various goals of individual executives, of the different divisions, and of the organization as a whole in the process of formulating the decision created a situation that may seem to those looking for one objective as inconsistent and lacking transitivity.

Fifth are the CONSTRAINTS. Any major decision in business involves a multitude of variables that could be investigated. Thus, a decision to build a plant in a foreign country necessitates search in many directions and the checking of a host of details. For instance, it involves an evaluation of the general political environment, the attitude of the foreign government, and the concessions that may be granted. It necessitates some knowledge of the legal system, the size of the market, the sociological and cultural backgrounds of the population, and the way this background influences its habits. It requires an evaluation of the location and the size of plant to be erected and of the production methods to be used. A decision must be made about which components should be procured and which should be produced. Land prices, wages, fringe benefits, behavior of trade unions, productivity of the workers, all must be evaluated. The best 'Product mix' should be examined from technological and marketing points of view. A capitalization scheme should be worked out and sources of funds must be tapped. Personnel should be checked and its availability ensured, etc.

Some of these variables – the political environment of the foreign country, for example – must, from the investor's point of view, be taken as given. Many can be changed at will. Many other variables may be changed after negotiations. Investors often negotiate such factors as special tax concessions, relaxation of various legal requirements, size of loans and the rate of interest to be paid on these loans, various guarantees, special rates of exchange, ban on imports or high customs duties on the product to be manufactured, and so on. The total number of plausible permutations and combinations of all these variables is almost infinite and each one of these combinations may give a different picture.

Thus, some investments may seem unprofitable if new machines are required, but they could be expected to show high profits if used machines are available; a highly mechanized process of production may create problems, but a labor-intensive process might be the answer. The size of the market could seem to be too small for a very large plant, but a smaller plant might be used and the profits could be high, even though the loss in larger scale economies might result in higher costs; or negotiations with the government might lead to a levy imposed on imports, thus making even a small-scale plant highly profitable.

But investigation costs money and management time. We have already pointed out that because of these factors businessmen are compelled to decide on the basis of crude indicators whether more thorough investigation may be worthwhile. Another plausible method to save money and management time is to assume some variables to be fixed, i.e., as having assigned values or a range of values. Instead of checking all possible permutations, only some crucial variables might be investigated and only incremental changes considered. No explicit recognition is given to the possibility of changes in some variables such as size of plant, and so on. Thus, the decision maker atones for gaps in his information and for the finiteness of his computational capacity by adopting 'strategies', 'decision rules', and policies, and by assuming some variables to be fixed.

Cyert and March (1963) have demonstrated that organizations accept precedents as binding and look at standard operating procedures as constraints in any problem-solving situation. This was found to be true in the case of the foreign investment decision process also. First, many organizations lacking the precedent of a foreign investment experience would refuse to consider such a possibility. Second, when such a possibility is considered, many previous 'policies' are taken as given and become constraints in the decision process. Under certain circumstances, however, certain constraints will not be binding and changes will be considered. The constraints and the conditions under which they will be changed are therefore another element in the decision process.

THE FOREIGN INVESTMENT DECISION

Investments in foreign countries are not within the sphere of interest of the overwhelming majority of businessmen in the United States. The possibility of looking for investment opportunities outside the United States (and Canada) simply does not occur to them. This way of thinking manifests itself in such expressions as, 'There are enough profitable opportunities in the United States. Why bother to go abroad?' When a foreign investment opportunity is brought before management, the burden of proof that such an opportunity should be considered (let alone decided upon) is on the proposer. It is not enough to show that the expected value of profits is high. It must be proved that 'it is worthwhile to go abroad'.

Investment decisions in business are based on the alternatives which are known to exist, or those which have emerged from previous activities of the business unit (such as those that are a result of research and development activities). Except for companies that already have made direct foreign investments, investments abroad are very rarely included in these alternatives.

Our analysis leads us to conclude that the most important question is: 'Who and what event posed the problem initially?' The first foreign investment decision is to a large extent a trip to the unknown. It is an innovation and development of a new dimension, and a major breakthrough in the normal course of events. There should be some strong force, some drastic experience that will trigger and push the organization into this new path. This trigger compels the organization to shift the focus of its attention and to look at investment possibilities abroad. It creates a situation that leads the decision maker to feel that an investment abroad may help him solve some urgent problem or carry on some activity that he has committed himself to maintain, or simply that such an investment may fulfill some important needs. The types of initiating forces are listed below.

Generally, the decision to look abroad is actually a specific one. It is a decision to look at the possibilities of a specific investment in a specific country, not a general resolution to look around the globe for investment opportunities. The most crucial decision is taken when the first venture abroad is considered. At this stage, the organization has had no experience whatsoever in the complicated field of foreign investment, although it often has had export experience. No standard operating procedure exists to give some guidelines in dealing with the problem. No one in the organization is explicitly responsible for dealing with this type of problem. In all these cases, quite a strong push is needed for making the decision to look abroad. When subsequent foreign investment decision processes are carried through, the company will benefit from its experience in previous investigations.

The initiating forces

The forces leading an organization to consider the possibility of launching a project outside the United States might be classified into those arising within the organization and those exogenous to it, stemming from its environment. In the first category are forces arising from a strong interest by one or several high-ranking executives inside the organization. In the second, we include the following:

1. An outside proposal, provided it comes from a source that cannot be easily ignored. The most frequent sources of such proposals are foreign governments, the distributors of the company's products, and its clients.
2. Fear of losing a market.
3. The 'band wagon' effect: very successful activities abroad of a competing firm in the same line of business, or a general belief that investment in some area is 'a must'.
4. Strong competition from abroad in the home market.

In any specific case it is generally very difficult, if not impossible, to pin down one reason for a decision to look abroad, or to find out precisely who was the initiator of a project. The decision results from a chain of events, incomplete information, activities of different persons (not necessarily in connection with the particular project) and a combination of several motivating forces, some of them working in favor of such a decision, some against it. The existence or the emergence of any one of these initiating forces might be looked upon as a necessary but not sufficient condition for the decision to look abroad. There is no simple functional relationship between any one force and such a decision. Thus, a company may lose a market and still not decide to look abroad. The impact of any one of these forces depends on the social system it encounters. It depends on various feelings and social and organizational structures, on previous events in the company's history, and on other problem areas facing the company at the time this force is encountered. In general, the decision to look abroad is brought about by the interaction of several forces – partly environmental and partly inside the organization – influencing different persons at different times. Generally, a decision to look abroad means only that an investigation will be made of some possibility abroad. It does not mean that an investment will follow. This decision means only that the investment will be considered on its own merits and will not be rejected *a priori* simply because it is an investment *abroad*. It also means that money and what is usually even more important management time, energy, and attention will be spent on investigation and data gathering. The next logical step is, therefore, *investigation*. The process of investigation is generally geared to a purpose. Individual investment opportunities are considered on their own merits, rather than as choices among many alternatives. The sequence of the investigation, the variables assumed as fixed, the nature of the data collected and their evaluation, depend to a large extent on the impact of the initiating force. In some cases, the force may have been so strong as to lead to an immediate decision to invest. In these cases the purpose of the investigation is to find a sufficiently good way to implement and execute this earliest decision. In other situations, there will be only a tentative decision to check possibilities. In some instances, much of the relevant data will be presented by the outsider who suggested the investment in the first place. If this is the case, information is collected to evaluate both the data presented and the person presenting them.

The investigation is generally carried out in stages and with various 'check points' built into the process. Depending on the strength of the force which initiated it, the investigation might be stopped at any time when one of these early benchmarks is perceived as unsatisfactory from the organization's point of view, or it might be carried on to find ways to circumvent this unsatisfactory sign. If this second alternative is followed, many conditions that were considered 'given' (such as production methods and techniques, size of the plant, or majority of control) or as *sine qua non* for the investment (such as monopoly in the market) might be changed.

The order of the investigation has therefore a crucial importance. Our field research shows that the first check point will be the 'risk involved'. Risks may be considered excessive because of a multitude of reasons, such as fear of war, a strong belief that the attitude of the foreign government is 'unfriendly to business', fear of expropriation, exchange restrictions, lack of adequate basic services, or labor problems.

Because of the lack of knowledge of foreign countries in general, and the lack of interest in direct foreign investments in particular, there is a general belief that the risks involved in foreign investments, particularly in the less developed countries, are excessive, that the probability of making mistakes is very high, and that such investments would require 'too much' management time. Often, the risks abroad are not specified. When they are enumerated, this is done in general terms and not in terms of their impact on a specific business situation.

If the risks are perceived to be too high and the force triggering the investigation is a weak one, the investigation is stopped. Otherwise, the next step will be taken: some crude idea of the size of the market will be developed. Again, depending on the investigator's perception about the size of the market on the one hand and the evaluation of the strength of the initiating force on the other hand, the investigation may or may not be carried on to check such other variables as cost, availability of labor, and so on.

Because information is not readily available, and because its acquisition is costly, decision makers are compelled to reach tentative conclusions, to operate on the basis of assumptions, and to be ready to alter their line of action or redefine the problem when more information becomes available. Partly because of past history, partly because of this necessarily roundabout way of looking at a problem, the decision maker finds himself engulfed by commitments he himself created, albeit unintentionally. Thus involved and getting in deeper and deeper, he seeks the best way out. The way commitments are created are now briefly discussed.

The decision to invest

It is natural to assume that after the investigation is completed, a report is written and a decision is reached as to whether an investment should be made. Unfortunately, things are not as simple as that. In general, it is virtually impossible to find out at what point and by whom a decision to invest was made. Even in those cases in which such a point can be defined, the decision to invest is not necessarily the last in a chain of decisions, nor is it always the outcome of the investigation process. Sometimes, as we have seen, the decision is made before the investigation begins, and the investigation is carried out with the specific aim of finding an optimal way of implementing it. Quite often, the investigation reveals additional facts and the original decision is changed, or problems are redefined. The investigation usually takes a long time and conditions may change both inside the company and in its environment, although not necessarily in direct connection with the specific project considered. These changes influence the decision process.

Creation of commitments during the investigation

The very fact that an organization is making an investigation creates new commitments. Some of these emerge because money and time are spent; executives apparently find it hard to look at this investment of scarce resources as a sunk cost. They resist the idea of abandoning the project. They feel an urge to persist, to find ways to overcome difficulties and 'to make a go of it'.

Thus, one executive, when asked to estimate the cost of investigation, a foreign investment, added the following revealing comment:

> When the negotiations become complicated, you get in deeper and deeper. You want to protect your initial investment, so you continue. . . . By that time you are stuck and have to go on. You have spent $25,000 and you do not want to lose it, so you invest another $10,000 to continue the negotiations, and then you are in even deeper.

In another case, a concern investigating an investment possibility found it would have to face a welter of problems if it wanted to invest: detailed examination revealed the existence of strong competition, and the foreign government did not agree to any one of the original proposals suggested. The respondent telling the history of the project was frustrated and exasperated. Still, it was crucially important to him to find some way to complete a deal. According to him: 'We had spent a lot of time on this thing and also money from our own pockets – and, having committed so much time and money, we decided to be stubborn.'

Commitments are created not only by financial investments. They may also emerge because of a psychic or social investment. Thus, the fact that a certain group of people – inside or outside the investigating organization – knows that an investigation is being carried on may also cause a feeling of commitment. It may be felt that once an investigation has begun, a decision to reject the investment proposal may create some psychologically or socially undesirable effects. The investigator may feel this will be interpreted as a failure; he may think this will hamper his relations with these people or his social standing among them, or will destroy further deals. The following examples may help to elucidate this point.

Consider first the case of the executive who felt his company should invest in Japan and finally got permission to investigate this possibility. It was only natural that he felt committed to negotiate conditions that would make investment in Japan acceptable to his organization.

An American Jewish businessman was approached by a friend and was asked to join in an investment in Israel. The businessman felt that he could not turn his friend down and began to investigate the details of the project. In the meantime, the friend decided not to go along with the project. The Jewish businessman, however, had made it known in his community that he was considering an investment in Israel. He was frequently asked by his Jewish friends about it. According to him, he simply felt he could not tell them that he had decided to pull out after his friend left. Therefore he decided to persevere.

In other cases, commitments emerged from negotiations with prospective partners or with financial institutions. When a decision is made by an organization, additional entangling situations are created by prior commitments of the organization as a whole and interrelationships among its various members. Each one of the organization's members has to take into account feelings, actions, powers, values and commitments of orders that are not necessarily related to the specific opportunity considered. Modifications have to be made not only to satisfy individual commitments, but also to assuage various members of the organization and to take a host of environmental factors into account. Somebody in the organization decides to invest, usually on the basis of the most cursory information. He tries to influence others by writing reports on or arguing orally the points that rationalize and support his conclusions. Depending upon relationships in the organization, others may or may not agree, often posing several more restraints as conditions for their agreement. Then, an effort is made to incorporate these new requests and point of view into the program. Often, the conclusion is a tentative one: it is agreed to open negotiations with a foreign government, prospective partners, financial institutions – or executives in the company itself – to hammer out a modified version of a project that, again, will help the organization keep as many commitments as possible. The negotiations, in time, may create new commitments and new problems, and a new round of bargaining inside and outside the organization.

When a decision is sought concerning a second foreign investment, the experience gained in the first decision process comes to bear. Gradually, the organization gains experience in foreign operations, and some persons in the organization are assigned roles in a newly created international division. The very creation of a particular division in an organization devoting all its time and energy to international operations creates forces that will drive the organization toward increasing involvement and expansion of this field. Thus an analysis of a decision cannot be separated from the history of the organization, from the personalities and roles of the various participants, or from the continuing stream of activities. It is a stream of events in many dimensions and therefore should be analyzed in terms of a total system that includes the self systems of various persons, the impact of the environment, and the characteristics of the organizational system.

SUMMARY

In summary, a foreign investment decision process is a very complicated social process, involving an intricate structure of attitudes and opinions, social relationships both in and outside the firm, and the way such attitudes, opinions and social relations are changing. It contains various elements of individual and organizational behavior, influenced by the past and the perception of the future as well as by the present. It is composed of a large number of decisions, made by different people at different points in time. The understanding of the final outcome of such a process depends on an understanding of all its stages and parts. The breakdown of this process into neat stages is done just for the convenience of presentation. The reader should keep in mind that in real-life situations these stages are not well defined. They may be blended one into the other; several investigations could be made at the same time by different people or the same person may continue other activities and thus find himself unable to devote as much time as he would like to in this specific investigation; there may be discontinuities in the process, etc. Only if we fully grasp the meaning of all the elements involved and discard any stereotyped notion of a simplified model of decision making can we proceed to observe how actual investment decisions in a busy organization emerge. Only if all the factors in the system are kept in mind can we hope to find some order and logic in what might seem at a first glance to be totally chaotic, and thus labelled as hopelessly 'irrational'. It should be reiterated that a human being is not a mathematical programming machine. He has limited faculties and limited ability to focus his attention. A multiplicity of reasonable alternatives always exist. His priorities in dividing his time and attention among them depend on many factors. The first question that should be posed is therefore: What factors make an organization veer off its 'normal' path and look abroad?

2

International Investment and International Trade in the Product Cycle

Raymond Vernon

Anyone who has sought to understand the shifts in international trade and international investment over the past twenty years has chafed from time to time under an acute sense of the inadequacy of the available analytical tools. While the comparative cost concept and other basic concepts have rarely failed to provide some help, they have usually carried the analyst only a very little way toward adequate understanding. For the most part, it has been necessary to formulate new concepts in order to explore issues such as the strengths and limitations of import substitution in the development process, the implications of common market arrangements for trade and investment, the underlying reasons for the Leontief paradox, and other critical issues of the day.

As theorists have groped for some more efficient tools, there has been a flowering in international trade and capital theory. But the very proliferation of theory has increased the urgency of the search for unifying concepts. It is doubtful that we shall find many propositions that can match the simplicity, power, and universality of application of the theory of comparative advantage and the international equilibrating mechanism; but unless the search for better tools goes on, the usefulness of economic theory for the solution of problems in international trade and capital movements will probably decline.

The present paper deals with one promising line of generalization and synthesis which seems to me to have been somewhat neglected by the main stream of trade theory. It puts less emphasis upon comparative cost doctrine and more upon the timing of innovation, the effects of scale economies, and the roles of ignorance and uncertainty in influencing trade patterns. It is an approach with respectable sponsorship, deriving bits and pieces of its inspiration from the writings of such persons as Williams, Kindleberger, MacDougall, Hoffmeyer, and Burenstam-Linder.[1]

Emphases of this sort seem first to have appeared when economists were searching for an explanation of what looked like a persistent, structural shortage of dollars in the world. When the shortage proved ephemeral in the late 1950s, many of the ideas which the shortage had stimulated were tossed overboard as prima facie wrong.[2] Nevertheless, one cannot be exposed to the main currents of international trade for very long without feeling that any theory which neglected the roles of innovation, scale, ignorance and uncertainty would be incomplete.

Reproduced with permission from *Quarterly Journal of Economics*, 1966, 80, 190–207.

LOCATION OF NEW PRODUCTS

We begin with the assumption that the enterprises in any one of the advanced countries of the world are not distinguishably different from those in any other advanced country, in terms of their access to scientific knowledge and their capacity to comprehend scientific principles.[3] All of them, we may safely assume, can secure access to the knowledge that exists in the physical, chemical and biological sciences. These sciences at times may be difficult, but they are rarely occult.

It is a mistake to assume, however, that equal access to scientific principles in all the advanced countries means equal probability of the application of these principles in the generation of new products. There is ordinarily a large gap between the knowledge of a scientific principle and the embodiment of the principle in a marketable product. An entrepreneur usually has to intervene to accept the risks involved in testing whether the gap can be bridged.

If all entrepreneurs, wherever located, could be presumed to be equally conscious of and equally responsive to all entrepreneurial opportunities, wherever they arose, the classical view of the dominant role of price in resource allocation might be highly relevant. There is good reason to believe, however, that the entrepreneur's consciousness of and responsiveness to opportunity are a function of ease of communication; and further, that ease of communication is a function of geographical proximity.[4] Accordingly, we abandon the powerful simplifying notion that knowledge is a universal free good, and introduce it as an independent variable in the decision to trade or to invest.

The fact that the search for knowledge is an inseparable part of the decision-making process and that relative ease of access to knowledge can profoundly affect the outcome are now reasonably well established through empirical research.[5] One implication of that fact is that producers in any market are more likely to be aware of the possibility of introducing new products in that market than producers located elsewhere would be.

The United States market offers certain unique kinds of opportunities to those who are in a position to be aware of them.

First, the United States market consists of consumers with an average income which is higher (except for a few anomalies like Kuwait) than that in any other national market – twice as high as that of Western Europe, for instance. Wherever there was a chance to offer a new product responsive to wants at high levels of income, this chance would presumably first be apparent to someone in a position to observe the United States market.

Second, the United States market is characterized by high unit labour costs and relatively unrationed capital compared with practically all other markets. This is a fact which conditions the demand for both consumer goods and industrial products. In the case of consumer goods, for instance, the high cost of laundresses contributes to the origins of the drip-dry shirt and the home washing machine. In the case of industrial goods, high labour cost leads to the early development and use of the conveyor belt, the fork-lift truck and the automatic control system. It seems to follow that wherever there was a chance successfully to sell a new product responsive to the need to conserve labour, this chance would be apparent first to those in a position to observe the United States market.

Assume, then, that entrepreneurs in the United States are first aware of opportunities to satisfy new wants associated with high income levels or high unit labour costs. Assume further that the evidence of an unfilled need and the hope of some kind of monopoly windfall for the early starter both are sufficiently strong to justify the initial investment that is usually involved in converting an abstract idea into a marketable product. Here we have a reason for expecting a consistently higher rate of expenditure on product development to be undertaken by United States producers than by producers in other countries, at least in lines which promise to substitute capital for labour or which promise to satisfy high-income wants. Therefore, if United States firms spend more than their foreign counterparts on new product development (often misleadingly labelled 'research'), this may be due not to some obscure sociological drive for innovation but to more effective communication between the potential market and the potential supplier of the market. This sort of explanation is consistent with the pioneer appearance in the United States (conflicting claims of the Soviet Union notwithstanding) of the sewing machine, the typewriter, the tractor, etc.

At this point in the exposition, it is important once more to emphasize that the discussion so far relates only to innovation in certain kinds of products, namely to those associated with high income and those which substitute capital for labour. Our hypothesis says nothing about industrial innovation in general; this is a larger subject than we have tackled here. There are very few countries that have failed to introduce at least a few products; and there are some, such as Germany and Japan, which have been responsible for a considerable number of such introductions. Germany's outstanding successes in the development and use of plastics may have been due, for instance, to a traditional concern with her lack of a raw materials base, and a recognition that a market might exist in Germany for synthetic substitutes.[6]

Our hypothesis asserts that United States producers are likely to be the first to spy an opportunity for high-income or labour-saving new products.[7] But it goes on to assert that the first producing facilities for such products will be located in the United States. This is not a self-evident proposition. Under the calculus of least cost, production need not automatically take place at a location close to the market, unless the product can be produced and delivered from that location at lowest cost. Besides, now that most major United States companies control facilities situated in one or more locations outside of the United States, the possibility of considering a non-United States location is even more plausible than it might once have been.

Of course, if prospective producers were to make their locational choices on the basis of least-cost considerations, the United States would not always be ruled out. The costs of international transport and United States import duties, for instance, might be so high as to argue for such a location. My guess is, however, that the early producers of a new product intended for the United States market are attracted to a United States location by forces which are far stronger than relative factor-cost and transport considerations. For the reasoning on this point, one has to take a long detour away from comparative cost analysis into areas which fall under the rubrics of communication and external economies.

By now, a considerable amount of empirical work has been done on the factors affecting the location of industry.[8] Many of these studies try to explain observed locational patterns in conventional cost-minimizing terms, by implicit or explicit reference to labour cost and transportation cost. But some explicitly introduce problems of communication and external economies as powerful locational forces. These factors were given special emphasis in the analyses which were a part of the New York Metropolitan Region Study of the 1950s. At the risk of oversimplifying, I shall try to summarize what these studies suggested.[9]

In the early stages of introduction of a new product, producers were usually confronted with a number of critical, albeit transitory, conditions. For one thing, the product itself may be quite unstandardized for a time; its inputs, its processing, and its final specifications may cover a wide range. Contrast the great variety of automobiles produced and marketed before

1910 with the thoroughly standardized product of the 1930s, or the variegated radio designs of the 1920s with the uniform models of the 1930s. The unstandardized nature of the design at this early stage carries with it a number of locational implications.

First, producers at this stage are particularly concerned with the degree of freedom they have in changing their inputs. Of course, the cost of the inputs is also relevant. But as long as the nature of these inputs cannot be fixed in advance with assurance, the calculation of cost must take into account the general need for flexibility in any locational choice.[10]

Second, the price elasticity of demand for the output of individual firms is comparatively low. This follows from the high degree of production differentiation, or the existence of monopoly in the early stages.[11] One result is, of course, that small cost differences count less in the calculations of the entrepreneur than they are likely to count later on.

Third, the need for swift and effective communication on the part of the producer with customers, suppliers, and even competitors is especially high at this stage. This is a corollary of the fact that a considerable amount of uncertainty remains regarding the ultimate dimensions of the market, the efforts of rivals to pre-empt that market, the specifications of the inputs needed for production, and the specifications of the products likely to be most successful in the effort.

All of these considerations tend to argue for a location in which communication between the market and the executives directly concerned with the new product is swift and easy, and in which a wide variety of potential types of input that might be needed by the production unit are easily come by. In brief, the producer who sees a market for some new product in the United States may be led to select a United States location for production on the basis of national locational considerations which extend well beyond simple factor cost analysis plus transport considerations.

THE MATURING PRODUCT[12]

As the demand for a product expands, a certain degree of standardization usually takes place. this is not to say that efforts at product differentiation come to an end. On the contrary; such efforts may even intensify, as competitors try to avoid the full brunt of price competition. Moreover, variety may appear as a result of specialization. Radios, for instance, ultimately acquired such specialized forms as clock radios, automobile radios, portable radios, and so on. Nevertheless, though the subcategories may multiply and the efforts at product differentiation increase, a growing acceptance of certain general standards seems to be typical.

Once again, the change has locational implications. First of all, the need for flexibility declines. A commitment to some set of product standards opens up technical possibilities for achieving economies of scale through mass output, and encourages long-term commitments to some given process and some fixed set of facilities. Second, concern about production cost begins to take the place of concern about product characteristics. Even if increased price competition is not yet present, the reduction of the uncertainties surrounding the operation enhances the usefulness of cost projections and increases the attention devoted to cost.

The empirical studies to which I referred earlier suggest that, at this stage in an industry's development, there is likely to be considerable shift in the location of production facilities at least as far as internal United States locations are concerned. The empirical materials on international locational shifts simply have not yet been analysed sufficiently to tell us very much. A little speculation, however, indicates some hypotheses worth testing.

Picture an industry engaged in the manufacture of the high-income or labour-saving products that are the focus of our discussion. Assume that the industry has begun to settle down in the United States to some degree of large-scale production. Although the first mass market may be located in the United States, some demand for the product begins almost at once to appear elsewhere. For instance, although heavy fork-lift trucks in general may have a comparatively small market in Spain because of the relative cheapness of unskilled labour in that country, some limited demand for the product will appear there almost as soon as the existence of the product is known.

If the product has a high income elasticity of demand or if it is a satisfactory substitute for high-cost labour, the demand in time will begin to grow quite rapidly in relatively advanced countries such as those of Western Europe. Once the market expands in such an advanced country, entrepreneurs will begin to ask themselves whether the time has come to take the risk of setting up a local producing facility.[13]

How long does it take to reach this stage? An adequate answer must surely be a complex one. Producers located in the United States, weighing the wisdom of setting up a new production facility in the importing country, will feel obliged to balance a number of complex considerations. As long as the marginal production cost plus the transport cost of the goods exported from the United States is lower than the average cost of prospective production in the market of import, United States producers will presumably prefer to avoid an investment. But that calculation depends on the producer's ability to project the cost of production in a market in which factor costs and the appropriate technology differ from those at home.

Now and again, the locational force which determined some particular overseas investment is so simple and so powerful that one has little difficulty in identifying it. Otis Elevator's early proliferation of production facilities abroad was quite patently a function of the high cost of shipping assembled elevator cabins to distant locations and the limited scale advantages involved in manufacturing elevator cabins at a single location.[14] Singer's decision to invest in Scotland as early as 1867 was also based on considerations of a sort sympathetic with our hypothesis.[15] It is not unlikely that the overseas demand for its highly standardized product was already sufficiently large at that time to exhaust the obvious scale advantages of manufacturing in a single location, especially if that location was one of high labour cost.

In an area as complex and 'imperfect' as international trade and investment, however, one ought not anticipate that any hypothesis will have more than a limited explanatory power. United States airplane manufacturers surely respond to many 'non-economic' locational forces, such as the desire to play safe in problems of military security. Producers in the United States who have a protected patent position overseas presumably take that fact into account in deciding whether or when to produce abroad. And other producers often are motivated by considerations too complex to reconstruct readily, such as the fortuitous timing of a threat of new competition in the country of import, the level of tariff protection anticipated for the future, the political situation in the country of prospective investment and so on.

We arrive, then, at the stage at which United States producers have come around to the establishment of production units in the advanced countries. Now a new group of forces is set in train. In an idealized form, Figure 1 suggests what may be anticipated next.

As far as individual United States producers are concerned, the local markets thenceforth will be filled from local production units set up abroad. Once these facilities are in operation, however, more ambitious possibilities for their use may be suggested. When comparing a United States producing facility and a facility in another advanced country, the obvious production-cost differences between the rival producing areas are usually differences due to scale and differences due to labour costs. If the producer is an international firm with producing locations in several countries, its costs of financing capital at the different locations may not be sufficiently different to matter very much. If economies of scale are being fully exploited, the principal differences between any two locations are likely to be labour costs.[16] Accordingly, it may prove wise for the international firm to begin servicing third-country markets from the new location. And if labour cost differences are large enough to offset transport costs, then exports back to the United States may become a possibility as well.

Any hypotheses based on the assumption that the United States entrepreneur will react rationally when offered the possibility of a lower-cost location abroad is, of course, somewhat suspect. The decision-making sequence that is used in connection with international investments, according to various empirical studies, is not a model of the rational process.[17] But there is one theme that emerges again and again in such studies. Any threat to the established position of an enterprise is a powerful galvanizing force to action; in fact, if I interpret the empirical work correctly, threat in general is a more reliable stimulus to action than opportunity is likely to be.

In the international investment field, threats appear in various forms once a large-scale export business in manufactured products has developed. Local entrepreneurs located in the countries which are the targets of these exports grow restive at the opportunities they are missing. Local governments concerned with generating employment or promoting growth or balancing their trade accounts begin thinking of ways and means to replace the imports. An international investment by the exporter, therefore, becomes a prudent means of forestalling the loss of a market. In this case, the yield on the investment is seen largely as the avoidance of a loss of income to the system.

The notion that a threat to the status quo is a powerful galvanizing force for international investment also seems to explain what happens after the initial investment. Once such an investment is made by a United States producer, other major producers in the United States sometimes see it as a threat to the status quo. They see themselves as losing position relative to the investing company, with vague intimations of further losses to come. Their 'share of the market' is imperilled, viewing 'share of the market' in global terms. At the same time, their ability to estimate the production-cost structure of their competitors, operating far away in an unfamiliar foreign area, is impaired; this is a particularly unsettling state because it conjures up the possibility of a return flow of products to the United States and a new source of price competition, based on cost differences of unknown magnitude. The uncertainty can be reduced by emulating the pathfinding investor and by investing in the same area; this may not be an optimizing investment pattern and it may be costly, but it is least disturbing to the status quo.

Pieces of this hypothetical pattern are subject to empirical tests of a sort. So far, at any rate, the empirical tests have been reassuring. The office machinery industry, for instance, has seen repeatedly the phenomenon of the introduction of a new product in the United States, followed by United States exports,[18] followed still later by United States imports. (We have still to test whether the timing of the commencement of overseas production by United States subsidiaries fits into the expected pattern.) In the electrical and electronic products industry, those elements in the pattern which can be measured show up nicely.[19] A broader effort is now under way to test the United States trade patterns of a group of products with high income elasticities; and, here too, the preliminary results are encouraging.[20] On a much more general basis, it is reassuring for our hypotheses to observe that the foreign manufacturing subsidiaries of United States have been increasing their exports to third countries.

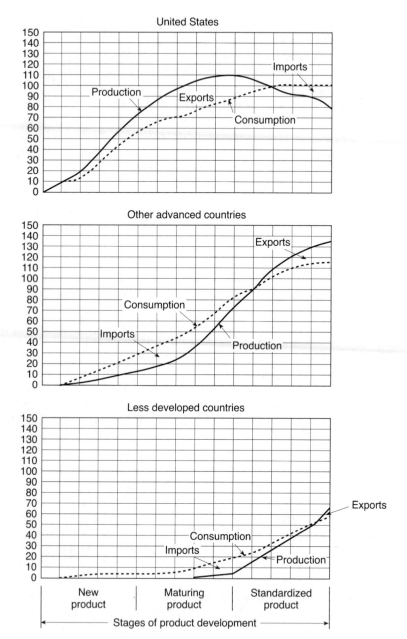

Fig. 1. Development of Production Units.

It will have occurred to the reader by now that the pattern envisaged here also may shed some light on the Leontief paradox.[21] Leontief, it will be recalled, seemed to confound comparative cost theory by establishing the fact that the ratio of capital to labour in United States exports was lower, not higher, than the like ratio in the United States production which had been displaced by competitive imports. The hypothesis suggested in this paper would have the United States exporting high-income and labour-saving products in the early stages of their existence, and importing them later on.[22] In the early stages, the value-added contribution of industries engaged in producing these items probably contains an unusually high proportion of labour cost. This is not so much because the labour is particularly skilled, as is so often suggested. More likely, it is due to a quite different phenomenon. At this stage, the standardization of the manufacturing process has not got very far; that is to come later, when the volume of output is high enough and the degree of uncertainty low enough to justify investment in relatively inflexible, capital-intensive facilities. As a result, the production process relies relatively heavily on labour inputs at a time when the United States commands an export position; and the process relies more heavily on capital at a time when imports become important.

This, of course, is an hypothesis which has not yet been subjected to any really rigorous test. But it does open up a line of inquiry into the structure of United States trade which is well worth pursuing.

THE STANDARDIZED PRODUCT

Figure 1, the reader will have observed, carries a panel which suggests that, at an advanced stage in the standardization of some products, the less-developed countries may offer competitive advantages as a production location.

This is a bold projection, which seems on first blush to be wholly at variance with the Heckscher-Ohlin theorem. According to that theorem, one presumably ought to anticipate that the exports of the less-developed countries would tend to be relatively labour-intensive products.

One of the difficulties with the theorem, however, is that it leaves marketing considerations out of account. One reason for the omission is evident. As long as knowledge is regarded as a free good, instantaneously available, and as long as individual producers are regarded as atomistic contributors to the total supply, marketing problems cannot be expected to find much of a place in economic theory. In projecting the patterns of export from less-developed areas, however, we cannot afford to disregard the fact that information comes at a cost; and that entrepreneurs are not readily disposed to pay the price of investigating overseas markets of unknown dimensions and unknown promise. Neither are they eager to venture into situations which they know will demand a constant flow of reliable marketing information from remote sources.

If we can assume that highly standardized products tend to have a well-articulated, easily accessible international market and to sell largely on the basis of price (an assumption inherent in the definition), then it follows that such products will not pose the problem of market information quite so acutely for the less-developed countries. This establishes a necessary if not a sufficient condition for investment in such industries.

Of course, foreign investors seeking an optimum location for a captive facility may not have to concern themselves too much with questions of market information; presumably, they are thoroughly familiar with the marketing end of the business and are looking for a low-cost captive source of supply. In that case, the low cost of labour may be the initial attraction drawing the investor to less-developed areas. But other limitations in such areas, according to our hypothesis, will bias such captive operations toward the production of standardized items. The reasons in this case turn on the part played in the production process by external economies. Manufacturing processes which receive significant inputs from the local economy, such as skilled labour, repairmen, reliable power, spare parts, industrial materials processed according to exacting specification, and so on, are less appropriate to the less-developed areas than those that do not have such requirements. Unhappily, most industrial processes require one or another ingredient of this difficult sort. My guess is, however, that the industries which produce a standardized product are in the best position to avoid the problem, by producing on a vertically-integrated self-sustaining basis.

In speculating about future industrial exports from the less-developed areas, therefore, we are led to think of products with a fairly clear-cut set of economic characteristics.[23] Their production function is such as to require significant inputs of labour; otherwise there is no reason to expect a lower production cost in less-developed countries. At the same time, they are products with a high price elasticity of demand for the output of individual firms; otherwise, there is no strong incentive to take the risks of pioneering with production in a new area. In addition, products whose production process did not rely heavily upon external economies would be more obvious candidates than those which required a more elaborate industrial environment. The implications of remoteness also would be critical; products which could be precisely described by standardized specifications and which could be produced for inventory without fear of obsolescence would be more relevant than those which had less precise specifications and which could not easily be ordered from remote locations. Moreover, high-value items capable of absorbing significant freight costs would be more likely to appear than bulky items low in value by weight. Standardized textile products are, of course, the illustration par excellence of the sort of product that meets the criteria. But other products come to mind such as crude steel, simple fertilizers, newsprint, and so on.

Speculation of this sort draws some support from various interregional experiences in industrial location. In the United States, for example, the 'export' industries which moved to the low-wage south in search of lower costs tended to be industries which had no great need for a sophisticated industrial environment and which produced fairly standardized products. In the textile industry, it was the grey goods, cotton sheetings and men's shirt plants that went south; producers of high-style dresses or other unstandardized items were far more reluctant to move. In the electronics industry, it was the mass producers of tubes, resistors and other standardized high-volume components that showed the greatest disposition to move south; custom-built and research-oriented production remained closer to markets and to the main industrial complexes. A similar pattern could be discerned in printing and in chemicals production.[24]

In other countries, a like pattern is suggested by the impressionistic evidence. The underdeveloped south of Italy and the laggard north of Britain and Ireland both seem to be attracting industry with standardized output and self-sufficient process.[25]

Once we begin to look for relevant evidence of such investment patterns in the less-developed countries proper, however, only the barest shreds of corroboratory information can be found. One would have difficulty in thinking of many cases in which manufacturers of standardized products in the more advanced countries had made significant investments in the less-developed countries with a view of exporting such products from those countries. To be sure, other types of foreign investment are not uncommon in the less-developed countries, such as investments in import-replacing industries which were made in the face of a threat of import restriction. But there are only a few export-oriented cases similar to that of Taiwan's foreign-owned electronics plants and Argentina's new producing facility, set up to manufacture and export standard sorting equipment for computers.

If we look to foreign trade patterns, rather than foreign investment patterns, to learn something about the competitive advantage of the less-developed countries, the possibility that they are an attractive locus for the output of standardized products gains slightly more support. The Taiwanese and Japanese trade performances are perhaps the most telling ones in support of the projected pattern; both countries have managed to develop significant overseas markets for standardized manufactured products. According to one major study of the subject (a study stimulated by the Leontief paradox), Japanese exports are more capital-intensive than is the Japanese production which is displaced by imports;[26] this is what one might expect if the hypothetical patterns suggested by Figure 1 were operational. Apart from these cases, however, all that one sees are a few provocative successes such as some sporadic sales of newsprint from Pakistan, the successful export of sewing machines from India, and so on. Even in these cases, one cannot be sure that they are consistent with the hypothesis unless he has done a good deal more empirical investigation.

The reason why so few relevant cases come to mind may be that the process has not yet advanced far enough. Or it may be that such factors as extensive export constraints and overvalued exchange rates are combining to prevent the investment and exports that otherwise would occur.

If there is one respect in which this discussion may deviate from classical expectations, it is in the view that the overall scarcity of capital in the less-developed countries will not prevent investment in facilities for the production of standardized products.

There are two reasons why capital costs may not prove a barrier to such investment.

First, according to our hypotheses, the investment will occur in industries which require some significant labour inputs in the production process; but they will be concentrated in that subsector of the industry which produces highly standardized products capable of self-contained production establishments. The net of these specifications is indeterminate so far as capital-intensiveness is concerned. A standardized textile item may be more or less capital-intensive than a plant for unstandardized petro-chemicals.

Besides, even if the capital requirements for a particular plant are heavy, the cost of the capital need not prove a bar. The assumption that capital costs come high in the less-developed countries requires a number of fundamental qualifications. The reality, to the extent that it is known, is more complex.

One reason for this complexity is the role played by the international investor. Producers of chemical fertilizers, when considering whether to invest in a given country, may be less concerned with the going rate for capital in that country than with their opportunity costs as they see such costs. For such investors the alternatives to be weighed are not the full range of possibilities calling for capital but only a very restricted range of alternatives, such as the possibilities offered by chemical fertilizer investment elsewhere. The relevant capital cost for a chemical fertilizer plant, therefore, may be fairly low if the investor is an international entrepreneur.

Moreover, the assumption that finance capital is scarce and that interest rates are high in a less-developed country may prove inapplicable to the class of investors who concern us here.[27] The capital markets of the less-developed countries typically consist of a series of water-tight, insulated, submarkets in which wholly different rates prevail and between which arbitrage opportunities are limited. In some countries, the going figures may vary from 5 to 40 per cent, on grounds which seem to have little relation to issuer risk or term of loan. (In some economies, where inflation is endemic, interest rates which in effect represent a negative real cost are not uncommon.)

These internal differences in interest rates may be due to a number of factors: the fact that funds generated inside the firm usually are exposed to a different yield test than external borrowings; the fact that government loans are often floated by mandatory levies on banks and other intermediaries; and the fact that funds borrowed by governments from international sources are often re-loaned in domestic markets at rates which are linked closely to the international borrowing rate, however irrelevant that may be. Moreover, one has to reckon with the fact that public international lenders tend to lend at near-uniform rates, irrespective of the identity of the borrower and the going interest rate in his country. Access to capital on the part of underdeveloped countries, therefore, becomes a direct function of the country's capacity to propose plausible projects to public international lenders. If a project can plausibly be shown to 'pay its own way' in balance-of-payment and output terms at 'reasonable' interest rates, the largest single obstacle to obtaining capital at such rates has usually been overcome.

Accordingly, one may say that from the entrepreneur's viewpoint certain systematic and predictable 'imperfections' of the capital markets may reduce or eliminate the capital-shortage handicap which is characteristic of the less-developed countries; and, further, that as a result of the reduction or elimination such countries may find themselves in a position to compete effectively in the export of certain standardized capital-intensive goods. This is not the statement of another paradox; it is not the same as to say that the capital-poor countries will develop capital-intensive economies. All we are concerned with here is a modest fraction of the industry of such countries, which in turn is a minor fraction of their total economic activity. It may be that the anomalies such industries represent are systematic enough to be included in our normal expectations regarding conditions in the less-developed countries.

Like the other observations which have preceded, these views about the likely patterns of exports by the less-developed countries are attempts to relax some of the constraints imposed by purer and simpler models. Here and there, the hypotheses take on plausibility because they jibe with the record of past events. But, for the most part, they are still speculative in nature, having been subjected to tests of a very low order of rigorousness. What is needed, obviously, is continued probing to determine whether the 'imperfections' stressed so strongly in these pages deserve to be elevated out of the footnotes into the main text of economic theory.

NOTES

The preparation of this article was financed in part by a grant from the Ford Foundation to the Harvard Business School to support a study of the implications of United States foreign direct investment. This paper is a by-product of the hypothesis-building stage of the study.

1. J. H. Williams, 'The Theory of International Trade Reconsidered,' reprinted as Chap. 2 in his *Postwar Monetary Plans and Other Essays*. (Oxford: Basil Blackwell, 1947); C. P. Kindleberger, *The Dollar Shortage* (New York: Wiley, 1950); Erik Hoffmeyer, *Dollar Shortage*. (Amsterdam: North-Holland, 1958); Sir Donald MacDougall, *The World Dollar Problem*. (London: Macmillan, 1957); Staffan Burenstam-Linder, *An Essay on Trade and Transformation* (Uppsala: Almqvist & Wicksells, 1961).

2. The best summary of the state of trade theory that has come to my attention in recent years is J. Bhagwati, 'The Pure Theory of International Trade,' *Economic Journal*, LXXIV (Mar. 1964), 1–84. Bhagwati refers obliquely to some of the theories which concern us here; but they receive much less attention than I think they deserve.

3. Some of the account that follows will be found in greatly truncated form in my 'The Trade Expansion Act in Perspective,' in *Emerging Concepts in Marketing*, Proceedings of the American Marketing Association, December 1962, pp. 384–89. The elaboration here owes a good deal to the perceptive work of Se'ev Hirsch, summarized in his unpublished doctoral thesis, 'Location of Industry and International Competitiveness,' Harvard Business School, 1965.

4. Note C. P. Kindleberger's reference to the 'horizon' of the decision-maker, and the view that he can only be rational within that horizon; see his *Foreign Trade and The National Economy* (New Haven: Yale University Press, 1962), p. 15 *passim*.

5. See, for instance, Richard M. Cyert and James G. March, *A Behavioral Theory of the Firm* (Englewood Cliffs, N.J.: Prentice-Hall, 1963), esp. Chap. 6; and Yair Aharoni, *The Foreign Investment Decision Process*, to be published by the Division of Research of the Harvard Business School, 1966.

6. See two excellent studies: C. Freeman, 'The Plastics Industry: A Comparative Study of Research and Innovation,' in *National Institute Economic Review*, No. 26 (Nov. 1963), p. 22 *et seq.*; G. C. Hufbauer, *Synthetic Materials and the Theory of International Trade* (London: Gerald Duckworth, 1965). A number of links in the Hufbauer arguments are remarkably similar to some in this paper; but he was not aware of my writings nor I of his until after both had been completed.

7. There is a kind of first-cousin relationship between this simple notion and the 'entrained want' concept defined by H. G. Barnett in *Innovation: The Basis of Cultural Change* (New York: McGraw-Hill, 1953), p. 148. Albert O. Hirschman, *The Strategy of Economic Department* (New Haven: Yale University Press, 1958), p. 68, also finds the concept helpful in his effort to explain certain aspects of economic development.

8. For a summary of such work, together with a useful bibliography, see John Meyer, 'Regional Economics: A Survey,' in the *American Economic Review*, LIII (Mar. 1963), 19–54.

9. The points that follow are dealt with at length in the following publications: Raymond Vernon, *Metropolis, 1985* (Cambridge: Harvard University Press, 1960), pp. 38–85; Max Hall (ed.), *Made in New York* (Cambridge: Harvard University Press, 1959), pp. 3–18, 19 *passim*; Robert M. Lichtenberg, *One-Tenth of a Nation* (Cambridge: Harvard University Press, 1960), pp. 31–70.

10. This is, of course, a familiar point elaborated in George F. Stigler, 'Production and Distribution in the Short Run,' *Journal of Political Economy*, XLVII (June 1939), 305, *et seq.*

11. Hufbauer, *op. cit.*, suggests that the low price elasticity of demand in the first stage may be due simply to the fact that the first market may be a 'captive market' unresponsive to price changes; but that later, in order to expand the use of the new product, other markets may be brought in which are more price responsive.

12. Both Hirsch, *op. cit.*, and Freeman, *op. cit.*, make use of a three-stage product classification of the sort used here.

13. M. V. Posner, 'International Trade and Technical Change,' *Oxford Economic Papers*, Vol. 13 (Oct. 1961), p. 323, *et seq.* presents a stimulating model purporting to explain such familiar trade phenomena as the exchange of machine tools between the United Kingdom and Germany. In the process he offers some particularly helpful notions concerning the size of the 'imitation lag' in the responses of competing nations.

14. Dudley M. Phelps, *Migration of Industry to South America* (New York: McGraw-Hill, 1963), p. 4.

15. John H. Dunning, *American Investment in British Manufacturing Industry* (London: George Allen & Unwin, 1958), p. 18. The Dunning book is filled with observations that lend casual support to the main hypotheses of this paper.

16. Note the interesting finding of Mordecai Kreinin in his 'The Leontief Scarce-Factor Paradox,' *The American Economic Review*, LV (Mar. 1965), 131–39. Kreinin finds that the higher cost of labour in the United States is not explained by a higher rate of labour productivity in this country.

17. Aharoni, *op. cit.*, provides an excellent summary and exhaustive bibliography of the evidence on this point.

18. Reported in U.S. Senate, Interstate and Foreign Commerce Committee, *Hearings on Foreign Commerce*, 1960, pp. 130–39.

19. See Hirsch, *op. cit.*

20. These are to appear in a forthcoming doctoral thesis at the Harvard Business School by Louis T. Wells, tentatively entitled 'International Trade and Business Policy'.

21. See Wassily Leontief, 'Domestic Production and Foreign Trade: The American Capital Position Re-examined,' *Proceedings of the American Philosophical Society*, Vol. 97 (Sept. 1953), and 'Factor Proportions and the Structure of American Trade: Further Theoretical and Empirical Analysis,' *Review of Economics and Statistics*, XXXVIII (Nov. 1956).

22. Of course, if there were some systematic trend in the inputs of new products – for example, if the new products which appeared in the 1960s were more capital-intensive than the new products which appeared in the 1950s – then the tendencies suggested by our hypotheses might be swamped by such a trend. As long as we do not posit offsetting systematic patterns of this sort, however, the Leontief findings and the hypotheses offered here seem consistent.

23. The concepts sketched out here are presented in more detail in my 'Problems and Prospects in the Export of Manufactured Products from the Less-developed Countries,' U.N. Conference on Trade and Development, Dec. 16, 1963 (mimeo.).

24. This conclusion derives largely from the industry studies conducted in connection with the New York Metropolitan Region study. There have been some excellent more general analyses of shifts in industrial location among the regions of the United States. See e.g., Victor R. Fuchs, *Changes in the Location of Manufacturing in the United States Since 1929* (New Haven: Yale University Press, 1962). Unfortunately, however, none has been designed, so far as I know, to test hypotheses relating locational shifts to product characteristics such as price elasticity of demand and degree of standardization.

25. This statement, too, is based on only impressionistic materials. Among the more suggestive, illustrative of the best of the available evidence, see J. N. Toothill, *Inquiry into the Scottish Economy* (Edinburgh: Scottish Council, 1962).

26. M. Tatemoto and S. Ichimura, 'Factor Proportions and Foreign Trade: the Case of Japan,' *Review of Economics and Statistics*, XLI (Nov. 1959), 442–46.

27. See George Rosen, *Industrial Change in India* (Glencoe, Ill.: Free Press, 1958). Rosen finds that in the period studied from 1937 to 1953, 'there was no serious shortage of capital for the largest firms in India.' Gustav F. Papanek makes a similar finding for Pakistan for the period from 1950 to 1964 in a book about to be published.

3

The Internationalization of the Firm:
Four Swedish Cases[1]

Jan Johanson and Finn Wiedersheim-Paul

INTRODUCTION

The widespread interest in multinational firms has given rise to many articles and books on various aspects of the international strategies of firms. Research has been concentrated on the large corporations, particularly the American.

Many firms, however, start international operations when they are still comparatively small and gradually develop their operations abroad. From our studies of international business at the University of Uppsala we have several observations indicating that this gradual internationalization, rather than large, spectacular foreign investments, is characteristic of the internationalization process of most Swedish firms. It seems reasonable to believe that the same holds true for many firms from other countries with small domestic markets. A related observation is that the type of development during the early stages is of importance for the following pattern. Similar observations have also been made about US firms and have been used as an argument in discussions of foreign investments and international marketing.[2]

In this paper we describe and analyse the internationalization of four Swedish firms – Sandvik, Atlas Copco, Facit and Volvo. All of them sell more than two-thirds of their turnover abroad and have production facilities in more than one foreign country. In Sweden[3] they are often used as examples and patterns in discussions of international operations. Usually such discussions only treat the operations of the firms during later years when they have already become large and international. Here we adopt a more longitudinal approach, describing and discussing the whole development which has led to their present international position.

Before the case descriptions we give an account of our view of the internationalization process, on which these descriptions are based, and discuss some patterns which follow from this view. In the concluding section we discuss some similarities and differences between the firms with respect to the internationalization.

THE INTERNATIONALIZATION PROCESS

The term international usually refers to either an attitude of the firm towards foreign activities or to the actual carrying out of activities abroad.[4] Of course there is a close relationship between attitudes and actual behaviour. The attitudes are the basis for decisions to undertake international ventures and the experiences from international activities influence these attitudes. In the case descriptions we have to concentrate on those aspects of the internationalization that are easy to observe, that is the international activities. We consider, however, these attitudes as interesting and important and the discussion of the internationalization process is basically an account of the interaction between attitudes and actual behaviour.

Our basic assumption is that the firm first develops in the domestic market[5] and that the internationalization is the consequence of a series of incremental decisions. We also assume that the most important obstacles to internationalization are lack of knowledge and resources. These obstacles are reduced through incremental decision-making and learning about the foreign markets and operations. The perceived risk of market investments decreases and the continued internationalization is stimulated by the increased need to control sales and the increased exposure to offers and demands to extend the operations. We are not trying to explain why firms start exporting[6] but assume that, because of lack of knowledge about foreign countries and a propensity to avoid uncertainty, the firm starts exporting to neighbouring countries or countries that are comparatively well-known and similar with regard to business practices etc. We also believe that the firm starts selling abroad via independent representatives, as this means a smaller resource commitment than the establishment of a sales subsidiary.[7]

Considering the development of operations in individual countries we expect a stepwise extension of operations. Of course it is possible to identify different types of steps and a different number of stages. We have chosen to distinguish between four different stages. They are:

1. no regular export activities
2. export via independent representatives (agent)
3. sales subsidiary and
4. production/manufacturing

We think these stages are important because

(a) they are different with regard to the degree of involvement of the firm in the market
(b) they are often referred to by people in business.

There are two aspects about the degree of involvement. The four stages mean successively larger resource commitments and they also lead to quite different market experiences and information for the firm. The first means that the firm has made no commitment of resources to the market and that it lacks any regular information channel to and from the market. The second means that the firm has a channel to the market through which it gets fairly regular information about sales influencing factors. It also means a certain commitment to the market. The third means a controlled information channel to the market, giving the firm ability to direct the type and amount of information flowing from the market to the firm. During this stage the firm also gets direct experience of resource influencing factors. The fourth stage means a still larger resource commitment.

We call the sequence of stages, mentioned above, the *establishment chain*.[8] We have, of course, simplified the matter somewhat by exaggerating the differences between the four steps. It is not always obvious whether a firm has established relations with an agent or not, while a joint venture with an earlier representative can be placed in the second or the third stage, etc.

Of course we do not expect the development always to follow the whole chain. First, several markets are not large enough for the resource demanding stages. Second, we could expect jumps in the establishment chain in firms with extensive experience from other foreign markets.

Considering the extension of activities to new markets, it is possible that the concept of psychic distance may prove useful.[9] This concept is defined as factors preventing or disturbing the flows of information between firms and market. Examples of such factors are differences in language, culture, political systems, level of education, level of industrial development, etc. For obvious reasons, psychic distance is correlated with geographic distance. But exceptions are easy to find. Some countries in the British Commonwealth are far apart geographically, e.g. England and Australia, but for different reasons they are near to each other in terms of psychic distance. The USA and Cuba are near to each other geographically, but, for political reasons, far apart with regard to psychic distance. As these examples indicate, psychic distance is not constant. It changes because of the development of the communication system, trade and other kinds of social exchange. In general we expect most changes to take place rather slowly.[10]

Psychic distance, however, is of course not the only important factor for international operations. In most textbooks about international business the size of the potential market is considered the most important factor for international operations. 'The first activity phase of export planning then, is identifying and measuring market opportunity.'[11] Thus we should expect that market size influences decisions in the internationalization process. We could expect either that the firm first starts operations in countries with large markets or that they prefer to start in smaller markets. In the latter case the argument may be that small markets are more similar to the domestic Swedish market and require a smaller initial resource commitment or have less competitive domestic industries.

But there are reasons to expect that the patterns of agency establishment differ from those of sales subsidiary establishments with respect to the two factors. The agency establishments, according to our view, are made primarily during the early stages of internationalization, which means that they could be expected to be more closely related to psychic distance than to the size of the market. The sales subsidiary establishments – and still more production – could be expected to be influenced primarily by the market size as it generally requires a larger minimum resource commitment than an independent representative. The production establishments are influenced by different forces; on one hand, by psychic distance, on the other, by factors such as, e.g. tariffs, non-tariff barriers and transport costs. As a result it is hard to observe any correlation between psychic distance and production establishments.

A third pattern which could be expected is that after the establishment of the first agency a phase follows when agencies are established in several markets. In the same way we could expect a separate phase dominated by the establishment of sales subsidiaries in several markets. Last, a phase with the establishment of production in several markets will follow. We assume that the three different phases in the internationalization of the firm are dependent on the development of the activity knowledge and the organizational structure of the firm. During the agent phase the firm builds an export department with the capability and responsibility for the establishment and maintenance of agencies. Establishment of sales subsidiaries means that units for the control of subsidiaries are organized. In the last phase, units for coordination of production and marketing in different countries are developed.

It should be noted that the discussion so far has dealt exclusively with the development of the marketing side of the firm. We do not regard this as a serious limitation. Marketing operations in this sense are predominant among the international activities of at least the Swedish firms.[12] Furthermore it has been shown that the marketing side is often a determining factor in the development of the firm.[13] Last, a similar development is likely when internationalization takes place on the purchasing side of the firm.[14]

THE INTERNATIONALIZATION PROCESS – FOUR CASES

Here we describe the internationalization of the four firms Sandvik, Atlas Copco, Facit and Volvo. The descriptions are based on various types of published data[15] about the firms which have been checked and supplemented by interviews with the firms. As we said before, we have chosen to use the moments when a firm establishes agencies, a sales subsidiary and production facilities as key factors in the process of internationalization. It has been possible to identify these moments with fairly high accuracy in most cases.

In order to help the reader we have constructed diagrams illustrating the 'establishment profiles' of the firms. These profiles show when the firm has started operations in twenty national markets. To standardize the case descriptions the countries are the same for all cases.

The analysis of the establishment patterns is based on a ranking of countries according to psychic distance.[16] As mentioned above, we believe that the psychic distance changes very slowly. Thus the rank order of countries according to the present psychic distance from Sweden, which is given in the 'establishment profiles' with a few exceptions, reflects the psychic distance fairly accurately even when the internationalization has taken a long time, as in our cases.

In order to compare the relations between establishments and the two kinds of market characteristics, we used a very crude indicator of market size, GNP 1960. As it is only used for the ranking of countries we do not think this crudeness is of much importance. Most market size indicators are fairly well correlated with GNP which also changes rather slowly.

Sandvik AB

Steel production in Sandviken started in 1862 in order to exploit the Bessemer process. During the first years the product line consisted mainly of industrial raw material: pig iron, ingot and blanks. These products became successively less important and were replaced by more manufactured special steel products, like cold-rolled strips, wire, tubes and saws; product groups that are still very important for Sandvik. In 1910 production of steel conveyors was started and in the 1940s hard metal products were introduced. The latter have been of great significance for the development of the firm during the last decades. At present about 40 per cent of the turnover comes from this product group and Sandvik is one of the biggest producers of hard metal products in the world. Another type of product which has been introduced during the 1960s is alloys used in nuclear reactors.

Of the four firms described Sandvik is the oldest and also the one which first started its internationalization course. The first contacts with representatives were established in the 1860s. Sandvik's early start with representatives in foreign countries was an innovation at that time. Until then the Swedish iron and steel exporting had mainly been undertaken by trading firms. A probable explanation of these early foreign representatives is that the founder of Sandvik, G. F. Göransson, had earlier been general manager in a trading firm with extensive connections abroad.

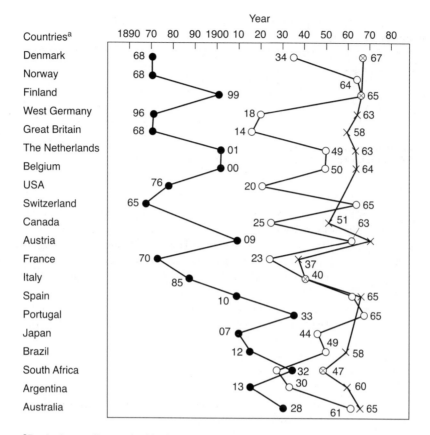

Fig. 1. Profiles of Establishments, Sandvik.

As can be seen from the profile for agency establishments they were set up in successively more distant markets. We computed the Spearman rank correlation coefficient between the time order of establishments and the order of psychic distance and market size respectively (see Table 1). Obviously there is high correlation between the order of agency establishments and distance. The coefficient of the market size factor should be interpreted with care as most of the establishments took place a long time ago. But it is remarkably low.

The same distance-related behaviour, as for the agencies, cannot be observed in the establishments of sales subsidiaries. As the profile shows, Sandvik did not establish the first subsidiaries in the nearest markets, the Nordic countries, but in the large industrial markets like Germany, Great Britain and the USA.

The reason for not establishing trading links in the Nordic countries and the big import markets like Switzerland and the Netherlands was probably that Sandvik had access to efficient representatives, in these markets, with well developed channels to the customers.

Table 1. Rank correlation (Spearman) between the order of Sandvik foreign establishments and psychic distance and market size

	Psychic distance[b]	Market size[b]
Agents	0.79 (0.001)[a]	0.24 (0.181)
Sales subsidiaries	0.16 (0.227)	0.66 (0.002)
Production	−0.01 (0.496)	0.06 (0.386)

[a] In this and all tables that follow, the probability of getting the coefficient or a more extreme value is shown in brackets after each coefficient. It is done in order to give the reader an indication of the 'strength' of the coefficients.
[b] The correlation between the measures of distance and size is only 0.06.

Establishments after 1940 have mainly been made in important markets where Sandvik until then lacked sales subsidiaries, e.g. the Nordic countries and EEC countries. During the 1950s Sandvik developed a policy to use subsidiaries in foreign marketing and, when entering new markets during the 1960s, sales subsidiaries were used from the beginning.

Table 1 also shows that the sales subsidiary establishments do not follow the same time pattern as the agency establishments. In this case the market size factor's highest correlation is with the order of establishments. This is in accordance with our expectations.

The patterns for the manufacturing subsidiaries is quite different from the other kinds of establishment. The first production establishments were made in distant markets. They were saw production in France, Finland and Italy and drill production in South Africa and Canada. There is no correlation at all between the order of production establishments and the factors of distance and size.

According to the establishment chain, described above, firms first make contacts with an independent representative in the foreign market. Later they set up sales subsidiaries and after that, in some cases, production. At the same time there is also a broadening to other markets. The internationalization course of Sandvik is well in accordance with this picture. On practically all markets, independent representatives have been the first connections. Then, after a considerable period of time, they have been replaced by sales subsidiaries. Canada is the only country where a subsidiary was not preceded by a representative. The reason was that Sandvik's representative in the USA and, later, the subsidiary there, performed the marketing in Canada as well.

In 1971, 85 per cent of the total turnover of around 1800 million Swedish kronor came from abroad. The main part of sales is made by the subsidiaries and the independent representatives are nowadays of little significance. The number of independent representatives reached its maximum about 1950 but, since then, has radically diminished.

Two new patterns can be seen in Sandvik's establishments during the last few years. First, Sandvik has developed a new organization of subsidiaries, especially intended to handle the marketing of conveyor bands. The head office of this group is situated in Stuttgart in West Germany and the manufacturing units are in the USA and West Germany. Second, several establishments during the last five years have been made as joint ventures. The products involved are those used in the nuclear industry in France, the USA and West Germany. One reason for these joint ventures is that a 'national connection' is very important as projects in this area are often characterized by 'buy national' behaviour. Another reason is that Sandvik alone cannot afford the heavy investments needed.

Atlas Copco

The firm started in 1873. At the beginning the production was railway material of various kinds. Soon, other products were added; steam engines for ships and machine tools. Production of pneumatic tools started in the 1890s and already at the turn of the century the marketing of rock drills was started. In 1905 Atlas produced the first air compressor of their own design. In 1917 the company was merged with another firm, producing diesel engines.

As early as in 1880 exports were substantial. Diesel engines were the dominant export products until some years after 1930, while the compressed air products were sold mostly on the domestic market. After World War II the selling of pneumatic products soon dominated and the diesel motor production was sold in 1948.

During the first years after the war the selling efforts were concentrated on 'the Swedish method' – lightweight rock drill equipment combined with Sandvik's rock drills. At the end of the 1950s the production and selling were changed towards heavier equipment, stationary compressors and pneumatic tools.

Atlas Copco is five years younger than Sandvik but started the internationalization process considerably later. The successive establishment of contacts with representatives on more and more distant markets, which the model predicts, is evident also for Atlas Copco but less clear than for Sandvik (see Figure 2).

The establishment of sales and production subsidiaries was not common until after World War II, when Atlas Copco sold off its production of diesel motors and concentrated on pneumatic products. During the first few years of the 1950s twenty-three sales subsidiaries were established. By concentrating on 'the Swedish method', Atlas Copco also concentrated on an active marketing strategy, including well developed sales organizations, storing and technical service in the local markets. Sales subsidiaries were considered necessary for this strategy.

The first manufacturing subsidiary abroad was started in Great Britain in 1939. Most important was the acquisition in 1956 of Arpic in Belgium. This firm was an important competitor of Atlas Copco. During the 1960s several establishments were made in more distant countries. The reasons for this expansion were mostly to overcome various barriers to trade.

The pattern of establishment is similar to Sandvik's but less pronounced. The agency establishments are correlated with the distance factor and the sales subsidiary establishments with the market size factor. The production establishments are correlated with neither.

The development in individual markets is illustrated in Figure 2. In most cases representatives have been used before subsidiaries. But many of these representatives were used in the marketing of diesel products. The selling of pneumatic products, being more method than product oriented, was from the start performed by subsidiaries in the important

Table 2. Rank correlation (Spearman) between the order of Atlas Copco foreign establishments and psychic distance and market size

	Psychic distance	Market size
Agents	0.40 (0.041)	−0.26 (0.123)
Sales subsidiaries	0.33 (0.072)	0.48 (0.018)
Production	0.16 (0.242)	−0.11 (0.312)

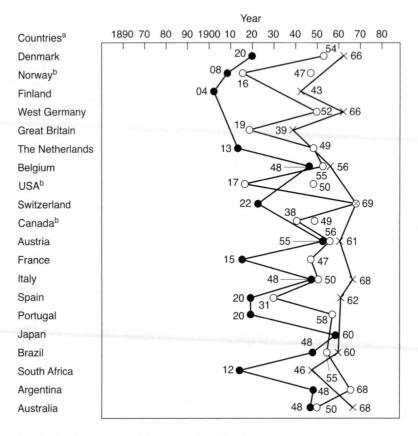

Fig. 2. Profiles of Establishments, Atlas Copco.

markets. Four of the sales subsidiaries were not preceded by representatives. Two of these were failures in so far as they soon had to close down (the USA and Canada).

One of them was not established until 1952 (West Germany). The late establishment in the German market was due to the fact that Atlas Copco met its strongest competition in this market, and it was considered too tough for selling. The first regular export to Germany did not occur until 1951, when the selling of the recently developed pneumatic equipment for mines started.

Selling abroad as a ratio of total turnover 1922 (1900 million Swedish kronor) was nearly 90 per cent. The majority of this selling is made by about thirty-five foreign subsidiaries, but Atlas Copco has representatives in more than 100 countries. There are manufacturing units in ten countries.

Facit

This firm was formed in a reconstruction in 1922. The new enterprise took over the production of a calculating machine from a bankrupt firm, AB Facit. In the beginning of the 1930s a new version of this machine was developed. The new product started Facit's expansion on foreign markets. Some figures of turnover illustrate this. During the period 1923–33 the turnover was constant, 2.5 million Swedish kronor. Until 1939 there was an increase to 10 million Swedish kronor. In 1939 the export ratio was 80–85 per cent and the number of export markets was about seventy.

The expansion also continued with the buying of other firms; viz. in 1939 a manufacturer of typing machines, in 1942 a manufacturer of calculating machines and in 1966 a manufacturer of accounting and calculating machines. In 1972, after a financial crisis, Facit merged with a well-known Swedish multinational firm, Electrolux.

The internationalization process in Facit is unlike Sandvik's and Atlas Copco's. About ten years after the reconstruction in 1922, contacts were established with independent representatives on a large number of markets at the same time. There was no tendency to start on neighbouring markets.

There was, however, a high negative correlation with the market size, indicating that Facit first established agency relations in small countries (see Table 3).

The establishment of subsidiaries, which started at the end of the 1940s, is less confined to a certain time period. They are highly correlated with the distance factor but not with market size. The reasons for substituting subsidiaries for representatives are numerous. For one thing, it became a policy for Facit to use sales subsidiaries. For specific market reasons, such as better control, the reinforcement of the selling organization and dissatisfaction with the representative were mentioned.

The motives for setting up manufacturing subsidiaries abroad have been mostly defensive in character. The foremost reasons for these establishments have been barriers to exporting to the markets concerned. This is also the case of those markets where licensing has been used. The general policy of Facit has not been to decentralize production geographically, but to export from Sweden.

In one case Facit has sold a sales subsidiary to the former representative on the market. This is the only example of a backward move in the 'establishment chain'. In all other cases the establishments have followed the 'chain' pattern.

In 1971 the turnover was about 950 million Swedish kronor. Forty-nine per cent of this turnover was sold through subsidiaries, 17 per cent through independent foreign representatives. The total export ratio was 66 per cent. The number of foreign subsidiaries was twenty, distributed among fourteen countries. Three of these were manufacturing units, two both manufacturing and sales and 15 sales.

Table 3. Rank correlation (Spearman) between the order of Facit foreign establishments and psychic distance and market size

	Psychic distance	Market size
Agents	0.25[a] (0.200)	−0.53[a] (0.040)
Sales subsidiaries	0.60 (0.004)	0.21 (0.179)

[a] Only fourteen observations were used due to difficulties in dating some agent establishments.

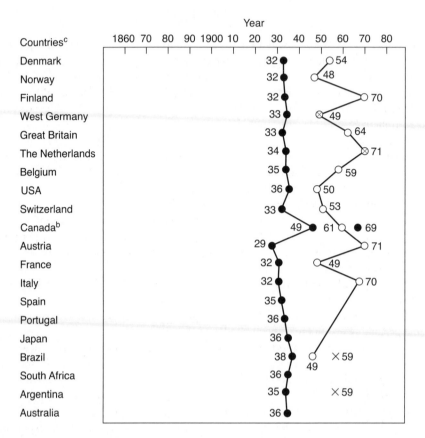

ᵃEstablishments of manufacturing subsidiaries are so few that they cannot be connected by a line.
ᵇThe subsidiary started in 1961, but in 1968 was sold to the former agent on the market.
ᶜRanked according to psychic distance from Sweden.

● agent   ✕ manufacturing subsidiary
○ sales subsidiary   ⊗ sales and manufacturing subsidiary

Fig. 3. Profiles of Establishments, Facitᵃ.

A new development, considered of great importance, is various agreements with foreign companies, often Japanese, on development and production of new products.

VOLVO[17]

The company started its activities in 1927, but the first product, a car, was already finished the year before. The production of cars appeared to be rather sensitive to seasonal variations and in 1928 Volvo started producing trucks as well, the sales of which were more evenly distributed throughout the year.

Export selling was a part of the first production plans and shortly after the start Volvo began establishing representatives abroad.

This was first done on neighbouring markets, Denmark and Norway and on less industrialized distant ones like Argentina, Brazil, Spain and Portugal. No attempt was made to sell to the large European markets until the 1950s. One reason for this behaviour was the hard competition from the domestic industries on these markets. From the start Volvo's policy was to not use its own affiliates or subsidiaries. However, early on Volvo had to break with its policy and establish selling subsidiaries in Finland and Norway, due to difficulties in finding retailers on these markets. A wave of establishments followed in the 1950s when Volvo started up new selling subsidiaries in most European countries, and in the USA and Canada.

This establishment pattern is very similar to Facit's with a high correlation between subsidiary establishments and distance and a negative correlation between agent establishments and market size.

The establishment of manufacturing units on most markets has not occurred before that of sales subsidiaries and the strategy has been to keep production in Sweden as long as possible. Establishments are said to be caused mainly by barriers to trade. Volvo has in such cases used assembly plants to avoid tariffs, import fees and other barriers. In Canada and Australia those plants were preceded by sales subsidiaries. This was not the case in Belgium. This plant was intended to produce for the EEC market. Besides the markets studied, Volvo also has its own assembly plants in Peru and Malaysia. As can be seen, assembly plants are often situated in distant countries.

The model's assumption that a firm starts selling to markets through representatives is correct for all countries except Finland. The two other very early establishments, in Norway and Argentina, were soon shut down, in Norway due to World War II and, in Argentina, because of barriers to import. A number of years thereafter the distribution was run by agents. When the markets again became important Volvo established new subsidiaries.

Special circumstances were at hand in the USA, West Germany and Switzerland. In the USA, Volvo had an agent for part of the market before establishing a subsidiary for the other parts. For a couple of years, an agency and a subsidiary were used side by side. Volvo thereafter took over and used a single subsidiary for the whole market. Also, in Switzerland, an agent was first used. After some years a subsidiary took over part of the market, but an agency is still used for the other parts. In West Germany two different local agents appeared, but their sales were of minor importance. Volvo therefore started a subsidiary in order to cover the whole market.

In 1973 Volvo has more than 100 export markets and the export ratio exceeds 70 per cent of the total turnover of about 7000 million Swedish kronor. In 1973 Volvo had manufacturing subsidiaries in five countries and sales subsidiaries in twelve. A new tendency in Volvo's international development in the last few years is a number of cooperation agreements and 'joint ventures' with various foreign companies regarding the construction and production of engines, gear boxes etc.

THE INTERNATIONALIZATION COURSE – SOME CONCLUDING REMARKS

First, compared to their present sizes the four firms were small when they started internationalization. Of course we have to be careful comparing sizes over so long a time period. However, they were not small in comparison with other Swedish firms in their

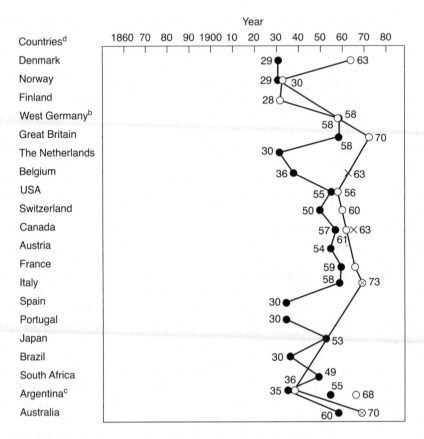

^aEstablishments of manufacturing subsidiaries are so few that they cannot be connected by a line.
^bEstablishment of agent and subsidiary in the same year.
^cThe subsidiary, which started in 1936, was closed down and substituted by an agent in 1955.
^dRanked according to psychic distance from Sweden.

- ● agent
- ○ sales subsidiary
- ✕ manufacturing subsidiary
- ⊗ sales and manufacturing subsidiary

Fig. 4. Profiles of Establishments, Volvo[a].

Table 4. Rank correlation (Spearman) between the order of Volvo foreign establishments and psychic distance and market size

	Psychic distance	Market size
Agents	0.23 (0.076)	−0.70 (0.001)
Sales subsidiaries	0.47 (0.021)	0.06 (0.386)

respective industries at that time. Sandvik had 300 employees and a sales value of 1 million Swedish kronor in 1870. Atlas Copco was of similar size when it started exporting in the 1880s. Facit and Volvo had sales values of 2–3 million Swedish kronor when they started exporting forty years later.

Two of the firms – Sandvik and Volvo – had export in mind when they were established. It is interesting to note that the founders of both these firms – Göransson and Gabrielsson – had long experience of selling abroad. Göransson had been general manager of a trading firm. Gabrielsson was a sales manager in SKF and had been employed at the SKF subsidiary in Paris.

The internationalization process was much faster in the firms that started latest. Sandvik, which established its first agency contact in 1868, needed sixty-five years to get agents in all twenty markets investigated. Atlas Copco, that established its first contact in 1904, needed fifty-five years, Volvo started in 1929 and needed thirty years and Facit, finally, with its first contacts in 1929 needed twenty years.

We expected to find a negative relationship between psychic distance and the establishments. At least we expected that agency relations should be established first in neighbouring and similar countries. To a certain extent we expected the establishment of sales subsidiaries to occur in the same order. Both kinds of establishments were expected to be influenced by the size of the market. In that case, however, we expected the relationship to be stronger with the sales subsidiary establishments.

To a certain extent the establishments have followed this course. However, there are obvious differences between the firms as shown in the following table (Table 5).

All the coefficients of distance have the expected sign and some of them are significant at the 0.05 level. But the differences between the firms are so large that there is reason to believe that they have followed different strategies of internationalization. This impression is strengthened when looking at the size of the coefficients which are rather low, with the exception of Volvo and Facit, which have significant negative coefficients. Whereas Sandvik and, to a certain extent, Atlas Copco could be described as having followed a course of establishing agency contacts in successively more distant countries, Volvo and Facit have started in the smaller countries and later extended to large countries. Atlas Copco has not followed any pronounced course with respect to the two country characteristics. This is not surprising as the product on which Atlas Copco based its main internationalization, drill equipment, has markets in countries with certain resources which need not be correlated with any of the above mentioned characteristics.

Looking at the sales subsidiary establishments the pattern is quite different (Table 6). It should be noted that the correlations between agency and sales subsidiary establishments are all lower than 0.30. The distance factor seems to have influenced Facit's and possibly Volvo's subsidiary establishments, whereas Sandvik's and Atlas Copco's are correlated with the

Table 5. Rank correlation (Spearman) between agency establishments and psychic distance and respective market size

	Sandvik	Atlas Copco	Facit	Volvo
Psychic distance	0.79 (0.001)	0.40 (0.041)	0.25[a] (0.200)	0.23 (0.076)
Size	0.24 (0.181)	−0.26 (0.123)	−0.53[a] (0.040)	−0.70 (0.001)

[a] Based on only fourteen observations due to lack of information on establishing years of agents.

Table 6. Rank correlation (Spearman) between subsidiary establishments and psychic distance and respective market size

	Sandvik	Atlas Copco	Facit	Volvo
Psychic distance	0.16 (0.227)	0.33 (0.072)	0.60 (0.004)	0.47 (0.021)
Size	0.66 (0.002)	0.48 (0.018)	0.21 (0.179)	0.06 (0.386)

market size. It seems reasonable to draw the conclusion that the firms have followed different internationalization strategies with respect to the two variables.

To a certain extent the establishing behaviour is similar within two groups, Sandvik and Atlas Copco in one and Facit and Volvo in the other one. A possible explanation of the difference between the two groups is that the members of the first group had started their internationalization process already at the end of the nineteenth century, while the two other firms did not start establishing until the late 1920s and the effects of the two factors may very well have changed during this long time period.

Another possible explanation of the difference between the two groups is that Sandvik and Atlas Copco manufacture and market more unique products than Facit and Volvo. The latter firms, according to that explanation, have had to avoid the domestic competitive situation in the big industrial countries, whereas the former have found gaps in those markets.

We may conclude that in order to be able to understand the patterns of different firms we have to develop some conditional model of internationalization. At the present stage we cannot formulate any such model, but we consider this a primary objective of our future research.

It should also be noted that the manufacturing establishments of Sandvik and Atlas Copco – the others have set up so few of such establishments – are not at all correlated with the two factors (−0.01 and 0.06 for Sandvik and 0.16 and − 0.11 for Atlas Copco).

The establishment chain – no regular export, independent representative (an agent), sales subsidiary, manufacturing – seems to be a correct description of the order of the development of operations of the firms in individual countries. This is illustrated in Table 7. Of sixty-three sales subsidiaries, fifty-six were preceded by agents and this pattern is the same for all the firms. With regard to the manufacturing establishments there is a difference between Sandvik and Atlas Copco on one hand, where twenty-two out of twenty-seven establishments were preceded by sales subsidiaries, and Facit and Volvo on the other, where five out of seven occurred without the firm having any sales subsidiary in the country. However, in no case has a firm started production in a country without having sold in the country via an agency or sales subsidiary before.

In all firms there have been periods of agency establishments, sales subsidiary establishments and, in the case of Sandvik and Atlas Copco, of manufacturing establishments. In two of the firms – Sandvik and Volvo – there has followed a period of international joint ventures for special purposes.

Considering the first establishment of sales subsidiaries it does not seem to have been a step in a conscious and goal directed strategy of internationalization – at least not in the case of Sandvik, Atlas Copco and Volvo. For various reasons they had to take over representatives or start subsidiaries. Gradually, when they had gained experience of setting up and managing subsidiaries they developed policies of marketing through subsidiaries in some of the firms. It should be noted that the firm Atlas Copco, which most consistently used subsidiaries for export marketing, did that when it got a new general manager, the former manager of a department store.

The manufacturing subsidiaries almost all manufacture for local or, in some cases, regional markets. They have finishing, assembly or component production which could be called marketing production. The only exception is Atlas Copco's factory in Belgium making stationary pneumatic equipment.

Generally the development of the firms seems to be in accordance with the incremental internationalization view discussed. In a few cases, notably Atlas Copco after World War II and Facit's agency establishments, the direction and velocity of internationalization has, however, been influenced heavily by strategic decisions.[18]

Table 7. Establishment patterns for the investigated firms

	Pattern				
	Sales subsidiary			Production subsidiary	
	n	a	n	a	s
Firm	↓	↓	↓	↓	↓
	s	s	p	p	p
Sandvik	2	18	0	2	13
Atlas Copco	3	14	0	3	9
Facit	0	14	0	2	3
Volvo	2	10	0	2	3
Total	7	56	0	9	28

n   no regular export activity
a   export via an agent
s   sales subsidiary
p   production subsidiary
An arrow denotes change from one state to another

NOTES

1. This study has been financially supported by the Swedish Council for Social Science Research and the Svenska Handelsbanken Foundation for Social Science Research. Appreciation is expressed to our colleagues in the international business research programme for their valuable comments.

2. See Gruber, W., Mehta, R. and Vernon, R., 'The R and D Factor in International Trade and International Investment of The United States', *Journal of Political Economy*, Vol. 75, No. 1, February 1967, pp. 20–37, and Caves, R.E., 'International Corporations: The Industrial Economics of Foreign Investment', *Economica*, Vol. 38, No. 149, 1971, pp. 1–27, in discussions of foreign direct investments; also Terpstra, V., *International Marketing*, New York: McGraw-Hill, 1972.

3. Since its crisis in 1971, Facit is not quoted as an example any longer.

4. These two aspects of the international process are discussed in Kindleberger, C. P., *American Business Abroad*, Boston: Yale University Press, 1969.

5. Cf. Vernon, R., 'International Investment and International Trade in the Product Cycle', *Quarterly Journal of Economics*, Vol. 80, pp. 190–207, 1966, May and Burenstam-Linder, S., *An Essay on Trade and Transformation*, Stockholm: Almqvist & Wicksell, 1961. Market and country are used interchangeably in this paper.

6. This question is investigated in a research project by F. Wiedersheim-Paul entitled 'Export Propensity of the Firm'.

7. A more detailed discussion of the internationalization process is given in Johanson, J. and Vahlne, J.E., 'The Internationalization Process of the Firm', *Mimeographed Working Paper*, Department of Business Administration, Uppsala, 1974.

8. Similar discussions of a stepwise extension of activities in individual countries can be found in, for example, Gruber, W., Mehta, R., Vernon, R., op. cit., and Caves, R.E., op. cit.

9. 'Psychic Distance' has been used by, for example Beckermann, W., 'Distance and the Pattern of Intra-European Trade', *Review of Economics and Statistics*, Vol. 28, 1956, Linnemann, H., *An Econometric Study of International Trade Flows*, Amsterdam: North-Holland, 1966, and Wiedersheim-Paul, F., *Uncertainty and Economic Distance – Studies in International Business*, Uppsala: Almqvist and Wicksell, 1972. Here we use the concept with the same meaning as in Wiedersheim-Paul, op. cit., 1972.

10. Of course, changes due to political decisions can be very fast, e.g. USA–Cuba.

11. Root, F.R., *Strategic Planning for Export Marketing*, Copenhagen: Elhar Hareks Forlag, 1964, p. 11.

12. See, information from 'A File of Swedish Subsidiaries Abroad', Centre for International Business Studies, Department of Business Administration, University of Uppsala.

13. Chandler, A.D., *Strategy and Structure*, Cambridge, Mass.: MIT Press, 1962.

14. Håkansson, H. and Wootz, B., 'Internationalization of the Purchasing Function of the Firm', *Mimeographed Working Paper*, Department of Business Administration, Uppsala, 1974.

15. Carlson, S., *Ett Halvsekels Affärer, in Ett Svenskt Fernverk (A Swedish Steel Mill)*, Sandviken, 1937, Gärdlund, T., Janelid, I. and Ramström, D., *Atlas Copco, 1873–1973*, Stockholm: 1973, and *Mimeographed Research Papers* by students at the Department of Business Administration, Uppsala.

16. The ranking, with minor modifications, is taken from Hörnell, E., Vahlne, J.-E. and Wiedersheim-Paul, F., *Export och Utlands-Etableringar (Export and Foreign Establishment)*, Stockholm, 1973.

17. The discussion below relates exclusively to the automobile manufacturing part of the company.

18. Three of the firms, after a period of international operation, changed their names to adapt to the international market. The only exception is Volvo.

4

The Internationalization Process of the Firm: a Model of Knowledge Development and Increasing Foreign Market Commitments

Jan Johanson and Jan-Erik Vahlne

INTRODUCTION

Several studies of international business have indicated that internationalization of the firms is a process in which the firms gradually increase their international involvement. It seems reasonable to assume that within the frame of economic and business factors, the characteristics of this process influence the pattern and pace of internationalization of firms. In this paper we develop a model of the internationalization process of the firm that focuses on the development of the individual firm and particularly on its gradual acquisition, integration, and use of knowledge about foreign markets and operations and on its successively increasing commitment to foreign markets. The basic assumptions of the model are that lack of such knowledge is an important obstacle to the development of international operations and that the necessary knowledge can be acquired mainly through operations abroad. This holds for the two directions of internationalization we distinguish, increasing involvement of the firm in the individual foreign country and successive establishment of operations in new countries. In this paper we will, however, concentrate on the extension of operations in individual markets.

We have incorporated in our model some results of previous empirical studies of the development of international operations, seeking theoretical explanation through the behavioural theory of the firm (Cyert and March, 1963). Specifically we believe that internationalization is the product of a series of incremental decisions. Our aim is to identify elements shared in common by the successive decision situations and to develop thereby a model of the internationalization process which will have explanatory value. Because we, for the time being, disregard the decision style of the decision-maker himself, and, to a certain extent, the specific properties of the various decision situations, our model has only limited predictive value. We believe, however, that all the decisions that, taken together, constitute the internationalization process – decisions to start exporting to a country, to establish export channels, to start a selling subsidiary, and so forth – have some common characteristics which are also very important to the subsequent internationalization. Our model focuses on these common traits.

We hope that the model will contribute to conceptualization in the field of internationalization of the firm and thus increase understanding of the development of international operations as described in the empirical studies. We hope, too, that it can serve as a frame of reference for future studies in the problem area and may also be useful as a tool in the analysis of the effects of various factors on the pattern and pace of internationalization of the firm.

In the first section we describe the empirical background of our study. Next we outline the model of the internationalization process defining the main variables and the interaction among them. We then sum up by discussing some implications of the model and suggesting some problems for future research.

EMPIRICAL BACKGROUND

The model is based on empirical observations from our studies in international business at the University of Uppsala that show that Swedish firms often develop their international operations in small steps rather than by making large foreign production investments at single points in time. Typically firms start exporting to a country via an agent, later establish a sales subsidiary, and eventually, in some cases, begin production in the host country.

We have also observed a similar successive establishment of operations in new countries. Of particular interest in the present context is that the time order of such establishments seems to be related to the psychic distance between the home and the import/host countries (Hörnell, Vahlne and Wiedersheim-Paul, 1972, Johanson and Wiedersheim-Paul, 1974). The psychic distance is defined as the sum of factors preventing the flow of information from and to the market. Examples are differences in language, education, business practices, culture and industrial development.

Studies of the export organizations of the Swedish special steel firms (Johanson, 1966) and of the Swedish pulp and paper industry (Forsgren and Kinch, 1970) have shown that almost all sales subsidiaries of Swedish steel companies and pulp and paper companies have been established through acquisition of the former agent or have been organized around some person employed by the agent. Most of the establishments were occasioned by various kinds of economic crises in the agent firms. Sales to a market by the agent had preceded establishment of a sales subsidiary in each of nine cases investigated by Hörnell and Vahlne (1972). Further case studies of the development of international activities by Swedish firms have allowed us to generalize our observations. Sales subsidiaries are preceded in virtually all cases by selling via an agent; similarly, local production is generally preceded by sales subsidiaries.

A summary of the results we reached in two studies follows. They are by no means meant to be statistically representative, but the results are typical of studies we know. The first example is a case study of the internationalization process of the second largest Swedish pharmaceutical firm, Pharmacia. At the time of the case study (1972) Pharmacia had organizations of its own in nine countries, of which three were performing manufacturing activities. In eight of these cases the development pattern was as follows. The firm received orders from the foreign market and after some time made an agreement with an agent (or sold licences regarding some parts of the product line). After a few years Pharmacia established sales subsidiaries in seven of those countries (and in the eighth they bought a manufacturing company bearing the same name, Pharmacia, that had previously served as an agent). Two of the seven sales subsidiaries further increased their involvement by starting manufacturing activities. It is interesting to note that even this production decision was incremental, the new production units began with the least complicated manufacturing activities and later successively added more complicated ones.

In the ninth country Pharmacia started a sales subsidiary almost immediately when demand from the market was discovered. But the company did not totally lack experience even in this case. The decision-maker had received parts of his education in the country in question, and before the decision he had become acquainted with the representative of another pharmaceutical firm who was later made the head of the subsidiary (Hörnell, Vahlne, and Wiedersheim-Paul, 1973).

In another study we investigated the internationalization of four Swedish engineering firms. Below we quote some of the conclusions of the study (Johanson and Wiedersheim-Paul, 1975).

The establishment chain – no regular export, independent representative (agent), sales subsidiary, production – seems to be a correct description of the order of the development operations of the firms in individual countries. This is illustrated in Table 1. Of sixty-three sales subsidiaries fifty-six were preceded by agents; this pattern holds for all the firms. With regard to the production establishments there is a difference between Sandvik and Atlas Copco on one hand, where twenty-two out of twenty-seven establishments were preceded by sales subsidiaries, and Facit and Volvo on the other, where five out of seven occurred without the firm having any sales subsidiary in the country. However, in no case has a firm started production in a country without having sold in the country via an agency or a sales subsidiary before.

Regarding the first establishment of sales subsidiaries, they do not seem to have been a step in a conscious and goal directed internationalization – at least not in Sandvik, Atlas Copco, and Volvo. For various reasons they had to take over representatives or start subsidiaries. As they gradually have gained experience in starting and managing subsidiaries, they have developed policies of marketing through subsidiaries in some of the firms. It should be noted that the firm Atlas Copco which most consistently used subsidiaries for export marketing did so when it acquired a new general manager, a former manager of a department store.

The producing subsidiaries almost all produce for local or in some cases regional markets. Their activity embraces finishing assembly or component works which could be called marketing production. The only exception is Atlas Copco's factory in Belgium making stationary pneumatic equipment.

Generally the development of the firm seems to be in accordance with the incremental internationalization view discussed.

Table 1. Establishment patterns for the investigated firms

| | Pattern | | | | |
| | Sales subsidiary | | | Production subsidiary | |
Firm	n ↓ s	a ↓ s	n ↓ p	a ↓ p	s ↓ p
Sandvik	2	18	0	2	13
Atlas Copco	3	14	0	3	9
Facit	0	14	0	2	3
Volvo	2	10	0	2	3
Total	7	56	0	9	28

n   no regular export activity
a   selling via agent
s   sales subsidiary
p   production subsidiary
An arrow denotes change from one state to another

This gradual internationalization is not exclusively a Swedish phenomenon, as the following quotations demonstrate.

> On its part exporting is a means also of reducing costs of market development. Even if investment is necessary in the future, exporting helps to determine the nature and size of the market. As the market develops, warehouse facilities are established, later sales branches and subsidiaries (Singer, National Cash Register, United Show Machinery). The record of company development indicates that the use of selling subsidiaries at an early stage reduced the later risks of manufacturing abroad. These selling affiliates permitted the slow development of manufacturing from repairing, to packaging, to mixing, to finishing, to processing or assembling operations, and finally to full manufacture (Behrman, 1969, p. 3).
>
> Within countries there is often a pattern of exports from the United States, followed by the establishment of an assembly or packaging plant, followed by progressively more integrated manufacturing activities (Vaupel, 1971, p. 42).

Without reference to any specific empirical observations Gruber, Mehta, and Vernon (1967) mention that 'one way of looking at the overseas direct investments of US producers of manufacturers is that they are the final step in a process which begins with the involvement of such producers in export trade'. Knickerbocker (1972) also refers to this process and explicitly distinguishes agents and sales subsidiaries as separate steps in the process. Lipsey and Weiss (1969, 1972) refer to a 'market cycle' model with similar characteristics. However, in none of these cases have the dynamics of this process been investigated. It has only been used as an argument in the discussion of related problems.

Specification of the problem

If internationalization indeed follows the pattern described above, how can we explain it? We do not believe that it is the result of a strategy for optimum allocation of resources to different countries where alternative ways of exploiting foreign markets are compared and evaluated. We see it rather as the consequence of a process of incremental adjustments to changing conditions of the firm and its environment (cf. Aharoni, 1966).

Changes in the firm and its environment expose new problems and opportunities. Lacking routines for the solution of such sporadic problems, the concern's management 'searches in the area of the problem' (Cyert and March, 1963). Each new discontinuity is regarded as an essentially unprecedented and unparalleled case, the problems and opportunities presented are handled in their contexts. Thus commitments to other markets are not explicitly taken into consideration, resource allocations do not compete with each other.

Another constraint on the problem solution is the lack of, and difficulty of obtaining market knowledge in international operations. That internationalization decisions have an incremental character is, we feel, largely due to this lack of market information and the uncertainty occasioned thereby (Hörnell, Vahlne and Wiedersheim-Paul, 1972, Johanson, 1970). We believe that lack of knowledge due to differences between countries with regard to, for example, language and culture, is an important obstacle to decision making connected with the development of international operations. We would even say that these differences constitute the main characteristic of international as distinct from domestic operations. By market knowledge we mean information about markets and operations in those markets, which is somehow stored and reasonably retrievable – in the mind of individuals, in computer memories and in written reports. In our model we consider knowledge to be vested in the decision-making system, we do not deal explicitly with the individual decision-maker.

THE INTERNATIONALIZATION MODEL

As indicated in the introduction a model in which the same basic mechanism can be used to explain all steps in the internationalization would be useful. We also think that a dynamic model would be suitable. In such a model the outcome of one decision – or more generally one cycle of events – constitutes the input of the next. The main structure is given by the distinction between the state and change aspects of internationalization variables. To clarify we can say that the present state of internationalization is one important factor explaining the course of following internationalization as in expression (1) below

$$\Delta I = f(I \ldots)$$

where

$$I = \text{state of internationalization}$$

The state aspects we consider are the resource commitment to the foreign markets – market commitment – and knowledge about foreign markets and operations. The change aspects are decisions to commit resources and the performance of current business activities. The basic mechanism is illustrated schematically in Figure 1.

Market knowledge and market commitment are assumed to affect both commitment decisions and the way current activities are performed. These in turn change knowledge and commitment (cf. Aharoni, 1966).

In the model, it is assumed that the firm strives to increase its long-term profit, which is assumed to be equivalent to growth (Williamson, 1966). The firm is also striving to keep risk-taking at a low level. These strivings are assumed to characterize decision-making on all levels of the firm. Given these premises and the state of the economic and business factors which constitute the frame in which a decision is taken, the model assumes that the state of internationalization affects perceived opportunities and risks which in turn influence commitment decisions and current activities. We will discuss the mechanism in detail in the following sections.

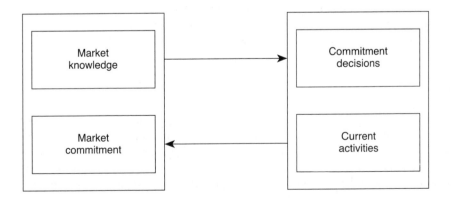

Fig. 1. The Basic Mechanism of Internationalization – State and Change Aspects.

State aspects

The two state aspects are resources committed to foreign markets – market commitment – and knowledge about foreign markets possessed by the firm at a given point of time. The reason for considering the market commitment is that we assume that the commitment to a market affects the firm's perceived opportunities and risk.

Market commitment

Let us first take a look at the market commitment concept. To begin with we assume that it is composed of two factors – the amount of resources committed and the degree of commitment, that is, the difficulty of finding an alternative use for the resources and transferring them to it. Resources located in a particular market area can often be considered a commitment to that market. However, in some cases such resources can be sold and the financial resources can easily be used for other purposes. The degree of commitment is higher the more the resources in question are integrated with other parts of the firm and their value is derived from these integrated activities. Thus, as a rule, vertical integration means a higher degree of commitment than a conglomerative foreign investment. An example of resources that cannot easily be directed to another market or used for other purposes is a marketing organization that is specialized around the products of the firm and has established integrated customer relations. However, resources located in the home country and employed in development and production of products for a separate market also constitute a commitment to that market. The more specialized the resources are to the specific market the greater is the degree of commitment. And even if such resources can easily be directed to development and production for other markets, as for example engineers in a central engineering department, they cannot always be profitably used there. Consider Volvo – the Swedish car manufacturer – with a large part of its production capacity employed in production of cars for the US market. Even if that capacity is not highly committed to the US production, it is not easy, at least in the short run, to use it for production for other markets. And although the engineers employed in adapting the car to the US requirements can probably be used for another purpose, it is not certain that they can be profitably employed there. On the whole, it seems reasonable to assume that the resources that are located in the particular market are most committed to that market, but we shall not disregard the commitment that follows from employing parts of the domestic capacity for a particular market.

The other part of market commitment – the amount of resources committed – is easy to grasp. It is close to the size of the investment in the market, using this concept in a broad sense, including investment in marketing, organization, personnel, and other areas.

Market knowledge

In our model, knowledge is of interest because commitment decisions are based on several kinds of knowledge. First, knowledge of opportunities or problems is assumed to initiate decisions. Second, evaluation of alternatives is based on some knowledge about relevant parts of the market environment and about performance of various activities. Very generally, the knowledge 'relates to present and future demand and supply, to competition and to channels for distribution, to payment conditions and the transferability of money, and those things vary from country to country and from time to time' (Carlson, 1974).

A classification of knowledge which is useful for us is based on the way in which knowledge is acquired (Penrose, 1966, p. 53). One type, objective knowledge, can be taught, the other, experience or experiential knowledge, can only be learned through personal experience. With experiential knowledge, emphasis is placed on the change in the services the human resources can supply which arises from their activity (ibid. p. 53), and '. . . experience itself can never be transmitted, it produces a change – frequently a subtle change – in individuals and cannot be separated from them' (ibid. p. 53) 'Much of the experience of businessmen is frequently so closely associated with a particular set of circumstances that a large part of a man's most valuable services may be available only under these circumstances' (ibid. p. 53).

We believe that this experiential knowledge is the critical kind of knowledge in the present context. It is critical because it cannot be so easily acquired as objective knowledge. In domestic operations we can to a large extent rely on lifelong basic experiences to which we can add the specific experiences of individuals, organizations and markets in foreign operations; however, we have no such basic experiential knowledge to start with. It must be gained successively during the operations in the country.

We believe that the less structured and well defined the activities and the required knowledge are, the more important is experiential knowledge. We think it is particularly important in connection with activities that are based on relations to other individuals. Managerial work and marketing are examples of such activities. Especially in the marketing of complex and soft-ware-intensive products, experiential knowledge is crucial.

An important aspect of experiential knowledge is that it provides the framework for perceiving and formulating opportunities. On the basis of objective market knowledge it is possible to formulate only theoretical opportunities, experiential knowledge makes it possible to perceive 'concrete' opportunities – to have a 'feeling' about how they fit into the present and future activities.

We can also distinguish between general knowledge and market-specific knowledge. General knowledge concerns, in the present context, marketing methods and common characteristics of certain types of customers, irrespective of their geographical location, depending, for example, in the case of industrial customers, on similarities in the production process. The market-specific knowledge is knowledge about characteristics of the specific national market – its business climate, cultural patterns, structure of the market system, and, most importantly, characteristics of the individual customer firms and their personnel.

Establishment and performance of a certain kind of operation or activity in a country require both general knowledge and market-specific knowledge. Market-specific knowledge can be gained mainly through experience in the market, whereas knowledge of the operation can often be transferred from one country to another country. It is the diffusion of this general knowledge which facilitates lateral growth, that is, the establishment of technically similar activities in dissimilar business environments.

There is a direct relation between market knowledge and market commitment. Knowledge can be considered a resource (or, perhaps preferably, a dimension of the human resources), and consequently the better the knowledge about a market, the more valuable are the resources and the stronger is the commitment to the market. This is especially true of experiential knowledge, which is usually associated with the particular conditions on the market in question and thus cannot be transferred to other individuals or other markets.

Change aspects

The change aspects we have considered are current activities and decisions to commit resources to foreign operations.

Current business activities

There is, to begin with, a lag between most current activities and their consequences. Those consequences may, in fact, not be realized unless the activities are repeated more or less continuously. Consider, for example, marketing activities, which generally do not result in sales unless they are repeated for some time. In many cases the time lag is considerable, and the marketing investment represents an important and ever-increasing commitment to the market. The longer the lag, the higher the commitment of the firm mounts. It seems reasonable to assume that the more complicated and the more differentiated the product is, the larger the total commitment as a consequence of current activities will come to be.

Current activities are also the prime source of experience. It could be argued that experience could be gained alternatively through the hiring of personnel with experience, or through advice from persons with experience. To clarify the roles of these alternative ways of integrating experience into the firm in the internationalization process, we distinguish between firm experience and market experience, both of which are essential. Persons working on the boundary between the firm and its market must be able to interpret information from inside the firm and from the market. The interpretation of one kind of information is possible only for one who has experience with the other part. We conclude that, for the performance of marketing activities, both kinds of experience are required; and in this area it is difficult to substitute personnel or advice from outside for current activities. The more the activities are production-oriented, or the less interaction is required between the firm and its market environment, the easier it will be to substitute hired personnel or advice for current activities, and consequently the easier it will be to start new operations that are not incremental additions to the former operations. It should be remembered, however, that even production activities are dependent on the general business climate, which cannot easily be assessed in ways other than performance of business activities.

To some extent it may be possible to hire personnel with market experience and to use them profitably after some time in the marketing activities. The delay is occasioned by the need for the new personnel to gain the necessary experience in the firm. But if the new personnel have already worked as representatives for the exporter, the delay may approach zero. Thus, the best way to quickly obtain and use market experience is to hire a sales manager or a salesman of a representative or to buy the whole or a part of the firm. In many cases this kind of experience is not for sale; at the time of entry to a market the experience may not even exist. It has to be acquired through a long learning process in connection with current activities. This factor is an important reason why the internationalization process often proceeds slowly.

Commitment decisions

The second change aspect is decisions to commit resources to foreign operations. We assume that such decisions depend on what decision alternatives are raised and how they are chosen. Regarding the first part we assume that decisions are made in response to perceived problems and/or opportunities on the market. Problems and opportunities – that is awareness of need and possibilities for business actions – are assumed to be dependent on experience. Like Penrose, we might even say that opportunities – and problems – are part of that experience. Firm experience, as well as market experience, is relevant. Problems are mainly discovered by those parts of the organization that are responsible for operations on the market and primarily by those who are working there. For them, the natural solution to problems will be the extension of the operations on the market to complementing operations. In any case we assume the solutions to market operations problems are searched for in the neighbourhood of the problem symptoms, that is in the market activities (Cyert and March, 1963). In the same way opportunities will be perceived mainly by those who are working on the market, and such opportunities will also lead to extension of the operations on the market. They will be related to those parts of the environment that the firm is interacting with (Pfeffer, 1974). Thus, whether decision alternatives are raised in response to problems or in response to opportunities, they will be related to the operations currently performed on the market. Alternative solutions will generally consist of activities that mean an extension of the boundaries of the organization and an increase in commitment to the market. We could speak of an opportunity horizon that – given the operations performed – describes the kind of activities that are likely to be suggested by those responsible for operations.

But opportunities are also seen by individuals in organizations with which the firm is interacting; these individuals may propose alternative solutions to the firm in the form of offers or demands. The probability that the firm is offered opportunities from outside is dependent on the scale and type of operations it is performing; that is, on its commitment to the market.

We distinguish between an economic effect and an uncertainty effect of each additional commitment. We assume that the economic effect is associated primarily with increases in the scale of operations on the market, and that the uncertainty effect concerns the market uncertainty, that is the decision-makers' perceived lack of ability to estimate the present and future market and market-influencing factors. We mean that this market uncertainty is reduced through increases in interaction and integration with the market environment – steps such as increases in communication with customers, establishment of new service activities or, in the extreme case, the take-over of customers.

Our thinking on this point is further illustrated by the system of relationships below:

R^* = maximum tolerable market (market i) risk = f (firm's resource position, firm's risk approach)

R = existing market risk situation = $C_i \cdot U$
    where C = existing market commitment
           U = existing market uncertainty

ΔR = incremental risk implied by an incremental addition to operations on market i

Scale increasing decisions are assumed to affect the size of C but not the size of U so that

$$\Delta R = U \cdot \Delta C_i > 0$$

Uncertainty reducing decisions are assumed to affect U, primarily so that

$$\Delta R = \Delta U (C + \Delta C) + \Delta C_i \cdot U_i < 0$$

Using this framework we say that scale-increasing decisions will be taken when $R < R^*$. The firm will incrementally extend its scale of existing operations on the market – in expectation of large returns – until its tolerable risk frontier (R^*) is met. Scale-increasing commitments may, for example, be occasioned by a decline in uncertainty about the market (U_i) incidental to gaining market knowledge acquired with experience. Such a decline in market uncertainty can be expected when the market conditions are fairly stable and heterogeneous. If market conditions are very unstable, experience cannot be expected to lead to decreased uncertainty. And, if market conditions are very homogeneous, experience is probably not a necessary requirement for market knowledge. Under such market conditions an optimal scale of operations can be chosen from the beginning. Market uncertainty can also decline as a consequence of a competitive – or political – stabilization of market conditions. Scale-increasing commitments may also follow a rise of the maximum tolerable risk level due to an increase in the total resources of the firm or a more aggressive approach toward risk. We can in any event say that large increases in the scale of operations in the market will only take place in firms with large total resources or in firms which feel little uncertainty about the market.

Uncertainty-reducing commitments on the other hand will be made when $R > R^*$. The firm will respond to this imbalance by taking steps to increase interactions and integration with the market environment. Such an imbalance may be the result of a decrease in the maximum tolerable market risk (R^*) or an increase in the existing risk situation on the market (R_i). The latter case may, in its turn, be occasioned by an increase in market commitment (C_i) or market uncertainty (U_i). Market commitments that increase risk are, according to our assumptions, those that increase the scale of existing operations on the market. Such increases are likely to be associated with current activities in an expanding market but can also be a consequence of the scale-increasing decisions discussed in the previous paragraph. Note that increases in the scale operations on the market can be expected to lead to uncertainty-reducing commitments, that is increased interaction and integration with the market environment. Market uncertainty (U_i) can be expected to rise as a consequence of experience in a dynamic market environment, showing that the original perception of the market was too simple. It may also rise because of a structural change in market conditions, for example, in connection with the entrance of new competitors on the market or introduction of new techniques. A typical example of the former is the change of the market situation of Swedish pulp and paper firms due to the entrance of North American producers on the European market (Kinch, 1974). However, increases in market uncertainty due to political changes cannot be expected to lead to the uncertainty-reducing commitments discussed here since such commitments cannot be expected to affect the political situation.

This discussion requires some further comments. First, it is very partial since we do not take into account how various factors other than scale may affect the economy of the market operations. The technology of the firm probably has a great impact on the economy of different types of market operations. Secondly, the variable 'firm's approach to market risk' is a very complicated factor. We can, for example, distinguish between three different strategies with respect to this factor. One may be that a high risk level on one market is compensated by a low risk level on other markets. Another is that the tolerable risk level is the same on all markets. A third is that risk taking on the market is delegated to those working on the market as long as decisions do not require additional resources from the firm.

We conclude this discussion of commitment decisions by observing that additional commitments will be made in small steps unless the firm has very large resources and/or market conditions are stable and homogeneous, or the firm has much experience from other markets with similar conditions. If not, market experience will lead to a step-wise increase in

the scale of the operations and of the integration with the market environment where st(
will be taken to correct imbalance with respect to the risk situation on the market. Mark
growth will speed up this process.

Empirical verification

We think that the general characteristics of the model fit nicely with empirical observations
given earlier. In order to validate it empirically we intend to make two kinds of empirical
studies. Firstly, we shall make one or two intensive case studies to see if the mechanism can be
used for explanation in empirical situations. In those case studies, we shall try to measure the
internationalization variables, market commitment and market knowledge, and investigate
how they develop during the internationalization of the firm.

Secondly, we intend to make comparative studies of the internationalization courses of
different firms. Assuming that such factors as firm size, technology, product line, home
country, etc., via the mechanism discussed affect the character of the internationalization in
different ways, we will investigate whether firms that differ with respect to those factors also
differ with respect to the patterns of internationalization. Such studies will require more
systematic discussions of the expected influence of the factors. The present model will
constitute the framework of such discussions.

Possible applications

In many countries various programmes to affect foreign trade and operations are designed
and carried out. Still more are discussed. Usually such programmes are based on models in
which prices of factors and products in different countries are the only explaining factors. We
think that our model can help in giving such discussions and programmes a better base. An
evaluation of a Swedish export stimulation programme showed that the 'export stimulation
measures affect firms' export behaviour in different ways due to differences in their degrees of
previous export experience' (Olson, 1975). Our model indicates how such experience can be
expected to affect the export behaviour. It also makes it possible to develop a better
understanding of foreign investment behaviour.

We also think that the model can be useful in planning and decision making in the firm
with regard to international operations. Many firms consider internationalization a
promising strategy. There are, however, numerous examples of firms which have started
international operations without success. We think that the importance of the experience
factor is often overlooked. The model indicates how it is related to other internationalization
variables thus giving a better base for planning and executing the internationalization
process.

And finally we hope, as do other students in the field, that our way of reasoning will add
something to the understanding of the process by which firms become international or even
multinational. Thus, many studies of international trade and investment have shown that
oligopolistic industries have the greatest international engagement. Such features as high
R&D intensity, advertising intensity and efforts at product differentiation characterized these
industries (Gruber, Mehta, Vernon, 1967; Hymer, 1960; Kindleberger, 1969; Caves, 1971;
Vaupel, 1971). Oligopolistic competition, however, lacks explanatory value at the firm level;
we have to look for other features to explain variations in the level of international
involvement among the several firms in a given oligopolistic industry (Horst, 1972;

53

). Perhaps our model of the internationalization process can help in
this explanation by stressing the importance of some factors affecting the
rocess.

ES

The Foreign Investment Decision Process. Boston, 1966.
J. Some Patterns in the Rise of the Multinational Enterprise. Chapel Hill, 1969.
S. Investment in Knowledge and the Cost of Information. Acta Academiae Regiae Scientiarum
    iensis, Uppsala, 1974.
, R.E. 'International Corporations: The Industrial Economics of Foreign Investment', Economics
    371) vol. 38.
rt, R.M., March, J.G. A Behavioral Theory of the Firm. Englewood Cliffs, 1963.
rsgren, M., Kinch, N. Foretagets anpassning till forandringar i omgivande system. En studie av massaoch
    pappersindustrin. Uppsala, 1970.
Gruber, W., Menta, R., Vernon, R. 'The R&D Factor in International Trade and International
    Investment of the United States'. Journal of Political Economy. February 1967.
Horst, T.O. 'Firm and Industry Determinants of the Decision to Invest Abroad: An Empirical Study'.
    Review of Economics and Statistics. 1972.
Hymer, S. 'The International Operations of National Firms. A Study of Direct Investment.' Doctoral
    dissertation, Mass. Institute of Technology. 1960.
Haakansson, F., Wootz, B. 'Supplier Selection in an International Environment – An Experimental
    Study,' Journal of Marketing Research. February 1975.
Hörnell, E., Vahlne, J.-E., Wiedersheim-Paul, F. Export och utlandsetableringar. Stockholm, 1973.
Johanson, J. (ed.) Exportstrategiska problem. Stockholm, 1972.
Johanson, J. 'Svenskt kvalitetsstål på utländska marknader.' Mimeographed licentiate dissertation. Dept.
    of Business Administration, Uppsala, 1966.
Johanson, J., Wiedersheim-Paul, F. 'The Internationalization of the Firm – Four Swedish Cases'. Journal
    of Management Studies. 1975.
Kinch, N. 'Utlandsetableringar inom massa-och pappers-industrin'. In Företagsekonomisk forskning kring
    internationellt foretagande, ed. by Jan-Erik Vahlne. Stockholm, 1974.
Kindleberger, C.P., American Business Abroad. New Haven, 1969.
Knickerbocker, F.T. Oligopolistic Reaction and Multinational Enterprise. Boston, 1973.
Lipsey, R.E., Weiss, M.Y. 'The Relation of US Manufacturing Abroad to US Exports. A Framework for
    Analysis', Business and Economics Section Proceedings. American Statistical Association, 1969.
Lipsey, R.E., Weiss, M.Y. 'Analyzing Direct Investment and Trade at the Company Level', Business and
    Economic Section Proceedings. American Statistical Association, 1972.
Olson, H.C. Studies in Export Promotion Attempts to Evaluate Export Stimulation Measures for the Swedish Textile
    and Clothing Industries. Uppsala, 1975.
Penrose, E., The Theory of the Growth of the Firm. Oxford, 1966.
Pfeffer, J. 'Merger as a Response to Organizational Interdependence'. Administrative Science Quarterly 6
    (1972).
Vaupel, J.V. 'Characteristics and Motivations of the US Corporations that Manufacture Abroad'.
    Mimeographed, Boston, 1971.
Williamson, J. 'Profit Growth and Sales Maximization'. Economica 33 (1966).

5

A Theory of International Operations

Peter J. Buckley and Mark Casson

This paper provides a theoretical framework for the explanation and prediction of the methods of market servicing (or 'sourcing policies') of multinational enterprises (MNEs).

1. THE DIVISION OF NATIONAL MARKETS

A national market for a final product can be served in four main ways: by indigenous firms, by subsidiaries of MNEs located in the market, by exports to the market from foreign locally owned firms and by exports from foreign plants owned by MNEs. The first two methods are distinguished from the second two by the 'location effect': the market is served by local production rather than export. The first method is distinguished from the second and the third method from the fourth by the 'ownership effect': production is owned and controlled by domestic nationals rather than by a foreign-owned international corporation.

Final goods markets cannot, however, be considered in isolation from the markets for the intermediate goods involved in the production process. Intermediate goods too are subject to ownership and location effects. In order to service a final product market it may be advantageous to locate different stages of production in different locations. Also the ownership of 'the good' may change as we move through the process – an example of this is licensing where essential proprietary knowledge to produce the final good is licensed from one product to another.

In order to examine these factors in detail the following sections deal firstly with location effects and then with ownership effects.

2. THE LOCATION OF PRODUCTION FACILITIES

Production in a multi stage process can be characterised as a sequence of distinct activities linked by the transport of semi-processed materials. The orthodox theory of location assumes constant returns to scale, freely available and therefore standardised technology and that firms are price takers in all factor markets. Given such assumptions, a firm chooses its optimal location for each stage of production by evaluating regional production costs and choosing the set of locations for which the overall average cost of production is minimised. Regional production costs vary only according to regional differentials in non tradeable goods (the price

Reprinted with permission from *European Research in International Business*, North-Holland, Amsterdam, 1979, 1–8 of tradeables is standardised by trade), the relative prices of tradeables and non tradeables and elasticities of substitution between pairs of non tradeables and between tradeables and non tradeables. Overall average production costs are minimised by the correct choice of the least cost 'route' from the location of raw materials through to the final destination.[1]

This location strategy is complicated in practice by a number of factors.

First, there are increasing returns to scale in many activities. Where only one destination is to be serviced, increasing returns means that location strategy may change in response to a change in the size of market. Where more than one destination is to be serviced, increasing returns in either production or transportation create an incentive to concentrate each stage of production at just a few locations. Increasing returns at any one stage of production or in the transport of any one semi-processed material may be diffused through the entire process, leading to the relocation of plants involved in quite remote stages of production, and to the reorganisation of the entire network of trade.

The second major factor is that modern businesses perform many activities other than routine production. Such activities require different inputs from production, but need to be integrated with the production process. They have a twofold influence on location: their own least cost location will differ from that of routine production because of their differing input requirements and secondly they will exercise a locational 'pull' on routine production. Two important non-production activities are marketing and research and development (R&D).[2] Both these functions represent an integral set of activities. Marketing has three main constituents: stockholding, distribution and advertising. The location of stockholding depends on the interplay between the better quality of service provided by decentralised stockholding and the declining costs of large, centralised stockholding and the declining costs of large, centralised warehouses. Only above a certain market size is local stockholding efficient. Routine advertising and distribution are generally located in the final market. The location of R&D will depend largely on the regional differentials in the price of the most important non traded input – skilled labour. However, this will be modified by information costs which play the same role as transport costs in routine production. Where a firm relies on the creation and internal use of productive knowledge from its own R&D department, there are strong reasons for centralising this creative function and integrating it closely with the more creative aspects of marketing and production.[3] Constant reworking of ideas through teamwork is necessary for least cost innovation and the importance of information flows will encourage the centralisation of these activities. However the more routine 'development' work may be much more diffused: the communications problem is not so great and local knowledge and inputs are more important. We conclude that the location strategy of a firm which integrates production marketing and R&D is highly complex. The activities are normally interdependent and information flows as well as transport costs must be considered. Information costs which increase with distance encourage the centralisation of activities where exchanges of knowledge through teamwork are of the essence. Such activities are the 'high level' ones of basic research, innovative production and the development marketing strategy; they require large inputs of skilled labour, and the availability of skilled labour will therefore exert a significant influence on the location strategy of such firms.[4]

The third factor which complicates the location strategies of firms is that in practice they operate largely in imperfectly competitive markets. This means that, in many cases, MNEs cannot be considered as price takers in intermediate and factor markets. Consequently, a firm which can force down input or factor prices in a particular region will tend to concentrate the production processes which are intensive in these inputs in that region. It has been argued that the explanation of monopsony power may also exert a significant influence on a firm's choice of production technique in a particular region.[5]

The fourth factor is government intervention. The influence of taxes and tariffs and other regulations such as preferential duties has been shown by many analysts to affect location[6] and it is unnecessary to elaborate on this here.

Finally, location decisions will be influenced by the ownership effect, or the extent to which the internalisation of markets in the firm modify the above considerations. This is examined in detail in the following section.

To sum up, the location decisions of firms in the international economy will in practice differ considerably from the predictions of the theory of the location of production under ideal competitive conditions where transport costs are the only barrier to trade. The possibilities of economies of scale in certain activities, the complexities of the activities, the extent of their integration, the type of market structure and the extent of Government intervention will all influence location strategy. We now examine ownership effects and the extent to which location strategy is dependent on the replacement of external markets by internal markets within the firm.

3. THE OWNERSHIP OF PRODUCTION

Having considered location effects in some detail, we can now turn our attention to the ownership of production, considering production locations unchanged. A strong case can be made for the contention that the major dynamic of the world economy is changing *ownership* effects which influence the pattern of distribution of production between MNEs and national firms. Resource endowments are to a large extent geographically fixed: copper, bauxite and oil reserves for instance. The question at issue is why US owned copper companies, US and Canadian aluminium producers and US and UK oil companies should dominate their markets. We argue here that the essence of the ownership effect can be explained in terms of the internalisation of key intermediate goods markets within firms of particular nationalities.

In a situation where firms are attempting to maximise profits in a world of imperfect markets, there will often exist an incentive to bypass imperfect markets in intermediate products. Their activities which were previously linked by the market mechanism are brought under common ownership and control in a 'market' internal to the firm. Where markets are internalised across national boundaries, MNEs are created.[7]

Benefits of internalisation arise from the avoidance of imperfections in the external market, but there are also costs. The optimum size of firm is set where the costs and benefits of further internalisation are equalised at the margin. We now go on to examine these costs and benefits and to consider how they apply in practice.

Benefits from 'internalisation' arise from five main types of market imperfection. Firstly, production takes time. Often activities linked by the market involve significant time lags and the relevant futures markets required for their coordination are inadequate or completely lacking. This creates a strong incentive for the creation of an internal future market. Secondly, the efficient explanation of market power may require discriminating pricing of a type not feasible in an external market – this will encourage the monopolist to integrate forward and the monopsonist to integrate backwards. Thirdly, internal markets remove – or prevent the growth of – bilateral concentrations of market power, and thus reduce the likelihood of unstable bargaining situations. The fourth type of imperfection occurs where there is inequality between buyer and seller with respect to the evaluation of a product. 'Buyer uncertainty' is prevalent where the product in question is a type of knowledge, which cannot be properly valued unless the valuer is in full possession of it. Buyer uncertainty is eliminated when buyer and seller are part of the same organisation. Fifth, internalisation may be a way of avoiding Government intervention. Prices reported in an organisation are much more difficult to monitor than those in an external market. Consequently government evaluation of tax and tariff payments and its enforcement of exchange control regulations becomes difficult, and the firm is able to exploit this through transfer pricing.

There are also costs of internalisation which may offset the benefits. Firstly some of the costs of operating a market – whether internal or external – are fixed independently of the volume of transactions, so that if a single external market is split up and internalised within a number of distinct firms the costs of market organisation for each firm will tend to rise. Secondly when a single external market is replaced by several internal ones it may be necessary for firms to adjust the scales of the activities linked by the markets to make them compatible; this may mean that some activities have to be operated on a less efficient scale than would be possible with a larger external market. Thirdly there may be increased communication costs. In an external market only price and quantity information is exchanged, but the demands of an internal market are normally greater because of the additional flows of accounting and control information. Finally internalisation costs have an international dimension arising from problems associated with foreign ownership and control. It should be noted that such problems can in varying degrees, be reduced or eliminated by *partially* internalising a market; for instance disposing of excess output on the open market or subcontracting outside the firm.

Having set out the general theory of the costs and benefits of internalising markets, we now turn to the application of the theory. It can be argued that the benefits of internalisation are particularly large in two cases. Firstly in industries where firms need to receive future supplies of vital raw materials and secondly in industries where flows of technical and marketing knowledge are important. The first phase of the growth of MNEs (up to the end of World War I) was concerned with maintaining and developing raw material supplies through vertical integration. However the major force in the world economy at the present time arises from the special advantages of internalising flows of knowledge. It is this factor to which we look to account for the continued strength of the ownership effect.

The production of knowledge (through R & D) is a lengthy process which requires careful synchronisation with other activities within the firm. Knowledge is a (temporary) 'natural monopoly' which is best exploited through discriminatory pricing. The buyers of knowledge are in many cases monopsonists, by virtue of control of regional distribution outlets, and so bilateral monopoly is likely if knowledge is licensed through an external market. Buyer uncertainty applies with particular force, for knowledge cannot be valued until it is in full possession of the valuer. Finally, because of difficulties of evaluation, knowledge flows provide an excellent basis for transfer pricing.

Internalisation across national boundaries of markets in knowledge-based products is clearly of great importance in accounting for overseas production by MNEs. Subsidiaries of MNEs are likely to be successful in taking a large share of foreign markets because of the 'branch plant effect' arising from subsidiary unit's access to the internal markets of MNEs. This access gives it a great advantage over those firms which have access only to (often inadequate) external markets. The greater the market imperfections, the more disadvantaged are 'national' firms in competing with MNEs.

Branch plant effect – the fact that subsidiaries of MNEs can out-perform national firms arise not from multinationality but from access to internal markets. This has two main aspects. Firstly, subsidiaries can obtain inputs which are simply not available in external markets. Most important among such inputs are proprietary knowledge (the output of past R & D), marketing know-how (arising from a worldwide intelligence system) and production experience. Secondly, branch plants can often obtain inputs more cheaply within the firm than their competitors can on the open market. This price differential arises, not from plant economies, but from access to the firm's internal futures markets, and from tax savings arising from transfer pricing.

Ownership effects may impinge on the location policies of MNEs. Firstly efficient transfer pricing normally involves giving the highest mark-up to operations in the lowest tax area. This policy may imply a complete change of location strategy within the scheme of section 2. Secondly, internalisation involves increased communication costs in the form of accounting and control information. As communication costs increase with geographical, social and linguistic 'distance', this will bias the location of internally coordinated activities towards a central region.

4. THE DIVISION OF NATIONAL MARKETS EXPLAINED

Combining both ownership and location effects allows us to give the reasons for the division of particular markets between domestic producers, local subsidiaries of MNEs, exports from foreign-owned plants and exports from MNEs. The division between exports and local servicing is largely the result of the economics of location. Least cost location, influenced by regional price differentials and by barriers to trade largely governs the proportion of a market serviced by exports. This however is modified by the economics of internalising a market, for not only can this affect the least cost location of any stage of production but the strategy of a MNE after having internalised a market may differ from that which external market forces would dictate. Consequently, the question of servicing a final market is inextricably bound up with the nature and ownership of internal markets – which will be dictated by the costs of benefits of internalisation.

In order to predict the division of national markets between the above groups we must have information relating to the following variables.

1. *Industry specific factors*: the nature of the product, the structure of the external market and the relation between the optimal scales of the activities linked by the market;
2. *Region specific factors*: factor costs in different regions, intermediate and raw material availability, the geographical and social distance between the regions involved;
3. *Nation specific factors*: the political and fiscal structures particularly of the nations involved;
4. *Firm specific-factors*: in particular the ability of management to communicate internally across national boundaries, and to cope with the legal and accounting complexities of international ownership.

From the above, the strategy of MNEs can be explained by combining our knowledge of locational influences with the opportunities of internalising markets profitably. Location and ownership effects are interdependent for the least cost location of an activity is at least partly determined by the ownership of the activities integrated with it.

NOTES

1. For a full exposition see Peter J. Buckley and Mark Casson *The Future of the Multinational Enterprise*, Macmillan London 1976. Chapter II Section 3.

2. R & D includes the innovative aspects of advertising.

3. Note the similarity of this argument with Raymond Vernon 'International Investment and International Trade in the Product Cycle', *Journal of Economics*, Vol. 80 (1966), pp. 190–207.

4. This agrees with Hymer's 'Law of Uneven Development': the centralisation of 'higher order activities' in the parent. See S. Hymer 'The Multinational Corporation and the Law of Uneven Development' in J.N. Bhagwati (Ed.), *Economics and World Order*, Macmillan, 1972.

5. See e.g. D.E. de Meza, Multinationals' Choice of Technique, *mimeo*, Reading 1975.

6. Notably T. Horst, 'The Theory of the Multinational Firm: Optimal Behaviour under Different Tariff and Tax Rates', *Journal of Political Economy*, Vol. 79, (1971), pp. 1059–1072.

7. Note the similarity of this argument with Stephen H. Hymer, *The international operations of national firms*, M.I.T. Press, Cambridge, Mass., 1976.

6

Trade, Location of Economic Activity and the Multinational Enterprise: A search for an eclectic approach

John H. Dunning

The main task of this article is to discuss ways in which production financed by foreign direct investment, that is, undertaken by MNEs, has affected our thinking about the international allocation of resources and the exchange of goods and services between countries. The analysis takes as its starting point the growing convergence between the theories of international trade and production, and argues the case for an integrated approach to international economic involvement, based both on the location-specific advantages of countries and the ownership-specific advantages of enterprises. In purusing this approach, the article sets out a systemic explanation of the foreign activities of enterprises in terms of their ability to internalize markets to their advantage. It concludes with a brief examination of some of the effects which the MNE is allegedly having on the spatial allocation of resources, and on the patterns of trade between countries.

We begin by looking at the received doctrine on international economic involvement. Until around 1950 this mainly consisted of a well-developed formal theory of international trade and a complementary but less well-developed theory of capital movements. With the notable exceptions of John Williams (1929)[1] and Bertil Ohlin (1933), international economists of the interwar years were less concerned with explanations of the composition of goods and factors actually traded across boundaries (and implicitly, at least, of the spatial distribution of economic activity) as with theorizing on what would occur if, in the real world, certain conditions were present. The Heckscher–Ohlin model, for example, asserted that, provided certain conditions were met, countries would specialize in the production of goods which required relatively large inputs of resources with which they were comparatively well endowed, and would export these in exchange for others which required relatively large inputs of factors with which they were comparatively poorly endowed. The conditions included that countries had two homogeneous inputs, labour and capital, both of which were: locationally immobile (i.e. they were to be used where they were located); inputs were converted into outputs by the most efficient (and internationally identical) production functions; all enterprises were price-takers, operating under conditions of atomistic competition; there were no barriers to trade and no transaction costs; and international tastes were similar.

The Heckscher–Ohlin model has been criticized in the literature on various grounds, including the unreality or inapplicability of its assumptions. Here, I would underline some of

Reprinted with permission from Drew, John (ed.) *Readings in International Enterprise*, London, 1995, 250–274.

the implications of three of these assumptions: factory immobility, the identity of production functions and atomistic competition. These are, first, that all markets operate efficiently; second, there are no external economies of production or marketing; and third, information is costless and there are no barriers to trade or competition. In such a situation international trade is the only possible form of international involvement; production by one country's enterprises for a foreign market must be undertaken within the exporting country; and all enterprises have equal access to location-specific endowments.

One of the deductions of the Heckscher–Ohlin theory is that trade will equalize factor prices. Replacing the assumption of factor immobility with that of the immobility of goods, it may be shown that movements of factors also respond to differential resource endowments. This was the conclusion of the early writings of Nurkse (1933), Ohlin (1933) and Iversen (1935) which explained international (portfolio) capital movements in terms of relative factor prices, or differential interest rates. For many years trade and capital theory paralleled each other, it being accepted that, in practice, trade in goods was at least a partial substitute for trade in factors. Eventually, the two were formally integrated into the factor price equalization theorem by Samuelson (1948) and Mundell (1957).

In the late 1950s there was a striking shift of direction in the interests of international economists brought on, *inter alia*, by the tremendous post-war changes in the form and pattern of trade and capital exports. Building on the empirical work of MacDougall (1951) and Leontief (1953 and 1956), and taking advantage of much improved statistical data, the 1960s saw the first real attempts to explain trade patterns as they were, rather than as they might be. Contemporaneously, the emergence of international production as a major form of non-trade involvement was demanding an explanation.

Over the past twenty years the positive theory of international economic involvement has 'taken off'. For most of the period it comprised two quite separate strands. The first concerned explanations of trade flows. Here, contributions were mainly centred on introducing more realism into the Heckscher–Samuelson–Ohlin doctrine. Basically, there were two main approaches. The first was that of the neofactor theories, which extended the two-factor Heckscher–Samuelson–Ohlin model to embrace other location-specific endowments (notably natural resources) and differences in the quality of inputs, especially labour. The second group of theories was more path-breaking, as it cut at the heart of the Heckscher–Samuelson–model by allowing the possibility of differences in the production function of enterprises and of imperfect markets. These theories, which included the neotechnology and scale economy models, were different in kind to the neofactor theories because they introduced new explanatory variables which focused not on the specific resource endowments of countries but on the exclusive possession of certain assets by enterprises. Sometimes, in addition to, but more often as a substitute for, orthodox theories, these new hypotheses of trade flows have been exposed to various degrees of testing. Yet as Hufbauer (1970) has shown, the predictive power of the neofactor and the neotechnology theories is scarcely better than that of the crude factor proportions theory. In his own words, 'No one theory monopolises the explanation of manufacturing trade'.

The second strand of research in the 1960s centred on explaining the growth and composition of foreign direct investment, or of production financed by such investment. At first causes were sought either from orthodox location theory (witness the plethora of microeconomic field studies and more macro-oriented econometric studies) or from neo-classical investment doctrine; but for various reasons, discussed elsewhere (Dunning, 1973a), neither approach proved very helpful. More rewarding were the attempts to identify the distinctive features of foreign direct investment in terms of ownership advantages of foreign firms. Though the gist of this idea was contained in the writings of Southard (1931) and Dunning (1958), it was left to Stephen Hymer in his seminal PhD thesis (Hymer 1960) to explore it in depth. Out of this approach, later refined and extended by Caves (1971, 1974a, 1974b) several hypotheses, focusing on particular kinds of ownership advantages of MNEs, were put forward: for example, access to superior technology (Johnson 1970), better capabilities for product differentiation (Caves 1971), underutilization of entrepreneurial and managerial capacity (McManus 1972; Wolf 1977), while a more behavioural perspective was taken by Vernon and his colleagues, notably Knickerbocker (1973), who chose to emphasize the role played by defensive oligopolistic strategy. These theories, too, have been subject to some testing,[2] but again it seems clear that no single hypothesis offers a satisfactory explanation of non-trade involvement.

Though these new theories of trade and production originated quite independently of each other, by the early 1970s it was clear that they were converging on, and even overlapping, each other. Though expressed differently, the same variables were being increasingly used to explain both trade and non-trade involvement. Comparable to the technological gap theory of trade was the knowledge theory of direct investment; analogous to monopolistic competitive theories of trade were theories of direct investment focused on product differentiation and multi-plant economies. Yet, with the exception of Vernon's early integration of trade and investment as different stages of the product cycle (Vernon 1966), which took as its starting point the innovative advantages of enterprises in a particular country, and the later discovery of Horst (1972) that the same variable – size of firm – which best explained foreign investment also explained investment plus trade, no attempt was made to integrate the two forms of involvement into a single theory, although the need for this had been discerned by Baldwin (1970) and others. Nor, indeed, was there any explicit recognition that, because the decisions to trade or engage in foreign production are often alternative options to the same firm, any explanation of one must, of necessity, take account of the other.

The last decade has seen the first, albeit faltering, attempts to do just this. In a paper published in 1973, this author suggested that only by considering trade and foreign production as alternative forms of international involvement in terms of ownership and location endowments could the economic implications of the UK joining the EEC be properly evaluated (Dunning 1973b). Hirsch (1976) formalized these concepts into a model that specifies, very clearly, the conditions under which foreign markets will be serviced by alternative routes. Parry (1975) applied these concepts to a study of the pharmaceutical industry; his contribution is especially noteworthy as he included licensing as a third form of economic involvement. Buckley and Dunning (1976) examined comparative US and UK trade and non-trade in these terms. Swedenborg (1979) uses a similar approach in her analysis of the international operations of Swedish firms. In the belief that this is a helpful route towards an eclectic theory of international economic involvement, I now explore it in more detail.

INTERNATIONAL ECONOMIC INVOLVEMENT

Exactly what is to be explained? Here an important point of taxonomy arises. A country's economic involvement outside its national boundaries may be perceived in two ways. First, it may mean the extent to which its own resources, that is, those located within its boundaries, are used by economic agents (irrespective of their nationality) to produce goods or services for sale outside its boundaries; or the extent to which it imports either resources or the products of resources located in other countries. This is the interpretation of orthodox international economics; *inter alia* it implies arm's length trade in inputs and outputs. But second, a country's involvement may mean the extent to which its own economic agents[3] service foreign markets with goods and services, irrespective of where the resources needed to do this are located or used, and the extent to which its own economic agents are supplied goods by foreign owned firms, irrespective of where the production is undertaken. Here, a country's economic space is perceived more in terms of the markets exploited by its institutions than of its geographical boundaries.

Like the distinction between gross national product and gross domestic product[4] which of the two interpretations is the more appropriate depends on the purpose for which it is being used. But for an evaluation of the contribution of a country's international economic involvement to the economic welfare of its citizens, the second has much to commend it, particularly where inward or outward investment account for a substantial proportion of its net capital formation.

Economic involvement by one country's enterprises in another may be for purposes of supplying both foreign and home markets. Production for a particular foreign market may be wholly or partly located in the home country, in the foreign market, in a third country or in a combination of the three. Similarly, production for the home market may be serviced from a domestic or a foreign location.

The capability of a home country's enterprises to supply either a foreign or domestic market from a foreign production base depends on their possessing certain resource endowments not available to, or not utilized by another country's enterprises. We use resource endowments in the Fisherian sense (Johnson 1968) to mean assets capable of generating a future income stream. They include not only tangible assets, such as natural resources, manpower and capital, but intangible assets, such as knowledge, organizational and entrepreneurial skills, and access to markets. Such endowments could be purely location specific to the home country, in other words they have to be used where they are located[5] but are available to all firms, or they could be ownership specific, that is, internal to the enterprise of the home country, but capable of being used with other resources in the home country or elsewhere.[6] In most cases, both location and ownership endowments affect competitiveness.

For some kinds of trade it is sufficient for the exporting country to have a location-endowment advantage over the importing country, that is, it is not necessary for the exporting firms to have ownership-endowment advantage over indigenous enterprises in the importing country. Much of the trade between industrialized and non-industrialized countries (which is of the Ricardian or H/O type) is of this kind. Other trade, such as that which mainly takes place between developed industrialized countries, is of high skill intensive or sophisticated consumer goods products, and is based more on the ownership advantages of the exporting firms;[7] but, observe, this presupposes that it is better to use these advantages in combination with location-specific endowments in the exporting rather than in the importing (or in a third) country. Where, however, these latter endowments favour the importing (or a third) country, foreign production will replace trade. Foreign production then implies that location-specific endowments favour a foreign country, but ownership endowments favour the home country's firms, these latter being sufficient to overcome the costs of producing in a foreign environment (Hirsch 1976). (Again we assume that transfer costs can be considered as a negative endowment of countries other than the country of marketing.)

From this it follows that any theory that purports to explain the determinants of any one form of international economic involvement is unlikely to explain the whole; nor, where that form is one of a number of possible alternatives, will it be adequately explained unless the forces explaining these alternatives are also taken into account. One should not be surprised, then, if trade theories of the neofactor brand, based on location-specific endowments, will not normally be able to explain trade in goods based on ownership-specific endowments. But neither should one be disquieted if the neotechnology and monopolistic competitive theories of trade, based on ownership specific endowments, are also inadequate where the use of such advantages is better exploited in conjunction with location specific endowments of foreign countries.

It may be reasonably argued, however, that this latter criticism would be better directed against the way in which data on international transactions are collected and presented, and the way in which the exported ownership advantages are priced. First, trade statistics usually give details of the gross output of goods exported. But where exports contain a high import content, their total value may tell us little about the use made of indigenous endowments. This deficiency can only be overcome by recording exports on a domestic value-added basis. Second, trade statistics either ignore, or classify completely separately, intermediary goods, such as technology, management and organization, which are exported in their own right. If these could be given a commodity classification, and their value added to the export of final products, then the ownership advantages of exporting enterprises would be better captured. Third, where trade takes place within the same enterprises the recorded prices may bear little resemblance to arm's length prices, and so to the value of factor inputs used. If these problems could be overcome, a combination of the neofactor, neotechnology and monopolistic competitive theories of trade would probably explain trade patterns very well.

MULTINATIONAL ENTERPRISES

So far the multinational enterprise has not been explicitly introduced into the discussion. MNEs are companies which undertake productive activities outside the country in which they are incorporated. They are, by definition, also companies which are internationally involved. The extent to which they engage in foreign production will depend on their comparative ownership advantages *vis-à-vis* host country firms, and the comparative location endowments of home and foreign countries.

Unlike location-specific endowments, which are external to the enterprises that use them, ownership-specific endowments are internal to particular enterprises. They consist of tangible and intangible resources, including technology, which itself dictates the efficiency of resource usage. Unlike location endowments many ownership endowments take on the quality of public goods, that is, their marginal usage cost is zero or minimal (hence, wherever a marginal revenue can be earned, but is not earned, they are underutilized); and although their origin may be partly determined by the industry or country characteristics of enterprises, they can be used anywhere.

What, then determines the ownership advantages which one country's enterprises possess over those of another? For our purposes, we distinguish between three kinds of advantage. The first comprises those which any firms may have over another producing in the same location. Here, Bain's (1956) classic work on the barriers to new competition provides the basic answer. Such benefits may lie in the access to markets or raw materials not available to competitors; or in size (which may both generate scale economies and inhabit effective competition); or in an exclusive possession of intangible assets, for example, patents, trademarks, and management skills, which enable it to reach a higher level of technical or price efficiency and/or achieve more market power. These advantages, then, stem from size, monopoly power and better resource capability and usage.

The second type of advantage is that which a branch plant of a national enterprise may have over a *de novo* enterprise (or over an existing enterprise breaking into a new product area), again producing in the same location. This arises because, while the branch plant may benefit from many of the endowments of the parent company, for example, access to cheaper inputs, knowledge of markets, centralized accounting procedures, administrative experience, R&D, at zero or low marginal cost, the *de novo* firm will normally have to bear their full cost. The greater the non production overheads of the enterprise, the more pronounced this advantage is likely to be.

The third type of advantage is that which arises specifically from the multinationality of a company, and is an extension of the other two. The larger the number and the greater the difference between economic environments in which an enterprise operates, the better placed it is to take advantage of different factor endowments and market situations. I shall return to this point later in the article.

Most of these benefits, both individually and collectively, have been used by economists to explain the participation of affiliates of MNEs in the output of industries in host countries. However, while recognizing that they are interrelated, there have been few explicit attempts to explain either the basis of interrelationship or why the more marketable of the advantages are sold directly to other firms. In consequence, not only has one of the fundamental attributes of MNEs been largely overlooked, but so also has the basis for much of the concern about the present international economic order. The substance of our thesis is not, in itself, new; it is more a reinterpretation and extension of an idea first formulated by Coase in 1937, and more recently resurrected in the literature by Arrow (1969, 1975), Williamson (1971, 1975, 1979), Alchian and Demsetz (1972), Furobotn and Pejovich (1972), McManus (1972), Baumann (1975), Brown (1976), Magee (1977a, 1977b) and, perhaps most systematically of all, by Buckley and Casson (1976).[8]

The thesis is that the international competitiveness of a country's products is attributable not only to the possession of superior resources and, in some cases, the necessity of its enterprises but also to the desire and ability of those enterprises to internalize the advantages resulting from this possession; and that servicing a foreign market through foreign production confers unique benefits of this kind. Where, for example, enterprises choose to replace, or not to use, the mechanism of the market, but instead allocate resources by their own control procedures, not only do they gain but, depending on the reason for internalization, others (notably their customers and suppliers prior to vertical integration, and their competitors prior to horizontal integration) may lose. Internalization is thus a powerful motive for takeovers or mergers, and a valuable tool in the strategy or oligopolists.

It has long been recognized that such gains may follow from vertical integration and, to a lesser extent, from horizontal integration of a firm's activities; and much of current antitrust legislation is designed to prevent or minimize abuses arising as a result. But much less attention has been paid to the type of internalizing practised by conglomerates, or that which reflects in the internal extension of a company's activities, or that associated with the internalization of resources, products or markets over geographical space.

Consider, for example, the areas in which the participation of MNEs, irrespective of their country of origin, is most pronounced in host countries. These include export-oriented primary goods sectors requiring large amounts of capital, for example, aluminium, oil, copper and/or those faced with substantial barriers to foreign marketing and distribution, for example, bananas, pineapples, coffee; technologically advanced manufacturing industries or those supplying branded consumer products with a high income elasticity of demand and subject to the economies of large-scale production; capital or skill intensive service industries, such as insurance, banking and large-scale construction; and activities in which the spatial integration of inputs, products or markets is essential to efficiency, for example, airlines, hotels. All of these not only require endowments in which MNEs have a comparative advantage, and which are difficult to acquire by *de novo* entrants, but, more pertinent to our argument, they are all sectors in which there is a pronounced propensity of firms to internalize activities, particularly across national boundaries.

What, then, are these incentives of firms to internalize activities? Basically they are to avoid the disadvantages or capitalize on the advantages of imperfections or disequilibria in external mechanisms of resource allocation.[9] These mechanisms are mostly of two kinds – the price system and public authority fiat. Where markets are perfectly competitive, the coordinating of interdependent activities cannot be improved upon; once imperfections arise or can be exploited through internalization, this becomes a possibility.

Market imperfections may be both structural and cognitive. Uncertainty over future market conditions in the absence of competitive future markets, or about government policies, is another kind of imperfection.

Structural imperfections arise where there are barriers to competition and economic rents are earned; where transaction costs are high; or where the economies of interdependent activities cannot be fully captured.

Cognitive imperfections arise wherever information about the product or service being marketed is not readily available, or is costly to acquire. The cost of uncertainty may be gauged by the risk premium required to discount it, which may differ quite significantly between firms. From the buyer's viewpoint, market imperfections to avoid include uncertainty over the availability and price of essential supplies, and lack of control over their delivery timing and quality. From the seller's viewpoint, the propensity to internalize will be greatest where the market does not permit price discrimination; where the costs of enforcing property rights and controlling information flows are high; where the output produced is of more value to the seller than the buyer is willing to pay (again, possibly because of ignorance on the part of the buyer),[10] or, in the case of selling outlets, where the seller, to protect his reputation, wishes to ensure a certain quality of service, including after-sales maintenance. For both groups of firms, and for those considering horizontal integration, the possession of underutilized resources, particularly entrepreneurial and organizational capacity, which may be used at low marginal cost to produce products complementary to those currently being supplied, also fosters internalization.

At the same time, to benefit from some of these advantages an enterprise must be of sufficient size. This prompts firms to engage in product diversification or integration, which, in turn, increases their opportunities to profit from other internalizing practices such as cross-subsidization of costs and predatory pricing. One suspects that many of the advantages of conglomerate mergers are of this kind; and it cannot be a coincidence that, in recent years, takeovers and mergers have been concentrated in areas in which advantages of internalization are most pronounced.[11]

Public intervention in the allocation of resources may also encourage enterprises to internalize activities. Many policy instruments of governments, however justified in the pursuance of macroeconomic (and other) goals, may create distortions in the allocation of resources which enterprises may seek to exploit or protect themselves against. Some of these provoke reactions from all enterprises; others from only those which operate across national boundaries.

Here the analysis will be confined to two kinds of government intervention especially relevant to the behaviour of MNEs. The first concerns the production and marketing of public goods, which are not only characterized by their zero marginal cost, but by the fact that their value to the owner may hinge on the extent to which others also possess them. Under these circumstances, an orthodox perfect market is impossible, unless the purchaser relies on the seller to withhold the sale of a good to other buyers, or not to price it lower.

Some commodities and services produced by private enterprises also have the characteristics of public goods. The major example is technology – an intermediary good which embraces all kinds of knowledge embodied in both human and non-human capital (Johnson 1970). The significance of technology in the modern world economy needs no elaboration: it is the main engine of development, a leading determinant of both absolute and relative living standards, and a controlling factor in the spatial allocation of resources. Its phenomenal growth since the Second World War, especially in the field of information and communications technology, has undoubtedly facilitated the internationalization of firms, just as the railroad, telegraph and telephone helped the creation of national enterprises a century ago.[12]

It is my contention that the need both to generate innovations and ideas and to retain exclusive right to their use has been one of the main inducements for enterprises to internalize their activities in the last two decades. Governments have encouraged this by extensively subsidizing R&D, continuing to endorse the patent system and recognizing that, in some industries, if the benefits of technological advances are to be fully exploited, not only may it be necessary to restrict the number of producers but that enterprises should be free to internalize their knowledge producing with their knowledge-consuming activities. Even without the intervention of governments, technology possesses many of the attributes for internalizing (or not externalizing) markets. At the time of its production, it is the sole possession of the innovator, who naturally wishes to exploit it most profitably; it is costly and takes time to produce but there is no future market in it; it is often difficult for a potential buyer to value as its usefulness can only be determined as it has been purchased. Yet often, for its efficient exploitation, it needs complementary or back-up resources. These qualities apply particularly to the kind of knowledge which cannot be patented, for example, financial systems, organizational skills, marketing expertise, management experience and so on.

The second example of government intervention is particularly relevant to the operations of MNEs. It both encourages such enterprises to internalize existing activities and to engage in new activities which offer the possibility of internalizing gains. It arises because of different economic policies of national governments which often lead to distortions in the international allocation of resources. Assume, for example, that an MNE wishes to maximize its post-tax profits and that corporate tax rates differ between countries. One way it can reduce its total tax burden is to capitalize on its intra-group transactions by manipulating its transfer prices so as to record the highest profits in the lowest tax areas. Other things being equal, the more internal transactions the company engages in the greater its opportunities for doing this – hence, in the case of MNEs, the added impetus to engage in a global strategy and to practise product or process specialization within its organization.

The MNE has other reasons for internalizing its operations across boundaries (Rugman 1980). These include the desire to minimize the risk and/or costs of fluctuating exchange rates; to cushion the adverse effects of government legislation or policy, for example, in respect to dividend remittances; to be able to take advantage of differential interest rates and 'leads' and 'lags' in intra-group payments; and to adjust the distribution of its short-term assets between different currency areas. Some of these benefits of internalization are now being eroded by government surveillance over transfer pricing and by the tendency for contractual arrangements between foreign and indigenous firms to replace equity investments of the former.

How far MNEs actually do manipulate intra-group prices to transfer income across national boundaries is still a matter for empirical research; so far the evidence collected is partial and impressionistic. Suffice to say there are many reasons why an MNE may wish to take advantage of such opportunities (Lall 1973), and that however vigilant the tax authorities may be in some areas, for example, the pricing of intangible assets, the difficulty of (1) estimating the extent to which a transfer of goods or services has taken place, and (2) assigning a value to them, is a very real one.

It has been illustrated, at some length, why firms, and MNEs in particular, gain from internalizing their activities, especially in respect of the production and marketing of technology. Another sector in which MNEs are particularly active is the capital intensive, resource based industries. Here, all the traditional reasons for vertical integration hold good, in addition to those which result from multinationality *per se*; the classic example is the oil industry. They imply, for the most part, a vertical division of activity of firms, though the operations may be horizontal as well, where similar products are produced. Here, too, the impetus to internalize transactions (as opposed to engaging in contractual arrangements) in the case of international vertical integration is likely to be greater than in the case of domestic vertical integration.

It must not be forgotten, however, that there are costs as well as benefits to internalizing economic activities; for an examination of these see Coase (1937) and Buckley and Casson (1976). As markets become less imperfect the net gains of internalization are reduced. The move towards externalizing the marketing of many raw materials, partly stimulated by the actions of governments, testifies to this. In his study of UK direct investment overseas, Reddaway *et al.* (1968) found that only 4 per cent of the output of UK plantation and mining affiliates, originally set up to supply the investing firms, was now directly imported by them.

It can be concluded, therefore, that the ownership advantages of firms stem from their exclusive possession and use of certain kinds of assets. Very often enterprises acquire these rights by internalizing those previously distributed by the market or public fiat, or by not externalizing those which they originate themselves. This will only be profitable in imperfect market conditions, and where it is thought the coordinating and synergizing properties of the firm to allocate resources are superior to those of markets or public fiat. It is possible to identify the source of such imperfections, both within countries and internationally, and to point to the types of activities which offer the greatest gains from internalization. Of these, the production and marketing of intangible assets and of essential location-specific resources are the two most important. Both happen to be areas in which MNEs are particularly involved; the fact that the ownership advantages are exploited by foreign production is partly explained by location-specific endowments of the foreign country, and partly by certain ownership advantages which accrue only when a firm produces outside its national boundaries.[13]

AN ECLECTIC THEORY OF PRODUCTION

What is the link between the above discussion and other explanations of international involvement? Simply this. The neotechnology theories of trade and the knowledge theories of direct investment both emphasize the possession of superior technology as an explanation of both trade and production. The monopolistic competitive theories concentrate on some aspect of arm's length imperfect competition as the explanation for trade and investment.

It is my contention that the two approaches should be treated as complementary aspects of an eclectic theory of international involvement, which should embrace not only the product but also the factor and intermediary goods markets, and should acknowledge that the ownership advantages arise not only from the exclusive possession of certain assets, but from the ability of firms to internalize these assets to protect themselves against the failure of markets (including the consequences of this failure for competitors' behaviour) and government fiat over the rest of their activities. Because it relates to the way in which the enterprise coordinates its activities, this approach may be called a systemic theory of ownership advantages, applied to both trade and international production.[14] In favouring such an approach admittedly I may be in danger of being accused of eclectic taxonomy. I also acknowledge the interdependence between technology, imperfect competition and the internalization process, and that it is not always easy to separate cause and effect.

But in the search for a composite measure of ownership advantage a systemic approach has something to commend it. Empirically, there can be little doubt of the increase in the vertical and horizontal integration of firms and of market and product diversification, which has enabled firms to benefit from the internalization of their activities. This is demonstrated both by the increase in the concentration of enterprises in industrial economies in the postwar period and by the growing importance of the pre- and post-production activities of firms. Other data suggest that about one half of all exports of MNEs are intra-group in character.

More generally, the eclectic model can be perceived as a general theory of international production in so far as it provides an analytical framework for explaining all forms of such production. This, however, is not to assert that particular forms of international production are to be explained by the same ownership, location of internalization characteristics. This is clearly not the case, and it is readily accepted that different types of international production may call for quite different explanations. But our contention is that these should be regarded as complementary, rather than alternative, interpretations of MNE activity and of the eclectic paradigm. For this reason, I have no difficulty in reconciling seemingly competing theories within this paradigm, as, more often than not, they are seeking to explain different things.

What, then, is the positive value of the eclectic theory of international production? The theory suggests that, given the distribution of location-specific endowments, enterprises which have the greatest opportunities for and derive the most from, internalizing activities will be the most competitive in foreign markets.[15] *Inter alia* these advantages will differ according to industry, country and enterprise characteristics. Hence, the ownership advantages of Japanese iron and steel firms over South Korean iron and steel firms will be very different from those of UK tobacco firms over Brazilian tobacco firms or US computer firms over French computer firms. Enterprises will engage in the type of internalization most suited to the factor combinations, market situations and government policies with which they are faced. For example, the systemic theory would suggest not only that research-intensive industries would tend to be more multi-national than other industries, but that internalization to secure foreign-based raw materials would be greater for enterprises from economies which have few indigenous materials than those which are self-sufficient; that the most efficient MNEs will exploit the most profitable foreign markets – compare, for example, the US and UK choice of investment outlets (Stopford 1976); that the participation of foreign affiliates is likely to be greatest in those sectors of host countries where there are substantial economies of enterprise size. This theory is consistent with Horst's conclusion (1972) that most of the explanatory variables of foreign direct investment can be captured in the size of enterprise; indeed, one would normally expect size and the propensity to internalize to be very closely correlated, and MNEs to be better equipped to spread risks than national multiproduct firms.

What does the eclectic theory predict that the other theories of international production do not? Taking the theories as a group, probably very little, except so far as the independent variables fail to capture the advantages of internalization. Indeed, it could be argued that this theory is less an alternative theory of ownership advantages of enterprises than one which pinpoints the essential and common characteristics of each of the traditional explanations. There is, however, one difference of substance. The eclectic approach would argue that it is not the possession of technology *per se* which gives an enterprise selling goods embodying that technology to foreign markets (irrespective of where they are produced) an edge over its competitors, but the advantage of internalizing that technology rather than selling it to a foreign producer for the production of those goods. It is not the orthodox type of monopoly advantages which give the enterprise an edge over its rivals – actual or potential – but the advantages which accrue through internalization, for example, transfer price manipulation, security of supplies and markets, and control over use of intermediate goods. It is not surplus entrepreneurial resources *per se* which lead to foreign direct investment, but the ability of enterprises to combine these resources with others to take advantage of the economies of production of joint products.

In other words, without the incentive to internalize the product and/or sale of technology foreign investment in technology-based industries would give way to licensing agreements and/or to the outright sale of knowledge on a contractual basis. Without the incentive to internalize market imperfections there would be much less reason to engage in vertical or horizontal integration, and again transactions would take place between independent firms. This, it could be argued, is the distinctiveness of this approach.

LOCATION

So far the discussion has concentrated on the ownership endowments of its enterprises as an explanation of a country's international competitiveness, whatever the form of the involvement. It has been argued that, although the advantages are enterprise specific, the fact that these may differ according to nationality of enterprise suggests that such advantages, though endogenous to the individual firms at that time, are not independent of their industrial structure, or of the general economic and institutional environment of which they are part. For example, US government science and education policy may be a key variable in explaining the technological lead of US firms in many industries, while, as Vernon (1974) has pointed out, innovations respond to factor endowment and market needs, which also influence the likely advantages of internalizing those innovations. The institutional arrangements by which innovations are rewarded are no less relevant.

But these country or industry variables affecting ownership advantages are not the same as the location specific endowments referred to earlier. With this interpretation, these comprise three components: the resources which can only be used by enterprises in the locations in which they are sited, unavoidable or non-transferable costs such as taxes, government constraints on dividend remission, and the costs of shipping products from the country of production to the country of marketing.

Each of these elements has received extensive attention in the literature of location theory, which usually assumes ownership endowments as the same between firms, and seeks to explain where they are exploited. Our concern here is a different one. Put in question form it is: given the ownership endowments, is the location of production by MNEs likely to be different from that of non-MNEs? The systemic theory suggests that it is, and for three reasons. First, there may be particular internalizing economies resulting from the friction of geographical space. Second, the location-specific endowments, which offer the greatest potential for internalization, are not distributed evenly between countries.[16] Third, where there are differences in the market imperfections or government policies of countries, then MNEs might be influenced by the extent to which they take advantage of these imperfections by internalizing their operations.

In elaboration of these points, four observations can be made. First, various studies have underlined the advantages of coordinating R&D activities of MNEs (Ronstadt 1977; Fischer and Behrman 1979; Lall 1979) and centralizing them in or near the markets which stimulate such activities (Michalet 1973; Creamer 1976). In the case of US-based MNE, this suggests, that for most kinds of R&D, both ownership and location endowments work in favour of a home R&D base.[17] In the case of MNEs from smaller home markets this tendency may not be so pronounced. By contrast, because the advantages of internalization are generally much less, it may be profitable to spatially disperse some kinds of manufacturing activities, especially where the production processes involved have become standardized (Vernon 1974).

Second, an MNE which produces in different market environments may well seek to coordinate its activities differently. The degree of uncertainty over local consumer tastes, future market conditions and government policy certainly varies between countries. For example, the less imperfect is the market for technology, the less likely is an enterprise to market technology-based products itself. Compare, for example, the role of foreign pharmaceutical companies in Italy, which does not recognize patent protection on drugs, with that of such companies in almost any other European country. By contrast, in some developing countries, MNEs may be reluctant to license local firms because they feel that the complementary technology is insufficient to ensure the quality control they need.[18]

Third, and perhaps most important, is the advantage that a diversified earnings base provides for an MNE to exploit differential imperfections in national or international markets and/or currency areas (Aliber 1970), *inter alia*, through transfer-price manipulation; the use of leads and lags in intra group transactions; the acquisition and monitoring of information; and the extension of benefits enjoyed by multi-plant national firms at an international level. These are some of the (potential) advantages of internalization afforded by international production, compared with international trade.

Fourth, there is the drive towards international production as part of oligopolistic behaviour (Knickerbocker 1973; Flowers 1976; Graham 1978). This is really a territorial extension of domestic strategy, and does not pose any new conceptual problems (but see Vernon 1974). Again, however, in so far as a company perceives its foreign interests to be part

of a global strategy, rather than as an independent entity, the internalizing advanta‸
crucial to the locational decision of both leaders and followers.

EFFECT OF MNEs ON INTERNATIONAL DISTRIBUTION

In the light of the above analysis, what might one expect the impact of the MNE to be on location of production, the international diffusion or transfer of technology and trade patterns?

There are many different views about the effect of MNEs on the international distribution of resources. Partly, these reflect differences in the perspective one takes, for example, that of a particular country or region, or that of all countries; or of the goals one is seeking to promote. We shall confine ourselves to economic issues viewed in a global context from two main viewpoints. The first is that MNEs promote a more efficient distribution of resources since, by internalizing imperfect markets, they are able to overcome distortions in the economic system such as barriers to the transfer of technology, import controls and inappropriately valued exchange rates. Moreover, in a world of uncertainty and information imperfections, their more efficient scanning and monitoring processes, and their flexibility to respond better to market signals, is a useful competitive stimulus. In short, this view extols the MNE as an integrating force in the world economy, surmounting national barriers, circumventing high transaction costs and improving the allocating of resources.

The second view asserts that, far from overcoming market imperfections, the MNEs are themselves a major distorting force in resource allocation; this is partly because they operate mostly in oligopolistic markets and partly because of their ability to bypass market mechanisms and/or government regulations (Hymer 1970). As a result, it is argued, they engage in restrictive practices, raise barriers to entry and, by their internalization and centralization of decision-taking, adversely affect the efficiency of resource allocation between countries. Far from promoting competition, the coordination of activities by entrepreneurs freezes existing production patterns, encourages agglomeration and makes it more difficult for countries to exploit their dynamic comparative advantages. Since MNEs do exert monopoly power, it is legitimate (on the lines of the optimum tariff argument) for home or host countries to impose restrictions on their activities.

The truth, in so far as it is possible to generalize, is obviously somewhere between these two extremes, with the balance steering one way or another according to:

1. the efficiency of the resource allocative mechanism prior to the entrance of the MNEs;
2. the market conditions under which MNEs compete – which will vary *inter alia* according to industry and country.

But there are certain effects of MNEs, however they may be interpreted, which do seem to have been reasonably well established in the literature, and we will now touch on three of these.

1. In some instances, MNEs have been an integrating force and have taken advantage of existing factor endowments, thus promoting the more efficient use of resources. The best example is where mobile resources of capital and technology are transferred from a capital- and technology-rich country and combined with immobile resources of labour and/materials in labour- and materials-rich countries, thereby helping these countries to exploit their dynamic comparative advantage. Other examples include what is currently

happening in Europe as a result of the EC, namely, that the MNEs are rationalizing their activities to take advantage of the economies of specialization. This is a slow process but no different, in principle, to the behaviour of multiregional (national) enterprises in the USA, which may well be one of the explanations of the greater specialization in the USA than within the EC, as demonstrated by Hufbauer and Chilas (1974).

2. There is some evidence of a spatial specialization of the activities of MNEs and, in particular, the centralization of R&D activities in the home country. Something over 90 per cent of the R&D activities of Swedish and US MNEs is undertaken in their home countries, and the proportion is probably not very different for most of the other leading investors. Hymer suggests that MNEs are encouraging the specialization of activities, not for technological as much as organizational or strategic reasons, most of which enhance the incentive to internalize R&D in the home country. But it does not necessarily follow that, without MNEs, the distribution of innovative activities would have been any the less centralized. R&D among Japanese and European enterprises has certainly been stimulated by the competition from US MNEs. The impact on the UK pharmaceutical and semiconductor industries are classic examples (Tilton 1971; Lake 1976). In the LDCs, because of the lack of indigenous competitors, the Hymer hypothesis probably holds more weight, though even here there are examples of MNEs setting up specialized R&D facilities (Behrman and Fischer 1980).[19]

3. In any analysis of the impact of MNEs on trade and location it is useful to distinguish between the different motives for foreign direct investment. Kojima (1978), for example, has distinguished between trade-oriented and anti-trade-oriented activities of MNEs. He suggests that current Swedish and Japanese investments are mainly made in areas in which the home countries are losing a comparative advantage and host countries are gaining it. These have been of two kinds; one to exploit natural resources not available indigenously, and the other to switch labour intensive activities from high labour cost to low labour cost locations. On the other hand, Kojima asserts that many foreign investments by US firms have been made to protect an oligopolistic position in world markets and in response to trade barriers, and have transferred activities from which they have a comparative advantage to where they have a disadvantage. Such investments, he claims, are anti-trade oriented and run against the principles of comparative advantage. Kojima cites here the extensive US foreign investments in the capital and technologically intensive industries.

The border between transferring a comparative advantage and creating a new one is a narrow one, and the Kojima distinction between trade-generating and trade-destroying investments is not altogether convincing. Moreover, his approach tends to be a static one and is couched in terms of first-best solutions. It also fails to consider vertical specialization within industrial sectors. Assuming technology (as an intermediate good) can be sold for a competitive price between independent parties, one might reasonably expect non-skilled labour intensive operations of high technology industries to be transplanted to those areas which possess such labour in abundance, and countries with an abundance of materials to utilize such materials with technology developed by nations which have a limited amount of materials. The Japanese and US patterns may be complementary to each other; their ownership and locational advantages may reflect country specific characteristics.[20] Evidence collected about the trading patterns of US MNEs (Lipsey and Weiss 1973) supports this view. The imports of US MNEs tend to be more capital intensive than those of other US firms, mainly because of the ability of MNEs to export capital and technology to undertake the labour intensive production processes of a capital intensive product in low labour cost areas.

From a normative viewpoint, the point of greater interest is the extent to which technology transfer through the coordination of the firm is preferable to that of the market, but, on this subject, there has been only limited research (Arrow 1969; Williamson 1979; Teece 1979). Yet this, as has been suggested, is a crucial issue, which both helps to explain the growth of MNEs (relative to non-MNEs) and their effect on the spatial distribution of economic activity. Assuming perfectly competitive markets are not generally feasible (nor, from viewpoints other than economic efficiency, necessarily desirable), under what circumstances is it preferable for the resource allocative process to be decided upon by markets or governments, however imperfect they may be, and under what circumstances by the internal governance of MNEs? For there is no *a priori* reason to suppose one form of resource allocation is preferable to the other. In remedying the imperfections and alleged distorting behaviour of MNEs, should not as much attention be given to removing some of the distortions of the environment in which they operate, so that they have less incentive to internalize their activities? To give a recent example, the replacement of fixed by flexible rates has decisively reduced the impetus for MNEs to engage in speculative or protective currency movements across boundaries. The candidate most in need of attention at the moments is technology. It is here that the present system of rewards and penalties leaves so much to be desired (Johnson 1970) and it is here that both the incentive to internalize by MNEs and the potential for distorting behaviour on their part in exploiting the benefits of that internalization arise.

In the last resort, however, we must acknowledge that it is not efficiency, and certainly not efficiency viewed from a global standpoint, that is the standard by which the relative merits of internalization of MNEs and imperfect markets of allocating resources is likely to be assessed. It is the effects of such patterns of resource allocation on the distribution of income between or within nations; on the relative economic powers of countries or of different groups of asset owners; on the sovereignty of one country to manage its own affairs. It is these matters which are at the centre of the arena of public debate at the moment; and it is on such criteria as these that the actions of MNEs are judged.

Some countries facing the choice offered above have clearly preferred to buy their resources in imperfect markets than through MNEs (Japan is the obvious example), while many LDCs are increasingly seeking to depackage the package of resources provided by MNEs in the belief that they can externalize the internal economies. Within the advanced countries the non-market route is generally accepted. But here, too, there are murmurings of concern, articulated not only in such polemics as *The Global Reach* (Barnet and Muller 1974) but in research studies done at the Brookings Institution (Bergsten *et al.* 1978) and by Peggy Musgrave (1975) on the effect of the (internalizing) advantages of international production on the domestic economic power of US corporations.

This particular area of the debate on the role of MNEs in trade and the transfer of technology and the location of production is still in its infancy. It is an area hazardous and not altogether attractive for the academic economist; the issues are controversial; the concepts are elusive; the data are not easily subject to quantitative manipulation and appraisal; and the standard of debate is often low. But, intellectually, it presents a great challenge, offering much scope for the collaboration not only of economists of different specialities and persuasions, but between economists and researchers from other disciplines. For these reasons alone, it deserves to attract our ablest minds.

NOTES

1. The following observation by Williams (1929) about industries which had expanded beyond their political frontiers is of interest to our discussion.

> They represent in some cases the projection by one country into others of its capital, technique, special knowledge along the lines of an industry and its market, as against the obvious alternative of home employment in other lines. They represent, in other cases, an international assembling of capital and management for world enterprises ramifying into many countries. They suggest very strikingly an organic inter-connection of international trade, movement of productive factors, transport and market organisation.

2. For further details see Dunning (1981) Chapter 3, p. 48.

3. Mainly enterprises: by a country's enterprises is meant those whose head offices are legally incorporated in that country.

4. Gross domestic product = incomes earned from domestic resources; gross national product = gross national product + income earned from assets abroad less income paid to foreigners on domestic assets.

5. Proximity to the point of same may be treated as a location specific endowment for these purposes; distance (implying transport and other transfer costs) is thus considered as a negative endowment.

6. See Lall (1980) for a discussion on the extent to which ownership advantages are mobile, that is, transferable across national boundaries.

7. For an elaboration of the complementarity between the neofactor and neotechnology theories of trade, see Hirsch (1974).

8. One of the most recent and stimulating contributions on these lines is contained in Swedenborg (1979). For a general reappraisal on the literature on internalization see Rugman (1980) and Teece (1981).

9. To avoid being subject to imperfections of markets when they are the weaker party to an exchange but to capitalize on imperfections when they are the stronger party.

10. Such as particularly applies in the case of transactions involving non-standard technology or information, and which are infrequent and conducted under uncertainty.

11. For a recent study of the applicability of the eclectic theory and the markets and hierarchies paradigm to the acquisition of foreign firms in Canada and that of domestic firms in the USA see Calvet (1980).

12. The transition from regional to national railroads in the nineteenth and early twentieth century was paralleled by the transition from national to multinational airlines after the Second World War.

13. We have not the space to deal with the role of internalization in prompting other forms of foreign direct investment; in some cases, the coordinating advantages of the firm clearly transcends that of the market for technological reasons, such as airlines; in others it is much more to do with controlling information among interdependent activities, such as advertising, and tourism; or as a form of oligopolistic strategy. In many cases, an investment based on technological innovation has managed to create its own barriers to entry through economies of size.

14. Licensing and other forms of contractual arrangements of intermediate products.

15. The points made in this paragraph are extended and set out in a rather different way in Tables 3.1 and 4.2 of Dunning (1981).

16. This point is elaborated in Chapter 4.

17. Lall (1979) suggests that in cases where major technological efforts on products and processes are not crucially linked to each other, international experience and cost advantages tend to promote greater reliance on foreign R&D. By contrast, in those sectors where innovation centres around product development and testing it is much more difficult to separate any major part of R&D activity from the main markets and centre of decision-taking. Michalet (1973), on the other hand, distinguishes between a specialized and imitative R&D strategy of MNEs, while Ronstadt (1977) adopts a more functional approach arguing that different types of R&D have different location needs. In a study of the overseas R&D activities of fifty-five US-based MNEs, Mansfield et al. (1979) found that such activities were increasing relative to those in the USA and were concentrated on product and process improvements and modifications rather than the discovery of new products and processes. The authors argued that one important reason – at least in the 1960s – for foreign R&D activities was that the cost of R&D inputs was considerably lower in Japan, Europe and Canada than in the USA.

18. See Chapter 5 of Dunning (1981).

19. Mainly in material processing or product adaptation to meet specialized local needs. Behrman and Fischer (1980) note that US enterprises have some R&D facilities in Hong Kong, Argentina, Colombia, Egypt, Philippines and Taiwan, whereas Argentina, Hong Kong and Singapore are among developing countries attracting such activities by European MNEs.

20. This point is further explored in Dunning (1981) Chapter 4. Here it is worth pointing out that vertical foreign direct investment often precedes horizontal foreign direct investment (as it did in the UK and USA)

and that the pattern of new Japanese investment in the late 1970s resembles much more that traditional US kind than it did in the 1960s.

REFERENCES

Alchian, A., and Demsetz, H. (1972), 'Production, information costs and economic organisation', *American Economic Review*, Vol. 62 (December).

Aliber, R. (1970), 'A theory of foreign direct investment', in C.P. Kindleberger (ed.), *the International Corporation* (Cambridge, Mass.: MIT Press).

Arrow, K.J. (1969), 'The organisation of economic activity: issues pertinent to the choice of market and non market considerations', in Joint Economic Committee, *The Analysis of Public Expenditures: the PPB System* (Washington, DC: US Government Printing Office).

Arrow, K.J. (1975), 'Vertical integration and communication', *Bell Journal of Economics*, Vol. 5 no. 1 (Spring).

Bain, J.S. (1956), *Barriers to New Competition* (Cambridge, Mass.: Harvard University Press).

Baldwin, R.E. (1970), 'International trade in inputs and outputs', *American Economic Review*, Vol. 60 (May).

Barnet, R.J., and Muller, R.E. (1974), *The Global Reach* (New York: Simon and Schuster).

Baumann, H. (1975), 'Merger theory, property rights and the pattern of US direct investment in Canada', *Weltwirtschaftliches Archiv*, Vol. 111, no. 4.

Behrman, J.N., and Fischer, W.A. (1980), *Overseas R and D Activities of Transnational Corporations* (Cambridge, Mass.: Oelgeschlager, Gunn and Hain).

Bergsten, E.F., Horst, T., and Moran, T.E. (1978), *American Multinationals and American Interests* (Washington DC: Brookings Institution).

Brown, W.B. (1976), 'Islands of conscious power: MNCs in the theory of the firm', *MSU Business Topics* (Summer).

Buckley, P.J., and Casson, M. (1976), *The Future of the Multinational Enterprise* (London: Macmillan).

Buckley, P.J., and Dunning, J.H. (1976), 'The industrial structure of US direct investment in the UK', *Journal of International Business Studies*, Vol. 7 (Summer).

Calvet, A.L. (1980), 'Markets and hierarchies: towards a theory of international business', PhD thesis, Sloane School of Management, Cambridge, Mass.

Caves, R.E. (1971), 'Industrial corporations: the industrial economics of foreign investment', *Economica*, Vol. 38 (February).

Caves, R.E. (1974a), 'Causes of direct investment: foreign firms' shares in Canadian and United Kingdom manufacturing industries', *Review of Economics and Statistics*, Vol. 56 (August).

Caves, R.E. (1974b), 'Industrial organisation', in J.H. Dunning (ed.), *Economic Analysis and the Multinational Enterprise* (London: Allen & Unwin).

Coase, R.H. (1937), 'The nature of the firm', *Economica*, Vol. 4 (November).

Creamer, D. (1976), *Overseas Research and Development by US Multinationals 1966–75* (New York: The Conference Board).

Davidson, W.H., and McFeetridge, D.G. (1980), *International Technology Transactions and the Theory of the Firm* (mimeo).

Dunning, J.H. (1958), *American Investment in British Manufacturing Industry* (London: Allen & Unwin).

Dunning, J.H. (1973a), 'The determinants of international production', *Oxford Economic Papers*, Vol. 25 (November).

Dunning, J.H. (1973b), 'The location of international firms in an enlarged EEC: an exploratory paper', Manchester Statistical Society.

Dunning, John H. (1981), *International Production and the Multinational Enterprise* (London: Allen & Unwin).

Fischer, W.A., and Behrman, J.N. (1979), 'The co-ordination of foreign R and D activities by transnational corporations', *Journal of International Business Studies*, Vol. 10 (Winter).

Flowers, E.B. (1976), 'Oligopolistic reaction in European and Canadian direct investment in the US', *Journal of International Business Studies*, Vol. 7 (Fall/Winter).

Furubotn, E.G., and Pejovich, S. (1972), 'Property rights and economic theory: a survey of recent literature', *Journal of Economic Issues*, Vol. 6 (December).

Graham, E.M. (1978), 'Transatlantic investment by multinational firms: a rivalistic phenomenon', *Journal of Post Keynesian Economics*, Vol. 1 (Fall).

Hirsch, S. (1974), 'Capital and technology confronting the neo factor proportions and neo-technology accounts of international trade', *Weltwirtschaftliches Archiv*, Vol. 110, No. 4.

Hirsch, S. (1976), 'An international trade and investment theory of the firm', *Oxford Economic Papers*, Vol. 28 (July).

Horst, T. (1972), 'Firm and industry determinants of the decision to invest abroad: an empirical study', *Review of Economics and Statistics*, Vol. 54 (August).

Hufbauer, G.C. (1970), 'The impact of national characteristics and technology on the commodity composition of trade in manufactured goods', in R. Vernon (ed.), *The Technology Factor in International Trade* (New York: Columbia University Press).

Hufbauer, G.C., and Chilas, J.G. (1974), 'Specialisation by industrial countries: extent and consequences', in H. Giersch (ed.), *The International Division of Labour: Problems and Perspectives* (Tubingen: Mohr).

Hymer, S. (1960), 'The international operations of national firms: a study of direct investment', unpublished doctoral thesis, MIT.

Hymer, S. (1970), 'The multinational corporation and the law of uneven development', in J. Bhagwati (ed.), *Economics and World Order* (New York: World Law Fund).

Iversen, C. (1935), *Aspects of International Capital Movements* (London and Copenhagen: Levin and Munksgaard).

Johnson, H. (1968), *Comparative Cost and Commercial Policy Theory for a Developing World Economy* (Stockholm: Almquist and Wiksell).

Johnson, H. (1970), 'The efficiency and welfare implications of the international corporation', in C.P. Kindleberger (ed.) *The International Corporation* (Cambridge, Mass.: MIT Press).

Knickerbocker, P.T. (1973), *Oligopolistic Reaction and the Multinational Enterprise* (Cambridge, Mass.: Harvard University Press).

Kojima, K. (1978), *Direct Foreign Investment* (London: Croom Helm).

Lake, A. (1976), *Transnational Activity and Market Entry in the Semiconductor Industry* and *Foreign Competition and the UK Pharmaceutical Industry* (National Bureau of Economic Research: New York, Working Papers Nos 126 and 155).

Lall, S. (1973), 'Transfer pricing by multinational manufacturing firms', *Oxford Bulletin of Economics and Statistics*, Vol. 35 (August).

Lall, S. (1979), 'The international allocation of research activity by US multinationals', *Oxford Bulletin of Economics and Statistics*, Vol. 41 (November).

Lall, S. (1980), 'Monopolistic advantages and foreign involvement by US manufacturing industry', *Oxford Economic Papers*, Vol. 32 (March).

Leontief, W. (1953), 'Domestic production and foreign trade; the American capital position re-examined', *Proceedings of the American Philosophical Society*, Vol. 97.

Leontief, W. (1956), 'Factor proportions and the structure of American trade: further theoretical and empirical analysis', *Review of Economics and Statistics*, Vol. 38.

Lipsey, R.E., and Weiss, M.Y. (1973), 'Multinational firms and the factor intensity of trade', National Bureau of Economic Research: New York, Working Paper 8.

MacDougall, G.D.A. (1951), 'British and American exports. A study suggested by the theory of comparative costs, Part I', *Economic Journal*, Vol. 61.

MacDougall, G.D.A. (1952), 'British and American exports. A study suggested by the theory of comparative costs, Part II', *Economic Journal*, Vol. 62.

McManus, J.C. (1972), 'The theory of the multinational firm', in G. Pacquet (ed.), *The Multinational Firm and the Nation State* (Toronto: Collier-Macmillan).

Magee, S.P. (1977a), 'Multinational corporations, the industry technology cycle and development', *Journal of World Trade Law*, Vol. XI (July/August).

Magee, S.P. (1977b), 'Technology and the appropriability theory of the multinational corporation', in J. Bhagwati (ed.), *The New International Economic Order* (Cambridge, Mass.: MIT Press).

Mansfield, E., Teece, D., and Romeo, A. (1979), 'Overseas research and development by US based firms, *Economica*, Vol. 46 (May).

Michalet, C. (1973), 'Multinational enterprises and the transfer of technology', unpublished paper for OECD, DAS/SPR/73.64.

Muller, R. (1975), 'Global corporations and national stabilisation policy: the need for social planning', *Journal of Economic Issues*, Vol. 9 (June).

Mundell, R.A. (1957), 'International trade and factor mobility', *American Economic Review*, Vol. 47 (June).

Musgrave, P.B. (1975), *Direct Investment Abroad and the Multinationals: Effects on the US Economy*. Prepared for the use of the Sub-Committee on Multinational Corporations of the Committee on Foreign Relations, US Senate, August (Washington DC: US Government Printing Office).

Nurkse, R. (1933), 'Causes and effects of capital movements', reprinted in J.H. Dunning, *International Investment* (Harmondsworth: Penguin Readings, 1972).

Ohlin, B. (1933), *Interregional and International Trade* (Cambridge, Mass.: Harvard University Press, rev. edn 1967).

Orr, D. (1973), 'Foreign control and foreign penetration in Canadian manufacturing industries', unpublished manuscript.

Owen, R.F. (1979), *Inter-Industry Determinants of Foreign Direct Investment. A Perspective Emphasising the Canadian Experience*, Working Papers in International Economics, Princeton University (May).

Parry, T.G. (1975), 'The international location of production: studies in the trade and non-trade servicing of international markets by multinational manufacturing enterprise', PhD Thesis, University of London.

Parry, T.G. (1980), *The Multinational Enterprise: International Investment and Host Country Impacts* (Greenwich, Conn.: JAI Press).

Reddaway, N.B., Potter, S.T., and Taylor, C.T. (1968), *The Effects of UK Direct Investment Overseas* (Cambridge: Cambridge University Press).

Ronstadt, R. (1977), *Research and Development Abroad by US Multinationals* (New York: Praeger).

Rugman, A.M. (1980), 'Internalisation as a general theory of foreign direct investment. A reappraisal of the literature', *Weltwirtschaftliches Archiv*, Vol. 116, no. 2.

Samuelson, P. (1948), 'International trade and equalisation of factor prices', *Economic Journal*, Vol. 58 (June).

Southard, F.A. (1931), *American Industry in Europe* (Boston: Houghton Mifflin).

Stopford, J. (1976), 'Changing perspectives on investment of British manufacturing multinationals', *Journal of International Business Studies*, Vol. 7 (Fall/Winter).

Swedenborg, B. (1979), *The Multinational Operations of Swedish Firms; An Analysis of Determinants of Effects* (Stockholm: Almquist and Wiksell).

Teece, D.J. (1979), *Technology transfer and R & D Activities of Multinational Firms: Some Theory and Evidence* (mimeo), Stanford University (November).

Teece, D.J. (1981), 'The multinational enterprise: market failure and market power considerations', *Share Management Review*, Vol. 22, no. 3.

Tilton, J.E. (1971), *International Diffusion of Technology: The Case of Semi-conductors* (Washington DC: The Brookings Institution).

Vernon, R. (1966), 'International investment and international trade in the product cycle', *Quarterly Journal of Economics*, Vol. 80 (May).

Vernon, R. (1974), 'The location of economic activity', in J.H. Dunning, (ed.), *Economic Analysis and the Multinational Enterprise* (London: Allen & Unwin).

Williams, J.H. (1929), 'The theory of international trade reconsidered', *Economic Journal*, Vol. 39 (June).

Williamson, O.E. (1971), 'The vertical integration of production market failure considerations', *American Economic Review*, Vol. 61 (May).

Williamson, O.E. (1975), *Markets and Hierarchies: Analysis and Antitrust Implications* (New York: The Free Press).

Williamson, O.E. (1979), 'Transaction-cost economics: the governance of contractual relations', *Journal of Law and Economics*, Vol. 22 (October).

Wolf, B.M. (1977), 'Industrial diversification and internationalisation: some empirical evidence', *Journal of Industrial Economics*, Vol. 26 (December).

Part II

The Internationalization Process

CONTENTS

7

Internationalization: Evolution of a Concept

Lawrence S. Welch and Reijo Luostarinen

Over the last two decades there has been growing interest in the international operations of business companies. Academic activity in the areas has both stimulated and been stimulated by the many strands of concern – for example, the business firms themselves, with a concern to make such operations more effective and efficient in a more competitive global environment; governments, with a concern to ensure that the overall process has a positive effect on the national interest; and trade unions, with a concern about the impact on working conditions, wages and their own power.

At the outset much academic interest and analysis focused on the multinational corporation. Studies such as Servan Schreiber's[1] American Challenge alerted governments and others to the already extensive international operations of these companies. Much of the academic research in the early stages was involved with documenting and explaining the spread of multinational corporations, and assessing their impact, with an emphasis on their foreign investment activities. This was reflected in a spate of studies of foreign investment in various recipient countries.[2,3,4]

However, much of the early research took the multinational, or at least foreign investment, as a starting point in the analysis, leaving many questions unanswered regarding the development process which preceded this stage, and undoubtedly affected the later steps. Horst,[5] for example, after finding that firm size was a significant factor in the firm's decision to invest abroad concluded that: 'The principal deficiency in this line of analysis, I believe, is the absence of dynamic considerations. Nowhere is there a description of how a firm came to acquire its current attributes . . . But if we are even to unravel the complexity of the foreign investment decision process, a systematic study of the dynamic behaviour of firms must be undertaken.' In essence a more longitudinal view, a process perspective, was called for.

Already though, a shift in this direction had begun with Aharoni's[6] study of the various steps involved in the foreign investment decision process. As well, Wilkins[7,8] had begun to delineate some of the dynamic factors contributing to the historical evolution of American multinational corporations.

This developing longitudinal approach was taken a stage further with a number of studies of the international operations of Nordic-based companies, studies which considered the expansion activity as an internationalization process.[9,10,11] Specifically, their research was important in advancing our knowledge of the process not only because of its identification of patterns of internationalization, and a method for examining them, but also because of the

Reprinted with permission from *Journal of General Management*, 1988, **14**(2), 36–64 attempt to outline the key dynamic factors which formed the basis of forward progress. In the Nordic case the overall pattern was one of gradual, sequential development of international operations.

At the same time as this overall longitudinal research was developing in the 1970s, an interest was growing in the analysis of specific steps which contribute to the ongoing process. Inevitably, the shift to a more longitudinal approach led to an interest in the earlier steps which formed a foundation for later moves. For example, considerable analysis of early exporting activity has been undertaken in a number of countries.[12,13,14,15,16] While each new step of the development of international operations can be considered unique, each nevertheless provides insight into the broader longitudinal forces at work.

In general therefore research into the process of internationalization has tended to be carried on at the level of specific decisions to increase involvement as well as overall patterns and dynamic causative factors. Nevertheless, although considerable progress has and is being made in unravelling the nature and cause of internationalization – much remains to be accomplished. The various contributions represent an incomplete patchwork. As Buckley[17] has noted: 'This development from naive entrant to established multinational has been inadequately modelled . . . and its implications for theory are as yet unassimilated.'

THE MEANING OF 'INTERNATIONALIZATION'?

At the very outset it is difficult to discuss a 'theory of internationalization' because even the term itself has not been clearly defined. Although widely used, the term 'internationalization' needs clarification. It tends to be used roughly to describe the outward movement in an individual firm's or larger grouping's international operations.[18,19,20] As a starting point this common usage could be broadened further to give the following definition: 'the process of increasing involvement in international operations.' An important reason for adopting a broader concept of internationalization is that both sides of the process, i.e. both inward and outward, have become more closely linked in the dynamics of international trade.

The growth of countertrade in its many forms, from pure barter to buy-back arrangements and offset policies, is indicative of the way in which outward growth has become tied in with inward growth.[21,22] In effect, countertrade has meant that, for many companies, success in outward activities is partly dependent on inward performance. This, in combination with supportive government action in some cases, has led to a number of large companies setting up trading arms to facilitate the process.[23,24] The inward-outward interlink is further illustrated in the growth of international viability of many companies through the ability to tie in cheap component/raw materials imports from international suppliers – from clothing manufacture through to sophisticated systems selling.[25,26,27] From a general perspective therefore, it seems to be inappropriate to restrict the concept of increasing international involvement merely to the outward side, given the growing inward-outward interconnection.

Having put forward a working definition of 'internationalization' it should be stressed that once a company has embarked on the process, there is no inevitability about its continuance. In fact the evidence indicates that reverse of 'de-internationalization' can occur at any stage, as the example of Chrysler and other disinvestments in the late-1970s illustrate, but is particularly likely in the early stages of export development.[28,29]

So far the concept of 'internationalization' has been couched in relatively broad terms deliberately, to cover a multitude of possibilities. However, to apply the concept, considerable elaboration is required. For example, on what basis can we assess the degree of internationalization of one firm versus another? What does the concept mean as an outcome? Perhaps the simplest objective basis for assessing the degree of internationalization is some measure of foreign sales relative to total sales. The proportion of total sales exported has often been used as an indication of export performance despite its drawbacks.[30] Such a measure can also be extended out to the national economy as exports/gross domestic product. Although this measure is attractive because of its simplicity and measurability it provides very little information about the nature of and capacity to conduct international operations. Given the diversity of international operations, types of markets, degree of organizational commitment and types of international offering, there is obviously a need for a broader framework for assessing the extent of 'increased international involvement' – i.e. on a number of different dimensions. An example of such a framework is presented in Figure 1. In general internationalization can be expected to be associated with, and perhaps dependent upon, developments along each of the dimensions shown:

Operation method (how)

Evidence indicates that as companies increase their level of international involvement there is a tendency for them to change the method/s by which they serve foreign markets,[31,32,33] The

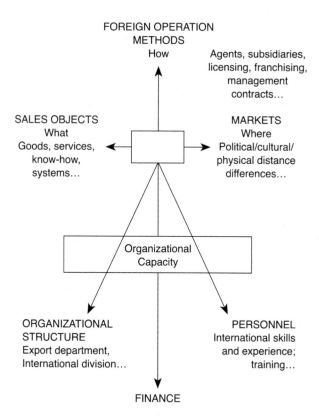

Fig. 1. Dimensions of Internalization

Nordic studies indicate that this change occurs in the direction of increasing commitment, a typical pattern being from no exporting, to exporting via an agent, to a sales subsidiary and finally to a production subsidiary. One of the reasons for the considerable attention on the operation method as a means of assessing a pattern of internationalization is that it does represent a clearly overt manifestation of the overall process.

As well as increasing commitment though, the pattern appears to be one of greater operational diversity as internationalization proceeds.[34] This appears to be related not only to the greater experience, skills, and knowledge of foreign markets and marketing which develops within the firm, but also to the exposure of a wider range of opportunities and threats. Sometimes the sheer success of one method of operation, for example exporting, causes the erection of import barriers by a foreign government thereby necessitating a shift to some other form such as licensing or foreign investment if a market presence is to be maintained. An Australian study found that outward foreign licensing was mainly adopted because of various constraints on the use of other, more preferred methods of operation in foreign markets.[34] The recent strong move by Japanese firms into foreign investment has been partly stimulated by the various forms of protection imposed in key markets.[35,36] In a similar manner, the exploitation of market opportunities in the socialist countries, because of the emphasis of their governments on counter-trade, is likely to force some shift towards operational diversity. Clearly, the degree of market diversity has an impact on the degree of operation diversity.

Thus, on the method of operation dimension we would expect internationalization to be reflected in both increasing depth and diversity of operational methods. At a global level, this is evident not just in the growth of foreign investment but also in the rise of countertrade in its various guises, of the technology trade, of franchising, of management contracts and so on. It is difficult, if not impossible, to go far in the internationalization process simply by using one preferred operational method. One can perhaps argue that the future international success of companies will partly depend on their ability to master and successfully apply a range of methods of foreign operation.

Sales objects (what)

As a company increases its involvement in international operations there is also a tendency for its offering to foreign markets to deepen and diversify.[37] This may occur at two levels:

- Expansion within an existing, or into a new, product line.[38]
- Change in the whole product concept to include 'software' components such as services, technology, know-how, or some combination. Over time the blending of hardware and software components is often developed into more packaged forms, representing project or systems solutions.[39]

Target markets (where)

As with sales objects and operation forms, it is difficult to develop internationally merely by concentrating on a limited number of countries. Expanded operations and offerings increasingly link with a wider range of foreign markets – typically more distant over time in political, cultural, economic and physical terms. There is a basic tendency for companies, particularly in the early stages of internationalization, to approach markets which appear simpler, more familiar and less costly to penetrate – and these are most commonly those which are closest in physical and cultural terms.[40,41] It is not uncommon for Australian firms to view operations in New Zealand as merely an extension of domestic activities, as also for Finnish firms moving into Sweden. A company's shift of activities to more 'distant' locations can therefore be seen as one indication of greater maturation in its internationalization process.

Organizational capacity

The internationalization process of a company is perhaps most overtly demonstrated by the preceding three dimensions: the further advanced a firm is along them the more 'internationalized' it may be regarded as being. For example, a Finnish company with a high export/total sales ratio of say 80 per cent but which is selling only one product, via an agent, to one country, Sweden would be regarded, according to the above framework, as still being only in the earliest stages of international development.

Nevertheless, although providing a broader-based assessment of internationalization, the first three dimensions concentrate on the components of actual foreign market activity. Such an approach leaves aside the variety of internal company changes which are consequent upon, and therefore reflect, the degree of internationalization but also form the foundation for additional steps forward in the overall process.[42] In the resources area finance and personnel are obviously important, but so also is the organization structure developed for handling foreign activities. In Figure 1, three of these areas – finance, personnel and organization structure – are noted because of their importance, but they are by no means exclusively so.

Personnel

The success of internationalization in any company depends heavily on the type of people both initiating and carrying through the various steps in the process, and on overall personnel policies. Lorange[43] has recently argued that 'the human resource function is particularly critical to successful implementation of (such) co-operative ventures (joint ventures, licensing agreements, project co-operation, . . .)'. In the initial exporting phase the background of the decision-marker, in such areas as work and foreign experience, education and language training, has been shown to be potentially important in the preparedness to commit a firm to the exporting activity.[44,45] At a general level though, internationalization both feeds upon and contributes to the development of international knowledge, skills and experience of the people involved.[46] While learning-by-doing appears to be a key part of the whole process, it is also possible to obtain some assistance through effective training and recruitment policies. Tung,[47] for example, concluded from a study of a number of US, European and Japanese companies that 'the more rigorous the selection and training procedures used, the less the incidences of poor performance or failure to work effectively in a foreign country.' Clearly, unless the people involved, through whatever means, become more international in their capacities and outlook, the ability to carry through any international strategy is bound to be severely constrained. International personnel development therefore remains as a prime indication of the internal extent to which a company has effectively become internation-alized, although it is perhaps more difficult to measure than the preceding three dimensions.

Organizational structure

As the administrative and organizational demands generally of carrying out international operations grow and diversify, the organizational structure for handling such demands ultimately needs to respond. A variety of formal and informal organizational arrangements have been used by companies in different countries to cope with the increasing amount and complexity of continuing internationalization.[48,49,50] The changes, and their sophistication, as the company seeks to improve the organizational mechanism and focus of international operations, provide a further signpost of the state of internationalization. Organizational changes are often a clear statement of commitment to the objectives of international involvement. In an Australian study the shift from experimental to committed exporting was often marked by the establishment of an export section or division in some form.[51]

Finance

The growth of international operations inevitably also places increasing demands on the availability of funds to support the various activities. The nature and extent of the company's financing activities for international operations provide a further indicator of the degree of internationalization. We might expect that the range of finance sources (both local and international) and the sophistication of financing techniques would develop with international growth. However, the relationship is by no means clear-cut – depending on such aspects as the type of product/service, operation methods and payment method, as well as the extent of government support.[52]

Framework overview

By examining the above six dimensions it is possible to derive a substantial overview of the state of internationalization of a given company, which could then form the basis of comparison to others. It is not the intention at this stage to consider scales of measurement along the different dimensions, although work has already taken place in this area – as for example in Luostarinen's[53] composite of business distance (including cultural, economic and physical distance). At a general level though it is possible to foresee the development of more precise composite measures along the various dimensions, providing a better basis for relative assessment of the internationalization progress of different companies. For example, the hypothetical patterns for two companies are presented in Figure 2. Comparing the two patterns it is clear that company 1 has gone further than company 2 in its foreign market activities, yet its internal development to support these is less developed than company 2. Perhaps this is a sign of potential problems for company 1.

PATTERNS OF INTERNATIONALIZATION

From the discussion so far it is clear that there is a wide range of potential paths any firm might take in internationalization. Nevertheless, are there any consistent patterns observable from the research? In answering this question a major contribution has been made by Nordic researchers.[54,55,56] Their work points generally to a process of evolutionary, sequential build-up of foreign commitments over time. Johanson and Wiedersheim-Paul studied the

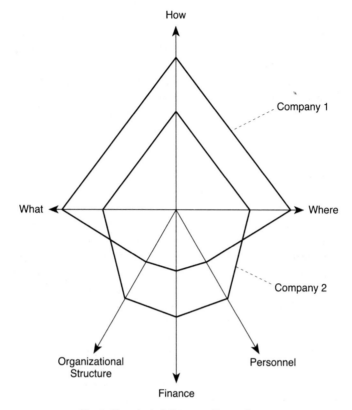

Fig. 2. Hypothetical Company Comparison

establishment chains of four large Swedish multinationals from the beginning of their operations. Typically the growth of foreign establishments was distinguished by a series of small, cumulative steps over time: the setting-up of a sales subsidiary was preceded by an agency operation in about three-quarters of cases.

This general pattern of evolutionary development was perhaps most strongly confirmed in Finnish research. In a study of around three-quarters of the population of Finnish industrial companies with foreign operations of any type Luostarinen found that, in 1976, 65 per cent of the companies had only non-investment marketing operations abroad, 33 per cent had production operations abroad which had been preceded by non-investment marketing operations, whereas in only 2 per cent of the total had production operations abroad begun without preceding operations. This result has apparently continued, although being less pronounced, according to a more recent examination of the shift to foreign direct manufacturing investment during the period 1980–82 by Finnish companies.[57] In only 13 per cent of cases did the shift occur without preceding alternative operations in the country concerned.

Luostarinen's research revealed a process of evolutionary development not only in terms of the depth of operational mode, but also in terms of the diversity of modes used, as well as in product offerings and the range of markets penetrated. For example, product offerings were divided into four categories: goods, services, systems and know-how. The offering to foreign markets consistently began in the simplest form – i.e. goods (for 99 per cent of companies) – while sales of services, systems and know-how came later, and approximately in that order.[58] The gradual development towards systems or package selling has also been noted in the growth of Swedish multinational corporations where skills and knowledge (software) were added to the hardware sale until a more complete problem-solving package was on offer.[59] This trend has broader implications as a growing software/service component clearly places greater stress on effective communication skills and understanding of user needs and the user's environment, which is a more demanding exercise once cultural and other distance barriers have to be surmounted, thereby reinforcing the impact of such distance variables on internationalization.

Research in other countries, although differing in sample size, period of study and subject of analysis, nevertheless has revealed a degree of consistency with the results of Nordic research. In examining Japanese foreign investment in South-East Asia, Yoshihara[60] found that 'the pattern of investment seems to substantiate the evolutionary theory of foreign investment'. This echoes a similar conclusion drawn from a longitudinal study of American direct investment abroad.[61] Small sample studies of first time UK smaller firm direct investors and of Continental European direct investors in the UK have confirmed the pattern of intermediate steps being used as a build-up to foreign investment.[62,63] While 15.4 per cent of cases involved a direct move to foreign investment 'over half of these firms were prevented from exporting by the nature of their product – transport cost barriers or a high 'service' element effectively ruled out exporting as a means of servicing the foreign markets'.[64]

The pattern is not completely consistent though as an Australian study of 228 outward direct investment cases revealed that in 39 per cent of these cases there was no pre-existing host country presence.[65] To some extent this can be explained by the high proportion (43.8 per cent) of service companies involved in the investment activity, given that it is often more difficult to operate with intermediate steps to the foreign investment stage in the services sector. However, service companies were only slightly under-represented (40.7 per cent) amongst those affiliates with a pre-existing presence.[66] Of particular note though is the fact that 65.5 per cent of the investments were undertaken during the period 1970–79. This is perhaps suggestive of a change in the rate at which firms have been accomplishing internationalization in more recent times, through leapfrogging of intermediate steps to the foreign investment stage in some countries. Further support for this development has been forthcoming in the more direct move to foreign investment by Swedish companies into the Japanese market from the early 1970s.[67] Perhaps a more general indication of the desire by companies to short-circuit the process of gradually building-up activities in foreign markets over time has been the switch in foreign investment towards acquisition and away from greenfield ventures.[68,69,70] Acquisition is not only a path to more rapid establishment in a given foreign market, which has become a more important consideration in the light of stronger global competition, but it is also potentially a means of obtaining faster access to a developed international network. For example, when the Australian company Wormald International purchased Mather and Platt in the UK it obtained as well a network of subsidiaries in Europe, Japan, Brazil, South Africa and New Zealand. The managing director commented that to have built such a network from scratch would have taken 20–30 years.[71,72]

Of course, it should be expected that observed patterns of internationalization will vary from country to country, and over time, because of environmental differences at the outset, as well as the inevitable changes in the environment. A combination of the more competitive international environment of the 1980s and the general demonstration effects of other companies' increased international efforts from different national environments has probably contributed to a less cautious approach to internationalization, at least in the latter stages.

It should also be stressed that the concept of a sequential, cumulative process of internationalization does not necessarily mean some smooth, immutable path of development. The actual paths taken are often irregular. Commitments are frequently lumpy over time, with plateaux while previous moves are absorbed and consolidated. Particular steps are affected by the emergence of opportunities and/or threats which do not usually arrive in a continuous or controlled manner. The outcome tends to be derived from a mixture of deliberate and emergent strategies.[73]

In fact, some of the argument which appears to be developing about the evolutionary or stages model of internationalization[74] seems to have occurred because of a lack of specification of what this process actually means for an individual company: does it mean evolution or a stepwise process for each individual foreign market or rather development of involvement in an overall sense? So far concentration has been on the former situation where the number and type of steps up to, for example, foreign investment are considered. A reduction in, or absence of, intervening steps in a foreign market is taken as some indication that the evolutionary or stages model is not functioning.[75] Such a result is of course more likely in particular markets where unique circumstances might apply, perhaps in the form of government policy. More importantly though it is probably more appropriate to analyse the process of international involvement at the company level, looking across total foreign market activities. As skills, experience and knowledge in the use of a more advanced form of operations are developed in some foreign markets we might expect that this will eventually allow a company to leapfrog some intermediate steps in others.[76] This proposition is illustrated in Figure 3. Taken on its own, company X's move directly to foreign investment in Foreign Market No. 6 might be regarded as a shift away from the sequentialist pattern revealed in other markets. However, when taken in the overall context of the steps taken in other markets it is certainly far removed from a leap into the unknown. Thus, leapfrogging moves in given markets should be examined as part of the overall operational pattern of the company before any definitive conclusions can be drawn about a 'shift' from the evolutionary pattern.

Likewise the concept of what is evolutionary could be related back to the type of preceding experience of international operations that key individuals in the company might have had. For example an Australian company with four years of operating and marketing experience in a small Australian city (Toowoomba) considered its first 'export' move as an attempt to penetrate a large Australian city 130 kilometres away (Brisbane). By contrast a Sydney company was exporting within three months of beginning operations and to 52 countries in three years. The differences in behaviour were strongly related to the owner-managers of each company. In the Toowoomba example the individual had very limited personal or company experience beyond the local area, whereas in the second case the manager was a migrant with over 20 years of international experience in the industry concerned which had exposed an unexploited market niche. His perception of the market place was international in character from the outset. In this context, the international moves of the Sydney company were less startling than at first sight. One person's (or company's) evolution often appears as a revolution to others.[77,78]

Overall then, the research has revealed a reasonable degree of consistency, at least up to the mid-1970s, that the pattern of internationalization for most firms has been marked by a sequential, stepwise process of development. More recently, limited evidence has been

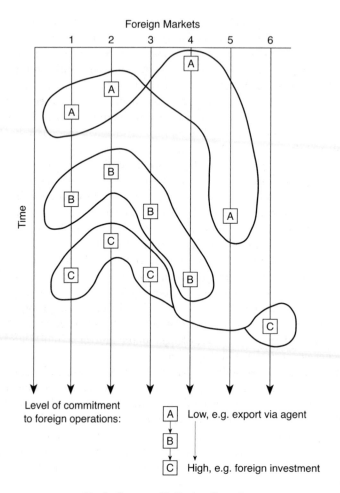

Fig. 3. Company X–Foreign Operations

emerging of a departure from the gradualist path as some firms seek to by-pass the steps to deeper commitment, resulting in a speeding up of the whole process. Just how widespread the change is can only be determined from further research, but pattern variation should be expected in response to the many environmental changes, both nationally and globally, which have occurred in the 1970s and 1980s.

WHY INTERNATIONALIZATION?

While we can expect continued debate on the nature of the shifting pattern of internationalization, an important question remains to be settled: why internationalization? What is it that drives the process, leading a firm from little or no involvement to, in some cases, widespread multinational investments? Obviously, if we are to understand the process then we have to explain why a company undertakes each particular step in an overt pattern.

As Starbuck[79] has noted, growth is not spontaneous, it is the result of decisions. As such, the separate analysis of these distinct steps contributes to our understanding of why and how the internationalization process is initiated and maintained. For example, the recent research on the export involvement decision has considerably elucidated how and why a company's internationalization begins, and what sort of base is established for subsequent forward moves, if any.[80,81,82] However, each of the decision points inevitably has a variety of unique causative elements as well as bearing the impact of any general on-going influential factors, as noted in Figure 4. In developing any overall explanation of internationalization it is important to examine those continuing influences which play such a key role in maintaining forward momentum – in building the company to the point where it is more receptive to the possibilities of increased involvement, and better prepared to respond to them. These dynamic factors also help to explain why there is some degree of consistency of internationalization patterns across countries because of their general effect. At the same time they represent reasons why so many companies feel constrained to a more gradual, sequential path of development, as revealed in the research noted earlier.

Overall pattern explanatory factors – resources availability

The ability to undertake any form of international operations is clearly limited by the means accessible to the firm to carry it out. For smaller firms, given their limitations in many areas, this is an obvious reason why less demanding directions of international development can be undertaken first, with major commitments only occurring well into the longer run. By the same token, this means that we should expect larger firms, based in large domestic markets, to reveal more advanced involvement far earlier, and generally to move through the overall process at a faster rate. While there is some argument about the research results which consider the impact of size, there does not appear to be any clear relationship between size of firm and export performance.[83,84] Instead of size, Czinkota and Johnston[85] concluded that 'what really does seem to make for export success is the attitude of management'. Some of the constraints which face companies of whatever size, when considering international expansion, particularly financial ones, are sometimes more apparent than real. Outside financial sources and creative funding of takeovers, have been used by some companies to permit faster expansion than directly accessible means would imply.[86] While resource availability may limit expansion at any given point in time, the constraint is not static, so that

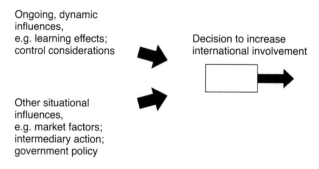

Fig. 4. Determinants of Forward Momentum

any action or developments which widen availability provide the basis for increased foreign operations over time.

Knowledge development

Clearly, there is something more to the resources question than just physical or financial capacity. A critical factor in the ability to carry out chosen international activities is the possession of appropriate knowledge: this includes knowledge about foreign markets, about techniques of foreign operation, about ways of doing business, about key people in buyer organizations, and so on. Such information and understanding is not easily, cheaply or rapidly acquired. Much of it is not readily acquired 'off-the-shelf' as it is developed through the actual experience of foreign operations.[87] The learning-by-doing process explains much in the evolutionary patterns of internationalization revealed in research.[88]

Communication networks

Personal contact and social interaction play an important part in the development of international markets – especially where more complex industrial products are concerned.[89] Networks between buyers and sellers which form the basis of effective communication must be established. Network establishment can be a demanding and time consuming process where the gap between buyer and seller is large due to an initial lack of knowledge of each other and is accentuated by physical and cultural distance barriers. There is considerable inertia amongst buyers who feel more secure with suppliers from familiar sources and locations. While this constrains the development of operations at the outset, the initial gaps are not necessarily static: they are susceptible to reduction over time. With wider experience, greater contact at all levels and more diverse cultural exposure on both sides, there is a potential for deeper and more long-standing relationships to evolve, forming the basis for deeper commitments.[90]

Risk and uncertainty

As foreign buyers are loath to establish networks with unknown foreign suppliers at the outset so too the foreign suppliers, because of initial lack of knowledge and experience, tend to feel uncertainty about taking on additional or new foreign operations, especially in unfamiliar locations. Inevitably there is a response of seeking ways to reduce the uncertainty exposure. It is not surprising therefore to find the pattern noted earlier that companies are attracted to foreign operations first in more familiar (culturally) and closer locations and that only small steps in operational commitments are undertaken initially thereby limiting exposure. This also allows experimentation without high risk and the time required to gather relevant knowledge and experience, before any deeper commitment is contemplated.

In general therefore the need to develop relevant knowledge and skills and communication networks, as well as to reduce risk and uncertainty exposure, interact and play a key role at given points in constraining international moves. Over time, however, the inevitable changes in these areas consequent upon foreign activities also change the capacity of the company to contemplate and carry through more involving commitments.[91]

Control

Given the limited foreign market knowledge and experience of many companies during the early stages of internationalization it is not surprising that they will often look to outside foreign intermediaries to assist in market penetration. With more experience, however, if a company's knowledge about a given market increases through active involvement, there is a tendency for it to scrutinize the activities of its foreign intermediary more closely, especially when sales potential has been proven by preceding operations. The concern about control is reflected in a variety of efforts to more closely direct the operations of the intermediary on its behalf. Sometimes this will result in 'positive' steps such as training or the provision of promotional materials. In other cases a more 'negative' approach will be adopted, leading to more stringent checks and guidelines. Under these changing circumstances, with the power positions being subtly reversed and the principal feeling less dependent on its foreign intermediary, it is not uncommon for dissatisfaction about perceived under-performance to grow. Ultimately, perhaps sparked by other developments, the principal may feel that the effective way of dealing with the 'problem' is for it to take over the running of the foreign operation itself, in some altered form. Inevitably this will mean increasing its commitment in the given foreign market. Thus, the control factor, interacting with knowledge development and risk perception, tends to be a growing influence over time which pushes a company towards increasing involvement in foreign operations. In general, increasing market control means increasing involvement and thereby greater cost and risk.[92]

Commitment

As international operations are developed there is necessarily a commitment of resources, and by people, to the process. This commitment is particularly strong when key management staff are involved in developing the international strategy.[93] It creates a need for fulfilment and provides strong forward momentum whereby justification is sought in further operations and deeper involvement along the same line.[94] The commitment factor therefore represents a further dynamic driving force in the overall internationalization process.

The above factors taken together help to explain the continued forward momentum of the internationalization process of individual companies and also why the evolutionary pattern has been found in so many studies in different countries.[95] In essence, these factors, apart from any general market size and potential considerations, help us to understand why for example a given environmental change – such as protectionist action by a foreign government or a change in foreign investment rules – is unlikely to cause a shift to foreign investment by a company with limited foreign experience but is more likely to do so at a later stage after the development of market knowledge, contacts, a sales organization, etc., as illustrated in Figure 5.

CONCLUSION

Taken overall the concept of internationalization has yet to be clearly developed as a research object. Nevertheless, considerable progress has been made in establishing its conceptual and empirical foundations, while the emerging debate about the 'stages thesis' or 'gradual internationalization' can be considered a healthy step in clarifying the subject.

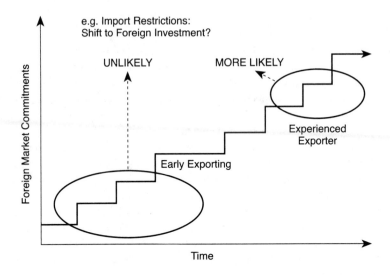

Fig. 5. Response to Environmental Change

Given the focus of the concept, a development process through time, much research remains to be conducted that is responsive to its longitudinal character. Inevitably this is a difficult activity: take for example the attempt to trace the impact of individuals and the evolution of communication patterns in the past. It can be expected however that research will continue along the dual lines of analysis of particular decisions or steps in the overall process and those elements which tie together total progress.

NOTES

1. Servan-Schreiber, J.J., *Le Defi American*, Editions de Noel, Paris, 1967.
2. Brash, D.T., *American Investment in Australian Industry*, Harvard University Press, Cambridge, Mass., 1966.
3. Safarian, A.E., *Foreign Ownership of Canadian Industry*, McGraw-Hill, Toronto, 1966.
4. Dunning, J.H., *American Investment in British Manufacturing*, Allen and Unwin, London, 1958.
5. Horst, T., 'Firm and Industry Determinants of the Decision to Invest Abroad', *Review of Economics and Statistics*, Vol. 54. 1972, pp. 264–5.
6. Aharoni, Y., *The Foreign Investment Decision Process*, Harvard University Press, Boston, Mass, 1966.
7. Wilkins, M., *The Emergence of Multinational Enterprise*, Harvard University Press, Cambridge, Mass., 1970.
8. Wilkins, M., *The Maturing of Multinational Enterprise*, Harvard University Press, Cambridge, Mass., 1974.
9. Johanson, J. and Wiedersheim-Paul, F., 'The Internationalization of the Firm – Four Swedish Cases', *Journal of Management Studies*, Vol. 12, No. 3, October, 1975.
10. Johnason, J. and Vahlne, J.-E., 'The Internationalization Process of the Firm', *Journal of International Business Studies*, Vol. 8, Spring/Summer, 1977.
11. Luostarinen, R., *The Internationalization of the Firm*, Acta Academic Oeconomica Helsingiensis, Helsinki, 1979.
12. Bilkey, W.J. and Tesar, G., 'The Export Behavior of Smaller Wisconsin Manufacturing Firms', *Journal of International Business Studies*, Vol. 8, Spring/Summer, 1977.
13. Welch, L.S. and Wiedersheim-Paul, F., 'Initial Exports – A Marketing Failure?' *Journal of Management Studies*, Vol. 17, October, 1980b.
14. Joynt, P., 'An Empirical Study of Norwegian Export Behavior', *Skriftserie*, No. 1, 1981.
15. Piercy, N., 'Company Internationalisation: Active and Reactive Exporting', *European Journal of Marketing*, Vol. 15, No. 3, 1981.

16. Denis, J.-E., and Depelteau, D., 'Market Knowledge, Diversification and Export Expansion', *Journal of International Business Studies*. Vol. 16, Fall, 1985.

17. Buckley, P.J., 'New Theories of International Business', in M. Casson (ed.), *The Growth of International Business*, Allen and Unwin, London, 1983, p. 48.

18. Johanson, J. and Wiedersheim-Paul, F., op. cit.

19. Piercy, N., op. cit.

20. Turnbull, P., 'Internationalisation of the Firm – A Stages Process or Not?', paper presented at the conference on Export Expansion and Market Entry Modes, Dalhousie University, Halifax, October 15/16, 1985.

21. Koury, S.J., 'Countertrade: Forms, Motives, Pitfalls, and Negotiation Requisites', *Journal of Business Research*, Vol. 12, No. 2, June 1984.

22. Huszagh, S.M. and Huszagh, F.W., 'International Barter and Countertrade', *International Marketing Review*, Vol. 3, No. 2, Summer, 1986.

23. Dizard, J.W., 'The Explosion of International Barter', *Fortune*, Vol. 107, No. 3, February 7, 1983.

24. Cohen, S.S. and Zysman, J., 'Countertrade, Offsets, Barter, and Buybacks', *California Management Review*, Vol. 28, No. 2, Winter 1986.

25. Carstairs, R., and Welsh, L.S., 'Australian Offshore Investment in Asia', *Management International Review*, Vol. 20, No. 4, 1980.

26. Hornell, E. and Vahlne, J.-E., 'The Changing Structure of Swedish Multinational Companies', Working Paper 1982/12, Centre for International Business Studies, University of Uppsala.

27. *Business Week*, 'The Hollow Corporation', March 3, 1986.

28. Boddewynn, J.J., 'Foreign Divestment: Magnitude and Factors', *Journal of International Business Studies*, Vol. 10, Spring/Summer, 1979.

29. Welch, L.S. and Wiedersheim-Paul, F., op. cit., 1980b.

30. Cavusgil, S.T. and Godiwalla, Y.M. 'Decision-Making for International Marketing: A Comparative Review', *Management Decision*, Vol. 20, No. 4, 1982.

31. Johanson, J. and Wiedersheim-Paul, F., op. cit.

32. Luostarinen, R., op. cit.

33. Luostarinen, R., op. cit., pp. 105–124.

34. Carstairs, R.T. and Welch, L.S., 'Licensing and the Internationalization of Smaller Companies: Some Australian Evidence', *Management International Review*, Vol. 22, No. 3, 1982, p. 35.

35. Roscoe, B., 'Getting round protectionism by the direct route', *Far Eastern Economic Review*, June 13, 1985, pp. 82–3.

36. Emmott, B., 'Japan: A Survey', *Economist*, December 7, 1985, pp. 26–30.

37. Luostarinen, R., op. cit., pp. 95–105.

38. Price Waterhouse Associates, *Successful Exporting*, Australian Government Publishing Service, Canberra, 1982, pp. 30–34.

39. Hornell, E. and Vahlne, J.-E., op. cit. p. 8.

40. Vahlne, J.-E. and Wiedersheim-Paul, F., 'Psychic Distance – An Inhibiting Factor in International Trade', Working Paper, 1977/2, Centre for International Business Studies, University of Uppsala, Sweden.

41. Luostarinen, R., op. cit., pp. 124–172.

42. Cavusgil, S.T. and Godiwalla, Y.M., op. cit.

43. Lorange, P. 'Human Resource Management in Multinational Cooperative Ventures', *Human Resource Management*, Vol. 25, No. 1, Spring, 1986, p. 133.

44. Reid, S.D., 'The Decision-Maker and Export Entry and Expansion, *Journal of International Business Studies*, Vol. 12, Fall, 1981.

45. Welch, L.S., 'Managerial Decision-Making: The Case of Export Involvement', *Scandinavian Journal of Materials Administration*, Vol. 9, No. 2, 1983.

46. Johanson, J. and Vahlne J.-E., op. cit.

47. Tung, R.L., 'Selection and Training of U.S., European and Japanese Multinationals, *California Management Review*, Vol. 25, No. 1, Fall 1982, p. 70.

48. Stopford, J.M. and Wells, L.T., *Managing the Multinational Enterprise*, Basic Books, New York, 1972.

49. Bartlett, C.A., 'Multinational Structural Change: Evolution Versus Reorganization, in L. Otterbeck (ed.), *The Management of Headquarters – Subsidiary Relationships in Multinational Corporations*, Gower, Aldershot, 1981.

50. Hedlund, G., 'Organization In-Between', *Journal of International Business Studies*, Vol. 15, Fall, 1984.

51. Welch, L.S. and Wiedersheim-Paul. F., op. cit., 1980b.

52. Price Waterhouse Associates, op. cit., pp. 56–62.

53. Luostarinen, R., op. cit., p. 151.

54. Johanson J. and Wiedersheim-Paul F., op. cit.

55. Luostarinen, R., op. cit.

56. Juul, M. and Walters, P., 'The Internationalization of Norwegian Firms: A Study of the U.K. Experience', *Management International Review*, Vol. 27, No. 1, 1987.

57. Larimo, J. 'The Foreign Direct Manufacturing Investment Behaviour of Finnish Companies', paper presented at the 11th European International Business Association Conference, Glasgow, December 15–17, 1985.

58. Luostarinen, R., op. cit., pp. 95–105.

59. Hornell, E. and Vahlne, J.-E., op. cit., p. 8.

60. Yoshirhara, K., 'Determinants of Japanese Investment in South-East Asia', *International Social Science Journal*, Vol. 30, No. 2, 1978, p. 372.

61. Wilkins, M., 1974, op. cit., p. 414.

62. Buckley, P.J., Newbould, G.D. and Thurwell, J., 'Going International – The Foreign Direct Investment Behaviour of Smaller U.K. Firms' in L.G. Mattsson and F. Wiedersheim-Paul (eds), *Recent Research on the Internationalization of Business*, Acta Universitatis Upsaliensis, Uppsala, 1979.

63. Buckley, P.J., Newbould, G.D. and Berkova, Z., 'Direct Investment in the U.K. by Smaller Continental Eurpoean Firms', Working Paper, University of Bradford, 1981.

64. Buckley, P.J., 'The Role of Exporting in the Market Servicing Policies of Multinational Manufacturing Enterprises', in M. Czinkota and G. Tesar (eds), *Export Management*, Praeger, New York, 1982, pp. 178–9.

65. Bureau of Industry Economics, *Australian Direct Investment Abroad*, Australian Government Publishing Service, Canberra, 1984, p. 115.

66. Bureau of Industry Economics, op. cit., p. 128.

67. Hedlund, G. and Kverneland, A., 'Are Establishments and Growth Strategies For Foreign Markets Changing?', paper presented at the 9th European International Business Association Conference, Oslo, December 18–20, 1983.

68. Hornell, E. and Vahlne, J.-E., op. cit.

69. Larimo, J., op. cit.

70. OECD, 'International Direct Investment: A Change in Pattern', *OECD Observer*, No. 112, September, 1981.

71. Korporaal, G. *Yankee Dollars: Australian Investment in America*, Allen and Unwin, 1986, ch. 12.

72. Department of Trade, 'Fire Protection firm sparks new sales in China, U.S.S.R.', *Overseas Trading*, Vol. 31, No. 10, 25 May, 1979, p. 345.

73. Mintzberg, H. and McHugh, A., 'Strategy Formation in an Adhocracy', *Administrative Science Quarterly*, Vol. 30, June, 1985.

74. Turnbull, P., op cit.

75. Hedlund, G. and Kverneland, A., op. cit.

76. Buckley, P.J., op. cit.

77. Welch, L.S. and Wiedersheim-Paul, F. 'Domestic Expansion: Internationalization At Home'.

78. Layton, R. (ed.), 'Magna Alloys and Research Pty, Ltd.', *Australian Marketing Projects*. Halstead Press, Sydney, 1969.

79. Starbuck, W.H., 'Organizational Growth and Development', in W.H. Starbuck (ed.), *Organizational Growth and Development*, Penguin, Harmondsworth, 1971.

80. Welch, L.S. and Wiedersheim-Paul, F., op. cit., 1980b.

81. Cavusgil, S.T., 'Organizational Characteristics Associated With Export Activity', *Journal of Management Studies*, Vol. 21, No. 1, Jan. 1984.

82. Yaprak, A., 'An Empirical Study of the Differences Between Small Exporting and Non-Exporting US Firms', *International Marketing Review*, Vol. 2, No. 2, Summer, 1985.

83. Czinkota, M.R. and Johnston, W.J., 'Exporting: Does Sales Volume Make a Difference', *Journal of International Business Studies*, Vol. 14, Spring/Summer, 1983.

84. Cavusgil, S.T., op. cit.

85. Czinkota, M.R. and Johnston, W.J., op. cit., p. 153.

86. *Euromoney*, 'Elders IXL', Supplement, August, 1985.

87. Johanson, J. and Vahlne, J.-E., op. cit.

88. Carlson, S., *How Foreign Is Foreign Trade*, Acta Universitatis Upsaliensis, Uppsala, 1975.

89. Hakansson, H. (ed), *International Marketing and Purchasing of Industrial Goods*, John Wiley, Winchester, 1982.

90. Ford, D., 'The Development of Buyer-Seller Relationships in Industrial Markets', *European Journal of Marketing*, Vol. 14, 5/6, 1980.

91. Johanson, J. and Vahlne, J.-E., op. cit.

92. Luostarinen, R., op. cit., p. 117.

93. Aharoni, Y., op. cit.

94. Johanson, J. and Vahlne, J.-E., op. cit.

95. Cavusgil, S.T. and Godiwalla, Y.M., op. cit.

8

Foreign Direct Investment by Small- and Medium-sized Enterprises: The Theoretical Background

Peter J. Buckley

1. DEFINITIONAL PROBLEMS

It is apparent that definitions of 'small firm' vary according to author and context. Definitions are not right or wrong, just more or less useful. Table 1 shows the definitions employed by the Wilson Committee and the UK 1981 Companies Act. On these definitions, the companies of our British study (worldwide turnover less than £10 millions) are relatively large (Buckley et al, 1988). However, when we examine the criteria used for instance in the Bolton Report based on 'economic' criteria, then we are justified in terming our firms 'smaller'. The Bolton Report took as its criteria: (1) Market share, the characteristic of a small firm's share of the market is that it is not large enough to enable it to influence the prices or national quantities of goods sold to any significant extent, (2) Independence, which means that the owner has control of the business himself – this rules out small subsidiaries of large firms, (3) Personalized management, which implies that the owner actively participates in all aspects of the management of the business and in all major decision making processes with little devolution or delegation of authority. On these grounds the 43 firms analysed in the study by Buckley et al (1988) qualify for the epithet 'smaller'. Further, on the world scale they are in the tail of the size distribution of international firms. The criterion of £10 million turnover was chosen so as to exclude large multinationals but to leave a population such that a viable sample could be chosen.

Comparable definitions for other countries relate to the size of the economy. A study of US 'midsized companies' defines midsized companies as those with sales between $25 million and $1 billion (Cavanagh and Clifford, 1983). An alternative US definition of a medium-sized company is 15–50 million US dollars in sales (Fierheller, 1980). A study of strategic planning in small and medium-sized companies in the Netherlands took lower limits of 50–75 employees, 3–10 million DF sales and 2–8 million DF in assets and higher limits of 300–500 employees, 25–100 million DF sales and 20–120 million DF assets (van Hoorn, 1979).

2. THE ANALYSIS OF FOREIGN DIRECT INVESTMENT BY SMALL FIRMS

There exists a variety of approaches to the analysis of small firm foreign direct investment. The economics of the firm's growth points to internal and external constraints on the growth of the firm. Questions about the size of firm may indeed be misplaced. Both the

Reprinted by permission of Kluwer Academic Publishers from *Small Business Economics*, 1989, 1, 89–100

Table 1. Definitions of small firms

A. Wilson Committee 1978 (cmnd. 7503)	
Manufacturing	200 employees or less
Retailing	Turnover 185 000 p.a. or less
Wholesale trades	Turnover 730 000 p.a. or less
Construction	25 employees or less
Mining and quarrying	25 employees or less
Motor trades	Turnover 365 000 p.a. or less
Misc. Services	Turnover 185 000 p.a. or less
Road transport	5 vehicles or less
Catering	All excluding multiples and brewery managed public houses

B. 1981 Companies Act

1. Medium-sized

A company may be classified as medium sized if, for the financial year and the one immediately preceding it, two out of the following three conditions apply:

   (i)   turnover did not exceed 5.75 m

   (ii)   balance sheet total did not exceed 2.8 m

   (iii)   average weekly number of employees did not exceed 250

2. Small

A company may be classified as small, if for the financial year and the one immediately preceding it, two of the following three conditions apply:

   (i)   turnover did not exceed 1.4 m

   (ii)   balance sheet total did not exceed 0.7 m

   (iii)   average weekly number of employed did not exceed 50

Balance sheet total means the total of all its assets without deduction of any liabilities.

underutilized resources approach (Penrose, 1959) and the internationalization approach (Buckley and Casson, 1976; 1985) suggest that the size of firm is merely a point of time view of a dynamic process of growth and that it is the growth process which is critical. The export literature has seen the foreign expansion of firms as part of a generalized view of deepening international commitment, with foreign direct investment as a final stage in an evolutionary process beginning with the 'pre export phase'. A specific hypothesis on foreign investment behaviour in the early post war period, the 'Gambler's Earnings Hypothesis' may be relevant to the explanation of the foreign operations of smaller firms. The corporate decision making approach exemplified by Yair Aharoni's *The Foreign Investment Decision Process* (1966) also represents a contribution to our understanding of decision making in first time foreign investors. Finally, the international business approach has been to attempt to define successful foreign operation and to relate this outcome to the subdecisions going into the investment decision. The following sections investigate these approaches in more detail.

2.1. The economics of the firm's growth

The economic theory of the multinational enterprise, drawing on industrial economics, international economics, the theory of finance and the economics of location has integrated and expanded concepts relevant to the growth of the firm (Buckley and Casson, 1976; 1985). Many of these concepts are relevant to the international expansion of smaller firms. (For a review of these concepts see Casson, 1983; and Buckley, 1983a, b.)

The role of management is central in this process. The function of management is to adjust to change. The faster the rate of change, the higher the demand for management. Foreign direct investment is (or should be) a management intensive activity because of the risks involved in the move and because of the necessity to collect and, crucially, to channel information in order to support effective decisions. Smaller firms are constrained by a shortage of management time and consequently frequently take short cuts in decision making and information gathering which can be disastrous. However, the exercise of entrepreneurial ability is often difficult to rationalize from an observer's viewpoint. Individual managers endowed with foresight, flair, imagination (or luck) may be able to cut through the planning process and achieve success.

The availability of managerial skills and their successful absorption may be important constraints on the growth of the firm (Penrose, 1959). Further constraints arise from technological and contractual factors. The optimum scale of a production plant is a constraint on operations in an individual location, not on the size of firm because optimum scale plants can be replicated at different locations (Scherer et al, 1975). The true constraints are co-ordination (via management) and contractual. The minimization of transactions costs are a major explanation of firm size. The difficulties of diversification and expansion out of a given sector and product are well known (Teece, 1983), as are barriers to entry and technological changes because they are not diversified and are often one product, one market companies. Thus, although the state of technology may not be a constraint on firm size, changes in technology may curtail or reverse the growth of individual firms.

Organizational issues are also important in the growth of the firm. A balance must be achieved between hierarchical control and co-operation which suits the unique situation of the firm (Casson, 1983). This problem is highlighted, for example, by the difficult choice of chief executive of the newly created foreign subsidiary. This is bound up with the issues of exercising adequate control at a distance. Our findings (Buckley et al, 1988) were that a British chief executive was chosen where hierarchical control was envisaged and a local national where a co-operative mode of operation was sought. Such a simplistic device did not, in many cases, succeed, but it illustrates a response to the organizational/management style problem which becomes more acute in international operations.

The availability of finance is often adduced to be a constraint on the expansion of small firms. Where external finance is not available, funds for expansion are limited to the profits generated by past investment. Beyond this, small firms must win the confidence of the market for funds. This confidence can be won by technological achievement, attempts at proof of future success, recruiting individuals who have the confidence of the market or astute political lobbying. In most cases financial constraints are secondary to managerial constraints. However the lack of funds for future investment in new products and processes (and for recruitment of managerial talent) is a constraint at particular points of time. As such, in a dynamic environment, they can be fatal by preventing the reduction of the vulnerability which besets smaller firms. A further corollary of lack of funds is that attempts to minimize outlays, e.g. on the acquisition of information, on salaries for key individuals and on product adaptation can be disastrous.

2.2. The evolutionary approach: internationalization

The export literature has seen exporting as an innovative strategy and as a first step in internationalizing, possibly a step which ends in failure. Thus exporting can be seen as launching a process of deepening international commitment, possibly leading to direct investment (for a full review of the literature, see Buckley, 1982).

This evolutionary approach is, to a degree, embodied in Figure 1. All but 7 of the 43 firms in the sample used by Buckley et al (1988) had exported prior to making their first direct investment in a particular country. This deepending investment, and the success which goes with having a number of intermediate states (exports, agency, sales subsidiary) before a production subsidiary is capable of two explanations. The first is that each stage allows a learning process to take place. The second explanation is that the unsuccessful firm can drop out at any one of the intermediate states and thus never appears as a direct investor. In other words, looking back in time from a position where a direct investment is established, 'failures' are weeded out (Buckley et al, 1988).

The internationalization approach has identified crucial interactions between internal and external pressures in the firm's development and, in particular, has highlighted the crucial role of management activity and awareness. All forms of international activity are management intensive, foreign investment particularly so. Information gathering, a crucial part of the feedback process, is particularly time intensive. The 1978 study shows the heavy costs of information gathering for a small firm with severe constraints on management time (Buckley et al, 1988).

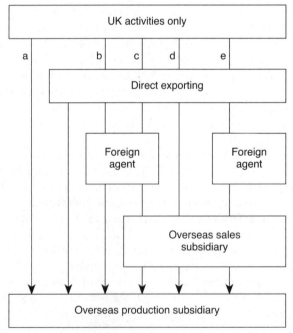

Licensing may be an additional, or alternative, intermediate state

Fig. 1. Routes to Investment in Production Facilities Overseas.

Information also plays a crucial role in reducing risk. One way of minimizing the risks arising from foreignness is to invest in a country as similar as possible to the home country. This suggests an expansion strategy based on 'psychic distance', investing in psychically 'nearby' countries first. The results of our study show that, often, psychic distance and physical distance are inversely correlated. It is unwise, however, to underestimate psychic distance between two ostensibly 'close' countries, as the 1978 study by Buckley et al (1988) and those of British investment in Australia show (Buckley and Mathew, 1979, 1980; Mathew, 1979).

The switch from exporting to direct investment is a crucial decision. Models of the switch, based on the different costs involved in these methods of market servicing, have been put forward by Vernon (1966) and Hirsh (1976). The more complex model of Buckley and Casson (1981) specifies the optimal timing of the switch by reference to the costs of servicing the market, demand conditions in the market and host market growth. This decision emerges as highly complex and in a highly uncertain world, its correct execution demands a great deal of management judgment.

Alternative modes of technology transfer can be incorporated into this model by considering licensing as an alternative intermediate stage. This should not imply that licensing is merely a step towards a direct investment in all cases – it can be a viable, permanent and optimal choice under certain circumstances (Buckley and Davies, 1981).

2.3. The 'gambler's earnings' hypothesis

The 'gambler's earnings' hypothesis was put forward in the mid-1950s to explain an empirical phenomenon associated with foreign direct investment. This phenomenon was the large ploughback of profits in foreign owned subsidiaries (notably in General Motors' Holden subsidiary in Australia). Consequently multinational firms were likened to gamblers who, beginning the game with a small stake (the initial investment, usually small) continually ploughed back their 'winnings' (profits) into the game until a real 'killing' was made. In foreign investment this meant that when a dividend repayment was eventually made to the parent firm, it was large in relation to the initial investment (Barlow and Wender, 1955; Penrose, 1956). Such behaviour poses adjustment problems for the host country because a large repayment can disrupt its balance of payments stability.

Underlying this behaviour are three features of interest. First, the subsidiary is assumed to be very largely independent of the parent. This may be because of distance (both physical and psychic), because of the need for local judgment or because of the lack of firm-wide policy co-ordination. Second, the differences in setting up a foreign rather than a domestic subsidiary are relevant. The rate of return on a foreign subsidiary needs to be higher in order to compensate for the greater risks. Moreover, foreign investment is often in the nature of an exploratory strategy in order to see if further foreign investment is desirable. Therefore, the risk averse firm is likely, initially at least to underinvest and to begin with a small stake. The small initial investment thus economizes on the costs of investigation and organization. Third, the process has a dynamic of its own. When the firm has a (small) successful foreign subsidiary, uncertainty is lower and the costs of search for further profit approximate to zero. The argument thus is that rather than scanning the world for further, possibly more profitable, opportunities, the firm will reinvest in its safe bet – the existing subsidiary. Thus, the investor will keep reinvesting long after this is justified by relative rates of return from other (unconsidered) alternatives. In other words, foreign investors are hypothesized to exhibit a bias in the allocation of investment funds towards existing, profitable subsidiaries. The 'gambler's earnings' hypothesis is no longer a valid explanation of the behaviour of large, diversified multinational firms used to monitoring worldwide opportunities, managerially integrated and often highly centralized. However, the hypothesis may hold for small firms where the costs of information and co-ordination are high. For first-time foreign investors in particular, the costs of decision making may make such behaviour optimal. However, in the longer run, 'gambler's earnings' behaviour results in missed opportunities, declining overall rates of return and lost gains from internationalization. It may be a phase in the development of an international strategy before full international co-ordination is justified, but for the successful firm it must not be more than this.

2.4. The corporate decision making approach

The corporate decision making approach sees foreign direct investment (by small firms) as a managerial process. It is exemplified by Yair Aharoni's *The Foreign Investment Decision Process* (1966). In this approach, competition is insufficiently perfect to prevent there existing an area in which managers can exercise discretion and pursue their objective function. Consequently, the objectives of managers, which may involve the search for an easy life, or concern for the share price, or managerial rewards, can be sought. Also included in the approach are the costs of information, the limited decision horizons of managers, conflicts within the firm and uncertainty of outcomes.

Aharoni's study based on a survey of US investors and non-investors in Israel suggests a five stage process as typical of the foreign investment decision. It is a basic finding of Aharoni's work that a strong 'initiating force' (Stage I) is necessary to propel an inert non-investor along the path towards a foreign direct investment. Such pressure may come from within the firm, an executive with an interest in such an investment perhaps, or from the environment, e.g. an outside proposal from a powerful source such as a client, distributor or government agency. Aharoni suggests that the existence of a profitable opportunity is not a sufficient stimulus, and the venture must have extra appeal. Given a sufficiently strong initiating force, Stage II is the investigation process. This is the beginning of the firm's search process. It is a biased search, however, carried out in a sequential way with built-in check points. If at one of these checks, a negative answer is found, the rest of the work is abandoned. Thus, the order of search is of crucial importance. The inexperienced foreign investor needs to know many factors in addition to those involved in its dramatic investment decisions. The phases of the search are: (1) general indicators, to establish the degree of risk, (2) on the spot indicators, and (3) presentation of a report. Before stage III 'the decision to invest' is reached, a process of building commitments in the firm takes place. The very fact of investigation is sufficient to create a commitment amongst the investigators, whence such a commitment diffuses throughout the decision makers. In Stage IV 'reviews and negotiations' a bargaining situation occurs where powerful groups within the firm impose their wishes and attempts to reduce uncertainty (and outlay) are made.

The first few stages of Aharoni's model then represent a description of short-run decision making under uncertainty. The fifth stage 'changes through repetition' adds a longer run element. In this stage, the firm changes organizationally so as to bring its foreign operation(s) within central control via, Aharoni suggests, an international division. The attitude to risk and uncertainty of foreign ventures alters radically, for the firm now finds them intrinsically little more risky than domestic ventures and the firm thus progresses to full international status.

2.5. The international business approach: defining 'success'

In discussing the foreign investment behaviour of smaller firms it is difficult to avoid normative statements. The observer is tempted to discuss 'what ought to be done' rather than the decisions which have been made. It was to avoid this difficulty that the methodology of the Bradford study was designed (Buckley et al, 1988). Briefly, the methodology is as follows. First, an attempt is made to define success. This is done by a 'success index' made up of measures of profitability, growth, managerial perception of success, synergy and an appraisal of the investment as a step towards full internationalization. Second, each investment is then rated on a five point scale or 'success index'. Third, each subdecision is then evaluated on the basis of the outcome in terms of average success of those investments making that subdecision. On this basis, a best practice set of decisions can be defined. Fourth, the findings of the success index are tested against external factors which may have influenced the outcome. For instance, longevity of investment may positively influence the success rating. Indeed Lupo et al (1978) showed that profitability of US multinationals in 1966 was strongly related to the ages of the subsidiary after controlling for the industry and country where the subsidiary was located. To eliminate such possibilities, the success rating is tested on these external factors which are shown not to be decisive. In view of this, the success index outcome is deemed to depend on managerial decision making. A variant of this model is also used in the companion volume (Buckley et al, 1983) to evaluate the direct investments of smaller European firms into the UK.

A similar approach is used by Sikander Khan (1978) to evaluate export ventures. In classifying firms' export ventures, he uses (1) objective criteria; profit and sales penetration, (2) semi-objective criteria; the degree to which expectations are met compared to the actual outcome with respect to costs, export volume and profitability, (3) subjective criteria; the firms' assessment of the degree of success and failure concerning individual export markets. No attempt was made to combine or aggregate these criteria and Khan notes (p. 220) that the objective and subjective evaluations were not significantly different.

3. SPECIAL ISSUES RAISED BY SMALL FIRM FOREIGN INVESTORS

A crucial issue arising from the above discussion is the extent to which small firms are at all different in their foreign investment behaviour. There are several key areas in which small firms are different and these raise a set of important conceptual and strategic issues.

In comparison with larger firms, two critical shortages may affect smaller firms: capital and management time (Buckley, 1979). The lack of pull in the capital market may lead to less than optimal arrangements. Decisions taken in order to minimize capital outlay sometimes have negative consequences. One example is entering into joint venture arrangements where they bring in finance but subsequently prove to be a serious liability. In raising capital, the small firm faces a 'Catch 22': how to raise finance without disclosing its competitive advantage secrets. Capital rationing can thus adverely affect small firms who therefore rely greatly on internally generated finance.

The shortage of skilled management in smaller firms is often a more serious liability. Small firms do not often have specialist executives to manage their international operations, nor do they possess a hierarchy of managers through which complex decisions can be sifted. Decision making is much more likely to be personalized involving *ad hoc*, short term reckoning based on individual perceptions and prejudice. Shortage of management time leads to firms taking short cuts without proper evaluation of alternatives. Linked to management shortage are the problems of information costs, which (like any fixed costs) bear heavily on small firms. Attempts to avoid these costs, for instance by making no attempt to appraise a potential joint venture partner, can be disastrous. The horizons of small firms are limited by managerial capacity and there is little 'global scanning' for opportunities. Therefore, when an opportunity appears, it is often taken without proper evaluation. Given this problem, why does the firm not recruit management from outside the firm? An important point here is the crucial phase of growth from a family firm to a wider management controlled organization (Casson, 1982). One issue is the desire to retain (family) control; the other is the difficulty in obtaining specialist knowledge of how to evaluate outsiders. Lack of these crucial skills constrains recruitment and makes endemic the burden on management. Consequently, small firms with inexperienced managers have an inevitable degree of naïvety because they lack the public relations skills, lobbying power and sheer economic muscle of larger firms. In the international sphere they lack knowledge of the local environment, the legal, social and political aspects of operating abroad.

Small firms face a high degree of risk in going international. It is likely that the proportion of resources committed to a single foreign direct investment will be greater in a small firm than a large one. Failure is more costly. It is arguable that owner-managers are greater risk takers than other types of decision makers.

The financial strategy of small firms also requires explanation. It is clear that the 'Gambler's Earnings Hypothesis' shows up an important empirical phenomenon. An explanation is given by analogy with ploughing and harvesting. A period of ploughing may be set by the firm (say 5 or 7 years). In this time it is given a great deal of leeway. After that it either generates a stream of income for the next project (the next ploughing) or it is sold off to obtain a return. The short horizon arises because of restricted capital and management time. Thus a target rate of return and payback period are discovered by trial and error.

It is important to distinguish two types of relationship between firm size and market size. In the first case we can envisage a small firm attempting to grow in a 'big-firm' industry, i.e. an industry where optimal scale is large in relation to market size. Secondly, there are many industries with few economies of scale where many small firms exist. Industries requiring a wide range of specialist intermediate inputs, in particular, present a situation of a small firm in equilibrium with a small market. In such a situation, foreign direct investment can enable a small firm to service optimally a growing market (Buckley and Casson, 1981). This role of small firms to fill a market niche is a major advantage and has been noted for Third World multinationals who are seen as versatile users of flexible equipment (Wells, 1983). There is an argument that disinternalization brought about by the need to decentralize in large companies and by the need for specialized services such as consultancies and oil industry services, makes this role loom larger on the world scale. However, in the first case, it is difficult for a small firm to grow in competition with large firms. In such situations, the vulnerability of small firms and the danger of becoming overstretched often lead to bankruptcy or selling out.

3.1. Synthesis

Several key points emerge from the theoretical literature. First is the importance of the relationship between firm and market. This is reflected in the crucial balance between firms size and market size. The growth of the firm by internalization of markets is a key to undersatnding the velocity and direction of the growth of small- and medium-sized firms. The importance of market niches is also of great potential in explaining the industrial distribution and pattern of the foreign activities of SMEs.

Second, the importance of constraints on the international activities of SMEs emerges from the literature. Both internal and external constraints can be seen to influence growth patterns. Internal constraints are shortages of capital and management and informational constraints. The acquisition of greater resources is impeded by the necessity to retain (family) control and institutional difficulties of borrowing and raising finance (capitalizing knowledge). External constraints arise from the market, from the dangers of takeover and from institutional restraints, both governmental and non-governmental.

Third, the role of uncertainty looms large in the decision making of SMEs. Partly, this can be offset by information acquisition, but this is costly and interacts with management shortages. Taking short cuts and inadequate evaluation of alternatives often result.

Fourth, the alternative forms of technology transfer must be evaluated. Licensing and other 'new forms' (Buckley, 1983b; also Chapter 3 in Buckley and Casson, 1985; Buckley and Davies, 1981; Oman, 1984) of industrial co-operation must be considered as alternatives to foreign direct investment. It is notable that technology transfer by SMEs via licensing was also significant (White, 1983, pp. 272–273; and White and Campos, 1986, where of 32 cases of technology transfer to Argentina and Brazil, 14 were arm's length technology agreements and 8 were minority foreign joint ventures, p. 72). Indeed, it has recently been hypothesized that smaller firms are likely to become important users of 'new forms of international co-operation' such as licensing, joint ventures, turnkey operations and production sharing (Oman, 1984). Whilst such operations economize on capital outlay, they tend to be management-intensive and this may choke off the ability of small firms to enter into the more complex forms of such arrangements (Buckley, 1983). Licensing and joint ventures remain viable options, although the 1978 study (Buckley et al, 1988) shows that the tolerance of small firms to joint venture arrangements can be low and that such arrangements can adversely affect success.

Fifth, the vulnerability of SMEs to technological, political, institutional and market changes must be stressed. Against this the flexibility of SMEs is often an important competitive advantage.

Sixth, the motives for foreign investment follow several patterns. (1) SMEs may be 'pulled' into foreign markets by larger firms, by government, e.g. tariff imposition, or other powerful influences. (2) They may be 'pushed' abroad by domestic conditions, e.g. a declining home market or avoidance of (foreign exchange) restrictions. (3) They may follow the classic motives of foreign direct investment – raw material or input control, market oriented or cost oriented. These forms of investment require very different types of analysis. Previous studies have shown that there are differences in predominant motives related to the nationality of SMEs. Ozawa (1985) found that many Japanese SMEs were investing in LDCs as offshore production platforms in order to export back to Japan whilst most Western European SMEs invest abroad in order to secure market access (Onida et al, 1985, for Italy; Buckley et al, 1988, for UK; Berger and Uhlman, 1984, for Germany; and Bertin, 1986, for France). See White and Campos (1986) for further elucidation. (4) SMEs are susceptible to 'spurious' investment based on inadequate evaluations of alternatives, over zealous actions in following up an approach from an external body or misinformation. (5) SMEs may invest abroad as a result of entrepreneurial foresight, which may or may not be rewarded.

Seventh, we should note that the large multinationals often have highly sector-specific expansion routes. This leaves market niches or 'interstices' for SMEs to exploit. It is in these 'small firm industries', not characterized by economies of scale where we should look for successful SMEs (see White and Campos, 1986).

Eighth, the international structure of industries should be examined. As well as industries population by small firms, we can often observe a 'fringe' of small firms in 'large firm industries'. This pattern should be investigated. Is it an historical legacy or a reaction to efficiency and optimum locational criteria?

The growth of the industry, too, is relevant. A cycle can be envisaged where in the early stages lots of small firm vie for position. As the industry matures, economies of scale become prevalent and dominance of the few ensues in an oligopolistic structure. Over time fragmentation takes place as new entry erodes the existing competitor's dominance. The role of SMEs over the life cycle of the industry needs to be examined.

Ninth, the location strategy of SMEs and multinationals is of great importance in determining the pattern of activity by both groups of foreign investors. Specifically, several forces are at work. (1) There are increasing returns to scale in many activities and this will affect location strategy and bias these activities towards large firm dominance. (2) The performance of many non-routine activities, such as research and development and marketing by modern firms, means that such activities will exercise a locational 'pull' on production. The inputs to these activities and the scale economies in their performance may dictate centralization within the firm. (3) Many (multinational) firms operate in imperfect markets and cannot be considered as price takers. Consequently, large firms can often force down input or factor prices and will concentrate their activities in countries or regions intensive in these inputs. Such distortions will have important effects on the opportunities for SMEs to compete with or supply such monopolistic multinationals. (4) Avoidance of government intervention at home or in the host country will affect location. Biases towards low interference countries and to the use of transfer pricing will distort location of both SMEs and multinationals away from what would be, in the absence of government interference, least cost location. (5) Communications costs within the firm dictate the centralization of high communication intensive activities and the decentralization of routine, low communication cost activities. These influences on location must be evaluated for SMEs as there is a differential impact on the activities of integrated multinationals and more loosely organized SMEs.

4. THE NATURE OF FOREIGN DIRECT INVESTMENT BY SMALL AND MEDIUM-SIZED ENTERPRISES

There are a number of suggestions in the literature as to the important factors in the existence of SMEs as direct investors. The range of industries and nature of production have been characterized in a number of studies.

Foreign investment by SMEs covers a wide range of industries. White (1983) characterizes the operations as 'highly specialized', covering one or two product lines, with short production runs, often serving the 'contractual markets' given by other industries (p. 274). Typical industries include metal working, capital goods production, textiles and clothing, food, furniture, ceramic products and non-metallic products. These industries are well represented in the sample of UK outward investors which have been studied in detail (Buckley et al, 1988).

UK smaller outward investors are largely engaged in the production of intermediate and component products and services for other firms. Thirty-six of the 43 investors studied made producer goods or services; only four were entirely engaged in consumer good production and four firms made both producer and consumer goods. A large proportion was engaged in the engineering and metal goods sectors (SIC orders VI, VII, VIII, IX, XI, XII) – fully 31 out of 43 (Buckley et al, 1988, Table 2.2, p. 9).

Medium sized firms investing in the UK were also concentrated in these sectors (SIC VI, VII, VIII, IX, XI, XII) which accounted for 21 out of 35 production subsidiaries. Textiles also was well represented with 5 production subsidiaries. Again producer goods were dominant – 27 production subsidiaries made only producer goods; 2 made both, and only 6 were consumer goods specialists (Buckley et al, 1983).

Smaller Japanese foreign investors cover a variety of labour intensive light manufacturing such as light metal articles, furniture, bags, footwear, apparel, toys, plastic products, etc. It is expected that the 1980s will see many more smaller firm foreign investors in electrical machinery, non-electrical machinery and transport equipment as smaller suppliers and subcontractors follow large enterprises abroad (UNCTAD, 1984).

Foreign direct investors from less developed countries (many of them SMEs) were largely small scale manufacturers, with high adaptability to local conditions (including input availability) and flexible users of capital equipment. Local procurement, small scale manufacturing, special products and access to markets were picked out as competitive advantages of 'Third World multinationals' (Wells, 1984). The existence of cross-national ethnic ties (e.g. overseas Chinese, expatriate Indian communities) should not be ignored.

These findings provide empirical support for the conjectures above supporting the hypothesis that balanced growth in 'small firm industries' is conducive to success.

4.1. The scale of UK SME foreign investment

In the case of United Kingdom foreign investors, according to the latest survey conducted for 1981, an estimated 1500 enterprises had 9100 foreign affiliates. Two thirds of these foreign investors (i.e. 1000 firms) with net foreign assets less than £2 million accounted for 0.8% of the total net book value of UK foreign direct investment at the end of 1981 (British Business, 2 March 1984) (see Figure 2). This is in sharp contrast to the 34 enterprises with net assets over £200 million and 1550 overseas affiliates which account for 55% of the total stock of British foreign investment.

When foreign investment in the UK is examined, it is found that about 3000 foreign countries had UK affiliates, three quarters (2150) of these had UK affiliates with a book value of less than £2 million; accounting in total for 2.4% of inward direct foreign investment in the UK (excluding oil, banking and insurance) (see Figure 3). In contrast, 21 foreign countries had assets valued at over £150 million in the UK, and account for one third of the total (British Business, 2 March 1984). Inward investment was less concentrated than outward: the 100 largest inward investors account for 60% of total direct investment; the 100 largest outward investors account for 80% (again excluding oil, banking and insurance).

4.2. The direction of UK foreign investment by SMEs

The study by Buckley et al (1988) examined first time foreign direct investors. None of these investments was in a middle income or developing country. However, the 52 firms (43 with

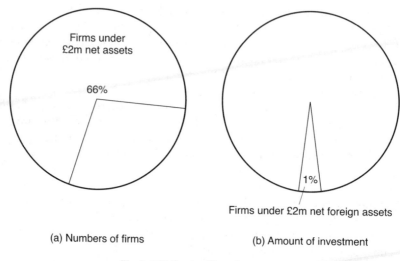

(a) Numbers of firms   (b) Amount of investment

Fig. 2. UK Foreign Direct Investment.

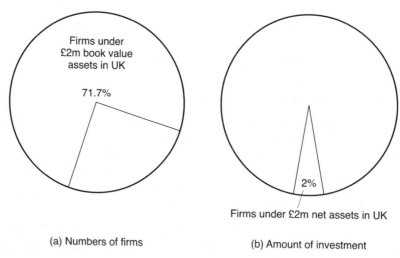

(a) Numbers of firms   (b) Amount of investment

Fig. 3. Inward Investment into UK.

foreign production subsidiaries and 9 with foreign sales subsidiaries) made a total of 39 further foreign investments – 33 production and 6 sales subsidiaries. Six production subsidiaries and two sales subsidiaries were in middle income and developing countries as Table 2 shows. This study also shows two marked shifts in overall UK foreign direct investment – one away from the old Empire and Commonwealth towards the countries of the European Communities dating from the late 1960s to late 1970s succeeded by a wave of investment to the USA. It appears, from very partial evidence that SMEs followed these general trends.

Table 2. Later foreign production and sales subsidiaries of the 52 UK smaller firms*

Location	Foreign production subsidiaries	Foreign sales subsidiaries
Developed countries		
South Africa	5	1
Australia	4	–
Netherlands	4	–
France	3	1
USA	3	–
Canada	2	2
New Zealand	2	–
Ireland	2	–
Belgium	1	–
Norway	1	–
Sub-totals	*27*	*4*
Middle income and developing countries		
Mexico	1	1
India	1	–
Nigeria	1	–
Malta	1	–
Spain	1	–
Portugal	1	–
Bahamas	–	1
Sub-totals	*6*	*2*
Totals	33	6

* 43 with foreign production subsidiaries, 9 with foreign sales subsidiaries.
Source: Derived from the research reported by Buckley, Newbould and Thurwell (1988).

5. CONCLUSION

The problems facing SMEs in foreign direct investment are most acute for first time investors. Risks are perceived to be great and the firm has no international experience on which to draw. Many firms in the 1978 study had unsuccessful first foreign ventures but went on to undertake later successful foreign investments. Learning from mistakes is a vital part of business progress. However, the dice are stacked by the type of industry and environment faced by the firm. SMEs have a natural constituency in industries characterized by insignificant economies of scale and specialized demand. In such industries there is no 'critical minimum scale' at which a firm can be expected to succeed in foreign direct investment. Attempts to move into areas of great potential demand where economies of scale are prevalent are fraught with danger and emphasize the vulnerability rather than the sensitivity of small firms.

The author would like to thank Mark Casson, Hafiz Mirza, Nick Wilson and Roger Brooksbank for constructive comments on an earlier draft.

University of Bradford Management Centre

REFERENCES

Aharoni, Y. (1966). *The Foreign Investment Decision Process*, (Boston, Mass: Graduate School of Business Administration, Harvard University.

Bain, J.S. (1956). *Barriers to New Competition*, (Cambridge, Mass: Harvard University Press).

Barlow, E.R. and Wender, I.T. (1955). *Foreign Investment and Taxation*, Englewood Cliffs, NJ: Prentice-Hall).

Berger, M. and Uhlman, L. (1984). *Auslandsinvestitionen kleiner und mittlerer Unternehmen*, IFO Schnelldienst 30/84 (Munich: IFO Institute).

Bertin, G.Y. (1986). Le Transfert de Technologie aux Pays en Developpement par les Petites et Moyennes Enterprises Françaises, Paris: Mimeo.

Buckley, P.J. (1979). 'Foreign Investment Success for Smaller Firms', *Multinational Business* **3**, 12–19.

Buckley, P.J. (1982). 'The Role of Exporting in the Market Servicing Policies of Multinational Manufacturing Enterprises: Theoretical and Empirical Perspectives', in M.R. Czinkota and G. Tesar (eds.), *Export Management: An International Context* (New York: Praeger).

Buckley, P.J. (1983a). 'A Critical View of Theories of the Multinational Enterprise', *Aussenwirtschaft* **36**, 70–87. Revised version in Buckley and Casson (1985) *op. cit.*

Buckley, P.J., (1983b). 'New Theories of International Business: Some Unresolved Issues', in Mark Casson (ed.) *The Growth of International Business*, (London: George Allen & Unwin).

Buckley, P.J., Berkova, K. and Newbould, G.D. (1983). *Direct Investment in the UK by Smaller European Firms* (London: Macmillan and New York: Crane Russak).

Buckley, P.J. and Casson, M. (1976). *The Future of the Multinational Enterprise* (London: Macmillan and New York: Holmes-Meier).

Buckley, P.J. and Casson, M. (1981). 'The Optimal Timing of a Foreign Direct Investment', *Economic Journal* **91**, 75–87.

Buckley, P.J. and Casson, M. (1985). *The Economic Theory of the Multinational Enterprise: Selected Papers* (London: Macmillan).

Buckley, P.J. and Davies, H. (1981). 'Foreign Licensing in Overseas Operations: Theory and Evidence from the UK', in A.G. Hawkins and A.J. Prasad (eds.), *Research in International Business and Finance*, Vol. 2 (New York: JAI Press).

Buckley, P.J. and Mathew, A.M. (1979). 'The Motivation for Recent First Time Direct Investment in Australia by UK Firms', *Management International Review* **19**(1): 57–69.

Buckley, P.J. and Mathew, A.M. (1980). 'Dimensions of the Market Entry Behaviour of Recent UK First Time Direct Investors in Australia', *Management International Review* 20(2), 35–51.

Buckley, P.J., Newbould, G.D., and Thurwell, J. (1988). *Foreign Direct Investment by Smaller UK Firms*, Macmillan, London. Previously published as Newbould, G.D., Buckley, P.J., and Thurwell, J., 1978, *Going International – The Experience of Smaller Companies Overseas* (London: Associated Business Press; New York: Halstead Press).

Casson, M. (1982). *The Entrepreneur: An Economic Theory* (Oxford: Martin Robertson).

Casson, M. (1983). 'Introduction: The Conceptual Framework', in M. Casson (ed.), *The Growth of International Business* (London: George Allen & Unwin).

Cavanagh, D.K. and Clifford, R.E. (1983). *The Winning Performance of the Midsized Growth Companies* (New York: McKinsey & Co Inc).

Fierheller, G.A. (1980). Jan/Feb, 'Planning in the Medium Sized Company', *Managerial Planning*, pp. 258–270.

Hirsch, S. (1976). 'An International Trade and Investment Theory of the Firm', *Oxford Economic Papers* **28**, 258–70.

Khan, S.M. (1978). *A Study of Success and Failure in Exporting* (Stockholm: Akademilitteratur).

Lupo, L.A., Gilbert, A., and Liliestedt, M. (1978). 'The Relationship between Age and Rate of Return of Foreign Manufacturing Affiliates of UK Manufacturing Parent Companies', *Survey of Current Business* **58**, 60–6.

Mathew, A.M. (1979). 'Recent Direct Investment in Australia by First Time UK Investors', Unpublished PhD thesis, University of Bradford Management Centre.

Oman, C. (1984). *New Forms of International Investment in Developing Countries* (Paris: OECD).

Onida, F., Balcet, G. *et al.* (1985). *Technology Transfer to Developing Countries by Italian Small- and Medium-Sized Enterprises* (Geneva: UNCTAD).

Ozawa, T. (1985). *International Transfer of Technology by Japan's Small and Medium Enterprises in Developing Countries* (Geneva: UNCTAD).

Penrose, E.T. (1956). 'Foreign Investment and the Growth of the Firm', *Economic Journal* **66**, 230–5.

Penrose, E.T. (1959). *The Theory of the Growth of the Firm* (Oxford: Basil Blackwell).

Savary, J. (1984). *French Multinationals* (London: Frances Pinter/IRM).

Scherer, F.M. *et al.* (1975). *The Economics of Multi-Plant Operation – an International Comparisons Study* (Cambridge, Mass: Harvard University Press).

Teece, D.J. (1983). 'Technological and Organisational Factors in the Theory of the Multinational Enterprise', in M. Casson (ed.), *The Growth of International Business* (London: George Allen & Unwin).

UNCTAD, (1984). International transfer of technology to developing countries by small and medium sized enterprises (Geneva: Report by UNCTAD Secretariat TD/B/C 6/119).

Van Hoorn, T.P. (1979). 'Strategic Planning to Small and Medium-Sized Companies', *Long Range Planning* **12** (April), 84–91.

Vernon, R. (1966). 'International Investment and International Trade in the Product Cycle', *Quarterly Journal of Economics* **80**, 190–207.

Wells, L.T. (1983). *Third World Multinationals: The Rise of Foreign Investment from Developing Countries* (Cambridge, Mass: MIT Press).

White, E. (1983). 'The Role of Third World Multinationals and Small and Medium Sized Companies in the Industrialization Strategies of Developing Countries', in *Industrial Development Strategies and Policies for Developing Countries* (Vienna: United Nations Industrial Development Organisation).

White, E. and Campos, J. (1986). *Alternative Technology Sources for Developing Countries: The Role of Small and Medium Sized Enterprises from Industrialized Countries* (Buenos Aires: Cederi Estudios).

9

Network Relationships and the Internationalization Process of Small Software Firms

Nicole Coviello and Hugh Munro

INTRODUCTION

Historically, research on the internationalization process has tended to focus on large manufacturing organizations, in spite of the importance of small service and/or knowledge-based firms to most economies. Such firms are of particular interest given they often possess limited capabilities and management resources (Erramilli and D'Souza, 1993; Buckley, 1989; O'Farrell and Hitchins, 1988). However, the success of these firms, particularly those pursuing niche strategies in small domestic markets, may depend on their ability to internationalize their operations (Luostarinen, 1989). If the firm is faced with increasing demand, sophisticated customers, and a volatile competitive market, as well as a product that is strategically important or unable to be standardised, successful internationalization may well require the firm to leverage the skills and resources of other organizations (Hara and Kanai, 1994). This is supported by McDougall *et al.* (1994) and Bell (1995), who highlight the potential impact of network relationships on small firm internationalization. More specifically, Coviello and Munro (1995) found that the conduct of international marketing activities of small firms was impacted by larger partners in their network. The conclusions of each of these studies call for further research on the role of networks in the internationalization process of small firms.

The purpose of this research is to further our understanding of how network relationships impact internationalization patterns and processes. More specifically, this research seeks to understand how network relationships influence the small firm's approach to internationalization, particularly in terms of foreign market and entry mode selection.

While the primary interest is on small firm processes, the research also focuses on software developers; firms characterised as high technology, knowledge-based, and service-intensive. This sector is similar to those examined by Bell (1995) and Coviello and Munro (1995), and provides an interesting contrast to much of the internationalization literature which focuses on traditional manufacturing organizations. Examination of high technology firms also allows for a deeper understanding of a global, fast-growing, and pervasive industry which is receiving increased attention in the international business literature (McDougall *et al.*, 1994; Oviatt and McDougall, 1994).

The paper proceeds with a review of the internationalization process literature, discussed in the context of small firms. This review highlights the need for research in the area, leading

Reprinted with permission from *International Business Review,* **6**(4), 1997, 361–386 to the identification of two research questions. This is then followed by a discussion of the research method and research findings. The paper concludes by offering an empirically-based framework describing the influence of network relationships on the internationalization process of small software firms, and a discussion of research and managerial implications.

LITERATURE REVIEW

Since Welch and Luostarinen's (Welch and Luostarinen, 1988) comprehensive analysis of the internationalization concept, a number of useful reviews have assessed and synthesised the general internationalization process literature (e.g. Johanson and Vahlne, 1990, 1992; Melin, 1992; Andersen, 1993). Each of these reviews seems to agree that efforts to encapsulate the internationalization concept in a definitive manner have been inadequate.

If it is accepted that internationalization is a dynamic concept (Johanson and Vahlne, 1992; Melin, 1992), then the definition of internationalization offered by Beamish (1990) is perhaps appropriate:

> . . . the process by which firms both increase their awareness of the direct and indirect influences of international transactions on their future, and establish and conduct transactions with other countries.

This view, like many others, is process-based, and incorporates: (1) the internal dynamics and learning of the firm as it expands internationally, and (2) the 'outward' pattern of international investment exemplified by market selection and mode of entry. Beamish's definition also allows for recognition of the fact that firms may begin the internationalization process through involvement in activities such as foreign sourcing or countertrade, i.e. reflecting an 'inward' pattern of internationalization (Welch and Luostarinen, 1988, 1993; Korhonen et al., 1995).

Efforts to understand the process of internationalization have been numerous. One area of the extant literature discusses an incremental approach to international market expansion, whereby a series of 'stages' of internationalization reflect the firm's increasing market knowledge and commitment over time. A second area suggests the internationalization process involves, and is influenced by, the set of connected relationships a firm develops as part of its 'network'. Both of these perspectives will be discussed in turn, including a review of the small firm research in each area.

Modes of incremental internationalization

The notion of a firm expanding to international markets in an incremental, stepwise manner is widely documented in the literature, with Johanson and Vahlne (1977) providing the most commonly cited conceptual and empirical base. Their research on the activities of large Swedish manufacturing firms emphasises managerial learning during the internationaliza-tion process, and shows that a series of 'stages' of internationalization occur in order of increasing commitment and investment in foreign markets. For example, the model offered by Johanson and Vahlne (1977) suggests that initial internationalization activities are targeted to 'psychically close' markets, i.e. markets having similar culture, language, political systems, trade practices, etc. Following initial expansion with low risk, indirect exporting to similar markets, firms improve their foreign market knowledge. Over time and through experience, firms then increase foreign market commitment and expand to more 'psychically distant' markets. This in turn enhances market knowledge, leading to further commitment, including equity investment in offshore manufacturing and sales operations. Overall, the Johanson and Vahlne model illustrates how managerial learning drives internationalization. At the same time, the model captures manifestations of the process in terms of market selection and the mechanisms used to enter foreign markets.

In addition to the Johanson and Vahlne model, other important research also reports an incremental approach to internationalization (e.g. Cavusgil, 1984; Czinkota, 1982; Reid, 1981; Bilkey and Tesar, 1977). For example, Cavusgil (1984) empirically identifies five stages (Preinvolvement, Reactive/Opportunistic, Experimental, Active, and Committed Involvement), reflecting differences in the firm's orientation and management attitude to international market expansion. As summarised by Andersen (1993) and Thomas and Araujo (1985), this type of incremental approach is a result of innovation adoption behaviour, whereby the perceptions and beliefs of managers' influence, and are shaped by, involvement in foreign markets. Like the Johanson and Vahlne model, these studies highlight the role of managerial learning in the internationalization process.

Models of incremental internationalization and the small firm

The general literature discussing incremental internationalization has led to a number of efforts to validate earlier work across different firm characteristics, including firm size. In a recent review of contemporary empirical research on small firm internationalization, Coviello and McAuley (1996) identified eight studies which either:

1. support the traditional view of incremental internationalization (Hakam et al., 1993; Calof and Viviers, 1995);
2. confirm a gradual process of internationalization, but note the prevalence of inward investment preceding outward investment and foreign market entry (Hyvaerinen, 1994);
3. redefine the traditional perspective by describing different 'stages' in the context of firm and market characteristics (Rao and Naidu, 1992);
4. identify a process of incremental commitment for small firms that may be different to that of larger firms (Lau, 1992);
5. identify stages of competitive strategy in the small firm internationalization process, but no linear relationships between these stages and the mechanisms used in internationalization (Chang and Grub, 1992); or
6. challenge the traditional view of incremental internationalization (Lindqvist, 1988; Bell, 1995).

As a result, while some recent small firm findings support the view that firms follow an incremental process of internationalization in terms of increasing knowledge, commitment, and investment, others do not. This apparent contradiction reflects patterns also found in the large firm literature, where empirical findings both identify and support the incremental approach (see Johanson and Vahlne, 1990; also Luostarinen, 1989; Buckley, 1989), while others challenge it (e.g. Whitelock and Munday, 1993; Millington and Bayliss, 1990; Turnbull, 1987; Sharma and Johanson, 1987).

Each of the studies examined by Coviello and McAuley (1996) provides a contribution in its own right, however the findings of Bell (1995) and Lindqvist (1988) are particularly interesting as they suggest that:

- the pace and pattern of international market growth and choice of entry mode for small firms is influenced by (for example) close relationships with customers (Lindqvist, 1988); and
- interfirm relationships (with clients, suppliers, etc) appear influential in both market selection and mode of entry for small firms (Bell, 1995).

These results are perhaps not surprising, as both Bell (1995) and Lindqvist network and relationships within current markets, than on market and cultural characteristics.

Overall, the network perspective goes beyond the models of incremental internationalization by suggesting that a firm's strategy emerges as a pattern of behaviour influenced by a variety of network relationships. As stated by Benito and Welch (1994):

> . . . the sometimes erratic character of internationalization for individual firms appears to be related to the seeming randomness with which opportunities and threats relevant to international activity arise in a company's external environment.

Such opportunities and threats may be presented to the firm by their network relationships. As such, these external contact systems or relationships may drive, facilitate, or inhibit a firm's international market development. Such relationships might also influence the firm's choice of foreign market and entry mode.

Networks and the small firm

Much of the small firm network research focuses on general network influences on firm behaviour (e.g. Tjosvold and Weicker, 1993; Dubini and Aldrich, 1991; Larson, 1991; Lorenzoni and Ornati, 1988). As noted previously however, certain studies highlight the potential role of networks in small firm internationalization (Lindqvist, 1988; McDougall et al., 1994; Bell, 1995).

Other findings also recognise the importance of networks to a small firm (e.g. Hanson et al., 1994; Hara and Kanai, 1994; Coviello and Munro, 1995; Kaufmann, 1995; Korhonen et al., 1995). For example, Korhonen et al. (1995) found that over half of Finnish SMEs started their internationalization process with 'inward' foreign operations, largely through the import of physical goods or services. From this, Korhonen et al. (1995) conclude that such inward operations allow for international network connections to be established, thus supporting Welch and Luostarinen (1993). Also, Coviello and Munro (1995) found that successful New Zealand-based software firms are actively involved with international networks, and outsource many market development activities to network partners.

Finally, Bonaccorsi's (1992) study of small Italian exporters suggests that 'access to external resources' (through for example, buyer–seller relationships) can play an important role in the firm's internationalization process. This view is also held by Welch (1992), who provides a thorough discussion of the potential use of alliances or cooperative arrangements by small firms in the internationalization process, concluding that while alliances are 'no panacea,' they can improve the potential for foreign market penetration by providing access to a network of additional relationships.

Overall, research examining network issues in the context of small firms is increasing. However, none of the above authors identify and examine specific network and relationship influences in any detail, in the context of the internationalization process. This weakness is particularly evident when considering the causes or drivers of internationalization, and how the process is manifested in terms of foreign market selection and the mechanisms used for market entry.

Summary and identification of research questions

Empirical research to date shows that the various models of incremental internationalization provide useful frameworks for analysis of international growth patterns, in terms of a firm's gradual learning and commitment to international markets. Similarly, there is a growing body of literature highlighting the potential influence of network relationships on the internationalization process. At the same time, while Johanson and Vahlne (1990) suggest that researchers should investigate how internationalization is related to surrounding processes, and more fully understand the influences on internationalization strategies, little empirical work has been done in this regard, in the specific context of small firms and networks.

Therefore, the purpose of this research is to empirically examine the internationalization process of small firms, integrating the incremental or 'stage' views of internationalization with the network perspective. Using the context of the software industry, the research seeks to understand:

1. how the internationalization process of small software firms is manifested in their choice of foreign market and mode of entry; and
2. how network relationships influence the small software firm's choice of foreign market and model of entry.

METHOD

To most effectively identify and understand detailed international growth patterns and processes, this research used multi-site case study methodology, following the principles of data collection established by Eisenhardt (1989) and Yin (1989). Multiple sources of evidence were used (depth interviews, documents, archival records), and a case study data base was created using four case sites.

The population from which the case sites were selected consists of New Zealand-based software developers. These firms are small by international standards, and have knowledge as a core competency. The industry is active internationally, serving diverse and complex markets from a small domestic base. While the findings of the study are perhaps limited to high technology firms, the choice of a single sector minimises the impact of inter-industry differences (as per Turnbull, 1987; Strandksov, 1986). Further, characteristics of the software industry are similar to other knowledge-based industries competing internationally, and are the same as those examined by Bell (1995) and McDougall *et al.* (1994). Thus, a basis for comparison is provided, enhancing theory development, and our understanding of the internationalization patterns and processes of an important business sector.

The case sites were chosen for theoretical rather than statistical reasons, to replicate and extend the emergent theory under examination. Sites were generated based on a number of different characteristics, as suggested by Eisenhardt (1989). For the purposes of this research, the case sites had differing product and market characteristics, and their histories included both success and failure in foreign markets. Individual sample elements were upper-level managers in the company, primarily the Managing Director/Chief Executive, and key informants identified by the Managing Director. These respondents were directly involved in decision-making for internationalization, and able to provide responses based on personal experience.

Data analysis was designed to identify patterns relevant to international market growth and the influence of network relationships on the case firms. The techniques of pattern-matching and explanation-building developed by Yin (1989) were used. This approach was aided by a variety of analytical tools applied within and across the cases, as suggested by Miles and Huberman (1984). For example, Checklists, Time-Ordered Matrices, and Event Listings were used to identify and chronicle critical events pertaining to growth, product-market and relationship development, and decision-making. As is consistent with qualitative research methods, no attempt was made to operationalize and measure concepts on an a priori basis. Rather, verbatim transcripts were content analysed, then interpreted and coded as a means for labelling dimensions which emerged in the process of data collection. In most instances, direct quotes from case informants were used, as they were believed to best reflect the phenomena under investigation.

Given the historical and longitudinal perspective of the research, all analysis was conducted chronologically as the basic sequence of cause/effect should not be inverted. Further, a major area of the literature base on the internationalization process focuses on sequential stages, thus chronological analysis was relevant. This approach is also supported by Axelsson and Johanson (1992) and Melin (1992), as appropriate to the study of the internationalization process and network development. Finally, the processes under examination may be context specific, requiring subjective and interpretative analysis. An inductive approach to the research is therefore warranted, following the relativist view (Hunt, 1991).

FINDINGS AND DISCUSSION

To address the research questions developed previously, the international growth patterns of the case firms will be presented, followed by a discussion of the influence of network relationships on the internationalization process. To begin, the case firm characteristics are briefly summarised.

At time of data collection, each case firm had extensive experience in the international software industry. All four firms were founded between 1978 and 1983, and had experienced significant growth. For example, firm size (at time of data collection) ranged from 25 employees located in one country to 140 employees in four countries. Annual turnover ranged from $2 million to approximately $15 million, and the number of countries served ranged from five to seventeen. The average per annum growth rate for these firms was 83%. Their products ranged from modular applications packages for the financial accounting market, to complex system programming software.

International growth patterns

The international growth patterns of the four case firms are summarised in Fig. 1 (below). This figure captures the internationalization process in terms of the firm's orientation toward international expansion, the time frame associated with internationalization, the foreign markets entered, and the modes of entry used.

Three 'stages' of international activity are apparent in the case findings. In terms of firm orientation, the small software firms had a largely domestic focus in the initial stage (Year 0–1), but clear intentions to internationalize. The second stage (Year 1–3) is characterised by the small firms becoming actively involved in their first foreign market. Managers also began to seriously evaluate potential market expansion opportunities. Finally, the third stage (beginning at Year 3) is evidenced by each of the four firms showing committed involvement across numerous markets, with international sales dominating their growth.

Interestingly, while certain internationalization stages are able to be identified, they do not fully match the extant literature. for example, only three stages of evolution are evident, and market expansion was not on a 'trial' or 'experimental' basis. Rather, the internationalization process began with management exploring the feasibility of international expansion from the time of firm inception. Thus, Fig. 1 depicts the compressed time frame in which the internationalization process occurs, with the small software firms commencing operations with a foreign market intention, and being 'committed' internationalists within three years. This supports Sullivan and Bauerschmidt (1990) and McDougall et al. (1994).

In terms of entry mode, the second stage of Fig. 1 shows that prior to entering their first market, some firms established a product development agreement with a large overseas partner. This in fact occurred for three of the four cases, impacting their future growth patterns in that the agreements provided them with development funding, and led to loose piggy-backing arrangements being established. These relationships quickly evolved to become formal distribution agreements,* in a psychically close market (Australia). While the expansion to close markets supports Johanson and Vahlne (1977) among others, the initial mechanisms for internationalization is different, and the resultant pattern therefore supports Welch and Luostarinen (1993), as well as the findings of Korhonen et al. (1995) and Hyvaerinen (1994). Of note, the psychically close market was also physically close, perhaps reflecting the importance of physical proximity for small firms that are geographically distant from potential markets.

The first stage of Fig. 1 highlights that based on their initial experience offshore, the case firms quickly began to develop more complex relationship structures (cf. Welch and Luostarinen, 1993). They made simultaneous use of multiple entry modes, including distributors, joint marketing and/or development agreements, piggy-backing, and joint ventures. In addition, the markets selected for international expansion in this phase were worldwide and psychically 'distant,' often reflecting little psychic similarity or physical proximity (e.g. Hong Kong, Spain). These patterns reflect the findings of Bell (1995).

Finally, two firms established a foreign sales office during the internationalization process, to support sales made through partner subsidiaries or establish regional headquarters in a distant market. This occurred relatively late in the internationalization process (e.g. Year 5–7), and reflects internalization of activities in order to better support existing relationships and increase control over marketing activities. Only one firm travelled the length of the internationalization process as described by Johanson and Vahlne (1977), by attempting to establish an offshore product development facility in the US. As this market was viewed as critical, and management believed their major partner was unable to provide the necessary market access, technology, or capital, a separate organization was established for introduction of a new product, independent of the partner. The subsidiary was closed within twelve months however, and all software development activities returned to New Zealand.

---

* While one firm attempted direct sales to its first market, it quickly realized it was unable to invest the effort and time required for market development, and due to its limited resource base, established a distributor.

Mode of Entry

Firm Orientation   **Year**

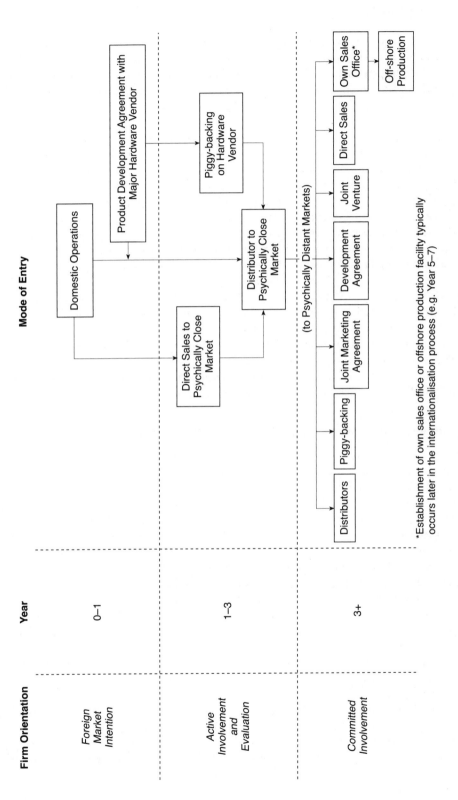

*Establishment of own sales office or offshore production facility typically occurs later in the internationalisation process (e.g. Year 5–7)

Fig. 1. The International Process of Small Software Firms

Overall, if management is expected to show a gradual awareness of, interest in, and involvement with foreign markets, the small software firm behaves differently to those represented by the general models of incremental internationalization. The case firms began their internationalization process with the intent to enter foreign markets, and although their first entry was to a psychically and physically close market, other relatively early expansion, was not.

Similarly, if the internationalization process of small software firms is examined in terms of entry mode, and increased learning and commitment is expected to result in the establishment of host country production, the internationalization process of small software firms is manifested differently from those patterns generally found in the literature. According to Johanson and Vahlne (1977, 1990) however, such patterns are typical only of firms: (1) with large resources; (2) with experience in other markets with similar conditions; or (3) competing in easily predictable market conditions. None of these parameters fit the small, young, software firm, competing in volatile markets with rapid growth and technological change.

Some of these findings are perhaps to be expected given the target market for these small firms is inevitably beyond New Zealand, and usually, is geographically distant. This, combined with the limited resource base of the small software firm at early stages of its lifecycle (when internationalization begins for these firms), would suggest that it would be different for such firms to expand international operations on their own. This in fact, was the situation in this research, and thus Oviatt and McDougall (1994), McDougall *et al.* (1994), and Bell (1995) are supported. That is, the small software firms show a pattern of externalising their activities during the internationalization process, often relying on network relationships for market selection as well as mode of entry. This will now be discussed.

The influence of networks on the internationalization process

As seen previously in Fig. 1, the small software firm's internationalization process is rapid, with the firm using a variety of mechanisms to enter a diverse number of foreign markets in as little as three years. This activity appears to be largely driven by existing network relationships. That is, the rapid and successful growth of the case firms appears to be a result of their involvement in international networks, with major partners often guiding foreign market selection and providing the mechanism for market entry. Thus, network relations may not only drive internationalization, but influence the pattern of market investment.

To understand this, critical incident listings were used to describe the pattern of international market development and network relationships in a chronological manner. Table 1 (below) provides a summary of each firm's internationalization process over time, including information on the sequence of foreign market development, the entry mode used for each market, and how the direct and indirect network relationships influence each firm's internationalization process.

Using one firm (FACT) as a representative example from Table 1, it can be seen that FACT's major relationship was with a Japanese multinational (Wang). In this relationship, FACT leveraged the market access provided by Wang, and Wang harnessed FACT's technological capabilities for product development. At a more subtle level, Wang played a significant role in directly or indirectly providing FACT with market development opportunities worldwide. For example, FACT's expansion to Australia was triggered by an informal contact generated indirectly by FACT's product development agreement with Wang.

Table 1. Market Selection and Mode of Entry Patterns for the Four Case Firms (Presented Chronologically)

Foreign Market Entry	CBA	DSR	FACT	MSL
A. Initial Foreign Market Entry	• following successful NZ distribution of product for a US MNC, CBA management was approached by a distributor in Australia (initiated by the US MNC both it and CBA represented) • Australian distributor signed*	• while identifying product and market opportunities, DSR's CEO met a New Zealander managing an Australian subsidiary of a Japanese MNC hardware vendor • contact led to a joint product development and marketing agreement for Australia	• following establishment of a product development agreement with a Japanese MNC, FACT was approached by a distributor in Australia (referred by a NZ-based industry contact) • first Australian distributor signed	• sold direct to major customer in Australia
B. Subsequent Market Entries	*All Products* • Australian distributor grew to include a dealer network across Australia • Singapore distributor for CBA's own range of products established, initiated by a member of the Australian dealer network • based on word-of-mouth, CBA was approached by two distributors in the UK, one of which distributed product for the same US MNC represented by CBA in NZ and Australia	*Product 1* • Australian partner helped establish a distributor relationship with the Japanese MNC's US subsidiary • DSR piggy-backed on Japanese MNC's distribution network to Canada, Europe, and the UK	*All Products* • interested UK distributor identified and signed • Australian sales office established • second Australian distributor signed; initiated through previous business contacts	*Product 1* • established agent in Australia through personal contact of MSL's CEO; agency agreement terminated after 1 year • selected a distributor in US (through active search) but distributor declared bankruptcy; MSL on verge of insolvency

Table 1. Continued

Foreign Market Entry	CBA	DSR	FACT	MSL
B. Subsequent Market Entries (continued)	• one UK firm signed for distribution and product enhancement; informal relationship established with the other firm (the distributor for the US MNC) • Malaysian distributor established, initiated through the family and business contacts of a member of the NZ dealer network.	*Product 2* • initially sold direct to Australia; success led to agreements with five agents and one distributor • Singapore distributor established, initiated through a personal contact of the DSR Product Manager • CEO and management team used industry contacts to identify two Scandinavian hardware manufacturers to act as distributors for Europe • joint marketing and development agreement also established with the two Scandinavian firms	• entered Hong Kong by piggy-backing on Japanese MNC's distributor • used Japanese MNC's contacts to establish US sales office (independent of the Japanese firm) • at Japanese MNC's direction, terminated first Australian distributor relationship, acquired second Australian distributor, and transferred UK distribution rights to Japanese MNC's UK subsidiary • entered Europe through Japanese MNC's German subsidiary, connected to subsidiaries in Holland, Belgium, Austria, and Poland • withdrew from the US	*Product 2* • approached several international hardware vendors for product development support, including a Japanese MNC • contact by NZ subsidiary of same Japanese firm, to establish a product development agreement with the Japanese firm's Australian subsidiary; development agreement evolved to include marketing activities • entered Malaysia and Spain by piggy-backing on sales of the Japanese MNC's Australian subsidiary • same Japanese MNC recommended an independent distributor for Japan; Japanese distributor signed • long-term product development agreement established with original Japanese MNC partner, for world markets

Table 1. Continued

Foreign Market Entry	CBA	DSR	FACT	MSL
		Product 3 • CEO and management team used industry contacts and advice from personal contact at Japanese MNC partner to establish distributors in Singapore, Hong Kong, Canada, and the US *Product 4* • UK distributor established, initiated through DSR's Product Manager and his industry	• Japanese MNC experienced financial difficulties • Japanese distributor established (independent of the Japanese MNC), initiated by one of the distributor's NZ-born employees • Indonesian distributor established, initiated by a major competitor of the initial Japanese MNC partner • reentered US with US venture capital, establishing a US-based marketing operation, independent of initial Japanese MNC partner	

* Australian distributor became a joint venture in Year 3, and then a wholly-owned sales subsidiary in Year 7.

Following expansion to Australia, FACT pursued the UK market independently of Wang. However, the Wang relationship ultimately impacted FACT's growth patterns in Australia and the UK in that the original distributor relationships in both countries were terminated at the request of Wang, and UK distribution rights were transferred to Wang's subsidiary. Beyond Australia and the UK, Wang offered FACT market access to Hong Kong, Europe, and the Eastern Bloc countries, through Wang's international subsidiaries. Thus, Wang influenced FACT's international market selection and also provided the entry mode.

A different pattern emerges for the US market in that FACT established a local sales office independent of Wang's subsidiary network. Nevertheless, the FACT office relied informally on Wang for market intelligence and support.

Of all the markets served by FACT, only Japan and Indonesia were entered through contacts outside the Wang network. For example, the Japanese relationship was initiated through previously established personal contacts (a New Zealander working for the Japanese firm). Entry to Indonesia resulted from an approach by another well-established hardware vendor: Compaq, a competitor to Wang. Thus, additional sets of network relationships were introduced to FACT.

Overall, FACT's internationalization process was driven and shaped by a complex set of network relationships, influenced by one large international partner. As commented by the General Manager:

> . . . you congregate around a particular honey pot, and in the past it was called Wang. So, we buzz around the Wang pot, and they [potential partners] buzz around, and Wang may put you in contact or you may bump into each other.

In a pattern similar to FACT, the other case firms were also linked to extensive, established international network at a very early stage of their life cycle. This presented the small software firms with new market opportunities and established organizations as potential partners, thus accelerating and shaping their internationalization efforts. More specifically, each firm's choice of foreign market and entry mode was clearly influenced by their early partner(s) and resultant network relationships. Through network contacts, all four case firms were well-established offshore within three years of company formation, and actively looking to further their international expansion through development of additional relationships. This supports Johanson and Vahlne's more recent views, recognising the influence of networks and multiple market relationships in the internationalization process.

Of note, the early partners of these small software firms tended to be large, internationally-established hardware vendors. As stated by FACT's General Manager, small software firms are undercapitalised and created on the efforts and strengths of only two or three people. Thus,

> . . . you have to be in some way associated with a hardware partner, or a substantial company.

In the case of MSL, a product development relationship was critical to the company's survival, and the Managing Director believed the only viable option for international growth was to develop a relationship with an overseas partner. As he commented:

> . . . if you have got a piece of the jigsaw they want, then you know its going to go very well because you're not fighting to sell your product in isolation.

Therefore, the findings of this study support Welch and Luostarinen (1993) and Korhonen et al. (1995) in that the initial product development relationship established with hardware vendors provided the catalyst and resources for international growth. That is, the 'inward' relationship facilitated 'outward' expansion.

This behaviour also supports the findings of McDougall *et al.* (1994) in that the small software firms externalised certain activities in order to minimise their financial and market risk during international expansion. Thus, network relationships facilitate international growth. However, while network relationships enhanced the internationalization activities of all four case firms, they also constrained the pursuit of other opportunities. Referring back to the FACT example, market access and international reputation was strongly associated with Wang. Thus, when Wang suffered financial difficulties in the late 1980s, FACT found it necessary to establish separate, independent relationships with parties outside the Wang network.

The case firms also experienced a number of difficulties associated with internationalising through a large firm, primarily related to market and product planning. For example, the Managing Director of MSL noted there was a degree of vagueness in the MSL-Fujitsu relationship:

> . . . in some ways we seem to be extremely lucky that we are part of Fujitsu's dream for the future, and they're feeding us a few bits and pieces of what that is [but] we don't actually have a blue-print of what we are going to be doing in five years time . . . there's just no detail.

These constraints and the associated fears of total dependence* on a major partner contributed to three of the firms developing new products for diversified markets, or establishing separate support/service facilities. For example, DSR's original product was strongly associated with their partner's brand name in international markets, and the initial products for FACT and MSL were developed specifically for their partner's hardware platform. Therefore, DSR began to develop products outside their partner's area of expertise, and FACT and MSL developed software that was compatible with other competitive systems. All three firms also established separate service and support facilities to decrease reliance on their partners for customer contact and support.

The case findings also reveal that as each firm experienced market success, it began to desire greater control in network relationships (i.e. more autonomy in its decision-making with respect to product and relationship development, market selection, and mode of entry). In two of the cases (CBA and FACT), technological and market success allowed the New Zealand-based firm to evolve over time to become the central firm in its network. DSR also increased in strength and negotiating influence within its network. For these three firms, the case findings suggest that managerial learning occurred, whereby market experience and success over time led to increased knowledge about both markets and managing relationships. This in turn led to increased commitment to foreign market development, and further learning. This pattern supports Johanson and Vahlne (1977, 1990).

Finally, as the three firms became more successful in international markets, they caught the attention of major organizations in their industry areas. In late 1990, FACT was acquired by a Canadian multinational outside their formal network, but part of a wider industry network. DSR was acquired in 1991 by a US company connected through product development to their formal network. In 1993, CBA was also acquired by a US firm which was part of CBA's informal industry network, and owned by a New Zealander familiar with the local market. Each of these New Zealand firms had felt increasingly vulnerable to acquisition due to their market success, and in fact, *chose* their new parent through existing network relationships rather than risk a buy-out by existing partners (e.g. FACT and DSR), or

---

* 'Dependence' was the term used by informants to reflect the percentage of sales attributed to a network partner.

firms that were unknown to them (e.g. CBA). For these three firms, it is apparent that the impact of network relationships went beyond the internationalization process per se, to affect their ownership structure (and, perhaps, future internationalization efforts).

In the case of MSL, the fourth firm, diversification efforts were made to minimise the risk in being associated solely with one large firm, as MSL's growth was limited to that of its partner. Also, the partner restricted MSL's direct access to existing and potential customers. These diversification efforts (into service and support areas) were halted by the partner however, and MSL remained positioned as a 'development arm' for the partner's network. This situation continued until 1993, when the 'long-term' product development agreement was completed, and the formal relationship between the two parties was terminated, in a decision made by the larger partner. This had a severe effect on MSL, causing it to downsize to half its employee base, and seek alternative product development opportunities and relationships.

Overall, the case findings indicate that the internationalization decisions and growth patterns of small software firms, particularly with respect to initial and subsequent market selection and mode of entry, are very much shaped by their network of formal and informal relationships. Thus, both Johanson and Vahlne (1992) and Johanson and Mattsson (1988) are supported, as are Benito and Welch (1994) who suggest that network development is one of a number of explanatory factors in the 'ability and preparedness of a company to expand its foreign market servicing commitments'. Further, the small firm empirical findings of Lindqvist (1988), Bonaccorsi (1992), Hansen *et al.* (1994), Bell (1995), and Kaufmann (1995) are also supported.

CONCLUSIONS

The general purpose of this research was to extend our understanding of the impact of network relationships on the internationalization patterns and processes of small firms, with particular interest in the influence of network relationships on the small firm's approach to foreign market selection and mode of entry. To achieve this, the international growth patterns of four small software firms were empirically assessed relative to their network relationships. Within the context of knowledge-based, non-manufacturing software developers, the findings suggest that our understanding of the internationalization process for small firms, at least small software firms, can be enhanced by integrating the models of incremental internationalization with the network perspective. The specific findings of this study are elaborated on below.

To begin, the internationalization process of small knowledge-based software firms differs from those typically discussed in the literature in that:

- it is very rapid, with firms becoming established and committed internationalists in as little as three years;
- it is characterised by only three 'stages', beginning with foreign market intention, and excluding extensive foreign market trial, experimentation, or evaluation; and
- it is characterised by the small firms making simultaneous use of multiple and different modes of entry; mechanisms which are part of a larger firm's international network.

These findings are perhaps explained by the fact that the case firms were 'international new ventures' (cf. Oviatt and McDougall, 1994), competing in a dynamic global market characterised by rapid market change and product obsolescence. Thus, these findings support McDougall *et al.* (1994) and Bell (1995).

Also, the case findings indicate that small software firms show a pattern of externalising their international market development activities through investment in network relationships. This is perhaps not surprising given the nature of the software industry and the need for small, resource-constrained, technically-oriented firms to leverage the complementary capabilities of other organizations (Hara and Kanai, 1994; McDougall *et al.*, 1994; Oviatt and McDougall, 1994). As seen in this study, network relationships can drive market expansion and development activities, including choice of market and entry mode. In addition, they can both facilitate and inhibit product development and market diversification activities.

Overall, this research has shown that we are better able to understand the internationalization process of small firms by expanding our research focus to integrate the models of incremental internationalization with the network perspective. Based on these findings, Fig. 1 (describing the basic internationalization process of the small software firm) is extended to include the role and influence of networks (Fig. 2 below). That is, the internationalization process of small software firms relative to surrounding network processes is superimposed on the three 'stages' of internationalization previously discussed.

This framework also reflects how the characteristics of the small software firm change as the firm moves through the internationalization process.

For these firms, the pattern of internationalization is depicted as evolving in the following manner:

1. the small firm commences operations with the intent to internationalise;
2. an initial relationship with a larger firm is developed in the first year of the small firm's lifecycle, often in an opportunistic or reactive manner, and usually for the purposes of product development. This relationship also provides a mode of entry to a psychically close market;
3. over time, a network of formal and informal contacts is developed. Usually facilitated by the small firm's initial relationship. This network provides market knowledge and potential access/mode of entry to markets around the world. Network relationships facilitate international market development and sales growth, with the small firm entering at least two foreign markets in as little as three years;
4. this growth then leads to increased visibility for the small firm in international markets, as well as an increase in both financial and human resource capabilities. Managerial experience in international markets continues to increase, leading to greater knowledge and confidence in market and relationship decisions;
5. increased experience with network relationships, combined with strong market performance, leads to the small firm desiring increased autonomy and control over their market development activities. At this point, one of two patterns may emerge:

- the small firm may begin to: (1) diversify from its core product areas, (2) proactively pursue new markets, and/or (3) establish its own sales and marketing offices overseas (all independent from existing network partners). The small firm may also actively pursue the development of new network relationships, or such relationships may emerge from product and market development activities. With the increased market visibility, the small firm may become a prime candidate for acquisition by another organization, often a larger firm within or peripheral to the small firm's main network (exemplified by the

FACT, DSR, and CBA, and consistent with Bell, 1995). This exposes the small firm to additional sets of network relationships and further growth opportunities;

OR

- although the small firm may desire increased autonomy from initial network relationships, the major network partner may have enough control over the small firm (e.g. financial control), to limit its product and market diversification opportunities (as in the case of MSL). Thus, the major partner continues to influence the small firm's internationalization process, and growth is restricted to the initial set of network relationships.

The contribution of this framework is that it presents the internationalization process in the context of: (1) the stages of internationalization evident in these small software firms, (2) their network relationships, and (3) their firm characteristics over time. By superimposing the three identified stages of internationalization onto the pattern of network influence, this framework complements the earlier description of the internationalization process (Fig. 1), and provides an understanding of how a firm's international growth patterns relate to surrounding network processes.

This integration is of particular importance given the network perspective introduces a 'more multilateral element' to the rather unilateral process found in the traditional models of incremental internationalization (Johanson and Vahlne, 1990). On one hand, the 'stages' view suggests an evolution to internationalization based on cognitive learning and competency development which increases, through experience, over time. That is, more of an internally-driven approach to internationalization in which firms expand their market scope and entry methods as managers gain confidence and learn from personal experience. On the other hand, the network perspective shows that international market development activities emerge from, and are shaped by, an external web of formal and informal relationships. From this network-driven behaviour, cognitive development also occurs, with learning focused on: (1) the markets entered, (2) the modes of entry used, and (3) the relationships developed during the process of internationalization. Therefore, both perspectives to internationalization encompass cognitive processes. Integration of these perspectives brings the internally and externally-driven views together, allowing a richer understanding of both the drivers of internationalization, and the emergent patterns of international market development activities.

Research implications

This research was context specific in that it examined the internationalization patterns and processes of small software firms. Such firms tend to be owned and managed by technical specialists who develop and market software; an offering more intangible than traditional manufactured goods, and requiring significant support and service to add value. At a market level, the ease with which software can be distributed electronically may affect both foreign market selection and mode of entry decisions. This is compounded by the fact that development and marketing agreements between hardware vendors and software developers is an industry norm, thus the industry is characterised by interfirm cooperation. Finally, the small software firms examined in this study are likely to be resource constrained, and serving a small domestic market. This may contribute to (1) outsourcing and leveraging the capabilities of other firms, and (2) managerial motivation to pursue international markets to

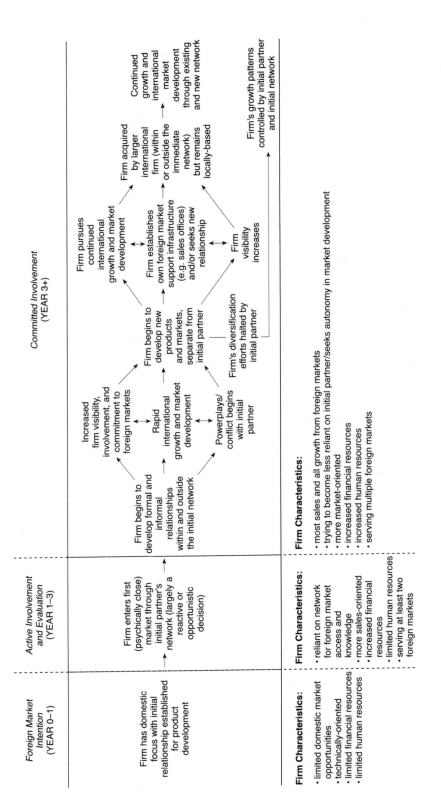

Fig. 2. Growth Patterns, Network Influences and Firm Characteristics through the Internationalization Process of Small Software Firms

sustain firm growth. Each of these factors may influence both the pattern and rate of internationalization.

Such contextual factors need to be considered when reviewing the results of this study, and it is important to recognise that while theory development specific to high technology firms is possible, the findings may not be generalisable to a wider population. Therefore, it is suggested that future research extend this investigation to other industrial contexts, including small firms which are:

- low technology and knowledge-based;
- low technology and manufacturing-based; or
- high technology and manufacturing-based.

Also, given the small software firms studied in this research may have been influenced by rapid industry growth, the findings of this study should be compared with the internationalization patterns of newer software firms; firms which began the process of internationalization in a maturing rather than new industry.

Future research should also incorporate the perspectives of multiple players in the network rather than just that of a single firm. This would yield richer insights into the shift of positions within a network of relationships over time. Network analysis may also be used to more fully examine the impact of specific types of network relationships on foreign market selection, the evolution of power and control in networks, and the specific effect of network relationships on the rate and success of international growth.

In terms of method, the use of case research provides a richness and depth of understanding to the internationalization process which is not possible with survey data. To enhance the qualitative approach in future, it is suggested that in-depth, longitudinal, 'in-process' methods be applied (cf. Benito and Welch, 1994).

Managerial implications

From a practical viewpoint, the findings of this research suggest that managers of small software firms need a better understanding of the impact of network relationships on their internationalization activities, and the potential for such relationships to provide entry to foreign markets. Further, managers should be aware of the speed at which internationalization can occur through network relationships, and that network partners may govern both market selection and mode of entry.

Given the apparent reliance on network relationships for international growth, more attention should be paid to how and with whom relationships are established, and what network management skills are required over time. Related to this, managers must understand the benefits and risks associated with externalising activities to network partners. This is important since managers of small software firms tend to sacrifice some managerial control for market access, potentially weakening their position in a relationship.

Management of established relationships also warrants more attention, particularly when larger partners tend to take control over the activities of smaller firms. Issues related to managing relationships with partners operating in different cultures must also be considered, as well as how best to manage multiple, complex relationship structures. Finally, it is important that managers continue to successfully position their firms such that they have a wide array of relationship options open to them. Their existing networks as well as their ability to establish new network relationships should be managed as a key competitive capability.

Acknowledgements

The authors gratefully acknowledge the constructive comments of Rod Brodie and two anonymous IBR reviewers, on earlier versions of this paper.

REFERENCES

Anderson, O. (1993) On the internationalization process of firms: a critical analysis. *Journal of International Business Studies* **24**(2): 209–231.

Axelsson, B. and Easton, G. (Eds.) (1992) *Industrial Networks: A New View of Reality.* Routledge, London.

Axelsson, B. and Johanson, J. (1992) Foreign market entry – the Textbook vs the Network View. In *Industrial Networks: A New View of Reality*, eds. B. Axelsson and G. Easton, pp. 218–234. Routledge, London.

Beamish, P.W. (1990) The internationalization process for smaller Ontario firms: a research agenda. In *Research in Global Strategic Management – International Business Research for the Twenty-First Century: Canada's New Research Agenda*, ed. A.M. Rugman, pp. 77–92. JAI Press, Greenwich.

Bell, J. (1995) The internationalization of small computer software firms – a further challenge to 'stage' theories. *European Journal of Marketing* **29**(8): 60–75.

Bemito, G.R.G. and Welch, L.S. (1994) Foreign market servicing: beyond choice of entry mode. *Journal of International Marketing* **2**(2): 7–27.

Bilkey, W.J. and Tesar, G. (1977) The export behaviour of smaller-sized Wisconsin manufacturing firms. *Journal of International Business Studies* **8**, 93–98.

Bonaccorsi, A. (1992) On the relationship between firm size and export intensity. *Journal of International Business Studies* **4**(4): 605–635.

Buckley, P.J. (1989) Foreign direct investment by small and medium-sized enterprises: the theoretical background. *Small Business Economics* **1**, 89–100.

Calof, J.C. and Viviers, W. (1995) Internationalization behaviour of small- and medium-sized South African enterprises. *Journal of Small Business Management* **33**(4): 71–79.

Cavusgil, S.T. (1984) Differences among exporting firms based on their degree of internationalization. *Journal of Business Research* **12**, 195–208.

Chang, T.L. and Grub, P.D. (1992) Competitive strategies of Taiwanese PC firms in their internationalization process. *Journal of Global Marketing* **6**(3): 5–27.

Coviello, N.E. and McAuley, N.A. (1996) Internationalization processes and the smaller firm: a review of contemporary research. Working Paper, Faculty of Management. University of Calgary.

Coviello, N.E. and Munro, H.J. (1995) Growing the entrepreneurial firm: networking for international market development. *European Journal of Marketing* **29**(7): 49–61.

Czinkota, M.R. (1982) *Export Development Strategies: US Promotion Policies.* Praeger, New York.

Dubini, P. and Aldrich, H. (1991) Personal and extended networks are central to the entrepreneurial process. *Journal of Business Venturing* **6**, 306–313.

Eisenhardt, K.M. (1989) Building theories from case study research. *Academy of Management Review,* **14**(4): 532–550.

Erramilli, M.K. and D'Souza, D.E. (1993) Venturing into foreign markets: the case of the small service firm. *Entrepreneurship Theory and Practice*, Summer, 29–41.

Hakam, A.N., Lau, G.T. and Kong, S.B. (1993) The export behaviour of firms in Singapore: an application of the stage of internationalization model. *Asia Pacific Journal of Marketing and Logistics*, Summer, 1–15.

Hansen, N., Gillespie, K. and Gencturk, E. (1994) SMEs and export involvement: market responsiveness, technology, and alliances. *Journal of Global Marketing* **7**(4): 7–27.

Hara, G. and Kanai, T. (1994) Entrepreneurial networks across oceans to promote international strategic alliances for small businesses. *Journal of Business Venturing* **9**, 489–507.

Hunt, S.D. (1991) *Modern Marketing Theory: Critical Issues in the Philosophy of Marketing.* Southwestern Publishing Company, Cincinnati.

Hyvaerinen, L. (1994) Internationalization of Finnish SMEs: commitment, internationalization paths and innovation. In *Internationalization, Networks, and Strategy*, ed. J.M. Veciana, pp. 76–100. Ashgate Publishing Ltd, Aldershot.

Johanson, J. and Mattsson, L.-G. (1988) Internationalization in industrial systems – a network approach. In *Strategies in Global Competition*, eds N. Hood and J.-E. Vahlne, pp. 287–314. Croom Helm, London.

Johanson, J. and Vahlne, J.-E. (1977) The internationalization process of the firm – a model of knowledge development and increasing foreign market commitment. *Journal of International Business Studies*, Spring/Summer, 23–32.

Johanson, J. and Vahlne, J.-E. (1990) The mechanism of internationalization. *International Marketing Review* **7**(4): 11–24.

Johanson, J. and Vahlne, J.-E. (1992) Management of foreign market entry. *Scandinavian International Business Review* **1**(3): 9–27.

Kaufmann, F. (1995) Internationalization via co-operation: strategies of SME. *International Small Business Journal* **13**(2): 27–33.

Korhonen, H., Luostarinen, R. and Welch, L. (1995) *Internationalization of SMEs: Inward–Outward Patterns and Government Policy.* Working Paper 7/1995, Department of Marketing/The Centre for International Management and Commerce, University of Western Sydney, Nepean.

Larson, A. (1991) Partner networks: leveraging external ties to improve entrepreneurial performance. *Journal of Business Venturing* **6**, 173–188.

Lau, H.F. (1992) Internationalization, internalization, or a new theory for small, low technology multinational enterprise. *European Journal of Marketing* **26**(10): 17–31.

Lindqvist, M. (1988) *Internationalization of Small Technology-Based Firms: Three Illustrative Case Studies on Swedish Firms.* Stockholm School of Economics Research Paper 88/15.

Lorenzoni, G. and Ornati, O.A. (1988) Constellations of firms and new ventures. *Journal of Business Venturing* **3**, 41–57.

Luostarinen, R. (1989) *Internationalization of the Firm* (first published 1979). Acta Academiae Oeconomicae Helsingiensis, Series A:30, Helsinki.

McDougall, P.P., Shane, S. and Oviatt, B.M. (1994) Explaining the formation of international new ventures: the limits of theories from international business research. *Journal of Business Venturing* **9**, 469–487.

Melin, L. (1992) Internationalization as a strategy process. *Strategic Management Journal* **13**, 99–118.

Miles, M.B. and Huberman, A.M. (1984) *Qualitative Data Analysis: A Sourcebook of New Methods.* Sage Publications Ltd, Beverly Hills.

Millington, A.I. and Bayliss, B.T. (1990) The process of internationalization: UK companies in the EC. *Management International Review* **30**(2): 151–161.

O'Farrell, P.N. and Hitchins, P.W.N. (1988) Alternative theories of small firm growth: a critical review. *Environment and Planning* **20**, 365–382.

Oviatt, B.M. and McDougall, P.P. (1994) Toward a theory of international new ventures. *Journal of International Business Studies* **25**(1): 45–64.

Rao, T.R. and Naidu, G.M. (1992) Are the stages of internationalization empirically supportable? *Journal of Global Marketing* **6**(1–2): 147–170.

Reid, S.D. (1981) The decision-maker and export entry and expansion. *Journal of International Business Studies*, Fall, 101–112.

Sharma, D. (1993) Introduction: industrial networks in marketing. In *Advances in International Marketing*, eds S.T. Cavusgil and D. Sharma, Vol. 5, pp. 1–9. JAI Press, Greenwich.

Sharma, D.D. and Johanson, J. (1987) Technical consultancy in internationalization. *International Marketing Review*, Winter, 20–29.

Strandksov, J. (1986) *Toward a New Approach of Studying the Internationalization Process of Firms.* WP 4/1986, Copenhagen School of Economics and Business Administration.

Sullivan, D. and Bauerschmidt, A. (1990) Incremental internationalization: a test of Johanson and Vahlne's thesis. *Management International Review* **30**, 19–30.

Thomas, M.J. and Araujo, L. (1985) Theories of export behaviour: a critical analysis. *European Journal of Marketing* **19**(2): 42–52.

Tjosvold, D. and Weicker, D. (1993) Cooperative and competitive networking by entrepreneurs: a critical incident study. *Journal of Small Business Management* **31**(1): 11–21.

Turnbull, P.W. (1987) A challenge to the stages theory of the internationalization process. In *Managing Export Entry and Expansion*, eds P.J. Rosson and S.D. Reid, pp. 21–40. Praeger, New York.

Welch, L.S. (1992) The use of alliances by small firms in achieving internationalization. *Scandinavian International Business Review* **1**(2): 21–37.

Welch, L.S. and Luostarinen, R. (1988) Internationalization: evolution of a concept. *Journal of General Management* **14**(2): 34–55.

Welch, L.S. and Luostarinen, R. (1993) Inward–outward connections in internationalization. *Journal of International Marketing* **1**(1): 46–58.

Whitelock, J. and Munday, P. (1993) Internationalization of the firm: two cases in the industrial explosives industry. *Journal of International Marketing* **1**(4): 19–30.

Yin, R.K. (1989) *Case Study Research: Design and Methods*, Sage Publications Ltd, Beverly Hills.

10

The Expansion of Foreign Direct Investments: Discrete Rational Location Choices or a Cultural Learning Process?

Gabriel R.G. Benito and Geir Gripsrud

The decision to undertake a foreign direct investment (FDI) in a particular country is the outcome of a decision process where projected revenues and costs are evaluated. Increased knowledge of a foreign country reduces both the cost and the uncertainty of operating in a foreign market (Buckley and Casson 1981), and should increase the probability of an investment being made in that country. Experience creates – and is sometimes the only way to achieve – increased market knowledge and uncertainty reduction, and experience is therefore considered an owner-specific advantage in the so-called eclectic theory of international production (Dunning 1981, 1988). While it is generally recognized in the literature that experience acts as a determinant of location decisions concerning FDIs, the types of experience that are relevant and the role experience plays in the evolution of FDIs over time, are less clear.

In this paper it is argued that two different perspectives on the role of experience in explaining the location of FDIs are offered in the literature. Mainstream economic theory is basically static and treats individual investment decisions as discrete phenomena. Lack of experience from a market is typically treated as a cost component in terms of the cost of controlling foreign operations (Hirsch 1976). An alternative approach is the process-oriented model advocated by Johanson and Vahlne (1977), which claims that the internationalization of the company should be interpreted as a learning process. Our interpretation of this model is that experience is not only related to costs, but also to the consideration set of locations which are evaluated by the decision makers. Initially, only culturally close markets are evaluated as potential locations, but as companies acquire more experience from operating in foreign markets, more distant markets will be regarded as potential locations for the next FDI. As a result, a stepwise expansion pattern of FDIs is expected to evolve for individual companies.

The aim of this article is to develop hypotheses from the internationalization process framework and to test them empirically. Based upon a short review of the literature, two hypotheses are deduced from the process approach to internationalization. These hypotheses are operationalized and tested on data from Norwegian FDIs in manufacturing. As opposed to most previous studies in this area, which are industry- or even company-specific, the database used contains by and large a complete set of the FDIs undertaken by Norwegian

We would like to thank Tom Stranger-Johannessen and Peggy Brønn for excellent assistance in the research process. The valuable comments to earlier versions of the article provided by three anonymous reviewers are also gratefully acknowledged.

Reprinted with permission from *Journal of International Business Studies*, Third quarter, 1992, 461–476 manufacturing companies in the time period covered. The empirical results do not provide support for the process model, thus suggesting that the choice of locations for FDIs is better explained by the competing economics framework.

THE LITERATURE

The economic theory of the multinational enterprise focuses on two fundamental aspects of international production; the *ownership* of assets employed in production activities in different countries and the *location pattern* of such activities. The question of why multinational enterprises own and control operations abroad has been analyzed by a number of authors using a transaction cost approach (Buckley and Casson 1976; Rugman 1981; Teece 1986). Similarly, the question of why production is undertaken in different countries has been treated as a question of minimizing what could be termed, in a broad sense, production costs (Vernon 1966). In both cases the explanation offered by the theory basically has to do with cost minimization.

Economic theory predicts that a company investing in production facilities will choose the location that minimizes total costs, given the distribution of demand in local (national) markets. Labour cost differentials, transportation costs, the existence of tariff and non-tariff barriers, as well as government policy (e.g., taxes affecting the investment climate in a given host country) are generally held to be important determinants of location choice. This basic framework has been extended by several authors. Aliber (1970) takes into account the size of foreign markets as well as the 'costs of doing business abroad,' and Hirsch (1976) includes the costs of controlling foreign operations. Such costs are likely to be less in familiar markets, that is, markets that are culturally similar to the home country or markets with which the company has previous experience.

Even if it is recognized that experience may have an effect on the perceived costs and uncertainty of operating in different markets, few empirical studies have explored the relationship between experience and location decisions. Davidson (1980) analyzed the effect of experience and country characteristics on the location of foreign direct investments for a sample of 954 individual new products introduced by fifty-seven U.S. firms in the period 1945–76. Pairwise 'entry frequencies' were calculated for twenty countries by determining the percentage of cases in which an FDI in an industry was initiated in one country before each of the others. By comparing subsets of entry frequencies dependent on prior experiences of the parent company in each of the countries involved, Davidson concluded that the presence of an existing subsidiary in a foreign market increases the firm's propensity to make subsequent investments in that market. Furthermore, according to Davidson (1980), the data indicates that 'firms in the initial stage of foreign expansion can be expected to exhibit a strong preference for near and similar cultures. Those in advanced stages of foreign operations will exhibit little if any preference for near and similar cultures' (Davidson 1980, p. 18). This conclusion is not, however, based upon any measure of cultural similarity or a formal statistical test.

Yu (1990) maintains that there are two types of experience that are relevant for firms engaged in international business: country-specific experience and general international operations experience. He estimates a logit model where the dependent variable is 1 if a firm has a manufacturing subsidiary in a given host country and 0 if otherwise. Independent variables include various host country-related factors, three firm-related factors, and the general international experience of the firm measured by the ratio of foreign sales to total sales. The general experience factor was only significant at the 5% level for FDIs of large companies in less developed countries. Country-specific experience was measured by proxy variables in this study. It is argued that if a company has subsidiaries in neighboring countries, its knowledge about the focal country increases. Based upon this assumption, Yu (1990) finds some support for the notion that country-specific experience exerts influence on the location of FDIs. However, since the validity of both types of experience measures is dubious, the experience effects indicated in this paper should be regarded as tentative.

Both Davidson (1980) and Yu (1990) make references to the seminal paper by Johanson and Vahlne (1977) in discussing the effect of experience and cultural similarity on location choices. The empirical studies conducted by these authors are not, however, based upon the theoretical framework suggested by the internationalization process approach. The framework originally developed by Johanson and Wiedersheim-Paul (1975) and Johanson and Vahlne (1977) explicitly regards the internationalization of the firm as a *process* consisting of a series of small steps, whereby firms gradually increase their international involvement. For most firms, and in particular those without international experience, decisions about expansion into international operations are characterized by a considerable amount of uncertainty. This uncertainty stems from a lack of knowledge about the workings of particular foreign markets in terms of customer behavior, institutional framework and so on, as well as the lack of general knowledge of how to run a given business operation in an unfamiliar setting. In both cases, the type of knowledge involved is typically accumulated through a process of 'learning by doing.' The framework depicts a process that evolves through an interplay between the development of knowledge about foreign markets and operations on the one hand, and an increasing commitment of a firm's resources to foreign markets on the other.

The process approach seeks to explain – and predict – two aspects of the internationalization of the firm. The first is the step-by-step fashion by which a firm's engagement in a specific country often develops. Although several stages are proposed in the literature, a typical establishment chain could begin with occasional exports, develop into regular exports through agents, followed by setting up sales subsidiaries, and end with fully-owned production facilities abroad. The second aspect is that firms are assumed to successively enter markets at an increasing 'cultural distance' from the home country, as measured by differences in language, values, political systems, etc. Thus, firms are predicted to start their internationalization by moving into those markets they can most easily understand, entering more distant markets only at a later stage.

The internationalization process model is firmly rooted in a behavioral decision making approach. Luostarinen (1980) discusses in detail the stages in the decision process, building upon Cyert and March (1963), and underlines the importance of 'lateral rigidity' between the stages in the decision process; limited perception of alternatives and selective search leads to confined choice. As more knowledge is acquired more alternatives will be considered, and foreign direct investments (as well as other modes of foreign operation) will gradually take place in more culturally distant countries.

A considerable amount of empirical research has been done that investigates the internationalization process model. However, the empirical support for the internationaliza-tion process model, and variants thereof, is mixed. While Welch and Luostarinen (1983) and Johanson and Vahlne (1990) point out the empirical support for the internationalization process model found in a number of studies, several studies fail to provide corroborative support for the model. Turnbull (1987) undertakes a critical survey of the theory and the empirical evidence, which in his opinion 'does not support the proposition that the pattern of export organizational development follows an evolutionary path' (Turnbull 1987, p. 36). Several recent studies cast additional doubt on the validity of the internationalization process model. In a cross-country study of the forest product industry, Sullivan and Bauerschmidt (1990) found no differences in the perceived barriers to or incentives to internationalization among managers of firms at various stages of internationalization. Engwall and Wallenstål (1988) found only mixed support for the process approach in a study of the international expansion of Swedish banks. In particular, their data did not support the hypothesis that companies tend to start their foreign operations in countries that are culturally close to their own.

Given the lack of support for the process model found in these studies, the generalizability of the model has been questioned along several lines. Recent changes in the nature of international competition may have weakened the explanatory power of the internationalization process model, suggesting that the theory is time bound (Sullivan and Bauerschmidt 1990). These authors also point out the possibility of 'cultural boundedness,' since the original formulation of the model drew upon observed patterns of internationalization by Swedish companies and much of the subsequent empirical work has been done in a Scandinavian (Nordic) setting. Engwall and Wallenstål (1983) question in particular the validity of the theory across industries. They argue that organizations with different tasks in different environments can be expected to operate in different ways. Thus, a theory originating from studies of the behaviour of industrial firms may have little to say about the behaviour of firms in other sectors of the economy.

A previous study of FDIs made by Norwegian manufacturing companies concluded that the 'findings fit in rather well with a cultural distance analysis of the internationalization process' (Walters 1979, p. 12). This conclusion was, however, drawn after investigating the overall pattern of Norwegian foreign direct investments, and with no explicit measure of cultural distance. Aggregate data for all FDIs are not suitable for testing the implications of the cultural hypothesis embedded in the process model. A more appropriate test is the one undertaken in this paper.

HYPOTHESES

The internationalization process model suggests that international expansion follows an expansion path, whereby companies move from close to more distant markets. This pattern is supposed to apply to all industries, and should therefore show up in a cross-industry study of FDIs over time. The economic theory of multinational production recognizes the experience factor and the costs of operating in an unknown environment. However, the cost of operating in a foreign environment does not necessarily dominate other factors, and even if such costs are increasing with cultural distance the location decision is only marginally affected by such costs.

The internationalization process approach suggests that the first foreign direct investment undertaken by a company typically takes place in a country that is culturally close to the home market, while later investments are made in more distant locations. Therefore, our first hypothesis based upon the process model is:

H1: The first FDIs undertaken are made in countries that are culturally closer to the home country than later FDIs.

The alternative hypothesis suggested by the economics framework, is that there is no particular tendency to make the first FDIs in locations closer to the home country than later FDIs.

The process approach to internationalization furthermore suggests that a particular company will tend to move further away from the home market as more experience is acquired. If some companies make their first FDI in relatively distant countries, H1 may not be supported. Still, a general movement away from the home country may take place as more investments are made. This hypothesis has been formulated as follows:

> H2: The cultural distance to the country where an FDI is made will increase with the number of FDIs previously undertaken by a given company.

Again, the economics framework suggests that there is no general tendency to move into more distant countries as accumulated experience grows. Each decision is made separately. The probability of investing in a particular country may not be independent of earlier location decisions due to the experience effect, but to the extent that this effect is present it would cause the next investment to be undertaken in the same country as the previous one or in a nearby country in terms of culture.

The two hypotheses put forward have been tested on data regarding the foreign direct investments undertaken by Norwegian manufacturing companies. This means that the test takes into account the alleged 'cultural boundedness' of the process approach, since the FDIs are all made by Scandinavian (Norwegian) companies. If the data from Norwegian FDIs do not support the hypotheses, the process approach is unlikely to provide a general explanation of the location pattern of FDIs over time.

CULTURAL DISTANCE

Culture, in a broad sense, refers to the social context within which humans live. Culture may be regarded as the set of attitudes and values that are common to a group of people, and that affects the ways that individuals perceive and respond to their environment. It is a kind of collective 'programming of the mind that distinguishes the members of one human group from another' (Hofstede 1980, p. 13). However, it is difficult to actually measure and quantify distances between cultures.

Luostarinen (1980) defines cultural distance as 'the sum of factors creating, on the one hand, a need for knowledge, and on the other hand, barriers to the knowledge flow and hence also for other flows between the home and target country' (1980, pp. 131–32).

Some studies have applied objective measures in order to group countries according to their cultural proximity. One example of this approach is provided by Luostarinen (1980) in his study of Finnish firms' international operations. He used indicators such as level of economic development, everyday language, and level of education, in order to operationalize cultural distance. Countries were classified into five groups by cluster analysis, and then assigned values ranging from 1 (very close) to 5 (very distant). Apart from the rough classification of different cultures, the validity of the indicators used may be questioned.

Other studies have used attitudinal data at the individual level in order to map similarities and differences between countries. Ronen and Shenkar (1985) review eight cross-cultural studies of work-related attitudes and values. The variables in these studies were grouped into four broad categories: (i) work goals importance, (ii) need deficiency, fulfillment and job satisfaction, (iii) managerial and organizational variables, and (iv) work role and interpersonal orientation. Ronen and Shenkar (1985) integrate the results of these studies, and classify countries into culturally similar clusters. Nine country groupings are identified, comprising a total of forty-six countries. The grouping is suggestive of differences between clusters. However, it does not measure cultural distances between clusters, i.e., *how* different the various clusters are.

The most comprehensive research to date on cultural dimensions relevant to work organization, is probably the work conducted by Hofstede (1980, 1984). Hofstede collected data within a large multinational enterprise, at first for its forty largest subsidiaries, and later for more than fifty subsidiaries (Hofstede 1984). Only employees in similar occupations were compared, and all respondents were employed by the same multinational company, thus controlling for bias from different occupational positions and organizational practices. Based on a factor analysis of thirty-two value statements, Hofstede found that differences in national culture vary along four dimensions. These dimensions were labeled uncertainty avoidance, individuality, power distance, and masculinity-femininity.

The internal as well as the external validity of Hofstede's findings have been questioned (Drenth 1983; Goodstein and Hunt 1981). However, this critique may be extended to most of the work done in this area (Drenth 1983). As Kogut and Singh (1988) point out, Hofstede's work has several appealing attributes, such as the size of the sample, the reliability of scores over time, its emphasis on work-related attitudes and values, and the codification of cultural traits along a numerical index. The last point is particularly important, as it makes it possible to compare the relative differences between countries along cultural dimensions.

In order to arrive at a measure of cultural distance among countries, Kogut and Singh (1988) constructed a composite index using Hofstede's indices. Their index is based on the deviation along each of the four cultural dimensions (i.e., uncertainty avoidance, individuality, power distance, and masculinity-femininity) from the score of a given focal (home) country for each country. The deviations are corrected for differences in the variance of each dimension and then arithmetically averaged. Algebraically, the Kogut-Singh index for cultural distance CD_j is given as:

$$CD_j = \sum_{i=1}^{4} \{(I_{ij} - I_{iN})^2 / V_i\} / 4,$$

where

I_{ij} = index value for cultural dimension i of country j;
V_i = variance of the index for dimension i;
N = home country (Norway in this case).

In the present study the Kogut-Singh index is used as a measure of the cultural distance between Norway and the countries where FDIs are made. The actual values of the indices of four cultural dimensions for the various countries are taken from Hofstede (1984). The only relevant country not included in Hofstede's study is Iceland. However, as the other Nordic countries show a considerable degree of similarity on all cultural dimensions, a proxy value for Iceland was computed as the average of the values for the other Nordic countries.

THE DATABASE

The database was compiled from a survey of Norwegian FDIs originally published by the magazine *Norges Industri*, and consists of the majority of foreign direct investments in manufacturing undertaken by Norwegian manufacturing companies up to mid-year 1982. Only foreign subsidiaries in operation at the time of publication were included in the survey and therefore in the database. A foreign direct investment is defined as ownership of 10% or more of the equity in a foreign company. However, in a majority of the actual cases the level of ownership is far higher, and 55% of the cases are wholly owned subsidiaries.

In total, the database consists of 201 cases representing investments undertaken by 93 Norwegian companies. The first investment dates back to 1910, but, as shown in Figure 1, the majority of investments were undertaken later, and in particular during the 1970s and '80s. The almost negligible number of investments undertaken before 1960, followed by the rapidly increasing number of investments in the 1960s and '70s, reflect the transformation of the Norwegian economy in the last decades. Norway was a poor country at the turn of the century. Economic development, fueled first by hydropower, and later by North Sea oil, has made Norway a prosperous country. Still, the country has few big companies by international standards, and though about 3000 Norwegian firms were engaged in exporting in the late 1980s, only a few of them were truly internationalized in the sense of operating a diverse set of international operations (Joynt 1989).

According to official statistics from the Bank of Norway, 291 cases of Norwegian foreign direct investment in manufacturing were registered by the end of 1982 (Norges Bank 1985). Our database contains 201 cases. However, since our database only covers investments up to the middle of 1982, the figures are not completely compatible. Bearing in mind that the outflow of investments increased steeply during the first part of the eighties, some of the discrepancy could be accounted for by the half-year difference in the termination dates of the two data collections. In sum, the data used in this study appear to give a satisfactory coverage of the actual number of manufacturing operations in foreign locations owned or partly owned by Norwegian manufacturing companies in 1982.

A further check of how representative the database is has been carried out by comparing the geographical distribution of the FDIs in our sample with official data. For this purpose the countries were divided into three groups. The first group encompasses other Nordic countries (Sweden, Denmark, Finland and Iceland). The second group includes other countries in Europe and North America, while the rest of the countries of the world were lumped together in the third group of countries.

Table 1 shows a comparison of the geographical distribution of FDIs in our database with the distribution of FDIs according to official data at the end of 1983. A similar geographical distribution was, unfortunately, not available for 1982. Apart from the remarkable increase in FDIs in 1983 (from 291 to 365 according to the official data), the table suggests that the geographical distribution at the end of that year is fairly consistent with the distribution in our sample.

The database lists the location and size of FDIs along with their mother companies. Based on the year of establishment of the FDIs, the sequence of FDIs for a particular company was determined. In addition, various variables relating to mother companies and FDIs have been compiled and included in the database. In the data analysis the export share of the mother company, the sales of the mother company, the mode of entry used (greenfield vs. acquisition), and the ownership percentage of the FDIs are introduced as control variables.

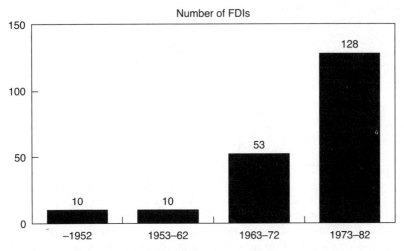

Fig. 1. Norwegian FDIs in Manufacturing by Year of Investment

Table 1. Geographical Distribution of Norwegian FDIs in Manufacturing

Region	This Study	Official Data*
Region 1	33%	39%
Region 2	47%	42%
Region 3	20%	19%
Total	100%	100%
	(N=201)	(N=365)

* 1983-data

RESULTS

After sorting the data for FDIs according to sequence of investment for individual companies, it turns out that we have ninety-three observations of the first foreign investment made by a company but only thirty-one observations of a second foreign investment. The number of companies having made more investments is rapidly decreasing with higher order investments. The highest number of FDIs made by one company is eighteen, while the second highest is eleven. The mean cultural distance to the foreign market by investment number is reported in Table 2. In this table, investment numbers 5 and higher have been collapsed into one category.

Table 2 shows that there are only minor differences in the cultural distances to the markets entered at different stages. Analysis of variance for the data in this table shows that sequence of investment is not related to the cultural distance from Norway to the markets ($F=.54$, $DF=4$, 196). Thus, across companies there is no general relationship between cultural distance to the market and investment sequence. Furthermore, Scheffe's test of pairwise group means indicate that no significant differences exist between any of the groups in Table 2. H1 suggests that the

Table 2. Average Distance of FDIs by Sequence of Investments

Investment Number	Mean Cultural Distance	Standard Deviation	Number of Cases
1	1.8162	1.4530	93
2	2.1631	1.2698	31
3	2.0711	1.5399	18
4	2.2758	1.9052	11
5 and higher	1.9608	1.3877	48
Total	1.9522	1.4392	201

first FDI undertaken is located closer to the home country than later FDIs. The database contains 93 observations of first investments and 108 observations of later investments. To test H1, the null hypothesis is that the mean cultural distance of the first investments is equal to the mean cultural distance of all later investments. The alternative hypothesis is that the mean cultural distance of later investments is larger than for first investments. A one-tailed t-test shows that the observed difference is not statistically significant at the 5% level ($t=1.25$; $p=0.11$). This means that across all observations in the database, there is no firm evidence that first investments are made closer to the home country than later investments.

The second hypothesis deals with the expansion pattern of FDIs after the first investment. The process approach suggests that a movement away from the home country should be observed as more experience is acquired, that is, an increasing number of investments are made. Table 2 suggests that such a movement is unlikely. However, these data reveal the location of all investments with a given number in the sequence of investments. A test of H2 requires that the location of investment n should be related to the location of investment $n-1$ for a particular company. The cultural expansion may, however, decrease as the number of investments increase. Based upon these considerations the test proposed for H2 involves estimating a simple regression model:

$$CD_n - CD_{n-1} = a + bI_n, \tag{1}$$

where

CD_n = cultural distance to location of investment number n for a given company;
CD_{n-1} = cultural distance to location of investment number $n-1$ for a given company;
I_n = investment number n for a given company;
a,b = coefficients.

The second hypothesis derived from the process model implies that the constant a (1) is positive. A decrease in cultural expansion as the number of investments grows means that the coefficient b in (1) is negative. In total, 108 investments in our database are preceded by another investment made by the same company. The estimation of (1) results in:

$$CD_n - CD_{n-1} = .116 - .003 \, I_n$$
$$(.43) \quad (-.08) \tag{2}$$

$$F = .94, \text{ Adj } R^2 = .00$$

While the sign of the constant in (2) is in accordance with H2, the t-values reported in the parentheses show that neither the constant (a) nor the coefficient for the number of investments (b) is significant. Thus, the empirical evidence indicates that the average change in cultural distance between two subsequent investments is not positive and does not vary with the number of investments previously undertaken by the company. This means that H2 is not supported.

The process approach maintains that a gradual penetration of more distant markets serves to reduce the uncertainty felt by managers. According to this approach the experience from nearby markets will reduce uncertainty and make more distant markets more appealing to managers. Our findings suggest that this process does not play a major role in the choice of locations for FDIs undertaken by Norwegian manufacturing companies. On the other hand, experience may still affect location choices by lowering the perceived cost of operating in well-known cultures. If this is the case, we would expect to find a strong correlation between the cultural distance to a country where an investment is made, and the cultural distance to the country where the *previous* investment by the same company was undertaken. This turns out to be the case, as the correlation between CD_n and CD_{n-1} is highly significant ($r=.40$, $n=108$; $p<.01$).

Since the locations of two consecutive investments are highly correlated, the direction and extent of any movement in cultural distance between two subsequent investments should be related to the location of the first of the two investments. If the starting point is a distant location, we may expect the location of the next investment to be closer to home while the opposite would be expected if the starting point is a culturally close location. A linear regression for the 108 observations preceded by another investment reveals the following relationship:

$$CD_n = 1.31 + .38 \ CD_{n-1}$$
$$\quad\quad (6.26) \quad\quad (4.53) \quad\quad\quad\quad\quad\quad\quad\quad (3)$$

$$F = 20.6, \text{ Adj } R^2 = .15$$

Equation (3) shows that there is a strong association between the location of an investment and the direction and extent of the next movement in cultural space. If the cultural distance of the previous FDI (CD_{n-1}) exceeds an index value of 2.13, the regression predicts that the next investment will be culturally closer. In the opposite case, the next investment will tend to take place in a more distant location. Separate regressions for investment number two (thirty-one observations) and all later investments (seventy-seven observations) reveal the same basic pattern.

A close inspection of the database does not reveal any industry-specific differences in the location sequences. Since the choice of location for the first FDI seems important, a number of variables have been investigated that might be correlated with the location of the first FDI. The only significant relationship found is that FDIs located in countries that are culturally distant, tend to be greenfield investments to a larger extent than for FDIs undertaken in culturally closer countries. The explanation is probably that culturally distant countries tend to be less developed countries where fewer opportunities exist to buy established companies. Export share, ownership percentage and size of the parent company are not correlated with the cultural distance to the country where the first investment was undertaken.

SUMMARY AND DISCUSSION

In this article hypotheses concerning the international expansion of foreign direct investments have been developed from the 'process' approach to internationalization. The process approach presents a rich framework for interpreting the internationalization of companies, and this paper covers only one aspect of the theory. Previous studies have tended to be case oriented, and more emphasis should be placed upon developing testable hypotheses.

Our findings do not provide support for the notion that FDIs are, in general, initially made in foreign markets close to the home country, and at a later stage are spread to more distant markets. Across all companies, there was only a weak tendency for the first investments to be made in countries that are culturally closer than those where later investments were made. Furthermore, for given companies, no evidence of an expansion into more distant markets was found as the number of FDIs increases. On the other hand, the locations of subsequent investments are interrelated. It seems that if the previous investment was made in a fairly distant location, there is a tendency to move into a less distant location the next time and vice versa.

In order to explain these findings, it has to be acknowledged that firms move into foreign markets for different reasons. For instance, firms making a foreign investment mainly to take advantage of low labor costs will probably not consider countries culturally close to Norway as viable alternatives. The first investments of such firms are likely to be in distant markets. Still, the question remains why such companies would tend to move to closer locations the next time. Obviously, there are limits to cultural expansion and the chance of selecting a closer location the next time is higher if the starting point is a distant one.

The pattern revealed suggests that the internationalization process does not manifest itself in a gradual expansion of FDIs into culturally more distant locations. Our findings support the notion that location choices are discrete rational choices, and not a cultural learning process. This does not preclude experience effects, but it is the nature of the business that defines the feasible locations. Within the set of such locations the company will expand, sometimes moving into more distant locations while at other times moving into locations closer to the home country.

It may be argued that the hypotheses derived in this paper give an inadequate representation of the internationalization process model. In the sense that the hypotheses are restricted to the expansion path of FDIs, they certainly do not provide a full test of the basic model. The depth of involvement in particular markets is not covered, but how the various stages in involvement should interact with the geographical expansion envisaged by the model is somewhat unclear. In an earlier study of Norwegian exporters (Gripsrud 1990), it was found that the nature of the products is a determinant of the exporters' attitudes towards a foreign market. In our opinion, this may be the case for FDIs as well in the sense that the evaluation of potential locations hinges on the nature of the products to be produced.

The study reported in this paper is certainly not without limitations. While, in principle, all FDIs undertaken up to mid-1982 and still in operation at that time are included, a number of FDIs may have been made that were no longer operated by Norwegian owners. Exits, due to closure or takeover by other owners, could represent a bias when it comes to the location pattern. It is, however, difficult to imagine why exits, if any, should represent a serious distortion of the locational pattern observed at the end of the period.

It would be interesting to conduct a study of the pattern that has evolved after 1982. Since the number of FDIs by Norwegian companies has increased rapidly in recent years, it would give a larger database for testing our hypotheses. This is particularly important when analyzing higher order investment numbers. In addition, it would make it possible to test any changes in the location pattern over time. Recent changes in communications, and the general tendency towards global markets, indicate that the impact of cultural and psychological distance is likely to decrease over time. In the 'global village,' cultural and psychological distances between countries are probably smaller than before, even if they still are not negligible. Since we did not find any support for the internationalization process model in the FDIs undertaken up to mid-1982, it is not likely that FDIs undertaken later are following the pattern envisaged by the process model.

A related line of reasoning deals with the organization of investment activities in MNEs. The 'internationalization process' approach deals mainly with the initial phase of foreign operations and direct investments. It is based upon the assumption that the activity is spreading from the parent company to ever more distant locations. Forsgren (1990) has pointed out that this framework is inadequate in interpreting the location decisions of large multi-center firms that have been operating internationally for a long period of time. In such cases each new investment is increasingly linked to a foreign-based center with its own investment program. Our database does not include such large multi-center firms, but the emergence of such firms would make it even less likely that more recent data would support the process model.

REFERENCES

Aliber, R.Z. (1970). A theory of direct foreign investment. In C.P. Kindleberger, editor, *The international corporation*. Cambridge, Mass.: MIT Press.

Buckley, P.J. and Casson, M. (1976). *The future of the multinational enterprise*. London: MacMillan Press.

——. (1981). The optimal timing of a foreign direct investment. *Economic Journal*, **91**(1): 75–87.

Cyert, R.M. and March, J.G. (1963). *A behavioral theory of the firm*. Englewood Cliffs, N.J.: Prentice-Hall.

Davidson, W.H. (1980). The location of foreign direct investment activity: Country characteristics and experience effects. *Journal of International Business Studies*, **11**(2): 9–22.

Drenth, P.J.D. (1983). Cross-cultural organizational psychology: Challenges and limitations. In S.H. Irvine and J.W. Berry, editors, *Human assessment and cultural factors*. New York: Plenum Press.

Dunning, J.H. (1981). Explaining the international direct investment position of countries: Towards a dynamic or developmental approach. *Weltwirtschaftliches Archiv*, 117: 30–64.

——. (1988). The eclectic paradigm of international production: A restatement and some possible extensions. *Journal of International Business Studies*, **19**(1): 1–31.

Engwall, L. and Wallenstål, M. (1988). Tit for tat in small steps: The internationalization of Swedish banks. *Scandinavian Journal of Management*, **4**(3/4): 147–55.

Forsgren, M. (1990). Managing the international multi-centre firm: Case studies from Sweden. *European Management Journal*, **8**(2): 261–67.

Goodstein, L.D. and Hunt, J.W. (1981). Commentary: Do American theories apply abroad: *Organizational Dynamics*, **10**(1): 49–62.

Gripsrud, G. (1990). The determinants of export decisions and attitudes to a distant market: Norwegian fishery exports to Japan. *Journal of International Business Studies*, **21**(3): 469–85.

Hirsch, S. (1976). An international trade and investment theory of the firm. *Oxford Economic Papers*, **28** (New Series): 258–70.

Hofstede, G. (1980). *Culture's consequences: International differences in work-related values*. Beverly Hills, Calif.: Sage Publications.

——. (1984). Cultural dimensions in management and planning. *Asia Pacific Journal of Management*, **1**(2): 81–99.

Johanson, J. and Vahlne, J.E. (1990). The mechanism of internationalization. *International Marketing Review*, **7**(4): 11–24.

———. (1977). The internationalization process of the firm: A model of knowledge development and increasing foreign market commitments. *Journal of International Business Studies*, **8** (Spring/Summer): 23–32.

Johanson, J. and Wiedersheim-Paul, F. (1975). The internationalization of the firm: Four Swedish cases. *Journal of Management Studies*, **12**(3): 305–22.

Joynt, P. (1989). International strategy: A study of Norwegian companies. In R.N. Farmer, editor, *Advances in international comparative management*, 4: 131–46. Greenwich: JAI Press.

Kogut, B. and Singh. H. (1988). The effect of national culture on the choice of entry mode. *Journal of International Business Studies*, **19**(3): 411–32.

Luostarinen, R. (1980). *Internationalization of the firm.* Helsinki: The Helsinki School of Economics.

Norges B. (1985). *Norske investeringer i uterolandsk næringsvirksomhet: En undersøkelse basert på regnskapsresultater 1982–83.* Oslo: Bank of Norway.

Ronen, S. and Shenkar, O. (1985). Clustering countries on attitudinal dimensions: A review and synthesis. *Academy of Management Review,* **10**(3): 435–54.

Rugman, A.M. (1981). *Inside the multinationals: The economics of internal markets.* London: Croom Helm.

Sullivan, D. and Bauerschmidt, A. (1990). Incremental internationalization: A test of Johanson and Vahlne's thesis. *Management International Review,* **30**(1): 19–30.

Teece, D.J. (1986). Transaction cost economics and the multinational enterprise: An assessment. *Journal of Economic Behavior and Organization*, **7**(1): 21–45.

Turnbull, P.W. (1987). A challenge to the stages theory of the internationalization process. In P.J. Rosson and S.D. Reid, editors, *Managing export entry and expansion.* New York: Praeger Publishers.

Vernon, R. (1966). International investment and international trade in the product cycle. *Quarterly Journal of Economics*, **80** (May): 190–207.

Walters, P.G.P. (1979). Norwegian overseas direct investments: Recent developments and trends. Paper presented at the 5th annual EIBA Conference, London, December 12–14.

Welch, L.S. and Luostarinen R. (1988). Internationalization: Evolution of a concept. *Journal of General Management*, **14**(2): 34–55.

Yu, Chwo-Ming J. (1990). The experience effect and foreign direct investment. *Weltwirtschaftliches Archiv,* **126**(3): 561–80.

11

The Internationalization of Service Firms: A Comparison with the Manufacturing Sector

Peter J. Buckley, C.L. Pass and Kate Prescott

INTRODUCTION

Much of the literature on international business has taken on a manufacturing perspective, often implicit rather than explicit. More recent literature has paid attention to the internationalization of service firms and this has necessitated paying attention to the thorny question of defining a service. This article seeks to integrate the various existing strands of literature on service industries in an attempt to understand the behaviour of internationalizing service firms. We begin by posing the question 'Are services different?' In doing so the characteristics that distinguish services from goods are highlighted, and classifactory systems for types of international activity are introduced. This is followed by a critical review of the eclectic theory of the multinational enterprise which is used as a framework for classifying factors with a particular bearing on the service industries. The article analyses the dynamics of the internationalization process and presents a summary and conclusions.

ARE SERVICES DIFFERENT?

Many writers have posed this question, and in an attempt to provide a satisfactory answer, have highlighted several factors which distinguish services from goods.

Characteristics of services

Marketing theorists generally propose five distinct features of services (Cowell, 1986):

- intangibility
- inseparability
- heterogeneity
- perishability
- ownership.

Intangibility refers to the fact that services, unlike goods, do not always consist of physical attributes which can be judged by consumers by sight, taste, smell or touch. Rather, they are 'experiences' which cannot be clearly assessed before consumption (Bateson, 1977; Berry,

Reprinted with permission from *Scandinavian International Business Review*, 1992, **1**(1), 39–56

1980; Rathmell, 1966). *Inseparability* of production and consumption refers to the fact that many services are supplied and consumed simultaneously. Thus, whereas goods are produced, sold and consumed, services are often sold and then produced and consumed at the same time (Grönroos, 1977; Regan, 1963; Zeithaml, *et al.* 1985). Personal contact between the producer and consumer is thus an important aspect of many services. Following on from this, as the production of a wide array of services is embodied in the firm's personnel there is, potentially, wide variation in the way the service is produced, and the quality of the service (Langeard *et al.* 1981). This *heterogeneity* poses problems of quality control, and of providing consistency in the service communicated to customers and in that ultimately delivered.

Some services are also *perishable* and cannot be stored (Berry, 1975; Lovelock, 1981; Thomas, 1978). For example, an empty seat on an airline flight is a lost sale and can never be recovered. This illustration also serves to highlight the issue of *ownership*. A consumer only has access to his seat on the aircraft, he does not own it. With many services the customer merely buys the right to use, to access or to hire the service.

Few services display all these features, although most exhibit more than one. Due to the heterogeneous nature of the service industry, it would be virtually impossible to identify a list of characteristics applicable to all sectors.

Implications for international business

Having characterized the distinctive attributes of services it could be concluded that services are different from goods. However, the problem of defining a service is complicated by the fact that there are few 'pure' goods or services. Many goods embody non-factor services in their production and distribution and many services involve some physical 'goods' in their make-up, both being supplied simultaneously at the point-of-sale (Dunning, 1989). The distinction between goods and services cannot be viewed as a simple black and white categorization. It rather depends on the extent to which the service is embodied in physical attributes within the overall 'package' implicitly based on the degree of tangibility/intangibility of the good or service. Shostack (1977) developed Rathmell's (1966) idea of a goods-service continuum to map out the combination of physical and experimental attributes in a range of goods and services contending that:

> The greater the degree of intangible elements in a market entity, the greater will be the divergence from product marketing in priorities and approach.

Although this continuum was designed to identify differences in approach to marketing functions, it would not be false to assume that the greater the degree of intangible elements the more likelihood there is of foreign expansion strategies differing from those traditionally associated with product manufacturing. From Shostack's model, therefore, the internationalization of, say, legal consulting would be expected to show a different pattern from that of soft drinks. This expectation is borne out by recent literature on the international activities of service firms. Boddewyn *et al.* (1986) classify types of international service according to their tradeability, based on the extent to which services are embodied in physical goods and the degree of inseparability in provision of the service:

1. service commodities, which are distinct from their production process, are tradeable across national boundaries and are thus exportable;

2. where production cannot be separated from consumption as in the case of legal advice, a foreign presence is necessary;
3. where services comprise a mix of distinct commodities and location-bound service elements, some location substitution is possible.

Sampson and Snape (1985) also take responsibility as the key distinguishing factor between goods and services. They categorize services according to their tradeability, proposing that 'separated' services, that is those which do not require direct contact between supplier and consumer, are the only services which can be exported as distinct from those which demand movement of factors of production to the consumer (e.g. repair services) or movement of the consumer to factors of production (e.g. tourism).

Building on these themes, Vandermerwe and Chadwick (1989) combine 'the relative involvement of goods' with the degree of consumer/producer interaction to develop a matrix of service industries wherein clusters of services can be distinguished according to the typical modes of market servicing most appropriate for international expansion. The three emergent clusters can be classified as follows:

> *Exporting*: This involves minimum presence and control, being most appropriate where a firm can export the good providing the service, or export the service through some physical embodiment included in the service 'package'. This can involve the firm employing the services of overseas intermediaries to distribute and sell the product in the foreign market.
> *Licensing/joint ventures*: Here, some degree of investment is needed in order that the company be represented abroad. Investment may be financial or may be in terms of management time. A presence is achieved through the third party (licensee, franchisee, majority joint-venture partner) whilst control is achieved through the supply of key assets (e.g. management know-how, training, brand names).
> *Foreign direct investment*: This is most appropriate where the service is 'people-embodied' and where there is a high degree of producer/consumer interaction. Control over delivery is therefore a key feature, achievable through the establishment of branches or subsidiaries, and mergers or acquisitions.

Although this classificatory matrix is somewhat simplistic and flawed in terms of its ability to explain the behaviour of all firms within the disparate industries (many of which operate across several categories of service), it does highlight the importance of the impact of the degree of service intangibility and inseparability on the foreign-market servicing decision of internationalizing firms.

In terms of the inter-mode options, services do not differ markedly from goods. There is evidence of a wide array of distribution arrangements – direct exporting, exporting via intermediaries (agents and distributors), licensing, franchising, management contracts, sales offices, sales subsidiaries, joint ventures and wholly owned production subsidiaries. The nature of the service may be a major influence on the form of market servicing. Foreign operations in services may also be conducted by non-service multinationals. Many manufacturing firms engage in service activities to support their manufacturing operations (e.g. transport, wholesaling, after-sales servicing and repairs). This further complicates the analysis of international service operations (Markusen, 1989). However, for the purpose of this assessment a distinction is drawn between service activities of multinational enterprises and the service sector, the latter forming the focus for analysis. In this article, we are perforce generalizing across a wide variety of service sectors and a great diversity of individual products. The product-specific elements in the market-servicing decision have been shown to be very important in manufacturing (Buckley, *et al.* 1990) and are also important in services (compare fast-food restaurants with high-technology consultancy). However, our purpose here is to seek commonalities across these product varieties whilst retaining the essential qualities of services as the focus of attention.

Foreign market servicing strategies and services

In terms of the equation for total foreign sales:

$$TFS = X + L + I$$

(i.e. total foreign sales are the sum of sales arising from exporting, licensing and other contractual arrangements and foreign direct investment), although the elements of the equation remain the same for service industries, it may be expected that the relative importance of the three generic elements will differ as a result of industry-specific factors (Buckley and Prescott, 1989). Hirsch (1986), addressing the implications of the inseparability of production and consumption characteristic of services, notes how the 'simultaneity factor' (that is the fact that services are produced and consumed at the same time) serves to retard export trade. The costs associated with satisfying the need for interaction between producer and buyer (in the case of engineering consultancy for example) are compounded by the high price of international travel and communications, and thus the exporting firm is at a cost disadvantage *vis-à-vis* its foreign competitors. When the costs of cultural distance, language, communication, nationalistic and legal barriers are added, the cost disadvantages are further heightened. Extending the notion of cultural distance, Edvinsson (1981) notes that foreign service providers, lacking any legitimacy and identity in the foreign market, require some kind of 'platform' and local support environment to operate successfully. Although this is also true for goods manufacturers operating abroad, the intangibility of services means that uncertainty about performance is higher and thus greater demands are placed on service firms to win the confidence of the consumer through strong referent promotion and a good local image. Edvinsson suggests that this is best achieved through co-operation with a local firm known and trusted by consumers.

Foreign involvement by service industries may be expected, therefore, to yield higher levels of licensing and other contractual arrangements and foreign direct investment at the expense of exporting. For the period 1975 to 1983, the average percentages of foreign sales of British manufacturers showed exporting to be the dominant mode (53.0 per cent) followed by foreign direct investment (37.7 per cent) and then licensing (9.2 per cent). For non-manufacturing investment (64.3 per cent) and licensing (7.5 per cent) (Buckley and Prescott, 1989). Interestingly, the period reveals a shift in emphasis from foreign direct investment to exporting in the non-manufacturing sector. This may possibly be attributable to the growing sophistication of communication systems and technology.

Vandermerwe and Chadwick (1989) found that information technology appears to lie in the intersection of the three clusters of foreign-market servicing: exporting, licensing and foreign direct investment, creating a new mode of market servicing in the service sector with the following characteristics:

- transactions are classified as exports as there is no physical movement by the service provider;

- transactions require an infrastructure in the foreign market – provided by host-market third parties, which may include customers;
- a market 'presence' is achieved through locating the technology abroad. Control is achieved via ownership of the technology, systems procedures and management arrangements.

This theory provides a possible explanation for the shift from foreign direct investment to exporting in the contribution to total foreign sales of British firms in the non-manufacturing sector. It does not explain, however, the low incidence of licensing. Here the loss of direct control over operations which compounds the problem of quality control due to the natural heterogeneity in the sale of people-supplied services may provide some explanation. Additionally, preference for joint ventures as a form of co-operation, as opposed to licensing contracts, which allows greater control over proprietary skills may shed further light on the low incidence of sales arising from licensing contracts. The data presented, whilst highly aggregated, and including operations other than those traditionally characterized as services, demonstrates a clear difference between manufacturing and non-manufacturing sectors. The poor data available on service firms, which fail to allow a clear analysis of exporting, licensing and foreign direct investment sales to be made, mean that whilst such an assessment is flawed they provide a general picture of patterns of business in the service sector. Another issue worthy of comment is the highly diverse nature of the services sector, which results in widely differing trade and investment patterns (Shelp, 1981). The picture provided does not therefore provide a universally applicable conceptual framework, but when considered in conjunction with the classificatory systems presented earlier, provides a basic foundation to explain the behaviour of internationalizing service firms.

Service firms as multinational enterprises

Many early definitions of multinational enterprise relied on foreign direct investment, the ownership of assets in more than one country, as the crucial characteristic. Such definitions, based on observation of the behaviour of early multinational firms, fail to take account of licensing and franchising arrangements which are of equal importance to many global firms as is foreign direct investment. Consequently, changes in definition have proved to be necessary to encompass the changing nature of global business. Boddewyn *et al.* (1986) highlight the amendment made by the United Nations to their definition of the multinational enterprise to cater for such change. In 1973 the UN referred to multinational enterprises as:

All enterprises which control assets – factories, mines, sales offices and the like – in two or more countries (1973, p. 5).

By 1984 this definition had been amended to:

An enterprise (a) comprising entities in two or more countries regardless of the legal form and fields of activity of those entries, (b) which operates under a system of decision making permitting coherent policies and a common strategy through one or more decision-making centres, (c) in which the entities are so linked, by ownership or otherwise, that one or more of them may be able to exercise a significant influence over the activities of the others, and, in particular, to share knowledge resources and responsibilities with others (1984, p. 2).

The relaxation both of the ownership and the control dimensions in the latter definition broadens the scope of the analysis to include forms of foreign market servicing other than foreign direct investment in the theoretical framework. This definition thus comes close to Casson's (1987) 'a firm which adds value in more than one country'. Taking this wider definition, it may be concluded that international service firms can be regarded as multinational enterprises and are thus open to scrutiny within the ambit of the multinational enterprise.

A CRITICAL REVIEW OF THE ECLECTIC THEORY AND SERVICE INDUSTRIES

Dunning's eclectic theory of the multinational enterprise provides a useful framework for the classification of factors governing the internationalization of service firms (Dunning, 1979). Both Dunning (1989) and Enderwick (1989) have used the framework to analyse the international activities of service firms.

The three classifying principles of the eclectic framework are (1) firm-specific advantages (2) internalization decisions and (3) location-specific factors. The following section presents the key forces governing the internationalization of service firms under these headings.

Firm-specific advantages and multinational service enterprise

The interpretation which Kindleberger (1969) put on Hymer's pioneering work (1960, published in 1976) suggested the multinational firms needed some compensating advantage in order to offset the costs of operating abroad. Thus some cost-reducing advantage was necessary in order to compensate for costs of foreignness. This is the origin of the search for firm-specific advantages.

The necessity of such an assumption for the existence of multinational enterprises in the presence of internalization decisions and differential location costs has been questioned extensively (for example Buckley (1983; 1988) and it is clearly no longer valid for established mature multinational enterprises.

Firm-specific advantages are, however, important from two perspectives. First, they provide the starting point for an analysis of a question which is different from that of the existence of multinational firms. That question is 'What makes a firm successful?' Second, because firm-specific advantages have public-good characteristics, internalization leads to *vertical* integration in the *intermediate* market for the advantage, but *horizontal* integration in the *final product* market, as different plants exploit the advantage in spatially differentiated markets (Casson 1991a). Internalization of markets in advantages enables the firm to overcome 'buyer uncertainty' about the quality of the advantage and it enables successful co-ordinated collusion among the subsidiaries of the unitary firm. This successful collusion is possible because of the barrier to entry which the internalized monopolistic advantage creates. Thus ownership advantages create a situation where quality uncertainty and opportunities for collusion allow internalization economies to flourish (Casson, 1991a). Thus the Hymer monopolistic advantages approach and the internalization approach are complementary in explaining the existence and competitive ability of the multinational firm (Buckley, 1990). It is however essential to remember that ownership advantages result from the investment policy of the firm (Buckley and Casson, 1976) and there must be continual reinvestment in these assets in order to generate competitive advantages and supernormal profits (i.e. maintain the barrier to entry). Ownership advantages must be defined in a dynamic, not a static sense (Buckley, 1983).

The remainder of this section follows Kindleberger's (1969) four-fold classification of internationally exploitable advantages with special reference to service industries:

1. imperfect competition in goods markets
2. imperfect competition in factor markets
3. economies of scale
4. government intervention.

Imperfect competition in goods markets

As has been noted, heterogeneity is an important aspect of many people-supplied services (Langeard *et al.* 1981) and quality variation is common. Consequently, service branding can be an important tool in creating and sustaining a strong brand image and goodwill amongst customers. Coupled with this, the brand image can provide important signals to customers about the nature of the service and performance expectations, which help to minimize consumer uncertainty stemming from the intangibility of the service. The scope for branding of services, and the success of brand image as a firm-specific advantage is highlighted by the success of the international franchise networks of many fast-food chains. Branding also serves to differentiate one producer's service from those of its competitors and, through advertising campaigns, convey information about the target market for the service. Enderwick (1989) notes how corporate image tends to result in specialization by service firms who capitalize on the image they have developed by concentrating on their core strengths. Although this does not preclude firms from following diversification strategies, it suggests that maximum benefits are accrued to those organizations diversifying into related business areas in which they may confidently draw on their recognized strengths.

Technological advantages and innovation in services, unlike goods manufacturing, offer little scope for sustained competitive advantage. This may be partly due to the fact that in many people-embodied services, technology merely provides a support function – an adjunct to the actual service provided – and whilst necessary to the efficient and effective delivery of the service, is not central to its quality. Furthermore, many service firms buy-in this support technology, and being freely available on the market, it does not provide a distinct firm-specific advantage. A further explanation arises from the fact that many services cannot be patented, and are often easily and rapidly copied by competitors. There is thus a very short lead time on innovations which means competitive advantages of this kind are not sustainable.

Imperfect competition in factor markets

A critical factor in the production of many services is information, differential access to which gives rise to competitive advantage. This partly depends on the spatial location of the firm – those firms with geographically dispersed subsidiaries gaining access to a wider pool of information. Thus multinationality reinforces the advantage and serves to create barriers to entry in service industries. The capability to gather, store, monitor, interpret and analyse information at the least possible cost can be the key intangible asset providing firm-specific advantages (Dunning, 1989). Enderwick (1989) points to the economies of learning in the scale and scope of information gathering and use, and the often high investment requirements for such indivisible assets. This reinforces the idea of specialization by service firms and economies of integration throughout the production process. Such economies can also provide first-mover advantages – those firms willing to invest in information accruing short-term benefits from its use and longer-term benefits from scale and scope economies.

Coupled with information is knowledge, which can be derived from investment in information, or which accrues as a result of the experience gained by the firm's personnel. Dunning (1989) argues that knowledge as a service (e.g. management, consultancy, legal services) is not necessarily perishable and can be repeatedly used by the producer at little or no cost. When the knowledge is invested in the personnel of the firm, the knowledge can be produced and sustained over time, the firm capitalizing on its innate firm-specific knowledge. Firms may acquire such knowledge by providing attractive employment packages to experienced personnel – knowledge transfer being dependent on the flow of people between different institutions and the ability of local education establishments to convey pertinent knowledge to students. Protecting firm-specific knowledge can thus be critically dependent on retaining key staff who are invested with experience and knowledge.

Economies of scale and scope

As with manufacturing, advantages can be gained from large-scale operations. As Dunning (1989) notes:

> Similarly, large international business consultants, the merchant and investment banks, and the hotel chains can profit from the economies of specialization of personnel and the economies of common governance arising from their ability to move people, money and information between different parts of the same organization, and to take advantage of differential factor costs and environmental flexibility. Often too, large service companies can gain from raising finance on favourable terms and buying goods and services at quantity discounts in exactly the same way as manufacturing firms.

Scale economies in production may, however, be harder to achieve as many services require customization to individual customer requirements. Consequently, although large-scale operations may be able to generate scale economies in management, finance and inputs there are limited benefits in centralizing production in large centres.

Scope economies are particularly pertinent in retailing sectors where the larger the range and volume of goods stocked the greater the retailers' bargaining power over suppliers and control over quality of goods supplied – benefits which the retailers can pass on to their customers. In other service sectors, however, conflict may exist between factors which induce specialization, and the desire to generate scope economies through broadening the range of services offered. This may lead firms to seek synergistic links with other organizations offering complementary specialisms, rather than diversifying away from sectors in which they can capitalize on their skill base. This has been the case in the UK retail financial services sector where banks and building societies have seen the benefits in establishing 'financial supermarkets' where customers can buy all their financial service requirements. Many firms, however, lacking experience in the insurance business, have negotiated ties with insurance providers, avoiding diversification away from core strengths.

Government intervention

Government intervention in particular industries frequently varies between countries, resulting in differential advantages for firms in countries with fewer restrictions. This is currently a critical issue for many firms operating out of those countries whose governments have taken an early stand in the liberalization and deregulation of service industries.

Internalization theory and service multinational enterprises

Licensing can be differentiated from exporting and investment by the externalization effect. Licensing involves a market sale of embodied knowledge, technical or managerial, to a host-country producer. With exporting and investment, flows of services from assets are internalized (Buckley and Casson, 1976; 1985). The choice of internalized versus externalized business structure rests on the costs and benefits of the two alternatives with the firm seeking to minimize transaction costs and maximize the advantages of internalizing markets, particularly in scarce resources. In the manufacturing sector and in tradeable services, costs are, to a large extent, volume related. However, there are prevailing costs associated with each structure necessary to overcome the inherent impediments. Coase (1937) identified the major source of these impediments as uncertainty (principally related to external markets) and the loss of managerial control (within the firm). More recently, Casson (1991b) has attributed lack of trust in intermediaries and foreign partners as a major motivating factor behind internalization.

It has already been suggested that there is a greater propensity for service firms to invest abroad rather than engage in international trade as a result of the inseparability factor. In addition, some light has been shed on the preference for foreign direct investment over contractual arrangements based on firms' desire to maximize control over operations. However, further explanation can be given in the light of the nature of firm-specific advantages which were identified in the previous section and the relative transaction costs associated with the different modes of market servicing.

In information-intensive sectors, where information is tacit and costly to produce, but where it can be replicated with ease, there are advantages of internalizing such competitive assets and protecting leakage of firm-specific knowledge derived from these assets. In such instances there is greater likelihood of firms pursuing foreign direct investment strategies as opposed to licensing contracts (Dunning, 1989; Enderwick, 1989). In addition, where imparted knowledge is an important element in the delivered service (for example, in the case of management consulting) the role of service provider includes educating the consumer, best achieved through vertical integration of production and sales (Enderwick, 1989). The importance of brand image can also lead to the firm internalizing operations in order to protect the quality of the delivered service and avoid the potentially damaging effect on corporate image caused by underperformance by the licensee. However, such an assumption is not universally applicable across all service sectors. Many firms, notably fast-food chains, have created and sustained an international brand image through franchising. Although they have externalized the selling arm of their operations, they are able to maintain control over the quality of the delivered service by drawing up strict contracts with the franchisees, and controlling inputs. Stopford and Wells (1972) suggest that firms choose entry modes which allow them maximum control over foreign activities. As control is often assumed to be proportionately related to the degree of resource commitment, this suggests that firms will follow high-involvement strategies, investing a large amount of resources in the foreign operation. However, such a decision is weighed against the amount of perceived risk and uncertainty associated with the venture (as well as the available resources of the firm). Erramilli and Rao (1990) suggest that firms are prepared to relinquish some of their control over the operation in return for lower uncertainty and risk. By teaming up with host-market intermediaries they are able to overcome the problem of lack of market knowledge, lack of business contacts and distribution structures.

Licensing may also be discounted on the grounds that there is no identifiable 'technology' or 'managerial' element in the service which can be packaged in such a way that it becomes saleable. If firm-specific advantages are embodied in the experience and knowledge of a firm's pool of personnel, licensing becomes a non-viable option. As in the manufacturing sector, there are also hidden costs associated with licensing, notably search and negotiation costs; failure to reap the full economic rent in the sale of assets on which it is hard to put a price, policing use of the assets, and controlling and monitoring performance. This may result in licensing being a less cost-effective option than first perceived. Costs of market transactions in services are also considered by Dunning (1989) to be higher in services than in manufacturing. He highlights five major reasons for this:

1. tailoring services to individual customer needs is an important factor in many sectors and production is highly idiosyncratic;
2. the human element in services results in variability of quality;
3. until recently, information gathering and the knowledge and experience required to evaluate and interpret information was tacit and non-codifiable;
4. as certain information may be inexpensive to replicate, the possibility of its use outside formalized contracts and its dissipation throughout the market poses a real threat;
5. markets for many services are highly segmented and opportunities exist for price discrimination within internal systems.

Overall, therefore, there is a preponderance of factors promoting internalization of activities and deterring firms from entering into contractual arrangements with host-country firms. This is not to say, however, that firms are averse to entering into agreements with host-country service firms, but rather that equity joint ventures with foreign firms may be perceived as a more satisfactory economic solution. One of the important advantages of joint ventures is the fact that they reduce capital risk (Dunning 1989; Enderwick, 1989). Enderwick goes on to suggest that the risks involved with internalization by service firms are greater than those experienced by manufacturing firms. This is partly due to the fact that many service firms do not lend themselves to incremental internalization, with the opportunity of gaining experience through exporting before embarking on equity investment or considerable investment in managerial time in the case of licensing. Furthermore, there are high rates of expropriation in many service sectors which compounds the risks of committing all the capital to a foreign venture. Joint ventures also give access to local specialized knowledge with which the foreign partner is invested and also complementary competitive assets such as established contacts with key buyers, a customer base and extensive distribution networks which would be costly for the foreign firm to establish from scratch, and which would result in the operation taking longer to produce returns.

Recent developments in the theory of joint ventures suggest that three key factors are in operation in the establishment of joint ventures (Buckley and Casson, 1988). These are:

1. net benefits from internalizing a market in one or more intermediate goods or services flowing between the joint venture and the parties' other operations;
2. indivisibilities, which prevent each party setting up its own separate operation rather than a joint venture;
3. net disadvantages to a complete merger.

In services, the markets which are likely to be internalized are those in information, be it market, skills, quality or delivery related. Indivisibilities are likely to be present because of the information intensity of services and difficulties of establishing spatial barriers between markets. Mergers are likely to be less satisfactory because of regulatory barriers and cultural differences (often in service delivery). Kogut and Singh (1988) found that cultural distance between source and host countries increased the probability of a joint venture over an acquisition or greenfield wholly owned subsidiary.

Both Dunning (1989) and Enderwick (1989) suggest that the recent trend towards internalized modes of foreign-market servicing can be partly explained by the liberalization of markets, and the recent trend of governments in both developed and developing countries to encourage inward investment in service industries. New information technologies are also seen as playing an important role in reducing the cost of co-ordinating operations across international boundaries and increasing the need for centralized control. Alternatively, both writers acknowledge the fact that these factors also serve to reduce market imperfections and communication barriers associated with licensing and other contractual arrangements. Other recent changes in market conditions conversely promote the likelihood of increased licensing or joint-venture activity. First, service specialization suggests that appropriately worked contracts can be drawn up to cover contractual agreements. Second, the cost of acquiring and processing information is such that co-operation between firms can reduce risks and maximize the advantages of combining information.

Location theory and the service multinational enterprises

Exporting can be differentiated from licensing and investment by the location effect, the bulk of value adding taking place in the domestic market, whereas in the case of licensing and investment such activities are conducted abroad. Location theory assumes that firms locate their production where immobile inputs are cheapest and average production costs can consequently be minimized.

The location choice for tradeable services, like that for many goods, is consequently greater than for location-bound services, choice being principally dependent on:

1. the need to adapt products to local market conditions;
2. transport costs including tariff barriers;
3. economies of scale in production;
4. availability of factor inputs (such as suitably qualified personnel);
5. the degree of vertical and horizontal integration within the firm;
6. government restrictions (Dunning, 1972).

For location-bound services, where interaction between supplier and customer is essential, location depends on the catchment area of customers. This suggests the location of many services will tend towards areas of high population density (Enderwick, 1989) that high agglomeration of service firms in densely populated areas is an important feature of many service sectors (e.g. restaurants, financial services, repair services) and that international location of service firms will exhibit a pattern of multiple representation and geographic inequality. As the growth of many personal service sectors has been linked to the growth in real income of consumers in many developed economies, location of activities also tends towards countries and regions which are economically stable and where consumers are relatively affluent (Dunning, 1989).

Unlike the manufacturing sector, where location of production is heavily dependent on transport costs and tariff barriers, location of many services is more concerned with closeness to customers and adaptation to customers' requirements. As the incidence of contact is high in such situations, further pressure is placed on the firm to locate activities in close proximity to the customer as personal contact is the most expensive form of interaction for firms exporting (trading) services across international frontiers, involving both time and the high cost of travel (Hirsch, 1986). However, Hirsch goes on to suggest that modern communication technology is reducing the need for face-to-face contact, making it possible for some service firms to centralize their activities and 'export' services internationally.

Summary of the application of the eclectic theory to service industries

As with manufacturing firms, firm-specific advantages are an important prerequisite for the successful operation for all forms of foreign market servicing. However, it does not necessarily follow that lower host market production costs are a necessary condition for foreign direct investment and licensing options. As a result of inseparability, characteristic of many service sectors, proximity to the market is a prerequisite of selling in foreign markets, and this factor supersedes cost considerations in the foreign market servicing decision. There are also greater incentives for service firms to internalize operations due to the non-codifiable nature of firms' competitive advantages. Information and people-embodied knowledge are critical firm-specific advantages for many service firms and as such competitive assets are non-patentable, difficult to package into a saleable form and easy to replicate or acquire through 'poaching' of staff. There is thus a greater propensity to invest in foreign markets rather than pursue contractual arrangements.

DYNAMICS OF FOREIGN-MARKET SERVICING IN SERVICE INDUSTRIES

One of the major limitations of the eclectic theory lies in its failure to shed any light on the dynamics of the foreign-market servicing decision. As markets and firms change over time, so do the market-servicing modes most appropriate to sustaining a competitive position in the foreign market. A dynamic analysis is therefore essential.

The models which are put forward to explain the dynamics of foreign-market servicing, notably the international product cycle (Vernon, 1966), the work of Hirsch (1976) and Horst (1971, 1972), Buckley and Casson's (1981) model of the timing of the switch from exporting to foreign direct investment and the behavioural models of Johanson and Wiedersheim-Paul (1975), Johanson and Vahlne (1977) and Bilkley and Tesar (1977), suggest a stepwise sequence from domestic production, through modes of exporting to foreign direct investment. For services which are embodied in tradeable goods, internationalization may follow a similar pattern, unless firm-specific advantages are best exploited through internal hierarchies, or where there are government restrictions on trade. Where production cannot be separated from consumption, however, and foreign direct investment and licensing are the only available options, the increased resource commitment involved in adopting these modes may slow down the process of internationalization. This argument is supported by Enderwick's (1989) suggestions that incremental internationalization is not possible in many service sectors as a result of the inseparability factor. Research exists, however, to counter this view. Terpstra and Yu's (1988) research on advertising agencies and Welch's (1990) research into the behaviour of Australian franchisors both exhibit evidence of incremental internationalization. Although low-investment exporting is not feasible in either industry, low financial commitment licensing and foreign direct investment options provide an alternative. In the advertising industry international expansion through joint ventures provides a relatively low-cost, low-risk mode through which firms can acquire knowledge before committing themselves to full foreign direct investment. Alternatively, the case of Australian franchisors exhibits an example of firms testing out market opportunities through licensing before proceeding to a committed franchise operation.

Recent research by the authors on internationalization by UK retail financial service firms also shows a high incidence of firms embarking on international expansion through joint ventures (Buckley, *et al.* 1992). Joint ventures are principally seen as being more advantageous than greenfield entry in that they offer not only lower capital outlay, but also access to established distribution networks. Arguably this latter issue is likely to be pertinent in oth service sectors. Where exporting is ruled out on the grounds of the inseparability facto the opportunities of accessing intermediaries' distribution networks are also removed. ' respect, joint ventures and contractual relationships such as licensing provid. 'doorways' into existing market networks.

Thus, Buckley and Casson's (1981) assertion that licensing should have a place in the internationalization model appears particularly pertinent. However, whereas their model is based on volume-related fixed and variable costs, for service firms it may be more appropriate to consider the different costings of internal and external modes. The risk of lost sales arising from leakage of competitive advantages in the case of licensing may make equity investment, particularly minority joint ventures, a more risk-averse method of gaining market knowledge. When the added advantages of pooled resources, which are a feature of joint ventures, are added into the equation, along with the long-term possibility of increasing the equity stake to achieve majority ownership, joint ventures appear to be a more favourable option.

The international behaviour of location-bound service firms may therefore be expected to follow a path from initial, low-risk contractual or joint ventures designed to gather market information and important learning experiences as a precursor to majority-owned or wholly-owned foreign direct investment options.

It should not be suggested, however, that all manufacturing firms religiously follow such a process of incremental expansion. Buckley *et al.* (1990), in an analysis of foreign-market servicing strategies of British manufacturing firms, found an unexpectedly high proportion of firms moving from little or no market involvement to foreign direct investment. Although this may be partly explained by their having experience of internationalization in other markets, the nature of the product (being bulky and too expensive to transport) and the need to gain a local identity and demonstrate commitment to the market precluded consideration of export strategies. These factors are not dissimilar to those determining foreign direct investment options in the service sector, that is, the nature of the service dictates production in close proximity to customers, and the need to generate a strong image and goodwill determines foreign investment. This suggests that whilst it is useful to identify features of many service industries which dictate particular modes of marketing servicing, the differences between manufacturing and service sectors should not be overstated. It is rather the greater number of instances where factors specific to the nature of services dictate foreign direct investment or some form of market presence which characterizes the service sector, rather than the fact that services, *per se*, are implicitly 'different'.

Initial market entry may, therefore, take the form of foreign direct investment. Given the arguments put forward earlier concerning the problems of accessing distribution networks, there are some grounds for supposing that takeovers are preferable to greenfield entry modes. Although takeovers characteristically involve firms relying on the skills of the incumbent staff and the ability of the new management to retain key personnel in whom the service provision skills are embodied, the internalization of the distribution network, a key competitive asset, may outweigh the perceived problems in the acquisition decision.

SUMMARY AND CONCLUSIONS

W   there are several factors which distinguish services from goods, in an international busi.   tract two features of services emerge which critically affect foreign market servicing decisic   / the process of internationalization. The first is the extent to which the service is embodic in physical goods, which determines the degree of tradeability of the service. Where the service supplied can be embodied in a tangible product, then it is possible for the firm to export the product, license or invest in the foreign market. Where, however, the provision of the service depends on people then the firm's personnel must either travel to the consumer, or be located in close proximity to the consumer. The second factor is the degree to which the production and consumption of the service can be spatially separated. Where production and consumption take place simultaneously (for example in the case of medical care), unless the consumer travels to the country of the service supplier, it is necessary for the firm to locate activities abroad, either through contractual arrangements with host-country suppliers or through foreign direct investment.

The 'people' element in the provision of services also suggests that the firm's personnel, invested with learning and experience, can be a critical source of firm-specific advantage. Leading on from this it is apparent that, in order to exploit such advantages, the firm must maintain control of these assets in its internationalization strategies. This often dictates a strategy of internalization.

It is important to note, however, that whilst the 'people' element and the inseparability factor, characteristic of many services, lead to a different balance in the equation of total foreign sales, exporting options giving way to international investment as the dominant form of market servicing, the theoretical explanation for firms' behaviour remains unchanged. The dominance of the nature of the product (service) and derived competitive advantages merely tip the scales in favour of foreign direct investment in much the same way that firms producing bulky products which are expensive to transport, for instance, are forced to consider only licensing and foreign direct investment options, or where a firm's success is dependent on discriminatory pricing and thus establishment of overseas subsidiaries is necessary to capitalize on their advantages. The contribution to the theory derived from separate analysis of service therefore stems from its ability to highlight specific factors which help to predict the behaviour of internationalizing service firms, not its ability to challenge traditional international business theory.

REFERENCES

Bateson, J.E.G. (1977), 'Do We Need Service Marketing?', in *Marketing Consumer Services: New Insights*, Marketing Science Institute. Report No. 77–115, December.

Berry, L.L. (1975), 'Personalizing the Bank: Key Opportunity in Bank Marketing', *Bank Marketing*, Vol. 8, April, pp. 22–5.

Berry, L.L. (1980), 'Service Marketing is Different', *Business*, Vol. 30 No. 3, pp. 24–9.

Bilkley, W. and Tesar, G. (1977), 'The Export Behaviour of Smaller-sized Wisconsin Manufacturing Firms', *Journal of International Business Studies*. Vol. 8 No. 2, pp. 93–8.

Boddewyn, J.J., Halbrich, M.B. and Perry, A.C. (1986), 'Service Multinationals: Conceptualization, Measurement and Theory', *Journal of International Business Studies*, Vol. 16 No. 3, pp. 41–57.

Buckley, P.J. (1983), 'New Theories on International Business: Some Unresolved Issues', in Casson, M. (Ed.), *The Growth of International Business*, George Allen & Unwin, London.

Buckley, P.J. (1988), 'The Limits of Explanation: Testing the Internalization Theory of the Multinational Enterprise', *Journal of International Business Studies* Vol. XIX No. 2, Summer, pp. 181–93.

Buckley, P.J. (1990), 'Problems and Developments in the Core Theory of International Business', *Journal of International Business Studies*, Vol. XXI No. 4, pp. 657–65.

Buckley, P.J. and Casson, M. (1976), *The Future of the Multinational Enterprise*, Macmillan, London.

Buckley, P.J. and Casson, M. (1981), 'The Optimal Timing of a Foreign Direct Investment', *Economic Journal*, Vol. 91, March, pp. 75–87.

Buckley, P.J. and Casson, M. (1985), *The Economic Theory of the Multinational Enterprise*, Macmillan, London.

Buckley, P.J. and Casson, M. (1988), 'A Theory of Co-operation in International Business', in Contractor, F.J. and Lorange, P. (Eds), Competitive Strategies in International Business, Lexington Books, Lexington, MA.

Buckley, P.J., Pass, C.L. and Prescott, K. (1990), 'The Implementation of an International Market Servicing Strategy in UK Manufacturing Firms', *British Journal of Management*, Vol. 1 No. 3, October, pp. 193–203.

Buckley, P.J., Pass, C.L. and Prescott, K. (1991), 'Foreign Market Servicing Strategies of UK Retail Financial Firms in Europe', in Young, S. (Ed.), *Europe and the Multinationals: Issues and Responses for the 1990s*, Edward Elgar, Cheltenham.

Buckley, P.J. and Prescott, K. (1989). 'The Structure of British Industry's Sales in Foreign Markets', *Managerial and Decision Economics*, Vol. 10, pp. 189–208.

Casson, M. (1987), *The Firm and the Market*, Basil Blackwell, Oxford.

Casson, M. (1991a), 'Economic Theories of International Business: A Research Agenda', mimeo. University of Reading.

Casson, M. (1991b), 'Beyond Internalization', in Buckley, P.J. (Ed.), *New Directions in International Business*, Edward Elgar, Cheltenham.

Coase, R.H. (1937), 'The Nature of the Firm', *Economica*, Vol. 4, November, pp. 386–405.

Cowell, D. (1986), 'The Marketing of Services', Institute of Marketing, Heinemann, London.

Dunning, J.H. (1972), 'The Location of International Firms in an Enlarged EEC: An Exploratory Paper', Manchester Statistical Society, Manchester.

Dunning, J.H. (1979), 'Explaining Changing Patterns of International Production: In Defence of the Eclectic Theory', *Oxford Bulletin of Economics and Statistics*, Vol. 161 No. 41, pp. 269–95.

Dunning, J.H. (1989), 'Multinational Enterprises and the Growth of Services: Some Conceptual and Theoretical Issues', *Service Industries Journal*, Vol. 9 No. 1, January, pp. 5–39.

Edvinsson, L. (1981), 'Some Aspects on Export of Services', working paper, University of Stockholm.

Enderwick, P. (1989), 'Some Economics of Service-sector Multinational Enterprises', in Enderwick, P. (Ed.), *Multinational Service Firms*, Routledge, London.

Erramilli, M.K. and Rao, C.P. (1990), 'Choice of Foreign Market Entry Modes for Service Firms: Role of Market Knowledge', *Management International Review*, Vol. 30 No. 2, pp. 135–50.

Grönroos, C. (1977), 'A Service-oriented Approach to Marketing of Services', *European Journal of Marketing*, Vol. 12 No. 8, pp. 588–601.

Hirsch, S. (1976), 'An International Trade and Investment Theory of the Firm', *Oxford Economic Papers*, Vol. 28, pp. 258–70.

Hirsch, S. (1986), 'International Transactions in Services and in Service Intensive Goods', working paper. Tel Aviv University.

Horst, T.O. (1971), 'The Theory of the Multinational Firm: Optimal Behaviour under Different Tariff and Tax Rates', *Journal of Political Economy*, Vol. 79, pp. 1059–72.

Horst, T.O. (1972), 'Firm and Industry Determinants of the Decision to Invest Abroad: An Empirical Study', *Review of Economics and Statistics*, Vol. 54, pp. 258–66.

Hymer, S.H. (1976), *The International Operations of National Firms: A Study of Foreign Direct Investment*, (PhD thesis, MIT, 1960), MIT Press, Cambridge, MA.

Johanson, J. and Vahlne, J.E. (1977), 'The Internationalization Process of the Firm – A Model of Knowledge Development and Increasing Foreign Market Commitments', *Journal of International Business Studies*, Vol. 8, pp. 23–32.

Johnason, J. and Wiedersheim-Paul, F. (1975), 'The Internationalization on the Firm: Four Swedish Cases', *Journal of Management Studies*, Vol. 12, pp. 205–22.

12

The Process of Internationalization in the Operating Firm

Timothy Clark, Derek S. Pugh and Geoff Mallory

INTRODUCTION

This article is concerned with the internationalization process of the firm. Firms seeking either to expand into foreign markets or to alter their existing arrangements have a choice between three general modes of foreign market servicing: exporting, foreign licensing and foreign direct investment (FDI) (Buckley, 1992; Buckley and Casson, 1976; Root, 1987; Terpstra, 1987). As Chandy and Williams (1994) show, a large proportion of the most cited articles in the international business field have sought to understand those factors which account for firms' choices between alternative modes of foreign market servicing. Despite the historical importance of the subject no common framework has emerged. Barkema *et al.* (1996) suggest that this is due to a range of factors which include the diversity of disciplines among researchers, the theoretical frameworks they adopt, the samples of organizations they investigate and the national origins of data they examine.

Some researchers adopt a static approach, while others focus on internationalization as an incremental and cumulative process. For example, Dunning (1981, 1988); Hennart (1982); Hill *et al.* (1990); Hymer (1960, 1976) and Teece (1981) generally examine a firm's foreign expansion as a series of static choices dictated by efficiency considerations and relative costs and benefits. In contrast, others view internationalization as a process of increasing involvement within and across national markets (e.g. Johanson and Weidersheim-Paul, 1975; Johanson and Vahlne, 1977, 1990). This article is anchored in the process-orientated literature, in particular the Uppsala Model, since it is concerned with examining on a longitudinal basis the increasing international involvement of 25 UK-based firms.

The Uppsala Model suggests that the process of internationalization is the consequence of the acquisition of experiential knowledge, in particular, market-specific knowledge. It is the knowledge gained by operating within a particular national market that enables a firm to increase its commitment to that market. Market-specific knowledge therefore underpins the shifts between different modes of foreign market servicing within a market.

In this article we wish to maintain that market-specific knowledge is not the only source of information available to a firm. As firms operate in foreign markets they develop in addition to networks of institutional arrangements a knowledge of the *processes* of internationalization.

Reprinted with permission from *International Business Review,* 1997, **6**(6), 605–609.

Account therefore has to be taken of the general knowledge obtained from operating internationally in understanding the management of the relationship between foreign operations. Consequently, the appropriate unit of analysis of the development of FDI is not the individual national market but the operating firm as a whole.

BACKGROUND

As Andersen (1993) and Barkema *et al.* (1996) point out there are two approaches to examining the process by which firms internationalize: (1) the group of Innovation-Related Internationalization Models; and, (2) the Uppsala Internationalization Model. All these models consist of a number of identifiable and distinct stages with higher level stages indicating greater involvement in a foreign market.

The first group of models are based on Rogers's stages of the adaption process (Rogers, 1962, pp. 81–86). Common to these models is the view that the internationalization process is a series of innovations for the firm. Their focus is exclusively on the export development process, in particular of small and medium sized firms (see Leonidou and Katsikeas, 1996, p. 529). This is conceived of as a number of fixed and sequential stages, although the number of stages identified varies considerably between models, ranging from as few as three to as many as six (Bilkey and Tesar, 1977; Cavusgil, 1980; Czinkota, 1982; Reid, 1981), Leonidou and Katsikeas (1996, pp. 524–525), on the basis of a comprehensive review of these models, identify three generic stages: the pre-export stage; the initial export stage; the advanced export stage.

The focus of this article is on the second model, the Uppsala Internationalization Model, since its distinctive feature is the stress on the different institutional forms that are associated with the growing dependence on foreign markets. As Reid (1983) notes, this model examines internationalization in terms of structural adjustments to foreign market servicing arrangements resulting from 'the level of export sales dependence' (p. 44). Foreign market servicing modes change once a certain threshold of dependency in the host country is reached.

The Uppsala Model seeks to explain and predict two aspects of the internationalization of the firm: (1) the step-by-step pattern of institutional development within individual national markets; and, (2) the expansion of firms across national markets as they move from nations which are proximal to those which are increasingly psychically distant. The focus of this article is on examining the first rather than the second aspect of the Uppsala Model. In other words it is concerned with the sequence of development within rather than across national markets. This aspect of the model predicts that because of the considerable uncertainties associated with operating internationally (e.g. consumer habits, rules and regulations, cultural and political differences, etc.), firms increase their commitments to individual markets in small incremental steps. A firm's involvement in a specific national market develops according to the following four stages, termed the 'establishment chain' (Johanson and Wiedersheim-Paul, 1975):

Stage 1:	No regular export activities.
Stage 2:	Export via independent representatives (agent).
Stage 3:	Establishment of an overseas sales subsidiary.
Stage 4:	Establishment of a foreign production/manufacturing facility.

These steps suggest that internationalization is a process of organizational learning characterized by the increasing degree of involvement of firms in specific foreign markets. Firms increase their presence in a foreign market by moving from Stage 1 through Stages 2 and 3 to Stage 4, by accumulating market-specific knowledge. This type of knowledge is experiential and refers to knowledge of the culture, customers, business and market structure, and so forth of individual markets. The establishment of a production facility is therefore dependent upon the knowledge that has been accumulated previously. Hence, prior experience of operating in a particular foreign market, in some way, is essential to the process of acquiring relevant market-specific knowledge. As Johanson and Vahlne (1990) write, 'a critical assumption is that market knowledge, including perceptions of market opportunities and problems, is acquired primarily through experience from current business activities in the market. This market experience is to a large extent country-specific, i.e. it can be generalised to other country markets only with difficulty' (p. 12).

A number of empirical studies have examined this aspect of the Uppsala Model. Reid (1984) has expressed surprise at the widespread acceptance of the stages approach to internationalization since it largely rests on a limited number of empirical studies: the initial research into the overseas expansion of four Swedish companies (Johanson and Wiedersheim-Paul, 1975), a case study of Pharmacia (cited in Johanson and Vahlne, 1977), and an Australian investigation which treated interstate expansion as analogous to overseas expansion (Wiedersheim-Paul et al., 1978). In addition, Luostarinen (1980) and Larimo (1985) have reported similar evidence for Finland. Finally, Yoshihara (1978) on the basis of an examination of Japanese foreign investment in Southeast Asia concluded that 'the pattern of investment seems to substantiate the evolutionary theory of foreign investment' (p. 372). In contrast, a number of other studies fail to corroborate the notion that firms increase their commitment to individual markets through the four successive stages of the establishment chain (Buckley et al., 1988; Hedlund and Kverneland, 1985; Millington and Bayliss, 1990; Turnbull, 1987; Turnbull and Valla, 1986; Young and Hood, 1976).

Given that there is a continuing debate concerning the predictive accuracy of the Uppsala Model in the international business literature this article makes three contributions. First, since a number of studies have presented evidence of firms diverging from the sequence of four stages posited in the Uppsala Model a logical model is presented of the full range of choices available to firms when first entering a foreign market and when subsequently altering the form of their foreign market servicing in that market. Second, the frequency with which each of these options is used is examined in relation to the international development of 25 UK-based firms. Third, in discussing the research results we suggest that the Uppsala Model places too great an emphasis on the accumulation of market-specific compared to general knowledge. The core proposition of the model is that increased market-specific knowledge will lead to increased market commitment, and vice versa. We wish to suggest that it is the general knowledge from operating internationally, plus the management of the relationship between already-established foreign operations (in conjunction with market-specific knowledge) which determines the shifts between different forms of foreign market servicing. This leads to at least two implications for the analysis of the internationalization process: (1) the need to place greater emphasis on the process at the firm rather than market level; and (2) the importance of the active management of the interdependencies between operating units.

A LOGICAL MODEL OF FOREIGN MARKET SERVICING

Figure 1 extends the model first proposed by Buckley *et al.* (1990, p. 130) and suggests 16 possible options beyond minimal involvement. The numbers indicate the actual direction and type of shifts it is logically possible for a firm to take when initially entering a foreign market and when subsequently adjusting its mode of operating in specific markets. These 16 shifts are listed in Table 1. Three general types can be distinguished: *between*, *within* and *mixed*. The *between* mode shift refers to forward (i.e. towards FDI) and backward (i.e. towards minimal involvement) movements between the three generic forms of market servicing: exporting, licensing and FDI (e.g. exporting to licensing). The *within* mode adjustment concerns shifts within any one of the three generic forms of market servicing (e.g. in export form, from agent to distributor). These can be simplified into four classes of moves, of which **initial entry, move to FDI** and **retrenchment** are *between* mode shifts, and for example, export adjustment is a *within* mode shift. The *mixed* mode shift concerns moves to operating in more than one mode simultaneously in a single foreign market. Each of these general shifts is considered in more detail below.

Between mode shifts

Initial entry

This refers to the first significant attempt by a firm to penetrate a foreign market. However, as Fig. 1 shows the first move is not confined to exporting, firms may initially engage in licensing and FDI, if they so choose. Although an experienced international firm may tend towards the latter, empirical evidence suggests licensing accounts for a small but nevertheless growing proportion of UK industry's foreign market sales (Buckley and Davies, 1981: Buckley and Prescott, 1989). Both studies indicate licensing, as a method of entry, is prevalent in markets which are difficult to penetrate by other, more common, means of market servicing, such as Italy, Japan and Spain.

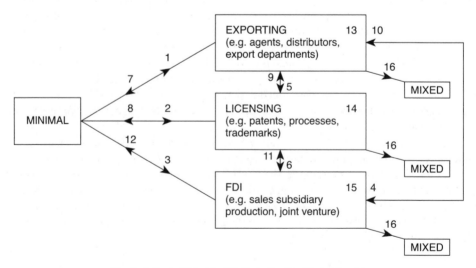

Fig. 1. A Logical Model of Shifts in Foreign Market Servicing

Move to FDI

We use an expanded definition of FDI to include any form of market servicing which involves direct investment in the host country. This leads to a distinction between direct investment in sales operations and direct investment in production facilities. Such a definition permits greater sensitivity to the variety of shifts involving FDI. This move may be likened to Cavusgil's (1980) 'committed involvement stage' where the firm has a long-run commitment to its international activities. The term 'global investment stage' (Young *et al.*, 1989, p. 33) is perhaps more precise since this recognizes the fact that any one firm may have a broad spread of international institutional arrangements. It is important to emphasize that unlike the Uppsala Model there is no assumption in Fig. 1 that the institutional arrangements adopted are the consequence of the stage in internationalization obtained. As Johanson and Wiedersheim-Paul (1975) write, 'the agency establishments, according to our view, are made primarily during the early stages of internationalization' (p. 18). Hence, exporting through agents is considered an initial stage of internationalization, whilst FDI is viewed as the final stage. In contrast, Fig. 1 suggests that firms with considerable experience and well-developed international institutional arrangements may continue to export extensively. It may be that FDI is achieved in a limited number of markets.

Retrenchment

This concerns the reduction of a firm's depth of involvement in a host country. A firm may continue to be present in the market, whether it be via export, licensing or a sales and marketing subsidiary, but its previous resource commitment, as represented by its marketing mode, is reduced. This does not imply that the market becomes less significant for the firm, rather its resource commitments within the individual market are reduced. Resources may be transferred to other more strategic markets within the firm's international network. Alternatively, a firm may choose to exit a market completely. In the original Uppsala study by Johanson and Wiedersheim-Paul (1975) only one instance of retrenchment was noted (i.e. a backward move in the 'establishment chain'). This was the sale by Facit of its Canadian sales subsidiary to its former agent. As a consequence, the Uppsala Model focuses exclusively on the increasing involvement of firms in foreign markets (i.e. moves that follow the 'chain' pattern). Moves that go in the opposite direction are not incorporated into the model.

Within mode adjustment

These can be as significant as between mode shifts. Essentially the firm retains its existing foreign market servicing mode, but adjusts the form this takes. In other words, it adjusts its institutional arrangements within *one* mode. Examples include changing from a distributor to an agent, exporting directly to end users instead of using distributors as intermediaries, changing agents (i.e. change in export form), and changing licence or joint venture partners (i.e. change in licensing and FDI form).

Mixed mode shifts

These occur when firms add additional modes to their existing marketing modes thereby adopting a mixed marketing approach. The various types of mixed marketing approaches are combinations of the modal shifts already noted. For example a firm can license a product initially then establish a manufacturing plant for other products in the same market, whilst the licensing agreement is allowed to continue. As with retrenchment above, this type of move is absent from the Uppsala Model.

RESEARCH METHODS

The empirical results presented in the next section of the paper are founded upon the UK element of an international collaborative research project – the International Organization Observatory (IOO). The common purpose of this international team of researchers is to conduct research which will help in understanding the management implications occasioned by developments within the European Union. The IOO research focus and research methods have been extensively described elsewhere (Clark, 1996; Clark and Mallory, 1992; Clark *et al.*, 1997). However, it is necessary to briefly enumerate the methods as they apply to this particular study.

The study examined the internationalization of 25 UK-based firms. The method by which organizations were selected was developed in order to overcome a number of deficiencies which attach to previous studies of the Uppsala Model. Three main problems can be identified.

1. Studies focus on different levels within the organization. Some focus on the firm as a whole, others on the operational units which comprise the organization. This distinction is critical since with the increasing importance to national economies of large multi-divisional/multiproduct firms the organizational unit being analysed may determine the extent and type of internationalization observed. Operational units may differ in their degree of international sales activity, number of foreign markets served, and institutional arrangements. Furthermore, some multiproduct firms may have distinct institutional arrangements for different product ranges. Overall, a firm may have a high percentage of export sales, but whilst some product ranges may mirror this others may be more domestic in their focus. Hence, the degree and complexity of internationalization can depend on whether the empirical focus is at the group, operational or product level.

2. The Uppsala Model is a theory of organizational learning. Learning occurs over the lifespan of an organization. Consequently, the original Uppsala study conducted by Johanson and Wiedersheim-Paul (1975) examined the internationalization of four Swedish firms (Atlas Copco, Facit, Sandvik and Volvo) from the year in which they were founded to the early 1970s. Therefore, a proper test of the Uppsala Model should examine the process by which a firm internationalizes over its lifespan. In general studies which sought to apply the Uppsala Model to the internationalization of firms have focused on particular periods in a firm's history. For example, Barkema *et al.* (1996) examined the internationalization of 13 large non-financial Dutch firms between 1966 and 1988. Their study, and those which adopt a similar approach (Turnbull, 1987; Turnbull and Valla, 1986), ignores the impact in this time period of accumulated knowledge which may have been built up as a result of expansion into foreign markets in earlier time periods.

3. Finally, and related to the previous point, a number of studies limit their investigation to the expansion of firms in particular markets. Hedlund and Kverneland (1985) examined the development of Swedish companies in Japan. Turnbull (1987) focused on the

expansion of 24 UK-based firms into France, Germany and Sweden. Millington and Bayliss (1990) concentrated on the expansion of UK-based firms into the European Union. By contrast the original Uppsala study included the 20 nations the four Swedish firms had entered. These are assumed to be all or the vast majority of their entries. If studies exclude the majority, or a proportion of markets in which a firm operates it is not possible to take full account of the impact of the transferability of learning between markets (i.e. general knowledge) which Johanson and Vahlne (1977) acknowledge may lead to jumps in the establishment chain. In other words it should be a historical study of all the national markets entered by a firm. Consequently, knowledge accumulated in other (i.e. excluded) nations may have an impact on the type of institutional arrangement found in those national markets which are the focus of the study, but its impact will be ignored.

Given these points the sample firms were selected in the following ways. We began by defining the population from which the sample is taken as the largest 1000 firms in the UK, as ranked by sales turnover, provided they manufactured in the UK. We then distinguished between two levels within these organizations: the holding company and the operating firm. Potential participants were approached at the operating firm level (i.e. the level at which it manufactured rather than just owned). Information was collected via in-depth interviews with senior managers of the organizations, including those responsible for international marketing and the management of international operations. This was supplemented by published information on the history of each operating firm. As a result we were able to obtain information on the pattern of international expansion of each operating firm in every market which they currently service, or had at one time, serviced.

RESEARCH RESULTS

This section analyses the form of foreign market servicing adopted by our sample of 25 UK companies when entering a foreign market and any subsequent modal shifts to these initial arrangements.

Table 1 shows which methods of operating firms adopted when first entering a foreign market and the subsequent changes to these. The numbers for each move (1–16) refer to those previously identified in Fig. 1. Four firms focused their marketing activities on their home market – the UK. However, at some time each company had responded to a foreign order. Hence, their position in these 16 markets was minimal since they had made no concerted attempt to internationalize. Each order was treated no differently to a domestic order.

The most frequent way that the companies entered a foreign market was by exporting (58% of first moves). The second most popular method was the establishment of a sales subsidiary (20% of first moves), the third was via a licensing agreement (11% of first moves) and the fourth was establishing a production facility (11% of first moves).

Of the 203 changes the firms made to their foreign market servicing arrangements, the most frequent was to move from export straight to FDI. This accounted for 63% of all subsequent shifts with 78 instances of a move from export to production, 26 cases of a move from export to establishing a sales subsidiary, and 17 moves from export to licensing.

The second most common subsequent change, accounting for 18% of cases, was the move to mixed marketing. There were a total of 36 instances in which companies combined two or more marketing modes simultaneously in a single foreign market. A number of classifications

Table 1. Changes to Foreign Operations in a Particular Market

Type of change	Number of moves
No move	
Minimal	16
BETWEEN MODE SHIFTS	
First move	
1. Minimal to export	391
2. Minimal to licence	78
3. Minimal to foreign direct investment (FDI)	
(i) Sales subsidiary	134
(ii) Production facility	76
TOTAL (first moves)	679
Move to FDI	
4. Export to FDI	
(i) Sales subsidiary	78
(ii) Production	26
5. Export to licensing	17
6. Licensing to FDI	
(i) Sales subsidiary	1
(ii) Production	6
Retrenchment	
7. Export to minimal	
8. Licensing to minimal	
9. Licensing to export	
10. FDI to export	
(i) Sales subsidiary	2
(ii) Production	1
11. FDI to licence	
(i) Sales subsidiary	
(ii) Production	2
12. FDI to minimal	
WITHIN MODE ADJUSTMENTS	
13. Change in export form	4
14. Change in licensing form	9
15. Change in FDI form	
(i) Sales subsidiary to production	20
(ii) Production to sales subsidiary	1
MIXED MARKETING SHIFTS	
16. Mixed marketing	36
TOTAL (subsequent changes)	203

Table 2. Types of Mixed Marketing Approaches and Their Frequency

Type mixed approaches*	Number of moves	Frequency (%)
EX+LIC	4	11
EX+JV		
EX+SSUB		
EX+MAN		
LIC+JV	10	28
LIC+SSUB	4	11
LIC+MAN	4	11
JV+SSUB	5	14
JV+MAN	2	6
SSUB+MAN	3	8
LIC+JV+SSUB	1	3
JV+SSUB+MAN	3	8
TOTAL	36	100

* EX=exporting; LIC=licensing; JV=joint venture; SSUB=sales subsidiary; MAN=manufacturing facility

of mixed marketing approaches have been propounded (Turnbull and Valla, 1986, p. 33; Young and Hood, 1976, p. 242), the approach adopted in this study is identified in Table 2. This indicates the various mixed marketing approaches adopted by companies in the sample. Whilst 12 combinations are possible, nine were used in the sample. The most frequent of these combinations includes licensing with the other three forms of foreign market servicing (50% of cases). The second most frequent solution (28% of cases) combines the use of joint ventures with sales and manufacturing subsidiaries. The next most frequent was the combination of exporting with other market servicing modes (11% of cases). Four instances (11% of cases) of markets being serviced by more than two modes are noted in Table 2. In one case a licensing agreement was combined with a joint venture agreement and a manufacturing facility; in the other three cases a joint venture, sales subsidiary and manufacturing facility were combined.

Two conclusions can be drawn from the above analysis: first, at some point firms in the sample found that a single mode of marketing their products was inappropriate and did not optimize their presence in the market; second, instead of changing from one mode to another (as suggested by the Uppsala Model of internationalization), firms preferred to complement existing marketing structures with additional servicing modes. Taken in isolation this finding does not support the idea of a sequential development of marketing modes in a national market. Rather a number of firms have sought to develop a more complex system by combining several forms of market servicing in a single market.

Retrenchment is defined by Buckley (1983) as a reduction of 'involvement' in the host country. The data in Table 1 indicate that the depth of involvement was reduced in five instances. In three instances firms moved to export from a neighbouring country, whilst in the other two cases they adopted a licensing approach. This evidence indicates that whilst this type of move is uncommon it nevertheless does occur.

A detailed analysis of the data presented in Table 1 indicates that the 25 firms in the study adopted four routes to establishing a production facility.

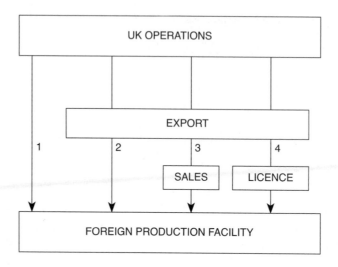

Fig. 2. Routes to Establishing a Foreign Production Facility

Figure 2, following Buckley *et al.* (1988), diagramatically represents each of these routes. The four identified routes are:

Route 1 – direct to foreign production;
Route 2 – export then foreign production;
Route 3 – export then sales subsidiary then foreign production; and
Route 4 – export then licence then foreign production.

The shortest and most direct path, Route 1, was followed most frequently accounting for 53% of cases. Route 2, the next most common route, was followed in 26 markets and accounted for 18% of cases. Route 3 was followed in 20 markets accounting for 14% of cases. Route 4 was the least popular occurring in 6 markets accounting for 5% of cases. For our sample of firms the shortest routes to FDI were therefore the most common. These results do not support the idea of a single incremental view of the process of internationalization since the stepwise path was the exception rather than rule.

When discussing the routes to production it should be remembered that this was the third most frequent way of operating in foreign markets. A greater number of markets were serviced via export and sales subsidiaries (see Table 1). In terms of the Uppsala Model, the sample made a greater number of moves from minimal to export to sales subsidiaries (58) than to production (20). Production was not a widespread form of operating. Two conclusions follow from this analysis. First, there is no single route to production. This contradicts the evolutionary stepwise development propounded by the Uppsala Model. Instead firms have a number of routes from which to choose. Second, even firms with considerable international experience continue to export to the majority of their foreign markets. A production facility is only established in a select number of markets.

DISCUSSION

The results of this study have confirmed previous research that the process of internationalization, when examined in relation to each individual market, is frequently not as the Uppsala Model predicts – a smooth and immutable series of small steps. The 'establishment chain' is one amongst several paths to FDI taken since firms often bypass the intermediate stages to FDI. Indeed, in our sample of firms the shortest and most direct paths were the most common.

A number of explanations for the failure of the Uppsala Model to consistently predict the pattern of internationalization have been offered. One suggestion is that the strongest and most consistent evidence for the 'establishment chain' has been found amongst Scandinavian firms, particularly Swedish and Finnish firms (Sullivan and Bauerschmidt, 1990). It may be that patterns of internationalization vary from country to country. In this respect the Uppsala Model may be a peculiarly Scandinavian model of internationalization. Yoshihara's (1978) study of Japanese foreign investment in Southeast Asia is the only non-Scandinavian evidence which supports the Uppsala Model.

A second, and related explanation is that the Uppsala Model represents a description of a particular period in the development of Swedish, or more generally Scandinavian, industry overseas. Hedlund and Kverneland (1985, p. 56) concluded on the basis of a study of Swedish firms operating in Japan that 'entry and growth strategies are changing toward more direct and rapid entry modes than those implied by theories of gradual and slow internationalization processes'. More than half the firms examined in their study went directly from a sales agent to FDI, rather than taking the route via a sales subsidiary.

We wish to develop a further explanation as to why the paths of internationalization in individual markets for our sample of firms diverge from the Uppsala Model. A critical assumption in the Uppsala Model is the notion that for every entrant, and each foreign market entered, there is an identical sequential development. The internationalization process is primarily treated as a step-by-step, country-by-country, repetition of an identical sequence of stages (agent then sales subsidiary then production facility). To explain the incremental character of internationalization, Johanson and Vahlne (1977, 1990) formulated a dynamic model in which the outputs of one set of decisions provide the inputs for the next. Briefly, the basic argument is that the process of internationalization is the consequence of the acquisition of experiential knowledge, in particular market-specific knowledge (i.e. knowledge of local demand and supply conditions, customers, culture, political and institutional systems, etc.). Incremental participation in a market increases the stock of this knowledge. Firms begin by exporting in neighbouring markets using simple, indirect methods such as agents. As knowledge and experience are accumulated they adopt more direct and resource demanding forms of foreign market servicing, such as sales subsidiaries or production facilities. This suggests that market-specific knowledge primarily underpins the development of foreign market servicing arrangements in a country. There is therefore a direct relationship between market-specific knowledge and market commitment. As Johanson and Vahlne (1977, p. 28) conclude, 'the better the knowledge about a market, the more valuable are the resources and the stronger is the commitment to the market'. The underlying assumption is that each entry decision and subsequent modal shift in a market is made in isolation of the decisions in other markets. Hence, decisions relating to market servicing are considered to be driven by market-specific factors. As a consequence the impact of general knowledge (i.e. of operating internationally) on the decision to increase market commitment is viewed as negligible. Even Johanson and Wiedersheim-Paul (1975) recognize that their model does not apply in every situation. They intimate the importance of general knowledge when they write 'We could expect jumps in the establishment chain in firms with extensive experience from other foreign markets' (p. 18).

However, we wish to make this more explicit by arguing that experiential knowledge from within a specific national market represents only one source of information for a firm. As Millington and Bayliss (1990, p. 153) argue, 'international experience, irrespective of the specific foreign market, represents transferable benefits'. This is an argument which has been most clearly articulated in the literature relating to international strategy. Agarwal and Ramaswami (1992) and Kim and Hwang (1992), for example, have argued that it is the knowledge of operating internationally, rather than in specific markets, which is of greater importance. Put differently, a firm's 'global strategic posture has a major impact on its entry mode choice' (Kim and Hwang, 1992, p. 30).

This approach has two important implications for the study of the internationalization process. First, the unit of analysis becomes the operating firm rather than the servicing units in individual countries. Second, the emphasis is on the active management of the interdependencies within the operating firms and between servicing units in each country.

The first point implies that the strategic relationship between foreign operations has an impact on the entry mode decision and subsequent modal shifts. Past experiences, resulting from entry into other markets, feeds into current decisions relating to the form of foreign market servicing adopted in individual markets. Hence, general knowledge of operating internationally has a critical impact on market servicing decisions in individual countries. As a consequence, firms do not necessarily develop incrementally along an identical continuum in each market they enter. This idea is further developed by Welch and Luostarinen (1988) who argue that any leapfrogging within individual markets should be viewed within the historical context of a firm's whole foreign market servicing development. If a firm initially enters different foreign markets via export, and subsequently enters other nations via sales subsidiaries, a move direct to FDI is not a fundamental deviation from an evolutionary model of internationalization. Rather, the sequential development has occurred at the firm level rather than within individual markets. Further reinforcing this point, Welch and Luostarinen (1988) write 'As skills, experience and knowledge in the use of a more advanced form of operations are developed in some foreign markets we might expect that this will eventually allow a company to leapfrog some intermediate steps in others' (p. 163). Thus, they implicitly recognize the importance of general knowledge to market servicing decisions. This suggests that direct moves to FDI within individual markets (i.e. Route 1 in Fig. 2) should not be considered in isolation to the development of operations in other markets. Two case studies from our research can be presented to illustrate this point.

Figure 3 illustrates how one company in the study developed its international operations between 1928 and 1992. In 1928 it entered its first foreign market by establishing a production facility in Ireland. In the 1940s it began exporting to a number of other European countries. Over the next 40 years resource commitments to each of these countries were gradually increased as the company established either a joint venture or sales subsidiary prior to installing a wholly owned production facility. Thus the direct moves to production (Foreign Markets 7 and 8) and sales subsidiaries (Foreign Markets 9 and 10) in the latter part of the 1980s cannot be regarded as a shift away from the sequentialist pattern internationalization. The pattern within individual markets may not be as neat and evolutionary as that indicated by the Nordic case studies, but nevertheless at the level of the

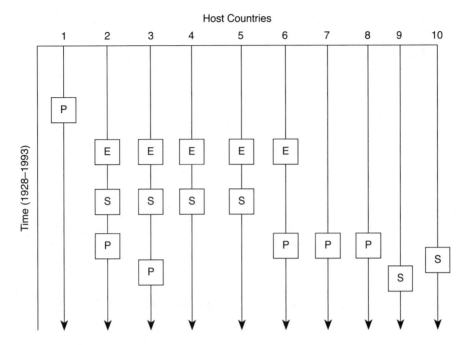

Fig. 3. FMS Development in Company A

operating firm, when account is taken of the institutional developments in all foreign markets, a stepwise pattern is observed.

Figure 4 shows a further example of sequential development at the operating firm level rather than within each market for an organization which is part of a large international group. In this instance the firm tended to enter foreign markets using modes of foreign market servicing which the stages model would regard as advanced operational forms, namely variants of FDI. This is possibly due to the ability of the unit of analysis to utilize knowledge and experience of operating internationally from the group of which it is a part. The firm began its international development with the purchase of a German company which owned production facilities in two further countries. In the 1970s the product technology acquired with the German company was licensed in a further eight foreign markets. In the 1980s these were translated into joint ventures in seven instances, and a wholly owned production facility in one case, as the company sought greater control over its product technology. During the mid to late 1980s the company also directly established three joint ventures (Foreign Markets 13, 14 and 15) and two wholly owned production facilities (Foreign Markets 16 and 17). As with the previous example, these latter four cases of initial entry occurred within a context of a move to modes of foreign market servicing which supported greater control. As Welch and Luostarinen (1988, p. 164) write, 'leapfrogging moves in given markets should be examined as part of the overall operational pattern of the company before any definitive conclusions can be drawn about a 'shift' from the evolutionary pattern'. This is clear support for the earlier suggestion that the focus of analysis should be on the unfolding of the foreign marketing strategy at the operating firm level rather than the servicing units within individual markets.

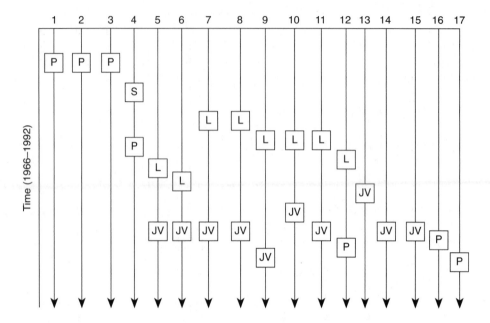

Fig. 4. FMS Development in Company B

The second implication arising from the international strategy literature is that interdependencies between foreign operations mean actions taken in one country have repercussions for units located elsewhere (Hamel and Prahalad, 1985; Kim and Mauborgne, 1988; Watson, 1982). In such instances the collection of institutional arrangements which characterizes a firm's foreign operations is continually assessed in terms of the situation within individual countries and the relationship between countries. There is thus an interplay between market-specific and general knowledge. Consequently, it is feasible that a shift in the mode of foreign market servicing within one country may be due to factors external to that country. Thus, varying the location of one activity has repercussions for activities in other national markets. For example, one firm in our study having already established its own production subsidiary in Spain then acquired a manufacturing company in France. The resulting overcapacity lead to the closure of the Spanish facility since the larger French facility was in a better position to supply both markets.

A related point is that when entering a foreign market firms may have 'motivations which go beyond the narrow calculus of choosing the most efficient entry mode; that is, they may have global strategic motivations' (Kim and Hwang, 1992, p. 35). These motivations range from establishing a competitive scanning post in an otherwise unprofitable market, to sacrificing the revenues of a subsidiary thereby limiting the cash flow of a global competitor and forestalling entry into the firm's domestic market (Hout *et al.*, 1982). The interdependencies between foreign operations mean the losses in one country are cross-subsidized by the profits generated in domestic or protected markets (Bartlett and Ghoshal, 1987).

An example from our research is the case of a UK-based horticultural products firm and its main French competitor. The French firm decided to expand into the UK by marketing its products at a lower price. Given the importance of the UK market to the UK-based firm's revenues, the French firm surmised that it would be unlikely to match its price reductions. Indeed, the UK firm did not react by reducing its prices in the UK. Rather, to use Hout *et al.*'s (1982) terminology, it 'parried' the French firm's attack by using its French sales subsidiary to conduct a massive sales push in the French market. Since the revenues from the French firm's home market were being used to subsidize its activities in the UK it was forced to turn its attention from the UK back to its domestic market and at the same time retract its UK pricing policy rendering its marketing tactic futile and costly.

Following from the previous discussion in seeking to explain the different paths firms take towards FDI, we wish to place greater emphasis on the operating firm level rather than country-specific factors. We suggest that in order to gain a more detailed understanding of the factors which determine the shifts between modes of foreign marketing, account has to be taken of general knowledge obtained from operating internationally, in addition to market-specific knowledge. Firms are repositories of various types of knowledge which assist them to learn about the nature of internationalization. Consequently they are able to pursue a range of options which are not conceivable within the limits of the Uppsala Model's establishment chain. Therefore, progress from exporting to FDI is neither inevitable nor unidirectional since decision making is at a firm rather than at a country-by-country level.

CONCLUSION

These results support the conception that two factors influence the understanding of the choice of, and subsequent shifts between, modes of foreign market servicing: (1) market-specific knowledge; and (2) the generalized knowledge from operating internationally. In the past the main emphasis has been placed on the first factor. In this article we have highlighted the importance of general knowledge which, in conjunction with market-specific knowledge, accounts for the choices and shifts between modes of foreign market servicing. In pursuing this argument we suggest an approach to understanding the process of internationalization which is at the level of the operating firm rather than that of the individual market. The decision of which mode of market servicing to adopt in a particular market is taken within the context of that market *but* more importantly also relates to the factors enumerated above. It is not the market *per se* which determines the institutional form adopted. Rather, as firms operate in foreign markets, they develop both knowledge of the process of internationalization in addition to networks of institutional arrangements. Conducting business in foreign markets is a learning process in which a firm increases its capabilities. This accumulated experience enables firms to bypass the incremental development posited by the Uppsala Model. In fact firms can take a number of routes to internationalization drawing upon their learned experience. In summary, the evidence suggests that understanding the process of internationalization requires an additional focus on the learning processes within the firm rather than a limited focus on the development of market-specific knowledge.

REFERENCES

Agarwal, S. and Ramaswami, S.N. (1992) Choice of foreign market entry mode: impact of ownership, location and internalisation factors. *Journal of International Business Studies* **23**, 1–27.

Andersen, O. (1993) On the internationalization process of firms: a critical analysis. *Journal of International Business Studies* **24**, 209–231.

Barkema, H.G., Bell, J.H.J. and Pennings, J.M. (1996) Foreign entry, cultural barriers and learning. *Strategic Management Journal* **17**, 151–166.

Bartlett, C.A. and Ghoshal, S. (1987) Managing across borders: new organizational responses. *Sloan Management Review* **29**, 43–53.

Bilkey, W.J. and Tesar, G. (1977) The export behaviour of small Wisconsin manufacturing firms. *Journal of International Business Studies* **8**, 93–98.

Buckley, P.J. (1983) New forms of international industrial co-operation: a survey of the literature and special reference to North–South technology transfer. *Aussenwirtschaft* **38**, 195–222.

Buckley, P.J. (1992) Alliances, technology and markets: a cautionary tale. *Studies in International Business*, ed. P.J. Buckley. Macmillan, London.

Buckley, P.J. and Casson, M. (1976) *The Future of the Multinational Enterprise*. Macmillan, London.

Buckley, P.J. and Davies, H. (1981) Foreign licensing in overseas operations: theories and evidence from the UK. In *Research in International Business and Finance*, eds R.G. Hawkins and A.J. Prasad. JAI Press, Greenwich, CT.

Buckley, P.J., Newbould, G.D. and Thurwell, J.C. (1988) *Foreign Direct Investment by Smaller UK Firms: The Success and Failure of First-time Investors*. Macmillan, London.

Buckley, P.J., Pass, C.L. and Prescott, K. (1990) The implementation of an international market servicing strategy in UK manufacturing firms. *British Journal of Management* **1**, 127–136.

Buckley, P.J. and Prescott, K. (1989) The structure of British industry's sales in foreign markets. *Managerial and Decision Economics* **1**, 189–208.

Cavusgil, S.T. (1980) On the internationalization process of firms. *European Research* **8**, 273–281.

Chandy, P.R. and Williams, T.G.E. (1994) The impact of journals and authors on international business research: a citation analysis of JIBS articles. *Journal of International Business Studies* **25**, 715–727.

Clark, T. (1996) *European Human Resource Management*. Blackwell, Oxford.

Clark, T. and Mallory, G. (1992) Cross-cultural organizational research: a methodological minefield. Paper presented to the International Organization Development Association 7th Annual World Conference, Coventry.

Clark, T., Ebster-Grosz, D. and Mallory, G. (1997) From a universalist to a polycentric approach to organizational research. In *Advancement in Organizational Behaviour: Essays in Honour of Derek S. Pugh*, ed. T. Clark, pp. 337–353. Ashgate, Aldershot.

Czinkota, M.R. (1982) *Export Development Strategies: US Promotion Policy*. Praeger, New York.

Dunning, J.H. (1981) *International Production and the Multinational Enterprise*. Allen and Unwin, London.

Dunning, J.H. (1988) *Explaining International Production*. Unwin Hyman, London.

Hamel, G. and Prahalad, C.K. (1985) Do you really have a global strategy? *Harvard Business Review* **63**, 139–148.

Hedlund, G. and Kverneland, A. (1985) Are strategies for foreign markets changing? The case of Swedish investment in Japan. *International Studies of Management and Organization* **15**, 41–59.

Hennart, J.-F. (1982) *A Theory of Multinational Enterprise*, University of Michigan Press, Ann Arbor, MI.

Hill, C.W.L., Hwang, P. and Kim, W.C. (1990) An eclectic theory of the choice of international entry mode. *Strategic Management Journal* **11**, 123–128.

Hout, T., Porter, M.E. and Rudden, E. (1982) How companies win out. *Harvard Business Review* **60**, 98–108.

Hymer, S. (1960) The international operations of national firms: a study of direct foreign investment, Ph.D. dissertation, Massachusetts Institute of Technology, Cambridge, MA.

Hymer, S. (1976) *The International Operations of National Firms: A Study of Direct Foreign Investment*. MIT Press, Cambridge, MA.

Johanson, J. and Vahlne, J.-E. (1977) The internationalization process of the firm – a model of knowledge development and increasing foreign market commitment. *Journal of International Business Studies* **8**, 23–32.

Johanson, J. and Vahlne, J.-E. (1990) The mechanism of internationalization. *International Marketing Review* **7**, 11–24.

Johanson, J. and Wiedersheim-Paul, E. (1975) The internationalization of the firm – four Swedish cases. *Journal of Management Studies* **12**, 305–322.

Kim, W.C. and Hwang, P. (1992) Global strategy and multinationals' entry mode choice. *Journal of International Business Studies* **23**, 29–53.

Kim, W.C. and Mauborgne, R.A. (1988) Becoming an effective global player. *Journal of Business Strategy* **January/February**, 33–37.

Larimo, J. (1985) The foreign direct manufacturing investment behaviour of Finnish companies. Paper presented to the 11th European International Business Association Conference, Glasgow.

Leonidou, L.C. and Katsikeas, C.S. (1996) The export development process: an integrative review of empirical models. *Journal of International Business Studies* **27**, 517–551.

Luostarinen, R. (1980) The internationalization of the firm. *Actua Academica Series A* **30**, Helsinki School of Economics, Helsinki.

Millington, A.I. and Bayliss, B.T. (1990) The process of internationalization: UK companies in the EC. *Management International Review* **30**, 151–161.

Reid, S. (1981) The decision-maker and export entry and expansion. *Journal of International Business Studies* **12**, 101–112.

Reid, S. (1983) Firm internationalization, transaction costs and strategic management. *International Marketing Review* **2**, 44–56.

Reid, S. (1984) Market expansion and firm internationalization. In *International Marketing Management*, ed. E. Kaynak, pp. 167–206. Praeger, New York.

Rogers, E.M. (1962) *History of Economic Analysis*. Free Press, New York.

Root, F.R. (1987) *Entry Strategies for International Markets*. Lexington Books, D.C. Heath and Co., Lexington, MA.

Sullivan, D. and Bauerschmidt, A. (1990) Incremental internationalization: a test of Johanson and Vahlne's thesis. *Management International Review* **30**, 19–30.

Teece, D.J. (1981) The multinational enterprise: market failure and market power considerations. *Sloan Management Review* **22**, 3–17.

Terpstra, V. (1987) *International Marketing*, 4th edn. Dryden Press, New York.

Turnbull, P.W. (1987) A challenge to the stages theory of the internationalization process. In *Managing Export Entry and Expansion*. eds P.J. Rosson and S.D. Reid, pp. 21–40. Praeger, New York.

Turnbull, P.W. and Valla, J.-P. (1986) *Strategies for International Industrial Marketing*. Croom Helm, London.

Watson, C.M. (1982) Counter-competition abroad to protect home markets. *Harvard Business Review* **60**, 40–42.

Welch, L.S. and Luostarinen, R. (1988) Internationalization: evolution of a concept. *Journal of General Management* **14**, 34–64.

Wiedersheim-Paul, F., Olson, H.E. and Welch, L.S. (1978) Pre-export activity: the first steps in internationalization. *Journal of International Business Studies* **9**, 47–58.

Yoshihara, K. (1978) Determinants of Japanese investment in South-East Asia. *International Social Science Journal* **30**.

Young, S. and Hood, N. (1976) Perspectives on the European marketing strategy of US multinationals, *European Journal of Marketing* **10**, 240–256.

Young, S., Hamill, J., Wheeler, C. and Davies, R.J. (1989) *International Market Entry and Development*. Harvester Wheatsheaf, Hemel Hempstead.

Part III

Methods of Foreign Market Servicing

CONTENTS

13

Modes of Foreign Entry: A Transaction Cost Analysis and Propositions

Erin Anderson and Hubert Gatignon

A firm seeking to perform a business function (e.g., production management, distribution) outside its domestic market must choose the best 'mode of entry' (institutional arrangement) for the foreign market. The would-be entrant faces a large array of choices, including: a wholly-owned subsidiary, a joint venture (in which the entrant could be majority, equal, or minority partner), or a nonequity arrangement such as licensing or a contractual joint venture.

The impact of entry modes on the success of foreign operations is great, leading Wind and Perlmutter (1977) to identify entry modes as a 'frontier issue' in international marketing. Entry modes differ greatly in their mix of advantages and drawbacks. The tradeoffs involved are difficult to evaluate and little understood. Several surveys of how firms actually make the entry mode decision (reviewed in Robinson 1978) indicate that few companies make a conscious, deliberate cost/benefit analysis of the options.

What is the best mode of entry for a given function in a given situation? Despite the existence of relevant evidence, the literature does not suggest how the manager should weigh tradeoffs to arrive at a choice that maximizes risk-adjusted return on investment. Instead, much of the literature contains many seemingly unrelated considerations, with no identification of key constructs. Often, a consideration is mentioned as part of a case study, with little indication of how the factor should affect other situations. Further, relevant work is scattered across books and journals in several disciplines, obscured by varying terminology, and separated by differences in problem setup, theory, and method.[1]

The objective of this paper is to develop a theory, expressed in testable propositions, for integrating the literature on entry into a unified framework. The theory which comes from industrial organization is explicitly concerned with weighing tradeoffs and with maximizing an economic criterion: long-term efficiency. In particular, the theory includes interactions between determinants of entry modes, interactions that help resolve contradictory arguments in the literature.

This review develops testable propositions concerning the following question: Under what circumstances is an entry mode the most efficient choice in the long run? Efficiency in general terms is the ratio of output to input. In the international context we mean the entrant's long-run return on its investment in an entry mode, adjusted for risk. Hence, we address the impact of a mode on both the numerator (returns) and denominator (investment) over the long-time horizon.[2]

Section one of this paper categorizes modes of entry into varying degrees of control by the entrant. Section two presents a transaction cost theory of entry modes, which generates a set of propositions. Entry mode research is reviewed in the context of these propositions. The paper concludes with suggestions for empirical research.

MODES OF ENTRY AND CONTROL

The classical approaches to long-term strategic decisions, such as entry mode choice, emphasize choosing the option offering the highest risk-adjusted return on investment in the feasible set. Yet, the literature on the entry mode choice makes little direct mention of risk or return. Instead, the issue is structured in terms of the degree of control each mode affords the entrant (Daniels, Ogram, and Radebaugh 1982, Robinson 1978, Robock, Simmonds, and Zwick 1977, Vernon and Wells 1976). But why such emphasis on control?

The preeminent role of control

Control (the ability to influence systems, methods, and decisions) has a critical impact on the future of a foreign enterprise. Without control, a firm finds it more difficult to coordinate actions, carry out strategies, revise strategies, and resolve the disputes that invariably arise when two parties to a contract pursue their own interests (Davidson 1982). Further, the entrant can use its control to obtain a larger share of the foreign enterprise's profits. In short, control is a way to obtain a higher return.

Yet control, while obviously desirable, carries a high price (Vernon 1983). To take control, the entrant must assume responsibility for decision-making, responsibility a firm may be unwilling or unable to carry out in an uncertain foreign environment. Control also entails commitment of resources, including high overhead. This in turn creates switching costs, reducing the firm's ability to change its institutional arrangement should its choice turn out to be suboptimal. Resource commitment also increases the firm's exposure, i.e., the possibility of losses due to currency changes (Davidson 1982). Thus, to assume control is also to assume some forms of risk.

Control, then, is the focus of the entry mode literature because it is the single most important determinant of both risk and return. High-control modes can increase return and risk. Low-control modes (e.g., licenses and other contractual agreements) minimize resource commitment (hence risk) but often at the expense of returns. Firms trade various levels of control for reduction of resource commitment in the hope of reducing some forms of risk while increasing their returns. Hence, focusing on control is consistent with the classical risk-adjusted return perspective.

The viewpoint adopted in this paper is that international entry mode choices are most usefully and tractably viewed as a tradeoff between control and the cost of resource commitments, often under conditions of considerable risk and uncertainty. Preserving flexibility should be a major consideration of most firms in making the tradeoff. Flexibility, the ability to change systems and methods quickly and at a low cost, is always an important consideration, particularly in lesser-known foreign markets (where the entrant is likely to change systems and methods as it learns the new environment). This view is consistent with Holton (1971), who argues that control, risk, and flexibility are principal considerations (Mascarenhas 1982).

Classifying modes of entry

The object of this review is to suggest major factors that determine what degree of control maximizes long-run efficiency. The theory of the efficiency of modes of entry treated in section two relies on the existence of a mapping to a control dimension but not on any particular mapping. For purposes of illustration, we suggest, in this section, a mapping from entry modes to the degree of control they afford the entrant.

As a caveat, there are many ways to gain control and many variations within any one form of entry mode (Kindleberger 1984, Hayashi 1978). For example, a minority partner might exercise influence out of proportion to ownership, due to such factors as a special contractual arrangement, expertise, or status as a government body. Hence our discussion is very general, and exceptions to our mapping can be found. Consequently, this discussion is intended to demonstrate the feasibility of a mapping, empirical tests of which are independent from the theory proposed in section two. Indeed, a valuable research contribution would be the development of a detailed theory of the relationship between control and governance structure.

A suggested clustering of entry modes

Although there is no tested, accepted theory as to how much control each entry mode affords, both the 'management' (Root 1983) and the 'economic' (Calvet 1981, Caves 1982) streams of research offer information as to the clustering of entry modes. Figure 1 illustrates how 17 entry modes can be grouped in terms of the amount of control (high, medium, low) an entrant gains over the activities of a foreign business entity.

As shown in Figure 1, dominant equity interests (wholly-owned subsidiary or majority shareholder) are expected to offer the highest degree of control to the entrant (Root 1983, Davidson, 1982, Bivens and Lovell 1966, Friedman and Beguin 1971, Killing 1982).

Balanced interests (plurality shareholder, equal partnership and balanced contracts) are shown as medium-control modes based on the notion of a 'credible commitment' (Williamson 1983) or 'hostage.' Firms forming a venture with a high likelihood of trouble (such as equal partnerships) will have difficulty locating a suitable partner. To attract a partner, the entrant may need to put up something to lose, a sort of good-faith collateral, known as credible commitment. For example, in a slightly unbalanced venture, the over 50%-partner may concede favorable contract clauses (such as veto power). These clauses can be so favorable that a firm may have more control with a 49% share than a 51% share (Friedman and Beguin 1971). Or the commitment may be the most critical positions in the foreign entity: the exposed partner can demand to fill them with its own personnel, a method preferred by Japanese multinationals (Hayashi 1978).

In a 50-50 relationship, the hostage is a peculiar one – the venture itself. Friedman and Beguin (1971) point out that equality in equity capital can 'lend a special feeling of partnership to the two partners' (p. 372), adding 'the risk of deadlock itself acts as a powerful incentive to the partners, encouraging them to find solutions to disagreements by discussion and compromise' (p. 377).

In certain nonequity modes, moderate control comes from daily involvement in the operation and from expertise. These modes include:

High-Control Modes: Dominant Equity Interests
Wholly-owned subsidiary
Dominant shareholder (many partners)
Dominant shareholder (few partners)
Dominant shareholder (one partner)

Medium-Control Modes: Balanced Interests
Plurality shareholder (many partners)
Plurality shareholder (few partners)
Equal partner (50/50)
Contractual joint venture
Contract management
Restrictive exclusive contract
  (e.g., distribution agreement, license)
Franchise
Nonexclusive restrictive contract
Exclusive nonrestrictive contract

Low-Contract Modes: diffused Interests
Nonexclusive, nonrestrictive contracts
  (e.g., intensive distribution, some licenses)
Small shareholder (many partners)
Small shareholder (few partners)
Small shareholder (one partner)

Fig. 1. Entry Mode Classified by the Entrant's Level of Control

- *Contract management* (an ongoing relationship) in which the entrant performs specified functions and in which the entrant has representation on the management committee that oversees the venture's activities,
- *Contractual joint ventures*,
- *Restrictive exclusive contracts*,
- *Franchising* (a form of licensing in which the use of a business system is granted).[3] Franchising offers medium control because the typical agreement includes incentives to adhere to the system's rules and allows a high degree of monitoring of the franchisee's activities.
- Contracts that are *exclusive but nonrestrictive* or *nonexclusive but restrictive*. Either restrictiveness or exclusivity give the entrant moderate control, though by different means. Restrictive contracts circumscribe the other party's freedom of action, while exclusive contracts (simultaneously a reward and a protection against competition) motivate the other party to cooperate (Stern and El-Ansary 1982).

Low-control modes are ones in which the entrant has diffused interests. These include nonexclusive, nonrestrictive contracts (multiple unrestricted licenses and intensive distribution) and minority equity positions.

We reiterate here that there are many ways to gain control. Our list is not exhaustive: In particular, we note that entrants may build stable relationships or networks with other parties in which the long-term interests of both parties allow the development of norms. Although this area has received relatively little research attention, developments have been made by Hakansson (1984) and Williamson (1985).

We now turn to propositions concerning the degree of control that is most efficient for a variety of conditions. Given a ranking of entry models on control, it is then possible to recommend an entry mode for a given entry situation.

A TRANSACTION COST ANALYSIS OF FOREIGN MODES OF ENTRY

What is the best entry mode for a given setting? Obviously, a large number of factors bear on the answer. The intent of this review is to propose constructs and mechanisms derived from a unified theoretical framework. This framework is similar to the general approach of several new theories of foreign investment (Kindleberger 1984, Caves 1971, 1982, Hennart 1982, Rugman 1982), which concern why multinational firms exist. In this paper, we develop these theories for one specific issue: choice of mode of entry. Our analysis builds on the existing literature by proposing detailed relationships between constructs corresponding to the ideas presented in the more general theories. As we develop these empirically testable propositions, we contrast them with predictions from other, frequently more well-known frameworks to suggest how they differ and to spur empirical research designed to sort out competing predictions. We also review findings that bear on each proposition.

Our mapping from governance structure to control (Figure 1) looks something like a progression from less integrated to more integrated. Williamson (1979) suggests that degree of integration proceeds from complete non-integration (classical marketing contracting between two parties) to complete integration (one entity 'contracts' internally to perform a function), passing through intermediate points. Underlying this progression is the transference of authority from paper (a contract) to entities (arbitrators, parties to a transaction), culminating in the consolidation of authority by one party. This progression of authority is a growing degree of control.

Control and integration are closely related, since integration gives a firm legitimate authority to direct operations. Hence, we employ a theory of vertical integration to generate propositions about the desirability of various modes of entry offering various degrees of control. The theory, transaction cost analysis, combines elements of industrial organization, organization theory, and contract law to weigh the tradeoffs to be made in vertical integration (and by extension, degree of control) decisions.

We begin with the assumption that the market being entered has at least enough potential that the firm can recoup the overhead of a high-control entry mode. If this is not the case, high-control modes are not worth considering (Williamson 1979). However, for markets large enough to break even on the fixed cost of a high-control mode, the entrant has a choice to make. In these circumstances, the efficiency of an entry mode depends on four constructs that determine the optimal degree of control, following a transaction cost analysis. These constructs are:

1. *transaction-specific assets*: investments (physical and human) that are specialized to one or a few users or uses;
2. *external uncertainty*: the unpredictability of the entrant's external environment;
3. *internal uncertainty*: the entrant's inability to determine its agents' performance by observing output measures;
4. *free-riding potential*: agents' ability to receive benefits without bearing the associated costs.

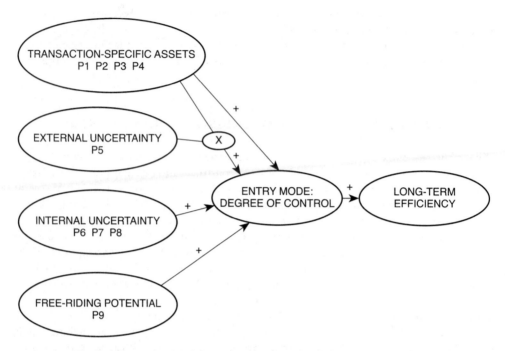

Fig. 2. A Transaction Cost Framework for Analyzing the Efficiency of Entry Modes

Figure 2 is an overview of the framework, which shows that these four factors should be positively associated with the entrant's degree of control. The four factors, their rationale, and their corresponding propositions about entry modes are discussed one by one in this section.

Figure 3 restates the propositions in a more accessible form and lists the conditions under which the modes in the high-control cluster are most appropriate.

TRANSACTION-SPECIFIC ASSETS

Transaction cost analysis approaches the entry mode question with the following promise: a low level of ownership is preferable until proven otherwise. We label this premise the 'default' hypothesis.

The default hypothesis accords with an assumption fundamental to economics, that is, that market outcomes tend to be efficient when competition is strong. Competitive pressures drive parties to perform effectively at low cost and to deal with each other in fairness, honesty, and good faith lest they be replaced. Hayashi (1978) gives the example of foreign sales agents competing to carry out distribution for a Japanese entrant. Hayashi finds that where competition among agents is active, the resulting business relationship is highly cooperative. In general, where suppliers of a good or service are readily available, a firm may take advantage of their expertise and economies of scope and scale in performing their specialized function by writing a contract with one supplier, confident that a new supplier may be found if the relationship is unsatisfactory (Williamson 1981b). Accordingly, firms are advised to avoid integration whenever the supplier market is competitive. In this way, the firm can have both a high return and low risk.

By not integrating (or investing directly), a firm avoids the drawbacks of a company division. Overhead is minimized, as is company politics, communication distortion, and the possibility that an inside division will become obsolete or inefficient because it is shielded from the pressures of daily competition for contracts (Williamson 1975).

Integration (or direct investment) is, however, justified when the market mechanism no longer encourages performance, i.e., when competitive pressure is low. Williamson (1979) argues that most transactions begin when competition is intense but some degenerate into lock in ('small numbers bargaining') when the contract partner becomes irreplaceable. Then the partner may extract new contract terms, become inflexible, and otherwise violate the letter and spirit of the agreement ('opportunistic' behavior, i.e., self-interest seeking with guile) with relative impunity.

Degeneration into lock in occurs when 'transaction-specific assets' of considerable value accumulate. These are investments (physical and human) that are valuable only in a narrow range of transactions, that is, specialized to one or a few users or uses (Williamson 1981b). An example of a physical transaction-specific asset is a stamping machine to make parts to the specifications of one manufacturer (Klein, Crawford, and Alchian 1972). Human transaction-specific assets include working relationships and knowledge of the idiosyncrasies of a firm and its activities. Transaction-specific assets usually develop over time, coming to assume a larger role the longer the transaction has continued. Frequently these experienced-based assets are not very valuable. But where they significantly contribute to performance, the partner who acquires them becomes hard to replace.

When transaction-specific assets are likely to become valuable, transaction cost analysis suggests that firms are better off either integrating the function (exerting maximum control) or redesigning tasks so that general purpose assets will suffice. If the firm integrates, it will still become locked in, but to employees rather than outsiders. Opportunism can be combatted by exercising legitimate authority, monitoring behavior, and offering more varied incentives than can be used with outsiders. If instead the firm redesigns the task, it loses the value generated by specialized assets. However, both small numbers bargaining and overhead can be avoided, which sometimes offsets the loss of specialization benefits.

The preceding discussion has focused on ownership as a means of exerting control. More recent developments in transaction cost analysis (see Williamson 1985 for a summary) have begun to stress other ways to gain control, ways that fall in the large zone between classical market contracting and vertical integration. Many of the arrangements found in international operations fall into this zone (relational contracting). Research that explores the development of relational contracts promises to make a valuable contribution to our understanding of modes of entry (see Hakansson 1984).

We now turn to four propositions applying the notion of transaction-specific assets to the entry mode decision. The appropriate entry mode is a function of a number of variables taken simultaneously. For clearer exposition, our propositions deal with one factor at a time.

When Dominant Entry Interests Are		When Balanced Interests Are		When Diffused Interests Are	
Conditions	**Based on**	**Conditions**	**Based on**	**Conditions**	**Based on**
Transaction-Specific Assets		_Transaction-Specific Assets_		_Transaction-Specific Assets_	
Products or processes highly proprietary	P1	Products or processes moderately proprietary	P1	Products or processes not proprietary (open knowledge)	P1
Products or processes unstructured, ill understood	P2	Products or processes semi-structured, moderately well understood	P2	Products or processes well structured, routinely understood	P2
Products highly customized to each user	P3	Products adaptable to user groups	P3	Products complete standardization	P3
Introductory and growth stages or product life cycle	P4	Later growth and early maturity stages of product life cycle	P4	Mature stage of product life cycle	P4
Interaction: Transaction-Specific Assets/External Uncertainty		_Interaction: Asset Specificity/External Uncertainty_		_Interaction: Transaction-Specific Assets/External Uncertainty_	
Products or processes highly proprietary _and_ political or economic instability acute	P5	Products or processes somewhat proprietary _and_ political or economic instability moderate	P5	Products or processes not proprietary _and_ political or economic instability acute	P5
Products processes unstructured, ill understood, _and_ political or economic instability acute	P5	Products processes semi-structured, moderately well understood, _and_ political or economic instability moderate	P5	Products or processes well structured, routinely understood, _and_ political or economic instability acute	P5
Products highly customized to each user _and_ political or economic instability acute	P5	Products adaptable to user groups _and_ political or economic instability moderate	P5	Products completely standardized _and_ political or economic instability acute	P5
Introductory and growth stages of product life cycle _and_ political or economic instability acute	P5	Later growth or early maturity stages of product life cycle _and_ political or economic instability moderate	P5	Mature stage of product life cycle _and_ political or economic instability acute	P5
Internal Uncertainty		_Internal Uncertainty_		_Internal Uncertainty_	
Firm has considerable international experience	P6	Firm has moderate degree of international experience	P6	Firm has little international experience	P6
Sociocultural distance is great	P7b	Sociocultural distance is moderate	P7a, P7b	Sociocultural distance is great	P7a
Benefits of doing business the entrant's way are large	P7c	Modest benefits to doing business the entrant's way	P7c	Small (if any) benefits to doing business the entrant's way	P7c
Foreign business community is very small	P8	Foreign business community is of substantial size	P8	Foreign business community is very large	P8
Free-Riding Potential		_Free-Riding Potential_		_Free-Riding Potential_	
Brand name is extremely valuable	P9	Brand name carries some value	P9	Brand name not valued	P9

Fig. 3. When a Mode of Entry is Most Efficient

Transaction-specific assets: proposition 1

The concept of transaction-specific assets suggests the following proposition:

P1:   Modes of entry offering greater control are more efficient for highly proprietary products or processes.

Proprietary knowledge is an important type of specialized asset. On the surface, proprietary products and processes would seem appropriate for a low level of control, licensing, because there is something of value to license (Root 1983). Indeed, firms with high R&D expenditures (which generate proprietary knowledge), do more licensing *per se* (Caves 1981). However, Calvet (1981) points out that proprietary knowledge is subject to hazards of transmission and valuation. Such knowledge is often ill codified and difficult to transmit across organizational boundaries. Furthermore, the classic problem of valuation of information arises: the buyer cannot know what the knowledge is worth (what bid to make) unless the knowledge is disclosed, at which point the acquirer need not pay for it. This obliges information-holders to exploit it themselves, resulting in high levels of ownership, and hence control, of a foreign business entity. Ownership has the added advantage of encouraging teamwork and keeping the (employee) team together (Williamson 1981b).

If a particular practice is efficient and an industry is competitive, we may expect to see firms that have survived in that industry following the efficient practice (Lilien 1979). Hence, systematic practices that firms follow constitute information about what mode is efficient. In the entry mode literature, it appears that firms do exert more control as proprietary content increases. Research and development expenditures (which generate proprietary knowledge) increase the extent of licensing (Telesio 1979) but increase the extent of direct investment even more (Davidson and McFetridge 1984, Caves 1982, Davidson 1982). Stopford and Wells find a negative relationship between research and development expenditures and the proportion of subsidiaries organized as joint venture rather than wholly-owned subsidiaries. This implies that firms tend to reserve proprietary knowledge for entry vehicles they control completely. In a similar vein, Coughlan and Flaherty (1983) study the use of wholly-owned distribution (high control) vs. independent distribution (low control) by U.S. semiconductor manufacturers operating in foreign markets. They find that high control is more often employed for technically sophisticated products, which tend to have higher proprietary content than unsophisticated products. This corresponds to a finding in the literature on intra-firm trading, which considers the extent to which a multinational firm manufactures its own inputs and markets its own outputs. Intra-firm trade indicates that a firm not only is integrated (common ownership) but acts integrated (is self-sufficient). Hence, the forces that drive integration (high control) should also drive intra-firm trading (Lall 1978). Lall (1978) and Helleiner and Lavergne (1979) find that intra-firm trading is strongly related to R&D spending, an oft-used proxy for proprietary content and technological sophistication.

Transaction-specific assets: proposition 2

Another implication of the concept of asset specificity is:

P2:   Entry modes offering higher degrees of control are more efficient for unstructured, poorly-understood products and processes.

It is particularly difficult to use low-control entry modes for more ill-structured, poorly-understood activities and knowledge. Teece (1976) refers to a 'common code' of understanding is a transaction-specific asset that is critical for amorphous functions (Johanson and Vahlne 1977). Teece (1976), in a path-breaking empirical study of technology transfer costs, strongly supports this idea. He finds that the costs of the entrant's first transfer across national boundaries are much higher than the costs of subsequent transfers. This occurs because the first transfer is ill understood. Thus, development personnel must interact heavily with production personnel to solve the inevitable unforeseen problems. Fortunately, the firm moves down the learning curve by developing and codifying solutions, which are applied to subsequent transfers of this technology. For such ill-structured, poorly understood activities as first transfers of technology, high-control entry modes are preferable to preserve and extend the common code of understanding.

Teece (1983) suggests complexity is a proxy for the degree to which products and processes are ill-structured and poorly understood. In accordance with proposition 2, Wilson (1980) finds licensing (low control) is more common for simpler products, while direct investment (higher control) is more common for complex products. Davidson and McFetridge (1984) find that radical new products are more likely to be transferred to a virtually wholly-owned affiliate (at least 95% equity) than to an independent firm (less than 5% equity).

Transaction-specify assets: proposition 3

P3:   Entry modes offering higher degrees of control are more efficient for products customized to the user.

Customized products demand considerable local knowledge. On the surface, this presents no difficulties, since the entrant can contract with a local independent entity that has that knowledge. But by the nature of customization, the entrant must work actively with the local entity to tailor the product to the user. Accordingly, working relationships must be developed between personnel from each company (contractor and contractee). Those relationships will include a knowledge of what to expect from individuals and of how to communicate. These working relationships constitute an asset specific to the contractor-contractee transaction. Holton (1971), Keegan (1974), and Kobrin et. al. (1980) note the strong reliance of decision-makers on such relationships when assessing other foreign opportunities, which underscores their importance. Since these relationships exist only with the current contractee, the entrant is locked in. Team effects have been created, and control is needed to preserve them (Williamson 1981b).

Johanson and Vahlne (1977) suggest that people-intensive tasks are particularly ill-structured. If so, we would expect such customized businesses as management consulting, banking, and advertising to be dominated by high-control entry modes. Caves (1981) surveys anecdotal evidence that service firms such as these are more likely than other firms to go abroad, often at the urging of domestic clients making their own international entries. Presumably, this occurs because clients want to preserve and extend the intimate knowledge and working relationship already built up with service firms. Weinstein (1974), in his survey of U.S. advertising agencies expanding abroad, finds over 60% of foreign affiliates are at least majority-owned by the parent agency. In distribution, Coughlan and Flaherty (1983) find high-control distribution methods used more often for products with high service requirements, a characteristic of customized products.

Transaction-specific assets: proposition 4

P4:   The more mature the product class, the less control firms should demand of a
      foreign business entity.

Immature product classes have a high proprietary content (Chandler 1977), raising the
transmission and valuation problems mentioned earlier. Further, technological and market
knowledge of a new product class is not yet common. Hence, only the innovator's
personnel know the product and its markets. To avoid becoming locked in to outsiders who
acquire that knowledge, control is required. Thus, newer technology is likely to be handled
by wholly-owned subsidiaries (high control) (Williamson 1979).

Specialized knowledge comes into the open market as the innovation diffuses. Over time
transaction-specific assets associated with an innovation become general purpose assets
associated with a well-established product. Chandler (1977) documents this diffusion for
products and processes that were an innovation in the U.S. in the nineteenth century. As this
diffusion occurs, we should expect to see less integration, as less administrative control is
needed. Hence, older technology is likely to be licensed or handled by a joint venture (lower
control) (Williamson 1979).[4]

In the international entry mode literature, Weinstein (1974) finds that U.S. advertising
agencies entered foreign markets beginning in 1915, when large-scale advertising was a novel
way of doing business. Consistent with P4, Weinstein finds that the first advertising agencies
going abroad were highly likely to start subsidiaries from scratch and to own them 100%. In
later years, when advertising became common, U.S. entrants became more likely to acquire
existing firms and to take less equity, often minority positions.

Teece (1976) finds that technology transfer costs (absorbed by transferor and transferee)
decline sharply in mature product classes (measured by the age of the technology and the
number of competitors using similar or competing technology). Because the requisite
knowledge is well codified and widely available for hire, the entrant does not need to
supplement the control offered by the market mechanism.

This product class effect has been suggested for various reasons in the entry mode
literature. One reason advanced is that the likely gains are lower with mature products, so
that management will prefer investing resources in more promising sectors (Bivens and Lovell
1966). Another explanation is that firms with immature products are in a better bargaining
position with local authorities. Because their product is difficult to duplicate, they can force
host governments and local partners to grant them more ownership and control and do not
need the expertise of partners (Bivens and Lovell 1966, Davidson 1982). As the product
matures, the advantage erodes, creating pressure to give up control. Vernon (1977) calls this
the 'obsolescing bargain.'

We now turn to propositions about the impact of external uncertainty, the second of the
four transaction cost constructs, on the viability of entry modes.

EXTERNAL UNCERTAINTY

External uncertainty is the volatility (unpredictability) of the firm's environment. Williamson
(1979) hypothesizes that firms should react to volatility by avoiding ownership, since it
commits them to one operation that may not be appropriate when the next environmental

shift occurs. Rather, firms should retain flexibility and shift risk to outsiders. This suggests that in the absence of transaction-specific assets, the default option, market contracting, is unchanged by volatility. We should not expect higher-control entry modes to be more efficient than lower-control modes in volatile settings.

But what if transaction-specific assets accumulate such that the entrant becomes locked in to a partner in a shifting environment? Then flexibility, the major reason not to integrate in the face of uncertainty, is lost anyway. Further, frequent shifts mean frequent negotiation of new arrangements, presenting the agent with many occasions to behave opportunistically and inflexibly. In short, uncertain environments aggravate the normal difficulty of working with irreplaceable agents, making the combination of uncertainty and specificity a potent double bind. This suggests that given some degree of asset specificity, control becomes more desirable as uncertainty increases.

This idea is represented in Figure 3. The horizontal line (no transaction-specific assets) indicates that without specificity (TSA), uncertainty should be unrelated to the degree of control sought. But given specificity, marked by an X, uncertainty increases the need for control. The strength of this relationship increases as specificity increases.

External uncertainty: proposition 5

In international operations, external uncertainty (unpredictability) is an important factor. External uncertainty is typically labeled 'country risk,' which can take many forms, e.g., political instability, economic fluctuations, currency changes (Herring 1983).[5] Some writers argue that firms react to unpredictability by exerting control to manage their volatile affairs and resolve disputes (Killing 1982, Bivens and Lovell 1966). Unfortunately, this commits the entrant to an operation that may turn out to be inappropriate as unforeseen circumstances develop (Root 1983). Further, in volatile environments, a product or technology may be obsolete by the time a high-control administrative mechanism is in place. Hence, firms may license in fast-changing industries simply to get their returns before they disappear (Caves 1981).

Transaction cost analysis suggests that in volatile environments, entrants are better off accepting low-control entry modes (the 'default option'). This not only avoids resource commitment but frees entrants to change partners or renegotiate contract terms and working arrangements relatively easily as circumstances develop and change.[6] Low control maintains flexibility – unless flexibility has already been lost through the accumulation of transaction-specific assets.

Hence:

P5:   The greater the *combination* of country risk (e.g., political instability, economic fluctuations) and transaction-specificity of assets (proprietary content, poorly understood products, customization, product class immaturity), the higher the appropriate degree of control.

This proposition is an interaction,[7] expressed as an X in Figure 2, and occurs in addition to the effect of asset specificity alone (propositions 1 through 4). An interaction implies that each source of unpredictability should interact to magnify (add to) the separate impact of each source of transaction-specific assets: the proprietary nature of products and processes (P1), ill-understood products and processes (P2), customizing products to the user (P3), and the immaturity of a product class (P4). An entrant in these circumstances is likely to find the problems of managing irreplaceable agents magnified, since the risky, changing environment presents numerous occasions for agents to shirk and to renegotiate to their advantage.

In a nutshell, proposition 5 suggests that environmental unpredictability plays a major role when asset specificity is high, magnifying the need for control that specificity creates. When specificity is low, unpredictability does not change the default option, low control, for the firm can deal with unpredictability by changing agents. Instead of exerting control (and assuming the corresponding risk), the entrant can retain flexibility and let the competitive market mechanism operate to generate returns (Mascarenhas 1982).

INTERNAL UNCERTAINTY

The third factor in the transaction cost framework is internal uncertainty. Internal uncertainty exists when the firm cannot accurately assess its agents' performance by objective, readily available output measures. This may occur when good measures of output are not available, or when the relationship between inputs and outputs is ill-understood (Ouchi 1977), making it difficult to specify what performance level to expect. Uncertainty internal to the firm makes control more desirable regardless of the level of asset specificity involved (Williamson 1981a). When performance cannot be specified or measured easily, firms can monitor inputs rather than evaluate outputs. Further, firms can use a variety of subtle incentives to develop goal congruence and loyalty. Thus, employees may act in the firm's best interest even if a firm cannot precisely specify what to do.

When internal uncertainty is high, control is needed to impose subjective judgement and to monitor inputs (behavior). This presupposes that management knows how people should behave and how to judge hard-to-quantify results. In the domestic environment, this is likely to be the case, as management has learned to manage over time. But the international setting is another matter. Entrants new to the international setting are unlikely to know how to overcome internal uncertainty. Further, firms that operate in competitive industries and try to exert control before they know how to use it will make serious errors that should depress efficiency (Teece 1976, p. 46).

Internal uncertainty: proposition 6

Accordingly,

P6:   The entrant's degree of control of a foreign business entity should be positively related to the firm's cumulative international experience.

Proposition 6 has been extensively discussed in the literature that describes what managers do (which may or may not be efficient). There is some indication that firms do behave according to this proposition. A popular conception in the international management literature is that of a firm as a humanlike entity, 'maturing' (Stopford and Wells 1972) as it acquires experience in international markets. The international neophyte fears the unknown, consequently overstating risks and understating returns of international markets (Davidson 1980). Overly conservative, the firm avoids setting up a foreign business entity and merely exports (Bilkey 1978). With the limited experience of exporting, the firm gains confidence and becomes more aggressive in nondomestic markets, moving toward more direct investment rather than export (Bilkey 1978, Weston and Sorge 1972) or licensing (Telesio 1979).

Still hesitant, the firm selects nearby, culturally similar countries (Engwall 1984, Davidson 1980, Bilkey 1978). With experience comes enhanced understanding, competence, and confidence, as well as more accurate perception of foreign risks and returns. The firm enters more distant, different countries (Davidson 1980) and with new adventuresomeness acquires a taste for control, for active management of the entity (Root 1983). Unlike the neophyte firm, content to let someone else run the international side of the business, the more experienced firm is confident, assertive, desirous of control, and willing to take risks to get it. Further, the firm has probably set up a headquarters staff for international operations and is eager to get the most from this overhead (Davidson 1980, 1982). Accordingly, experience should lead to more control, which proposition 6 suggests is the most efficient outcome.

Proposition 6 is not without controversy in the descriptive literature. Conceivably, the relationship between international experience and the *observed* degree of ownership is negative, i.e., that inexperienced firms demand higher ownership levels than do more experienced firms. This argument is based on the ethnocentric orientation of many international neophytes. Ethnocentrism leads inexperienced firms to demand to have their own nationals in key positions, which is easier to achieve via ownership than negotiation (Weichmann and Pringle 1979). Over time, firms become comfortable with local differences, develop working relationships with local people, and become confident that they can use local expertise to their advantage. At this point, firms are more willing to delegate control (Shetty 1979), which is reflected in lower degrees of ownership.

This counter-argument is a market power proposal: it assumes that firms have the latitude to follow their preferences even if the result is inefficient. In contrast, transaction cost analysis assumes inefficient practices are extinguished by market pressures. This implies that in noncompetitive industries, we may observe that the entrant's degree of control is negatively related to the firm's international experience. In other words, an inefficient practice may be observed where managers have the slack to implement their preferences at the sacrifice of long-term results.

Internal uncertainty: proposition 7

A particularly potent form of internal uncertainty is created by socio-cultural distance. The difference between home and host cultures, although difficult to measure, has intrigued researchers in the international area. It is often argued that the greater the sociocultural difference between home and host countries, the lower the degree of control an entrant should and does demand. This is explained by the higher uncertainty executives perceive in cultures that are truly 'foreign' to them. Not knowing, being comfortable with, or even agreeing with the values and operating methods of the host country, executives may shy away from the involvement that accompanies ownership (Root 1983, Davidson 1980, 1982, Richman and Copen 1972). Uncertainty due to sociocultural distance may also cause executives to undervalue foreign investments (Root 1983). Further, transferring home management techniques and values is difficult where the operating environment is very dissimilar to that of the home country (Richman and Copen 1972, Alpander 1976). Finally, sociocultural distance also creates high information costs, which firms may avoid by turning management over to partners or licensees (Root 1983).

Goodnow and Hansz (1972) support this viewpoint in an empirical study of how much control large U.S. firms exert when going overseas. Via cluster analysis, they sort 100 countries into three groups that roughly correspond to increasing sociocultural distance from the United States. Goodnow and Hansz also group entry modes into three types: strong control/high investment, moderate control/modest investment, and weak control/low investment. They find firms reduce their control and investment as they move away from socioculturally similar countries.

Not all writers agree. The Conference Board (Bivens and Lovell 1966) suggests that some firms react to sociocultural distance by demanding rather than avoiding ownership so that they may impose their operating methods. Such firms do not trust local management or non-local partners and prefer the control to 'do it their way.' Richman and Copen (1972) point out that being foreign gives a firm latitude to be different, to break the rules of the local culture to a point, because foreigners are expected to do things differently. Hymer (1976) contends that local firms, because they do not have the disadvantage of operating in a foreign culture at a distance, will always outperform foreign firms unless the entrants have a distinctive advantage. On occasion operating methods that do not fit local culture will constitute the necessary advantage that enables foreigners to compete with locals on their home ground.

In short, the entry mode literature conflicts concerning the impact of sociocultural distance. Transaction cost analysis suggests both views are correct for the following reason. Sociocultural distance makes internal uncertainty very high, since the environment is unknown. Furthermore, an entrant transferring its operating procedures and methods to a very different setting will have to train its agents heavily. Once they learn the entrant's ways, agents will have acquired valuable knowledge and relationships that are of little use to other firms in that country, making these assets transaction-specific (see Richman and Copen for examples). Given that the management problems created by sociocultural distance are now aggravated by specificity, an entrant is better off to demand control.

Alternatively, the entrant may decide to give up the benefits of employing its own methods, design an operation that uses local (general purpose) methods, and have little control. This is the design reaction to the prospect of specific assets. With specificity designed out, the problems of socio-cultural distance can be managed by transferring risk to external agents, thereby reducing flexibility. If the foregone specialization benefits are not too large, designing out specificity is the efficient solution.

Which is the more efficient reaction to sociocultural distance: creating specificity and using a high-control mode or designing out specificity ('going native') and using a low-control mode? The answer depends on the gains from doing business in unconventional foreign ways for a given culture. Transaction cost analysis suggests the effect of cultural differences is as follows:

P7:   When sociocultural distance is great:
    a: Low-control levels are more efficient than intermediate levels;
    b: High-control levels are more efficient than intermediate levels;
    c: High-control levels are more efficient only when there is a substantial advantage to doing business in the entrant's way.

Proposition 7c suggests that when operating in a very different environment, 'our way' is not automatically the best way. Put differently, the default option, low control, should not be given up without a reason. Proposition 7b reflects the control reaction to sociocultural distance: a firm running an operation in a very different culture is bound to manage 'our way,' therefore creating specificity. The control that created lock in is now needed to manage it, but the firm benefits from its freedom to operate unconventionally. In contrast, proposition

7a reflects the design reaction to sociocultural distance: lacking control, a firm manages 'as it's done here,' losing specialization benefits but avoiding lock in. Intermediate levels of control are undesirable because they offer the worst of both possibilities – neither freedom to be unconventional nor low commitment to be flexible.

As a corollary, entrants are unlikely to write contracts with outsiders that impose the entrant's style on the contractee. By so doing, the entrant would enter small numbers bargaining without gaining much control over the partner. A testable implication is that franchising, which by nature imposes a management style on an independent, should decline as sociocultural distance increases.

Internal uncertainty: proposition 8

Richman and Copen (1972) point out that the problems of sociocultural distance can diminish over time even if the culture is stable. This occurs because as more foreign firms enter the country, the pool of local personnel trained in these methods grows. Not only do firms train managers, but their presence arouses awareness, which in turn causes host-country nationals to obtain a business education abroad. The process is slow but has a cumulative effect (which Richman and Copen detail in the case of India). Eventually, the pool is large enough that an entrant finds enough local contractees available to constitute an open market in management skills. In short, these skills have diffused to become general purpose and readily available rather than narrowly available and specific to the few companies using them. This suggests:

> P8:   The larger the foreign business community in the host country, the lower the level of control an entrant should demand.

Proposition 8 occurs because over time the entrant will find multinational management skills widely available, in spite of sociocultural distance (Seidler 1972 details this process for the transfer of American-style accounting methods to less developed countries). This diffusion of skills removes a major barrier to licensing (a low-control mode), which is the unavailability of 'suitable' local firms (Caves 1981). Hence, management of the foreign entity can be contracted out to a pool of knowledgeable personnel, not necessarily employees, who can be controlled by the threat of replacement. In this vein, Contractor (1984) finds evidence that licensing becomes more lucrative relative to direct investment as a country's indigenous technical capability increases.

FREE-RIDING POTENTIAL

A potential control problem arises whenever one party can 'free ride' on the efforts of others, receiving benefits without bearing costs. For example, McDonald's has charged its French franchisee with riding on the company's international goodwill and recognition to attract customers without maintaining the cleanliness standards that support the company name (*Time* 1981). Transaction cost analysis suggests that ceteris paribus, where the potential for free-riding ('demand externalities') is high, entry modes offering higher control are more efficient.

Free-riding potential: proposition 9

This suggests:

P9:   Entry modes offering higher degrees of control are more efficient the higher the value of a brand name.

When a brand name is valuable, short-term gains can be had at the expense of the long term. Firms will take control to protect their brand name from degradation by free-riders (Davidson 1982) or to prevent the local operation from using the name in an inconsistent manner, thus diluting or confusing the international positioning of the brand (Holton 1971). Caves (1981) highlights the danger of local partners, who have less to lose from degrading a brand than does the entrant. Caves reviews both anecdotal and survey evidence that firms demand higher ownership levels when standardization of the product's design, style, quality, and name is part of the entrant's strategy. Since the strategy depends on assurance of all the name connotes (a 'goodwill asset' or 'reputation effect'), quality control is critical and free-riding is especially damaging.

These findings suggest high control is appropriate for heavily advertised brands. However, there is some contradiction in the empirical literature. Lall (1978) and Helleiner and Lavergne (1979) find that high advertising levels are associated with low intra-firm trading (low integration, low control), suggesting that valuable brand names can be efficiently marketed via low-control entry modes. Their explanation is that heavily advertised products tend to be unsophisticated consumer goods, which many agents are capable of handling, making low control appropriate. This explanation is consistent with propositions 1 through 4 concerning transaction-specific assets.

Yet heavy advertising does make free-riding more likely and control more desirable. This situation illustrates the value of the default option (low control) in transaction cost analysis. Beginning from low-control modes, a firm is advised to exert more control for valuable brand names (e.g., more heavily advertised brands). Hence, a firm is better off franchising its heavily advertised brands rather than merely licensing them in non-restrictive, non-exclusive fashion. However, the firm may not need to go so far as a joint venture or majority-owned affiliate. Proposition 9 proposes that more restraints be added (higher-control entry modes) as brand value increases, rather than proposing that high control is always appropriate. Hence proposition 9 fits the empirical literature and illustrates the control-flexibility tradeoff.

STRATEGIES FOR EMPIRICAL TESTS

The measurement strategy used by researchers to date has largely consisted of using single-item measures that are themselves proxy variables (e.g., R&D spending to indicate the construct 'extent of proprietary information'). This approach, which is practical in light of the difficulty of obtaining international data, has yielded promising results. Clearly, hypothesis testing would be even stronger if psychometric methods were used to develop composite measures of each construct, thereby reducing reliance on single-item measures of complex constructs.[8] One advantage of this method is that the interpretability of findings using proxy variables would be greatly enhanced if they were embedded in a composite measure. Further, the proxy variable approach would be a stronger test if researchers were able to rule out alternative explanations by controlling for the impact of a greater range of covariates than is typical in entry mode studies.

These suggestions are particularly useful for researchers designing their own data collection instruments, which allows them greater degrees of freedom in their approach and provides a closer correspondence between theory and data (Williamson 1985). Outside the entry mode field, some research involving primary data collection has resulted in multi-item measures of transaction cost constructs. These measures are described in Walker and Weber (1984), Anderson (1985), and Anderson and Coughlan (1985).

An empirical test of transaction cost propositions is incomplete without the inclusion of two classes of predictor variables. One class concerns government restrictions, which narrow the feasible set of entry modes (Teece 1984). The other class concerns 'production cost' factors, e.g., taxes, labor costs, and transportation costs. Ultimately, an efficient entry mode is based on the sum of production and transaction (governance) costs, given the feasible set. Production cost factors correlated with transaction cost factors will bias estimates of effects unless included as covariates. Further, a more complete picture of entry modes emerges when production factors are considered (Williamson 1985).[9]

A direct test of the long-term efficiency of an entry mode would be difficult to make. Efficiency data are highly proprietary and, even if obtainable, reflect potentially large short-run effects. We suggest that an appropriate and more tractable empirical research approach is to study prevailing practice (usage of entry modes) in competitive industries, which tend to extinguish inefficient choices (Lilien 1979). An example would be to predict the impact of explanatory variables on the odds of choosing a higher-control mode over a lower-control mode at a given point in time.

An approach that is even closer to the long-term nature of the propositions is to study what practices survive over time (e.g., using a hazard rates model). Although the time dimension introduces new variables, it does approximate the working out of inappropriate choices.

CONCLUSION

The transaction cost propositions advanced here are not suggested as an all-inclusive answer. Other factors will of course enter and may be very powerful in some settings. As indicated earlier, the framework applies to an entry decision where the choice is real. For a firm already operating in a foreign market with an existing mode of operation, the concepts discussed in this paper are certainly relevant. However, additional factors related to switching costs must be considered. The proposed framework also has limited value in situations where governmental, competitive, or information restrictions eliminate a large number of options. Nonetheless, the transaction cost approach is a useful way to structure the issues. This is particularly helpful when dealing with poorly understood issues and a long list of potentially relevant variables whose direction of effect is difficult to predict.

Simplification is a critical first step when dealing with complex problems. Our analysis ignores or downplays considerations that play a major role in some settings. In particular, we assume that an entrant, having decided to operate in a given market, has a choice of entry modes. This ignores possible government restrictions and assumes the entrant is contemplating a volume of business sufficient to carry the overhead of a high-control entry mode, at least over the long run (Williamson 1979). Further, we do not consider possible interactions between decision to enter and choice of entry mode.

Finally, we assume the entrant wants to operate a profitable business venture in the host country. To the extent that a foreign operation's objectives may be subordinate to the strategy needs of a parent multinational, other objectives may take precedence. In turn, the multinational's need to trade off subsidiary profits for system profits obliges the MNC to exert more control than the transaction cost default option suggests (Caves 1982). In general, higher degrees of control are more appropriate for entrants that closely coordinate global strategies.

Given these limitations, what can be gained from the framework proposed here? Much of the literature on modes of entry does not suggest hypotheses but considerations. The pros and cons of, say, licensing, are weighed against an alternative that is usually unspecified. Hence, predictions are difficult to make. In contrast, the framework presented here yields testable propositions based on the control-resource commitment tradeoff. A notable advantage of transaction cost analysis in this regard is the 'default' hypothesis: low-resource commitment is preferable until proven otherwise. The presence of a default hypothesis is especially helpful for theory testing because it provides a testable prediction.

Transaction cost analysis has been extended in recent years to cover a range of control rather than the extremes of integrate or contract out (Williamson 1985). In this form, transaction cost analysis brings to the entry mode problem an emphasis on the growth of ties that bind, on uncertainty, on the balancing of risks (credible commitments) and on the scale of operations. These constructs have been used to bring together many of the diverse ideas (such as the effect of sociocultural distance) expressed in the managerial and economic literatures and order them into testable propositions under a consistent rationale. Some of these propositions are new (e.g., the effect of the foreign business community), while others serve to clarify debates in the literature (e.g., the effect of sociocultural distance). The propositions also emphasize the interactions derived from the transaction cost analytical framework. Other interactions could be observed in empirical work in the sense that the joint effect of two variables could be greater than the sum of their independent effects. However, the rationale for these interactions goes beyond a transaction cost analytical framework. While the approach is incomplete, it is a useful starting point in examining tradeoffs among modes of entry.

In this paper we have developed a systematic approach to the entry mode issue. The propositions summarized in Figures 2 and 3 are testable. It is hoped, these propositions will encourage empirical research into an important area, as well as provide guidelines to management about how to match entry modes with their situations.

NOTES

1. Caves (1982) and Hennart (1982) undertake ambitious surveys of both the economic and international business research on multinational enterprise, including the entry mode issue. This paper builds on their works. We develop testable propositions (involving tradeoffs and interactions) as to when each mode of entry is likely to be effective. This is made possible by adopting an explicit criterion of long-term efficiency and employing a transaction cost perspective.

2. The purpose of developing the theory presented here is to help managers choose which form of entry to employ in a foreign market. Therefore, the theory concerns only situations where there is a set of options from which to choose. Further, the long-term orientation confines us to durable entry modes. We do not address short-term contracting (e.g., nonrenewable one-year licenses). The long-term efficiency criterion does not apply to a short-term arrangement. Consequently, this analysis does not offer insight about the length of contract. Nonetheless, the long-term perspective is necessary when the firm makes a long-term commitment to a market. See Kindleberger (1984) for a discussion of long vs. short-term contracts.

3. Franchising arrangements are frequently exclusive as well.

4. A product class may have reached the mature stage in the entrant's home country but not the host country. Hence, indigenous capability is not yet widely available, and the entrant who contracts with and

trains a local independent entity is creating transaction-specific assets. The relevant level of product maturity, therefore, is in the host country.

5. For practical purposes, risk and uncertainty are synonymous (Herring 1983).

6. Many firms choose to retain low resource commitment but trade off the renegotiation aspect of flexibility by writing long-term licenses.

7. Interactions are typically operationalized as a multiplication of two terms (here, specificity and uncertainty). The multiplicative term is high when both factors are high (combined presence) and low when either factor is low (lack of combined presence). Of course, both terms must be positive for the interaction to meanfully express the combined presence of two factors.

8. Nunnally (1978) is perhaps the most cited reference on psychometric methods and offers concrete suggestions for overcoming the data limitations that are bound to arise in conducting field research.

9. Accounting for production costs is particularly important when considering introducing a new product line into a foreign market where the firm has an ongoing operation. While product addition is an entry, it is an incremental decision. Hence, it is the incremental costs that are relevant. For example, Davidson and McFetridge (1984) find that if firms have an affiliate in place, they are more likely to add product to the affiliate's line than to seek other arrangements. This is because the fixed costs of the affiliate have already been incurred; the additional operation generates only marginal costs.

ACKNOWLEDGEMENTS

The authors gratefully acknowledge the financial support of the Wharton Center for International Management Studies. The comments of Yoram Wind, Jean-Francois Hennart, and three anonymous reviewers, as well as Charles Goodman and Leonard Lodish, are greatly appreciated, as is the assistance of Shari Powell.

SELECTED REFERENCES

Alpander, G.G. (1976). Use of Quantitative Methods in International Operations by U.S. Overseas Executives, *Management International Review* **10**(1): 71–77.

Anderson, E. (1985). The Salesperson as Outside Agent or Employee: A Transaction Cost Analysis, *Marketing Science* **4** (Summer), 234–254.

——. and Coughlan, A.T. (1985). Distribution of Industrial Products Introduced to Foreign Markets: Independent Versus Integrated Channels, Working Paper 85–033, Department of Marketing, The Wharton School.

Bilkey, W.J. (1978). An Attempted Integration of the Literature on the Export Behavior of Firms, *Journal of International Business Studies*, **9** (Spring–Summer), 33–46.

Bivens, D.K. and Lovell, E.B. (1966). *Joint Ventures with Foreign Partners*, New York: the National Industrial Conference Board.

Calvet, A.L. (1981). A Synthesis of Foreign Direct Investment Theories and Theories of the Multinational Firm, *Journal of International Business Studies*, **12** (Spring–Summer), 43–59.

Caves, R.E. (1982). *Multinational Enterprise and Economic Analysis*, Cambridge: Cambridge University Press.

——. (1971). International Corporations: The Industrial Economics of Foreign Investment, *Economica*, **38**, 1–27.

Chandler, A.D. (1977). *The Visible Hand: The Managerial Revolution in American Business*, Cambridge, Mass.: The Belknap Press.

Contractor, F.J. (1984). Choosing Between Direct Investment and Licensing: Theoretical Considerations and Empirical Tests, *Journal of International Business Studies*, **15** (Winter), 167–188.

Coughlan, A.T. and Flaherty, T.M. (1983). Measuring the International Marketing Productivity of U.S. Semiconductor Companies. In D. Gautschi, ed., *Productivity and Efficiency in Distribution Systems*, 123–149, Amsterdam: Elsevier Science Publishing Co., Inc.

Daniels, J.D., Ogram, E.W. Jr., and Radebaugh, L.H. (1982). *International Business: Environments and Operations*, 3d edition, Reading, Mass.: Addison Wesley.

Davidson, W.H. (1982). *Global Strategic Management*, New York: John Wiley and Sons.

——. (1980). The Location of Foreign Direct Investment Activity: Country Characteristics and Experience Effects, *Journal of International Business Studies*, **11** (Fall), 9–22.

Davidson, W.H. and McFetridge, D.G. (1984). International Technology Transactions and the Theory of the Firm, *The Journal of Industrial Economics*, **32** (March), 253–264.

Eiteman, D.K. and Stonehill, A.I. (1973). *Multinational Business Finance*, Reading, Mass.: Addison-Wesley.

Engwall, L. (1984). ed., *Uppsala Contributions to Business Research*, Uppsala, Sweden: Acta Universitatis Upsaliensis.

Evan, W.M. (1965). Toward A Theory of Inter-Organizational Relationships, *Management Science*, **11** (August), B-217-B-230.

Friedmann, W.G. (1972). The Contractual Joint Venture, *Columbia Journal of World Business*, **7** (January–February), 57–63.

Friedmann, W.G. and Beguin, J.-P. (1971). *Joint International Business Ventures in Developing Countries*, New York: Columbia University Press.

Goodnow, J.D. and Hanz, J.E. (1972). Environmental Determinants of Overseas Market Entry Strategies, *Journal of International Business Studies*, **3** (Spring), 33–50.

Hackey, D. (1976). The International Expansion of U.S. Franchise Systems: Status and Strategies, *Journal of International Business Studies*, **7** (June), 65–75.

Hakansson, H. (1984) ed., *International Marketing and Purchasing of Industrial Goods*, New York: John Wiley and Sons.

Hayashi, K. (1978). Japanese Management of Multinational Operations: Sources and Means of Joint Venture Control, *Management International Review*, **18**(4): 47–57.

Helleiner, G.K. and Lavergne, R. (1979). Intra-Firm Trade and Industrial Exports to the United States, *Oxford Bulletin of Economics and Statistics*, **41** (November), 297–311.

Hennart, J.-F. (1982). *A Theory of Multinational Enterprise*, Ann Arbor: The University of Michigan Press.

Herring, R.J., ed. (1983). *Managing International Risk*, Cambridge: Cambridge University Press.

Holton, R. (1971). Marketing Policies in Multinational Corporations, *California Management Review*, **13**(4): 57–67.

Hymer, S. (1976). *The International Operations of National Firms*, Cambridge: MIT Press.

Johanson, J. and Vahlne, J.-E. (1977). The Internationalization Process of the Firm – A Model of Knowledge Development and Increasing Foreign Market Commitment, *Journal of International Business Studies*, **8** (Spring–Summer), 23–32.

Keegan, W.J. (1974). Multinational Scanning: A Study of the Information Sources Utilized by Headquarters Executives in Multinational Companies, *Administrative Science Quarterly*, **19** (September), 411–421.

Killing, P.J. (1982). How to Make A Global Joint Venture Work, *Harvard Business Review*, **60** (May–June), 120–127.

Kindleberger, C.P. (1984). *Multinational Excursions*, Cambridge: The MIT Press.

Klein, B., Crawford, R.G. and Alchian, A.A. (1972). Vertical Integration, Appropriable Quasi-Rents, and the Competitive Contracting Process, *Journal of Law and Economics*, **21** (October), 297–325.

Kobrin, S. J. (1976). The Environmental Determinants of Foreign Direct Manufacturing Investment: An Ex Post Empirical Analysis, *Journal of International Business Studies*, **7** (Fall–Winter), 29–42.

Kobrin, S.J., Basek, J. Blank, S. and La Palombara, J. (1980). The Assessment and Evaluation of Noneconomic Environments by American Firms: A Preliminary Report, *Journal of International Business Studies*, **11** (Spring–Summer), 32–46.

Lall, S. (1978). The Pattern of Intra-Firm Exports by U.S. Multinationals, *Oxford Bulletin of Economics and Statistics* **40** (August), 209–222.

Lee, W.-Y. and Brasch, J.J. (1978). The Adoption of Export as an Innovative Strategy, *Journal of International Business Studies*, **9** (Spring–Summer), 85–93.

Lilien, G.L. (1979). ADVISOR 2: Modeling the Marketing Mix Decision for Industrial Products, *Management Science*, **25** (February), 191–204.

Mascarenhas, B. (1982). Coping With Uncertainty in International Business, *Journal of International Business Studies* **13** (Fall), 87, 98.

Newbould, G.D., Buckley, P.J. and Thurwell, J.C. (1978). *Going International: The Experience of Smaller Companies Overseas*, New York: John Wiley & Sons, Inc.

Nunnally, J.C. (1978). *Psychometric Theory*, Second Edition, New York: McGraw-Hill.

Puxty, A.G. (1979). Some Evidence Concerning Cultural Differentials in Ownership Policies of Overseas Subsidiaries, *Management International Review*, **19**(2): 39–52.

Richman, B.M. and Copen, M. (1972). *International Management and Economic Development*, New York: McGraw-Hill.

Robinson, R.C. (1978). *International Business Management: A Guide to Decision Making*, 2nd edition, Hinsdale, Ill.: The Dryden Press.

Robock, S.H., Simmonds, K. and Zwick, J. (1977). *International Business and Multinational Enterprises*, Homewood, Ill.: Richard D. Irwin.

Root, F.J. (1983). *Foreign Market Entry Strategies*, New York: AMACON.

Rugman, A.M. (1982). *New Theories of the Multinational Enterprise*, New York: St. Martin's Press.

Rummel, R.J. and Heenan, D.A. (1978). How Multinationals Analyze Political Risk, *Harvard Business Review*, **56** (January–February), 67–76.

Seidler, L.J. (1972). Nationalism and the International Transfer of Accounting Skills. In A. Kapoor and P.D. Grubb, eds., *The Multinational Enterprise in Transition*, 233–242, Princeton: The Darwin Press.

Shetty, Y.K. (1979). Managing the MNC: European and American Styles, *Management International Review*, **19**(3): 39–48.

Stern, L.W. and El-Ansary A. (1982). *Marketing Channels*, Englewood Cliffs, N.J.: Prentice Hall.

Stopford, J.M. and Wells, L.T. Jr. (1972). *Managing the Multinational Enterprise*, New York: Basic Books.

Teece, D.J. (1983). Technological and Organizational Factors in the Theory of the Multinational Enterprise. In M. Casson, ed., *The Growth of International Business*, 51–62, New York: George Allen and Irwin.

——. (1976). *The Multinational Corporation and the Resource Cost of International Technology Transfer*, Cambridge: Ballinger Publishing.

Telesio, P. (1979). *Technology Licensing and Multinational Enterprises*, New York: Praeger.

Time (1981). Big Mac Attack, (September 14), 56.

Vernon, R. (1983). Organizational and Institutional Responses to International Risk. In R.J. Herring, ed., *Managing International Risk*, 191–216, Cambridge: Cambridge University Press.

——. (1977). *Storm Over the Multinationals*, Cambridge: Harvard University Press.

——. (1966). International Trade and International Investment in the Product Life Cycle, *Quarterly Journal of Economics*, (May), 190–207.

——. and Wells, L.T. (1976). *Manager in the International Economy*, Englewood Cliffs, N.J.: Prentice Hall.

Walker, G. and Weber, D. (1984). A Transaction Cost Approach to Make-or-Buy Decisions, *Administrative Science Quarterly*, **29** (September), 373–391.

Weichmann, U, and Pringle, L. (1979). Problems that Plague Multinational Marketers, *Harvard Business Review*, **57**(4): 118–124.

Weinstein, A.K. (1974). The International Expansion of U.S. Multinational Advertising Agencies, *MSU Business Topics*, **10** (Summer), 29–35.

Weston, F.J. and Sorge, B.W. (1972). *International Managerial Finance*, Homewood, Ill.: Richard D. Irwin.

Williamson, O.E. (1985). *The Economic Institutions of Capitalism*, New York: Free Press.

——. (1983), Credible Commitments: Using Hostages to Support Exchange, *American Economic Review*, **83** (September), 519–540.

——. (1981a). The Economics of Organization: The Transaction Cost Approach, *American Journal of Sociology*, **87**(3): 548–577.

——. (1981b). The Modern Corporation: Origins, Evolution, Attributes, *Journal of Economic Literature*, **19** (December), 1537–1568.

——. (1979). Transaction Cost Economics: The Governance of Contractual Relations, *Journal of Law and Economics*, **22** (October), 233–62.

——. (1975). *Markets and Hierarchies: Analysis and Antitrust Implications*, New York: The Free Press.

Wilson, B.D. (1980). The Propensity of Multinational Firms to Expand Through Acquisitions, *Journal of International Business Studies*, **11** (Spring–Summer), 59–65.

Wind, Y. and Perlmutter, H. (1977). On the Identification of Frontier Issues in International Marketing, *Columbia Journal of World Business*, **12** (Winter), 131–139.

Wind, Y., Douglas, S.P. and Perlmutter, H.V. (1973). Guidelines for Developing International Marketing Strategies, *Journal of Marketing*, **37** (April), 14–23.

14

Differences Among Exporting Firms Based on Their Degree of Internationalization

S. Tamer Cavusgil

An overwhelming majority of the investigations of company export behaviour have utilized data obtained from all types of firms in a sample. An alternative approach would involve disaggregating the sample into some meaningful groups and contrasting company characteristics across the subsamples of firms. This study attempts to delineate differences among exporting firms when firms are classified by their degree of internationalization. Three types of exporters are identified in light of the internationalization hypothesis: experimental exporters, active exporters, and committed exporters. These firms are then contrasted with each other with respect to measurable company characteristics, domestic market environment, nature of international business involvement, marketing policy aspects, and export market research practices. The analysis in the paper is based upon data gathered through personal interviews with the executives of 70 midwestern manufacturers. The study reveals significant differences among the three types of exporters and provides further insights into the export marketing behavior of firms.

Too many studies of export marketing behavior have averaged results from all types of firms in a sample, when insight would require classifying them into some meaningful groups and then comparing average group responses.[1] The present discussion illustrates the use of the latter strategy in analyzing data; firms are first grouped by their degree of internationalization and then analyzed for significant differences among them. Three categories of exporting firms (experimental, active, and committed) are contrasted with respect to measurable company characteristics, domestic market environment, nature of the company's international business involvement, marketing policy aspects, and foreign market research practices. The findings provide partial support for the stages of internationalization framework and generate insights into the export marketing practices of firms which would not be possible from a study which aggregated all firms into one large sample.

METHOD

Data collection procedures

The data base for this investigation is derived from a series of personal interviews with 70 manufacturing companies from Wisconsin and Illinois. These firms were selected system-

Reprinted with permission from *Journal of Business Research*, 1984, **12**, 195–208
Copyright © Elsevier Science Publishing Co., Inc.

atically from the directories of the Milwaukee World Trade Club and Chicago World Trade Club. Initially, a larger number of firms were identified and contacted in order to gain their cooperation. Through an advance letter typed on the University of Wisconsin–Whitewater letterhead, those executives principally responsible for international marketing were asked to participate in a study of exporting. Those companies that indicated a willingness to participate were then contacted by phone in order to schedule an interview with a key executive.

Personal interviews took place during the latter part of 1981. In all cases, the respondent was the executive principally responsible for international business activities of the firm. The interviews lasted from one to two hours and covered a variety of topics including past history of international involvement, current international activity, international market research activities, background company characteristics, and other issues. A semistructured data collection instrument was used to guide the interviews, all of which were tape-recorded for later analysis.

Stages of internationalization framework

Most scholars now agree that firms tend to exhibit an evolutionary process in the way they become involved in international business.[3,4,6,7,9,10,11] Several stages can be identified along this gradual involvement process, including preinvolvement, reactive involvement, limited experimental involvement, active involvement, and committed involvement.[3,5] Clearly, not all firms will travel the entire internationalization path. Many firms, for example, find it desirable to restrict their international involvement to an opportunistic strategy by responding primarily to unsolicited orders from foreign customers or distributors.

The sequential nature of the internationalization process can be attributed to greater perceived risk associated with international business decisions, tentative nature of managerial expectations, and greater genuine uncertainty. These circumstances generate a very cautious type of management, one that makes incremental rather than total commitments for taking advantage of export market opportunities. As the firm gains more international experience, management may develop higher expectations, more rational and comprehensive policies concerning international business, as well as new organizational procedures for handling the new tasks.

In the present study we focus on only three stages of the internationalization process. These are experimental involvement, active involvement, and committed involvement. *Experimental involvement* characterizes the behavior of those managements who exert little commitment to overseas market development. Entry into exporting is typically prompted by unsolicited inquiries. The company responds to these inquiries in a passive (reactive) manner and treats international business as marginal business. Export sales in many of these firms may not account for more than 10% of total business. Often a few foreign markets (customers) are involved. Furthermore, experimenting exporters will often employ product and pricing strategies that are a simple extension of the domestic marketing mix. They will allocate managerial and financial resources and production capacity to export markets with some degree of reluctance. Short-term objectives will prevail over long-term goals.

Active involvement occurs when management recognizes the important contributions international business can make toward accomplishing corporate goals. Managers are now willing to make a long-term commitment to cultivating export markets. International business opportunities and problems now capture the attention of those decision makers higher up in the organization. Unused capacity may be allocated to only export orders. Products are designed to meet the specific needs of overseas customers; pricing policies are revised to secure effective penetration of foreign markets. In the active involvement stage, firms will have expanded their exporting activity to a number of key markets. Export activity is no longer considered to be marginal business, and it is conducted on a regular basis rather than sporadically. An export marketing department may be formed, usually as a spin-off of the domestic marketing/sales department.

Committed involvement represents the final stage firms may reach in the evolutionary process of internationalization. A committed exporter searches for business opportunities worldwide, not restricting itself to the traditional markets. The distinction between domestic and foreign sales may now appear artificial. This ultimate stage in the internationalization process usually brings about other types of international involvement, such as direct investment in overseas production facilities, sales subsidiaries, worldwide sourcing arrangements, and so on. An overseas division will usually be set up to assume responsibility over these operations. In the committed involvement stage, it is not unreasonable to find a company assessing opportunities in the global market much more systematically than before.

Procedure for classifying firms

The procedure for classifying the 70 firms into experimental, active, and committed involvement stages was primarily judgmental. A group of 25 graduate business students along with the principal researcher classified each firm into one of the three categories after considering *all* available information about the company, and in light of the conceptual framework of internationalization stages discussed above. A consensus had to be reached in the group before a firm was classified as an experimental, active, or committed exporter. Also, the judges refrained from using a single criterion (such as firm size or export sales/total sales ratio) to classify the firms. The classification was based on a multitude of characteristics in harmony with the conceptual framework. This was done in order to shed light on the validity of the internationalization hypothesis. To the extent that such a classificatory framework produces significant differences among the three groups of firms, we would have evidence pointing to the usefulness of the framework. Such an approach is also consistent with previous research efforts that attempted to validate the internationalization hypothesis.[2,5,8]

Using the above procedure, the judges characterized 28 of the firms as experimental exporters, 18 firms as active exporters, and the remaining 24 firms as committed exporters. A greater proportion of the experimental and committed exporters turned out to be industrial goods manufacturers, whereas the majority of active exporters were primarily consumer goods producers.

FINDINGS

Relating the stages of internationalization to measurable company characteristics

Is progression through the internationalization process a function of company size? Do committed exporters tend to be larger than experimental and active exporters? The findings in this respect were not consistent. When firm size was measured by the number of full-time employees and related to internationalization stages, no statistically significant relationship emerged. When firm size was measured by annual sales, however, there was a statistically significant relationship at the 0.00 level (see Table 1). In particular, experimental firms were more likely to have annual sales of less than $10 million; committed exporters sales in excess of $100 million; and active exporters somewhere in between. The strength of the relationship is moderate at best, however, as implied by lambda of 0.31 (index of predictive association has an upper limit of 1.00). A tentative conclusion to be drawn from these results is that there is a tendency for larger-volume companies to have progressed more along the internationalization process. This relationship does not appear to be strong, however, implying that a company's internationalization is not greatly influenced by its size, especially when the latter is measured by number of employees. The direction of casuality is also subject to speculation.

When the company's length of experience in exporting is cross-tabulated with its internationalization stage, a weak level of association is found (see Table 2). Although there are directional tendencies for experimental firms to have less than 20 years of export experience and for committed exporters to have more than 20 years of experience, export experience is not a strong predictor of internationalization. This finding implies that a 'natural' progress over time from experimental to active to committed stages is not necessarily a certainty. Many firms may find it desirable to maintain their involvement at the experimental level, despite greater experience gained over the years. Lack of top management interest or the presence of accessible sales potentials domestically may be responsible for the firm's less than full commitment to exploiting foreign market potentials.

The data in Table 3 suggest a weak-to-moderate relationship between export intensity of the firm, as measured by exports/total sales ratio, and the stages of internationalism. Again, there is a tendency for experimental exporters to export less than 10% of their output and for committed exporters to export more than 40% of total output. Export intensity, however, fails to emerge as a perfect correlate of internationalization. One may argue that true internationalization cannot be measured by a single dimension such as export intensity; perhaps it is the result of other concomitant changes in the organization, including certain attitudinal changes among management personnel.

There seems to be a stronger relationship between export profits as a percentage of total company profits and the stage of internationalization (Table 4). Here export profits emerge as a moderately strong predictor of a company's internationalization. More than two-thirds of experimental exporters generate less than 10% of their profits from foreign sales. In contrast,

Table 1. Test of Significant Relationship Between Company Sales and Degree of Internationalization

Annual Company Sales	Number of Firms in Each Stage		
	Experimental	Active	Committed
Less than $10 million	13	4	3
$10 million to $100 million	6	10	5
More than $100 million	5	4	13

Chi-square test statistic, $\chi^2 = 18.09$, with 4 degrees of freedom is significant at the 0.00 level.
Index of predictive association, $\lambda = 0.31$, with company sales as the predictor variable.

almost one-half of the committed exporters derive more than 40% of their profits from overseas sales. It appears that progression over the experimental/active/committed exporter stages is enhanced by greater degree of reliance in foreign markets as a source of profits. In addition, the latter variable appears to be a better predictor of internationalization than export intensity.

The degree of internationalization was related to one additional company characteristic – the scope of the domestic market for the company. Previous research had suggested that having already established a broad-based domestic market, a company might find it easier to expand into international markets.[10] The expectation is that with 'extra-regional expansion' or 'internationalization at home,' the firm will be in a better state of readiness to penetrate foreign markets. We were not able to confirm this expectation since almost all of the experimental, active, and committed exporters were found to be actively marketing in the

Table 2. Crosstabulation of Company's Export Experience with Degree of Internationalization

	Number of Firms in Each Stage		
Length of Company Experience in Exporting	Experimental	Active	Committed
Less than 10 years	12	4	2
10 to 20 years	5	5	5
21 to 40 years	4	4	7
More than 40 years	6	2	8

Index of predictive association is λ = 0.14, with export experience as the predictor.

Table 3. Crosstabulation of Export Intensity with Degree of Internationalization

	Number of Firms in Each Stage		
Export Sales as a Percentage of Total Company Sales	Experimental	Active	Committed
Less than 10%	16	7	3
10% to 19%	4	6	5
20% to 39%	4	4	6
More than 40%	1	1	10

Index of predictive association is λ = 0.31, with export intensity at the predictor.

Table 4. Crosstabulation of Export Profits with Degree of Internationalization

Profits Derived from Exporting as a Percentage of Total Company Profits	Number of Firms in Each Stage		
	Experimental	Active	Committed
Less than 10%	17	6	2
10% to 19%	3	7	2
20% to 39%	4	4	8
More than 40%	–	1	11

Index of predictive association is λ = 0.46, with export profits as the predictor.

entire U.S. market. The scope of the domestic market was not necessarily narrower in the case of experimental or active exporters.

Domestic market environment of the firms

Firms in the sample were questioned as to the nature and extent of their competition in the U.S. market as a way of understanding their motivations for being interested in international market opportunities. The majority of the firms indicated that they encountered 'moderate competition' in the home market (see Table 5). This response was consistent across the three groups of firms. Of the firms that had a 'below average level of competition,' most were in the experimental exporting stage. This may be reasonable because the firms in the experimental involvement stage tended to be smaller firms who had carved a specific niche in the market with their products, and therefore encountered less competition for their specific products.

Firms in the experimental involvement stage identified 'growing home markets' as their key opportunity in the immediate future. Exporting to world markets and using additional distributors were also mentioned. A significant proportion of committed exporters (47%), on the other hand, singled out export markets as their best opportunity. This reflects a greater awareness of foreign market opportunities and a greater significance attached to foreign markets. In addition, saturation of the domestic market is a driving factor for committed exporters in seeking additional foreign markets. Many of the executives of committed exporters were blunt about the fact that their domestic market was mature or declining, and that exporting was their only source of real growth. Consequently, they appeared eager to develop an aggressive exporting, licensing, and investment stance.

Table 5.   Domestic Market Environment of the Firms

Characteristics of Domestic Market	Percentage of Firms in Each Stage		
	Experimental	Active	Committed
Intensity of Competition in the U.S.			
Low level of competition	31	13	14
Moderate competition	65	73	76
Substantial competition	4	14	10
Major Opportunity Facing the Firm			
Growing market at home	29	12	21
Growing market abroad	24	25	47
Expansion of product lines	18	25	21
Acquiring new foreign distributors	18	–	–
Other	11	38	11
Major Challenge Encountered Domestically			
Pressures on price/profit margins	50	36	43
Maturing industry	7	7	22
Threats posed by larger competitors	29	29	7
High interest rates	14	14	21
Unfavorable aspects of demand	–	14	7

Nature of international business involvement

Needless to say, firms in different internationalization stages had different types of international involvement. For 79% of *all* firms, the principal international activity was exporting, but this varied among the firms (see Table 6). This is in line with the expectation that exporting is the initial strategy to penetrate foreign markets. As the firm travels the internationalization path, it will also become involved in licensing and foreign production.

When asked how the firm had its *initial* involvement in exporting, the answers varied depending upon the internationalization stages. Firms in the experimental and active involvement stages indicated that they simply responded to unsolicited foreign orders (40% and 25% respectively). Firms in the committed involvement stage suggest that they actively sought out foreign orders as their first international involvement. An explanation for this discrepancy may be that firms in the committed involvement stage have been exporting for a long time (usually more than 20 years) and, therefore, really cannot recall their initial international involvement. It would probably be safe to say that even these committed firms had their interest piqued by unsolicited orders or inquiries, or by a chance meeting of foreign buyers.

Both the desire for profits and the desire to achieve sales growth were cited as the major motivation for initial involvement in exporting by the majority of firms. Staying competitive, diversification as a way of achieving stability, and using excess manufacturing capacity accounted for the remaining responses. After the firms had become more involved in exporting, however, they appeared to be more interested in seeking profits and less interested in fulfilling other objectives. This may be a logical pattern for companies to take. As a firm begins its involvement with exporting, it knows it will take a few years to get established and to recover its original costs; hence one of the major motivations is sales growth and market share. Then, as the firm progresses into the higher exporting categories, it will want to see some of the efforts pay off, and will become more conscious of profits. This is especially true among committed exporters.

Table 6. The Nature of Company's International Business Involvement

Facets of International Involvement	Percentage of Firms in Each Stage		
	Experimental	Active	Committed
Primary form of involvement is exporting	92	81	68
Initial exporting was prompted by unsolicited orders	48	36	14
Initial motivation for export start was primarily profit-related	50	19	42
Major motivation *now* for exporting is profits	50	50	58
The most troublesome problem in exporting is:			
Working with foreign distributors	42	7	17
Exchange rate risks	25	53	59
Cultural and economic differences	16	–	12
Political instability, etc.	–	13	12
Redtape, regulatory restrictions, etc.	8	7	–
Other	9	20	–

For firms experimenting with exporting, the most pressing problem is working with foreign distributors. At this stage of internationalization, these firms have not committed sufficient resources to provide for a wide distribution network abroad. Therefore, finding, selecting, and training a distributor in large part determines the amount of sales they receive from foreign markets. In a sense, these firms are helpless without the commitment of the distributor. The most significant exporting problem for both active and committed exporters, on the other hand, is fluctuations in the value of foreign currencies. This is natural as these firms derive a higher percentage of company revenues from foreign sales. Therefore, an unfavorable currency fluctuation affects their bottom line more than it would a firm with a relatively small share of profits from exporting.

Marketing policy aspects of international involvement

Sixty-two percent of the exported products were considered 'not unique' by company executives. A greater proportion of active exporters classified their products as unique when compared to competition (see Table 7). When asked to describe their principal export product, one-third of all executives indicated that their products were of high quality. Twenty-two percent stated that they produced a 'traditional product that gave good value for the money.' Twenty-one percent described their product as highly technical, but this included such products as bull semen and diesel engines which may not be characterized as highly complex by others. The interviews seem to suggest that, regardless of internationalization stage, a company does not need a stupendous new product to be successful in exporting. Typically, a high-quality product seems to be sufficient.

Table 7. Marketing Policy Aspects of International Involvement

Features of Marketing Policy	Percentage of Firms in Each Stage		
	Experimental	Active	Committee
Principal export product is the same product sold domestically	80	69	67
Principal export product is 'unique'	36	50	26
Principal export market is Canada/Mexico/Western Europe	51	70	61
Organizational arrangement used for exports is a special export division	58	68	73
Major export channel includes a foreign distributor	56	47	50
Face-to-face contacts with foreign distributors take place:			
Once every 2 years or less frequently	37	12	8
Once a year	36	50	8
Twice a year or more often	27	38	84
Support provided for distributors includes:			
Sales aids	41	29	15
Initial sales and technical training	29	36	45
A formal sales and payment policy exists	11	40	75
A formal payment policy exists	44	60	79

With respect to choice of export markets, no differences emerged among the three types of exporters. For all firms, Western Europe was the primary export market, followed by Canada/Mexico, Latin America, Far East, and Australia/New Zealand. This is in contrast to initial expectations that the experimental and active exporters would concentrate on 'psychologically close' countries such as Canada, and that the committed exporters would exhibit a greater propensity to venture into nontraditional markets. This expectation was not confirmed, as we found no differences among the firms with respect to foreign market preferences.

In considering the types of organizational arrangement firms developed for export operations, we do find that a firm is more likely to have a special export division the greater is its degree of internationalization. Furthermore, firms appear to develop additional policies concerning exporting as they progress through internationalization, and they tend to formalize them to a greater degree. It is also evident that top executives of experimental exporters become more directly involved in exporting decisions than the executives of active and committed exporters.

With respect to relationships with foreign distributors, it was found that the experimental firms have face-to-face contact with their distributors least often and provide primarily sales aids. Active exporters and committed exporters visit overseas distributors more often and provide sales and technical training as well for their distributors. In addition, market research assistance, volume discounts, and temporary personnel for starting up a new operation may also be provided.

Foreign market research practices

As the firms progressed through the internationalization stages, foreign market research became much more important to them, as evidenced by the commitment of financial and managerial resources to the tasks involved. The percentage of executives who stated that the analysis of foreign market potentials is 'at least as important' as the domestic marketing research varied substantially for the three types of exporters (see Table 8). As the commitment of the company for foreign markets increased, a more thorough analysis of potentials was required. In addition, management took time more frequently to assess foreign market potentials.

As a company progresses through the internationalization stages, it becomes more likely to use a *variety* of informational sources in foreign market research. It was found that dependence on a limited number of sources was replaced by a tendency to utilize a multitude of information sources. In the experimental and active exporting stages, the most important source of data for export market research was perceived to be industry/business publications and contacts made at trade shows. Information obtained from other firms in the industry was the second most helpful source for experimenting and active exporters, and most helpful for committed exporters. Information obtained from the U.S. Department of Commerce, although it appears to be helpful to experimenting exporters, becomes less useful during the active and committed involvement stages. This is probably because of the nature of the information assistance provided by the U.S. Department of Commerce. Its 'broad' and 'basic' nature serves the needs of the experimental firms well. Information needs become much more specific, however, with passage into the active and committed stages. The company now finds it necessary to develop an internal 'information system' for foreign market research purposes. It can also be expected that, with greater experience, managers become more proficient in searching for and maintaining satisfactory sources of information.

Table 8. Foreign Market Research Practices of Companies

Foreign Market Research Practices	Percentage of Firms in Each Stage		
	Experimental	Active	Committed
Foreign market research is perceived to be equally as important as domestic marketing research	17	63	77
Analyzing foreign market opportunities is a frequent task (conducted several times a year)	14	17	57
Foreign market opportunity analysis is a fairly formalized process with written reports	–	7	30
The task is perceived to be complex and requires a high level of data analysis	4	14	26
Computerized data bases are regularly used in foreign market opportunity analysis	13	29	42
The most important source of data used in foreign market research is:			
Government (U.S. Dept. of Commerce, etc.)	24	13	13
Industry/business publications and reports	36	34	22
Other firms	32	27	30
Internal company sources	8	13	17
Other	–	13	18
The most important problem associated with foreign market data:			
Too broad to be useful	25	30	18
Not reliable; biased	25	50	41
Out of date	8	10	–

CONCLUSION

This study attempted to reveal differences among exporting firms at varying levels of internationalization. The results suggest that experimenting, active, and committed exporters can be distinguished in terms of measurable characteristics: company size as measured by sales and the percent of profits derived from exporting. Beyond that, significant differences exist among the three types of exporters in terms of their domestic market environment, the nature of international business involvement, policy aspects of international marketing, and foreign market research practices.

The present study represents a useful background for designing a more comprehensive investigation of the issues using a cross section of firms. Future investigators may also consider classifying firms by alternative criteria in addition to stages of internationalization. These criteria may include SIC codes, international orientation of company management, choice of foreign markets, and other meaningful dimensions. Such specific investigations of exporting are bound to generate richer insights than otherwise possible.

The findings do offer some implications for public policy concerning stimulation of export activity among firms. Most significantly, there is a need to view exporting firms as a heterogeneous rather than a homogeneous group. Depending upon the degree of internationalization, companies differ in terms of intensity of export activity, interest and commitment in pursuing international opportunities, information and assistance needs, and most importantly, their export potential. Therefore, if an immediate and substantial increase is desired in the level of U.S. exports, it would be best to focus promotional and assistance efforts on the active and committed exporters rather than on experimental exporters. This research delineated ways in which active and committed exporters differ from experimental exporters. Such an understanding is imperative for designing promotional and assistance efforts in exporting.

The author wishes to acknowledge the financial support of this research through a State Research Grant from the University of Wisconsin System. Thanks are expressed to Professors Warren J. Bilkey and John R. Nevin of the University of Wisconsin–Madison for their valuable comments on an earlier draft of this article.

NOTES

1. Bilkey, Warren J. An attempted integration of the literature on the export behavior of firms. *Journal of International Business Studies*. **9**, 33–46 (Spring/Summer 1978).

2. Bilkey, Warren J., Tesar, George. The export behavior of smaller sized Wisconsin manufacturing firms. *Journal of International Business Studies* **8**, 93–98 (Spring/Summer 1977).

3. Cavusgil, S. Tamer. On the internationalization process of firms. *European Research* **8**, 273–281 (November 1980).

4. Cavusgil, S. Tamer. On the nature of decision making for export marketing. In: Hunt, S.D., Bush, R., eds. *Marketing Theory: Philosophy of Science Perspectives*. American Marketing Association (1982) pp. 177–180.

5. Cavusgil, S. Tamer. Some observations on the relevance of critical variables for internationalization stages. In: Czinkota, M.R., Tesar, G., eds. *Export Management*, New York: Praeger (1982) pp. 276–286.

6. Cavusgil, S. Tamer, Nevin, John R. Internal determinants of export marketing behavior: An empirical investigation. *Journal of Marketing Research* **28**, 114–119 (February 1981).

7. Chisnall, Peter M. Challenging opportunities of international marketing. *European Research* **5**, 12–34 (February 1977).

8. Czinkota, Michael R., Johnston, Wesley J. Segmenting U.S. firms for export development. *Journal of Business Research* **9**, 353–365 (December 1981).

9. Johanson, J., Vahlne, J. The internationalization process of the firm – A model of knowledge development and increasing foreign commitments. *Journal of International Business Studies* **8**, 23–32 (Spring/ Summer 1977).

10. Welch, Lawrence S., Wiedersheim-Paul, Finn. Domestic expansion: Internationalization at home. *Essays in International Business*, No. 2. Center for International Business Studies, University of South Carolina, (December 1980).

11. Wiedersheim-Paul, Finn, Olson, Hans C., Welch, Lawrence S. Pre-export activity: the first step in internationalization. *Journal of International Business Studies* **9**, 47–58 (Spring/Summer 1978).

15

Outward Foreign Licensing by Australian Companies

Lawrence S. Welch

1. INTRODUCTION

There has been limited study of outward foreign licensing by Australian firms as a method for developing international operations. Two recent empirical studies have provided some aggregate statistics on outward licensing as a component of technology transfer. As part of an investigation of technology flows and foreign firms, Parry and Watson (1979) examined the extent of outward licensing by foreign-owned subsidiaries in Australia to affiliate and non-affiliate companies. In a study of research and development by Australian enterprises, the Australian Bureau of Statistics (1979b) obtained broad data on receipts from overseas for the sale of technical know-how. However, while these studies present an overall picture of the extent of outward foreign licensing by Australian companies, they provide little insight into the process of licensing. It is to this latter issue that this study has been directed.

The general objective was to analyse and assess the role of outward foreign licensing in the internationalization process of Australian companies. An important aspect of this objective was the consideration of licensing's role at the marketing level. It is hoped that, through an examination of the way in which Australian firms have utilized licensing in international business, other firms might gain useful insights into the possibilities of this relatively neglected mode of international operations – as well as some valuable lessons as to strategy and operational methods.

Outward foreign licensing has tended to be regarded as a secondary internationalization strategy by most firms within Australia and overseas. Based on evidence presented before it, an Australian government committee has recently commented that 'Too few companies in Australia seem capable of engaging in R and D with a view to recovering some of the costs through licensing later on' (Senate Standing Committee, p. 106). The findings of studies in other countries seem to confirm this pattern. In a study of US medium-sized firms, Tesar (1977, p. 1) found that 'the majority of firms do not consider licensing as a viable alternative'. Likewise from an investigation of virtually all Finnish manufacturing firms, Luostarinen (1979, p. 103) concluded that 'physical goods are, almost without exception, the first sales object to be introduced into foreign markets'.

Written specially for this volume and based on a report for the Industrial Property Advisory Committee and the Licensing Executives Society of Australia, 1981

2. METHODOLOGY

The original objective was to survey all Australian companies licensing overseas. This task is difficult as the population of companies is not known with certainty. In 1976/77, the Australian Bureau of Statistics (ABS) estimated that 124 companies were in receipt of royalties. Since then, it is known that the number of companies licensing overseas has grown but it is believed that the number falls short of 500. (This impression was gained from conversations with patent attorneys and other practitioners in the field.) From two lists, one compiled by the Australian Government's Department of Trade and Resources and the other compiled by the researchers, 502 companies were contacted. Of these, 30 firms indicated that they were not licensing. Of the remainder, 43 stated that they were licensing, giving a response rate of 9%. However, this estimate is likely to be well under the true response rate as many companies were not licensing and there was some overlap between the two lists. This could not be verified as the names on the Department of Trade and Resources' list could not be revealed to the researchers because of confidentiality reasons.

A breakdown with regard to size; number of agreements and company size; the proportion of private and public companies; and the proportion of foreign controlled companies is set out below.

Compared to the ABS Statistics the group of firms surveyed is biased towards small to medium-sized Australian owned companies. Over 70% of the companies were small to medium-sized and only 25.6% were foreign controlled (compared to 42% from the ABS Statistics). In addition, 79% of the companies held less than six agreements.

With regard to the survey results, findings for companies with one to five agreements, are more relevant for the small to medium-sized companies whereas findings for companies with greater than five agreements are more relevant to the larger companies.

The degree of representatives, however, cannot be measured with any accuracy. It is accepted that the very small firms and inventors and the very large (particularly foreign owned companies) are not represented adequately. As the survey was investigating the process of licensing rather than attempting to accurately predict given magnitudes for the population of licensing firms as a whole, this is not seen as critical.

Table 1. Characteristics of the group of companies surveyed

Number of agreements and company size				
	Small	Medium	Large	Total
One Agreement	5 (38.0%)	7 (54.0%)	1 (8.0%)	13
2–6 Agreements	10 (47.6%)	6 (28.6%)	5 (23.9%)	21
6–20 Agreements	2 (25.0%)	1 (12.5%)	5 (62.5%)	8
> 20 Agreements	0	0	1 (100%)	1
Total	17	14	12	43

Size: Small   below 200 employees   17   39.5%
       Medium   200–1000 employees   14   32.5%
       Large   more than 1000 employees   12   28.0%
Public and private companies: public (55.8%), private (44.2%)
Foreign control (>25% foreign equity): 25.6% of the companies were foreign controlled.

The survey was conducted in two phases. First, the questionnaires were sent to the two company lists. Second, respondents were followed up wherever possible with interviews. Twenty-nine companies (67.4%) were interviewed. In addition, patent attorney practices were surveyed in order that checks could be conducted on some of the information generated by companies. Of the 29 practices in existence at the time replies were received either through the mail/or interview from representatives of seven practices. Also one licensing consultant was interviewed.

Some companies responding to the questionnaire were attempting to license overseas for the first time. Five were interviewed. While their responses have not been included in the tabulations, their experience provided useful insight into how companies initially entered licensing arrangements.

3. THE ROLE OF LICENSING IN THE INTERNATIONALIZATION PROCESS OF THE FIRM

3.1. The adoption process

3.1.1. The licensing choice

Other studies have shown that outward foreign licensing is frequently adopted as a secondary or residual international strategy. Where foreign markets are too small or risky, or the firm has limited resources or experience to develop foreign markets by exporting or foreign investment, licensing may well appear as a feasible and simpler alternative. In a US study, Budack and Susbauer (1977, p. 17) noted that the common view of licensing at the outset is that it is relatively easy to implement. In many cases too, the licensing option is virtually forced on the firm if it is not prepared to risk the foreign investment step, because the imposition of various types of import restrictions constrain the ability to service a foreign market.

In the survey, firms were requested to indicate the most important factors involved in the decision to license overseas. Difficulties associated with exporting to a foreign market, combined with an unpreparedness to undertake foreign investment, were considered to be the most important by the respondents. Table 2 shows the most important factors (in order)

Table 2. Licensing decision factors

Factors in decisoin to license	Proportion of firms mentioning each factor
High costs of shipping goods	53.5%
Tariff and non-tariff barriers	41.9%
High production costs in Australia	25.6%
Difficulties in selling goods overseas (e.g. poor distribution)	23.3%
High risk associated with foreign investment	18.6%
Lack of finance	11.6%

Number of respondents = 43.

mentioned by the proportion of firms noting them. In the main, licensing was not adopted because of a positive view of its value as a strategy for developing foreign markets.

A typical example of the operation of the export difficulties factor was the case of a firm with 120 employees which had signed six foreign licensing agreements. The general manager, and instigator of the licensing programme, pointed out that the company had a preference for exporting but the attempt to export had not been successful. He stated that the combination of actions by foreign governments (import restrictions) and the cost of shipping bulky items made licensing the only feasible path for earning foreign income, given that foreign investment had never been seriously entertained.

The emphasis on barriers to exports created by government intervention is to some extent a result of the geographical orientation of Australian international expansion activity – at least in the earlier stages. Of the 18 firms which mentioned these barriers as a factor in causing an interest in licensing, 15 (or 83%) had licensed to New Zealand, suggesting that New Zealand's traditional barriers to exports of manufactures have resulted in firms looking to licensing.

The 'residual' market approach to the use of licensing was stressed in a small number of cases. It was the assessment that a given foreign market lacked sufficient size and potential which led these firms to opt for licensing, indicating an inherent judgment that licensing was inappropriate as a basis for servicing primary markets. In addition, two firms used licensing as a strategy to sell 'residual' (non-mainstream) technology. Patentable technology was developed as a result of researching solutions to operating problems within the firm. In one case, the technology developed was only subsidiary to the main income earning activities. In the first case, licensing allowed the company to earn 'some additional income' from the invention while the mining company seemed to have almost gone into the attempt to sell technology, despite its 'nuisance value', as an outlet for its younger research personnel who were particularly keen to see this area of the company's operations develop.

For those companies licensing overseas subsidiaries, licensing tended to be used as an additional means of extracting income and, in general, maintaining control.

3.1.2. *International involvement preceding licensing*

In explaining the adoption of licensing as an internationalization strategy, an important background factor is the preceding level of foreign involvement. Responses to a survey question on the type of international activity preceding each foreign licensing agreement are shown in Table 3. In general, licensing to particular foreign markets was preceded by either no involvement or exporting. In only a small number of cases was there a direct association with foreign investment reported by respondent firms. The mainly small to medium-sized firms in the sample appeared to enter licensing as a separate internationalization strategy rather than as an element of a foreign investment strategy. This is undoubtedly related to them being at an earlier stage of international development.

In all but eight cases, however, licensing was not the first form of international involvement by the firm. It was generally preceded by, if not exporting to the particular foreign market, at least by exporting to other foreign markets.

Preceding international selling experience was found to make a contribution to the initial licensing step in various ways:

(a) At a general level the development of skills, understanding and knowledge about selling in international markets could be applied to some extent in the exercise of selling technology.

Table 3. Type of international involvement preceding licensing

| | Foreign licensing agreements | | | | | | | |
| | Total | | 1–5 | | 6–20 | | >20 | |
	No.	%	No.	%	No.	%	No.	%
No involvement	119	56.9	38	48.1	61	77.2	20	39.2
Exporting beforehand	38	18.2	31	39.2	7	8.9	0	—
Foreign investment beforehand	12	5.7	4	5.1	5	6.3	3	5.9
Licensing and foreign investment in package	29	13.9	1	1.3	0	—	28	54.9
Other	11	5.3	5	6.3	6	7.6	0	—
Total	209	100	79	100	79	100	51	100

Number of respondents = 42.

Not all international knowledge and skills can be readily transferred to activities which are licensing specific, but some were – for example, experience in finding and selecting suitable overseas agents provided a useful background in approaching the task of finding, selecting and negotiating with suitable licensees.

(b) The large proportion of cases where exporting was directly replaced by licensing in a given foreign market necessarily means that firms developed varying degrees of market-specific knowledge and skills. Such knowledge obviously provides a basis on which to make the decision about choice of licensee. The market experience may throw up a potential licensee so that much of the search process can be short-circuited, and perhaps the selection and assessment phases.

In addition, the basis of the licensing arrangement may have been effectively created by the exporting activity in the market concerned. As an example, in the survey one firm was very successful in exporting to the Thai market but was eventually blocked out by various import restrictions.

However, because its name had become so well established in the market, it was able to license some know-how and, in the main, its trade mark to a local manufacturer. In this case the very basis for the licensing deal was established by the preceding export activity. A large number of other cases fell into a similar category in that exports established and proved a foreign market which was then threatened by various external developments (for example, import restrictions). As a result, not only did the Australian firm become interested in licensing but the end-product of the licensing exercise had been proven to potential licensees, who sometimes made the first approach to the Australian firm.

(c) The channel which was previously used for the exporting activity or for carrying on production was sometimes transferred to a licensee basis, in which case most of the pre-agreement activities were no longer necessary. The exporter to Thailand noted in (b) above is a case in point. Its Swiss export agent in Thailand became its licensee, undertaking manufacture locally. It was interesting to note the Australian firm's perception of this licensing deal as a 'riskless, troublefree income source – although still inferior to the preferred exporting mode'. In such cases then, licensing can be relatively simple and with little cost involved. It is clear however that most firms are not in a position to make such simple transfers between modes of representation in a given foreign country.

Rather than using licensing as a means of channel transfer, a small number of firms had used licensing in order to achieve some channel expansion – that is, they already had a majority-owned subsidiary or joint-venture partner within the foreign market and the formal relationship was extended by one or more licensing agreements covering various forms of technology transfer (including marketing). In all but one of these examples the purpose was to provide another means of extracting income from a New Zealand subsidiary. The odd case involved an attempt to provide a broader basis of control and income generation with respect to a joint venture partner in Malaysia where the Malaysian government had restricted the Australian firm's equity level to 40%. Control over the activities of the joint venture operation was written into the licensing agreement such that the Australian company was able to determine any important strategic decisions of the Malaysian operation.

(d) Preceding international selling operations also frequently led to organizational and resource allocation changes within the firm, as well as creating a degree of international orientation which further assisted the ultimate move into international licensing activity.

It is clear then that preceding international selling activity, in whatever form, provides an important foundation for the move into licensing and explains why some firms are able to accomplish the move with relative ease. Nevertheless, there are other forms of international involvement which can contribute to the ability and likelihood of adoption of licensing.

An important form of foreign licensing experience for Australian firms arises from the activity of licensing from foreign sources. The derivative nature of Australian technology is reflected in the reliance on technology obtained via licensing into Australia. In an earlier study, Stubbs (1968, p. 92) found that 'about four-fifths of companies in the study had signed (inward) licence agreements'. A 1976–7 survey by the Australian Bureau of Statistics (1979) revealed that licensing payments overseas were almost ten times greater than receipts while the number of firms making payments overseas far exceeded those earning receipts. The experience gained in such aspects as negotiation, drawing up of agreements, etc., can be readily applied to outward licensing activities. Certainly, given the greater prevalence of inward licensing by Australian companies, foreign licensing skills are likely to be frequently developed through this avenue. The effect of licensing into the country also seems to be useful in developing an awareness of the possibilities of using the licensing mode. While there were only four firms in the survey that specifically mentioned the contribution of inward licensing to the later outward licensing step, their experience confirms that this was not only important in producing an awareness of licensing but also provided a frame of reference for outward licensing agreements ultimately devised. Clearly the international technology purchasing exercise can feasibly open up foreign market possibilities like more outward-looking international selling modes and has more direct application to the mechanics of licensing.

Other forms of international purchasing can likewise expose licensing possibilities, although obviously not producing the same awareness of the licensing mode. There were two cases in the survey of Australian firms importing first from their eventual licensees.

Overall then, the type of international involvement which precedes the move into international licensing emerges as a key influence on the nature of the adoption process. There are a number of ways in which preceding international experience can make a contribution to removing some of the barriers associated with outward foreign licensing as a new form of international operations. International experience in its various forms has a positive effect on licensing through the development of relevant skills and knowledge, which enhance the process of risk and uncertainty reduction in the new venture. Without such experience, it can be a long road from invention to international commercial exploitation via licensing. When an inventor enters the international sphere for the first time, unless he uses an intermediary, there is not only the need to acquire licensing-specific skills but also international marketing skills.

3.1.3. Industrial property protection as a barrier to licensing

For the smaller firm or individual inventor, even the patenting stage, as a prelude to licensing, can pose a major hurdle. Particularly for the individual inventor, the establishment of ownership rights to industrial property is a crucial exercise as he tends to be less reliant on know-how. As a result, he is more exposed to any breach of his industrial property rights and more concerned about any actual or latent challenge to them. Any defence ties up the operational capacity of the inventor (and small firm), stretches his liquidity and constrains his ability and preparedness to proceed to international patenting and ultimately licensing. There were only a few firms in the sample which could be classed as inventors only (3 licensing, 1 attempting). Three small firms were also interviewed whose approach to patenting and licensing seemed to reflect similar problems to those faced by individual inventors. Two of the individual inventors and one of the small firms had faced patent litigation problems within Australia. In these cases it is clear that the threat to their industrial property rights tended to divert attention and funds away from the prospects of international patenting and licensing. Thus, the ability to exploit technology via licensing in other countries is affected by an inventor's or company's path through the patenting process.

Any concern about the viability of industrial property protection in foreign countries, whether directly related to problems experienced within Australia or not, acts as an important constraint on the activity of marketing technology internationally. Threat of patent breach and involvement in some form of patent litigation is one aspect of this concern, which is heightened in foreign countries where the problems of policing industrial property are usually seen to be greater. This concern is further accentuated where no form of protection of industrial property has been taken out in a given foreign country. For all investors, individuals or companies, early in the life of the Australian patent decisions must be made about the international extent of patent protection to be sought. Judgments must be made in advance about the likely extent of exploitation, and the cost of carrying a large international portfolio of patents is usually prohibitive for most inventors and small firms.

Thus, it is frequently the case that inventors and small firms find themselves with inadequate foreign industrial property protection and a heightened concern about the possibility of breach of industrial property rights by foreign companies. Two instances from our sample illustrate the constraining effect these influences may have on the foreign marketing of technology. In the first case, the company had faced patent litigation within Australia and, as a result, had neglected to seek patent protection within the United States until after the expiry time for such applications. In lieu of the patent, it had registered its trade mark because of interest in US market possibilities. After undertaking some advertising in trade journals there, 25 inquiries had been received from potential US licensees, but after a year no response to these had been made. The company was not prepared to send a brochure explaining its product for fear of the concept being copied.

The second firm had registered its designs in the UK and Denmark and had undertaken a small level of exporting via a Danish agent. The company had also been visited by South Korea's chief licensing officer who was prepared to arrange a licensing deal by taking drawings of designs back to South Korea and finding appropriate licensees to undertake production. The owner of the firm had responded as follows: 'Send a potential (Korean) licensee to me and we can then discuss the prospects of a licensing agreement. I shall not send my drawings outside the country so that they can be copied.' A joint-venture proposal by the Malaysian authorities had also been turned down.

In both these examples, there were clear proposals for the sale of technology via licensing arrangements but the approach to them was constrained by a lack of official industrial property protection and a concern about how the technology could nevertheless be protected in the foreign country. However, without full access to the technology it is difficult for a foreign company to be convinced about the value of a licensing relationship. Disclosure or secrecy agreements do not appear to have filled this void.

While the problems involved in the establishment of industrial property rights are sometimes perceived to be sufficiently large to prevent foreign licensing, there are nevertheless many inventors who carry through the exercise to completion. The commitment of the inventor to his invention and belief in its ultimate commercial success is a powerful motivation towards exploitation. This drive seemed to produce two types of responses amongst inventors in the survey:

(a)   There was a continued effort to sell the invention despite a host of problems which might have provoked withdrawal. A number of inventors contacted had faced difficulties such as patent litigation and had incurred expenses to the point where their basic liquidity was in jeopardy, yet they continued on to complete the task of achieving commercial success for their invention.

(b)   In other cases, the inventors continued onwards into a world marketing exercise without any real knowledge of the potential problems, convinced of the invention's worth and that it would therefore sell. An understanding of the real demands of licensing came afterwards. In one example, the inventor attended a conference of manufacturers of his product in the US and was offered a licensing arrangement on the spot by one manufacturer. Only then did the real assessment of licensing take place. The offer was turned down, the inventor returned to Australia, advertised in a US trade magazine and, after a number of offers, spent some time negotiating a more acceptable agreement with the original interested party.

Thus, the background of a company or inventor is important in explaining the likelihood and form of initial outward foreign licensing involvement, and in this respect the patenting process particularly, and protection of industrial property generally, can be a crucial phase leading up to the licensing step. However, the experience of the inventors and small firms mentioned could not be generalized to other firms in the sample. Larger firms, although recognizing the importance of patents did not appear to display the same level of 'concern' about the protection issue. Perhaps this is because the patent is embedded in a far stronger overall framework including know-how, etc. In general, they appeared to be less reliant on the patent per se and were therefore less exposed to patent breach. It was interesting to note the examples of larger firms having a high degree of confidence in the inability of other firms to copy their essential know-how, or more importantly, confidence in the unpreparedness of other firms to incur the cost involved in attempting to reproduce the concept in a viable manufacturing operation.

3.2. The impact of licensing in the longer run

In the following section the impact of the adopted licensing strategy on the development of a firm's international operations over time is examined. The impact of licensing in the longer run is determined in part by the role to which it is initially assigned and the circumstances surrounding adoption, frequently as a residual or second-line strategy. There is clearly a danger of firms merely looking to short-run returns rather than viewing licensing as a long-run investment in international development. Where licensing is only adopted as a secondary strategy there is a danger that this will lead to insufficient development and exploitation of the foreign markets involved. Licensing tends to be a more passive form of international operations, so that it is easy to slip into an arrangement whereby the market is totally left to the licensee to develop. For example, one respondent company had commented: 'It (the licensing deal) is a good arrangement. There is no work for us to do. The income just keeps on flowing in.' In this case, the firm was undertaking no information gathering or any other activity in the licensed foreign market. The market had been left completely to the licensee. The licensor was almost totally passive in the arrangement.

There are a variety of areas of co-operation with the licensee which will be necessary in order that the technology is effectively transferred and utilized by the licensee. If there is a passive involvement by the licensor, beyond the basic demands of negotiating and policing the licence, then it is likely that the firm will become a dependent partner. As a by-product, it will only have a limited degree of control over the success of the licensing venture.

In fact, the concern that licensing produces a loss of control over a firm's technological knowledge and its foreign exploitation is enough to discourage many firms from entering into any licensing arrangements at all, except with affiliated companies. Budack and Susbauer (1977, p. 21) concluded that: 'The loss of control has, for many firms, been the fundamental reason for not entering licensing agreements.' However, the more passive the involvement in the licensing arrangement, the greater the loss of control.

This problem is accentuated for the smaller firm which has limited capacity to develop marketing activities on a broad scale. It may have gone into licensing arrangements with limited exporting experience or other international background and been stretched to the limit of its resources in the patenting, licensee search and selection, and negotiation phases leading up to licensing. The small firm particularly tends to be more susceptible to dependency on the licensee and often the only form of control tends to be that which it is able to build into the licensing agreement. This represents a partial solution, but the firm still relies on other parties for international development, while it tends to remain in a relatively passive position.

It is interesting to note that, in responses to the survey question regarding 'drawbacks of licensing', information flow and control problems emerged as paramount. These drawbacks are of course interrelated as lack of information tends to be a contributory factor to the feeling of loss of control.

Of course, not all firms used licensing as the main means of developing a particular foreign market. In a small number of cases it acted in a supportive role to a joint venture operation. For example, one company entered into a licensing arrangement when it was forced to accept only a 30% equity in the UK joint venture operation rather than the preferred 50% level. The licensing agreement was a means of ensuring an adequate return on the technology transferred as well as controlling the utilization of the technology. Another company used two licensing agreements, one covering management assistance, the other technical assistance, in order to effect control of a 40%-owned joint venture in Malaysia as well as extract income. In other words, in the joint venture situation licensing becomes an important part of the armoury of control, rather than being a reason for loss of it as in normal licensing exercises.

In the longer run, however, the concern about lack of control in licensing may act as one of the factors causing a company to move to another mode of representation in a given foreign market. No examples were encountered in our survey where foreign market channel transfer could be said to have been induced by the control problem, but many of the companies had effected various measures, some via the licensing agreement itself, to ensure a degree of effective control. Some of the approaches were positive in nature (for example, via training schemes, frequent visits and early transfer of new technology) to ensure that the licensee operated as efficiently as possible and thereby generated acceptable returns to the licensor.

3.2.1. Licensing and knowledge development

The secondary, and passive, role to which licensing is commonly assigned is, in one sense, not surprising given some of its more obvious drawbacks as an internationalization strategy when compared to exporting and direct investment. It has, for example, been argued that 'the alternative of licensing a foreign producer can match the profitability of direct investment only in certain cases' (Caves, 1972, p. 272). The 'deficiencies' of licensing are chiefly related to the limited involvement in the foreign market that it usually implies. There tends to be reduced international marketing activity when compared to exporting or foreign investment. This restricts, or removes, the growth of experience in and knowledge about foreign markets, which form such key elements in the ability to extend foreign commitments. Johanson and Vahlne (1977, p. 23) have developed and partially confirmed a model of the internationalization process of the firm 'that focuses on the development of the individual firm, and particularly on its gradual acquisition, integration and use of knowledge about foreign markets and operations, and on its successively increasing commitment to foreign markets. The basic assumptions of the model are that lack of such knowledge is an important obstacle to the development of international operations and that the necessary knowledge can be acquired mainly through operations abroad.' If we accept the validity of this model, it does lead to the conclusion that, because licensing is usually a less involving form of international operations, it will tend to be less effective in advancing internationalization.

Information flows relating to foreign markets tend to be reduced in licensing relative to other international marketing strategies (Vernon, 1972, p. 216). Once the foreign licensing agreement has been signed and the technology effectively transferred (which may include training) there is less pressure on the licensor to maintain any further involvement in the foreign market.

3.2.2. Licensing as an interaction process

Notwithstanding the fact that licensing tended to be adopted as a secondary strategy, it was clear that most interviewees had, with experience, come to recognize the importance of licensing as an interactive operation. This was expressed in terms of the need to develop an effective 'working relationship' with the licensee. The emphasis on developing a 'licensing relationship' appeared to arise from a concern to ensure that licensing succeeded and the business developed as well as providing a means to achieve a degree of control over the nature and technological quality of the licensee's operations. Many firms commented that a 'hit-and-run' attitude to licensing ensured that there would be little future in the licensing business. It was not enough merely to transfer the technology under the terms of the agreement and leave it at that. It was stressed that the success of the licensor depended on the success of the licensee and that it was therefore in the interests of the Australian company to provide the best possible service to the licensee. This included frequent updating of the technology available. By such means, the licensee was made more dependent on the licensor, while the continuing royalty payments appeared as less of a millstone and there was less incentive to break the terms of the licensing agreement. A frequent comment in interviews was that a satisfactory two-way relationship could never be guaranteed by a legal document.

Thus, in time, the elements of a more positive approach to licensing seemed to emerge, with a more longitudinal view of its role and an emphasis on the effectiveness of interaction with the licensee. A general assessment of the experience of companies in the survey would be that failure to recognize the interactive nature of licensing put the long-run viability of the licensing strategy at risk.

The return benefits of effective interaction with the licensee can be considerable. For example, in response to a question about the long-run benefits of licensing, the three most commonly expressed items were (in order): return flow of technology and other information from the licensee; contribution to foreign market knowledge and skills; and exports of equipment to the licensee. In one case, the Australian company had participated in a joint venture in a third country with its licensee, while in another the Australian licensor had begun importing machinery from its US licensee in order to widen its local product range. There were also benefits in the expansion of consultancy services to the host country for a small number of firms. Such positive effects emphasize the potential role of licensing as a means of penetrating a foreign market and opening up wider market possibilities beyond licensing itself. A study of Finnish companies found that exports of related equipment to independent licensees (in aggregate) were more than double the value of licensing income (Oravainen, 1979, p. 99).

3.2.3. Licensing as a stepping stone strategy

From a longitudinal perspective, licensing is a phase in internationalization which may well create other marketing possibilities. In the long-run, it can become a springboard or bridge to these other openings, operating positively as a means of risk and uncertainty reduction. In some cases, the licensing arrangement opens up the possibility of takeover or a joint-venture relationship at a later stage. As such, foreign licensing can be viewed as a feasible experimentation phase by which a more direct involvement with, or takeover of, an existing manufacturer can be tested. Particularly in the early stages of internationalization, when a firm is often restricted by limited resources in its expansion activity, licensing can operate as an indirect means of securing a manufacturing base in a foreign market until it is better equipped to undertake direct investment. However, for such an approach to be effective, licensing has to be planned and adopted within a framework of the future potential for an altered marketing mode in the foreign market. In other words, if licensing is to operate as a stepping stone in the internationalization process, it should be seen not as an end point but as potentially a creative phase for developing alternative international possibilities.

The survey revealed few cases where licensing was utilized positively as a stepping stone strategy to other international marketing modes. The general impression was that the strategic role of licensing in the firm's internationalization process had not been clearly planned. Licensing tended to be adopted without consideration of its ultimate role. Although small in number, responses to the question regarding termination of licensing agreements tend to indicate that rather than being the subject of a planned disengagement from licensing to more effectively service a foreign market, termination tended to have been forced by outside circumstances and was generally not replaced by other modes of representation.

Even in cases where manufacturing companies have embarked on a licensing-only strategy for internationalization, there will be a tendency in the long-run to shift to other forms of international operations. Over time, the expanding licensing company will have developed international skills and is likely to have exposed new opportunities which are not exploitable by licensing alone.

In this sense, it is not the limitations of licensing per se that lead to an interest in an alternative approach, but rather that opportunities emerge *because* of the licensing activity. The success of licensing opens up and supports the move into hitherto uncharted territory. In the long run, an excess capacity for international operations beyond licensing is created within the firm at the same time as the uncertainty of new ventures is reduced. In individual foreign markets, market-specific skills and knowledge can often be best exploited by advancing to a more involved form of operations than licensing. By this means, a return is obtained on these other skills as well as on the original technological advantage.

A case in point is the Australian firm, Rocla Industries, which has extensively internationalized through the sale of technology embodied in licensing arrangements and in machinery. The initial stimulus to overseas operations came as a result of Rocla's patented invention, the roller suspension concrete pipe-making machine. This was developed in the 1940s and quickly sparked overseas interest. Rather than invest directly

Table 4. Reasons for termination of licensing agreements

Reason given	Number of firms
Licensee unwilling to renew agreement	2
Problems with licensee (e.g. licensee ceased operations, unsatisfactory performance)	6
Change in foreign market conditions	2
Product did not sell	1
Total	11

Table 5. Replacement activity where licensing agreement terminated

Replacement activity	Number of firms
Company has ceased to operate in host country	7
Another licensee adopted	1
Licensing replaced with exporting	3
Total	11

overseas, which would have required scarce capital and involved some risk, Rocla decided to market the patent via a licensing system. Capital was needed for Australian use. From 1948 onwards, Rocla began to sell the licence together with concrete pipe-making machinery. Since that time, it has steadily expanded the number of licensing agreements with foreign producers to the point of having now achieved near-global coverage. As a result, despite the market contact and knowledge 'deficiencies' normally associated with licensing, over such a long period Rocla developed considerable international knowledge, expertise and contacts and established its international reputation in the field. It was in a better position to perceive and act upon opportunities outside the normal licensing techniques. As the company has noted:

> Licensee arrangements can lead to investment opportunities in joint ventures, either for special contracts or normal production. In Northern Ireland, a licence agreement led to a joint venture operation for a major pipeline contract and then, eventually, to Rocla's own investment in Britain (Department of Overseas Trade, 1974, p. 363).

3.3. Overview

The mainly small to medium-sized companies in this investigation tended to utilize licensing because of various constraints on the use of other international marketing techniques, rather than because of a positive preference for licensing as such. Despite its adoption in a secondary or residual manner, though, many firms were still able successfully to expand their international operations via licensing. A key factor in the success of licensing appeared to be the development of effective interaction with the licensee in a long-run relationship. Effective interaction not only contributed to the commercial viability of the licensee but also produced return benefits for the licensor of technological and market information as well as exports of equipment and components and co-operation in other ventures in some cases. Few firms however, were able to develop the positive potential of licensing as a stepping stone strategy to other, more involving, forms of international market commitment. Perhaps this requires an altered strategic assessment of the potential for expanded international activities flowing from a more effective utilization of the licensing phase.

4. MARKETING ISSUES

4.1. The relative roles of patents, know-how and other forms of industrial property

There are various forms of technical and commercial technology (industrial or intellectual property in the broad sense) which may be the object of licensing overseas. Both in Australia and overseas, there appears to be a growing realization of the important roles which different elements in the licensing package can play in strengthening the process of marketing technology overseas. By tying the various elements together into a cohesive package, the position of the licensor is strengthened.

Patents and technical know-how are the most common objects of licensing and the most important basis of income generated. The Australian Bureau of Statistics (1979a) only made a separation between patent licence fees and royalties, and other technical know-how. Out of the total of $7.5 million received by the manufacturing sector, $4.3 million (57.3%) was for patents and $3.2 million (42.7%) for know-how.

There is some evidence, however, that once foreign-owned companies and cases of licensing to overseas affiliates are removed from consideration, the proportionate importance of patents is reduced. In a recent investigation of *all* Finnish firms engaged in outward licensing, it was found that out of the total of agreements with independent licensees, only 48.0% included patents as one form of industrial property transferred, whereas 96.1% included technical know-how. Other proportions were trade marks 36.4%, designs 5.2%, management know-how 11.7%, and marketing know-how 24.7% (Oravainen, 1979, p. 35). It is interesting to note the emerging separate importance of commercial, rather than technical, technology as an object of licensing. This area has probably been ignored or underrated in past considerations of licensing.

In this survey, companies were requested to provide a proportional breakdown of their licensing receipts between the main objects of licensing-patents, know-how, and other (trade marks, copyright, etc.). The results are shown in Table 6.

The clear message in responses to this question, taken overall, was that sale of know-how represented the principal element in licensing agreements signed. Only three out of the total of 34 respondent firms (8.8%) had not sold any know-how as part of their licensing agreements, whereas the corresponding figure for patents was 20 out of 34 companies (58.8%) and 28 out of 34 (82.4%) for the 'other' category. At the other end of the scale for 55.9% of respondent companies the know-how component constituted 80% or more of the licensing arrangement whereas the corresponding figure for patents was 11.8% and the 'other' category 3.0%. The overall breakdown was: patents 20.1%, know-how 69.8% and other 9.9%.

This pattern was further confirmed in responses to the question concerning overseas patenting, as shown in Table 7.

It is perhaps somewhat surprising that patents emerged as being of relatively minor overall importance in the responses. The breakdown does of course mask a great deal of variation on a company-to-company basis. While it might have been expected that smaller firms would have shown far greater reliance on patents – as is inevitably the case for individual inventors – the responses show otherwise. When the results shown in Table 7 are related to company

Table 6. Licensing receipts by object of licensing

Percentage of Licensing Receipts	Object of Licensing					
	Patents		Know-how		Other	
	No. of Firms	%	No. of Firms	%	No. of Firms	%
0	20	58.8	3	8.8	28	82.4
1–19	3	8.8	1	2.9	0	0
20–49	3	8.8	4	11.8	3	8.8
50–79	4	11.8	7	20.6	2	5.9
80–100	4	11.8	19	55.9	1	2.9
Total	34	100	34	100	34	100

Table 7. Has your company attempted to file for patents overseas?

	Number of agreements				
	1	2–5	6–20	>20	Total
No. of firms 'Yes'	7	10	11	1	29 (67.4%)
No. of firms 'No'	5	9	–	–	14 (32.6%)

size, and individual inventors removed, they reveal that about half of the small and medium-sized firms had not attempted to file for overseas patents whereas only one of the large firms had not done so. Although the supply of patentable technology is clearly a factor in the ability to patent overseas, the above results seemed to be a strong reflection of attitudes towards patenting held within respondent companies.

Larger firms seem to have recognized more clearly the marketing value of patents in the process of selling technology overseas, whereas many small to medium-sized firms have not only had a poor view of the value of patents but have been unprepared to commit finance to the investment in international patents. Nevertheless, it appears that the role of patents in the licensing process is currently subject to an important change, especially for small to medium-sized firms, the result of which is likely to be a greater emphasis than is indicated in the current results. This judgment is based on the interview process.

There were two cases where high technology companies had begun to pay greater attention to patenting after attaining some international experience. One company commented that while it originally did not take out patents it had learnt from that 'mistake' and now 'patented everything'. The other company noted that it had a limited understanding of patents in the 1960s leaving it with only know-how to license. It began to patent during the 1970s but had 'learnt that it was not as strong as it should be in the area and intended to become more competent'. The company was facing a court action in the US over breach of patent by an inventor who had taken out a patent on an idea which had already been developed, but not patented, by the Australian company.

A number of patent attorneys who were involved in outward foreign licensing activity on behalf of client companies were interviewed. One of these commented that there was a growing concern amongst companies that know-how is too easily lost through the movement of employees. As a result he said that companies were becoming more reluctant to buy straight know-how. He was in fact advising clients not to rely on know-how itself, but rather to use it as part of an overall package.

Thus, while there were many cases encountered of a negative or passive attitude towards the role and usefulness of patents, it was possible to discern a change in attitude within a number of firms towards a more positive approach. There appeared to be two sets of forces producing this development – technological 'push' and the 'pull' of international marketing. As a result of the involvement by firms in R&D activity, new technological know-how was being developed, some of it in patentable form, and so there was a natural defensive response of attempting to protect the ownership of the resultant industrial property. On the other side though, involvement in international marketing exercises, particularly via licensing, had produced, in many cases, a new recognition of the value of patents. Beyond the concern for protection of industrial property in foreign markets, patents have come to be viewed as an important element in strengthening the marketability of the licensing package to foreign licensees, of strengthening the hand of the licensor in the negotiation process and in ensuring compliance to the terms of agreement in the operative phase.

In general it would seem that, as Australian companies become more involved in international licensing, the value of patents and other forms of industrial property will become more apparent.

4.1.1. The know-how component

The passive approach towards patents by some companies partly reflects the importance placed on non-patented know-how. The way in which the interrelationship between patents and know-how influences judgments about patents was aptly illustrated by the experience of one manufacturer in the survey who was licensing two products overseas. One product was a component part which incorporated an idea that, once disclosed, could be readily copied. It required no back-up services to effect the transfer of technology. As a result, the manufacturer regarded the patents taken out overseas as being absolutely crucial to the generation of income from licensing. The other product being licensed overseas was a relatively complex machine used in hospitals. A high level of back-up services had to be provided to overseas manufacturers, in the form of supportive manufacturing know-how, so that the patent was considered to be a far less important factor in licensing.

The latter example is illustrative of the fact that effective international transfer of technology in a commercialized form via licensing normally requires far more than just the transfer of patent rights. In order that patent information be applied successfully, it commonly requires a 'software' element involving, in the main, the transfer of various forms of know-how. A training component of most licensing agreements tends to be an important medium for the transfer of manufacturing know-how. Pengilley has noted that:

> In a great number of patents, the patent does not necessarily tell anybody how the invention will work in a practical manner in actual operation. This disclosure is something different. It is 'know-how' . . . (a) United States survey undertaken by George Washington University showed that about 50 per cent of United States patents studied had to be supplemented by 'know-how' details before the patent became viable. Persons in industry with whom I have discussed this statistic give the uniform reply that they feel it overstates the position, that is they feel that far fewer inventions would be practically workable in the absence of 'know-how' details (Pengilley, 1977, p. 201).

Not only does the know-how factor complicate the technology transfer package, and therefore the negotiations surrounding commercialization via licensing agreement, but it also has important implications for the bargaining position of the licensor. To begin with, a strong know-how component strengthens the position of the licensor when selling the patent – he becomes less liable to patent breach, because the patent of itself is not enough to enable another manufacturer to go ahead with production, without considerable development cost and manufacturing experimentation. One inward licensor in the survey stressed that know-how was far more important than the patent because it could design around a patent, but it was far cheaper to purchase the licence, and thereby the manufacturing know-how, rather than attempt to replicate the development process itself. Given that much know-how tends to be developed through manufacturing experience, the individual inventor is at a significant disadvantage when compared to a manufacturing firm that is seeking to exploit an invention. The individual inventor is far more dependent on the patent – and is therefore far more exposed to patent breach. Should a large manufacturer be required to undertake considerable design and development work to make a licensed invention not only marketable but amenable to large-scale manufacturing techniques, it becomes questionable whether the invention is the same at the end of this process as the one originally offered. As a result, it is not surprising that proprietary rights are sometimes questioned. In fact, many manufacturers are not prepared to enter into patent licensing arrangements, as licensee, unless the product of the patent has already been commercialized, obviating the need for design work etc., and avoiding any potential problems regarding proprietary rights to any new technology developed. As a result, the individual inventor faces a difficult exercise when relying solely on the patent and attempting to sell technology overseas.

In contrast, a larger manufacturing company, with R&D facilities, normally has a strong know-how component to support the basic patent, as well as the ability to gain from technology swap arrangements, sell some related plant and equipment, etc. The availability of R&D facilities enhances the position of a manufacturer as a licensor because of the possibility of creating a more permanent flow of technology and back-up technological support. As Limbury (1979, p. 19) notes, 'it is usually the totality of the know-how concerning the use, manufacture and marketing of the item which is given the greatest weight by the potential licensee, particularly if the licensor is able to update it regularly'. The large manufacturer is therefore in a relatively stronger position by selling a technology 'package' rather than simply a patent. The returns will not only tend to be greater, but the patent is effectively secured within the total package.

Thus, while the patent can play an important role in strengthening the total package for licensing purposes, it appears that, not only does the know-how component perform a similar role, but it is the crucial element in most cases of effective technology transfer via licensing.

4.1.2. Other components

While patents and know-how are the major components of most licensing packages, other elements – mainly trade marks and designs – also play a part. For some industries, as noted earlier, and for certain companies they play a vital role in the ability to license overseas and obtain a degree of industrial property protection where patenting is not possible or could be readily bypassed. In fact in interviews both design and trade mark protection emerged as far more important components of industrial property protection overseas than was indicated by responses to the questionnaire. For example, one company mentioned that it was indicated by responses to the questionnaire. For example, one company mentioned that it was interested in expanding its overseas licensing activities beyond the one outward agreement currently held. However, it held few patents – none of these being overseas – and yet it had registered designs and product names in a number of prospective overseas markets as a basis for future licensing possibilities.

Trade marks can be a useful contributory factor in the development of a market via licensing. In this context Limbury (1979, p. 19) has noted that 'licensees usually can be required to use the licensor's trademark in relation to the licensed products or processes and this develops good-will attaching to the licensor rather than to the licensee. Should it ever be necessary to change licensees, the licensor's identity in the market, through its trademark, will already be established.' Likewise, when licensing occurs subsequent to a period of exporting, exporting having led to goodwill associated with the registered trade mark, the licensor may be able to make the trade mark an important element of the licensing package. The trade mark tends to be elevated as a component of the company's industrial property and improves the marketability of the total package. In one case a trade mark established via a successful exporting programme subsequently became the principal object of an enforced switch to licensing. However, it appeared that, for those firms in the survey licensing trade marks, trade marks were a relatively unimportant basis for generating licensing income in most instances.

While know-how emerged as the principal component of technology transfer via licensing, there is a clear trend that the elements within the licensing package are expanding, with the result that the licensing package in the future is likely to involve a more complex amalgam of elements than is presently the case. Not only will this tend to strengthen the basis of protection of the package but will enhance its marketability and widen the basis of income generation. As a by-product of the greater use of licensing in international marketing, it can be argued that a greater recognition of the useful contributory role which can be played by even the more minor components of the total package is likely to emerge. Overseas evidence suggests a further spread in the types of know-how being licensed, with an increase in emphasis on commercial 'technology'.

4.2. The timing factor

An important factor in the success of licensing is the timing of the attempt to sign up overseas licensees relative to the stage of technical and commercial development of an invention or other form of new technology. In most cases in the survey, there was relatively limited attention to this question because the timing move was determined by outside forces. Since licensing generally followed exporting, the technology was normally relatively well developed and had been effectively commercialized before the licensing step. The decision to license was promoted by a variety of commercial and strategic considerations which had little to do with a planned assessment of the most appropriate phase in the life of the technology to exploit it overseas via licensing. Similarly, a recent US investigation found that US innovations were more likely to be exploited internationally via licensing in the second five years after commercialization than in the initial five years (Mansfield et al, 1979, p. 56).

For most firms in the survey then, the timing was not strategically determined. Nevertheless, there was a fortuitous benefit in this situation, as the Australian licensors were able to approach licensees with generally proven technology – proven in both commercial and technical senses. For a licensee there is obviously a greater attraction in being able to utilize such technology because there tend to be limited risks in adoption, while the costs of further development and design work are saved. As Limbury (1979, p. 19) has noted:

> The most favourable environment in which to grant licenses is where the licensor is already successfully exploiting the products in his home market. Potential licensees can thus realistically evaluate the operating conditions they are likely to encounter . . . If the licensor has already solved his manufacturing and marketing problems he would possess a body of know-how which would enable the licensee to start promptly . . . A potential licensor is often better advised to postpone attempts to market a relatively untried patent until he can simulate actual operational conditions when negotiating with potential licensees.

One relatively large and successful licensor in the survey commented that while it was always a problem of when to offer technology for sale, it erred on the side of commercializing the product first. While most respondent companies went into licensing with established technology, it is clear that not all companies are in a position to license in such an evolutionary way because of, for example, rapid technological progress. In fields of rapid introduction of new ideas, long periods of commercial and technical development may jeopardize later attempts to license internationally. In such situations interest may be shown by potential licensees who are seeking early solutions to technological competition within their home markets. Licensing new technology is an attractive alternative to the time and cost which would be taken up in a firm's own R&D efforts (Stubbs, 1968, pp. 92–6). In industries where there is a certain fashion element to product designs, such as the furniture industry, there is considerable pressure on companies to exploit any newly developed technology as rapidly as possible. Thus, it may be necessary to advance the timing of the attempt to sell technology overseas to the phase of early commercial experimentation, despite the clear advantages in selling a well-proven product or process. McInnes (1979, p. 128) has argued that:

> Typically in the life of a patent the first five years are spent bringing the idea to an initial commercial level . . . Obviously and especially in a market as small as Australia's it is not logical to wait until the process is obsolescent before introducing it to the larger market overseas . . . For this reason I advocate taking technology overseas at the stage of pilot commercial development.

In a number of cases in the survey, companies were licensing principally to middle-income or developing countries in the Asian and African regions. The technology involved was well established, but more 'appropriate' to the developing countries and there was minimal danger of technological obsolescence. As a result, there seemed to be virtually no pressure on the companies to seek rapid exploitation of the technology. It is therefore in fields of high and/or rapidly changing technology where other technically advanced countries are the principal markets that the timing question becomes a critical issue. In these situations though, the risks involved in advancing the timing of sale of technology are reduced when the licensee is a well established overseas client, perhaps involving the broadening of an already established licensing relationship.

With regard to the commercial implications of selling technology before proving commercial success, Limbury (1979, p. 19) maintains:

> More difficult to conclude are successful licenses where the licensor merely has a pilot plant or prototype to offer for demonstration purposes to licensees. Lack of actual commercial success is usually reflected in less satisfactory royalty terms since the licensee requires recognition of the risks and delays in pioneering.

The timing problem for individual inventors with no manufacturing base is even more acute. Inventors have difficulties not only in demonstrating commercial feasibility but also in proving technological operation under manufacturing conditions. Such difficulties tend to be accentuated when the technology concerns an industrial process or a large item of capital equipment where scaling up is important. One inventor in the sample attempted to license his building systems technology to a Middle-Easter market but, while interest was shown, prospective clients were not prepared to consider seriously a licensing arrangement without evidence of its use within the housing and construction industry within Australia. The inventor has since switched to a programme of active commercial exploitation within Australia. Clearly he has attempted to sell the technology overseas too early in its life given that the idea involved a major departure from existing systems and included a large machine whose operation could not be readily demonstrated overseas.

This case was in direct contrast to the experience of another inventor whose product was very small, and consumer oriented. From conception to first sample the product had only taken six months, and was licensed soon thereafter to a Hong Kong toy manufacturer for world distribution. The idea used in the product was simple and its operation could be readily demonstrated. Given that the commercial life of the product was likely to be relatively short, there was considerable pressure on the inventor to seek maximum exploitation as quickly as possible.

Thus, while it is sometimes suggested that the attempt to license overseas by inventors should proceed immediately after the provisional patent application has been lodged, the small number of case studies examined in the survey indicate that the appropriate time to begin the attempt to license overseas for individual inventors as with manufacturing companies, relates to such broader questions as the rate of change of technology, the extent of departure from existing technology and the complexity of the product.

In general though, for both individual inventors and manufacturing firms, the strongest pressure in regard to the timing of exploitation of technology via international licensing appears to lie in the direction of some technical and commercial proving beforehand, at least within the home market. The marketing exercise is likely to be significantly more difficult without such background, unless there is strong commercial pressure on a potential licensee in the foreign market in favour of the early adoption of new technology.

4.3. Selection of the licensee

Interviews with companies revealed that there was considerable variation in the criteria used to select licencees. However, a picture emerged of companies taking greater care in the selection process as they increased the number of agreements. There seemed to be a strong consensus that the selection of a good licensee was far more important than a tight legal document. The terms most commonly used were 'trust' and 'confidence'.

Many companies put considerable time and resources into assessing the market first before finding licensees. The following were seen as important:

- the depth of political stability. Frequent changes of government were not as worrisome if the basic administrative structure was stable.
- the existence of a US or British legal system. Some companies would not license unless a strong British system existed.
- the end uses of the licensor's product and any peculiar requirements which may favour or disadvantage the product. For example, provision for insulation is necessary in external building panels in Scandinavia.
- establish what competitive product lines exist in the country.

One company even went to the trouble of having more than one executive travel through the country making independent assessments before embarking on the selection process.

With regard to short-listing several techniques were used. Some companies would not short list potential licensees unless they were already known to the licensor. However, for most, licensors were prepared to investigate previously unknown companies. A common technique was to advertise both in host country newspapers and other trade journals. Also, exhibitions during the short-listing period proved to be useful.

Uppermost in firms' minds in selecting licensees was the problem of competition. Even though much of the licensing which had taken place was in countries to which the licensor could not export, care was taken not to license firms that were able to compete in other markets and also not to license companies which produced competitive lines. The emphasis was on complementarity. Complementarity was also seen as important where there was considerable trade in technology. In these situations, licensees sought were those keen and able to participate in technology interchange.

In the selection process a number of characteristics of potential licensees seemed to have been examined closely:

4.3.1. Size

The largest companies were frequently avoided because of a concern that the technology offered would be relatively minor or unimportant to them. It was material that the technology make an important contribution to the licensee's operation an that the licensee was prepared to push the products. Small private firms tended to be avoided because they could quite easily close down and re-open under another name still holding the technology.

4.3.2. Distribution

The ability to distribute and market the licensor's product was considered paramount. This factor is of course partly connected to the size and extent of the licensee's operation.

4.3.3. Growth

Notwithstanding the above factors, in general companies preferred to select licensees which were keen to grow.

Finally, compatibility was seen as significant. The licensee needed to have the capacity to manufacture the product. Where firms were selected which were not producing competitive products it was still important that the firm had been working with similar materials. Compatibility was also strengthened if the licensee possessed quality technical staff and if necessary quality design staff. In general, there was a strong emphasis on the technical side.

Overall then, the selection of the licensee emerged as a crucial phase in the licensing process. The investment of considerable time and resources in the selection process was common and was justified by the fact that the licensee effectively becomes the long term representative of the licensor in the designated foreign market and ultimately determines the success of the licensing venture.

4.4. Negotiation

Having selected a target group of potential licensees, the next step for the licensor is the negotiation of an acceptable licensing agreement. In approaching a potential licensee, an important issue at the outset is the extent of information disclosure. This is a difficult area as the potential licensee must be aware of what is being offered before he can begin to make an assessment. Often licensors do not think out carefully what is to be offered and how it is to be protected. Negotiations can be aborted if the licensor needs to divulge confidential information but is not prepared to waive company secret status. If the licensor desires the potential licensee to sign a secrecy agreement the information must be clearly identifiable and separable from public information and information already in the potential licensee's possession. The interviews indicated that secrecy agreements were generally not used and licensors tended to take calculated risks after carefully choosing targets. With smaller companies often too much information was divulged in the early stages.

To sell the technology some licensors felt it necessary to collect intelligence on the potential market for the product embodying the technology and prepare cost estimates.

Accuracy was considered to be important to ensure that the licensor was not vulnerable in negotiations.

Companies saw it as rewarding to leave the potential licensee with a list of questions which should be answered before further rounds of negotiation took place. These questions were seen to serve two purposes:

(a) force more people in the recipient company to become involved in the agreement, and;
(b) provide more information to the licensor.

Companies were also careful to stress the need to take particular care over key clauses in the agreement. In assessing royalties licensors had to be able to calculate the likely savings or likely profits which would arise from adopting the technology.

Notwithstanding these calculations the most common royalty rate was 5%.[1] The royalty rate was varied by turnover, the need for warranties and servicing, and the field of activity. Pharmaceuticals, chemicals and engineering products (with low turnover) appeared to attract higher royalties.

Of curse all companies desired an up-front lump sum payment. Clearly, the firm must be able to bargain from a position of strength if it hopes for a lump sum payment as well as a reasonable royalty payment.

This is highlighted by the survey data. Those firms with only one licence agreement had had no lump sum payments included in their agreements. Out of the 11 companies which indicated that they had only one agreement (10 or 91%) received royalties based on sales levels alone. The remaining agreements attracting lump sum payments tended to increase for firms holding a larger portfolio of agreements. After taking into account conjointness with other forms of payment for firms holding 2–5 agreements 30.3% of agreements included lump sum payments. The proportion rose to 38% for firms holding 6–20 agreements.

It was stressed that licensors must realize that they are negotiating with individuals rather than companies at the negotiating table. Executives tend to be wary of committing their companies to high expenditure as such a decision may rebound against them in future promotional rounds.

Throughout weight was given to the need to be 'reasonable'. Notwithstanding the recognition that minimum royalties were important and perhaps more important than performance clauses, it was accepted that minimum royalties must be practical. Insufficient allowance for a settling-in period can destroy an agreement. Furthermore, exclusivity was seen in a similar light. 'It is unreasonable to expect a licensee to buy technology without exclusivity' was a common view.

Finally, most companies attempted to draw up a tight agreement. This was done not so much to keep two hostile parties together but rather to serve as a reminder or point of reference for both parties in the event that key personnel leave and in case a dispute requiring litigation arises.

5. COSTS

A common view in economic literature is that the marginal cost of transferring technology will be very low once the set-up cost associated with developing technology has been incurred. This view is naïve in practice, albeit because of the premise upon which it is based; that transfer involves no more than the provision of blueprints already developed. Indeed, if we accept this premise, we could go further and say that where a patent is involved no transfer is necessary as the specifications are on file in the host country and for a patent to be granted the specifications must be capable of being used successfully by an independent manufacturer. But the above view is discredited in practice by the complexity of the transfer. Often a transfer will require a composite of patents, unpatented know-how (technical, managerial and marketing), designs (both registered and unregistered) and sometimes trade marks and copyrights. The assignment of rights to use a patent is more complicated too. First, the specifications in the patent may be insufficient as they have been necessarily restricted to cover very narrow claims. Second, negotiations often take placed during the pre-publication period. Consequently, supplementary procedures are necessary. Third, many patents do require additional know-how for others to activate them.

Two overseas investigations add support to the above rebuttal. Teece (1977) analysed the cost of transfer of technology by US multinationals. His general conclusions were that there was a decline in the cost of transfer with each new transfer but on average his costs amounted to 19% of the total project cost associated with new technology acquired by the transferee. In the study by Oravainen (1979) which is perhaps more relevant to the Australian situation, there is a measure of all explicit and implicit costs[2] associated with establishing an agreement. Having acquired information on all Finnish firms licensing to independent licensees, he calculated that in 1977 the average total cost per agreement was 456,000 Finnish marks or approximately 100,000 Australian dollars.

5.1. Evidence from interviews

Because of the sensitivity of Australian companies to the release of cost data, it was not possible to obtain information on absolute costs. However, it became readily apparent in the interviews that the transfer process was a costly exercise. Many companies were surprised at the time, cost and difficulty of entering into licensing agreements. The opportunity costs associated with this exercise are highlighted where a small firm with an owner/manager is involved. He must make a decision as to where he devotes his time and his financial resources.

The costs and time scale associated with the initial phases of licensing appeared to be related to three main factors:

(a)   The necessity to undergo a considerable amount of learning about the process of licensing. Where authority cannot be delegated as in the case of smaller firms this is a major problem.

(b)   The location and assessment of suitable licensees. This cost is often increased as licensors became more aware of the importance of 'getting things right at the outset'. It was observed with some of the more successful licensors that considerable time was taken assessing the licensee, his market and the general economic environment, and;

(c)   the negotiation was often very costly in time and airfares as the licensor needed to negotiate in the host country rather than his own country.

Some of the smaller firms had attempted to circumvent these costs by using agents. To date it is difficult to assess how successful and cost effective this alternative has been. The use of outside assistance from government was certainly looked upon favourably. However, licensors could go little further than use these services for general information and some contacts.

5.2. Survey results

Licensors were asked to indicate the relative importance of particular costs. This required them to apportion total costs, costs associated with establishing an agreement and costs associated with maintaining agreements. The results are set out in Table 8.

Table 8(a) indicates that establishment costs were seen as the most important. However, the breakdown demonstrates that if the absolute costs are significant for the company then protection of industrial property and maintenance cannot be ignored. The high level associated with protection is perhaps a consequence of the desire on the part of many companies to patent wherever they saw potential for foreign sales. Of the 29 companies which filed for patents overseas, 16 (55.2%) had done so in countries where they adjudged a potential for licensing, export or foreign investment. As a result, some of the industrial property costs may in fact be connected with exporting and foreign investment. The relative importance of maintenance is also interesting. This indicated that many agreements are not 'one off' but require servicing, a natural outcome of the licensor's desire to build a licensing relationship.

Table 8(b) shows that well over half the expenses are involved in discovering, and striking an agreement with, the licensee. The relatively low figure for adaptation and testing may be partly explained by the fact that a high proportion of licences were struck after the firm had been exporting to the market. In addition much of the adaption could have been implemented by personnel training by the licensor.

Finally, in Table 8(c) there is a breakdown of the maintenance costs. Here we can see the outcome of the licensing relationship emerging quite strongly. A number of firms stressed that a large part of this figure is attributable to frequent visits to the licensee.

The relatively low figure for on-going market research is also interesting. Perhaps it indicates that even though much is being spent on building a licensing relationship relatively little is being spent on attempting to forge the next step in the internationalization process. Clearly then, the costs of transferring technology via licensing are significant, and greater than many firms embarking on a licensing strategy realize. The establishment costs of licensing are particularly significant, but if a licensing agreement is to be effectively maintained, substantial continuing costs must also be incurred. Over the longer run, the general pattern is for the cost of each new licensing agreement to decline.

For this to occur though, some economies need to be effected in each establishment phase. In this respect the beneficial effects of learning-by-doing in licensing have been reported for one Australian company:

> Rocla gained most of its know-how about licensing in overseas countries the hard way. Since it began in 1948, the company has found there are pitfalls as well as benefits. The license agreement now incorporates clauses to overcome the problems experienced during the life of its early arrangements (Department of Overseas Trade, 1974, p. 363).

6. CONCLUSION

In this study of outward foreign licensing by Australian companies the role of licensing in the internationalization process of individual firms was examined, along with important aspects of the associated marketing exercise. The emphasis has been on the use of licensing as an international business strategy other than as part of the transfer flows of a foreign affiliate network.

In general it was found that licensing tended to be utilized as a second-line or residual international marketing mode because external pressures constrained or prevented the use of exporting to particular foreign markets. As a result, there was limited assessment and planning of the longer term role of licensing. Nevertheless, many firms had recognized the need to work closely with their licensees over time in order to ensure that the licensing arrangement worked successfully and that it generated satisfactory returns. In some cases the development of an effective working relationship with the licensee had led to spin-off benefits in terms of technical interchange and co-operation beyond the confines of the licensing arrangement.

However, few firms appeared to have a clear perception of the positive potential of licensing as an international penetration strategy – either in the form of complementary operations built around licensing or as a bridge to alternative, deeper forms of market involvement.

The study does show that licensing has a positive role to play in extending and deepening the international operations of individual firms. For licensing to fulful this role though, it must be employed with far more strategic purpose, involving a longer term perspective of a company's foreign market involvement. In addition, to secure any long-term benefits from licensing, considerable care needs to be taken in the timing of technology transfer; the choice of foreign market; the selection of licensee; the negotiation process; and assembly of the contents of the licensing package to be offered.

Table 8. The relative costs of licensing overseas

		%
(a)	*Breakdown of total costs of licensing overseas*	
	Protection of industrial property	24.8
	Establishment of a licensing agreement	46.6
	Maintenance of licensing agreement	29.0
(b)	*Breakdown of establishment costs*	
	Search for suitable licensees	22.8
	Communication between involved parties	44.7
	Adaption and testing of equipment for licensee	9.9
	Training personnel for the licensee	19.9
	Other (additional marketing activity and legal expenses)	2.5
(c)	*Breakdown of maintenance costs*	
	Audit of the licensee	9.7
	On going market research in the market of the licensee	7.2
	Backup services for the licensee	65.0
	Defence of industrial property rights in the licensee's territory	11.0
	Others	7.1

This reading is based on a report for the Industrial Property Advisory Committee and the Licensing Executives Society of Australia, December 1981.

NOTES

1. The royalty was usually based on the licensee's invoice value for the products associated with the techniques less: (a) Sales tax; (b) Agent's commission; (c) Cash discounts; (d) Packaging, freight and delivery charges; (e) Site installation costs.

2. The Oravainen study involved probably the most comprehensive effort yet to assess the implicit costs associated with licensing. An import component of costs which is generally ignored is managerial time. The Finnish licensing executives provided details of their own and subordinates' activities concerning licensing, and the time spent in each. The time spent was valued at the appropriate salary level. Not only did these 'time costs' constitute a major component of the total licensing costs, but they caused most early licensing agreements of the Finnish firms to be unprofitable.

REFERENCES

Australian Bureau of Statistics (1979a) *Foreign Control in Research and Experimental Development: Private Enterprises, 1976–77*, Canberra.

Australian Bureau of Statistics (1979b) *Research and Experimental Development: Private Enterprises, 1976–77*. Canberra.

Budak, P.R., Susbauer, J.C. (1977) International Expansion Through Licensing: Guidelines for the Small Firm. *Journal of Small Business Management* **15**(1): 17–21.

Caves, R.E. (1972) International Corporations: The Industrial Economics of Foreign Investment. In J.H. Dunning (ed) *International Investment*, Penguin, Harmondsworth.

Department of Overseas Trade (1974) Rocla Builds Business Through Licensing. *Overseas Trading* July 25, 1974: 363–364.

Johanson, J., Vahlne, J.E. (1977) The Internationalization Process of the Firm – Model of Knowledge Development and Increasing Foreign Market Commitments. *Journal of International Business Studies* **8**(1): 23–32.

Limbury, A. (1979) Manufacturing Licence Deals Can Produce Export Profits. *Overseas Trading* January 19, 1979: 19.

Luostarinen, R. (1979) *The Internationalization of the Firm*, Acta Academiae Oeconomicae Helsingiensis, Helsinki School of Economics: Helsinki.

McInnes, A.D. (1979) Now Is the Time To Market Technology. *Overseas Trading* March 2, 1979, 128.

Mansfield, E., Romeo, A., Wagner, S. (1979) Foreign Trade and US Research and Development. *Review of Economics and Statistics* **61**(1): 49–57.

Oravainen, N. (1979) *Suomalaisten Yritysten Kansainvaliset Lisenssi – Ja Know-How – Sopimukset* (International Licensing and Know-How Agreements of Finnish Companies). Helsinki School of Economics, FIBO Publications, No. 13: Helsinki.

Parry, T.G., Watson, J.F. (1979) Technology Flows and Foreign Investment in the Australian Manufacturing Sector. *Australian Economic Papers* **18**(6): 103–118.

Pengilley, W. (1977) Patents and Trade Practices – Competition Policies in Conflict. *Australian Business Law Review* **5**(3): 172–203.

Senate Standing Committee (1979) *Industrial Research and Development in Australia*. Australian Government Publishing Service: Canberra.

Stubbs, P. (1968) *Innovation and Research: A Study in Australian Industry*. Cheshire: Melbourne.

Teece, D.J. (1977) Technology Transfer by Multinational Firms. *Economic Journal* **87**(346): 242–261.

Tesar, G. (1977) Corporate Internationalization Strategy Through Licensing Arrangements in Industrial Marketing. Paper presented at the annual meeting of the Academy of Marketing Science, Akron, Ohio, May 4–6, 1977.

Vernon, R. (1972) *The Economic Environment of International Business*. Prentice-Hall: Englewood Cliffs.

16

Joint Ventures and Global Strategies

Kathryn Rudie Harrigan

As business risks soar and competition grows more fierce, firms will embrace joint ventures with increasing frequency. This should not be surprising. Joint ventures have long been used by entrepreneurial firms to expand into new markets, particularly with newly industrializing nations. But what of the use of joint ventures within mature economies? What of the firms whose markets are being invaded by global competitors? Little attention has been devoted to other uses of joint ventures, and this is a serious shortcoming. Joint ventures represent a significant change in industry structures and in competitive behaviour. They can be a more versatile competitive tool than earlier studies have indicated.[1] They could help domestic firms to enter the global milieu or find a new way of competing. This article sketches firms' uses of 'operating joint ventures' in light of the pressures created by international competition. It presents a framework for predicting how parent firms might configure joint ventures to achieve these competitive purposes.

OPERATING JOINT VENTURES DEFINED

This definition suggests a defensive approach. 'Operating joint ventures' are partnerships by which two or more firms create an entity, a 'child,' to carry out a productive economic activity. Each partner takes an active role in decision-making, if not also in the child's operations. Operating joint ventures do not include passive financial investments made by parties who are not involved in the new entity's strategic business decisions. Nor do they include interfirm arrangements that do not create a separate entity.

Operating joint ventures could include manufacturing arrangements, such as the titanium steel mill of Allegheny International, Sumitomo Metal, and their partners. They could include distribution arrangements, like that of Coca-Cola Bottling and Seagram, or research and development arrangements, like those formed by a consortium of electronics firms. Each party to the operating joint venture makes a substantial contribution in the form of capital and technology, marketing experience, personnel or physical assets. But most importantly, partners contribute access to distribution networks. If neither partner controls market access, it will be more difficult for the joint venture to succeed, particularly within industries where other firms have longer track records. This will be so because of the nature of global competition and the greater difficulties encountered in hurdling entry barriers when an industry's structure is well-established. Similarly, when a nation's

Reprinted with the permission of the *Columbia Journal of World Business*, 1988, **14**(2), 36–64 economy is mature, distribution infrastructures will be better established, and more costly to duplicate.

GLOBAL STRATEGIES DEFINED

'Global strategies' are those which recognize that competition can no longer be confined to a single nation's boundaries. Industries become global for many reasons, and firms need an approach appropriate to meet new challenges when this change occurs.[2] When this occurs, firms must re-examine their assumptions concerning how competitive advantage can be gained by integrating the operations of diverse geographic locations. This is a novel suggestion. Although firms will often think of production scale economies, technological innovation, and new sourcing arrangements as a means of meeting the global challenge, fewer firms may recognize the advantages of joint ventures. Yet operating joint ventures offer a means of leveraging firms' advantages to succeed within global industries. As is explained below, competitive advantages could be gained through operating joint ventures.

A JOINT VENTURE FRAMEWORK

What determines the viability and durability of joint ventures? How should firms design and run them? This section presents a framework that predicts, from the parent firm's perspective, how the joint venture bargain might be struck. The framework is dynamic, as Figure 1 indicates, and it involves external forces as well as the considerations detailed below.

In Figure 1, competitive forces combine with the interests of two or more parent firms to make a joint venture feasible. (Figure 2 details these forces.) The combination of strategic needs and parent firm resources determine the configuration of the child. The configuration – the control mechanisms, vertical integration relationships and other points of the bargaining agreement – may change over time, due to many stimuli, as depicted in Figure 2.

The ultimate success (or failure) and disposition of the resources committed to the joint venture are also determined by these stimuli. A brief explanation of the framework follows. The forces giving parent firms more (or less) bargaining power to forge particular joint venture configurations are discussed more fully below.

Parent firm considerations

In Figure 2, Parent Firms A and B desire certain (1) benefits from their joint venture. These are their reasons for co-operating with other firms. They recognize that co-operation in joint ventures entails (2) costs, which some firms may consider too significant to accept. In such cases, their negotiations to form joint ventures will be fruitless or will take other forms, instead. If a joint venture can be negotiated, each potential partner has resources and skills which could serve as (3) inputs to the joint venture. Paradoxically, the greater firms' resources, the greater their (4) bargaining power. But the greater their (5) need to co-operate, the less their bargaining power will be in negotiating the configuration of the joint venture. The magnitude of the opportunity costs or other disadvantages firms perceive in co-operating will determine the height of their (6) barriers to co-operation. It is necessary to overcome these barriers if a joint venture is to be formed. Later, if asymmetries develop

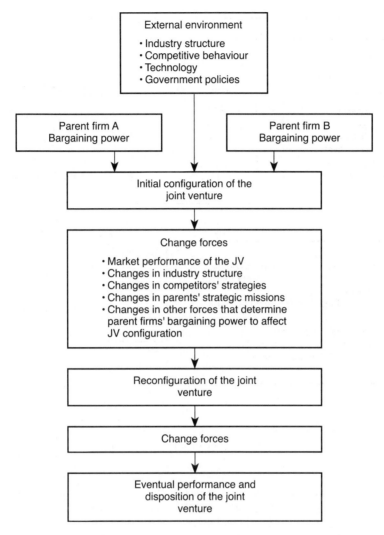

Fig. 1. A Dynamic Model of Joint Venture Activity.

between joint venture partners, exit barriers must be overcome to change the terms of the bargaining agreement, which is discussed below. Thus there are barriers in forming and in re-configuring joint ventures.

Child firm considerations

In Figure 1, the (7) child, or joint venture (JV), is the result of the bilateral bargaining power of its parents. Its form, inputs, outputs, and control mechanisms are defined by a (8) bargaining agreement. This agreement, which defines the child's domain of activities, specifies its (9) outputs, and it may specify its customers, as well. The purpose of the joint venture's existence is usually defined by these outputs. The bargaining agreement specifies

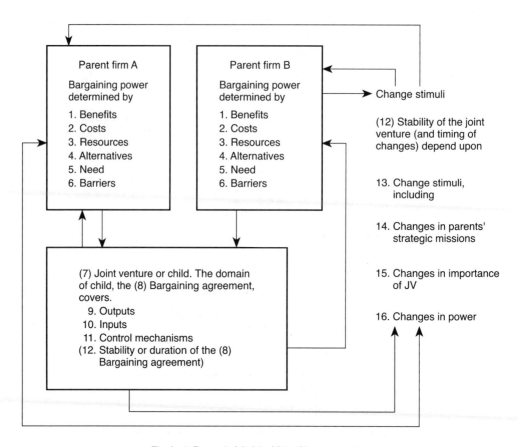

Fig. 2. A Dynamic Model of Joint Venture Activity.

the (10) inputs necessary for the joint venture to attain its objectives. These resources may be provided for by its parents through a variety of vertical integration arrangements, or they may be obtained from outsiders. The child cannot be viable, however, if its parents do not provide for an economic source of (or means of attaining) these inputs. The bargaining agreement also specifies the (11) control mechanisms its parents will use to ensure that the benefits they desired were received. These control mechanisms should also provide for the (12) stability of the joint venture.

Change stimuli

Both the formation and the stability of a joint venture agreement depend upon the nature of the bargaining agreement that can be struck between parents and the impact of (13) change stimuli upon the perceived attractiveness of the joint venture agreement. Joint ventures are formed within dynamic environments. Environmental conditions may change. Parent firms may change, and the child itself will evolve over time.[3]

A joint venture's (17) performance within its markets will affect its attractiveness to its parents. An industry's structure can change due to past competitive behaviours, and with it, change the potential for future profitability. Competitive conditions may change within the child's industry due to technological, political or other uncontrollable changes. The child's abilities to command resources or satisfy its customers may deteriorate or improve, depending upon its past performance. Another part of the child's performance is determined by the suitability of its strategy for serving its customers, and by its effectiveness in implementing its chosen strategy (past performance will be, in part, the source of the child's current market power). Since this strategy must accommodate the dynamics of at least three entities, the joint venture's relationship with one or both of its parents may change due to changes in their strategies.

These or other (13) stimuli may force the joint venture's parents to renegotiate the terms of the bargaining agreement. The timing of changes in the bargaining agreement will depend upon the forces motivating a particular parent to co-operate or modify the terms of co-operation (and whether they can overcome (6) the barriers which constitute impediments to their strategic flexibility). The re-configuration and ultimate disposition of the child will depend upon its parents' (14) strategic missions, (15) the strategic importance they attach to the child, and the alternatives parents possess to attain the same benefits which their joint venture may have provided in other ways. Possessing alternatives gives parents a new source of bargaining power that may be strong enough for them to change their bargain and hurdle inertia barriers. The sources of these barriers are sketched in the discussion of parent firm bargaining power which follows.

DETERMINANTS OF PARENT FIRM BARGAINING POWER

Firms will co-operate in forming joint ventures only if the needs of each partner are great enough and if they can add resources which are complementary to the other's attributes. The resources firms possess will give them the basis for bargaining power when entering joint ventures, but if their needs for co-operation are great enough this potential power will be mitigated.[4] The balance between these opposing forces will be realized in the form the joint venture takes. It will be apparent in the control mechanisms partners use to control their interests in the JV, in the vertical relationships they maintain with the JV, and with its stability. The stability of joint ventures will be affected by a variety of forces. This section discusses the net impact of parent firms' resources upon the ultimate bargaining agreement that determines the child's configuration, alternatives for attaining the benefits joint ventures promise, needs to co-operate and barriers to forming (and dissolving) joint ventures.

Successful joint ventures serve their purpose without disrupting their parents' strategic well-being. The key to successful joint ventures will be a meeting of minds.[5] Effective joint ventures depend upon trust, but they are often forged as a compromise between two or more parent firms who would rather own the child wholly.[6] Like a marriage, they tolerate their wayward partners to attain some advantage that satisfies their needs. They key to forging mutually satisfactory joint ventures will be realistically assessing firms' strengths (and weaknesses) in the proposed venture. It is also necessary to assess potential partners' commitments to the venture's success and their willingness to contribute resources (or provide a market for outputs) in a manner that accommodates their partners' needs.[7] Joint ventures may be transitory organizations firms embrace to attain an advantage faster, but the most stable joint ventures will be those where the child can stand on its own economically.

Benefits of joint ventures

Parent firms embrace joint ventures because they are ways to implement changes in their strategic postures or to defend current strategic postures against forces too strong for one firm to withstand.[8] They allow each partner to concentrate their resources in those areas where they possess the greatest relative competence, while diversifying into attractive but unfamiliar business arenas. Joint ventures should not be seen as a way to hide weaknesses. Rather, if they are used prudently, joint ventures are a way of creating strengths.

Managers have often disparaged joint ventures in the past, believing them to be too complex, too ambiguous or too inflexible.[9] But as the challenges of global competition increase, as projects grow larger and more risky, and as technologies become too expensive for one firm to afford, managers must learn how to use joint ventures, even in their firms' home markets. They have been an important structural trait within emerging national economies; joint ventures will become an important way to cope with uncertainties in established national economies, as well.

Often firms cannot afford to acquire the resources and competences they need.[10] Frequently, the knowledge and assets they seek cannot be purchased.[11] As an intermediate option (between acquisition or internal development and dependence upon outsiders) joint ventures represent a special, highly flexible means of enhancing innovation or achieving other strategic goals which managers should not overlook as their industries become global.[12] Joint ventures offer firms a window on promising new technologies, such as genetic engineering, videotext and synfuels.[13] They can be a means of utilizing a new manufacturing process (such as continuous casting in the steel industry), a by-product (as in many chemical processes), or a new capability (such as transmitting services over existing communications lines). Joint ventures offer salvation for firms within older global industries (such as automotive, farm equipment and petrochemicals), as well. Given the political realities of offsets and co-production requirements in order to conduct international trade, joint ventures among partners of different nationalities are becoming imperative.[14] Joint economies, co-production, common procurement and other aspects of joint ventures are being used to ward off competitors which are making inroads into firms' key markets.[15]

In brief, joint ventures offer many internal, competitive and strategic benefits. They provide firms with resources for which there are no equally efficient and available substitutes.[16] Some projects would never be undertaken without this means of spreading costs and risks.[17] Some firms could not retain their positions, given the rapid pace of change in global competition, without joint ventures.[18] Timing will be an important part of competitive strategy in this situation because firms which move first can gain access to better partners. If the ventures are 'exclusive' (explained below), firms could gain a competitive advantage which late entrants could not capture as easily. Joint ventures could be a means of pre-empting suppliers (or customers) from integrating to become competitors, and they could blunt the abilities of ongoing firms to retaliate as firms expand their domains.[19] By binding potential rivals to them through joint ventures, firms can make them allies.[20]

The benefits firms perceive from using joint ventures will differ according to whether they are 'insiders' or 'outsiders' with regard to the activities in question. Firms which are new to the market or activity ('outsiders') may see joint ventures as an insurance policy against domestic trade barriers or as a way to diversify.[21] Firms which are already in the market or engaged in the activity ('insiders') may see joint ventures as a way to curb potentially tough competitors or gain technological assistance. They must find some benefit in opening their markets to outsiders, else they would not consider joint ventures. Moreover, they must retain control over the enduring competitive advantage their market access gives them. Insiders should not trade away too much of this advantage for fleeting technological benefits.

Costs of joint ventures

Joint ventures are not without risks. Some industrialized nations, like the United States, have strict antitrust laws that prohibit those joint activities which function like monopolies.[22] When firms plan joint ventures within such environments, it will be particularly important to show a pro-competitive design and an antitrust-sensitive explanation of the need for the joint venture.[23] This justification must include a convincing portrayal of the inability of *either* parent to go it alone.[24] Parents may differ in their time horizons, the synergies they see with the joint venture, and other operating details. The objectives of host governments are not always the same as those of joint venture partners.[25] Decisions regarding whether to license knowledge or form joint ventures cannot follow the traditional patterns of technology transfer if host governments (or local partners) exert substantial bargaining power.[26] If partners possess such power, they could disrupt the schedule by which firms had intended to transfer the sources of their competitive advantage within global systems.[27]

Joint ventures can result in deadlocks if partners have not created equitable mechanisms for resolving day-to-day deadlocks in decision-making.[28] If deadlocks are not overcome, firms will suffer from foregone opportunities, loss of control over invested capital, technical resources, and proprietary information.[29] If the reasons for forming the joint venture were poorly conceived, if partners were not chosen carefully, or if the agreements and systems used to manage the venture were inadequate, firms may be worse off than they were before entering the joint venture.[30]

Firms' needs to co-operate

Firms' strategic missions determine their need to co-operate with others. If a business is close to firms' technological cores, they will often be less willing to enter joint ventures in those businesses, particularly if they distrust potential partners' motives. The technological core of many firms is the essence of their corporate strategies and business purpose. Their unwillingness to bare their technological cores to partners who could not protect this knowledge adequately from technological bleed-through makes them want majority control, if not full ownership.[31] It also makes them hover over every decision the child might make. Paradoxically, autonomous joint ventures have been more prolific innovators than JVs which were not allowed to operate in their own rights.[32] Yet parent firms are often reluctant to grant JVs the freedom to develop into viable entities.

Resources

By contrast, some firms use joint ventures pre-emptively to protect turf that is of great value to them. They form joint ventures with aggressive outsiders in businesses which are important to them in order to co-opt outsiders.[33] Their secret seems to be their awareness that they control crucial resources. Access to technology and market are the key bargaining chips in negotiations leading to joint-venture creations, reconfigurations and terminations. Firms' preferences concerning how many joint ventures to form (and with whom) depends on which resources they control. Market access permits firms to absorb aggressive outsiders. This approach seems to work best, for example, where domestic firms understand the importance of their control over market access and can prevent their joint-venture partners from gaining this resource. To do so, they configure the joint venture to prevent it from ever becoming a competitor. They may form parallel, in-house entities that duplicate the joint venture's activities and learn from its mistakes. Or they may form a spider's web of joint-venture relationships on the basis of their market power.

Alternatives

The balance of power ultimately agreed upon between firms will not necessarily be symmetrical because some partners will accept a lesser degree of control in order to achieve other objectives. Recognition of others' strategic needs and resource strengths can suggest how much latitude domestic firms will have in forming ventures that play off competing firms against each other.

'Spider's Web' joint ventures link many firms to one pivotal partner.[34] Depending upon the need to be satisfied and the sensitivity of information and resources to be exchanged, a domestic firm could forge a variety of patterns for co-operation that keep outsiders at bay while strengthening its own position. This approach is appropriate early in an industry's development when it is unclear which firm's technological standards will be adopted. It is the opposite of an approach whereby firms pick a future industry champion early and bet all resources on it through an 'exclusive' joint venture.

Where firms possess bargaining power over outsiders, spider's web joint ventures are more likely to result, unless the resources in question are so sensitive that neither firm wants to share information with others. Less powerful firms can only accept the terms dictated to them, so their ability to form multiple alliances is by mutual consent of the ongoing joint-venture partners.

Barriers

Joint ventures should be used to fortify parent firms' weaknesses in the face of global competition. Recognition of this and other weaknesses does not come easily to complacent firms.[35] Their unwillingness to see that their industries have become global creates barriers to firms' uses of joint ventures or other adaptive strategies.

The principal barriers to forming joint ventures are strategic in nature. Uncertainties regarding their abilities to manage operating joint ventures also erect barriers to joint-venture formation. Briefly, the strategic costs (detailed above) are valued more highly than the benefits firms believe they can attain. The high entry barriers that would normally deter a single firm from penetrating a new market or learning about a new technology are reasons to band together in forming joint ventures in the face of global competition.

Externally-imposed barriers to joint ventures include political restrictions on ownership, patent restrictions, competitor retaliation or other conditions. These may be easier to overcome than firms' own attitudinal barriers. For example, the comparative costs of off-shore manufacturing would inevitably drive domestic firms to relocate unless governments permitted them to join forces with efficient world-scale firms. Furthermore, joint ventures allow firms whose technologies have grown obsolete to replenish themselves.

USING JOINT VENTURES

Successful joint ventures require the correct choice of partners and symmetrical parent outlooks, but since most parents have diverse strategic outlooks and their strategies evolve dissimilarly, the inevitable tensions which develop must be managed. It is unreasonable to expect that joint ventures can preserve the relationships that existed when they were first created. Sometimes a change in managers is sufficient to change how a parent firm values its child. Joint ventures may be terminated, or they may be turned into a new opportunity to co-operate. The key to successful use of these tensions for competitive advantage lies in remembering the parent firm's sources of bargaining power.

It is useful to recall the inherent fragility of joint ventures when choosing partners to bring into one's home markets.[36] Today's partners could become tomorrow's competitors. Joint ventures are often reconfigured when partners have gained knowledge of markets which they previously did not understand. Thus it is important for domestic firms to avoid losing their competitive advantages to their partners. Providing for joint-venture disposition is also important, lest firms encounter difficulties in recovering the value of their investments in their child. One would expect that a market existed for the resources they had committed, but the ability to exit can be ensured better if firms manage for this contingency. Given firms' fundamental aversions to joint ventures, they would be expected to press to renegotiate their agreement into a fully-owned acquisition which they can control more fully. The flaw in this attitude is its assumption that the joint venture was sub-optimizing in its decisions while it was jointly-owned. If, instead, the child were given the freedom to make the best economic decisions, its profitability potential will not change after its ownership changes, unless its new owner imposed a *strategy* change on the child. The joint venture that is integrated well into its parents' global networks can be divested with greater ease should one of its parents' orientations change. Then 'fade-out' provisions can be exercised in a manner that permits firms to part amicably.[37]

CONCLUSION

Joint ventures are assuming greater importance in global strategies because product lives are shorter, cost advantages are becoming more pronounced and greater numbers of firms who formerly operated only in domestic markets are becoming international competitors. These changes have ominous ramifications for non-global firms, for they are likely to be offered partnership in joint ventures by firms who covet their strengths (transitory though they may be). A timely analysis of how joint ventures fit the interests of such firms could help them to forge configurations which leave them better off.

In the past, joint ventures have often been read as a signal of lesser corporate commitment to the project in question (unless firms purposely signalled high commitment to the markets in question in other ways). Firms have been particularly loath to use joint ventures where local governments did not require them as a condition of entry for domain-expanding multinationals. In environments of scarce resources, rapid rates of technological change and massive capital requirements, however, joint ventures may be the best way for some underdog firms to attain better positions in global industries which they consider to be important. Joint ventures may be used as pre-emptive manoeuvres to ensure that access to distribution channels, suppliers and technology in promising industries are not foreclosed to them because they ventured too late. They are also a way of ensuring that potential entrants do not team up with more dangerous opponents. As long as firms recognize the dangers and limitations of joint ventures and manage these shortcomings, there will be a chance for joint ventures to play a useful role in global strategies.

NOTES

1. Berg, Sanford V. and Friedman, Philip, 'Corporate Courtship and Successful Joint Ventures,' *California Management Review*, Vol. 22, No. 2, Spring 1980, pp. 85–91.

2. Porter, Michael E., *Competitive Strategy: Techniques for Analyzing Industries and Competitors*, (New York: Free Press, 1980) and Hout, Thomas; Porter, Michael E. and Rudden, Eileen, 'How Global Companies Win Out', *Harvard Business Review*, Vol. 60, No. 5, Sept.–Oct. 1982, pp. 98–108.

3. Edström, Anders, 'The Stability of Joint Ventures,' (working paper, University of Gothenburg, 1975b).

4. Fowaker, Lawrence E. and Siegel, Sidney, *Bargaining Behavior*, (New York: McGraw-Hill, 1963).

5. Riker, W.H., *The Theory of Political Coalitions*, (New Haven: Yale University Press, 1962).

6. Schermerhorn, John R., Jr., 'Determinants of Interorganizational Cooperation,' *The Academy of Management Journal*, Vol. 18, December 1975, pp. 846–956 and 'Openness to Interorganizational Cooperation: A Study of Hospital Administrators,' *Academy of Management Journal*, Vol. 19, June 1976, pp. 225–236.

7. Schelling, Thomas C., *The Strategy of Conflict*, (Cambridge: Harvard U. Press, 1960) and Telser, L.G., *Competition, Collusion and Game Theory*, (New York: Addine-Atherton, 1972).

8. Edström, Anders, 'Acquisition and Joint Venture Behavior of Swedish Manufacturing Firms,' (working paper, University of Gothenburg, 1975a) and Pfeffer, Jeffrey, and G.R. Salancik, *The External Control of Organizations: A Resource Dependence Perspective*, (New York: Harper & Row, 1978).

9. Killing, J. Peter, 'How to Make a Global Joint Venture Work,' *Harvard Business Review*, Vol. 61, No. 3, May–June 1982, pp. 120–127, and Wright, Richard W., 'Canadian Joint Ventures in Japan,' *Business Quarterly*, Autumn 1977, pp. 42–53.

10. Pfeffer, Jeffrey, 'Merger as a Response to Organizational Interdependence,' *Administrative Science Quarterly*, Vol. 17, 1972, pp. 382–394, and Pfeffer, Jeffrey and P. Nowak, 'Joint Ventures and Interorganizational Interdependence,' *Administrative Science Quarterly*, Vol. 21, No. 3, September 1976, pp. 398–418.

11. Williamson, Oliver, *Markets and Hierarchies: Analysis and Antitrust Implications*, (New York: Free Press, 1975).

12. Gullander, Stefan, 'Joint Ventures and Corporate Strategy,' *Columbia Journal of World Business*, Vol. XI, No. 1, September 1976, pp. 104–114.

13. Drucker, Peter, *Management: Tasks, Responsibilities, Promises*, (New York: Harper & Row, 1974), Hlavacek, James D. and Victor A. Thompson, 'The Joint Venture Approach to Technology Utilization,' *ILEE Transactions on Engineering Management*, Vol. EM-23, No. 1, February 1976, pp. 35–41, and Berg, Sanford V. and Philip Friedman, 'Corporate Courtship and Successful Joint Ventures,' *California Management Review*, Vol. 11, No. 2, Spring 1980.

14. Vernon, Raymond, *Storm Over the Multinationals*, (Cambridge, MA: Harvard University Press, 1977).

15. Harrigan, Kathryn Rudie, *Strategies for Declining Business* (Lexington, MA: D.C. Heath & Company, 1980), Harrigan, Kathryn Rudie, 'Deterrents to Divestiture,' *Academy of Management Journal*, Vol. 24, No. 2, June 1981, pp. 306–323, and Orski, C. Kenneth, 'The World Automotive Industry at a Crossroads: Cooperative Alliances,' *Vital Speeches*, Vol. 47, No. 3, November 15, 1980, pp. 89–93.

16. Bachman, Jules, 'Joint Ventures in the Light of Recent Antitrust Developments: Joint Ventures in the Chemical Industry,' *Antitrust Bulletin*, Vol. 10, Jan.–April 1965, pp. 7–23, and Brodley, Joseph F., 'Joint Ventures and the Justice Department's Antitrust Guide for International Operations,' *Antitrust Bulletin*, Vol. 24, Summer 1979, pp. 337–356.

17. Ballon, Robert J., ed., *Joint Ventures and Japan*, (Tokyo: Sophia University, 1967), and Franko, Lawrence G., *Joint Venture Survival in Multinational Corporations*, (New York: Praeger Publishers), 1971.

18. Bivens, Karen Kraus and Enid Baird Lovell, *Joint Ventures with Foreign Partners*, (New York, National Industrial Conference Board, 1966).

19. MacMillan, Ian C., 'Preemptive Strategies,' *The Journal of Business Strategy*, Vol. 4, No. 2, Fall 1983, pp. 16–26, and Harrigan, Kathryn Rudie, *Strategies for Vertical Integration*, (Lexington, MA: D.C. Heath & Company, 1983).

20. Harrigan, Kathryn Rudie, 'Strategies for Domestic Joint Ventures,' (book-length manuscript, forthcoming, 1985).

21. Meehan, James W., 'Joint Venture Entry in Perspective,' *Antitrust Bulletin*, Vol. 15, Winter 1970, pp. 693–711, and Daniels, John D., *Recent Foreign Direct Manufacturing Investment in the United States: An Interview Study of the Decision Process*, (New York: Praeger Publishers, 1971).

22. Mead, W.J., 'The Competitive Significance of Joint Ventures,' *Antitrust Bulletin*, Vol. 12, Fall 1967, pp. 819–849, Davidow, Joel, 'International Joint Ventures and the US Antitrust Laws,' *Akron Law Review*, 10, Spring 1977, and Rowe, Frederick M., 'Antitrust Aspects of European Acquisitions and Joint Ventures in the United States,' *Law and Policy in International Business*, Vol. 12, No. 2, 1980, pp. 335–368.

23. Marquis, Harold L., 'Compatibility of Industrial Joint Research Ventures and Antitrust Policy,' *Temple Law Quarterly*, Vol. 38, No. 1, Fall 1964, pp. 1–37.

24. Treeck, Joachim, 'Joint Ventures and Antitrust Law in the United States, Germany and the European Economic Community,' *Journal of International Law and Politics*, Vol. 3, No. 1, Spring 1970, pp. 18–55, Brodley, Joseph F., 'Joint Ventures and the Justice Department's Antitrust Guide for International Operations,' *Antitrust Bulletin*, Vol. 24, Summer 1979, pp. 337–356, and Ewing, K.P. Jr., 'Joint Research, Antitrust and Innovation,' *Research Management*, Vol. 24, No. 2, March 1981, pp. 25–29.

25. Vernon, Raymond, *Sovereignty at Bay: The Multinational Spread of US Enterprise*, (New York: Basic Books, 1971), Wright, Richard W. and Colin S. Russel, Joint Ventures in Developing Countries: Realities and Responses,' *Columbia Journal of World Business*, Vol. X, No. 2, Summer 1975, pp. 74–80; and Gregory, Gene, 'Japan's New Multinationalism: The Canon Giessen Experience,' *Columbia Journal of World Business*, Vol. XI, No. 1, Spring 1976, pp. 122–126.

26. Vernon, Raymond, 'International Investment and International Trade in the Product Cycle,' *Quarterly Journal of Economics*, Vol. 53, No. 2, May 1966, pp. 191–207, Gabriel, Peter P., *The International Transfer of Corporate Skills*, Boston: Harvard Business School, Division of Research, 1967, and Harrigan, Kathryn Rudie, 'Innovations by Overseas Subsidiaries,' *Journal of Business Strategy*, Vol. 5, Summer 1984 B, pp. 47–55.

27. Franko, Lawrence G., *The European Multinationals*, (London: Harper & Row, 1976), Vernon, Raymond and Louis T. Wells, Jr., *Manager in the International Economy*, (Englewood Cliffs, NJ: Prentice-Hall, Inc., 1976), and Young, G. Richard and Standish Bradford, Jr., 'Joint Ventures in Europe – Determinants of Entry,' *International Studies of Management and Organizations*, Vol. 1–2, No. 6, 1976, pp. 85–111.

28. March, J.G. and H.S. Simon, *Organizations*, (New York: Wiley, 1958).

29. Friedman, W., and G. Kalmanoff, *Joint International Business Ventures*, (New York: Columbia University Press, 1961), Picard, Jacques, 'How European Companies Control Marketing Decisions Abroad,' *Columbia Journal of World Business*, Vol. XII, No. 2., Summer 1977, pp. 113–121.

30. Tractenberg, Paul, 'Joint Ventures on the Domestic Front: A Study in Uncertainty,' *The Antitrust Bulletin*, Nov.–Dec. 1963, pp. 797–841. Ray, Edward John, 'Foreign Direct Investment in Manufacturing,' *Journal of Political Economy*, Vol. 85, No. 2, April 1977, pp. 283–297, and Davies, Howard, 'Technology Transfer Through Commercial Transactions,' *Journal of Industrial Economics*, Vol. XXVI, No. 2, Decembher 1977, pp. 161–175.

31. Killing, J. Peter, 'Technology Acquisition: License Agreement or Joint Venture,' *Columbia Journal of World Business*, Vol. 15, No. 3, Fall 1980, pp. 38–46.

32. Franko, Lawrence G., *Joint Venture Survival in Multinational Corporations*, (New York: Praeger Publishers, 1971).

33. March, J.G., 'The Business Firm as a Political Coalition,' *Journal of Politics*, Vol. 24, 1962, pp. 662–678.

34. Gullander, Stefan O., 'An Exploratory Study of Inter-firm Cooperation of Swedish Firms,' (doctoral dissertation, Columbia University, 1975).

35. Harrigan, Kathryn Rudie, *Strategies for Declining Business*, (Lexington, MA: D.C. Heath & Company, 1980), and Harrigan, Kathryn Rudie, *Strategies for Vertical Integration*, (Lexington, MA: D.C. Heath & Company, 1983).

36. Franko, Lawrence G., *Joint Venture Survival in Multinational Corporations*, (New York: Praeger Publishers, 1971); Gullander, Stefan O., 'An Exploratory Study of Inter-Firm Cooperation of Swedish Firms,' (doctoral dissertation, Columbia University, 1975); Gullander, Stefan, 'Joint Ventures and Corporate Strategy,' *Columbia Journal of World Business*, Vol. XI, No. 1, September 1976, pp. 104–114; and Young, G. Richard, and Standish Bradford, Jr., 'Joint Ventures in Europe – Determinants of Entry,' *International Studies of Management and Organizations*, Vol. 1–2, No. 6, 1976, pp. 85–111.

37. Meeker, Guy B., 'Fade Out Joint Venture: Can It Work for Latin America?' *Inter-American Economic Affairs*, Vol. 24, 1971, pp. 25–42.

REFERENCES

Bachman, J., 'Joint Ventures in the Light of Recent Antitrust Developments: Joint Ventures in the Chemical Industry,' *Antitrust Bulletin*, Vol. 10, Jan.–April 1965, pp. 7–23.

Ballon, R.J., ed., *Joint Ventures and Japan*, (Tokyo: Sophia University, 1967).

Berg, S.V., Duncan, J., Jr., and Friedman, P., *Joint Strategies and Corporate Innovation*, (Cambridge, MA: Oelgeschlager, Gunn & Hain, Publishers Inc., 1982).

Berg, S.V. and Friedman, P., 'Corporate Courtship and Successful Joint Ventures,' *California Management Review*, Vol. 22, No. 2, Spring 1980, pp. 85–91.

Bivens, K.K., and Lovell, E.B., *Joint Ventures with Foreign Partners*, (New York, National Industrial Conference Board, 1966).

Bourgeois, L.J. III and Singh, J., 'Organizational Slack and Political Behavior Within Top Management Terms,' (working paper, Stanford University, December 1982, presented at 1983 National Academy of Management Meetings, Dallas).

Brodley, J.F., 'Joint Ventures and the Justice Department's Antitrust Guide for International Operations,' *Antitrust Bulletin*, Vol. 24, Summer 1979, pp. 337–356.

Cyert, R.M. and March, J.G. *A Behavioral Theory of the Firm*, (Englewood Cliffs, NJ: Prentice-Hall, 1963).

Daniels, J.D., *Recent Foreign Direct Manufacturing Investment in the United States: An Interview Study of the Decision Process*, (New York: Praeger Publishers, 1971).

Davidow, J., 'International Joint Ventures and the U.S. Antitrust Laws,' *Akron Law Review*, 10, Spring 1977.

Davies, H., 'Technology Transfer Through Commercial Transactions,' *Journal of Industrial Economics*, Vol. XXVI, No. 2, December 1977, pp. 161–175.

Drucker, P., *Management: Tasks, Responsibilities, Promises*, (New York: Harper & Row, 1974).

Duncan, W.J., 'Organization as Political Coalitions: A Behavioral View of the Goal Formulation Process,' *Journal of Behavioral Economics*, Vol. 5, No. 1, 1976, pp. 25–44.

Edström, A., 'Acquisition and Joint Venture Behavior of Swedish Manufacturing Firms,' (working paper, University of Gothenburg, 1975a).

Edström, A., 'The Stability of Joint Ventures,' (working paper, University of Gothenburg, 1975b).

Ewing, K.P. Jr., 'Joint Research, Antitrust and Innovation,' *Research Management*, Vol. 24, No. 2, March 1981, pp. 25–29.

Filley, A.C., House, R.J. and Kerr, S., *Managerial Process and Organizational Behavior*, (Glenview, IL: Scott Foresman, 1976).

Fouraker, L.E. and Siegel, S. *Bargaining Behavior*, (NY: McGraw-Hill, 1963).

Franko, L.G., *The European Multinationals*, (London: Harper & Row, 1976).

Franko, L.G., *Joint Venture Survival in Multinational Corporations*, (New York: Praeger Publishers, 1971).

Friedman, W., and Kalmanoff, G., *Joint International Business Ventures*, (New York: Columbia University Press, 1961).

Gabriel, P.P., *The International Transfer of Corporate Skills*, (Boston: Harvard Business School, Division of Research, 1967).

Gregory, G., 'Japan's New Multinationalism: The Canon Giessen Experience,' *Columbia Journal of World Business*, Vol. XI, No. 1, Spring 1976, pp. 122–126.

Gullander, S.O., 'An Exploratory Study of Inter-Firm Cooperation of Swedish Firms,' (doctoral dissertation, Columbia University, 1975).

Gullander, S., 'Joint Ventures and Corporate Strategy,' *Columbia Journal of World Business*, Vol. XI, No. 1, September 1976, pp. 104–114.

Hambrick, D.C. and Mason, P.A., 'Upper Echelons: The Organization as a Reflection of Its Top Managers,' (working paper, Columbia University, 1982).

Harrigan, K.R., 'Deterrents to Divestiture,' *Academy of Management Journal*, Vol. 24, No. 2, June 1981, pp. 306–323.

Harrigan, K.R., 'Innovations by Overseas Subsidiaries,' *Journal of Business Strategy*, Vol. 5, Summer 1984, pp. 47–55.

Harrigan, K.R., *Strategies for Declining Business*, (Lexington, MA: D.C. Heath & Company, 1980).

Harrigan, K.R., 'Strategies for Domestic Joint Ventures,' (book-length manuscript, forthcoming, December 1984).

Harrigan, K.R., *Strategies for Vertical Integration*, (Lexington, MA: D.C. Heath & Company, 1983).

Hlavacek, J.D. and Thompson, V.A., 'The Joint Venture Approach to Technology Utilization,' *ILEE Transactions on Engineering Management*, Vol. EM-23, No. 1, February 1976, pp. 35–41.

Killing, J.P., 'How to Make a Global Joint Venture Work,' *Harvard Business Review*, Vol. 61, No. 3, May–June 1982, pp. 120–127.

Killing, J.P., 'Technology Acquisition: License Agreement or Joint Venture,' *Columbia Journal of World Business*, Vol. 15, No. 3, Fall 1980, pp. 38–46.

MacMillan, Ian C., 'Preemptive Strategies,' *The Journal of Business Strategy*, Vol. 4, No. 2, Fall 1983, pp. 16–26.

March, J.G., 'The Business Firm as a Political Coalition,' *Journal of Politics*, Vol. 24, 1962, pp. 662–678.

March, J.G. and Simon, H.S., *Organizations*, (New York: Wiley, 1958).

Marquis, H.L., 'Compatibility of Industrial Joint Research Ventures and Antitrust Policy,' *Temple Law Quarterly*, Vol. 38, No. 1, Fall 1963, pp. 1–37.

Mead, W.J., 'The Competitive Significance of Joint Ventures,' *Antitrust Bulletin*, Vol. 12, Fall 1967, pp. 819–849.

Meehan, J.W., 'Joint Venture Entry in Perspective,' *Antitrust Bulletin*, Vol. 15, Winter 1970, pp. 693–711.

Meeker, G.B., 'Fade Out Joint Venture: Can It Work for Latin America?' *Inter-American Economic Affairs*, Vol. 24, 1971, pp. 25–42.

Orski, C.K., 'The World Automotive Industry at a Crossroads: Cooperative Alliances,' *Vital Speeches*, Vol. 47, No. 3, November 15, 1980, pp. 89–93.

Pfeffer, J., 'Merger as a Response to Organizational Interdependence,' *Administrative Science Quarterly*, Vol. 17, 1972, pp. 382–394.

Pfeffer, J. and Nowak, P., 'Joint Ventures and Interorganizational Interdependence,' *Administrative Science Quarterly*, Vol. 21, No. 3, September 1976, pp. 398–418.

Pfeffer, J. and Salancik, G.R., *The External Control of Organizations: A Resource Dependence Perspective*, (New York: Harper & Row, 1978).

Picard, J., 'How European Companies Control Marketing Decisions Abroad,' *Columbia Journal of World Business*, Vol. XII, No. 2, Summer 1977, pp. 113–121.

Porter, M.E., *Competitive Strategy: Techniques for Analyzing Industries and Competitors*, (New York: Free Press, 1980).

Ray, E.J., 'Foreign Direct Investment in Manufacturing,' *Journal of Political Economy*, Vol. 85, No. 2, April 1977, pp. 283–297.

Riker, W.H., *The Theory of Political Coalitions*, (New Haven, CT: Yale University Press, 1962).

Rowe, F.M., 'Antitrust Aspects of European Acquisitions and Joint Ventures in the United States,' *Law and Policy in International Business*, Vol. 12, No. 2, 1980, pp. 335–368.

Schelling, T.C., *The Strategy of Conflict*, (Cambridge, MA: Harvard University Press, 1960).

Schermerhorn, J.R. Jr., 'Determinants of Interorganizational Cooperation,' *The Academy of Management Journal*, Vol. 18, December 1975, pp. 846–956.

Schermerhorn, J.R. Jr., 'Openness to Interorganizational Cooperation: A Study of Hospital Administrators,' *Academy of Management Journal*, Vol. 19, June 1976, pp. 225–236.

Shubik, M., *Strategy and Market Structure*, (New York: Wiley, 1959).

Telser, L.G., *Competition, Collusion, and Game Theory*, (New York: Aldine-Atherton, 1972).

Tractenberg, P., 'Joint Ventures on the Domestic Front: A Study in Uncertainty,' *The Antitrust Bulletin*, Nov.–Dec. 1963, pp. 797–841.

Treeck, J., 'Joint Research Ventures and Antitrust Law in the United States, Germany and the European Economic Community,' *Journal of International Law and Politics*, Vol. 3, No. 1, Spring 1970, pp. 18–255.

Vernon, R., 'International Investment and International Trade in the Product Cycle,' *Quarterly Journal of Economics*, Vol. 53, No. 2, May 1966, pp. 191–207.

Vernon, R., *Sovereignty at Bay: The Multinational Spread of U.S. Enterprise*, (New York: Basic Books, 1971).

Vernon, R., *Storm Over the Multinationals*, (Cambridge, MA: Harvard University Press, 1977).

Vernon, R. and Wells, L.T. Jr., *Manager in the International Economy*, (Englewood Cliffs, NJ: Prentice-Hall, Inc., 1976).

Von Neumann, J. and Morgenstern, O. *Theory of Games and Economics Behavior*, (Princeton, NJ: Princeton University Press, 1944).

Williamson, O., *Markets and Hierarchies: Analysis and Antitrust Implications*, (New York: Fress Press, 1975).

Wright, R.W., 'Canadian Joint Ventures in Japan,' *Business Quarterly*, Autumn 1977, pp. 42–53.

Wright, R.W. and Russel, C.S., 'Joint Ventures in Developing Countries: Realities and Responses,' *Columbia Journal of World Business*, Vol. X, No. 2, Summer 1975, pp. 74–80.

Young, G.R. and Bradford S. Jr., 'Joint Ventures in Europe – Determinants of Entry,' *International Studies of Management and Organizations*, Vol. 1–2, No. 6, 1976, pp. 85–111.

17

Interfirm Diversity, Organizational Learning, and Longevity in Global Strategic Alliances

Arvind Parkhe

On March 6, 1990, West Germany's Daimler Benz ($48 billion in sales) and Japan's Mitsubishi Group ($200 billion in sales) revealed that they had held 'a secret meeting in Singapore to work out a plan for intensive cooperation among their auto, aerospace, electronics, and other lines of business. However, combining operations of the two companies seems remote: Daimler's orderly German corporate structure doesn't mesh well with Mitsubishi's leaderless group management approach' (Business Week 1990b).

This example illustrates an important paradox in international business today. On one hand, global strategic alliances (GSAs) are being used with increasing frequency in order to, inter alia, keep abreast of rapidly changing technologies, gain access to specific foreign markets and distribution channels, create new products, and ease problems of worldwide excess productive capacity. Indeed, GSAs are becoming an essential feature of companies' overall organizational structure, and competitive advantage increasingly depends not only on a company's internal capabilities, but also on the types of its alliances and the scope of its relationships with other companies. On the other hand, GSAs bring together partners from different national origins, with often sharp differences in the collaborating firms' cultural and political bases. As in the above illustration, there may also exist considerable diversity in *firm-specific* characteristics that may be tied to each firm's national heritage. Interfirm diversity can severely impede the ability of companies to work jointly and effectively (Adler and Graham 1989; Harrigan 1988; Perlmutter and Heenan 1986), since many GSA partners – relative newcomers to voluntary cooperative relationships with foreign firms – have yet to acquire the necessary skills to cope with their differences. Not surprisingly, the rapid growth of GSAs is accompanied by high failure rates (Hergert and Morris 1988; Porter 1986).[1]

Before probing the nexus between diversity and alliance performance, however, it is fruitful to begin with the recognition that (1) in GSAs, significant interfirm diversity is to be expected, and (2) this diversity can be analytically separated into two types. Type I includes the familiar interfirm differences (interdependencies) that GSAs are specifically created to exploit. These differences form the underlying strategic motivations for entering into alliances; an inventory of such motivations is provided, for instance, by Contractor and Lorange (1988: 10). Thus. Type I diversity deals with the reciprocal strengths and complementary resources furnished by the alliance partners, differences that actually facilitate the formulation, development, and collaborative effectiveness of GSAs.

Type II diversity, the major focus of this paper, refers to the differences in partner characteristics that often negatively affect the longevity and effective functioning of GSAs. Over the life of the partnership, the dynamics of Types I and II are very different, since the two types are differentially impacted by the processes of organizational learning and adaptation. In the case of Type I, learning through the GSA may enable one partner to acquire the skills and technologies it lacked at the time of alliance formation, and eventually rewrite the partnership terms or even discard the other partner. Thus, the GSA becomes a race to learn, with the company that learns fastest dominating the relationship and becoming, through cooperation, a more formidable competitor. Conversely, organizational learning and adaptation can progressively mitigate the impact of Type II differences, thereby promoting longevity and effectiveness. To summarize, a minimum level of Type I differences are essential to the formation and maintenance (raison d'être) of an alliance, and their erosion destabilizes the partnership, Type II differences, though inevitably present at the initiation of an alliance, may be overcome by iterative cycles of learning that strengthen the partnership.

A large number of previous studies have examined how Type II interfirm differences can play a major role in frustrating the joint efforts of GSA partners. For example, Adler and Graham (1989) found that cross-cultural negotiations are more difficult than intra-cultural negotiations. Several other studies have also established that negotiations between business people of different cultures often fail because of problems related to cross-cultural differences (Adler 1986; Black 1987; Graham 1985; Tung 1984). Harrigan (1988) studied the influence of sponsoring-firm asymmetries in terms of strategic directions (horizontal, vertical, and relatedness linkages with the venture) on performance. Hall (1984) analyzed the effects of differing management procedures on alliances. Still other researchers have examined the influence of variations in corporate culture (Killing 1982) and national setting (Turner 1987) on successful collaboration. This brief overview, while not exhaustive, conveys the basic directions in which research to date has progressed.

Unfortunately, the usefulness of these important studies in an overview assessment of international interfirm interactions is limited, since they examine the impact of selected aspects of interfirm diversity on cooperative ventures in a piecemeal fashion. The academic literature thus remains fragmented at different levels of analysis, with no overarching theme cohesively pulling together the various dimensions of interfirm diversity in systematic theory-building. Therefore, the main contributions of this paper will be to extend current theory (1) by developing and justifying a typology of the major dimensions of interfirm diversity in the context of GSAs; and, (2) by examining diversity's impact on alliance outcomes through a dynamic model rooted in organizational learning theory. For this purpose, the following questions will be addressed: What are the theoretical dimensions of diversity between GSA partners? In what ways and under what circumstances does each dimension, individually or collectively, translate into reduced collaborative effectiveness? To what extent can deliberate learning/adaptation actions by firms deter expensive alliance failures and promote longevity?

A PREFATORY NOTE ON TERMINOLOGY

It is important at the outset to define terminology. Interfirm cooperative relationships have previously been defined by Borys and Jemison (1989), Schermerhorn (1975), Nielsen (1988), and Oliver (1990). However, the conceptual domain of GSAs must include the additional properties of being international in scope, mixed-motive (competitive + cooperative) in nature, and of strategic significance to each partner, i.e., tied to the firms' current and anticipated core businesses, markets, and technologies (commonly referred to as the corporate mission). Thus, GSAs are the relatively enduring interfirm cooperative arrangements, involving cross-border flows and linkages that utilize resources and/or governance structures from autonomous organizations headquartered in two or more countries for the joint accomplishment of individual goals linked to the corporate mission of each sponsoring firm. This definition delineates GSAs from single-transaction market relationships, as well as from unrelated diversification moves, while accommodating the variety of strategic motives and organizational forms that accompany global partnerships. For example, GSAs can be used as transitional modes of organizational structure (Gomes-Casseres 1989) in response to current challenges as firms grope to find more permanent structures including, sometimes, whole ownership after the GSA has achieved its purpose. Often, however, longevity is an important yardstick of performance measurement by each parent company (Harrigan 1985; Lewis 1990).

It must be clearly noted that longevity is an imperfect proxy for 'alliance success.' Longevity can be associated, for instance, with the presence of high exit barriers. And in some alliances, success can also be operationalized in terms of other measures such as profitability, market share, and synergistic contribution toward parent companies' competitiveness (cf. Venkatraman and Ramanujam (1986)). Yet, achievement of these latter objectives can be thwarted by premature, unintended dissolution of the GSA. Furthermore, objective performance measures (e.g., GSA survival and duration) are significantly and positively correlated with parent firms' reported (that is, subjective) satisfaction with GSA performance and with perceptions of the extent to which a GSA performed relative to its initial objectives (Geringer and Hebert 1991), so that for many research purposes the use of longevity as a surrogate for a favorable GSA outcome is probably not too restrictive. With the above limitations acknowledged, we focus mainly on the subset of GSAs where longevity (not planned termination) is sought by each partner, but is threatened by problems stemming from Type II interfirm diversity; however, inasmuch as planned termination represents an important potential alliance outcome involving the deliberate erosion of Type I diversity, it is treated as a special case of a more general diversity/longevity dynamic model later in the paper.

Interfirm diversity refers to the comparative interorganizational differences on certain attributes or dimensions (Molnar and Rogers 1979) that continually shape the pattern of interaction between them (Van de Ven 1976). In sum, this paper examines the interorganizational interface at which inherent interfirm diversity between GSA partners often makes effective management of pooled resource contributions problematic.

THE PROBLEM OF DIVERSITY

Just as modern business organizations are complex *social* entities (and therefore studied in the ambit of the social sciences), GSAs represent an emerging *social institution*. As researchers in sociology, marketing, and interorganizational relations theory have long noted, dissimilarities between social actors can render effective pairwise interactions difficult, and vice versa.

Evans' (1963) 'similarity hypothesis,' for example, maintains that 'the more similar the parties in a dyad are, the more likely a favorable outcome.' The proposed mechanism is:

Similarity leads to attraction (sharing of common needs and goals), which causes attitudes to become positive, thus leading to favorable outcomes (McGuire 1968). Likewise, Lazarsfeld and Merton (1954) identify the tendency for similar values and statuses to serve as bases for social relationships, as a basic mechanism of social interaction. These same principles may explain the characteristics of linkages between organizations (Paulson 1976). And Whetten (1981: 17) argues that 'potential partners are screened to reduce the costs of coordination that increase as a function of differences between the collaborating organizations.'

Although the above literatures primarily focus on problems of surmounting communication difficulties and establishing a common set of working assumptions, a broader set of dimensions is crucial in understanding GSA interactions, given the nature of GSAs as defined above. These dimensions are developed next.

DIMENSIONS OF INTERFIRM DIVERSITY IN GSAs

The major dimensions of Type II interfirm diversity in global strategic alliances are described below: Table 1 summarizes this discussion.[2] In a departure from previous studies that have focused on limited aspects of interfirm diversity, Table 1 spans multiple, critical levels of analysis that are indispensable in providing a fuller understanding of the factors that may lead to friction and eventual collapse of the GSA. In addition, the following discussion also includes an analysis of how each diversity dimension can influence ongoing reciprocal *learning* within the partnership, an important consideration in the study of alliance longevity and effectiveness. Table 1 distinguishes between levels of conceptualization and levels of phenomena. Levels of phemonena refer to dimensions of interfirm diversity that can, with arguable intersubjectivity, be observed and measured. (Hofstede (1983), for example, operationalized culture in four dimensions.) Conceptual levels deal with ideas and theories about phenomena. Thus, the social behavior of interfacing managers from each GSA partner firm is an output of the managers' respective societal (meta), national (macro), corporate-level (meso), and operating-level (micro) influences. While the actual behaviors can be observed, appreciating the often significant differences between them requires an abstraction to the underlying conceptual level of analysis. Finally, it is noted that the dimensions in the typology are often interrelated, and therefore cannot be treated as mutually exclusive.

Societal culture

The influence of a society's culture permeates all aspects of life within the society, including the norms, values, and behaviors of managers in its national companies. The cross-cultural interactions found in GSAs bring together people who may have different patterns of behaving and believing, and different cognitive blueprints for interpreting the world (Kluckhohn and Kroeberg 1952; Black and Mendenhall 1990). Indeed, Maruyama (1984) argues that cultural differences are at the epistemologic level, that is, in the very structure of perceiving, thinking, and reasoning.

Excellent examples of the deep impact of culture on GSA management can be found in the partners' approaches to problem solving and conflict resolution. In some cultures, problems are to be actively solved: managers must take deliberate actions to influence their environment and affect the course of the future. This is the basis for strategic planning. In contrast, in other cultures, life is seen as a series of preordained situations that are to be fatalistically accepted

Table 1. Interfirm Diversity in GSAs: A Summary

Conceptual Level	Phenomenological Level	Dimension of Diversity	Sources of Tension	Coping Mechanisms	Proposition
Meta	Supranational	Societal culture	Differences in perception and interpretation of phenomena, analytical processes	Promote formal training programs, informal contact, behavior transparency	1a, 1b
Macro	National	National context	Differences in home government policies, national industry structure and institutions	Emphasize 'rational' (i.e., technological and economic) factors	2
Meso	Top management	Corporate culture	Differences in ideologies and values guiding companies	Encourage organizational learning to facilitate 'intermediate' corporate culture	3
Meso	Policy group	Strategic direction	Differences in strategic interests of partners from dynamic external and internal environments	Devise flexible partnership structure	4
Micro	Functional management	Management practices and organization	Differences in management styles, organizational structures of parent firms	Set up unitary management process and structures	5

(Moran and Harris 1982). Similarly, GSA partners must routinely deal with conflicts in such areas as technology development, production and sourcing, market strategy and implementation, and so on (Lynch 1989). In some cultures, conflict is viewed as a healthy, natural, and inevitable part of relationships and organizations. In fact, programmed or structured conflict (e.g., the devil's advocate and dialectical inquiry methods) has been suggested as a way to enhance the effectiveness of strategic decision-making (cf. Cosier and Dalton (1990)). But in other cultures, vigorous conflict and open confrontation are deemed distasteful. Embarrassment and loss of face to either party is sought to be avoided at all costs by talking indirectly and ambiguously about areas of difference until common ground can be found, by the use of mediators, and other techniques.

Effective handling of such cultural differences must begin with developing an understanding of the other's modes of thinking and behaving. For example, reflecting on the failed AT&T-Olivetti alliance, AT&T group executive Robert Kavner regretted, 'I don't think that we or Olivetti spent enough time understanding behavior patterns' (Wysocki 1990). Avoidance of such preventable mistakes may become increasingly essential, and investments in sophisticated programs to promote intercultural awareness may become increasingly cost-effective, given the accelerating trend of GSA formation and the often enormous losses stemming from failed GSAs.[3] Ethnocentric arrogance (or cultural naivete) and GSAs simply do not mix well.

Nonetheless, Black and Mendenhall (1990) report from their survey of twenty-nine empirical studies that the use of cross-cultural training (CCT) in U.S. multinationals is very limited. Essentially, American top managers believe that a good manager in New York or Los Angeles will be effective in Hong Kong or Tokyo, and that a candidate's domestic track record can serve as the primary criterion for overseas assignment selection. Such a culturally insensitive approach is particularly unfortunate in light of CCT's proven success in terms of enhancing each of its three indicators of effectiveness: cross-cultural skill development, adjustment, and performance (Black and Mendenhall 1990: 115–20). Clearly, CCT can be a powerful catalyst not only in enhancing intrafirm foreign operations, but also toward overcoming cultural diversity between GSA partners and facilitating ongoing mutual learning that promotes alliance longevity, more formally:

> Proposition 1a: Societal culture differences will be negatively related to GSA longevity. However, this relationship will be moderated by formal training programs that enhance intercultural understanding.

Furthermore, bridging the culture gap between GSA partners may be facilitated by effective communication at all interfacing levels. This suggests the need to improve behavior transparency at each level, including effective recognition, verification, and signalling systems between the partners.

> Proposition 1b: The relationship between differences in societal culture and longevity of the alliance will be further moderated by structured mechanisms that improve behavior transparency.

National context

A company's national context primarily includes surrounding industry structure and institutions, and government laws and regulations. The great diversity that exists in the national contexts of global companies can hamper effective collaboration. For instance, disparities in the national context differentially impact global companies' ability to enter and operate GSAs. Of central relevance to this paper are national attitudes about simultaneous competition and cooperation. As noted below, however, national differences notwithstanding, important common patterns may be emerging internationally.

Japanese context

In Japan, companies have a long history of cooperating in some areas while competing in others, a practice that can be traced primarily to two factors: direction from the Ministry of International Trade and Industry (MITI), and *keiretsu*, or large industrial groups of firms representing diverse industries and skills. However, driven by recent trends in the competitive and political environments, Japanese companies are increasingly entering into GSAs, in the process forsaking their traditionally close *keiretsu* ties. In the context of this paper, the significant implications can be summed up as follows: (1) traditional Japanese industrial associations are in a state of flux; (2) a gradually diminishing role of the *keiretsu* in the future and a greater focus on the individual company; and (3) greater opportunities to enter into GSAs with Japanese firms.[4]

U.S. context

In the U.S., the federal government has traditionally viewed cooperation between companies with suspicion, particularly if they competed in the same markets. The environment of strict antitrust regulations spawned companies with little experience in successfully managing interfirm cooperation. More recently, however, in an attempt to help correct structural problems in mature industries and to promote international competitiveness in high-tech industries, the U.S. government has adopted more favorable attitudes toward interfirm cooperation, as reflected in its patent, procurement, and anti-trust policies. For example, the National Cooperative Research Act of 1984 holds that cooperative ventures between companies are permissible when such arrangements add to the companies' overall efficiency and benefit society at large.

Though intended primarily to benefit U.S. firms, these changes in American national attitudes and policies regarding interfirm cooperation may also have spillover benefits for non-U.S. firms, in that the latter may have greater opportunities to enter into GSAs with U.S. companies.[5] Recent developments in the U.S. may also mean that the ability of U.S. companies to spot, structure, and manage interfirm cooperative relationships will improve over time.

European context

In Europe, interfirm cooperation historically has been hampered by fragmented European markets, cultural and linguistic differences, diverse equipment standards and business regulations, and nationalist and protectionist government policies. Only in the past several years has the impending threat of a European technology gap against U.S. and Japanese competition compelled European governments to promote the integration of European firms, such as the European Strategic Programme in Information Technologies (ESPRIT). However, such efforts to build a more dynamic, technologically independent Europe do not diminish the fact that Europe is too small to support the risky, multibillion dollar commitments required in many new industries.[6] As Ohmae (1985) argues, companies also need to establish a strong presence in U.S. and Japanese markets to survive.

Three major points emerge from the preceding discussion. First, firms from the Triad regions are heavily influenced by their unique national contexts. Second, cooperating in GSAs may be rendered difficult by the significant differences in national contexts. And third, while these differences are likely to persist, as seen above, they may be progressively overwhelmed by powerful technological and economic factors.

> Proposition 2:   Differences in partner firms' national contexts and GSA longevity will be negatively related. The effects of these differences on longevity will be moderated by the technological and economic imperatives facing global firms.

Before concluding this discussion of national contexts, it is essential to broach one question that may have a significant bearing on global firms' future partnering abilities and success patterns: Will experience in managing linkages within a firms' home base provide an advantage in building linkages with foreign organizations (cf. Westney (1988))? As just seen, Japanese firms have greater domestic experience in interfirm cooperation than U.S. and European firms, though the latter are also accumulating more local experience. But is this experience transferable to GSAs, where partners typically have more widely varying characteristics? Insufficient evidence currently exists to answer this question: however, systematic research may yield important insights into the differential organization learning patterns of companies weaned in different domestic contexts.

Corporate culture

Corporate culture includes those ideologies and values that characterize particular organizations (Beyer 1981; Peters and Watersman 1982). The notion that differences in corporate culture matter, familiar to researchers of international mergers and acquisitions (BenDaniel and Rosenbloom 1990), is also crucially important in GSAs. Such firm-specific differences are often interwoven with the fabric of the partners' societal cultures and national contexts, as reflected in the phrases: European family capitalism. American managerial capitalism, and Japanese group capitalism.

Harrigan (1988) argues that corporate culture homogeneity among partners is even more important to GSA success than symmetry in their national origins. (She maintains, for example, that GM's values may be more similar to those of its GSA partner, Toyota, than to those of Ford.) However, studies have shown that a corporation's overall organizational culture is not able fully to homogenize values of employees originating in national cultures (Laurent 1983), indicating the transcending importance of meta- and macro-level variables relative to corporate culture. Although the relative importance of these dimensions must be determined empirically, it is clear that each dimension can be instrumental in erecting significant barriers to effective cooperation.

For example, strikingly different temporal orientations often exist in U.S. versus Japanese corporations. The former, pressed by investors and analysts, may tend to focus on quarterly earnings reports, while the latter focus on establishing their brand names and international marketing channels, a sine qua non of higher order advantage leading to greater world market shares over a period of several years. Thus, Japanese partners may give GSAs more time to take root, whereas their U.S. counterparts may be more impatient.

Significant differences may also exist on the issues of power and control. As Perlmutter and Heenan(1986) assert. Americans have historically harbored the belief that power, not parity, should govern collaborative ventures. In contrast, the Europeans and Japanese often consider partners as equals, subscribe to management by consensus, and rely on lengthy discussion to secure stronger commitment to shared enterprises.

For effective meshing of such diverse corporate cultures, each GSA partner must make the effort to learn the ideologies and values of its counterpart. For managers socialized into their own corporate cultures (Terpstra and David 1990), openness to very different corporate orientations may be difficult. Yet, new forms of business often necessitate the acquisition of new core skills. Among some U.S. firms, for instance, this may mean a reduced emphasis on equity control and an acceptance of slower payback periods on GSA investments in the interest of future benefits over longer time horizons. Among Japanese firms, this may mean a keener recognition of the demands on U.S. managers to show quicker results, with possible modifications in the goals of the GSA and the means used to achieve those goals. Turner (1987) found some support for the emergence of 'intermediate' corporate cultures – those characterized by priorities and values between those of the sponsoring firms – as GSA partners made mutual adjustments. However, he did not relate his findings to alliance longevity, and his study was limited to U.K.-Japanese alliances. More empirical work is needed to test the following proposition:

> Proposition 3:   Corporate culture differences will be negative related to alliance longevity. This relationship will be moderated by the development of an intermediate corporate culture to guide the GSA.

Finally, corporate culture has a circular relationship with learning in that it creates and reinforces learning and is created by learning; as such, it influences ongoing learning and adaptation within and between GSA partners, Miles and Snow (1978) demonstrate, for example, that a firm's posture (defender, prospector, etc.) is tied closely to its culture, and that shared norms and beliefs help shape strategy and the direction of organizational change. These broad norms and belief systems clearly influence the behavioral and cognitive development that each GSA partner can undergo; in turn, learning and adaptation in organizations often involves a restructuring of these norms and belief systems (Argyris and Schon 1978).

Strategic directions

As Harrigan (1985) observes, 'asymmetries in the speed with which parent firms want to exploit an opportunity, the direction in which they want to move, or in other strategic matters are destabilizing to GSAs' (p. 14). Partner screening at the alliance planning stage tests for strategic compatibility by analyzing a potential partner's motivation and ability to live up to its commitments, by assessing whether there may exist probable areas of conflict due to overlapping interests in present markets or future geographic and product market expansion plans. Yet, a revised analysis may become necessary as the partners' evolving internal capabilities, strategic choices, and market developments pull them in separate directions, diminishing the strategic fit of a once-perfect match. Strategic divergence is particularly likely in environments characterized by high volatility, rapid advances in technology, and a blurring and dissolution of traditional boundaries between industries.[7]

One key to managing diverging partner interests may be to build flexibility into the partnership structure, which allows companies to adjust to changes in their internal and external environments. Flexible structures may be attained, for example, by initiating alliances on a small scale with specific, short-term agreement (such as cross-licensing or second sourcing), instead of huge deals that can pose 'lock-in' problems with shifting strategic priorities. In a gradually developed relationship, areas of cooperation can be expanded to a broader base to the extent that continuing strategic fit exists. Alternatively, flexibility can be attained by entering into a general (or blanket) cooperative agreement which is activated on an as-needed basis. For example, RCA and Sharp have a long-established cooperative agreement within which they have worked on a series of specific ventures over the years, including a recent $200 million joint venture to manufacture complementary metal oxide semiconductor (CMOS) integrated circuits.

> Proposition 4: Divergence in the parents' strategic directions will be negatively related to GSA longevity. The relationship between divergence and longevity will be moderated by structural flexibility that permits adaptation to shifting environments.

Strategy can affect organizational learning, and through learning alliance longevity, in various ways. Since strategy determines the goals and objectives and the breadth of actions available to a firm, it influences learning by providing a boundary to decisionmaking and a context for the perception and interpretation of the environment (Daft and Weick 1984). In addition, as Miller and Friesen (1980) show, a firm's strategic direction creates a momentum for organizational learning, a momentum that is pervasive and highly resistant to small adjustments.

Management practices and organization

The wide interfirm diversity in management styles, organizational structures, and other operational-level variables that exists across firms from different parts of the world can largely be traced to diversity along the first four dimensions discussed above. In turn, these differences, illustrated by the Daimler Benz versus Mitsubishi contrast at the outset of this paper, can heighten operating difficulties and trigger premature dissolution of the GSA. An important issue in this regard is the problem of effectively combining the diverse systems of *autonomous* international firms, each accustomed to operating in a certain manner.

Many researchers in international cooperative strategies have tended, perhaps unwittingly, to focus solely on this final dimension of interfirm diversity (e.g., Dobkin (1988); Hall (1984); Pucik (1988)). Among the major differences that have been noted are the style of management (participatory or authoritarian), delegation of responsibility (high or low), decisionmaking (centralized or decentralized), and reliance on formal planning and control systems (high or low). To prevent problems of unclear lines of authority, poor communication and slow decisionmaking, GSAs may need to set up *unitary* management processes and structures, where one decision point has the authority and independence to commit both partners. Implementation of this recommendation is difficult in cases where both partners are evenly matched in terms of company size and resource contributions to the GSA (cf. Killing (1982)).[8] Yet, agreement on the streamlining of tough operational-level issues must be reached *prior* to commencement of the GSA.

> Proposition 5: Diversity in the sponsoring firms' operating characteristics will be negatively related to longevity of the GSA. This relationship will be moderated by the establishment of unitary management processes and structures.

Though structure is often seen as an outcome of organizational learning, it plays a crucial role in determining the learning process itself (Fiol and Lyles 1985). This observation can be important in the context of GSAs, where one firm's centralized, mechanistic structure that tends to reinforce past behaviors can collide with another firm's organic, decentralized structure that tends to allow shifts of beliefs and actions. More broadly, different management practices and organizational structures can enhance or retard learning, depending upon their degree of formalization, complexity, and diffusion of decision influence.

Theory and practice are linked in Table 2, which illustrates how significant Type II differences between GSA partners can impact the entire spectrum of alliance activities. For the sake of brevity, Table 2 outlines only a select number of characteristics that are derived from the typological dimensions of Table 1. Yet, a review of Table 2 clearly indicates that: (1) the extent of interfirm diversity in global strategic alliances may be high; and (2) as stressed earlier, the various dimensions of diversity are not distinct and unrelated, but rather share a common core that touches GSAs.

Furthermore, Type I and Type II diversity can undergo distinctly different patterns over time, generating different alliance outcomes. The dynamic model of longevity presented in the next section suggests that a pivotal factor in the interfirm diversity/alliance outcome link is organizational learning and adaptation to diversity by the GSA partners.

LONGEVITY IN GSAs: A LEARNING-BASED DYNAMIC MODEL

Organizational theorists (Lyles 1988; Fiol and Lyles 1985) define learning as 'the development of insights, knowledge, and associations between past actions, the effectiveness of those actions, and future actions,' and adaptation as 'the ability to make incremental adjustments.' Learning can be minor, moderate, or major. In stimulus-response terms, in minor learning, an organization's worldview (tied to its national and corporate identity) remains the same, and choice of responses occurs from the existing behavioral repertoire. In moderate learning, partial modification of the interpretative system and/or development of new responses is involved. And in major learning, substantial and irreversible restructuring of one or both of the stimulus and response systems takes place (Hedberg 1981). This conceptualization parallels Argyris and Schon's (1978) single-loop (or low-level) learning that serves merely to adjust the parameters in a fixed structure to varying demands, versus double-loop (or high-level) learning that changes norms, values, and worldviews, and redefines the rules for low-level learning.

Using a contingency theory perspective, we may expect the extent of learning (minor, moderate, or major) necessary for a given level of GSA longevity to be commensurate with the extent of interfirm diversity. Highly similar partners would require relatively little mutual adjustment for sustained collaborative effectiveness. Highly dissimilar partners would need to expend greater (double-loop) efforts and resources toward learning, absent which longevity may be expected to suffer.

Moreover, Type I and Type II diversity may shift dynamically along different phases of alliance development. Regarding the former, Porter (1986) observes that:

> Coalitions involving access to knowledge or ability are the most likely to dissolve as the party gaining access acquires its own internal skills through the coalition. Coalitions designed to gain the benefits of scale or learning in performing an activity have a more enduring purpose. If they dissolve, they will tend to dissolve into merger or into an arm's-length transaction. The stability of risk-reducing

Table 2. Selected International Differences and Impacted Areas of GSA Management

Characteristic	Value	Country Examples	Description	Impacted Areas of GSA Management
Ownership of Assets	Private	'Free World' Countries	Factors of production predominantly privately owned.	Sourcing strategy, pricing flexibility, quality control, technology transfer, profit repatriation
	Public	East Bloc Countries[1] Communist China[2]	Factors of production predominantly publicly owned.	Sourcing strategy, pricing flexibility, quality control, technology transfer, profit repatriation
Coordination of National Economic Activity	Market	'Free World' Countries	Consumer sovereignty; freedom of enterprise, equilibration of supply and demand of resources and products by market forces.	Sourcing strategy, pricing flexibility, quality control, technology transfer, profit repatriation
	Command	East Bloc Countries, Communist China[2]	Centralized planning of production quotas, prices, and distribution. Pyramidal hierarchy of control.	
Perceived Ability to Influence Future	Self-determination	USA	Individuals and firms can take actions to influence their environment and improve prospects for the future.	Long-range planning, production scheduling
	Fatalistic	Islamic Countries	People must adjust to their environment. Life follows a preordained course.	
Time Orientation	Abstract, Lineal	USA	The clock serves to harmonize activities of group members. Punctuality is important. Time is money.	Productivity, joint project deadlines
	Concrete, Circular	Argentina, Brazil	Activities are timed by recurring rhythmic natural events such as day and night, seasons of the year.	
Communication	Low Context	USA	Most information is contained in explicit codes, such as spoken or written words. Articulation ('spelling is out') is important.	Initial negotiations, ongoing communications
	High Context	Saudi Arabia	Sending and receiving messages is highly contingent upon the physical context and non-verbal communication.	
Information Evaluation	Pragmatic	U.K.	Emphasis on practical applications of specific details in light of particular goals.	Structure of the GSA management
	Idealistic	Soviet Union	Utilization of abstract frameworks for structuring thinking processes which are molded by a dominant ideology.	

Table 2. Continued

Characteristic	Value	Country Examples	Description	Impacted Areas of GSA Management
Conflict Management Style	Confrontation	USA	Openness and directness in work relations is promoted. Conflict resolution is preferred over conflict suppression.	Conflict management
	Harmony	Japan	Wa (maintaining harmony in Japanese) is important. Saving face is important. Saving face is preferred over direct confrontation.	
Decisionmaking[3]	Autocratic	South Korea	Decisions fully formulated before being announced, either individually or with input from experts.	Negotiation and bargaining
	Group	Japan	Information is shared with subordinates, whose input is sought before decisions are made.	
Leadership Style	Task Oriented	West Germany	Enforcement of rules and procedures. Focus on technological aspects.	Decisionmaking, leadership
	People Oriented	Japan	Greater attention to human factors, including morale and motivation. Utilization of group dynamics to reach organizational goals.	
Problem Solving	Scientific	Most Occidental Countries	Logic and scientific method are the means of solving new problems. Accurate data are more important than intuition.	Decisionmaking process
	Traditional	Most Oriental Countries	Solutions to new problems are derived by sifting through past experiences.	
Employment Duration	Variable	USA	Employees can quit to accept better jobs. Employers can terminate low-performing employees.	Human resources management
	Lifetime	Japan	Employees are a 'family' which cannot be abandoned. Termination causes enormous loss of prestige and must be avoided.	
Power Distance[4]	Low	Austria	Relative quality of superiors and subordinates. Greater participation of subordinates in decisionmaking.	GSA structure and communication
	High	Mexico	Distinct hierarchical layers with formal and restricted interactions. Emphasis on ranks. Top-down communication.	

Table 2. Continued

Characteristic	Value	Country Examples	Description	Impacted Areas of GSA Management
Uncertainty Avoidance[4]	Low	Denmark	Uncertainties are a normal part of life. Business risks are judged against potential rewards. Flexibility and innovation are emphasized.	Choice of projects tackled, information and control systems
	High	South Korea	Business risks lead to high anxiety, leading to mechanisms that offer a hedge against uncertainty; written rules and procedures, plans, complex information systems.	
Individualism[4]	Individualistic	Canada	Reliance on individual initiative, self-assertion, and personal achievement and responsibility	Accountability, performance evaluation systems
	Collectivistic	Singapore	Emphasis on belonging to groups and organizations, acceptance of collective decisions, values, and duties.	
Masculinity[4]	Masculine	Italy	Machismo attitudes. Valued ideals are wealth, power, decisiveness, growth, bigness, and profits. Compensation in monetary rewards, status, recognition, and promotion is expected in proportion to achievement of ideals.	Organizational design, reward systems
	Feminine	Netherlands	Nurturing attitudes. Care of people, interpersonal relations, quality of life, service, and social welfare are valued ideals. Members seek cooperative work climate, security, and overall job satisfaction.	

[1] The situation in the East Bloc countries is in a state of flux, with political reform toward democratization and economic reform embracing free markets and private property. However, Western companies rushing to enter into cooperative ventures with these countries are likely to encounter considerable inertia from past practices (see *Business Week* (1990a)); as such, managers must remain aware of fundamental differences and their implications for alliances.

[2] The international business environment in Communist China has deteriorated considerably following the Tiananmen Square Massacre, forcing corporate strategists to reassess their commitments in the PRC and Hong Kong (see *New York Times* (1990)).

[3] From Kolde (1985).

[4] From Hofstede (1983).

coalitions depends on the sources of risk they seek to control. Coalitions hedging against the risk of a single exogenous event will tend to dissolve, while coalitions involving an ongoing risk (e.g., exploration risk for oil) will be more durable. (p. 329).

Thus, Type I strategic motivations and organizational learning interact to shape alliance stability and outcome. Similarly, the impact of Type II diversity on alliances can be dynamically altered by organizational learning that itself is an outcome of certain types of deliberate management investments during different phases of alliance development. The pattern of these investments may be a function of the configuration of Type II diversity, i.e., the *degree* and *type* of interfirm differences. If the relatively stable dimensions of societal culture, national context, or corporate culture constitute salient interfirm differences, then organizational learning becomes a threshold condition for alliance success, and management attention must be targeted at the relevant dimensions during the earliest phases of alliance development (such as partner screening and pre-contractual negotiations). In cases where significant diversity arises from the relatively more volatile dimensions of strategic direction and management practices and organization, later adaptive learning under new partner circumstances is a necessary pre-condition for GSA longevity.

It is evident, then, that the magnitude and timing of Type I and Type II diversity shifts contribute to different alliance outcomes. Specifically, when Type I diversity (mutual interdependency) is larger than Type II diversity, ceteris paribus, longevity will be high. In this situation, additional alliances between the GSA partners become more likely, and ongoing organizational learning in repeated successful collaborative experiences may further reduce Type II diversity, reinforcing the alliancing process.

But when Type II diversity is larger than Type I diversity, ceteris paribus, longevity will be low. This situation can arise in one of two ways: shrinkage of Type I diversity, or escalation of Type II diversity. The first way represents the stepping-stone strategy (planned termination), in which one partner rapidly internalizes the skills and technologies of the other; after the process is completed, that is, when Type I diversity vanishes, little incentive remains for the internalizer firm to remain in the partnership. The second way represents untimely dissolution of the GSA, as a lack of learning and adaptation exacerbates problems of social interaction among managers from the alliance partners. Such unplanned termination is more likely when the partner firms are working together for the first time and have yet to establish a history of prior successful collaborative experiences; differ sharply on one or more of the Type II dimensions; and the efforts and resources committed to learning and adaptation are not commensurate with this diversity.

Thus, the relationship between diversity and longevity is dynamic, and is strongly influenced by the amount of learning and adaptation occuring between the GSA partners. The greater the amount of learning, the greater the negative impact of Type I diversity on longevity, but the smaller the negative impact of Type II diversity on longevity.

IMPLICATIONS AND CONCLUSIONS

The process model of longevity proposed in this paper, drawing upon learning-based management of differences in the properties of the partners, offers rich and exciting opportunities for improved research and practice in GSAs. Only a few of these are touched upon below.

First, there is a need for inductive theory-building (following covariance structure modeling and empirical research) on the relative importance, patterns of interconnectedness, and tension-inducing capacity of the typological dimensions of diversity in a variety of partnering situations, especially in longitudinal studies focusing on the phases of alliance development. Such research will be timely and useful for developing ex post alliance performance generalizations as well as ex ante partner selection criteria. Although preliminary work has been done in both of these areas, as noted above, the research has been fragmented and theory-building in GSAs has been slow, reflecting the lack of systematic conceptualization of a typology of interfirm diversity, much less a dynamic link between diversity and longevity.

The propositions and model developed here draw attention to the crucial aspect of *learning* among interfacing managers of GSA partners; important corollary implications flow from this emphasis. For example, faced with rapid internationalization and even faster growth of interfirm cooperation, how best can global firms quickly enlarge the severely limited cadre of culturally sophisticated, internationally experienced managers (cf. Strom (1990); Hagerty (1991))? Since coping with interfirm diversity (e.g, formal training programs) is not costless, how are (or methodologically should be) the costs and benefits of such coping efforts assessed by managers or researchers? Fledgling attempts toward institutionalizing learning within the company and enhancing the cumulativeness of cooperative experiences with other companies are already evident, such as General Electric Company's establishment of GE International in 1988. Created as a special mechanism to efficiently handle the swift growth of GSAs and facilitate organizational learning, GE International's primary roles are to identify and implement GSAs, to promote enhanced international awareness within GE, and to permit the sharing of international partnership expertise throughout the company.

In conclusion, as global firms' technological, financial, and marketing prowess increasingly becomes tied to the excellence of their external organizational relations, 'GSA sophistication' – the ability to diagnose important differences between partners and fashion a productive partnership by devising novel solutions to accommodate the differences – is likely to become an imperative. GSAs represent a type of competitive weapon, in that they involve interorganizational *cooperation* in the pursuit of global *competitive* advantage. Sharpening the edge of this competitive weapon may require the adoption of multifirm, multicultural perspectives in joint decisionmaking, a process rendered difficult by the perceptual blinders imposed by culture-bound and corporate-bound thinking (e.g., respectively, the 'ugly foreigner' mentality and the NIH, or not invented here, syndrome).[9] Thus, future research on GSA longevity and performance must take into account the partners' cognition of, and adaptation to, the important dimensions of diversity that is an integral, inescapable part of such alliances.

NOTES

1. Although other factors, such as hidden agendas and conceptually flawed logic of the GSA may also account for a portion of these failures, interfirm diversity remains a prime culprit. Moreover, as noted shortly, dissolution of a GSA does not necessarily constitute failure. When GSAs are used as 'stepping stones,' their termination may be viewed by the parents as a success, not a failure.

2. This typology is suggested as a parsimonious framework to be built upon in future research on GSAs, not as the comprehensive final word. For instance, differences in industry-specific considerations and firm sizes can be significant factors in some cases; these factors are not explicitly considered here.

3. GSAs typically involve commitment of substantial resources on both sides, in cash and/or in kind. Failure can result in a loss of competitive position far beyond merely the opportunity cost of the resources deployed in the GSA itself; synergistic gains and expected positive spillover effects for the parent firm may not be realized.

4. However, the speed with which these changes may occur should not be overestimated, in light of the deeply embedded industry structure and institutions in Japan.

5. One example is the GM-Toyota alliance called New United Motor Manufacturing, Inc. (NUMMI). NUMMI was approved despite strenuous objections from Chrysler and others, whose traditional (antitrust-based) arguments were rejected by the U.S. Department of Justice.

6. This is likely to remain true even after taking into account (a) the move toward a more genuine Common Market in 1992, which creates an integrated economy of 320 million consumers, and (b) the increase in the size of the market arising from East Bloc upheavals.

7. For example, the growing inseparability of data transmission and data processing has created hybrid businesses among companies in computers, telecommunications, office products, modular switchgears, and semiconductors. Similarly, auto firms, driven by cost, quality, and efficiency considerations, increasingly invest in electronics, new materials, aerodynamics, computers, robotics, and artificial intelligence.

8. GSAs must ultimately be guided by careful consideration of the respective management practices and organization of the parents, as well as the operational needs of the venture, such as response time to market developments and management information systems that accurately reflect the magnitude and scope of the alliance.

9. This problem may be particularly severe for Japanese companies, whose overseas activities until recently strongly emphasized exports and direct investments in wholly owned subsidiaries. The historically closed nature of Japan's society and corporations makes integrating outsiders – even other Japanese – difficult.

REFERENCES

Adler, N.J. (1986). *International dimensions of organizational behavior.* Boston, MA: Kent.
——. and Graham, J.L. (1989). Cross-cultural interaction: The international comparison fallacy? *Journal of International Business Studies,* Fall: 515–37.
Argyris, C. and Schon, D.A. (1978). *Organizational learning.* Reading. MA: Addison-Wesley.
BenDaniel, D.J. and Rosenbloom, A.H. (1990). *The handbook of international mergers and acquisitions.* Englewood Cliffs. NJ: Prentice-Hall.
Beyer, J.M. (1981). Ideologies, values, and decision making in organizations. In P.C. Nystrom and W.H. Starbuck, editors, *Handbook of organization design.* New York: Oxford University Press.
Black, S.J. (1987). Japanese/American negotiation: The Japanese perspective. *Business and Economic Review,* **6**, 27–30.
——. and Mendenhall, M. (1990). Cross-cultural training effectiveness: A review and a theoretical framework for future research. *Academy of Management Review,* **15**, 113–36.
Borys, B. and Jemison, D.B. (1989). Hybrid arrangements as strategic alliances: Theoretical issues in organizational combinations. *Academy of Management Review,* **14**, 234–49.
Business Week. (1990a). Big deals run into big trouble in the Soviet Union. March **19**, 58–59.
——. (1990b). A waltz of giants sends shock waves worldwide. March **19**, 59–60.
Contractor, F.J. and Lorange, P. (editors). (1988). *Cooperative strategies in international business.* Lexington, MA: Lexington Books.
Cosier, R.A. and Dalton, D.R. (1990). Positive effects of conflict: A field assessment. *International Journal of Conflict Management,* January: 81–92.
Daft, R.L. and Weick, K.E. (1984). Toward a model of organizations as interpretation systems. *Academy of Management Review,* **9**, 284–95.
Dobkin, J.A. (1988). *International technology joint ventures.* Stoneham. MA: Butterworth Legal Publishers.
Evans, F.B. (1963). Selling as a dyadic relationship – a new approach. *American Behavioral Scientist,* **6** (May): 76–79.
Fiol, M.C. and Lyles, M.A. (1986). Organizational learning. *Academy of Management Review,* **10**, 803–13.
Geringer, M.J. and Hebert, L. (1991). Measuring performance of international joint ventures. *Journal of International Business Studies,* **22**, 249–64.
Gomes-Casseres, B. (1989). Joint ventures in the face of global competition. *Sloan Management Review,* Spring: 17–26.

Graham, J.L. (1985). The influence of culture on the process of business negotiations: An exploratory study. *Journal of International Business Studies*, **16**, 81–95.

Hagerty, B. (1991). Firms in Europe try to find executives who can cross borders in a single bound. *The Wall Street Journal*, January **25**, B1, B3.

Hall, D.R. (1984). *The international joint venture*. New York: Praeger.

Harrigan, KR. (1985). *Strategies for joint ventures*. Lexington, MA: Lexington Books.

———. (1988). Strategic alliances and partner asymmetries. In F.J. Contractor and P. Lorange, editors, *Cooperative strategies in international business*. Lexington, MA: Lexington Books.

Hedberg, B. (1981). How organizations learn and unlearn. In P.C. Nystrom and W.H. Starbuck, editors, *Handbook of organizational design*. New York: Oxford University Press.

Hergert, M and Morris, D. (1988). Trends in international collaborative agreements. In F.J. Contractor and P. Lorange, editors, *Cooperative strategies in international business*. Lexington, MA: Lexington Books.

Hofstede, G. (1983). National cultures in four dimensions. *International Studies of Management and Organization*, **13**, 46–74.

Gilling, P.J. (1982). How to make a global joint venture work. *Harvard Business Review*, May–June.

Goide, E.-J. (1985). *Environment of international business*. Boston: PWS-Kent Publishing Co.

Guckhohn, C. and Kroeberg, A.L. (1952). *Culture: A critical review of concepts and definitions*. New York: Vintage Books.

Killing, P.J. (1982). How to make a global joint venture work. *Harvard Business Review*, May–June.

Laurent, A. (1983). The cultural diversity of management conceptions. *International Studies of Management and Organization*, Spring.

Lazersfeld, P.M. and Merton, R.K. (1954). Friendship as a social process. In Monroe Berger. Theodore Abel and Charles Page, editors, *Freedom and control in modern society*. New York: Octagon Books.

Lewis, M.A. (1988). Learning among joint venture-sophisticated firms. In F.J. Contractor and P. Lorange, editors, *Cooperative strategies in international business*. Lexington. MA: Lexington Books.

Lynch, R.P. (1989). *The practical guide to joint ventures and alliances*. New York: Wiley.

Maruyama, M. (1984). Alternative concepts of management: Insights from Asia and Africa. *Asia Pacific Journal of Management*, **1**(2): 100–11.

McGuire, W.J. (1968). The nature of attitudes and attitude change. In L. Gardner and G. Aronson, editors, *The handbook of social psychology*. Reading. MA: Addison-Wesley.

Miles, R.E. and Snow, C.C. (1978). *Organizational strategy, structure and process*. New York: McGraw-Hill.

Miller, D. and Friesen, P.H. (1980). Momentum and revolution in organization adaptation. *Academy of Management Journal*, **23**, 591–614.

Molnar, J.J. and Rogers, D.L. (1979). A comparative model of interorganizational conflict. *Administrative Science Quarterly*, **24**, 405–24.

Moran, R.T. and Harris, P.R. (1982). *Managing cultural energy*. Houston: Gulf Publishing Co.

New York Times. (1990). Bush distressed as policy fails to move China. March 11: 1, 11.

Nelsen, R.. (1988). Cooperative strategy. *Strategic Management Journal*, **9**, 475–92.

Onmae, K. (1985). *Triad power*. New York: The Free Press.

Oliver, C. (1990). Determinants of interorganizational relationships: Integration and future directions. *Academy of Management Review*, **15**, 241–65.

Paulson, S. (1976). A theory and comparative analysis of interorganizational dyads. *Rural Sociology*, **41**, 311–29.

Perlmutter, H.V. and Heenan, D.A. (1986). Cooperate to compete globally. *Harvard Business Review*, March–April: 136–52.

Peters, T. and Waterman, R.H. (1982). *In search of excellence*. New York: Warner Books.

Porter, M.E., editor. (1986). *Competition in global industries*. Boston: Harvard Business School Press.

Pucik, V. (1988). Strategic alliances with the Japanese: Implications for human resource management. In Farok Contractor and Peter Lorange, editors, *Cooperative strategies in international business*. Lexington. MA: Lexington Books.

Schermerhorn, J.R., Jr. (1975). Determinants of interorganizational cooperation. *Academy of Management Journal*, **18**, 846–56.

Strom, S. (1990). The art of luring Japanese executives to American firms. *New York Times*, March 25: F12.

Terpstra, V. and David, K. (1990). *The cultural environment of international business*. Cincinnati: Southwestern-Publishing Co.

Tung, R. (1984). *Key to Japan's economic strength: Human power.* Lexington. MA: Lexington Books.

Turner, L. (1987). *Industrial collaboration with Japan.* London: Routledge and Kegan Paul.

Van de Ven, A.H. (1976). On the nature, formation, and maintenance of relations among organizations. *Academy of Management Review,* **2**, 24–36.

Venkatraman, N. and Ramanujam, W. (1986). Measurement of business performance in strategy research: A comparison of approaches. *Academy of Management Review,* **11**, 801–14.

Westney, E.D. (1988). Domestic and foreign learning curves in managing international cooperative strategies. In F.J. Contractor and P. Lorange, editors, *Cooperative strategies in international business.* Lexington. MA: Lexington Books.

Whetten, D.A. (1981). Interorganizational relations: A review of the field. *Journal of Higher Education,* **52**, 1–28.

Wysocki, B. (1990). Cross-border alliances become favorite way to crack new markets. *Wall Street Journal,* March 26: A1, A12.

Part IV

Organizing the Multinational Firm

CONTENTS

18

Options Thinking and Platform Investments: Investing in Opportunity

Bruce Kogut and Nalin Kulatilaka

The world is witnessing a new era of competition with the development of new principles of organizing work, radical technologies, and globalization. For many firms, these transformations have biased managerial action towards myopic behavior and indecision. These transformations are similar to the changes that swept across the world at the turn of the century. In the United States and other countries, success was achieved through the willingness of entrepreneurs, firms, financial institutions, and government to invest capital for long-term payoffs. The building of the infrastructure in telecommunications, roadways, and electrical grids required massive amounts of invested capital. Organizing workers in the new ways of rationalized production required extensive experimentation and financial expense.

It is ironic that this willingness to invest is not validated by many of the financial criteria presently taught in business schools and practiced in industry. The problem is not that financial criteria have come to dominate decision making, but that there is a systematic bias towards the short term in the kind of decision heuristics that managers and financial analysts apply to evaluating major investments. Even popular strategic planning tools, such as industry structural analysis, bias action away from making investments with long-term payoffs. The myopia that currently plagues American industry has its source in the financial criteria, planning tools, and especially in the incentives attached to managers' performance.

Over the past few years, there have been two streams of thought aimed at correcting this bias. One has been the formulation of strategic investments as real options. By real, it is meant that the investment is in physical and human assets, as opposed to financial instruments. This stream of thinking has its origins in Stewart Myers' observations that the cash flows of many investments consists of income from the assets in their current use, plus a growth option to expand into new markets in the future.[1]

The second stream consists of recent works on organizational capabilities and core competence.[2] This approach seeks to redirect the orientation of strategic planning from the exploitation of current resources to an emphasis on the creation of capabilities with long-term payoffs. It is, in fact, a prominent feature of current competitive conditions that the battle for survival in many industries concerns the speed by which new organizational practices are adopted (e.g. quality programs, kanban systems, or value-based activity analysis).

The formal apparatus of option valuation has been criticized as being too narrow and demanding to be applied practically to strategic decisions. In contrast, the notion of organizational capabilities has been accused of being too vague to further useful analysis. We

Reprinted with permission from the *California Management Review*, 1994, **36**(2), 200–216 seek to bridge these two streams of thought by developing a set of heuristics that view an organization's capabilities as generating platforms to expand into new but uncertain markets. These capabilities are considered options because they are investments in opportunity. Without making the initial stake, the firm would be unable to act to its advantage when opportunity does strike. Furthermore, these options are valuable for a broad range of applications. The techniques for analyzing platforms as options have developed rapidly over the past ten years. The problem is not so much analytical as it is conceptual.

PLATFORM INVESTMENTS AS OPTIONS

Over the past few years, a wide body of applications of mathematical techniques has been developed to evaluate financial options. These techniques permit a price to be calculated for the value of the flexibility to exercise a given right, such as that of being able to buy the stock of a company at a fixed price in the case of a call option. This flexibility is, obviously, more valuable when there is more uncertainty about the best investments to make.

Consider the case of a biotechnology company and an electric company. The shares of both companies are selling at a price of $30. If an investor were to be given the right to buy shares of either company at $32 within 30 days, holding the option to buy the stock of a biotechnology company is more valuable than that to buy the stock of an electric company. Either stock may finish the period at below $32; the worst the investor can do is not exercise and receive, effectively, a payment of 0 for holding the option. In this case, the option has turned out to be of no value. But the biotechnology stock, because its price is more variable, has a better chance to be 'in the money'; that is, its price has more upside potential because it is more volatile. The option on the biotechnology company is a more valuable play on the upside potential, with the worst case being not to exercise at all, as in the case of the electric company option.

A common observation has been that the techniques used for valuing financial options of this sort are particularly well-suited to analyzing the complex and uncertain investment decisions facing managers. Indeed, many decisions have a straightforward option interpretation. Should a major oil company pump to full capacity today? If it pumps today, it has less oil in the future. If prices should rise, it would have oil to sell and to exploit the opportunity. Since more volatile oil prices increase the likelihood that it may pay to wait until the market takes off, the 'option to wait' is more valuable when there is more price uncertainty.

Many options of this nature are *inherent* in an investment. If you are running a business, you have the option to abandon it. Should you abandon it now or wait? Obviously, it pays to wait if there is a higher chance that the market will be more valuable tomorrow and if it costs too much – as it always does – to close down an operation. If it turns out to be worse, the option to abandon is always there; it is inherent in any operating business.

We are concerned in this article with a more *proactive* kind of option, one that is not inherent but must be designed and planned. We call such options 'platform investments' in order to cover two types of investment decisions. The first is the question of the design of an operating flexibility, such as whether it pays to buy robotics in order to automate a factory to produce many kinds of models depending on (uncertain) demand. The second is the growth option, as discussed earlier, which gives a firm the right to expand in the future into new product or geographic markets. This kind of investment captures the importance of investing rapidly in the opportunities critical to the growth and success of new business.

Platform investments are options on the future. This simple insight suggests that their value will be determined by the same factors that determine the price of a financial options. But because platform investments are real options, there are a few additional considerations which, in practice, turn out to be very messy for the purpose of arriving at easy methods of valuation. For example, whereas financial market expectations regarding the level and volatility of future oil prices can be easily gleaned from accessible trading data on crude oil future contracts, such data must be generated by the informed guesses of operating and staff managers for most kinds of investments. Many major investments, because they have an option-like quality, are more valuable than they appear in terms of simple discounted cash flows.[3] Such undervaluations are to be expected when the investments are in new ways of doing things.

THE PROBLEM OF MYOPIC HEURISTICS

Applying option models to operating and investment decisions would not be as difficult if there existed a set of explicit methods by which to evaluate option opportunities. Such methods could then be embodied in the strategic planning tools and decision rules that serve as heuristics reflecting the prevailing wisdom on how to arrive at 'best' performance. By heuristics, we mean the techniques used to identify and analyze problems. 'Choose the project which has the highest net present value' is one heuristic; 'enter markets only when you can win the most share of sales' is another.

There is no strategy that is best for all industries or at all times, but heuristics are often surprisingly robust. The choice of a heuristic is a compromise between ease of use and accuracy. Not everything can be measured and analyzed. Consequently, this compromise reflects the understanding of what rules support the achievement of best practices.

A common problem is that the notion of best practice changes more quickly than decision heuristics. Thomas Johnson and Robert Kaplan argue that accounting systems were developed during the first third of this century to track the cost of labor in the new mass systems of production.[4] Even though the importance of labor expenditure relative to quality and speed of production has fallen dramatically since then, many managerial accounting systems still emphasize direct labor costs as a primary concern of measurement.

There is good reason to suspect that today's heuristics are biased towards the short-term due to the evolution of particular institutions, ways of organizing, and rules developed during this century. Consequently, they ignore or undervalue platform investments. While these practices made good sense at one time, alterations are now required.

The following four sources of myopia are the most telling.[5]

Financial institutions

A common complaint of managers is that financial institutions compel boards of directors and top management to focus on short-term profits. This complaint has, until recently, received little credence among academics convinced that equity markets properly weigh current and expected cash flows. Moreover, this skepticism has been reinforced by the gradual emergence in the U.S. and Japan of similar patterns of equity financing with financial institutions (e.g. through pension fund management) as the dominant holders of equities. Today, both Japan and the United States have approximately the same levels of debt to equity financing.[6]

The analysis of the short-sightedness of American financial institutions has, however, become more subtle. The issue is not so much the differences in the cost of finance among countries (especially since capital costs are much more similar among countries in today's environment of integrated financial markets); rather, the factors affecting managers' investment horizons lie more in the differences among countries regarding the role of financial institutions (especially banks) in the governance of corporations. In this regard, Japan and Germany look very different from the United States. In these two countries, banks and insurance companies are permitted to hold substantial positions in the debt and equity of industrial corporations.

In Japan, a 'main bank' serves as the primary adviser to firms belonging to an industrial group. Estimates for holdings in 133 Japanese manufacturing firms in 1984 show that the largest debtholder (either a bank or insurance company) owns on average 22.3 percent of the debt and 6.2 percent of the equity. Because the main bank and institutions hold debt and equity positions in each other, consideration of the crossholdings would increase the centrality of the main bank.[7]

In Germany, three banks serve as the largest sources of capital to industry. Due to a custom whereby individuals give proxy voting rights to banks ('Depotstimmrecht'), their influence is substantially enhanced beyond their direct ownership of equity and debt. This influence is further strengthened by the veto rights of any major investment given to minority owners controlling more than 25 percent of the votes. In 1975, the three major banks controlled 43.2 percent of the voting rights for the 74 largest non-financial corporations with traded stocks; all banks (including investment companies) controlled 92.5 percent. Since little debt is raised through bonds (and when it is, banks are often the issuers), most firms rely upon loans from banks. Banks serve as the primary provider of loans to firms, and own and control equity positions in the largest companies.[8]

The concentration of financial power in Japan and Germany has certain benefits. One, it more clearly aligns the interests of debt and equity holders. In the U.S., in the event of bankruptcy, dissolution of assets will first be used to cover senior debt, which is often held by banks; hence, there is less incentive to maintain the firm as a going concern and bankruptcy is used as a way for senior claimants to recover the value of their loans. Two, banks have not only greater access to information, but they also disseminate information which improves the quality of strategic decisions. As a result, Japanese firms belonging to a *keiretsu* (industrial grouping) are less financially constrained than other independent Japanese firms.[9]

While the Japanese and German financial systems are not without their pitfalls, the incentives for investing for a longer horizon is greater in these two countries. Prior to regulations limiting the equity shares of banks and insurance companies in the United States, certain investment houses (such as J.P. Morgan) played a similar role in the American economy at the turn of the century to the one of German and Japanese banks today.[10] At the present, the U.S. is struggling to change the current regulatory framework of financial institutions.

Budgeting rules

The method of discounted cash flows (DCF) diffused widely among corporations in the post World War II period. While there is no doubt that DCF is superior to such alternatives as pay-back or internal rate of return as ways to evaluate investments, DCF also has severe problems. The principal problem is that DCF provides the wrong answer in the wrong direction just when the need for a good way to evaluate an investment is the greatest. In stable environments, DCF provides an easy and instructive way to analyze the decision whether to commit resources to a new investment. It is mostly likely to fail in cases where the investment presents a platform for future expansion in highly uncertain environments. As shown below, the weakness of DCF is its failure to account for how uncertainty, rather than implying a higher discount rate, can increase the value of an investment.

Strategic planning

One of the activities encompassed by strategic planning is the application of heuristics by which to identify profitable businesses for investment and expansion. One of the most well-known tools is the Boston Consulting Group (BCG) growth matrix, which was developed in the 1960s. In this matrix, an attractive business is indexed by its growth rate. Competitive advantage is driven by the share of the market held by a firm. Market share is a proxy measurement of a firm's cost position; thus, due to scale economies and experience effects, a firm with the largest market share will have the lowest costs.

This planning heuristic has the advantage of being simple; it is easier to measure relative market share than actual costs. Its success was driven by its compatibility with the expansion of mass-production systems into new industries and markets. Volume strategies and low cost positions are inevitably linked to the concept of relative market share.

The technique of industry structural analysis, which was developed and diffused in the 1970s and 1980s, is more sophisticated.[11] By emphasizing the unique constellation of competitive pressures from rivals, suppliers, and buyers in a particular industry, this technique encourages the consideration of a wider menu of strategies. This approach focuses on exploiting a firm's resources in the context of specific market structures.

No matter how faulty the BCG growth matrix may be for some industries, it has the merit of encouraging the allocation of resources to new business for the long-term purpose of eventual market domination. Industry structural analysis places the stress more upon the exploitation of resources in a given market structure than upon the creation of new capabilities. It tends to underestimate, however, the importance of developing generalized resources (which not only provide entry into future markets, but also shape their evolution).

Strategic business units

Along with the development of planning techniques for the analysis of discrete businesses, corporations have created corresponding organizational divisions. These divisions, called 'strategic business units' (SBUs), are delegated responsibility for the formulation of business strategy and for operations. The managers of the SBUs usually have their compensation linked to performance.

Though there are many merits to SBUs, they frequently lead to an underinvestment in projects with long-term growth. This problem may be more acute for many American firms than for their international counterparts, since the higher turnover rates among managers in the United States conflicts with the tracking of results over a long period of time. The recent trends towards strengthening divisionalization by 'flattening' the organization and by increasing the role of short-term incentives in compensation have exacerbated this orientation towards the short-term.

A more subtle problem is that the divisionalization of business will interfere with the identification and exercise of the underlying growth options. An SBU may view an investment as unattractive, even though it creates a platform valuable for other businesses. There is less incentive in this system to invest if the value of the platform accrues to other SBUs.

The SBU structure discourages the development of 'corporate assets.' New technologies are invariably valuable for many different businesses. Product divisions conflict with the broad implications of developing new capabilities. In many cases, no SBU can make the case for investment in expensive and risky new technologies. A corporate 'buy in' is required to relieve any single SBU of bearing the burden of developing corporate-wide capabilities. The failure is not of the SBU system itself, it rests instead with corporate management.

UNDERINVESTMENT

In some industries, myopic rules may be reasonable. What works today will work tomorrow; the extra cost of planning for the future may drown out the minor benefits. However, most industries do not fall in this category, and myopic biases will hurt when it matters the most. As a rule, the hard-nosed policy of accepting projects only on the basis of a hurdle rate will guarantee failure in any fast-growth industry.

The competitive implications of myopia can be seen through a simple simulation. Consider two firms in the same industry: one myopic and one far-sighted. The myopic firm uses the distribution of next period's net cash flows to forecast the future. The far-sighted firm recognizes that the decision to invest creates a platform to expand in the future. We let each firm increase its investment capacity by one unit, and we let supply equal demand, a not unreasonable assumption for fast-growing industries.

We trick the simulation to look as if there is an option to expand by using a log normal distribution of net cash flows. The log normal has the property of a fat upper tail, which is a good way to represent the 'option' value as a play on the upside. This tail also increases for the projection of cash flows further out in time, which captures the importance of looking into the more distant future. In the simulations, the far-sighted firm decides to invest or not depending upon a forecast which incorporates a forecast of the value of the investment if the market should grow rapidly. The myopic firm forecasts the future on the basis of next period's cash flows.

In a stable environment, the performances of myopic and far-sighted firms do not differ. In Figure 1, the simulated relationship between volatility of net cash flows and market share is graphed. Setting the volatility to 0, there is no difference in market shares after ten periods. These results underline the intuition that myopic behavior does not pay a penalty in stable and certain environments.

As the volatility of the net cash flows is allowed to increase, the penalty attached to myopia curves dramatically upward. With a volatility set to 50 percent of mean cash flows, the myopic firms are eliminated from the market. Far-sighted firms, even though constrained to invest only by increments, quickly come to dominate the market. Platform investments, like financial options, are more valuable in volatile environments.

What generates these results? The primary culprit is the aggregate underinvestment by the myopic firms in an industry where early investments generate the potential to expand and to earn increasing profits in later periods. In this industry, uncertainty actually favors more rather than less investment.

The issue is not that myopic policies fail under uncertainty; they fail when uncertainty represents opportunity. If the worse a firm can do is receive 0 net cash flows, then there is a

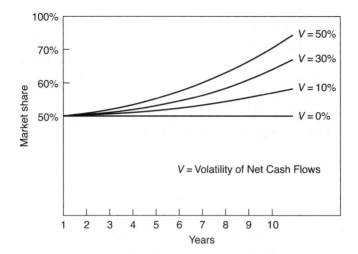

Fig. 1 Market share of firms with foresight

fundamental asymmetry in profits and losses. The greater the uncertainty, the more likely will be the chance that the market will generate large profits; the worst case always remains 0. The only way to exploit this opportunity is to invest in the first place.

These results provide an interesting insight into two heuristic rules. In growing but uncertain markets, a heuristic that says accept projects that promise to pay 20 percent on invested assets (or on operating income) conveys the message, 'Exit the market when uncertain.' The heuristic that says 'invest to capture dominant market share' is simple-minded but consistent with a far-sighted vision of the evolution of industry profits.

But is the rule to grab dominant share always right when there is high uncertainty? The answer is obviously no. This is a bad rule if there is no advantage to early investment. And it is a bad rule if all competitors blindly follow the same policy. Ignoring competitors is trading one kind of myopia for another.

HEURISTICS FOR PLATFORM INVESTMENTS FORMULATION

Rules must be developed for the identification of potential platforms in investment alternatives. Sometimes these rules can be formalized to arrive at rather exact valuations. More often, however, they will serve to guide how opportunities should be identified and framed for analysis.

Platforms, as options, are valuable due to four conditions: uncertainty, opportunity, time dependence, and discretion (see Figure 2). Obviously, flexibility is valuable only when there is uncertainty, yet understanding the source and properties of the uncertainty is a substantial problem. For example, it is difficult to describe the probabilities attached to the arrival of new technologies.

The value of a platform is related directly to the breadth of opportunities. It stands to reason that an investment with many potential applications is more valuable than one with a narrow set of opportunities. At the same time, some opportunities are more valuable than

- *Uncertainty*

- *Venue into multiple opportunities*
  A broad opportunity set
  Customers' perception of the value of derived products and services

- *Time dependence*
  Proprietary and difficult to imitate
  Risk of preemption

- *Managerial discretion to exercise the option*

Fig. 2 What determines the value of a platform?

others because their potential market is more lucrative. An investment in some platforms leads to products and services that are more valued by customers.

A more subtle feature is time dependence. The application of option analysis to investments is important, because it captures the value in the dependence of decisions over time. Having the ability to switch production from one kind of vehicle to another is only possible if an investment has been made earlier in flexible manufacturing systems. The issue of time dependence is one of the most complex problems in understanding the value of a platform investment. If the investment strategy can be quickly imitated, then there is no advantage for investing early. Similarly, if there is a high chance that a competitor will act first by preempting a market, then the value of investing in an option runs the threat of being eradicated over night.

A critical issue in the valuation of a platform is whether the investment is accompanied by the discretion to exercise the option. Many firms complain that they have more technologies than they use. It is not uncommon to hear the complaint that the benefits of investment in a technology were reaped by other firms. Witness the efforts of Texas Instruments and Honeywell, both of whom had to resort to the courts to collect on patented technologies. Competitors can sometimes have better incentives and information on how to apply a company's own technology to new markets.

Firms investing in platforms frequently face 'windows of opportunities' during which they must act to exploit their investments. Appropriate information systems are necessary to identify these opportunities in a timely way. Incentives must be in place in order to reward managers for acting promptly. Failure to benefit from platform investments is often due to deficiencies in the design of information flows and managerial incentives. New heuristics without proper information and incentives are of no value.

PLATFORM INVESTMENTS AS CAPABILITIES

Organizational capabilities – e.g. creating quality, being more flexible, and responding to the market quickly – are the most important platforms that a firm can build, because they support investment strategies into a wide spectrum of opportunities.

Investing in opportunity is important in businesses where the capability to expand is not easily acquired. The capability to expand is linked to reputation and to technologies. Reputation is hard to build quickly; similarly, the ownership of particular technologies is not easily attained. It is easy to advise a firm that it should compete by increasing the perceived quality-to-price performance; the hard part is learning 'how' to achieve the reputation for performance. Similarly, the important aspect of technological expertise is not simply the possession of a patent, but the capability to engineer new products consistently over time. Capabilities represent the accumulated skills of what corporations become best at doing.

These observations lead to a very simple point. The value of platforms as options ultimately comes down to viewing organizational capabilities as investments in learning and acquiring a broad-based expertise.[12] Prahalad and Hamel have suggested that these capabilities be understood as 'core competencies' in particular technologies.[13] These capabilities need not be restricted to technologies, but to the wider organizational capacity to develop new products and services, to bring them quickly to the market, or to market and distribute them effectively.

Organizational capabilities essentially consist of how a firm develops the expertise of its employees, through the way in which they are organized and rewarded and through the way in which information is gathered and disseminated. As shown in Figure 2, these capabilities represent the most important kind of options. They provide a platform into a wide number of opportunities. The ability to create new technologies is likely to generate a more vast potential than the opportunity associated with any one technology.

Organizational capabilities are important because they are hard to imitate or preempt. A competent group of engineers can reverse engineer and imitate many kinds of technologies. The hard part is learning how to build this group and coordinate product delivery to market. This capability is difficult to acquire, as it is often poorly understood and inadequately described in operating manuals.

The difficulty many corporations have had with adopting new capabilities has been that the benefits are often hard to measure. The benefits of new quality programs have been especially difficult to gauge, with estimates rarely being made and usually varying widely. No wonder that efforts to implement programs often appear as missionary. Not only are the data missing; there is not an understanding of what costs and benefits need to be measured to evaluate the investment in quality programs.

Four examples

Organizational capabilities are unlikely to be subject to the careful financial evaluation of other kinds of investments. Often, new capabilities are learned due to survival pressures. Most firms in the auto industry have adopted the capability to lower inventories by just-in-time systems and to speed product delivery by reliance on external sourcing. Yet, the investing in new capabilities and platforms is often delayed or neglected due to the failure to understand the option value. Consider the following examples.

Core technologies

A popular Silicon Valley adage is that certain products are important as 'technology drivers.' The manufacturing of memory semiconductors has played the role of driving the accumulation of experience in design and high-volume production. Learning that is gained in the product development of one memory generation serves as a basis for lowering the costs of subsequent generations.

This experience is not only useful for subsequent memory products, but also serves as a platform for diversification into other industries. In a study of the diversification of start-up companies in the semiconductor industry, Dong-Jae Kim found that firms with experience in the design of memory devices expanded significantly into other related areas. Start-ups in certain markets, such as application-specific integrated circuits (ASICs), not only did not diversify; they were also far more likely to fail or be acquired.

These results fit well with what we know of larger semiconductor firms that withdrew from memory production to stem their losses in this highly competitive market, only to discover the harmful effects on their other products. In the case of Motorola, it withdrew and later reentered. Other firms withdrew and continued on a downward spiral. However, even if a firm makes the decision to reenter, the competition has already moved on.

Technology drivers are platforms. They generate proprietary learning and they serve as points for expansion into other markets. The failure to recognize core technologies can lead to devastating results. A large electronics firm scrapped its cellular business in the 1980s, only to reenter by acquisition a few years later. If it had kept the option 'alive' by maintaining a small research and development activity, the capability to expand when the market turned-up would have been in place. The operating costs to keep the group running would have been low, at least in comparison with the high premium paid for the subsequent acquisition.

Joint ventures

An alternative to scrapping a project is to share the costs of running the activity with a partner. Frequently, the advantage of a joint venture is that the partners bring different capabilities to the cooperation. Motorola's reentry into the manufacturing of memory semiconductors was aided through a joint venture with Toshiba in exchange for microprocessor technology. As the Nummi joint venture between General Motors and Toyota indicates, the learning of new skills is facilitated by replicating the organization in the form of a joint venture.[14]

There is one complicating feature to joint ventures: they often do not last very long. The median life of a manufacturing joint venture in the United States is about 6 years. This gloomy figure is misleading, however, for most of these ventures terminate by acquisition. Figure 3 illustrates the relationship between profitability and the acquisition of the venture. The line indicates the expectation of profit based on a historical growth rate. (In this sense, this line corresponds to the expectation of the myopic firm, given in our earlier simulation.) Joint ventures tend to terminate when the industry begins to show unusual growth and the profits to early entrants increase. In this case, the joint ventures are not dissolved, but rather are acquired by one of the partners. When the industry does poorly, however, the partners neither dissolve nor acquire it. They maintain a hold position since there is no reason to throw away an already-bought option and since it is often better (if the holding and operating costs are not too high) to wait and see what opportunities present themselves in the future.

Joint ventures often carry an important option value. They are frequently used in high growth markets when neither partner has the necessary skills nor wants to bear the full risk. When the industry begins to grow quickly, the partners must invest more in order to exercise the option to expand with the market. It is at the moment of new investment that the partners realize they put different valuations on the opportunity. One partner buys it; the other one is bought out with capital gains.

These kinds of joint ventures are platform investments. They transfer and develop capabilities which serve as points of entry into uncertain markets. That they are so frequently acquired underscores their value for the development of organizational capabilities.[15]

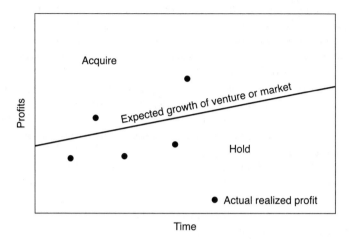

Fig. 3 Timing of exercise to acquire joint venture

Flexible manufacturing systems

One of the most important dimensions of competition is the capability to respond flexibly. There are many ways to achieve flexibility, from sub-contracting policies to product design. Some investments are made, however, with the sole purpose of achieving the flexibility to respond to uncertain markets. Flexible manufacturing systems are an example of a decision to purchase the ability to reprogram industrial machinery in order to increase the variety produced by the same capital equipment. This flexibility makes it possible to respond to shifts in customer demand as well as to offer greater customization of the product.

Installing flexible manufacturing systems appears to be relatively easy. The number of vendors willing to sell the hardware and provide software services is staggering. Yet, the experience with flexible manufacturing systems has often proven to be disappointing.

Robert Stempel of General Motors has commented:

> We've tried automation without knowledgeable workers, and it doesn't work . . . We put a tremendous amount of automation and electronics into our Cadillac plant in Hamtramck. And we couldn't run it because our people didn't understand what we were asking them to do.[16]

The difficulty of FMS is that the flexibility of the physical assets is nested in the organizational capability of the firm to operate flexibly. Physical equipment promising flexibility can be easily bought on the market. The more important platform value is the development of the capability to know how to run a plant flexibly, and then to expand this organizing heuristic to other operations.[17]

Country platforms

In the home country, managers take for granted that when a new product is launched, the customer already knows the brand label, the distribution channels are in place, and the salesforce knows the product and buyer. The product manager evaluating a new proposal need not calculate the cost of establishing these invisible assets of goodwill and acquired know-how.

An iron law of competing internationally, however, is that the first investment overseas will lose money. An investment in a foreign market underscores dramatically the value of owning platforms for sequential product launches. There may be few corporate and business assets established in the country. Because of the SBU incentive system, the costs of launching a single product appears as exorbitantly too high.

This view is clearly myopic, for the first investment establishes a country platform for the future. By establishing distribution channels and learning how to do business in a country, the initial entry generates the capability to launch subsequent products from this platform. The investment as a stand alone project may look unattractive, but the platform value is especially large for the first entry.

The importance of this platform is reflected in the debate on whether the product should carry a corporate label or be uniquely advertised. The corporate label establishes a platform by advertising the firm; advertising the product will result in higher market penetration. The choice comes down to evaluating the option value in the corporate label against the foregone revenues by not advertising the product.

The bias in a myopic approach is frequently revealed in country risk analysis. When confronted with a choice between investing in a developing country with a volatile market and a developed country, a manager is often advised to slap down a risk premium on the developing country project. Yet, if the initial investment is largely important for establishing a platform, the higher variance of the developing country should actually be seen as attractive. The upside of a Mexican investment is much larger for many products than the most optimistic scenario of an investment in the U.S. or other developed countries.

There is reason to be cautious, however. As shown in Figure 2, a platform investment is only valuable when acting today provides the capability to seize an opportunity in the future. Investing in the country carries no platform value if there is no advantage for early investment. For many firms already exporting to Europe, the 1992 policies of the European Community presented exactly this dilemma. With brand labels and distribution channels in place, the argument to invest before 1992 as a platform is *not* persuasive. Table 1 illustrates why this case is not a platform. For this analysis, the project with the plant in Europe against the export operation should be compared. We make the assumption that a new plant can be built in a year for a cost of 200. If a policy raising tariffs is imposed, the export operation pays a penalty of no sales until a European plant comes on stream. If the plant investment costs 200, the project with the new plant earns a net cash flow of -100 in the first year (investment costs plus the 100 from continued exports). The export project only builds the plant if barriers are imposed, and pays the investment costs of 200, with no export earnings for one year while the plant is being built. The cash flows for exporting should then be weighted by the probability of such a policy imposition.

Table 1 Cash flows of European plant versus export

	1990	1991	1992	1993	1994	1995
European plant	-100	100	100	100	100	100
Export						
If no barrier	100	100	100	100	100	100
If barrier	100	100	-200	100	100	100

This analysis is standard in any capital budgeting procedure; no platform value need be considered. As long as the option to invest in the future remained open, an early investment in a manufacturing plant generates little in the way of a platform; there is no time dependence. We could, of course, make the case that the plant builds goodwill with the Community which serves future product entries. But our point is that the case for such a platform has to be made and evaluated against the costs; it cannot be simply assumed and used to rationalize every investment.[18]

SHORT-RUN ACCOUNTABILITY FOR LONG-RUN RESULTS

The last example of the burden on a SBU in making a first investment in a country points to the importance of a corporate vision. If a country is deemed as vital, the corporate office should be willing to underwrite part of the investment. The criticism of this kind of proposal is the charge of the loss of accountability (which is the mirror image of the problem of discretion noted in Figure 2). There can be little doubt what the response from a room of SBU managers will be if corporate headquarters states that losses will be underwritten for investments into country X. The only problem will be sorting out which manager has the right to lose the money first.

A policy of funding platforms must resolve the problem of accountability. If the investment were to be in a financial stock option, prices of the security could be tracked even if a market for the option did not exist. Such markets do not exist by which to compare an investment in long-term capabilities. What, then, should be the criteria by which to monitor the platform value?

Most companies implicitly monitor this value. Figure 4, provides an example for evaluating a joint venture. The performance of the venture is measured along two lines. The first is the net cash flows (including dividends, transfer payments, and other fees) from assets currently in place. The second is a set of criteria for examining the progress of the venture along other lines. If the purpose is to learn new manufacturing techniques, the rate of what is to be learned over time should be established and then performance measured against this benchmark. The extent to which brand labels are recognized or knowledge of government regulatory bodies is improved can also be measured and evaluated on a year-by-year basis against the goals established at the time of the venture formation. The hard part, however, is understanding that these investments are valuable only if discretion is exercised; so every evaluation must also have an understanding of the menu of opportunities that should have been exploited.

In some cases, the evaluation can be made more exacting by estimating the value of the option over time. Reasonable benchmarks have been suggested for the evaluation of the option value of oil drilling, flexible manufacturing, and other investments whose value depends upon a price of a commodity or instruments traded in markets. For example, the value of establishing two plants with excess capacity in two countries with the option to switch overtime between them is primarily a function of exchange rate (or relative price) movements. This type of option is amenable to formal evaluation.

Ultimately, accountability rests with managers, who must gather the appropriate information for measurement and must understand the sources of uncertainty for defining when discretion should be taken. It may be difficult to break away from using the standard

Profits from venture as is:
- Fees
- Dividends
- Margins on sales to venture

Evaluation of platform:
- Brand label recognition
- Transfer of skills to other businesses
- Acquisition of contacts with new customers
- Improved relations with government regulatory bodies

Fig. 4 Evaluation of a joint venture

financial criteria of hurdle rates. Neglecting other forms of measurement will cause the evaluation system to tend inevitably toward myopic measurements.

MARKET STRUCTURE AND THE RISK OF PREEMPTION

The emphasis upon organizational capabilities and platforms should not lead to an underestimation of the competitive environment. Since platform investments can dramatically alter the structure of a market, it is important to understand how strategy itself influences the evolution of the industry. Clearly, the decision to invest in a country will generate competitive responses, which then influence an array of strategic variables such as prices, retaliation, and increases in output. The most difficult aspect of the analysis of platforms is incorporating the actions and responses of competitors.

It is important to understand how these investments influence a firm's commitment to a market. Too much flexibility can send the wrong signal in industries where entry is imminent. The option to wait before launching a new product that cannibalizes existing sales is attractive for a leader, until someone else enters and exploits the opportunity.

Though these are difficult issues, a few heuristics can be given with confidence. A common piece of advice has been that it is better to wait than to commit too early to a technology when there is high uncertainty over what customers want. Yet, at the same time, early commitment to a technology is often the way in which uncertainty is resolved; by early commitment, a firm can influence the evolution of the industry to favor their platform. As a rule, early commitment in such industries will tend to dominate the advantages of waiting.

Of course, there are cases when early commitment is not advisable. A good example is the restriction on the sale of cellular phones and services by some governments. In Japan, one electronics company developed what its managers felt were advanced proprietary technologies. This investment raised the costs of development and, consequently, the price of the phone. Offering less expensive but still high-quality systems, Motorola and NTT won the two licenses granted by the ministry for telecommunications to serve a particular region in Japan.

If not for the government restrictions, the investment in new cellular technologies may have proved worthwhile. The high costs of the technologies would cause initial losses, but there were anticipated benefits. Learning how to apply, develop, and manufacture products using the technology is earned over time; customers may then identify the technology with the firm (e.g. Xerox or Velcro). But neither benefit can be gained without experience selling to a market; government regulation eradicated the value of this platform.

THE LUXURY OF LOSING MONEY

It is important for financial institutions and corporate management to underwrite losses in the short run if there are to be any long-term advantages. Of course, Keynes's dictum that 'we are all dead in the long run' has a peculiar implication. Firms unable to finance these losses get locked in a vicious cycle, whereby concerns over surviving the threat of bankruptcy dominates the ability to invest in the long run. In the meantime, firms with sufficient foresight and resources are on a virtuous cycle of investments in capabilities which build the platforms for years to come. Not surprisingly, firms that begin their lives during difficult times have a hard time catching up; they never had the luxury of being able to invest for tomorrow.[19]

It has been a point of contention over the past few years that trends such as leveraged buyouts forebode a brighter future – the resulting debt burden forces management to bear down on the fundamentals of making money. However, the evidence shows that too severe pressure on cash flows drains money from R&D and other investments with long-term payoffs.[20] In industries with substantial growth opportunities, Keynes' dictum will be proven right just because the short-run question of survival dominates the necessity of foresight.

The United states and many other countries have now emerged from a decade of excess that centered on the short run. Many corporations are flatter and more focussed than ever. If they face a danger, it is the failure to develop heuristics to guide investments for future growth. The idea of a platform investment is directed at developing such heuristics to aid the understanding of how capabilities must be built in anticipation of the future. Flexibility is of no value in the absence of the resources required for execution. Learning new capabilities is ultimately the most critical investment in opportunity for the long haul.

NOTES

1. See Stewart Myers 'Determinants of Corporate Borrowing,' *Journal of Financial Economics*, **5** 147–75; see also S. Myers, 'Finance Theory and Financial Strategy,' In A. Hax (ed.) *Readings on Strategic Management*, Cambridge, MA: Ballinger, 1984. These ideas have been expanded by Carl Kester, 'Today's Options for Tomorrow's Growth,' *Harvard Business Review* (March/April 1984); William Hamilton and Graham Mitchell, 'What Is Your R&D Worth,' *The McKinsey Quarterly* (1990), pp. 150–60; and Tom Copeland and Jon Weiner, 'Proactive Management of Uncertainty,' *The McKinsey Quarterly* (1990), pp. 133–52; Leon Trigeorsis and Scott Mason, 'Valuing Managerial Flexibility,' *Midland Corporate Finance Journal* (1988, pp. 14–21.

2. See Jay Barney, 'Strategic Factor Markets: Expectations, Luck, and Business Strategy,' *Management Science*, **32** (1986): 1231–41; Richard Rumelt, 'Towards a Strategic Theory of the Firm,' in Robert Boyden Lamb (ed.) *Competitive Strategic Management*, Englewood Cliffs, NJ: Prentice Hall, Inc., 1984; Sidney Winter, 'Knowledge and Competence as Strategic Assets,' in D. Teece (ed.) *The Competitive Challenge – Strategies for Industrial Innovation and Renewal*, Cambridge, MA: Ballinger, 1987; and David Teece, Gary Pisano, and Amy Shuen, 'Resource-Based View of the Firm,' mimeo, 1991.

3. There are more technical obstacles to the application of exact formulations, with a principal problem being the strong assumptions of 'risk-neutral' valuations in the absence of arbitrage opportunities. Techniques, such as Monte Carlo simulations or decision trees, generally ignore entirely the option value, even they treat uncertainty explicitly.

4. Johnson and Kaplan (1987) *Relevance Lost: The Rise and Fall of Management Accounting*. Boston, MA: Harvard Business School Press.

5. For two explanations, see Michael Dertouzos, Richard Lester, and Robert Solow, *Made in America: Regaining the Productive Edge*, Cambridge, MA: MIT Press, 1989; and Michael Porter (ed.) *Investment Horizons in American Business*, Boston, MA: Harvard Business School Press.

6. Useem and Gottlieb estimate the share of institutions holding equity in the U.S. to have risen from 29 percent in 1980 to 46 percent in 1990. See Michael Useem and Martin Gottlieb, 'Corporate Restructuring, Ownership-Disciplined Alignment, and the Reorganization of Management,' *Human Resource Management*, **29** (1990), 285–306. Unpublished data from the Tokyo Stock Exchange shows financial institutions holding 38.5 percent of Japanese equity in 1980 and 42.5 percent in 1988. For an overview, see Michael Porter, 'Capital Disadvantage: America's Failing Capital Investment System,' *Harvard Business Review* (September/October 1992), pp. 65–82.

7. Stephen Prowse (1990) 'Institutional Investment Patterns and Corporate Financial Behavior in the United States and Japan,' *Journal of Financial Economics*, **27**, pp. 43–66; Michael Gerlach, 'The Japanese Corporate Network: A Blockmodel Approach,' *Administrative Science Quarterly*, **37** (1992), 105–139; and Erik Berglof and Enrico Perotti, 'The Japanese Financial Keiretsu as a Collective Enforcement Mechanism,' working paper 91–09, MIT Japan Program, 1991.

8. The data are summarized in Bruce Kogut, 'Capital Structure and Financial Institutions in the Federal Republic of Germany,' unpublished manuscript, 1982; primary data are drawn from Studienkommission, *Grundsatzfragen der Kreditwirtschaft*, Bericht der Studienkommission, Ministry of Finance, Bonn: Wilhelm Stollfuss Verlag, 1979; reliance on short-term debt is described in Charles Calomiris, 'Regulation, Industrial Structure, and Instability in U.S. Banking: An Historical Perspective,' mimeo, Wharton School, University of Pennsylvania, 1992.

9. Takeo Hoshi, Anil Kashyap, and David Schaftstein (1990) 'Bank Monitoring and Investment: Evidence from the Changing Structure of Japanese Corporate Banking Relationships,' in R. Glenn Hubbard (ed.) *Information, Investment, and Capital Markets*, Chicago, IL: University of Chicago.

10. J. Bradford Long (1991) 'Did J.P. Morgan's Men Add Value?' in Peter Temin (ed.) *Inside the Business Enterprise: Historical Perspectives on the Use of Information*, Chicago, IL: University of Chicago Press.

11. Michael Porter's *Competitive Strategy* (New York, NY: Free Press, 1980) represents the most well-known statement of this approach.

12. See Bruce Kogut and Udo Zander (1992) 'Knowledge of the Firm, Combinative Capabilities, and the Replication of Technology,' *Organization Science*, **3**, 383–97. Carliss Baldwin and Kim Clark. ['Capabilities and Capital Investment: New Perspectives on Capital Budgeting,' working paper 92–004, 1991, Harvard Business School] develop in detail the link between options and capabilities.

13. Prahalad, C.K. and Hamel, G. (1990) 'The Core Competence of the Corporation,' *Harvard Business Review* (May–June), pp. 79–91.

14. See the fascinating account by Paul Adler, 'The Learning Bureaucracy: New United Motor Manufacturing,' in B. Staw and L. Cummings (eds) *Research in Organizational Behavior*, Greenwich, CT: JAI Press.

15. See also, Bruce Kogut 'Joint Ventures and the Option to Acquire and to Expand,' *Management Science* (1991), pp. 19–33.

16. *Fortune*, 1992, p. 60; cited by Bernard Wolf and Steven Globerman, 'Strategic Alliances in the Automotive Industry: Motives and Implications,' mimeo, York University, 1992.

17. See also, Nalin Kulatilaka (1993) *The Value of Flexibility: The Case of a Dual-fuel Industrial Steam Boiler*, Financial Management Association, pp. 271–80.

18. See also, Bruce Kogut and Nalin Kulatilaka, 'Operating Flexibility, Global Manufacturing, and the Option Value of a Multinational Network,' *Management Science* (forthcoming).

19. See Glenn Carroll and Michael Hannan (1989) 'Density Delay in the Evolution of Organizational Populations: A Model and Five Empirical Tests,' *Administrative Science Quarterly*, **34** (3).

20. See Bronwyn Hall (1991) 'Corporate Restructuring and Investment Horizons,' Working Paper 3794, National Bureau of Economic Research.

19

Organizing for Worldwide Effectiveness: The Transnational Solution

Christopher A. Bartlett and Sumantra Ghoshal

The enormous success of Japanese companies that burst into the international competitive arena in the 1960s and 1970s has triggered a barrage of analysis and advice in the Western business press. Most of this analysis highlighted the convergence of consumer preferences worldwide, the impact of changing technologies and scale economies on international industry structures, and the emergence of increasingly sophisticated competitive strategies that have led to a rapid process of globalization in a large number of worldwide businesses.[1]

As Western companies have searched for the source of the newcomers' incredible ability to sell everything from automobiles to zippers, one conclusion has gained increasing credibility: companies that are unable to gain firm strategic control of their worldwide operations and manage them in a globally coordinated manner will not succeed in the emerging international economy. There are few senior managers in the West who are unaffected by the implications of this message.

The concerns of top managers in Japan, however, have been quite different and have focused on the forces of localization that have also been gathering strength in the recent past. Like their Western counterparts, they have been sensitized not only by their own experiences, but also by stories in the Japanese business press, which have been focused on the growing barriers to trade and, most recently, the impact of a strengthening yen in offsetting the efficiencies of global-scale Japanese plants. These managers are much more sensitive to the flip side of globalization – the growing demand of host governments for local investments, the building resistance of consumers to standardized homogenized global products, and the changing economics of emerging flexible manufacturing technologies that are making smaller-scale production and more tailored products feasible.

In the course of a study of some of the world's leading Japanese, European, and American multinationals, we found that these globalizing and localizing forces are working simultaneously to transform many industries.[2] But for historical reasons, few companies have built the organizational capabilities to respond equally to both of these forces.

Many of the European- and American-based companies had well-established networks of fairly independent and self-sufficient national subsidiaries – 'decentralized federations' we call them. Those with such organizations had little difficulty in responding to the increased demands from their host governments or adapting to shifts in consumer preferences worldwide, and their strategic posture was often literally multinational – multiple national positions, each highly sensitive to its local market. The problem with this strategy and the

Reprinted with permission from *California Management Review*, 1988, **31**(1), 1–21.

organizational structure that supported it was that it was difficult to coordinate and control these worldwide operations in order to respond to the global forces.

Most of the Japanese companies we studied had the opposite problem. Their operations tended to be concentrated in the home country – we term them 'centralized hubs' – and this gave them the ability to capture the opportunities presented by the global forces. Indeed, the strategic posture of these companies was literally global – the world was considered as an integrated whole. Such an approach made these companies less successful in building worldwide operating units that were sensitive and responsive to the countervailing forces of localization.[3]

THE CONSTRAINT OF A COMPANY'S HERITAGE

As the international operating environment became more complex over the past decade or so, the great temptation for companies was to try to imitate the organizational characteristics and strategic postures of their competitors. For example, in the United States, multinational managers are being advised to 'rein in far-flung autonomous subsidiaries, produce standardized global products, and pull decision-making power back to the home office,' with the reminder that 'this is a formula that, not coincidentally, many Japanese companies have used for years.'[4]

But the appropriate response to the developing international demands cannot be captured in a formula – and certainly not one that is imitative of companies in totally different situations. The problem is that while a company's tasks are shaped by its external environment, its ability to perform those tasks is constrained by what we term its 'administrative heritage' – the company's existing configuration of assets, its traditional distribution of responsibility, and its historical norms, values, and management style.[5] This internal organizational capability is something that cannot be changed overnight or by decree, and one of the important lessons for management is to shift its attention from a search for the ideal organization structure to a quest for ways in which to build and leverage the company's existing capabilities to make them more responsive to the ever-changing external demands.

That is not to deny that there are lessons to be learned from other companies – indeed our research indicates quite the opposite. However, the important lesson is that either blind imitation simply to eliminate obvious differences or wholesale adoption of another company's organizational approach or strategic posture is likely to end in failure. In the first part of this article, we distil some of the important transferable lessons that *can* be learned from companies that manage global coordination effectively and from those that have been most successful in developing and managing a responsive and flexible localized approach. Although the lessons are drawn from a broader study, we will emphasize the importance of a company's administrative heritage by comparing and contrasting the approaches of two leading consumer electronics companies and suggesting ways in which they can learn from each other.

But while such lessons are helpful, they do not provide the full solution. Today's operating environment in many worldwide businesses demands more than efficient central management and flexible local operations – it requires companies to link their diverse organizational perspectives and resources in a way that would allow them to leverage their capabilities for achieving global coordination and national flexibility simultaneously. In response to this need, a few companies have evolved beyond the simpler multinational or global approach to international business and developed what we term a *transnational* capability – an ability to manage across boundaries.[6] In the final part of the article, we will describe some of the characteristics of such an organization, and will suggest some steps that can be taken to build these capabilities.

MAKING CENTRAL MANAGEMENT FLEXIBLE: LESSONS FROM MATSUSHITA

For companies that expanded internationally by establishing fairly independent and self-sufficient subsidiary companies around the world, the task of imposing some kind of global direction or achieving some measure of coordination of activity is often a Herculean challenge. The problem that has confronted successive generations of top management at Philips is typical. The Dutch-based electronics giant has built a justifiable reputation as one of the world's most innovative companies, yet has continually been frustrated in its attempt to deliver its brilliant inventions to the world's markets. The recent failure of its VCR system is a classic example.

Despite the fact that it was generally acknowledged to be technologically superior to the competitive VHS and Beta formats, the Philips V2000 system failed because the company was unable to commercialize it. Within the company there is no shortage of theories to explain the failure: some suggest that those who developed the product and its competitive strategy were too distant from the market; others feel the barriers between research, development, manufacturing, and marketing led to delays and cost over-runs; and another group points to the fact that worldwide subsidiaries were uninvolved in the project and therefore uncommitted to its success. All these explanations reflect organizational difficulties and have some element of truth.

On the other hand, Matsushita Electric Company, Philips' archrival in consumer electronics, has built the global leadership position of its well-known Panasonic and National brands on its ability to control its global strategy from the center in Japan – yet it has been able to implement it in a flexible and responsive manner throughout its worldwide operations. As we tried to identify the organizational mechanisms that were key to Matsushita's ability to provide strong central direction and control without becoming inflexible or isolated, three factors stood out as the most important explanations of its outstanding success:

- gaining the input of subsidiaries into its management processes;
- ensuring that development efforts were linked to market needs; and
- managing responsibility transfers from development to manufacturing to marketing.

By examining how these core mechanisms work in Matsushita, managers in other companies may see ways in which they can gain more global coordination without compromising local market sensitivity.

Gaining subsidiary input: multiple linkages

The two most important problems facing a centrally managed multinational company are that those developing the new product or strategy may not understand market needs or that those required to implement the new direction are not committed to it. Matsushita managers are very conscious of these problems and spend much time building multiple linkages between headquarters and overseas subsidiaries to minimize their impacts. These linkages are designed not only to give headquarters managers a better understanding of country level needs and opportunities, but also to give subsidiary managers greater access to and involvement in headquarters decision-making processes.

Matsushita recognizes the importance of market sensing as a stimulus to innovation and does not want its centrally driven management process to reduce its environmental sensitivity. Rather than trying to limit the number of linkages between headquarters and subsidiaries or to focus them through a single point (as many companies do for the sake of efficiency), Matsushita tries to preserve the different perspectives, priorities, and even prejudices of its diverse groups worldwide and tries to ensure that they have linkages to those in the headquarters who can represent and defend their views.

The organizational systems and processes that connect different parts of the Matsushita organization in Japan with the video department of MESA, the U.S. subsidiary of the company, illustrate these multifaceted interlinkages. The vice president in charge of this department has his career roots in Matsushita Electric Trading Company (METC), the organization with overall responsibility for Matsushita's overseas business. Although formally posted to the United States, he continues to be a member of the senior management committee of METC and spends about a third of his time in Japan. This allows him to be a full member of METC's top management team that approves the overall strategy for the U.S. market. In his role as the VP of MESA, he ensures that the local operation effectively implements the agreed video strategy.

At the next level, the general manager of MESA's video department is a company veteran who had worked for 14 years in the video product division of Matsushita Electric, the central production and domestic marketing company in Japan. He maintains strong connections with the parent company's product division and is its link to the local American market. Two levels below him, the assistant product manager in the video department (one of the more junior-level expatriates in the American organization) links the local organization to the central VCR factory in Japan. Having spent five years in the factory, he acts as the local representative of the factory and handles all day-to-day communication with factory personnel.

None of these linkages is accidental. They are deliberately created and maintained and they reflect the company's open acknowledgement that the parent company is not one homogeneous entity, but a collectivity of different constituencies and interests, each of which is legitimate and necessary. Together, these multiple linkages enhance the subsidiary's ability to influence key headquarters decisions relating to its market, particularly decisions about product specifications and design. The multiple links not only allow local management to reflect its local market needs, they also give headquarters managers the ability to coordinate and control implementation of their strategies and plans.

Linking direction to needs: market mechanisms

Matsushita's efforts to ensure that its products and strategies are linked to market needs does not stop at the input stage. The company has created an integrative process that ensures that the top managers and central staff groups are not sheltered from the pressures, constraints, and demands felt by managers on the front line of the operations. One of the key elements in achieving this difficult organizational task is the company's willingness to employ 'market mechanisms' for directing and regulating the activities located at the center. Because the system is unique, we will describe some of its major characteristics.

Research projects undertaken by the Central Research Laboratories (CRL) of Matsushita fall into two broad groups. The first group consists of 'company total projects' which involve developing technologies important for Matsushita's long-term strategic position and that may be applicable across many different product divisions. Such projects are decided jointly by the research laboratories, the product divisions, and top management of the company and are funded directly by the corporate board. The second group of CRL research projects consists of relatively smaller projects which are relevant to the activities of particular product divisions. The budget for such research activities, approximately half of the company's total research budget, is allocated not to the research laboratories but to the product divisions. This creates an interesting situation in which technology-driven and market-led ideas can compete for attention.

Each year, the product divisions suggest research projects that they would like to sponsor and which would incorporate their knowledge of worldwide market needs developed through their routine multiple linkages to subsidiaries. At the same time, the various research laboratories hold annual internal exhibitions and meetings and also write proposals to highlight research projects that they would like to undertake. The engineering and development groups of the product divisions mediate the subsequent contracting and negotiation process through which the expertise and interests of the laboratories and the needs of the product divisions are finally matched. Specific projects are sponsored by the divisions and are allocated to the laboratories or research groups of their choice, along with requisite funds and other resources.

The system creates intense competition for projects (and the budgets that go with them) among the research groups, and it is this mechanism that forces researchers to keep a close market orientation. At the same time, the product divisions are conscious that it is their money that is being spent on product development and they become less inclined to make unreasonable or uneconomical demands on R&D.[7]

The market mechanism also works to determine annual product styling and features. Each year the company holds what it calls merchandising meetings, which are, in effect, large internal trade shows. Senior marketing managers from Matsushita's sales companies worldwide visit their supplying divisions and see on display the proposed product lines for the new model year. Relying on their understanding of their individual markets, these managers pick and choose among proposed models, order specific modifications for their local markets, or simply refuse to take products they feel are unsuitable. Individual products or even entire lines might have to be redesigned as a result of input from the hundreds of managers at the merchandising meeting.

Managing responsibility transfer: personnel flows

Within a national subsidiary, the task of transferring responsibility from research to manufacturing and finally marketing is facilitated by the smaller size and closer proximity of the units responsible for each stage of activity. This is not so where large central units usually take the lead role, and Matsushita has built some creative means for managing these transitions. The systems rely heavily on the transfer of people, as is illustrated by the company's management of new product development.

First, careers of research engineers are structured so as to ensure that most of them spend about five to eight years in the central research laboratories engaged in pure research, then they spend another five years in the product divisions in applied product and process development, and finally they spend the rest of their working lives in a direct operational function, usually production, wherein they take up line management positions. More important, each engineer usually makes the transition from one department to the next along with the transfer of the major project on which he has been working.

The research project that began Matsushita's development of its enormously successful VCR product was launched in the late 1950s under the leadership of Dr Hiroshi Sugaya, a young physicist in the company's Central Research Laboratory. As the product evolved into its development stage, the core members of Dr Sugaya's team were kept together as they transferred from CRL to the product development and applications laboratory located in the product division. After a long and difficult development process, the product was finally ready for commercial production in 1977, and many of the team moved with the project out into the Okanyama plant.[8]

In other companies we surveyed, it was not uncommon for research engineers to move to development, but not with their projects, thereby depriving the companies of one of the most important and immediate benefits of such moves. We also saw no other examples of engineers routinely taking the next step of actually moving to the production function. This last step, however, is perhaps the most critical in integrating research and production both in terms of building a network that connects managers across these two functions, and also for transferring a set of common values that facilitates implementation of central innovations.

Another mechanism that integrates production and research in Matsushita works in the opposite direction. Wherever possible, the company tries to identify the manager who will head the production task for a new product under development and makes him a full-time member of the research team from the initial stage of the development process. This system not only injects direct production expertise into the development team, but also facilitates transfer of the innovation once the design is completed. Matsushita also uses this mechanism as a way of transferring product expertise from headquarters to its worldwide sales subsidiaries. Although this is a common practice among many multinationals, in Matsushita it has additional significance because of the importance of internationalizing management as well as its products.

As with the multiple linkages and the internal market mechanisms, this organizational practice was a simple, yet powerful tool that seemed to be central to Matsushita's ability to make its centrally driven management processes flexible, sensitive, and responsive to the worldwide opportunities and needs. More important, these three organizational mechanisms are simple enough to be adopted, probably in some modified form, by other companies. They meet the needs of those trying to build an organization process that allows management at the center more influence and control over worldwide operations, without compromising the motivation or operating effectiveness of the national units.

MAKING LOCAL MANAGEMENT EFFECTIVE: LESSONS FROM PHILIPS

If Matsushita is the champion of efficient centrally coordinated management, its Netherlands-based competitor, Philips, is the master of building effective national operations worldwide. And as surely as Philips' managers envy their Japanese rival's ability to develop products and strategies in Osaka that appear to be implemented effortlessly around the globe, their counterparts in Matsushita are extremely jealous of Philips' national organizations that are not only sensitive and responsive to their local environments, but are also highly innovative and entrepreneurial.

For example, the company's first color TV set was built and sold not in Europe, where the parent company is located, but in Canada, where the market had closely followed the U.S. lead in introducing color transmission; Philips' first stereo color TV set was developed by the Australian subsidiary; teletext TV sets were created by its British subsidiary; 'smart cards' by its French subsidiary; a programmed word processing typewriter by North American Philips – the list of local innovations and entrepreneurial initiatives in the company is endless.

While Matsushita has had no difficulty in establishing effective sales organizations and assembly operations around the .world, top management has often been frustrated that its overseas subsidiaries do not exhibit more initiative and entrepreneurial spark. Despite pleas to its overseas management to become more self-sufficient and less dependent on headquarters for direction, the company has found that the decentralization of assets that accompanies its 'localization' program has not always triggered the kind of independence and initiative that had been hoped for.

Out of the many factors that drive Philips' international organization, we were able to identify three that not only appear central to the development and maintenance of its effective local management system, but also may be adaptable to other organizations that are trying to promote national innovativeness and responsiveness within a globally integrated organization:

- Philips' use of a cadre of entrepreneurial expatriates;
- an organization that forces tight functional integration within a subsidiary; and
- a dispersion of responsibilities along with the decentralized assets.

A cadre of entrepreneurial expatriates

Expatriate positions, particularly in the larger subsidiaries, have been very attractive for Philips' managers for several reasons. With only 7% or 8% of its total sales coming from Holland, many different national subsidiaries of the company have contributed much larger shares of total revenues than the parent company. As a result, foreign operations have enjoyed relatively high organizational status compared to most companies of similar size with headquarters in the United States, Japan, or even the larger countries in Europe. Further, because of the importance of its foreign operations, Philips' formal management development system has always required considerable international experience as a prerequisite for top corporate positions. Finally, Eindhoven, the small rural town in which corporate headquarters is located, is far from the sophisticated and cosmopolitan world centers that host many of its foreign subsidiaries. After living in London, New York, Sydney, or Paris, many managers find it hard to return to Eindhoven.

Collectively, all these factors have led to the best and the brightest of Philips' managers spending much of their careers in different national operations. This cadre of entrepreneurial expatriate managers has been an important agent in developing capabilities of local units, yet keeping them linked to the parent company's overall objectives. Further, unlike Matsushita where an expatriate manager typically spends a tour of duty of three to six years in a particular national subsidiary and then returns to the headquarters, expatriate managers in

Philips spend a large part of their careers abroad continuously working for two to three years each in a number of different subsidiaries.

This difference in the career systems results in very different attitudes. In Philips, the expatriate managers follow each other into assignments and build close relations among themselves. They tend to identify strongly with the national organization's point of view, and this shared identity makes them part of a distinct subculture within the company. In companies like Matsushita, on the other hand, there is very little interaction among the expatriate managers in the different subsidiaries, and most tend to see themselves as part of the parent company temporarily on assignment in a foreign country.

One result of these differences is that expatriate managers in Matsushita are far more likely to take a custodial approach which resists any local changes to standard products and policies. In contrast, expatriate managers in Philips, despite being just as socialized into the overall corporate culture of the company, are much more willing to be advocates of local views and to defend against the imposition of inappropriate corporate ideas on national organizations. This willingness to 'rock the boat' and openness to experimentation and change is the fuel that ignites local initiative and entrepreneurship.[9]

Further, by creating this kind of environment in the national organization, Philips has had little difficulty in attracting very capable local management. In contrast to the experience in many Japanese companies where local managers have felt excluded from a decision-making process that centers around headquarters management and the local expatriates only, local managers in Philips feel their ideas are listened to and defended in headquarters.[10] This too, creates a supportive environment for local innovation and creativity.

Integration of technical and marketing functions within each subsidiary

Historically, the top management in all Philips' national subsidiaries consisted not of an individual CEO but a committee made up of the heads of the technical, commercial, and finance functions. This system of three-headed management had a long history in Philips, stemming from the functional backgrounds of the founding Philips brothers, one an engineer and the other a salesman. Although this management philosophy has recently been modified to a system which emphasizes individual authority and accountability, the long tradition of shared responsibilities and joint decision making has left a legacy of many different mechanisms for functional integration at multiple levels. These integrative mechanisms within each subsidiary in Philips enhance the efficiency and effectiveness of local decision making and action in the same way that various means of cross-functional integration within Matsushita's corporate headquarters facilitates its central management processes.

In most subsidiaries, integration mechanisms exist at three organizational levels. First, for each product, there is an article team that consists of relatively junior managers belonging to the commercial and technical functions. This team evolves product policies and prepares annual sales plans and budgets. At times, subarticle teams may be formed to supervise day-to-day working and to carry out special projects, such as preparing capital investment plans, should major new investments be felt necessary for effectively manufacturing and marketing a new product.

A second tier of cross-functional coordination takes place at the product group level, through the group management team, which again consists of both technical and commercial representatives. This team meets monthly to review results, suggest corrective actions, and resolve any interfunctional differences. Keeping control and conflict resolution at this low level facilitates sensitive and rapid responses to initiatives and ideas generated at the local level.

The highest level coordination forum within the subsidiary is the senior management committee (SMC) consisting of the top commercial, technical, and financial managers in the subsidiary. Acting essentially as a local board, the SMC provides an overall unity of effort among the different functional groups within the local unit, and assures that the national unit retains primary responsibility for its own strategies and priorities. Again, the effect is to provide local management with a forum in which actions can be decided and issues resolved without escalation for approval or arbitration.

Decentralized authority and dispersed responsibility

While Matsushita's localization program was triggered by political pressures to increase local value added in various host countries, the company had also hoped that the decentralization of assets would help its overseas units achieve a greater measure of local responsiveness, self-sufficiency, and initiative. To management's frustration, such changes were slow in coming.

Philips, on the other hand, had created such national organizations seemingly without effort. The difference lay in the degree to which responsibility and authority were dispersed along with the assets. Expanding internationally in the earliest decades of the century, Philips managers were confronted by transport and communications barriers that forced them to delegate substantial local autonomy to its decentralized operating units. The need for local units to develop a sense of self-sufficiency was reinforced by the protectionist pressures of the 1930s that made cross-shipments of products or components practically impossible. During World War II, even R&D capability was dispersed to prevent it from falling into enemy hands, and the departure of many corporate managers from Holland reduced the parent company's control over its national operations abroad.

In the postwar boom, while corporate managers focused on rebuilding the war-ravaged home operations, managers in foreign units were able to capitalize on their well-developed autonomy. Most applied their local resources and capabilities to build highly successful national businesses, sensitive and responsive to the local needs and opportunities. In doing so, they achieved a degree of local entrepreneurship and self-sufficiency rare among companies of Philips' size and complexity.

Although it would be impossible for another company to replicate the historical events that resulted in this valuable organizational capability, the main characteristics of their development are clear. First, it must be feasible for offshore units to develop local capabilities and initiative, and this requires the decentralization of appropriate managerial and technological resources along with the reconfiguration of physical assets.

While this is necessary, it is not sufficient, however, as Matsushita and many other companies have begun to recognize. Local initiatives and entrepreneurial action must not only be feasible, they must also be desirable for local managers. This requires the legitimate delegation of responsibilities and authority that not only gives them control over the decentralized resources, but rewards them for using them to develop creative and innovative solutions to their problems.[11] Only when the decentralization of assets is accompanied by a dispersion of responsibilities can local management develop into a legitimate corporate contributor rather than simple implementers of central direction.

BUILDING TRANSNATIONAL CAPABILITIES: LESSONS FROM L.M. ERICSSON

In multinational corporations, the location of an opportunity (or threat) is often different from where the company's appropriate response resources are situated. This is so because environmental opportunities and threats are footloose, shifting from location to location, while organizational resources, contrary to the assumptions of many economists, are not easily transferable even within the same company. Further, the location of a company's strategic resources – plants and research centers are good examples – is related not only to actual organizational needs and intentions, but also to the idiosyncrasies of the firm's administrative history. The result is a situation of environment-resource mismatches: the organization has excessive resources in environments that are relatively noncritical, and very limited or even no resources in critical markets that offer the greatest opportunities and challenges.

Such environment-resource mismatches are pervasive in MNCs. For many historical reasons, Ericsson has significant technological and managerial capabilities in Australia and Italy, even though these markets are relatively unimportant in the global telecommunications business. At the same time, the company has almost no presence in the United States, which not only represents almost 40% of world telecommunications demand but is also the source of much of the new technology. Procter & Gamble is strong in the United States and Europe, but not in Japan where important consumer product innovations have occurred recently and where a major global competitor is emerging. Matsushita has appropriate technological and managerial resources in Japan and the U.S., but not in Europe, a huge market and home of archrival Philips.

Rectifying these imbalances in the configuration of their organization resources is taking these companies a long time and, since the relative importance of different environments will continue to change, the problem will never be fully overcome. The need, therefore, is not simply to make adjustments to the geographic configuration or resources, but also to create organizational systems that allow the spare capacity and slack resources in strong operating units to be redirected to environments in which they are weak.

Simply creating effective central and local management does not solve this mismatch problem, and to succeed in today's demanding international environment, companies must develop their organizational capabilities beyond the stages described in the first part of this article. The limitation of companies with even the most well-developed local and central capabilities is that the location of resources also tends to determine the locus of control over those resources. whether organizationally mandated or not, local management develops strong influence on how resources available locally are to be used. Further, organizational commitments are usually hierarchical, with local needs taking precedence over global needs. Consequently, at the core of resolving the problem of environment-resource mismatches is the major organizational challenge of loosening the bonds between ownership and control of resources within the company.

Among the companies we studied, there were several that were in the process of developing such organizational capabilities. They had surpassed the classic capabilities of the *multinational* company that operates as decentralized federation of units able to sense and respond to diverse international needs and opportunities; and they had evolved beyond the abilities of the *global* company with its facility for managing operations on a tightly controlled worldwide basis through its centralized hub structure. They had developed what we termed *transnational* capabilities – the ability to manage across national boundaries, retaining local flexibility while achieving global integration. More than anything else this involved the ability to link local operations to each other and to the center in a flexible way, and in so doing, to leverage those local and central capabilities.

Ericsson, the Swedish telecommunications company, was among those that had become most effective in managing the required linkages and processes, and we were able to identify three organizational characteristics that seemed most helpful in facilitating its developing transnational management capabilities:

- an interdependence of resources and responsibilities among organizational units;
- a set of strong cross-unit integrating devices; and
- a strong corporate identification and a well-developed worldwide management perspective.

Interdependence of resources and responsibilities

Perhaps the most important requirement of the transnational organization is a need for the organizational configuration to be based on a principle of reciprocal dependence among units. Such an interdependence of resources and responsibilities breaks down the hierarchy between local and global interests by making the sharing of resources, ideas and opportunities a self-enforcing norm. To illustrate how such a basic characteristic of organizational configuration can influence a company's management of capabilities, let us contrast the way in which ITT, NEC, and Ericsson developed the electronic digital switch that would be the core product for each company's telecommunications business in the 1980s and beyond.

From its beginnings in 1920 as a Puerto Rican telephone company, ITT built its worldwide operation on an objective described in the 1924 annual report as being 'to develop truly national systems operated by the nationals of each company.' For half a century ITT's national 'systems houses' as they were called within the company, committed themselves to integrating into their local environments and becoming attuned to national interests and market needs. All but the smallest systems houses were established as fully integrated, self-sufficient units with responsibility for developing, manufacturing, marketing, installing, and servicing their own products.

With the emergence of the new digital electronic technology in the 1970s, however, this highly successful strategic posture was threatened by the huge cost of developing a digital switch. Since no single systems house would be able to muster the required technological and financial resources on its own or recoup the investment from its market, the obvious solution was for ITT to make the System 12 digital switch project a corporate responsibility. However, given their decade of operating independence, the powerful country unit managers were unwilling to yield the task of developing the new switch to the corporate R&D group – and indeed, little expertise had been gathered at the center to undertake such a task.

By exercising their considerable influence, the European systems houses were able to capture the strategic initiative on System 12, but then began disagreeing about who should take what role in this vital project. Many of the large systems houses simply refused to rely on others for the development of critical parts of the system; others rejected standards that did not fit with their view of local needs. As a result, duplication of effort and divergence of specifications began to emerge, and the cost of developing the switch ballooned to over $1 billion.

The biggest problems appeared when the company decided to enter the battle for a share of the deregulated U.S. market. Asserting its independence, the U.S. business launched a major new R&D effort, despite appeals from the chief technological officer that they risked developing what he skeptically termed 'System 13.' After further years of effort and additional hundreds of millions of dollars in costs, ITT acknowledged in 1986 it was withdrawing from the U.S. central switching market. The largest and most successful international telecommunications company in the world was blocked from its home country by the inability to transfer and apply its leading edge technology in a timely fashion. It was a failure that eventually led to ITT's sale of its European operations and its gradual withdrawal from direct involvement in telecommunications worldwide.

If effective global innovation was blocked by the extreme independence of the organizational units in ITT, it was impeded in NEC by the strong dependence of national subsidiaries on the parent company. The first person in NEC to detect the trend toward digital switching was the Japanese manager in charge of the company's small U.S. operation. However, his role was one of selling corporate products and developing a beachhead for the company in the U.S. market. Because of this role, he had a hard time convincing technical managers in Japan of a supposed trend to digitalization that they saw nowhere else in the world.

When the U.S. managers finally were able to elicit sufficient support, the new NEAC 61 digital switch was developed almost entirely by headquarters personnel. Even in deciding which features to design into the new product, the central engineering group tended to discount the requests of the North American sales company and rely on data gathered in their own staff's field trips to U.S. customers. Although the NEAC 61 was regarded as having good hardware, customers felt its software was unadapted to U.S. needs. Sales did not meet expectations.

Both ITT and NEC recognized the limitations of their independent and dependent organizations systems and worked hard to adapt them. But the process of building organizational interdependence is a slow and difficult one that must be constantly monitored and adjusted. In our sample of companies, Ericsson seemed to be the most consistent and experienced practitioner of creating and managing a delicate balance of interunit interdependency. The way in which it did so suggests the value of a constant readjustment of responsibilities and relationships as a way of adapting to changing strategic needs while maintaining a dynamic system of mutual dependence.

Like ITT, Ericsson had built, during the 1920s and 1930s, a substantial worldwide network of operations sensitive and responsive to local national environments; but like NEC, it had a strong home market base and a parent company with technological, manufacturing and marketing capability to support those companies. Keeping the balance between and among those units has required constant adjustment of organizational responsibilities and relationships.

In the late 1930s, management became concerned that the growing independence of its offshore companies was causing divergence in technology, duplication of effort, and inefficiency in the sourcing patterns. To remedy the problem they pulled sales and distribution control to headquarters and began consolidating responsibilities under product divisions. While worldwide control improved, the divisions eventually began to show signs of isolation and short-term focus. Thus, in the early 1950s the corporate staff functions were given more of a leadership role. It was in this period that the central R&D group developed a crossbar switch that became an industry leader. As the product design and manufacturing technology for this product became well-understood and fully documented, however, Ericsson management was able to respond to the increasing demands of host governments to transfer more manufacturing capacity and technological know-how abroad. Once again, the role of the offshore subsidiaries increased.

This half a century of constant ebb and flow in the roles and responsibilities of various geographic, product, and functional groups allowed Ericsson to build an organization in which all these diverse perspectives were seen as legitimate and the multiple capabilities were kept viable. This multidimensional organization gave the company the ability to quickly sense and respond to the coming of electronic switching in the 1970s. Once it had prevented the emergence of strong dependent or independent relationships, product development efforts and manufacturing responsibilities could be pulled back to Sweden, without great difficulty. Where national capabilities, expertise, or experience could be useful in the corporate effort, the appropriate local personnel were seconded to headquarters. Having established overall strategic and operational control of the digital switching strategy, however, corporate management at Ericsson was then willing to delegate substantial design, development, and manufacturing responsibilities to its internal subsidiaries, resulting in a reinforcement of the interdependence of worldwide operations.

Sourcing of products and components from specialized plants have long provided a base of interdependence, but recently that has been extended to product development and marketing. For example, Italy is the company's center for global development of transmission system development, Finland has the leading role for mobile telephones, and Australia develops the company's rural switch. Further, headquarters has given some of these units responsibility for handling certain export markets (e.g., Italy's responsibility for developing markets in Africa). Increasingly, the company is moving even advanced core system software development offshore to subsidiary companies with access to more software engineers than it has in Stockholm.[12]

By changing responsibilities, shifting assets, and modifying relationships in response to evolving environmental demands and strategic priorities, Ericsson has maintained a dynamic interdependence among its operating units that has allowed it to develop entrepreneurial and innovative subsidiary companies that work within a corporate framework defined by knowledgeable and creative headquarters product and functional groups. This kind of interdependence is the basis of a transnational company – one that can think globally and act locally.

Interunit integrating devices

Although the interdependence of resources and responsibilities provides a structural framework for the extensive use of interunit cooperation, there is a need for effective organizational integrating mechanisms to link operations in a way that taps the full potential of the interdependent configuration.

Compared to some companies in our study where relationships among national companies were competitive and where headquarter-subsidiary interactions were often of an adversarial nature, the organizational climate in Ericsson appeared more cooperative and collaborative. The establishment and maintenance of such attitudes was important since it allowed the company's diverse units to work together in a way that maximized the potential of their interdependent operations. We identified three important pillars to Ericsson's success in interunit integration:

- a clearly defined and tightly controlled set of operating systems;
- a people-linking process employing such devices as temporary assignments and joint teams; and
- interunit decision forums, particularly subsidiary boards, where views could be exchanged and differences resolved.

Ericsson management feels strongly that its most effective integrating device is strong central control over key elements of its strategic operation. Unlike ITT, Ericsson has not had strong or sophisticated administrative systems (it introduced strategic plans only in 1983), but its operating systems have long been structured to provide strong worldwide coordination. Knowing that local modifications would be necessary, the company designed its digital switch as a modular system with very clear specifications. National units could custom-tailor elements of the design to meet local needs without compromising the integrity of the total system design. Similarly, Ericsson's global computer-aided design and manufacturing system allowed the parent company to delegate responsibility for component production and even design without fear of losing the ability to control and coordinate the entire manufacturing system.

Rather than causing a centralization of decision making, management argues that these strong yet flexible operating systems allow them to delegate much more freely, knowing that local decisions will not be inconsistent or detrimental to the overall interests. Rather than managing the decisions centrally, they point out they are managing the parameters of decisions that can be made by local units, thereby retaining the flexibility and entrepreneurship of those units.

But in addition to strong systems, interunit cooperation requires good interpersonal relations, and Ericsson has developed these with a long-standing policy of transferring large numbers of people back and forth between headquarters and subsidiaries. It differs from the more common transfer patterns in both direction and intensity, as a comparison with NEC's transfer process will demonstrate. Where NEC may transfer a new technology through a few key managers, Ericsson will send a team of 50 or 100 engineers and managers from one unit to another for a year or two; while NEC's flow is primarily from headquarters to subsidiary, Ericsson's is a balanced two-way flow with people coming to the parent not only to learn, but also to bring their expertise; and while NEC's transfers are predominantly Japanese, Ericsson's multidirectional process involves all nationalities.[13]

Australian technicians seconded to Stockholm in the mid-1970s to bring their experience with digital switching into the corporate development effort established enduring relationships that helped in the subsequent joint development of a rural switch in Australia a decade later. Confidences built when a 40-man Italian team spent 18 months in Sweden in the early 1970s to learn about electronic switching, provided the basis for the subsequent decentralization of AXE software development and the delegation of responsibility for developing the corporate transmission systems to the Italian company.

But any organization in which there are shared tasks and joint responsibilities will require additional decision-making and conflict-resolving forums. In Ericsson, often divergent objectives and interests of the parent company and the local subsidiary are exchanged in the national company's board meetings. Unlike many companies whose local boards are pro forma bodies whose activities are designed solely to satisfy national legal requirements, Ericsson uses its local boards as legitimate forums for communicating objectives, resolving differences and making decisions. At least one, and often several senior corporate managers are members of each board, and subsidiary board meetings become an important means for coordinating activities and channelling local ideas and innovations across national lines.

National competence, worldwide perspective

If there is one clear lesson from ITT's experience, it is that a company cannot manage globally if its managers identify primarily with local parochial interests and objectives. But as NEC has learned, when management has no ability to defend national perspectives and respond to local opportunities, penetration of world markets is equally difficult. One of the important organizational characteristics Ericsson has been able to develop over the years has been a management attitude that is simultaneously locally sensitive and globally conscious.

At the Stockholm headquarters, managers emphasize the importance of developing strong country operations, not only to capture sales that require responsiveness to national needs, but also to tap into the resources that are available through worldwide operation. Coming from a small home country where it already hires over a third of the graduating electrical and electronics engineers, Ericsson is very conscious of the need to develop skills and capture ideas wherever they operate in the world. But, at the same time, local managers see themselves as part of the worldwide Ericsson group rather than as independent autonomous units. Constant transfers and working on joint teams over the years has helped broaden many managers' perspectives from local to global, but giving local units systemwide mandates for products has confirmed their identity with the company's global operations. It is this ability for headquarters and subsidiary managers to view the issues from each other's perspective that distinguishes the company that can think globally yet act locally.

CONCLUSION: ORGANIZATIONAL CAPABILITY IS KEY

There are few companies that have not recognized the nature of the main strategic tasks facing them in today's complex international business environment. Philips' managers have understood for years that they need to build global scale, rationalize their diverse product lines, and establish a more integrated worldwide strategy. And while their counterparts at Matsushita have recently made localization a company watchword, this is just the culmination of years of effort to build more self-sufficient and responsive national subsidiaries which the company recognizes it will need to remain globally competitive. If changes have been slow in coming to both companies, it is not for the lack of strategic clarity about the need for change but for want of the organizational ability to implement the desired change.

In the course of our study, we found that managers engaged in a great deal of cross-company comparison of organizational capabilities. And the managerial grass inevitably looked greener on the other side of the corporate fence. Philips' managers envied their Japanese competitors' ability to develop global products, manufacture them centrally, and have them launched into markets worldwide on a time cycle that would be virtually impossible in their own organization. On the other hand, as Matsushita's managers face growing pressure from host governments worldwide, and as they feel the vulnerabilities of their central sourcing plants in an era of the strong yen, they view Philips' worldwide network of self-sufficient, well-connected, and innovative national organizations as an asset they would dearly love to have. But the apparently small step from admiration to emulation of another company's strategic capabilities usually turns out to be a long and dangerous voyage.

What we suggest is that managers ignore battle cries calling for 'standardization, rationalization, and centralization' or any other such simplistic quick-fix formulas. What is needed is a more gradual approach that, rather than undermining a company's administrative heritage, both protects and builds on it. Having built flexible central and local management capabilities, the next challenge is to link them in an organization that allows the company to do what it must to survive in today's international environment – think globally and act locally. For most worldwide companies it is the development of this transnational organizational capability that is key to long-term success.

NOTES

1. See for example, Theodore Levitt, 'The Globalization of Markets,' *Harvard Business Review* (May/June 1983), pp. 92–102; Michael Porter, 'Changing Patterns of International Competition,' *California Management Review*, 28/2 (Winter 1986): 9–40; and Gary Hamel and C.K. Prahalad, 'Do You Really Have a Global Strategy,' *Harvard Business Review* (July/August 1985), pp. 139–148.

2. The research on which this article is based consisted of a three-year-long in-depth study of nine leading American, Japanese, and European multinational companies in three diverse industries. We interviewed over 235 managers in the headquarters and a number of different national subsidiaries of these companies to uncover how these companies with their diverse national backgrounds and international histories were adapting their organizational structures and management processes to cope with the new strategic demands of their operating environments. The companies studied were Philips, Matsushita, and General Electric in the consumer electronics industry; Ericsson, NEC, and ITT in the telecommunications switching industry; and Unilever, Kao, and Procter & Gamble in the branded packaged products business. The complete findings of this study will be reported in our forthcoming book *Managing Across Borders: The Transnational Solution* to be published by the Harvard Business School Press.

3. For a more detailed explication of the decentralized federation and centralized hub forms of multinational organizations, see Christopher A. Bartlett, 'Building and Managing the Transnational: The New Organizational Challenge,' in Michael E. Porter, ed., *Competition in Global Industries* (Boston, MA: Harvard Business School Press, 1986).

4. 'Rebuilding Corporate Empires – A New Global Formula,' *Newsweek*, April 14, 1986, p. 40.

5. The concept of administrative heritage is explained more fully in Christopher Bartlett (op. cit.) and also in Christopher Bartlett and Sumantra Ghoshal, 'Managing Across Borders: New Strategic Requirements,' *Sloan Management Review* (Summer 1987) pp. 7–17.

6. The organization we describe as the transnational has a long but discontinuous history in the international management literature. The concept of such an organizational form was manifest in Howard Perlmutter's celebrated paper, 'The Torturous Evolution of the Multinational Corporation,' *Columbia Journal of World Business* (January/February 1969), pp. 9–18. Similarly, C.K. Prahalad and Yves Doz's idea of a multifocal organization is described in *The Multinational Mission: Balancing Local Demands and Global Vision* (New York, NY: The Free Press, 1987); Gunnar Hedlund's definition of the heterarchy in 'The Hypermodern MNC – A Heterarchy?' *Human Resource Management* (Spring 1986), pp. 9–35; and Roderick White and Thomas Poynter's description of the horizontal organization in 'Organizing for Worldwide Advantage,' presented at the seminar on Management of the MNC at the European Institute for Advanced Studies in Management, Brussels, on June 9–10, 1987, are conceptually similar to what we describe as the transnational organization, though the models differ significantly in their details.

7. Westney and Sakakibara have observed a similar system of internal quasi-markets governing the interface between R&D and operating units in a number of Japanese computer companies. See Eleanor Westney and K. Sakakibara 'The Role of Japan-Based R&D in Global Technology Strategy,' *Technology in Society*, No. 7, (1985).

8. See Richard Rosenbloom and Michael Cusumano, 'Technological Pioneering and Competitive Advantage: Birth of the VCR Industry,' *California Management Review*, 29/4 (Summer 1987): 51–76, for a full description of this interesting development process.

9. See John Van Mannen and Edgar H. Schein, 'Toward a Theory of Organizational Socialization,' in Barry Staw, ed., *Research in Organizational Behavior* (Greenwich, CT: JAI Press, 1979) for a rich and theory-grounded discussion on how such differences in socialization processes and career systems can influence managers' attitudes towards change and innovation.

10. See Christopher Bartlett and Hideki Yoshihara 'New Challenges for Japanese Multinationals: Is Organizational Adaptation Their Achilles' Heel?' *Human Resource Management*, 27/1 (Spring 1988): 1–25, for a

fuller discussion of some of the personnel management implications of managing local nationals in a classic centralized hub Japanese organization.

11. The need for both feasibility and desirability for facilitating innovativeness of organizations has been suggested by Lawrence Mohr, 'Determinants of Innovation in Organizations,' *American Political Science Review*, 63 (1969).

12. For a detailed discussion of how managers make such choices and how new responsibilities and relationships are developed, see Christopher Bartlett and Sumantra Ghoshal, 'Tap Your Subsidiaries for Global Reach,' *Harvard Business Review* (November/December 1986), pp. 87–94.

13. The effectiveness of personnel transfers as an integrative mechanism in multinational companies has been highlighted by many authors, most notably by E. Edstrom and J.R. Galbraith, 'Transfer of Managers as a Coordination and Control Strategy in Multinational Organizations,' *Administrative Science Quarterly* (June 1977).

20

New Structures in MNCs Based in Small Countries: a Network Approach

Pervez Ghauri

INTRODUCTION

Much of the literature on multinationals deals with structural development of MNCs from domestic to global structure. Stopford and Wells (1972) introduced a 'stage model' for organizational structure for international firms. Their study of 187 US-based international companies states that international companies typically adapt different structures at different levels of their internationalization (Figure 1). They use two variables, 'foreign product diversity' and 'foreign sales as percentage of total sales'.

The model states that at an early stage of foreign expansion, companies manage foreign operations through an international division. If a company decides to expand abroad by increasing its foreign sales in different markets, it manages its foreign operations through area

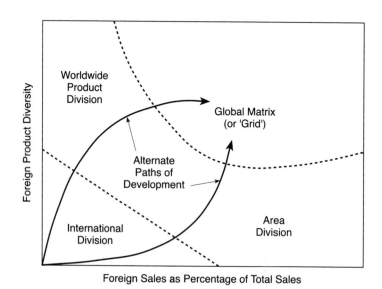

Fig. 1. Stopford & Wells' International structure stage model (1972)

Reprinted with permission from European Management Journal, 1992, **10**(3), 357–364
Copyright © 1992 *European Management Journal*

division, while a company that expands through product diversity manages through a worldwide product division structure. However, if the company expands through both foreign sales and foreign product diversity, it manages through a global matrix. In other words, this study leads to discussion on product- or geography-based structures and centralization or decentralization. In the past it was thought that global structure was the right form of structure for an international company, where line managers report simultaneously to another group of managers e.g. product or area. But companies which adapted to this solution faced more conflict than co-operation within their organization and barriers of distance, language, time and culture were unhelpful (Bartlett and Ghoshal, 1989).

In a recent study, Bartlett and Ghoshal (1989) presented their 'transnational solution'. They believe that until now there have been three main types of business or structure. They present characteristics of these three under multinational, international and global structures, considering that these are both chronological and specific for companies coming from different continents.

The multinational organizational model

The multinational Organizational model is the classic model used by prewar companies; these companies allowed their foreign offices (subsidiaries) to manage economic, political and social issues in their respective markets.

In other words 'decentralized federation'. This form was often considered a European management style, where control was exercised through personal relationships and informal contacts rather than formal structure and reporting systems. It was a decentralized system which was controlled through financial control systems as well as personal coordination.

The international organizational model

The international organizational model is a typically early postwar structure where international companies were supposed to transfer knowledge and technologies to foreign markets. The foreign offices (subsidiaries) were more dependent on their head office for development, new products and processes. More control and coordination was exercised by the head office than in multinational structures. It was classified as a 'coordinated federation'. This was, according to Bartlett and Ghoshal, a typical structure for American international firms. The head office always considered itself more superior than its international offices as it was the head office which had capabilities and resources. The subsidiaries were more dependent on the head office and control was exercised by formal systems.

The global organizational model

The global organizational model is the earliest global corporate form, where companies produce standard products to be shipped worldwide with a very 'tightly controlled central strategy'. It was adapted by Henry Ford, John Rockefeller, and later by the Japanese in the 1970s and 1980s. The model states that resources and capabilities are centralized at head offices while foreign offices (subsidiaries) are opened to access markets. Their role is limited to sales and service. Although in some countries, economic and political issues forced these companies to start assembly plants, the purpose is still sales and service. They do not have any freedom to develop or modify products. The term is 'central hub'. Decision-making and control are central and overseas subsidiaries depend on the centre for resources and directions. The flow of goods, resources and support is one way. This is typically a Japanese organizational structure.

The transnational model

According to Bartlett and Ghoshal (1989) today's companies, instead of demanding efficiency, or responsiveness, or ability to develop and exploit knowledge for success, should have all three capabilities. To achieve this, they must adopt the transnational organizational model. Innovations can be generated at several places so the company can make selective decisions, instead of being centralized or decentralized. For example, resources and capabilities can be centralized abroad. This kind of centralization would lead to scale economics.

A transnational distributes and centralizes some resources at home and some abroad, in different national operations. The company 'integrates dispersed resources through strong interdependencies', which are reciprocal. The distribution of transnational assets and resources are represented as an 'integrated network' (Figure 2).

This is an over-simplification of a complex issue. First, it is unrealistic to relate structures as different as European, American and Japanese; we can find firms from Europe following the international or global model, and many Japanese firms following the international or multinational model. Second, by the 1970s and 1980s, several firms were adopting the 'transnational solution', i.e. different resources and capabilities centralized at different places. Firms like Philips, Shell and Unilever are good examples. The 'integrated network' is rather misleading. The network approach, developed at Uppsala, is used in a different context than the above. It is more a question of a network of relationships between the firm and its environment, e.g. suppliers, distributors, competitors, etc., than a network relationship between the head office and its subsidiaries. This 'integrated network' or 'transnational model' does not include responsiveness to the local market (network) which is one of the three

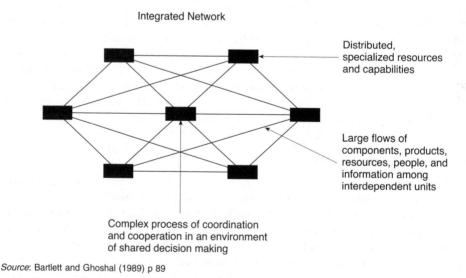

Source: Bartlett and Ghoshal (1989) p 89

Fig. 2. The transnational model

capabilities a firm managing across borders should have. To understand the complex problem of managing across borders, one should take into consideration other issues and complexities faced by international or multinational companies.

Here, we consider an evolutionary phenomenon where foreign subsidiaries become more prominent than the parent firm. Using a network approach, it is assumed that a foreign subsidiary has a three-dimensional relationship: (1) with the head office, (2) with local authorities, and (3) with the local network. Data on Swedish firms operating in Southeast Asia support the assumption that a new form of MNC structure is emerging: foreign subsidiaries are becoming more influential and independent than the parent firm. Furthermore, the emergence of a 'centre–centre' relationship suggests that some regional subsidiaries become the centre for a number of subsidiaries around them.

Here, we attempt to understand and analyse how the subsidiaries are dealing with these three-dimensional relationships and to see if there is any factual basis for this behaviour. We try to explain how subsidiaries are dealing with issues and policies of the head office which conflict with demands of the local network.

The study is based on primary data gathered from all Swedish firms having wholly- or partly-owned subsidiaries in Thailand, The Philippines and Indonesia. The data was collected through personal interviews with area managers at the head office of each firm in Sweden and with the managing director of each subsidiary in the respective foreign country. In some cases, the marketing managers of the subsidiaries were also interviewed. Firms such as Atlas Copco, Electrolux, Nitro Nobel, Swedish Match, Sandvik, ASEA (now Asea Brown Boveri) and Volvo are included. We believe that our conclusions regarding the independence of foreign subsidiaries/affiliates of Swedish MNCs are likely to be conservative, as they are based on data for Asian subsidiaries. Subsidiaries in large economies like the US are likely to be even more independent.

THE SWEDISH MODEL

The involvement of Swedish firms in international markets dates as far back as the 1870s. By the 1890s, several firms such as AGA, Alfa Laval, Nitroglycerin, and Ericsson, were manufacturing abroad. The decades immediately after World War II were a golden era for Swedish international business activities and by the 1960s most of them were involved in international marketing. Innovation capabilities and a well-established network of relationships have been important factors in their success.

The literature on multinational firms focuses on traditional firms from large countries such as the US (Franko, 1976, Kindleberger, 1979, Aggarwal, 1988). Research on Swedish firms and their international marketing activities is rather limited (Johanson and Wiedersheim-Paul for the internationalization process, 1975), Kaynak and Ghauri, for export behaviour, 1987). There have been some studies on Swedish firms and their activities in Western Europe (Jagren and Horwitz, 1984). In them it has been stated that subsidiaries of major European multinationals (e.g. Siemens, Philips, Nestlé) overwhelm their parent firms (Eliasson, 1988).

The phenomenon of subsidiaries becoming more influential and independent has not been systematically studied. In the early 1980s there was a government committee report (1983) on the impact of inward and outward foreign direct investment. Hedlund and Aman (1984) following Stopford and Wells (1972) and Franko (1976) looked at the structural development of multinational companies and explained how the structure of these firms developed from domestic to global. Hedlund and Aman (1984) presented a 'Swedish model' of managing foreign subsidiaries, containing the following key strategic and structural components:

- Swedish firms were competing on the basis of advanced technology, superior products, and premium prices.
- They had been producing for industrial buyers.
- Early internationalization.
- Low product diversity, expansion only in related areas.
- International expansion through 'green-field' investments.
- Mother-daughter structure, with subsidiaries reporting directly to the president of the parent company.
- More autonomy for subsidiary managers as compared to subsidiaries from other countries.
- Extended personal networks of close contacts between headquarters, and important foreign subsidiaries.
- Informal personalized control through information sharing and common experience.
- Strong position of managers with a technical/manufacturing background.

INTERNATIONAL GROWTH OF SWEDISH FIRMS

Initially, Swedish firms found an early market in Europe where countries needed Swedish raw materials and other products to rebuild their infrastructure after the Second World War. This was not the only factor in the success of Swedish firms abroad, however. Strong demand in the European market and abolition of trade restrictions after the war, helped Swedish firms expand internationally.

In 1965, 82 Swedish firms had 800 overseas manufacturing and sales subsidiaries with 170,000 employees. However, in the growth of Swedish multinationals, the 1970s and 1980s were crucial. Their ability to serve foreign markets through exports alone declined, and they had to increase activities involving FDI to protect these markets. In terms of expansion, there were two groups of firms: (1) those that started international activity long before the two World Wars, such as AGA, Alfa Laval, SKF, ASEA, and Swedish Match (Johanson and Wiedersheim-Paul 1975), (2) those which began after World War II, such as Volvo, Electrolux, and Saab.

Most Swedish firms such as ASEA, Atlas Copco, Sandvik, Nitro Nobel, and Volvo, became international in a traditional way. They started their activities first in the adjacent markets of Europe and later on went to Southeast Asia. They followed traditional modes of internationalization, starting first with an agent which was then converted into a sales subsidiary and only later into a manufacturing subsidiary. Swedish firms are generally among the world leaders in their product areas. Evidence from our studies reveals that the firms' knowledge of the market and relationship with all the actors are more important elements of competitive strategies than low cost production (Swedenborg 1982).

The foreign operation of larger Swedish firms, even in the 1970s, illustrates the above point. Table 1 provides a list of the 30 largest Swedish firms ranked in terms of their total sales and the part/percentage of sales derived from foreign markets.

Table 1. Largest Swedish firms in terms of 1986 sales (Millions of SEK)

Rank	Name	Sales	Foreign Sales	%FS
1	Volvo	84,090	70,604	84
2	Electrolux	53,090	43,434	82
3	Asea	46,031	33,447	73
4	Saab-Scania	35,222	23,247	66
5	Ericsson	32,278	25,177	78
6	KF	29,476	4,185	14
7	ICA	28,469	na	–
8	Televerket	26,340	na	–
9	Carnegie	20,411	na	–
10	SKF	20,232	19,220	95
11	SJ	16,431	na	–
12	Skanska	16,103	2,632	16
13	SCA	15,303	10,406	68
14	Procordia	15,299	4,950	32
15	Nordstjernan	15,251	7,000	46
16	Vattenfall	15,207	na	–
17	Stora	13,238	6,863	52
18	SSAB	13,010	5,204	40
19	Sandvik	12,721	11,652	92
20	Boliden	12,384	6,232	50
21	Postverket	11,956	na	–
22	Systembolaget	11,922	na	–
23	A. Johanson & Co	11,543	na	–
24	Nobel Industries	11,535	6,865	60
25	Esselte	11,251	7,421	66
26	Swedish Match	10,912	7,976	73
27	Flakt (Asea)	10,352	8,075	78
28	Atlas Copco	10,351	na	–
29	Alfa-Laval	10,300	na	–
30	ABV	9,661	1,700	18

Notes: na: not available
%FS: Foreign sales as a percent of total sales
SEK: Swedish krona
Source: Veckans Affärer No. 38/17 (September 1987 and Company Annual Reports)

These firms are large compared to other international firms. Most of them produce special products for relatively small international market niches where a network of relationships is more important than the price.

The major part of Swedish FDI is undertaken by larger firms with more than 500 employees abroad. The 30 largest firms have between 2,000 and 60,000 employees outside Sweden. According to Swedenborg (1982), approximately one-third of the 118 Swedish firms having manufacturing abroad, accounted for 90% of the employees of these firms outside of Sweden. Table 2 shows the 1965–1985 trend in employment by Swedish affiliates abroad.

Table 2. Employment abroad in foreign subsidiaries of Swedish firms

Year	1965	1970	1978	1981	1985
Number of employees (thousands)	171	122	301	326	329
Percentage of employment in manufacturing industry in Sweden	1	24	33	39	43

Source: Government Proposition 1986/1987. Central Bank of Sweden, 74, app. 3, p. 299.

There has been considerable growth in Swedish FDI. These firms have expanded their activities abroad and at home.

THE NETWORK APPROACH

Here, we examine the operating characteristics and recent evolution of Swedish MNCs using a framework based on the network approach. According to this approach, a firm has to develop various relationships to acquire raw material, components, and other factors of production. It also has to sell and distribute its products. These relationships have to be developed and nurtured, both before and after the firm operates in the production chain, with sub-contractors, suppliers, distributors, and wholesalers. The firm also has to develop relationships (liaison) with other organizations in the same network, such as competitors, local authorities and other third parties working in the same industry (Johanson and Mattsson, 1988 and Ghauri, 1988).

In the existing literature, multinationals (MNCs) are portrayed as working with a strong head office that controls and coordinates its subsidiaries around the globe (Swedenborg, 1982 and Hedlund and Aman 1984). Top management in these firms is, therefore, assumed to formulate an overall strategy and control for all the units. According to this view the MNC functions with a strong head office, 'centre', and a number of subsidiaries, 'peripheries', as illustrated by Figure 3.

A new stage of multinational structure is emerging after the global stage, as noted by Stopford and Wells (1972) and also the head office/subsidiary relationship is changing. This is contrary to Bartlett and Ghoshal (1989). The changing relationship is a step further in the internationalization process of the firm. The concept was introduced earlier by Ghauri (1990) and Aggarwal and Ghauri (1989), and we can see the emergence of a number of centres within the same firm. Due to their size and importance some regional subsidiaries have started functioning as centres. However, this picture is also changing, as illustrated by Figure 4.

The phenomenon is different from regional headquarters, where the head office itself delegates some of its decision-making to regional headquarters to encourage better coordination (Eliasson, 1988). It is a further step in the internationalization process, which may not be initiated according to the policies of headquarters.

Here, a number of subsidiaries such as A, B and C, are functioning as centres for other subsidiaries. In some cases the subsidiaries may or may not have contacts with the head office. As a result, a 'centre–centre' structure is emerging. Hedlund and Aman (1984) also concluded that interdependencies vary among the head office and its subsidiaries, depending upon the degree and experience of different markets. The subsidiaries, through adaptation to local markets, acquire a prominent position in the local network.

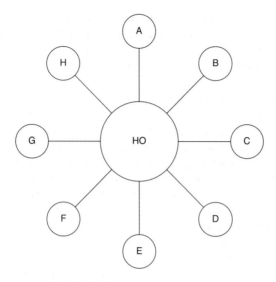

HO = Head office
A–H = Subsidiaries in different foreign markets

Fig. 3. Traditional head office/subsidiary relationship

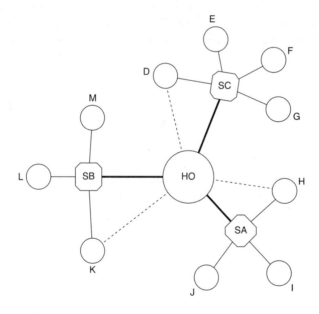

——— = Strong relationship
----- = Moderate relationship
HO = Head office
SA = Subsidiary A in a foreign market
SB = Subsidiary B in a foreign market
SC = Subsidiary C in a foreign market
D–M = Different subsidiaries in foreign markets

Fig. 4. 'Centre–centre' relationship in multinational firms

In the case of MNCs, the subsidiaries in the foreign markets are a part of the parent company's network as well as having their own network in the local market. These subsidiaries have to function and survive in the local market and must comply with the demands of the local network. At times, these demands may be counter to the policies of the parent company. Subsidiaries thus come to have a three-dimensional relationship: (1) there is the hierarchical relationship with the head office; (2) their activities are limited by the rules and regulations of the local government; and (3) they have to comply with the demands of other actors in the local network. This is illustrated by Figure 5.

The traditional head office/subsidiary relationship is strong, while the local network is weak. In the early stages of establishing the subsidiary, the head office directs the subsidiary in all matters, including how it manages its relationship with local government and the local network. However, as the subsidiary gains more experience in the local market, it may acquire a stronger position in the local network. It may also become resourceful enough to cope with the rules and regulations of local government, and eventually, its relationship priorities tend to change as illustrated by Figure 6.

The most important relationship for the subsidiary at this stage, is with other organizations in the local network; it has to abide by the rules and regulations of local government. The relationship with head office becomes less important. According to the network approach, the most important relationship for the subsidiary is the local network in which it has to operate. It is interesting to see how these firms are dealing with the issues and policies of the head office which conflict with the demands of the local network. We assume here that the subsidiary takes care of its own interests (i.e. the demands of the local network) and acts contrary to the policies of the head office. This depends upon several factors such as the size of the local market and the position of the subsidiary in the local network.

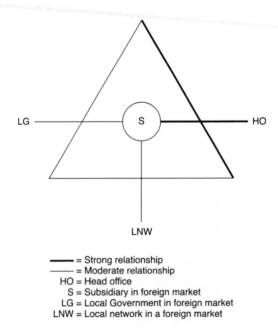

Fig. 5. The three dimensional relationships for a foreign subsidiary

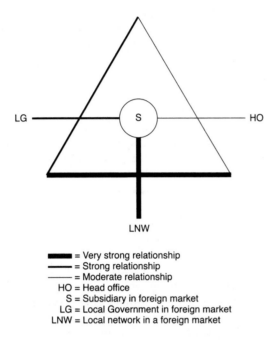

Fig. 6. Emerging head office/subsidiary relationship

The stronger the position, the more inclined it is to have its own policies, and not consider itself dependent on head office. Similarly, the bigger the size of the market (bigger than the parent company's market) the greater the chances are that the subsidiary becomes independent. These inferences are based on data gathered from Swedish firms having wholly- or partly-owned subsidiaries in Thailand, the Philippines, and Indonesia.

HEAD OFFICE-SUBSIDIARY RELATIONSHIP

Importance of regional centres

There are several examples where subsidiaries have become larger than the parent firm in terms of sales and number of employees. Considering the size of the home market, it appears to be natural in the case of Swedish firms. They now have their own R&D as well as product development programmes. In some cases, a number of subsidiaries have been grouped together into regional networks. This mode has been popular in the case of Swedish firms in Southeast Asia with Singapore being the regional headquarters. These regional offices work as independent firms which are many times more powerful than head office.

For example, Sandvik's subsidiary in the Philippines, although all the components emanate from Sweden, always sends its requisitions to Singapore. All the materials are channelled through Singapore. Some of the components used are not available from Sandvik group firms and are bought from other foreign firms; even so, these components are bought and delivered by the regional office in Singapore. The payments for all these components are also made to Singapore, not to head office or the suppliers. Singapore has jurisdiction over the Southeast Asia region, that is, Sandvik subsidiaries in Thailand, Malaysia, Singapore, Indonesia, the Philippines, Hong Kong, and Taiwan. All financial reports are sent to the regional office which later on consolidates all the returns and reports to head office. For head office, it is the performance of the regional office that counts, not the individual subsidiary.

Subsidiaries that grow through foreign operations meet problems, as illustrated by a Danish study (Rørsted 1985). The largest farm equipment company established ten sales subsidiaries in major overseas markets during the 1970s as outlets for its home production. Soon, these sales subsidiaries began to modify the parent company products in order to adapt them to local demands. This eventually evolved into local production. In some cases, the production facility even led to facilities for the development and manufacturing of new products. Most of these subsidiaries started buying parts and components from local suppliers in order to compete successfully with other international companies such as Massey Ferguson, John Deere, International Harvester, and Caterpillar. One subsidiary in England was buying 65 per cent of its components and parts from local suppliers, which was a clear violation of head office policy.

These developments eventually led to conflicts between the parent company and its overseas subsidiaries over sourcing and the optimal product mix. The parent company believed that the affiliates should purchase from each other. Some of the products offered by competitors were at prices and in quality hard to beat. Head office wanted to focus resources and know-how on product lines with higher technological content. Yet, purchasing policies and product mix strategies of subsidiaries were dictated by local networks and not by head office.

The head office/subsidiary conflict is illustrated by the Electrolux subsidiary in the Philippines. During 1979/1980, the subsidiary was importing all of its components from the parent company, and from affiliated sister companies around the world. As it gained more experience and a better position in the local network, it not only started buying from local suppliers but it helped local suppliers develop their own technical competence so they could supply to Electrolux's specification. In 1987, the local subsidiary was buying more than 85 per cent of its components locally and the vacuum cleaner manufactured in the Philippines was quite different from the one Electrolux was manufacturing at its subsidiaries in Europe. Another example of how the product mix adapted to the local market is illustrated by the Philippines water purifiers which were not even sold in the home market.

It is the same with the Nobel Industries subsidiary in the Philippines. The local firm purchases almost all of its components and raw materials from the local (Japanese and American) suppliers; only a small portion of the material being bought from Sweden. In 1984, the subsidiary started its own R&D department. As far as marketing was concerned, in 1984 when the market was shrinking in the Philippines, the subsidiary started exporting to nearby countries. This conflicted with sister firms from countries where the subsidiary wanted to export. Head office decided to establish a common sales subsidiary to sell to Indonesia and Thailand, countries where Nobel had no subsidiary.

Tetra Pak, which sells machines and raw materials for liquid packings, is another example. Its Philippine subsidiary imported all the machines and tools from Sweden and leased these machines to four different packers of milk and juices. Tetra Pak Philippines has a leasing contract for the service and maintenance of machines. The producers using Tetra Pak's machines are not allowed to use any materials other than those supplied by Tetra Pak. The subsidiary is nonetheless importing all the material they sell in the Philippines from

Singapore where Tetra Pak has a manufacturing subsidiary. Here too, we see the emergence of a strong regional office – Tetra Pak, Singapore, supplying the material to all subsidiaries in Southeast Asia. The development was not anticipated by head office.

Swedish Match, which wholly or partly owns 150 subsidiaries in about 40 countries, has 73 per cent of its total sales and 55 per cent of its production outside Sweden. It started international production with manufacturing subsidiaries in markets in India, Thailand, and the Philippines as early as the 1920s and 1930s. Although they are wholly-owned by Swedish Match, they work autonomously, purchasing their material from local suppliers and even the imported material is not necessarily bought from parent or sister firms. Most of the imported material comes from Germany, Japan, China, and Finland, often from competitors of Swedish Match. In the Philippines the subsidiary had two factories at two different locations, one in Cebu and one in Manila. In 1977, it sold one and bought 50 per cent shares of one of the suppliers of raw materials. It was considered more important to have a secure local supply of raw materials than to have a greater market share, although this goal was clearly against the policy of the head office.

CONCLUSION

The concept of centre and periphery, and the interdependence between the two are diminishing in importance in MNCs. In many cases, several centres in the same company have emerged, as for Tetra Pak and Sandvik, the Singapore unit is emerging as a centre for subsidiaries in Southeast Asia. The 'centre' or head office for these subsidiaries is Singapore, and not the parent company located in Sweden. The Electrolux subsidiary in the Philippines is working independently, has excellent manufacturing facilities, and exports to other Electrolux subsidiaries operating in the region – Thailand and Indonesia. Knowing the independent status of the Philippines subsidiary, and also accepting the fact that it is one of the most successful subsidiaries for the whole concern, the parent company has chosen not to have any say in their business with other regional companies and in their purchasing policies. For Electrolux subsidiaries in that geographical area, the Philippines subsidiary is the resource 'centre'. The product manufactured in that subsidiary is more suitable for them than the products manufactured in Sweden, or in any other European subsidiary.

We may conclude that changes in head office-subsidiary relationships are gradual. Our evidence suggests that this relationship changes with time and depends upon the position of the subsidiary in the local network. These changes can be shown, in theory, as going through three different stages (Figure 7).

The first stage, is at the start of internationalization, which is the most important relationship with head office. In the second, the subsidiary gives equal importance to head office, the local network, and local government. Finally, in the third, the subsidiary gains in experience, knowledge, and power in the local network and the relationship becomes pivotal. In some cases, the subsidiary's relationship with head office is replaced by its relationship with a regional office (centre). We believe it is not easy to control or enforce different structures from head office. In practice, it would be difficult for MNCs, especially those coming from small economies, to adapt the 'transnational solution' advocated by Bartlett and Ghoshal (1989). The three capabilities a transnational should have – efficiency, responsiveness to the local market and innovation, are best met by our network approach. In fact the transnational model ignores responsiveness to the local market.

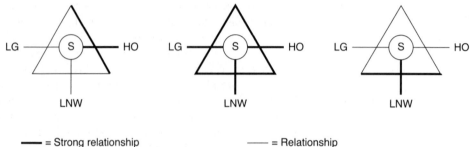

- ▬▬ = Strong relationship
  S = Subsidiary in a foreign market
  HO = Head office

- ──── = Relationship
  LG = Local Government in a foreign market
  LNW = Local network in a foreign market

Fig. 7. The process of changing head office/subsidiary relationship

We highlight the emerging concept of regional centres in MNCs based in small economies like Sweden. Foreign units are likely to become independent, or regional 'centre'-oriented as they overtake the parent firm in size and influence. Swedish cases from Southeast Asia are consistent with recent developments in foreign direct investment. We hope that more practical work will throw light on this intriguing developing and changing relationship between head office and its subsidiaries.

ACKNOWLEDGEMENT

The author thanks 'Handelsbankens Forskningsstiftelser', Sweden, for financing the study and travel to Southeast Asia for data collection.

REFERENCES

Aggarwal, R. (1988). Multinationals of the South. *Journal of International Business Studies*, **19**(1): 140–143.
Aggarwal, R., and Ghauri, P.N. (1989). *The Evolution of Multinationals from Small Economies: A Study of Swedish Firms in Asia*. Paper presented in UK meeting of Academy of International Business, University of Bath, April 7–8.
Bartlett, C.A., and Ghoshal, S. (1989). *Managing Across Borders: The Transnational Solution*. Boston: Hutchinson Business Books.
Eliasson, G. (1988). *De Utomlandsetablerade Foretagen och den Svenska Ekonomin, Forskningsrapport nr. 26*, IUI, Stockholm: Almquist & Wiksell.
Forsgren, M. (1989). *The Internationalization Process of Swedish Firms*. London: Routledge.
Franko, L.G. (1976). *Joint Venture Survival in Multinational Enterprise*. New York: Praeger.
Gates, S.R., and Egelhoff, W.G. (1986). Centralization in Headquarters–subsidiary Relationships. *Journal of International Business Studies*, 17, 71–92.
Ghauri, P.N., (1988). Marketing Strategies: Swedish Firms in South-East Asia. In R. Varaldo (ed.), *International Marketing Cooperation*. Pisa, Est.: Editirce.
Ghauri, P.N., (1990). Emergence of New Structures in Swedish Multinationals in S.B. Prasad (ed) *Advances in International Comparative Management*, JAI Press. Vol. 5 pp. 227–243.
Hedlund, G., and Aman, P. (1984). *Managing Relationships with Foreign Subsidiaries*, Vastervik: Sveriges Mekan Forbund.
Hornell, E., and Vahlne, J.E. (1986). *Multinationals: The Swedish Case*. London: Croom Helm.

Jagren, L., and Horwitz, E.C. (1984). *Svenska Marknadshandelar* (Swedish marketing) (Working Paper). Stockholm: IUI.

Johanson, J., and Wiedersheim-Paul, F. (1975). The Internationalization of the Firm. Four Swedish Cases. *Journal of Management Studies*, October, 205–231.

Kaynak, E., and Ghauri, P.N. (1987). Export Behaviour of Smaller Swedish Firms. *Journal of Small Business Management*, **25**(2): 26–32.

Kindleberger, C.P. (1979). *American Business Abroad*. New Haven, CT: Yale University Press.

Prahlad, C.H., and Doz, Y.L. (1981). An Approach to Strategic Controls in MNCs. *Sloan Management Review*, **22**(4): 5–13.

Robock, S.H., and Simmonds, K. (1989). *International Business and Multinational Enterprises*. Homewood, IL: Irwin.

Rørsted, B., (1985). 'Defining, Planning and Evaluating Subsidiary Competitive Profiles – an Empirical Investigation'. Conference Paper at the Fifth Annual Strategic Management Society Conference, Barcelona.

Stopford, J.M., and Wells, L.T. (1972). *Managing the Multinational Enterprise*. New York: Basic Books.

Swedenberg, B. (1982). *Svensk Industri i Utlandet*. (Swedish Industries Abroad). Stockholm: IUI.

21

Strategic Evolution Within Japanese Manufacturing Plants in Europe: UK Evidence

Neil Hood, Stephen Young and David Lal

INTRODUCTION

Although still relatively small, Japanese manufacturing investment in the EC has been growing very rapidly in the past decade. It has been largely import substituting investment, oriented towards Europe as a whole rather than to any particular national market. For both these sets of reasons it has been geared towards gaining the benefits of, and avoiding the potential barriers associated with, European economic integration. In terms of geographical location, the UK has historically dominated as a preferred entry point for Japanese foreign direct investment (FDI) in manufacturing, with Germany a close second. The background to this has been extensively examined in the literature (Dunning, 1986; Oliver and Wilkinson, 1983; Hood and Truijens, 1993).

The particular purpose of this paper is to explore the relationship between the strategic intentions behind the establishment of manufacturing plants in Europe and the directions in which these plants have evolved. It is evident that the timing of much of this investment activity reflects the threat of EC protectionist measures against selected Japanese imports, and that in most cases it is designed to protect existing market shares already held prior to the commitment to a manufacturing presence. As such, the investments are invariably strategic and long term, yet are often undertaken in the uncertainty as to how manufacturing competitive advantage can be transferred into Europe (Hood and Truijens, 1993; Burton and Saelens, 1987). The UK government and its regional development organisations have consistently pursued supportive policies to assist this transition for all foreign investors, and there is little doubt that these have been material in establishing the high UK market share of Japanese FDI. Since the early 1980s several UK regions have benefited from this inflow, and the empirical component of this paper is based on one of these, namely on data collected from Japanese manufacturing plants operating in Scotland.

While there is a growing body of academic literature on Japanese investment in Europe, the link between the underlying strategies of the parent companies, plant characteristics, plant performance and the evolution of the manufacturing operation as a whole has not been widely examined. In part this is because of the recent date of entry of the companies, but it is also because this issue is difficult to study without considerable assistance from them. In the case of this project, it was possible to bring two perspectives to most of the cases, namely that of the company at plant level and that of the development agency which had been closely

Reprinted with permission from *International Business Review*, 1994, **3**(2), 97–122 involved in attracting the investors and which had therefore had extensive discussions at the company headquarters level in Japan regarding European strategy. The survey which forms the core of this paper was thus undertaken with the following objectives in mind.

1. To determine the characteristics of a recently established sample of Japanese manufacturing subsidiaries.
2. To relate these to the strategic intentions of the parent, as revealed at both corporate and plant level.
3. To identify the development path along which each plant has progressed, especially in the light of the performance criteria which had been set for it.

In pursuit of these issues, this paper is in four main parts. The first briefly considers some contextual characteristics of Japanese FDI in Europe. The second reviews a selection of the relevant academic literature which has a bearing on this issue, and in particular that related to subsidiary strategies, subsidiary development, and performance evaluation. The following section sets out the methodology and findings of the company survey; thereafter conclusions and policy implications are drawn out in the final section.

JAPANESE DIRECT INVESTMENT IN EUROPE

At one level, Japanese manufacturing investments in Europe is both recent and reluctant (Trevor, 1983; Dunning and Cantwell, 1991). It has lagged behind that in the UK to a considerable degree (Yoshida, 1987). Its timing, distribution and scale can be attributed to the three inter-dependent motivating factors of globalisation, countering trade friction and the comparative advantage of local production (Kume and Totsuka, 1991). While the asset value of manufacturing is spread over a range of industrial sectors, electronics, electrical equipment and transport equipment dominate on both an asset and employment basis.

Much of the context in which this investment has occurred would lead to the expectation of Japanese investors having little to fear as they plan to commence manufacturing in Europe. Yet it is evident that the locational decision making process is a lengthy and deliberate one, within which the parent companies record uncertainties of many kinds (Hood and Truijens, 1993). Evidence from investment attraction agencies in Europe would emphasise this in several ways. For example, relatively few of the Japanese corporations commencing manufacturing in Europe have experience of production of any kind within that environment. Indeed several would claim to lack international production experience in western economies as a whole, although most have some executives who have set up plants in the US. For these, and associated cultural reasons, Japanese companies are among the most rigorous when it comes to the evaluation of an investment environment for manufacturing, paying meticulous attention to each detail which could affect plant performance; and conscious of the corporate responsibility to supply their own marketing systems with quality products. Two of the most common elements of this which are both consistently reported concern the quality and adaptability of the labour force and the capabilities of sub-contractors. In short, there is consistent evidence from attraction agency sources that the fulfilment of the strategic intention of local manufacturing has the highest priority once decisions have been made; and specifically that the achievement of local content requirements to ensure recognition as being technically a European product, together with market acceptance on grounds of quality, are the early twin peaks of achievement.

MULTINATIONAL ENTERPRISE STRATEGY AND SUBSIDIARY DEVELOPMENT

The strategies underlying the successes of Japan's world class firms, her Kaisha, have of course been the subject of much study and have generated many different theoretical approaches. Smothers (1990), for example, identifies three components of a meta-pattern of Japanese strategies. These are knowledge-based strategies within which there is a constant drive to make better products and, thereby, to create value; alliance-based strategies formed with both external and internal stakeholders, but not with competitors, in order to create mutual gains and to decrease overhead control costs; and productivity-based strategies, where productivity gains are a top-priority goal at all times. For some time it has become clear to observers of Japanese business that one of its distinctive features lies in its ability to consistently combine and implement groupings of strategies, described for example by Kotler *et al.* (1985) as 'sequence market development'; and by Abegglen and Stalk (1986) as a 'winner's competitive cycle'. Smothers (1990) and others see this as a sequenced and combined framework, expressed in terms such as 'deploy, improve, redeploy' in a manner which suggests systematic patterns of behaviour. In these terms the strategies considered in this paper reveal elements of all three of the basic strategic components considered above, within a timeframe where the companies involved have been redeploying resources overseas.

This study has therefore to be viewed in this context, as providing an insight into a continually developing strategic process within which the (largely) new decision to redeploy resources into European manufacturing has been recently initiated and is its formative years. The rather narrower aim of this particular section is, however, to establish an empirical base of related academic work in order to allow the proper interpretation of the findings of this study. As a starting point, the evidence on the types of subsidiary roles which MNEs specify for their operations is critical, since these provide tangible evidence of the implementation of grand strategies towards the European market. Thereafter some comment is made on the trajectories of subsidiary development, especially in the light of what is known about Japanese subsidiaries. The final part of this section briefly considers the measurement of subsidiary performance since this is one of the fundamental determinants of the strategic evolution of units within any multinational enterprise (MNE) network.

Subsidiary strategies

As regards the classification of subsidiary strategies, a model developed in Canada by White and Poynter (1984) has been shown to be of relevance in the setting of MNE strategies within the UK and directed towards European market penetration (Young *et al.*, 1988). The model (see Appendix 1) identifies five basic subsidiary groupings ranging (in terms of product and market franchise, and plant managerial maturity) from the marketing satellite to the strategic independent. The details of the alternative strategies will be considered at a later stage. It is sufficient in this section to suggest that the global strategic intentions of companies will to some considerable degree be reflected in the subsidiary strategies of their manufacturing units. Clearly this relationship may not always be a direct one. It is however more likely to be the case in recent Japanese affiliates given the trade environment in which they have been established and recalling the existing European market shares of many of the Japanese brands concerned. This working assumption was thus made in the design of the company survey and the White and Poynter framework was utilised.

There is much evidence to suggest that whatever the subsidiary strategy chosen at point of entry to Europe, the progression towards higher value added and more integrated plant structures in Japanese manufacturing investments in Europe will be much dependent on local sourcing. In the terminology used above, this points to an extension of alliance-based strategies. Thus initial assembly operations are transferred, followed by component part suppliers (Dunning and Cantwell, 1991), while quality, availability and continuity of supply will be critical determinants of localisation programmes and key success factors for the operations as a whole (Oliver and Wilkinson, 1988; Ozawa, 1991). It is evident, however, that the pressure for local sourcing within Europe, principally for local content and supply chain efficiency reasons, has to be balanced against an opposite force pulling towards global sourcing. In effect this is part of the tension of implementing productivity-based strategies on a global scale.

There has been considerable academic debate about the global-local sourcing balance, most of which is out with the scope of this paper. For the purposes of this study on the strategic evolution of manufacturing plants, there are however two aspects which are of importance. The first concerns the strategic linkages between product policy and manufacturing which is acknowledged to lie at the heart of much of Japanese manufacturing competitiveness and would be expected to feature considerably in the planning of subsidiary development. Some of the work which has been undertaken on strategic linkages has emerged out of studying Japanese FDI. For example, Kotabe (1990), examining European and Japanese MNEs in the US showed that, although they were not yet engaging in outsourcing as extensively as US firms, a negative relationship was suggested between outsourceability and the magnitude of process innovations by the foreign multinationals. This is a tentative, but interesting finding, and of importance for this study. At one level it poses a series of questions as to whether the Japanese FDI focus on outsourcing at new locations is only a relatively short-term one, or whether their capacity to manage these processes and maintain product innovation far exceeds that of their competitors, irrespective of the mix of global production and sourcing locations.

The second aspect of global–local sourcing balance concerns the ability of any production location (in this case, the UK) selected by a Japanese MNE to support the local component of its chosen strategy. In view of the fact that Japanese FDI in the UK mainly dates from the mid 1980s and that Japanese manufacturers have effectively passed on their EC local content pressures to their supply base, this appears to have been a critical locational determinant (Hood and Truijens, 1993). The nature of Japanese buyer–supplier relations has, of course, been widely studied, including ways in which these have been adapted to western contexts (Morris and Imrie, 1991). The process of adjustment within the UK to the rigorous standards set by Japanese companies has not always been easy. There is now consistent evidence that this has improved considerably in the UK through extensive collaboration programmes of supplier development supported by corporate and public interests (Trevor and Christie, 1988; Morris and Imrie, 1991). As will be observed in the empirical section, much attention has been given to this by the sample companies and it is regarded as a central factor in determining market share retention, volume growth, product transfer to Europe, and so on.

Subsidiary development

The discussion in the last few paragraphs has explored only one set of variables which might exert an influence on the development path of a particular manufacturing facility. There are clearly many others and it is evident that plants progress through different roles within categorisations such as that of White and Poynter, and others. This issue is considered in greater detail in the empirical section, since it is central to the subject matter of this paper. At this stage two related matters are examined, namely an illustration of plant progression as provided by Sony and a broader consideration of the early characteristics of Japanese manufacturing plants in the UK. Both will aid the interpretation of the survey data.

Table 1 sets out the Sony model for its European manufacturing in broad terms as declared by the company. It is important not to infer a causal relationship between these stages, since it is evident that many factors will influence the direction and timing of such progressions. Moreover, it may not always be possible to infer a common pattern even within any one company, or in any location. For example, trade restriction and local content issues have strongly influenced many companies, including Sony, in the way they have developed their European plants. Nor is it possible to infer that any given plant facility will be given the opportunity to progress along the route to full integration. Much more will be said on this issue in the survey section, with reference to the White and Poynter framework.

Relatively little work has been undertaken in the UK by way of longer term comparisons of strategic development and plant evolution. One such (Dunning, 1985) provides some relevant context for this study. Dunning examined the similarities and contrasts between US manufacturing affiliates in the UK in the early 1950s and those from Japan in the early 1980s. Among the points to emerge was that the Japanese affiliates exercised closer influence and control over general managerial philosophy and style than did their US counterparts in the 1950s, this being partly a function of type and activity, pattern of ownership and age of affiliate. Dunning expressed the view that it was perhaps largely due to the more holistic approach adopted by the Japanese to decision making. For example, the US subsidiaries had more freedom to introduce new products or adapt existing ones; however, there was less insistence in the meeting of the quality standards in the US case. The lack of any willingness to compromise on such matters, together with rigid standards and inspection procedures at all levels in the value added chain were marked features of the Japanese plants. By way of an overview, Dunning concluded that, while both waves of investment were mainly import substituting, the perceived asset advantages of the two groups were different and strongly reflected in the contemporary comparative advantage of the resource endowments of the home country. He drew attention to the fact that the Japanese investment in the UK was part of a consciously planned regional strategy.

These findings are an important backdrop to this study. They highlight many features which emerged in the survey work and stress the strategic regional role of early Japanese manufacturing operations within the UK. They also suggest that there would be an expectation of rapid evolution of key subsidiaries wherever the conditions were found to sustain such development. This in turn points towards the centrality of performance, hence the following section.

Subsidiary performance

Several studies have reported that many US-based MNEs evaluate foreign subsidiaries on virtually the same basis as domestic subsidiaries (Robbins and Stobaugh, 1973) and that they do so by processes which are shared with many other corporate contexts (Schoenfeld, 1986). It is, of course, evident that in certain basic areas of evaluation, considerable differences in approach would be expected. Thus, for example, financial evaluations of initial foreign

Table 1. Sequence of Sony Manufacturing in Europe

1.	Export of knock-down kits for local assembly
2.	Moves to local manufacture with some procurement of electrical and mechanical components
3.	Certain design facilities are localised, so that local components can be designed into products
4.	Total design in Europe and manufacturing moves to a just-in-time philosophy. As a result an R&D centre is required
5.	Specialisation by plant within Europe, controlled by Sony Europe HQ

Source: MD, Sony UK Ltd (1988).

investments using traditional cash flow techniques are not relied upon as heavily as in domestic investments because of greater perceived business, political and foreign exchange risks (Eiteman, Stonehill and Moffett, 1992).

The academic literature has frequently commented on the conceptual and practical problems associated with the evaluation of foreign subsidiary operations. For example, studies on the interaction of financial statement translation and performance evaluation have highlighted the paucity of adequate performance evaluation systems for appraising subsidiaries and their managers (Morsicato and Radebaugh, 1979). Other studies (such as Choi and Czechowicz, 1983) have found strong evidence pointing towards the importance of non-financial criteria in the evaluation process, stressing the role of increasing market share as the single most important non-financial variable for US MNEs, while other MNEs ranked productivity improvement as equally important. It is interesting to note that Japanese investors are rather distinctively regarded as having a long-term approach to both subsidiary strategy and evaluation, and thus perhaps being capable of taking a more rounded view of performance (Dunning, 1986; Yoshida, 1987). At the same time attention has been drawn to the fact that research on these aspects of MNE strategy has tended to neglect routines in spite of their importance in the process of co-ordination and control, being allegedly too concentrated on formal mechanisms such as departmentalisation and centralisation (Martinez and Jarillo, 1989; Kilduff, 1992). Such work emphasises the peculiar difficulties faced by many MNEs in co-ordination through the transmission of system-wide standard routines. Yet it is in this area where much of the efficiency gain of Japanese FDI networks resides, not least through their commitment to transferring their own unique production technology. Thus, for example, foreign production data on Honda, Sony, Matsushita and other Japanese pioneers of internationalisation show little difference in productivity among employees in their plants in Japan, Europe and North America (Ohmae, 1987).

There is little doubt that the criteria set for subsidiary performance will at any point in time be derived from the priorities which the parent sets for it. Thus the competitive priorities of Japanese MNEs will determine both the subsidiary priorities and performance measures. Over the recent past, there have been many studies on the different types of competitive priorities which emerge from MNEs in similar environmental conditions. For example, De Meyer *et al.* (1987) identified certain priorities as characterising Japanese, European and US companies in a major manufacturing study. Thus it is evident in this particular context that low cost, rapid design and volume changes were ranked higher by Japanese firms, which the authors suggested might reflect the importance which Japanese companies attach to set-up time reduction, small batch quantities and flexibility. Although undertaken in a quite different context, and not a comparative study, this project generates evidence of similar interests in recently established Japanese manufacturing units where a high priority was placed on establishing a flexible, quality European production base for the first time and, invariably, at considerable speed. Stated another way, many of the sample companies in this project were established in a situation where early manufacturing success was of a strategic importance for the parent which far exceeded the scale of the initial investment. This being the case, the relationship between subsidiary strategy, competitive priorities and performance criteria would be expected to be critical in determining the medium-term future of the local operation. As indicated earlier, there is little work on these relationships as they apply to recently established Japanese manufacturing plants in Europe, hence the motivation for this study.

SURVEY EVIDENCE

Methodology

When this project was undertaken in summer 1992 there were 24 Japanese companies listed by Government sources as manufacturing in Scotland, all of whom were contacted to seek their participation. In fact, two recent entrants had not yet commenced manufacture since their plants were under construction, and six of them declined to co-operate. Interviews were subsequently held during May and June 1992 with the senior plant management in the remaining sixteen, representing 72.7% of the Japanese companies manufacturing in Scotland at that time. Over the past decade Scotland, along with Northern England, Wales, Telford and Milton Keynes, has emerged as one of a number of locations within which Japanese manufacturing FDI in the UK has clustered. In all cases the regional development authorities have been very active in promoting these areas for inward investment as part of Government regional development policy. Being thus based on a high response rate from within one of these clusters, this study gives some important insights into certain operational aspects of Japanese manufacturing in the UK as a whole. To preserve undertakings which were given on confidentiality, the companies are not named.

Sample characteristics

Eleven of the 16 plants (68.7%) were established in the period 1987–1993 and the remainder between 1977 and 1986. As regards sector, eleven were in electronics products or components. This concentration is interesting, since UK estimates show that some 40% of projects are electronics or related, while the JETRO estimates for Europe are about 25%. This may be partially explained in the Scottish case by the fact that Japanese investment was attracted to Scotland as a result of the existence of long established, diversified electronic industry which already had substantial US and European MNE involvement within it.

In terms of employment, the plants were initially set up on a small scale, but several have built up rapidly over a short period. Thus the total number of employees in the sample companies after one year of establishment was 701, with a mean figure of 44; the mid 1992 figure was 4337, and the mean 271. Most of the sample expected this growth to be maintained over the next few years as the facilities were expanded through the addition of further product ranges.

Findings

Subsidiary mission and strategy

Since this study is primarily concerned about the early results associated with strategic manufacturing investments, it is essential to examine the ways in which this was translated into operational activity. As communicated to, or perceived by, senior local management there were three groupings of subsidiaries. Nine (56.3%) cited the support of the European market which already existed for the parent's products as being their primary mission. In that sense their view was a defensive one. Six (37.5%) regarded themselves as representing a more aggressive strategy reflecting the parent company's drive for world leadership in their product/technology; while the remaining one was located in Scotland at the request of a major adjacent Japanese customer which had specialist requirements for plastic injection moulding.

In order to begin to address the importance of the subsidiary mission. Table 2 relates it to a range of characteristics which might be expected to be indicative of plant standing. The early development stage of these facilities must be borne in mind, in that the average plant age was 5.3 years. The first issue in Table 2 concerns subsidiary strategy, based on the White and Poynter model. This classification system has two polar positions, namely the marketing satellite at the stage before the miniature replica, and the strategic independent as the development beyond the product specialist. Neither of these two are represented in the sample, the former because it is located elsewhere in the (invariably) well developed European sales and marketing facilities of the parent; the latter for a number of reasons including plant and managerial maturity, judgements on risk, policy on R&D allocation, and so on. The survey showed that eight (50%) of the plants were set up as rationalised manufacturers; and by 1992 only one had progressed into the product specialist role. In reality all of the rationalised manufacturers could more accurately be described as rationalised assemblers when they were established, consistent with the first stage of the Sony

Table 2. Subsidiary Mission, Strategy and Operating Characteristics

Subsidiary	Mission (no. of companies)	Subsidiary strategy[a] (no. of companies)	No. of products At est	No. of products 1992	Location of European Hq[b] (no. of companies)	R&D[b]
European market support	9	(RM: 6) (MR: 3)	41	202	S: 3 OUK: 5 E: 1	J: 9
World leadership	6	(PS: 4) (RM: 1)	11	268	S: 4 OUK: 1 E: 1	S: 4 J: 2
Local Japanese customer support	1	MR: 1	6	30	S: 1	J: 1
	16	16	28[c]	216	16	16

a. Subsidiary Strategies: RM, rationalised manufacturer; PS, product specialist; MR, miniature replica.
b. Locations: S. Scotland; OUK, other parts of UK; E, continental Europe; J, Japan.
c. Overall averages.
Source: Survey data.

model (Table 1). One of the initial miniature replica plants had progressed to a product specialist effectively doubling the number from two to four by 1992.

Before leaving this introduction to subsidiary strategies, it is worth noting that the miniature replicas were the smallest and youngest plants with a mean employment of 90 and period of establishment ranging from two to six years. The equivalent rationalised manufacturer figures were 420, and two to 13 years; and for product specialist 236, over one to 15 years.

The data in Table 2 on subsidiary strategies are for 1992. It is notable that the most advanced subsidiary role is only represented in the plants where world leadership missions were quoted. The interpretation of this issue is important and can be illustrated from one of the sample companies. In this case, the corporate strategy underlying its establishment of manufacturing in Scotland was related to its plan to build a three centred global network with Japanese plants supplying Asia; US plants, the Americas; and the Scottish facility, which started production in 1988, as the centre for Europe. The intention is that each of these three nodes will have three core activities, namely R&D, sales/distribution and manufacturing. Outside Japan, the US was established as a model from the early 1980s, with both west and east coast operations in each of the core activities. That model is now being extended to cover each of the three main product groupings which in this case are telecommunications equipment, data products and semi-conductors. Although under consideration for some time, this model has only been applied to Europe over the past five years. It was effectively launched through the sample plant being set up as a corporate facility, namely not as a unit for any one of the product divisions. It is therefore in that sense that its role is strategic in manufacturing terms and designed to represent a major step forward towards what the parent regards as world leadership in its products and technologies. By the time of this survey this plant had revenues of some £140m; was selling 25% to UK, 35% to Germany and 15% to Scandinavia; and had moved from a position where all material inputs were imported to one where 55% by value came from European sources. This case is that of a product specialist, growing and absorbing products from Japan, and set up to begin to be the focus for the third leg of its parent's global strategy.

Turning back to Table 2, it is difficult to imagine that the pursuit of global missions could be associated with plants remaining in either the miniature replica or rationalised manufacturer categories. Examining the other variables associated with this group, it is clear that as a whole the growth in the number of products being manufactured is much more rapid than in either of the others, and equally that the Scottish operations have more substantial roles as both European headquarters and R&D centres. In situations such as those illustrated in the earlier example, this is not entirely surprising, but should be interpreted with care. The manufacturing strategies of these companies towards Europe are not mature and while in some instances they were conceived over a long period, they were often implemented at short notice. Initial manufacturing investments in a market might well be allocated product and market franchises (and occasionally development responsibilities) as a holding operation and much change in the distribution of such functions is to be expected over time if past precedents are considered (Hood and Young, 1980, 1983).

The other major subsidiary mission grouping in Table 2 is associated with European market support. It is evident that many Japanese electronics companies have well-established brand names and substantial market shares in Europe before they commenced local manufacturing. However, there are also examples of relatively long established plants in this group where a more gradual and iterative growth trajectory has been pursued, with various experiments in marketing, distribution and production over several years. One such example is in sporting goods. It was set up as a joint venture in Scotland in 1977 as a substitute for Japanese and Taiwanese production. The joint venture with a UK business whose interests included sporting goods lasted only three years for manufacture, but twelve years for distribution. Over that period it closed a French plant in 1987 and bought equipment and production to Scotland as part of a rationalised manufacturing strategy. From a small R&D base in 1982, the plant is now home to European R&D for a key product group, which has a 35% market share in the UK. Its product range was 40 strong in 1978, but had developed to 450 by mid 1992; recording productivity levels at 90% of the Japanese parent and on a par with a sister Taiwanese plant. In the terminology used in this paper it had moved from a miniature replica to a rationalised manufacturer.

As Table 2 suggests, the predominant subsidiary strategy under this mission is the rationalised manufacturer, with the miniature replicas generally being younger plants. Again the product range growth is striking, but lower than that of the world leadership group. Probably because these groups had powerful marketing operations in Europe long before manufacturing commenced, a relatively small proportion have European headquarters in Scotland. The London area and South East England region account for most of the locations in the 'Other parts of the UK' category. Perhaps most noteworthy is that this group all record the source of R&D as Japan, even though, as in the example cited, some plants might have a measure of responsibility for European R&D.

Subsidiary strategy & local sourcing

The significance of the quality and availability of local sourcing for Japanese manufacturers entering Europe in the last decade has already been emphasised and analysed in detail elsewhere (Hood and Truijens, 1993). According to the company claims the existence of local sourcing was not in itself at the top of their selection criteria in the Scottish case. However, there is little doubt that component sourcing capability is closely related to the transfer of Japanese competitiveness to Europe in industries such as electronics, a sector strongly represented in this study.

Table 3 sets out some of the more important survey findings on strategy and sourcing. The first item to stress is that seven (44%) of the companies were under the 20% local sourcing figure, although this group had been established for an average of 2.7 years in Scotland. This figure needs to be interpreted with care for several reasons. All of these are electronics companies which, as part of their locational search processes, undertook detailed studies of local sub-contracting capability throughout UK. The locational choices made were thus informed ones. Further, although established for 2.7 years, several of these companies have been in production for a much shorter period and when they did commence, it was largely on the basis of assembling pre-packed kits for components and material from other plants in South East Asia. Thus, although firms were under 20% local content in Table 3 and this may appear to be a high figure, the investments were at an early stage and the data in the table suggests that age of plant is a factor related to increased levels of local sourcing. Further inspection of the data confirms this. For the firms established between 1977 and 1984, three quarters have over 60% local sourcing.

In common with similar UK surveys, several companies within this sample expressed a level of frustration about the inability to increase local sourcing as rapidly as they would have liked to. The predominant reason for lack of local sourcing lay in the non-availability

Table 3. Local Sourcing and Subsidiary Strategy

Local % range	Sourcing[a] No. of companies	Subsidiary strategies[b]			Average no. of years since establishment
81–100	3	PS: 1	RM: 1	MR: 1	4.0
61–80	5	PS: 2	RM: 3		6.6
41–60	0				—
21–40	1	PS: 1			c
0–20	7		RM: 3	MR: 4	2.7
—	16	4	7	5	—

    a. Local sourcing percentages are on a cost basis and cover purchases from within the EC as a whole. There is considerable controversy about such measurements and they can only be regarded as indicative. Japanese industry tends, for example, to include assembly labour costs of imported parts and components, local transportation costs, etc., and thus overstate 'real' local content.
    b. Categorisation as in note to Table 1.
    c. Number not disclosed since only one company is involved.
    Source: Survey data.

of material, with high cost of locally-sourced goods and concerns over quality as secondary issues but some way behind the supply availability. Experience in dealing with Japanese manufacturers suggests that, while the concept of 'local sourcing' is technically that from within the EC, the desire to develop quality suppliers at a much more regional level, for all the well known reasons associated with Japanese manufacturing practices, means that experience at that level tends to dominate responses. At the same time it will be remembered from earlier comments that the local (Scottish) supply base was not cited high among the reasons for plant establishment. It is interesting to note in this survey that even when providing reasons for a slower build up of local sourcing than was strategically desirable, some of the companies with the lowest levels pointed out that, due to the low levels of duty on imported kits coming into the UK, it would not be prudent to source more locally in the short term. Further, in these instances it was claimed that further local sourcing in such a situation would require additional overheads in inspection and supplier development. Clearly such judgements have to be made against the necessity for increased local content to meet the requirements for a European product, and such hesitancy for these reasons might be short-lived and company-specific. Outwith this context, it was evident in the survey that considerable effort was being directed at supplier development, frequently with the direct involvement of Scottish Enterprise and other economic development agencies.

Performance evaluation – Criteria

In the light of the strategic intentions behind the establishment of these manufacturing plants, the survey examined the performance criteria by which the parent company was measuring their performance. Based on a review of criteria employed in similar contexts Japanese MNEs, the executives were provided with a listing of 28 measures in seven distinct groupings as set out in Appendix 2. They were invited to rank the criteria within each group which were deemed to be of primary importance as part of the internal performance assessment of the plant. The overall response is in itself interesting, in that there were on average seven criteria selected for each of the 16 respondents, with a range from three to nine, the findings are summarised in Table 4.

While all of the companies responded, not all featured in the four predominant groupings of quality, financial, productivity and market/product development criteria. For example, there were two sample companies where quality measures did not explicitly feature, and the primary evaluation criteria were in the financial and productivity categories. Overall, however, the weight of emphasis in Table 4 reflects the characteristics of these plants which have been previously outlined. They are still largely production units in the process of rapidly absorbing products from other group operations in the Far East. Although criteria related to market development feature in 12 of the sample, it is generally a responsibility shared with marketing teams located in other parts of Europe as part of the corporate measurement of overall regional performance. The latter aspect is evident in the low level of comments on customer criteria, in that the plant priority is quality product, implicitly satisfying customers. Most Japanese MNEs would regard the requirement for explicit customer satisfaction criteria as an admission of failure. The same could be said for the personnel measures. The relevance of labour related variables in the locational choice was noted earlier and quality performances would be expected to flow from a combination of effective locational choice and good management. The fact thus that neither personnel not customer criteria emerge in Table 4 should not be misinterpreted. As regards the process criteria, again the plant age and responsibilities have to be remembered, as a result of which most are recipients of technology and process engineering. It is interesting to note, for example, that two of the larger rationalised manufacturer plants which have respectively moved from 150 to 830 and 30 to 530 products since establishment have process improvements as one of their primary criteria, thus reflecting the greater maturity and sophistication of these operations.

Relating the performance criteria to subsidiary missions, Table 5 shows the first ranked criteria for the four main groupings in Table 4. There would be no immediate expectation for these to be substantially different since performance by the standard criteria are essential ingredients of fulfilling any of these missions. The only issues to emerge, upon which commentary must be tentative, is that there is a tendency for the world leadership group to have rather different and broader criteria on both markets and productivity. Thus they have evidently more accountability for market share, cost leadership (on both productivity and finance criteria) and output measures associated with their more offensive role, than does the European market support group.

Table 4. Performance Criteria at Plant Level

Criteria groupings[a]	Sample no.	Companies %	No. of measures
Quality	14	87.5	28
Financial	13	81.2	25
Productivity	14	87.5	27
Market/product development	12	75.0	19
Process	3	18.7	5
Personnel	2	12.5	4
Customer	3	18.7	4

a. As detailed in Appendix 2.
Source: Survey data.

In order to obtain a closer appreciation of the manner in which the competitive priorities for the plant were translated into operational priorities, respondents in the companies were invited to rank these according to a schematic employed for similar purposes by De Meyer *et al.* (1987). The results of this exercise, categorised by subsidiary strategy, are shown in Table 6, based on a ranking of the arithmetic means of the respective responses from each grouping of subsidiaries. The consistent theme once again emerges as quality for a whole variety of reasons. Among these is the strategic issue related to the need for effective import substitution from high performing source plants, the desire to defend and develop European market share through quality indigenous production, and so on. Some of the relative priorities in Table 6 are consistent with previous findings in this survey. Thus, for example, high performance products would be expected to be a priority in the product specialists; as would dependable deliveries for both this group and the nationalised manufacturers. It is also consistent with the product specialist that rapid volume changes are not high on the list. Quality, price, performance and speed of deliveries are of greater importance to the miniature replica group. This would be expected, given the role which they play. Equally for them, and others to a lesser degree, rapid design changes are much less important.

Table 6 also provides the aggregate priorities for this survey as a whole to allow these to be compared with the Japanese companies in the study by De Meyer *et al.* From this it is evident that the priorities of the two sample groups are rather different. This may be a reflection of the recent foundation of many of the Scottish based plants where quality, high performance products and dependable deliveries are dominant issues, in what are largely manufacturing units rather than strategic business units. Thus, the timing and context of trade-restriction motivated investment would be expected to rank both low prices and rapid design changes as less important in the short term. If the Scottish sample is considered to have the characteristics of a 'bridge head' type of manufacturing investment for the EC, then it is likely that the operational priorities might be less directed to areas where high performance will be regarded as axiomatic in the medium term. Into this category might fall the three lowest ranking issues of design and volume change, and after sales service.

Outcomes

The evaluation of performance against the established criteria is clearly no easy matter for a number of reasons. Companies, even under a guarantee of confidentiality, are understandably reluctant to reveal too much detail on this issue. Equally, it is inevitable that shorter term issues such as the effects of recession in Europe on financial performance become intertwined with the longer term, more strategic measures. Bearing these issues in mind. Appendix 3 sets out a summary of the individual company responses. They are presented in this way in order to give an impression of the overall flavour of the way in which the various criteria were regarded in practice, rather than in concept as previously discussed. Of all the other plant characteristics considered in this study, the one deemed most likely to be material to the development of performance is the length of time the plant has been established, and the sample is grouped to reflect this.

A number of dominant themes emerge from the data in Appendix 3. Firstly, quality and productivity measures are usually equal to or better than those in Japan, though not always so when compared to other parts of SE Asia. The relatively favourable position across these and other variables is seen to hold for all of the 1977–1983 plants. It is notable that in this group of plants, there was little short term, recession-related comment on financial

Table 5. Subsidiary Mission and First Ranked Performance Criteria

Subsidiary mission	No. of companies	Quality			Finance			Productivity				Markets	
		1	2 %	5	1	2 %	3	1	2 %	3	4	1	2 %
European market support	9	21.5	7.1	–	23.1	15.4	7.7	28.5	7.1	7.1	–	41.6	–
World leadership	6	50.0	7.1	–	38.5	–	15.4	7.1	21.4	14.3	7.1	33.3	25.0
Local Japanese customer supplier	1	–	–	7.1	7.7	7.7	–	7.1	–	–	–	–	–
No. of Cos.		14 (100%)			13 (100%)			14 (100%)				12 (100%)	

a. Categories as detailed in Appendix 2, with the components within each of the four main headings as coded in the Appendix. The % figures are related to the numbers in each category. Because of rounding, they may not added up to 100%.
Source: Survey data.

Table 6. Competitive Priority Ranking by Subsidiary Strategy

Competitive priorities	Subsidiary strategies			Total sample (16 companies)	De Meyer results
	Miniature replica (five companies)	Product specialist (four companies)	Rationalised manufacturer (seven companies)		
Low prices	2	4	8	5	1
Rapid design change	8	6	6	6	2
Consistent quality	1	1	1	1	3
Dependable deliveries	5	3	2	3	4
Rapid volume changes	7	8	4	6	5
High performance products	3	2	3	2	6
Fast delivery	4	7	7	6	7
After sales service	6	5	5	4	8

Source: Survey data, based on the categorisations employed in De Meyer et al. (1987).

performance or capacity utilisation. As such, these examples probably reflect the long term nature of both the parent and local executive perspective. For the purposes of this exercise, they are styled as 'consolidators'. The second group, the 'builders', established over the 1984–1989 period, record a greater variety of operational experience. While invariably performing in line with expectations, several are below benchmarks adopted elsewhere, against which they are ultimately measured. This is the case with quality and productivity measures; and to a lesser degree as regards market share and development. However, the overall impression in these seven cases was of consistent progress being made in the plants and no fundamental performance concerns emerged in the interviews. In that sense they are still within the first five to ten years of establishment, building up operations and playing an increasing role in the parent companies' EC market strategies.

The third group of 'developers' are at an even earlier stage, generally experiencing rapid growth in physical space, employment and product range. In particular there are positive signs on quality, rather less so on productivity to date, and encouraging evidence on market shares. It should be stressed that while this initial experience gives critical feedback to the parent, it is based on a rather short time scale. Having said that this group is not materially different from the performance mix recorded for the builders.

The classification system used has its foundation in another set of considerations. It is reasonable to assume from the other evidence that the plans which these plants will be allowed to bring forward for future investment and further development of their role, will be much influenced by the performance record established at local level as compared to other group and industry benchmarks. The companies were thus invited to comment on the major elements in the next stage of their development as this was being considered within the corporation. It goes without saying that there are some risks in such a line of enquiry since it may reflect local managerial aspirations rather than corporate intentions. At the same time, it is probable that the responses are reflective of the discussion agendas between parent and subsidiary, and give some insight into the strategy of the former. It also points to some tentative evidence as to how the plant team as a whole is regarded.

The four oldest plants listed in the consolidators category cited the expansion of product families within the Scottish operation (in two cases); the bringing in of R and the expansion of production facilities. The first two of these are reflective of a more mature plant where new products and processes are sought rather than further transfer from within the partial range which they handle for Europe. Equally, R&D is unlikely to flow at earlier stages and the evidence within development agencies suggests that such transfers are particularly difficult for Japanese manufacturers at the early stages of their European strategy. In terms of subsidiary strategy three of these are rationalised manufacturers and one is a product specialist plant.

The builders show some rather different planning concerns. Two of the plants indicated the setting up of a satellite plant in Eastern Europe and another UK (or Continental European) production plant as forthcoming corporate events in which they would be expected to play a role. All of the others were still at the stage of expressing their plans in terms of adding new products from existing families, establishing a wider range of the parents' products in the market, raising capacity utilisation, and so on. Again this is consistent with the earlier observations made about this group in terms of solid progress with many of the functional aspects of a fully fledged plant yet to be internalised. However, it is interesting to note the diversity of subsidiary strategy characterising this group in that it contains product specialists (two); rationalised manufacturers (three); and miniature replicas (two). The later two are younger plants, and list further UK/European plants and the addition of tool making capacity as their planning priorities.

It would be expected that the developers group would have more immediate concerns about adding people and premises. the survey evidence confirms this. They are small, and in some ways embryonic operations, all of whom were dealing with short-term capacity recruitment and training plans. The longer term considerations of market development and R&D only featured at the margins. This is largely a miniature replica group (three), but has a rationalised manufacturer and a product specialist within it where it might be anticipated that these more strategic considerations would emerge in the next few years.

Before concluding this discussion of subsidiary performance criteria and outcomes, it is useful to relate back to some of the earlier comments in the literature. This survey confirms the expectation of common measures across emerging subsidiary networks and the active use of forms of benchmarking to chart progress against subsidiary missions. Equally the importance of non-financial criteria emerges quite strongly, with the Japanese parent companies evidently evaluating performance in a rounded manner and with longer term intentions in view. In the context of this particular study, the evidence points to the majority of the operations conforming to their subsidiary missions at this early stage in their life. Few as yet have sister European plants and little intra-EC competition for investment funds or development projects. There is some limited evidence that this is in the pipeline. However, several of the sample companies are some considerable distance from the stage where they might be expected to have an integrated network of development, manufacturing and marketing in Europe in each of the Triad areas (Ohmae, 1985).

CONCLUSIONS AND POLICY IMPLICATIONS

This paper has been concerned with the early stages in the strategic evolution of a sample of Japanese manufacturing affiliates established in a region of the UK, largely within a time frame associated with trade friction between the EC and Japan. For many of the sample companies these were the first European manufacturing plants to be established. It is evident, both in terms of the overall motivating forces behind Japanese manufacturing within Europe and in the light of the relatively low asset base which Japan has in Europe when compared to that in both the US and Asia, that the significance of Europe will increase considerably over the 1990s. However, it is possible to argue that trade friction is likely to decline in importance as a driving force behind Japanese FDI in Europe and that anti-dumping has passed its peak. In reality in one of its most vigorous phases between 1980 and 1988 only about 8% of the anti-dumping measures initiated were against Japanese firms, compared to 41% against products from state trading nations. While this Japanese figure roughly conformed to the country's share of EC imports, it has been highly visible and has had a profound influence on FDI trends. It is, however, likely that Japanese companies will move to less defensive strategies towards Europe and into more positive EC market oriented strategies, both in terms of locations and products – linking both of these into a global management framework.

It has been suggested that major Japanese electronics corporations are moving towards a situation in Europe where they will progressively add more value, not least by the transfer of more engineering and R&D to draw on foreign expertise in areas such as software, and to increase the international opportunities for indigenous management (McKinsey, 1988). For example, Hitachi and Fujitsu are among the companies to set up UK software centres in recent years. Equally, the persistent effort directed towards the development of multiple, high responsive medium- and small-sized component suppliers is part of the same process. In the short term, as evidenced, this may be driven by local content requirements, but in the more strategic sense it is an intrinsic part of Japanese competitive style. Many electronics companies rely more on frequent new product introduction and rapid production build-up, than they do on long-term plans based on exhaustive market research. This study has merely picked up the beginnings of these processes for recent entrants, not all of whom are of a scale where major strategic development on a pan-European scale can be expected.

However, it is not unreasonable to suggest that the locus of early manufacturing entry might continue to play an important role as such strategies evolve. This study confirms the findings for other parts of the UK, namely that the environment has proved to be one within which the most stringent performance measures set by the parent can be achieved or bettered through time. But experience elsewhere has led Japanese companies to expect that this would be the case, thus reinforcing the value of the diligence which goes into their choice of plant locations. In effect, given conformity to a series of carefully researched external variables, the corporations are confident of their own managerial and technical capabilities. The evidence in this sample points in this direction. In some instances, the plants have conformed to desired standards over a short time period, recognising that these are being progressively recalibrated. Equally, others have proved to be capable of absorbing new products while growing rapidly and have done so without detriment to performance measures. All of this was no more than was expected of them.

From the perspective of the Japanese companies entering the UK with considerable government encouragement and invariably with its financial support, the net outcome to date would appear to be positive on most counts. In most cases it is too early in the evolutionary process to determine whether this will lead to well-developed and integrated product specialist units, with wide market and product franchises for Europe and beyond. While it has been observed that early plant performance is a necessary condition for such transitions to begin to occur, it may not be a sufficient condition. More positive EC strategies, such as was suggested above, might well combine with the logistics of market servicing and with political pressures to add value within the major markets, thus leading to a much lesser role being played by UK manufacturing than at present. This may happen even within a Single European Market environment. However, there is little doubt that the sample plants examined were largely European in both concept and reality, which gives at least the basis of a platform for wider development centred in the UK.

Viewed from the angle of those promoting Scotland in an increasingly competitive European environment for foreign investment, there is much which is positive in this detailed look at performance and strategy. There would have to be some caution exercised about assuming all signs are equally favourable, in that in a multi-variable performance setting, there will always be some leading and lagging variables. Not all of these are controllable at plant level in that these are both external and internal (group) environmental factors which can obscure the fundamentals of how a plant is regarded by its parent. However, the very dynamic situation in these relatively young plants is evident and the actual trajectories for development are not easy to predict. Some tentative planning priorities did emerge, but the existence of a range of options open to Japanese parents on European recovery from recession is such that close attention should be paid both to aftercare for this group of plants and to the emergence of group strategy towards Europe.

As a final comment, it would, of course, be naive to suggest that the process of market entry and the transference of competitive skills in the context considered in this study has been universally smooth and problem free. There is consistent evidence to the contrary in many different environments as issues of managerial culture, organisation forms and production methods are addressed (Tackiki, 1991; Kidd, 1991; Dirks, 1992). While these were not matters which were within the objectives set for detailed examination in this study, such evidence as did emerge pointed to high levels of workforce and managerial flexibility being reported, and effective consultative mechanisms operating. In many cases this was perhaps assisted by the relative youth of the labour forces, the high emphasis placed on training both in the UK and in Japan, and the demand for employment in the region as a whole.

REFERENCES

Abegglen, J. and Stalk, G. (1986). The Japanese Corporation as Competitor. *California Management Review*, Vol. 28, No. 3, pp. 9–27.

Burton, F. and Saelens, F. (1987). Trade Barriers and Japanese Foreign Direct Investment in the Colour Television Industry. *Managerial and Decision Economics*, Vol. 8. No. 4, pp. 285–293.

Choi, F.D.S. and Czechowicz, I.J. (1983). Assessing Foreign Subsidiary Performance: A Multinational Comparison. *Management International Review*, Vol. 23, No. 4. pp. 14–25.

De Meyer, A., Nakaie, J., Miller, J.F. and Ferdows, K. (1987). Flexibility: the Next competition Battle. *Manufacturing Roundtable Research Report Series*, Boston.

Dirks, D. (1992). After the Investment: Organisational Development in Japanese Overseas Subsidiaries. Global Kaisha Conference, Manchester Business School, June.

Dunning, J.H. (1985). US and Japanese Manufacturing Affiliates in the UK; Some Similarities and Contrasts. University of Reading Discussion Papers in *International Investment and Business Studies*, No. 90, October.

Dunning, J.H. (1986). *Japanese Participation in British Industry.* Croom Helm, London.

Dunning, J.H. and Cantwell, J.A. (1991). Japanese Direct Investment in Europe, in Burgenmeier, B. and Muccheilli, J.L., *Multinationals and Europe 1992*, pp. 155–184, Routledge, London.

Eiteman, D.K., Stonehill, A.I. and Moffett, M.H. (1992). *Multinational Business Finance*, 6th Edition, Addison Wesley, New York.

Hood, N. and Truijens, T. (1993). European Locational Decisions of Japanese Manufacturers: Survey Evidence on the Case of the UK. *International Business Review*, Vol. 2, No. 4, pp. 39–63.

Hood, N. and Young, S. (1980). *European Development Strategies of US Owned Manufacturing Companies Located in Scotland.* HMSO, Edinburgh.

Hood, N. and Young, S. (1983). *Multinational Investment Strategies in the British Isles.* HMSO, London.

JETRO (1992). *8th Survey of European Operations of Japanese Companies in the Manufacturing Sector.* Japan External Trade Organisation, March.

Kidd, J.B. (1991). Globalisation through Localisation: Reflections on the Japanese Production Subsidiaries in the United Kingdom, in *Proceedings of the 1991 Symposium of the Euro-Asia Management Studies Association*, INSEAD.

Kilduff, M. (1992). Performance and Interaction Routines in Multinational Corporations. *Journal of International Business*, Vol. 23, No. 1, pp. 133–145.

Kotabe, M. (1990). Corporate Product Policy and Innovative Behaviour of European and Japanese Multinationals: An Empirical Investigation. *Journal of Marketing*, Vol. 54, pp. 19–23.

Kotler, P., Fahey, L. and Jatusripitak, S. (1985). *The New Competition.* Prentice-Hall, Englewood Cliffs, NJ.

Kume, G. and Totsuka, K. (1991). Japanese Manufacturing Investment in the EC: Motives and Locations, Sumitomo-Life Research Institute, with Yoshitomi, M., *Japanese Direct Investment in Europe.* Avebury, England.

Martinez, J.I. and Jarillo, J.I. (1989). The Evolution of Research on Co-ordination Mechanisms in Multinational Corporations. *Journal of International Business Studies*, Fall, pp. 489–514.

McKinsey & Co. (1988). *Performance and Competitive Success, Strengthening Competition in UK Electronics.* Report for the Electronics Industry Sector Group, NEDO, London.

Morris, J. and Imrie, R. (1991). *The End of Adversarialism – The Adaptation of Japanese-style Buyer–Supplier Relations in a Western Context.* Macmillan, London.

Morsicato, H.G. and Radebaugh, L.H. (1979). Internal Performance Evaluation of Multinational Enterprise Operations. *International Journal of Accounting*, Vol. 15, No. 1, pp. 77–94.

Ohmae, K. (1985). *Triad Power: the Coming Shape of Global Competition.* New York Free Press, Collier Macmillan, London.

Ohmae, K. (1987). Japan's Role in the World Economy: a New Approach. *Californian Management Review*, Spring, pp. 42–58.

Oliver, N. and Wilkinson, B. (1988). *The Japanization of British Industry.* Blackwell, Oxford.

Ozawa, T. (1991). Japanese Multinationals in 1992, in Burgenmeier, B. and Muccheilli, J.L., *Multinationals in Europe 1992*, pp. 135–154. Routledge, London.

Robbins, S. and Stobaugh, R. (1973). The Bent Measuring Stick for Foreign Subsidiaries, *Harvard Business Review*, Sept–Oct. pp. 80–88.

Schoenfeld, H.M. (1986).The Present State of Performance Evaluation in Multinational Companies, in Holzer, H.P. and Schoenfeld, H.-M. (Eds), *Managerial Accounting and Analysis in Multinational Enterprises*, pp. 50–65. De Gruyter, Berlin.

Smothers, N.P. (1990). Patterns of Japanese Strategy: Strategic Combinations of Strategies. *Strategic Management Journal*, Vol. 11, pp. 521–533.

Tackiki, D.S. (1991). Japanese Management Going Transnational. *Journal for Quality and Participation*, December, pp. 96–107.

Trevor, M. (1983). *Japan's Reluctant Multinationals.* Francis Pinter, London.

Trevor, M. and Christie, R. (1988). *Manufacturers and Suppliers in Britain and Japan.* PSI, London.

White, R.E. and Poynter, T.A. (1984). Strategies for Foreign Owned Subsidiaries in Canada. *Business Quarterly*, Summer, pp. 59–69.

Yoshida, M. (1987). *Japanese Direct Manufacturing in the United States.* Praeger, New York.

Young, S., Hood, N. and Dunlop, S. (1988). Global Strategies, Multinational Subsidiary Roles and Economic Impact in Scotland. *Regional Studies*, Vol. 22, No. 6, pp. 487–497.

APPENDICES

Appendix 1.

Subsidiary strategy	Features
– Marketing satellite	Marketing a standard product whether at regional, UK or wider level. No development role.
– Miniature replica	Produces some of the parent's products/services in the local plant. Activity ranges from adopting, adapting or involving some innovation to the product/service offering.
– Rationalised manufacturer	Designated set of products produced locally for a European or global market. Development generally still with the parent company, but some local and growing. Marketing usually with the parent.
– Product specialist	Develops, produces and markets a limited product line for multi-country or global markets. Much more self-sufficient in most areas.
– Strategic independent	Plant has both the freedom and resources to develop lines of business, normally for a multi country or global market.

Source: White and Poynter (1984).

Appendix 2. Performance Criteria

Description	Code
Quality criteria	
Quality output level	1
Parts per million	2
On-time delivery ratio	3
Yield	4
% Defect ratio	5
Reliability	6
Average quality level	7
Financial criteria	
Profit	1
Orders/sales/turnover	2
Cost reduction	3
Budget	4
Return on investment	5
Productivity criteria	
Standard time per unit	1
Cost/unit	2
Output	3
Efficiency	4
Market/product criteria	
Market development	1
Market share	2
Product development	3
Process criteria	
Improvements in process	1
Cycle-time	2
Noise reduction	3
Local material content	4
Personnel criteria	
Labour turnover	1
Attendance	2
Overall employment relationships	3
Customer satisfaction criteria	
Customer complaints	1
Enquiries-to-orders ratio	2

Appendix 3. Performance Evaluation

Period of establishment	No. of companies	Outcomes, by company
Consolidators: 1977–1983	4	– Quality higher and cost per unit lower than Japan. Taiwan subsidiary ahead of Scotland. Turnover and profit ahead of forecast. Market share increasing and on target.
		– Quality levels rising but still lower than both Japan and targets. Productivity considerably above Japan; market share and market development on target.
		– Quality levels equal to Japan; productivity levels close to Japan, and both ahead of target. Cost reductions on schedule, market development behind target.
		– Quality levels ahead of Japan; financial performance marginally ahead of forecast.
Builders: 1984–1989	7	– Quality better than Japan and US plants, but productivity lower. Market share and development growing, but behind target.
		– Both quality and productivity lower than Japan and lower target. Profitability ahead of plans.
		– Productivity and financial criteria showing improvements, but marginally under plan. Market share and product development ahead of target.
		– All quality, market and product performances below target.
		– All productivity and market development measures ahead. All measures, except cost per unit, ahead of Japan.
		– Quality levels under Japan and Taiwan, but on target; productivity level equal to Japan, but lower than Taiwan. Financial side under budgets.
		– Quality levels on target, but lower than Japan; productivity below Japan and target. Financial criteria improving, but under target.
Developers: 1990–1992	5	– All criteria better than all other subsidiaries, and ahead of targets.
		– Quality/yield comparable to Japan and ahead of plan. Efficiency lower than Japan, but improving. All productivity measures higher than expected in first year of trading. Finance, behind budget but return on investment (ROI) as expected.
		– Quality levels slightly lower than SE Asia; productivity also lower, but both improving on target. Profit and revenues both ahead of plan, as is market share.
		– Quality levels better than Japan, but productivity less than expected. Market development and share ahead of target.
		– Quality, finance and productivity measures all ahead of target; the productivity and quality better than Japan. Market share ahead.

Source: Survey data.

Part V

The Impact of Culture on Internationalization

CONTENTS

22

Psychic distance and buyer–seller interaction

Lars Hallén and Finn Wiedersheim-Paul

1. INTRODUCTION

There is always a distance between a selling and a buying organization, both in a geographical and in a mental sense. There are distances in both these dimensions also between actors in the same organization. These distances will cause difficulties for the different types of flows between buyer and seller: flows like information, products, and money. Disturbances in the flows of products and money have been discussed by several authors, but less so factors disturbing or preventing the flows of information. In this article we will formulate definitions of different types of psychic distance and also state a dynamic model of psychic distance and its development.

Psychic distance is particularly important in the interaction approach to the study of marketing exchanges, where the creation and maintenance of long lasting links between buyer and seller are basic assumptions.

Below we will discuss some aspects of this distance or closeness between buyers and sellers. The idea of closeness in industrial markets is seen as connected with the situation (or 'atmosphere') within specific buyer-seller dyads. The concept has also been analysed and defined on more general levels, however. Our discussion therefore will be focused on distance at different levels of specificity, i.e. with respect to the degree of individualization of the identification of the parties.

2. PSYCHIC DISTANCE – DEFINITION AND EXAMPLES

The internationalization of firms often takes place gradually. When the need to go beyond the local market develops, expansion is often initiated by selling to customers that are situated closely to the local market. Initially the growth is a type of 'internationalization at home', i.e. a domestic expansion process. Later on exports will occur.

As mentioned above, it is not just the geographical distance but also other factors that are of importance when measuring distance. On an inter-country level concepts and measurements have been developed by Vahlne and Wiedersheim-Paul (1973, Chs 3 and 4). They use the term 'psychic distance' to denote those factors which inhibit trade between countries in a wide sense. As indicators they have used the level of development and its

Reprinted with permission from Hallén, Lars and Wiedersheim-Paul, Finn, *Organisasjon, Marked og Samfund*, 1979, **16**(5), 308–324.
Copyright © Organisasjon, Marked og Samfund

difference to the selling country, the level of education and its difference to the selling country and the difference in business and everyday languages. These factors have been selected due to the observation that the levels of development and education must have reached a certain minimum level in order to allow trade to take place. Furthermore it has been observed that trade is favoured between countries of roughly the same level of development (Burenstam-Linder, 1961), i.e. the difference between them should not be too big, and this is also the case regarding the effects of the language differences. By means of statistical analysis a great number of countries have been ranked with respect to this psychic distance from Sweden.

So far we have not made a strict definition of psychic distance. In order to do so we first need a definition of marketing. We define marketing in a general sense as the activities used for 'bridging the gap' between buyer and seller. This gap can be defined in several ways. We have chosen to utilize *different perceptions*:

1. the buyer's perception of his own need (i.e. his 'ideal solution');
2. the buyer's perception of the seller's offer;
3. the seller's perception of his own offer;
4. the seller's perception of the buyer's need.

In these definitions we have assumed that the different perceptions do exist, i.e. the seller has a perception (a picture) of the buyer's need in a specific situation. The 'perception' is really a package of perceptions in different dimensions such as product quality, service, price, and ability to deliver.

We have not assumed that the buyer's and the seller's perception packages will contain the same dimensions. Rather incongruity between the packages will be an important feature of the gaps discussed below.

This means that Figure 1 (below) only is intended as a very simple illustration of the rare case when the perceptions only exist in one common dimension or when it has been possible to translate them to one dimension.

Using the four definitions of perceptions given above we can now define two types of gaps:

- marketing gaps
- psychic distance.

These gaps are illustrated in Figure 1.

As indicated in Figure 1 there are two types of marketing gaps

- *marketing gap* (S) which denotes the difference between perceptions 3 and 4 above and indicates the gap between buyer and seller as perceived by the seller.
- *marketing gap* (B) which denotes the difference between perceptions 1 and 2 above and indicates the gap between buyer and seller as perceived by the buyer.

Marketing gap (S) will form the basis for the seller's marketing behaviour. It is not a correct basis, because the buyer's buying behaviour will be influenced by marketing gap (B).

In this article we are not going to discuss these marketing gaps and their consequences for marketing behaviour in any detail. Instead we will concentrate on the 'marketing disturbance component' labelled psychic distance. The difference between the two marketing gaps is explained by the psychic distance which is defined as consisting of two components:

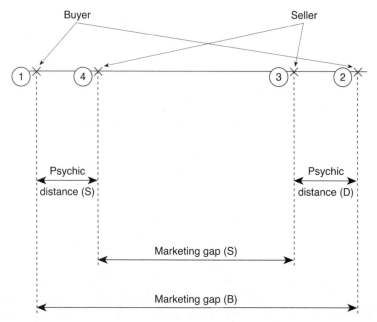

This figure illustrates the very specific situation where the perceptions can be transformed to one dimension. In all real situations a multidimensional illustration would be necessary. The numbers refer to the four different perceptions defined in the text.

Fig. 1. Illustration of Gaps Between Perceptions

A. DIFFERENT PERCEPTION OF NEEDS

The difference between the seller's perception of the buyer's need and the buyer's perception of his own need (4 and 1).

This is psychic distance with particular relevance for the seller, *psychic distance (S)*.

B. DIFFERENT PERCEPTION OF OFFERS

The difference between the buyer's perception of the seller's offer and the seller's perception of his own offer (2 and 3).

This is psychic distance with particular relevance for the buyer, *psychic distance (B)*.

It will be obvious from these definitions that psychic distance is a measure of the difficulty a seller has to perceive or estimate the needs of a buyer or the corresponding difficulty a buyer experiences in perceiving the seller's offer.

Psychic distance (S) and psychic distance (B) will be labelled *inter-firm distances*. On the analogy of their definition we will also create two other measures:

- *inter-country distances*, which will denote the psychic distance between two countries, i.e. the difference between the perceptions of an average firm in one country as seen by foreign and by domestic businessmen.

- *intra-firm distances* which will denote the psychic distances between any two actors in each of the organizations, i.e. the difference between the perceptions of a counterpart as seen by different people in the same firm.

It should be observed, that psychic distances will occur within organizations as well as between organizations. This follows from the fact that we have defined psychic distance as a difference in perceptions.

These three definitions of psychic distance will later in this article form the basis for a dynamic model of psychic distance. But let us first give some more examples of psychic distance 'in action', which will indicate the type of factors causing psychic distances to occur.

Inter-country and inter-firm distances – an example

Within the framework of established international buyer-seller relationships there is not necessarily a correspondence between the intercountry psychic distance and the distance or closeness that characterizes the inter-firm relationship. The relationship between a Swedish equipment producing firm and its French supplier of a certain quality of steel may exemplify this. Compared to other major countries in Western Europe France is perceived by many Swedish businessmen as a country which it is difficult to deal with. There are not only language difficulties (Swedes seldom speak French, and Frenchmen often give the impression of just reluctantly accepting other languages than their own), but there are also differences in business culture (e.g. Frenchmen are believed to favour centralized and formal procedures, whereas Swedes are seen to be more flexible and informal). Furthermore, both Swedes and Frenchmen sometimes have a tendency of considering their own technical standards self-evidently superior to foreign ones and consequently mistrusting other solutions. (See Hallén 1980.)

The Swedish firm of our example has bought its raw material from the French supplier – one of the major French steel works – since the mid 60's. On the average one third of the Swedish firm's needs has been covered by deliveries from the French steel works, but lately it has expanded its share of the Swedish firm's needs to 100%. This is against the will of the French firm – they want to reduce their share to 50% in order not to make the Swedish firm too dependent. The relationship runs extremely smoothly: the Swedes have almost never made any complaints, deliveries arrive regularly every month, and there are good personal contacts both between the marketers and purchasers and between the technical and laboratory personnel of the two firms. There is a long-term contract between the firms since 1974, but previously there were no contracts. The purchasing manager of the Swedish firm considers this contract unnecessary and means that the situation could be handled as well also before the contract was concluded. 'Contracts', he said, 'are papers that are intended for people who are not honest. Instead of legal procedures we rely upon common sense.' The inter-firm atmosphere thus renders the cultural differences unimportant. 'We do not speak French', the Swedish purchasing manager said. 'We can just say, "je t'aime", and that is sufficient.'

Inter-country distance: the firm-to-country difference

The method of analysis used by Vahlne and Wiedersheim-Paul (1973) implies that the study focuses on the impact on company behaviour of conditions on the national level. This approach is of special interest when the analysis is concerned with processes that cover long time spans, e.g. the internationalization process of Swedish firms in the 20th century. The inter-firm differences are suppressed in the analysis, and this may be a correct way of handling the problem given that no crucial inter-firm differences are present. This is in a way so: looking at a long perspective it is clear that once a firm had e.g. no exporting experience, which makes it comparable to other inexperienced firms in that respect.

Utilizing the measures developed by Vahlne and Wiedersheim-Paul (1973), the internationalization process of individual firms, i.e. the order in which establishments of selling and producing subsidiaries have taken place in various countries, has been compared to the computed values of psychic distance to the countries in question. Similarities and dissimilarities in the internationalization process of individual firms were observed and analysed (see Johanson and Wiedersheim-Paul, 1975).

Håkansson and Wootz (1975) have examined the selection of suppliers in an international context. Purchasers have chosen suppliers for certain products in a quasi-experimental situation. The suppliers have been identified with information about size and address etc, and based on the purchasers' decisions conclusions have been made regarding the tendency to select suppliers from countries at different psychic distances when certain variations in price and quality separate the offers from each other. The psychic distance between the purchasing firms in Sweden and their foreign suppliers is analysed on the company level, but it is only the buying firms, i.e. the firms where the participants of the experiment are to be found, that are actual ones: the counterpart is an abstraction, with whom the buyers thus have no personal experience. The analysis of the psychic distance is inferred from the purchasers' reactions to the relative importance of price and quality differences when buying from abroad. Their behaviour is considered to be based upon their general experience of foreign suppliers. It can thus be argued that the analysis is made on the company level as seen from the buying side but on the country level as seen from the selling side.

The conclusions of the study by Håkansson and Wootz are compatible with Vahlne and Wiedersheim-Paul's results insofar as the domestic market and Britain/Germany were considered to be closer to Sweden than France/Italy. This is what might have been expected, as the counterpart is defined abstractly, although using different indicators.

Inter-firm distances and total image

The interaction approach to the study of buyer-seller relationships in industrial markets implies that there is an interaction process between individual identified parties. This forms the buying and the selling behaviour. The trust that may have developed between the parties within a specific relationship due to previous contacts in connection with deliveries or other activities before or after earlier transactions has a profound influence on behaviour. These processes have been studied in an international setting by the researchers participating in the IMP Project (see Håkansson, 1980). The distance between sellers and buyers are here studied at two different levels. Firstly, the opinions of counterparts in general in five Western European countries are mapped. Secondly, the relation to one specific supplier or purchaser is investigated. The number of relationships mapped in this way exceeds 900.

An analysis of distance between buyers and sellers based on the first of the two approaches that are used in the IMP Project is reported by Hallén (1980). In contrast to the mentioned studies by Vahlne and Wiedersheim-Paul (1973) and Håkansson and Wootz (1975) the analysis here deals with actual firms on the perceiving as well as on the perceived side. But as the respondents have expressed their opinions of their actual suppliers or customers in general, total images are obtained. The experience of incidents and episodes within one specific buyer-seller relationship, which certainly has formed the opinion to a high extent, still cannot be observed directly. The counterpart is an aggregate, although an aggregate of actual firms.

A rather crude measure has been applied in the determination of the psychic distance in this context. The respondent's opinions of difficulties in communication due to language problems, of difficulties to make friends with the personnel in the other firm, and their feeling of being understood by their customers/suppliers in the other country were expressed on a five-point scale and added with each other into an index. The five-country design of the study gives the opportunity to analyse this distance also from other viewpoints than Sweden. This analysis shows that some countries seem to be more 'distant' than others both according to their own opinions and according to the opinion of their foreign business partners. Thus Italy seems to be the most isolated country of the group of five countries (Sweden, W. Germany, Britain, France, and Italy), and Sweden actually seems to be most integrated in the group, although the other four are members of the European Communities and Sweden is not. Another observation from the analysis is that purchasers generally consider the distance to be shorter than the marketers. A possible reason for this is that marketers more often take upon them the task to bridge the gap between buyer and seller than purchasers do, which might make the marketers more aware of the distance that may exist. Also, the observation stresses the important fact that psychic distance between two parties is asymmetrical.

Inter-firm distance and atmosphere

For a deeper understanding of the psychic distance in an international setting it is probably necessary to conduct the analysis on a firm-to-firm level. The interaction between buyer and seller leads to the development of an 'atmosphere', which can be described in terms of closeness/distance, conflict/co-operation, and power/dependence. The closeness or distance between the parties in a buyer-seller dyad is conditioned by characteristics of the interacting firms and the interaction processes as well as environmental factors. In the approaches described above these environmental factors have played quite a dominating role, but their importance in the company specific analysis is reduced to one factor group amongst others. Its importance for the development of an atmosphere characterized by 'closeness' between the parties is often secondary to the effects of the interaction processes, e.g. the adaptations and the role institutionalization that takes place within an ongoing relationship. A Swedish firm may experience a greater distance to another Swedish firm than to an established British supplier, in spite of the language and spatial gaps between Sweden and Britain. The access to informal communication channels to the foreign firm may be an indication of such 'closeness'.

Interaction processes between marketers and purchasers of the two firms in a buyer-seller dyad may bring these individuals together in a way that makes them feel as representatives of a common buying-selling organization rather than of their respective firms. Thus, the inter-firm distance, i.e. the distance between the two firms, in certain situations is shorter than the intra-firm distance between the selling or buying function and other involved functions of the concerned firms. The phenomenon of 'side-changing' mentioned by Ford (1979) where employees of one company in a buyer-seller dyad act in the interest of the other company may be seen as an extreme example of short inter-firm distance coupled with certain intra-firm distances.

Inter-firm and intra-firm distances – an example

In order to further clarify the various concepts of distance we will use a case description of the relations between a Swedish firm ('Nya Mekaniska Verkstaden', NMV) and a large French mining company, which we may call 'Union des Montagnes Métallifères', UMM. The Swedish firm is rather small and is specialized in the production of capital equipment for use in the mining industry. In 1962 the first drilling equipment was sold by NMV to UMM as a result of an ambitious campaign by NMV to establish itself as a company with world-wide sales. Based on advertising in professional journals all over the world NMV wanted to create a basis for expanded production by means of acquiring sales in other countries than the domestic market, to which most of its sales had gone before. This general approach to export marketing turned out to be too resource demanding, and therefore NMV decided to concentrate its marketing efforts to some ten countries. One of these countries was France, where a sales subsidiary was established in order to take care of contacts with prospective buyers of NMV's products. As the number of mining companies in France is rather limited (NMV believes that there are about 50 firms) contacts have been established with almost all of them, and about 20 firms in France more or less regularly buy NMV's drilling equipment. But a very large share of NMV's total sales to the French firms is bought by its largest French customer: UMM. Between 25 and 50 per cent of NMV's French sales have during the last years gone to UMM.

From the very beginning NMV tried to get into contact with technicians and production managers in UMM rather than to negotiate through UMM's purchasing department. NMV considers its product to have two major advantages compared to competing equipment: it considerably improves the working environment for the miners, and it increases the speed of the operations. Both these arguments impress upon production managers, NMV believes.

During the period between 1962 and 1975 NMV thus established what they considered to be a strong position as a supplier of mining equipment and spare parts to UMM. But during 1975 and 1976 production costs rose in Sweden, and NMV raised their prices by more than 80% during the three years 1975/77. This did not at all please the purchasing department at UMM. As far as NMV was able to find out, a decision was made centrally by the top management at UMM that NMV should be 'black-listed', i.e. nothing was to be bought from NMV, neither complete units nor spare parts.

This decision created problems for two of the involved parties. First of all it naturally worried the marketers at NMV. But it also annoyed the production department at UMM. They needed spare parts from NMV for their equipment, and they did not want to change from NMV's equipment to substitutes as UMM's technicians considered those inferior. Therefore, they continued to order from NMV, and after some time they also resumed purchasing new equipment. The black-listing may still formally be in force, but it seems to have turned into a dead letter. At present, UMM buys two or three units of equipment every year from NMV, and there are good relations between the firms, particularly between NMV's marketers and UMM's technicians. NMV tries to obtain a situation where decisions are made at the purchasing department in UMM, but as a NMV marketer put it: 'We would not make any extreme efforts in order to get hold of one of their purchasers.'

An analysis of this mini-case shows us that factors relating to 'distance' have been of importance in several instances. Firstly, there is the inter-country distance. The Swedish firm NMV did not inform UMM in advance of their plans to raise prices, and they also let these prices rise so as to compensate Swedish cost increases fully. It did not occur to the Swedes to negotiate this with the French purchasing unit, probably because they felt that the 'real' decision-makers in the French firm were not the purchasers but the production engineers. The Swedish marketers characterized the French purchasers of UMM as 'very French Frenchmen', and by this they meant that they found them aloof and secretive. Thus, there are clear differences in behaviour and expectations between the Swedes and the Frenchmen, and this may have been one of the major reasons to the development that led up to the black-listing.

Secondly, there is the inter-firm distance – the state of the inter-firm relationship in terms of conflict/co-operation, closeness/distance, and power/dependence. The production engineers of UMM seemed to consider themselves to have interests that were compatible with NMV's, and they were also dependent on NMV for spare parts for uninterrupted production.

In terms of closeness/distance UMM's production unit can be said to be rather close to NMV, as five of roughly ten persons from UMM with regular contacts with NMV were technicians. Only one regular contact came from UMM's purchasing unit. The total atmosphere of the relationship was thus characterized not only by cultural differences but also by similarities in terms of perceived needs of co-operation and of dependence. The inter-firm distance was shorter than the inter-country distance.

Thirdly, the case gives an example of the difference between intra-firm and inter-firm distances. As seen from NMV (which is the source of information) the purchasing department of UMM had not very good contacts with their own production people, although the purchasing unit was believed to have a high status in the French firm. The outcome of the crisis seems to indicate that the purchasing unit of UMM with its 'black-listing' were more distant from the actual decision-making and actions of their own organization than NMV's marketers were.

3. A DYNAMIC MODEL OF PSYCHIC DISTANCE

We are now in a position to develop a model of psychic distance and its implications for firms, based on the definitions given earlier and the different examples presented above. In this model we will study the changing impact of psychic distance in the development process of a buyer-seller relation where the parties are located in different environments. In order to simplify the discussion we assume that these environments are two different countries. The development of different types of psychic distance is of course a continuous process but in order to simplify the discussion below we have chosen to identify the following three stages:

pre-contact stage
initial interaction stage
maturing interaction stage.

During the first stage the seller has not yet any contacts with the buyer. In the extreme case when the seller is in the position to enter the export market for the first time the inter-country distance will be the relevant measure of psychic distance. This means that the difference between the buyer's and the seller's perception of the relevant need of the buyer (psychic distance (S)) will mainly be determined by factors on a national level, e.g. differences in language, level of development and level of education between the countries in question.

The same would be true for a potential buyer; his perception of the unknown seller's offer would be determined by his perception of the seller's country of origin (unless the buyer has some previous experience of other sellers in this country).

In those cases where the seller has exported to the specific country or to other countries the psychic distance will consist not only of the intercountry component but also to some extent of distance more on the interfirm level. Two cases would be rather common:

- The seller has other customers in the specific country. In this situation a kind of *halo* effect will occur; the new customer belongs to the same family, as it were.
- The seller has a representative/agent selling to the specific country. In this case much of the psychic distance between seller and potential customer will consist of the inter-firm distance between seller and representative/agent.

This latter case contains a number of sub-cases: the representative/agent is located in the same country as the seller or the representative/agent is located in the specific foreign market. These situations will reflect a choice, intentional or unintentional, in locating the psychic distance. In the first situation most of the psychic distance will occur between representative/agent and the market, in the second situation most of the distance will occur between seller and representative/agent. It is of course impossible to state *the* best solution, but the discussion in Johanson (1972) will give some indication.

A related case is when the seller uses a representative in a third country for marketing in a specific country. An example would be the use of trading houses in London for approaching present or former Commonwealth countries. It is to be expected that this deviation via a third country would result in a shorter psychic distance than if a representative in the seller's or the buyer's country were chosen.

In the initial interaction phase there has been a first contact between seller and buyer and this contact has resulted in a purchase. The psychic distance between the two firms will consist of a mixture of inter-country and inter-firm distances. The impact of the inter-country distance will still be comparatively strong but the importance will gradually shift to the inter-firm distance at the same time as this factor changes. The process is illustrated in Figure 2.

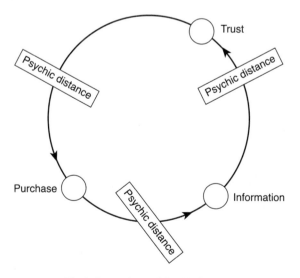

Fig. 2. Interaction and Psychic Distance

According to this illustration the interaction between buyer and seller may start with any of the factors: purchase, information or trust. A 'normal' course of events would perhaps start with information, leading to trust, leading to purchase. The psychic distance plays different roles in this process. Apart from disturbing or preventing the start of the process, it slows down or prevents information from resulting in trust and trust in leading to purchase. But if the barrier between information and trust or between trust and purchase has been passed it will in itself be changed.

In some cases the psychic distance will increase, causing the interaction process to end. In other cases it will decrease leading to a more intensive interaction process. The development of the inter-firm psychic distance will also have an impact on the inter-country distance; the 'image' of a country will improve if there are improving relations with a firm in that country.

If the initial contacts between two firms will develop into an interaction process (and if so at what speed) also depends on the buyer's perception of the initial state and the subsequent changes of the uncertainty variables: need uncertainty, market uncertainty, and transaction uncertainty (Håkansson, Johanson and Wootz, 1977). High need uncertainty, indicating a considerable perceived difficulty for the buyer to interpret the exact nature of the need for which a functional solution is required, would thus mean a large initial inter-firm psychic distance and a slow decrease in this distance. We will not penetrate these problems here, however.

If the relations between buyer and seller continue we will gradually move into the maturing interaction stage. In this phase, it is assumed that the elements that are exchanged within the transaction episodes (the product and/or service, the information, the means of payment, the social elements) eventually will lead to adaptations between the parties in terms of e.g. product modifications, special inventories, changed administration routines or the establishment of informal communication channels and the development of liking and trust between individuals of the concerned firms. This development will cause the inter-firm distance between buyer and seller to decrease but other effects will also occur. The informal contacts and the trust that may be present within well established relations often have the effect of raising barriers to entry against new partners, i.e. the inter-firm distances towards these potential sellers will increase.

The close relation between buyer and seller may result in the intra-firm distances becoming important, e.g. employees in the selling firm working in close contact with the buying firm may feel split loyalties between the two parties. In this maturing interaction stage the different perceptions illustrated in Figure 1 tend to be close together but not totally coinciding. A coincidence would be impossible due to differences between individuals and the continuous change in the problem situation.

4. CONCLUDING REMARKS

Our discussion of the different 'levels' or 'approaches' to the concept of inter-country and inter-firm psychic distance and degree of closeness in the interaction atmosphere is intended to illuminate when these differently defined concepts are applicable. In this concluding section we will focus upon two categories of marketing situations, viz. (1) the differences between the marketing of consumer goods and the marketing of industrial goods and (2) the difference between the initiation and the continuation of buyer-seller relationships in markets for producer goods.

The inter-country differences are likely to be more important in consumer goods marketing than in industrial marketing, whereas the inter-firm distance to a higher extent affects industrial marketing. Cultural idiosyncrasies probably are of considerable importance for the purchasing decisions of households and other end-consumers. Here subtle aspects of marketing such as design, ways of distribution and 'image' may mean the difference between success and failure, and thus it may be difficult to operate in a culturally distant market. As mass marketing is the norm for consumer goods the necessary 'feeling' for the right approach to the market cannot be replaced by the development of special relations to selected customers. For an analysis of consumer goods situations the concept of 'psychic distance' on the intercountry level thus may prove useful.

It is an over-simplification, however, to state that the dividing line between the applicability of the 'general' level of distance as opposed to the 'specific' distance within the framework of a buyer-seller dyad coincides with the dividing line between marketing to individual end consumers and marketing to organizations. The interaction approach to marketing deals primarily with the development of existing customer relations; the initiation of a relationship is seen as a 'special case'. Before there is any relation between the firms, there is not either any 'atmosphere' that may act to compensate for cultural differences between the seller and his prospective buyer. Thus, the general concept of 'psychic distance' also is applicable for the analysis of the industrial marketing problem in new markets. The studies of the internationalization process of Swedish firms mentioned above take as a starting point the situation when most firms were domestically oriented and the gradual penetration of foreign markets is analysed against the background of inter-country differences. This first phase of future interaction processes with customers abroad is often approached with marketing tools that can be classified as belonging to the marketing mix 'tool kit'. The Swedish firm NMV of our final example above approached the French market with advertisements in professional journals. Here the psychic distance in a general sense may affect the outcome of the attempts to market entry. But in later stages of buyer-seller relationships the inter-firm aspects may turn into the dominant feature of the distance/ closeness question. Here an analysis of the marketing problems may better be conducted using the interaction approach.

The ongoing discussion in Sweden whether Swedes are bad international marketers or not is to a large extent a question of psychic distance between Swedish marketers and their foreign customers. Consequently, the discussion would improve if a distinction was made between the ability to create a new relation and the ability to maintain a stable relation. According to recent studies (Phillips-Martinsson, 1979 and Hallén, 1980) the first mentioned ability is perhaps inferior to the second one. If this is correct it may cause considerable difficulties in the long run, as the ability to create new relations may become comparatively more important. This is one aspect of the domain problem of the firm, i.e. the problem to select the directions of future expansion: new customers, new knowledge, new products or what? (Wiedersheim-Paul and Erland, 1979; Wiedersheim-Paul, 1979).

There may also develop new types of distance problems, viz. the perception of possible internal distances within each firm. The institutionalization of roles, e.g. the boundary-spanning roles of the purchasers and marketers of the two organizations involved in a transaction, may create a feeling that they represent their common 'buyer-seller unit' rather than their respective firms. A reduction of inter-company distance may be obtained at the expense of intra-firm distances.

REFERENCES

Burenstam-Linder, S. (1961), *An Essay on Trade and Transformation*. Almqvist and Wiksell, Uppsala.

Ford, D. (1980), Developing Buyer-Seller Relationships in Export Marketing. *Organisation*, Marknad och Samhälle, Vol. 16, No. 5.

Håkansson, H., (ed.), 1980, *Industrial Marketing and Purchasing in Europe. An Interaction Approach*. Forthcoming.

Håkansson, H. and Wootz, B. (1975), Supplier Selection in an International Environment. *Journal of Marketing Research*, Vol. XII (Feb), pp. 46–5l.

Håkansson, H., Johanson, J. and Wootz, B. (1977), Influence Tactics in Buyer-Seller Processes. *Industrial Marketing Management*, Vol. 5, pp. 319–332.

Hallén, L. (1980), Sverige på Europamarknaden. *Studentlitteratur*, Lund.

Johanson, J. (1972), Fasta affärsförbindelser vid export. En jämförelse mellan olika exportkanaler. In: Johanson, J. (ed), *Exportstrategiska problem*. Stockholm.

Johanson, J. and Wiedersheim-Paul, F. (1975), The Internationalization of the Firm – Four Swedish Cases. *Journal of Management Studies*, October.

Phillips-Martinsson, J. (1979), *Cross-Cultural Relations in International Marketing*. Stockholm.

Vahlne, J.-E. and Wiedersheim-Paul, F. (1973), Ekonomiskt avstånd–modell och empirisk undersökning. In: Hörnell, E., Vahlne, J.-E. and Wiedersheim-Paul, F. *Export och utlandsetableringar*. Almqvist and Wiksell, Stockholm.

Wiedersheim-Paul, F. (1979), Towards a Model of International Marketing. In: Ståhl, I. (ed.), *Forskning, utbildning, praxis*. EFI, Stockholm.

Wiedersheim-Paul, F. and Erland, O. (1979), Technological Strategies and Internationalization. In: Mattsson, L.-G. and Wiedersheim-Paul, F. (eds.), *Recent Research on the Internationalization of Business*. AImqvist and Wiksell, Uppsala.

23

The effect of national culture on the choice of entry mode

Bruce Kogut and Harbir Singh

Foreign direct investment into the United States has grown dramatically since the early 1970s. Accompanying this increase has been a growth of academic work studying the phenomenon.[1] Whereas impressive information concerning foreign direct investment in the United States in general is available, there has been surprisingly few statistical investigations concerning the choice of entry modes.

The objective of this article is two-fold. First, original data regarding the choice of entry mode by foreign firms is described in terms of country and industry patterns. Second, the factors that influence the choice between joint ventures, wholly owned greenfield (i.e., start-up) investments, and acquisitions are analyzed statistically. In particular, the statistical investigation seeks to explain a striking difference among countries regarding their propensities to enter by acquisition versus other modes. These differences in country propensities towards acquisitions are examined in a framework which relates aspects of a nation's culture to preferences regarding the governance of foreign operations.[2]

This article represents the first statistical test of the relationship between culture and entry choice as an explanation of country patterns of entry modes while controlling for firm- and industry-level variables. Because our measure of culture is derived from the indices of Hofstede [1980], the results validate the usefulness of his constructs, though this was not our primary intention. Moreover, the findings suggest that transaction cost explanations for mode of entry choice must be qualified by factors stemming from the institutional and cultural context.[3]

A PREFATORY NOTE ON TERMINOLOGY

It is important at the outset to define terminology. This article looks at three kinds of entry modes: acquisitions, joint ventures, and greenfield investments. Acquisitions refer to the purchase of stock in an already existing company in an amount sufficient to confer control. All of the acquisitions in our study consist of a controlling equity share with the remaining shares dispersed across many investors. A joint venture is the pooling of assets in a common and separate organization by two or more firms who share joint ownership and control over the use and fruits of these assets.[4] A greenfield investment is a start-up investment in new facilities. Such an investment can be wholly owned or a joint venture. For purposes of simplifying the exposition, we classify all start-up investments which are wholly owned under greenfield and those which involve shared ownership under joint venture.

Many studies, as discussed later, have treated greenfield and acquisition as representing alternative entry modes, with joint ventures being only a question of the degree of ownership. This approach implies that entry and ownership involve two sequential decisions, the first deciding whether to invest in new facilities or to acquire existing ones, the second one on how ownership should be shared. Whereas such an approach is clearly defensible on both theoretical and empirical grounds, we treat joint ventures as a choice made simultaneously with other alternative modes of entry.

Our reasoning can be tersely summarized as follows. Conceptually, it could well be argued that joint ventures are not merely a matter of equity control, but represent a set of governance characteristics appropriate for certain strategic or transaction cost motivations or for the transfer of tacit organizational knowledge [Kogut 1987]. Joint ventures are vehicles by which to share complementary but distinct knowledge which could not otherwise be shared or to coordinate a limited set of activities to influence the competitive positioning of the firm. Empirically, the evidence on whether managers consider joint ventures sequential to, or simultaneous with, other entry choices is slim. It is of interest, therefore, that Gatignon and Anderson [1987], whose results are described in more detail later, find that their statistical model of entry choice discriminates well between wholly owned and shared control choice of entries, but not between wholly owned and the *degree* of shared control. This finding suggests that managers perceive the choice as between wholly owned and joint venture (and possibly other entry modes), with degree of ownership being explained by other factors, such as perhaps the bargaining power of the parties.[5] Consequently, due both to the above conceptual and empirical reasons, we frame the joint venture choice as made simultaneously in consideration with other entry alternatives.

THEORETICAL FRAMEWORK

The theory underlying our approach reflects in some ways a return to an older line of thought in the work on foreign direct investment. Since the publication of Stephen Hymer's thesis in 1960, the economic theory of foreign direct investment has been driven not by country-level variables, such as differences in interest rates, but by industry- and firm-level variables [Hymer 1960]. Industry-level variables reflect barriers to entry and patterns of oligopolistic behavior. Firm-level variables are related to the concept of transaction costs, whereby the transfer of specialized assets between firms is impeded by market failures, thus necessitating the expansion of the firm (in some cases across borders) in order to internalize the transfer. To the extent that the same variables influence whether to enter by foreign direct investment, licensing, or exporting, the choice of the mode of entry is jointly and simultaneously determined.[6]

Because our emphasis in this article is upon country patterns in the entry mode propensities, we do not seek to develop a full theory of entry choice. Rather, we concentrate on only those factors likely to affect national patterns. Observations on differences among countries in their propensities to joint venture, acquire, or invest in greenfield sites have been made by Robinson [1961], Brooke and Remmers [1972], Franko [1976], and Stopford and Haberich [1978] in relation to the lower frequency of overseas joint venture activity by American firms compared to that by European firms. In his study on foreign acquisitions,

Wilson [1980] found that there were significantly different patterns of acquisition among American, British and Japanese corporations.

A number of previous studies lend theoretical and empirical support to the relationship between a firm's country of origin and the mode of entry. Two studies, in particular, isolate the influence of culture on entry mode patterns. The investigations by researchers at the University of Uppsala related foreign direct investment patterns to the 'psychic distance' between countries.[7] By psychic distance, it is meant the degree to which a firm is uncertain of the characteristics of a foreign market. Psychic distance, they reasoned, would be influenced by differences in the culture and language of the home and target countries. Similarly, Puxty [1979] speculated on the relationship between cultural differences and ownership policies regarding overseas subsidiaries. Neither of these studies, however, laid out systematically how cultural differences influence entry choices, or provided large-sample statistical evidence.

We seek to explain differences in country propensities in the choice of entry modes from the point of departure that differences in cultures among countries influence the perception of managers regarding the costs and uncertainty of alternative modes of entry into foreign markets. Assuming revenues constant across alternatives, managers will choose the entry mode which minimizes the perceived costs attached to the mode of entry and subsequent management of the subsidiary. Because differences in national cultures have been shown to result in different organizational and administrative practices and employee expectations, it can be expected that the more culturally distant are two countries, the more distant are their organizational characteristics on average [Bendix 1956; Lincoln, Hanada and Olson 1981]. If cultural factors influence differentially the perceived or real costs and uncertainty of the mode of entry, there should exist country patterns in the propensity of firms to engage in one type of entry mode as opposed to others.

Due to the difficulty of integrating an already existing foreign management, cultural differences are likely to be especially important in the case of an acquisition. Indeed, empirical studies on mostly domestic acquisitions have shown that post-acquisition costs are substantial and are influenced by what Jemison and Sitkin [1986] call the organizational fit of the two firms. They define organizational fit as 'the match between administrative practices, cultural practices, and personal characteristics of the target and parent firms' [Jemison and Sitkin 1986, p. 147]. Sales and Mirvis [1984] document in detail the administrative conflicts following an acquisition when both firms differ strongly in their corporate cultures.

In contrast to the integration costs of an acquisition, a joint venture serves frequently the purpose of assigning management tasks to local partners who are better able to manage the local labor force and relationships with suppliers, buyers, and governments [Franko 1971; Stopford and Wells 1972]. Thus, a joint venture resolves the foreign partner's problems ensuing from cultural factors, though at the cost of sharing control and ownership. Unquestionably, a joint venture is affected by the cultural distance between the partners. But such conflict should not obscure the original motivation to choose a joint venture because the initial alternative of integrating an acquisition appeared more disruptive than delegating management tasks to a local partner. Of course, a joint venture may be troubled not only by the cultural distance of the partners, but also due to concerns over sharing proprietary assets. A wholly owned greenfield investment avoids both the costs of integration and conflict over sharing proprietary assets by imposing the management style of the investing firm on the start-up while preserving full ownership.[8]

For this reason, we expect that the use of acquisitions by foreign firms entering the United States should be dissuaded, the more distant the culture of the country of origin.[9] The following analysis tests the relationship of cultural factors to country patterns in entry mode choice under two different hypotheses:

1. The greater the cultural distance between the country of the investing firm and the country of entry, the more likely a firm will choose a joint venture or wholly owned greenfield over an acquisition.
2. The greater the culture of the investing firm is characterized by uncertainty avoidance regarding organizational practices, the more likely that firm will choose a joint venture or wholly owned greenfield over an acquisition.

Hypothesis 1 is derived from the premise that firms from culturally distant countries will attach greater costs to the management of acquisitions relative to joint ventures or to wholly owned greenfield investments than firms from culturally similar countries.[10] These costs may be perceptual only or accurate appraisals of the increased difficulties of managing a foreign workforce in a culturally distant country. Hypothesis 2 is derived from the premise that acquisitions confront firms with greater uncertainty over the management of foreign operations.[11] Therefore, firms from countries characterized by relatively high uncertainty avoidance in their organizational practices will tend towards joint ventures or greenfield investments.

LITERATURE REVIEW

There have been several previous studies which have found that entry choice is influenced by the firm's uncertainty over the characteristics of the targeted countries. In this section, the central findings are reviewed. These studies differ in terms of which entry modes are being compared and are, as a result, complex to compare. The implications for the choice of entry mode are sorted out more clearly in a subsequent section when discussing the relationship of the explanatory variables.

A common theme in a number of studies has been the identification of perceived uncertainty as a function of a firm's experience in a country. In developing their theory of internationalization based on the Uppsala school's work on psychic distance, Johanson and Vahlne [1977] attributed the evolutionary process by which a firm advances from exporting to joint venturing and wholly owned subsidiaries to the reduction in perceived risk regarding the foreign market as a firm gains in experience. They did not, however, explore the implications for country patterns in entry mode behavior from psychic distances between countries, nor stipulate clearly how the experience of the firm mitigates perceived uncertainty arising from differences in cultures.

The influence of firm experience on entry choice has played a prominent role in several of the studies employing the Harvard Multinational Enterprise Data Base. In their pioneering study on the ownership structure of American multinational firms, Stopford and Wells [1972] found joint ventures, relative to wholly owned activities, were less likely to be chosen, the more central the product to the core business of the firm and more experience the firm had in the relevant country. Similarly, they found that marketing and advertising intensity, as well as research and development intensity, discouraged the use of joint ventures.

Dubin [1975] turned to an investigation of the determinants of foreign acquisitions by American firms over the period of 1948 to 1967. Using bivariate cross-tabulations without statistical testing, he found that the tendency to acquire fell with the size of the firm, its foreign experience, and if the target country was an LDC. His findings, thus, suggest an increasing use of acquisitions the lower the cultural and physical barriers between the home and host countries and the more experience the firm has in the foreign market.

Davidson [1980] analyzed a version of the Multinational Enterprise Data Base which was updated from 1967 to 1975 and traced the establishment of foreign subsidiaries from their inception. Through the identification of statistically significant correlations, he found three patterns: 1) that firms will more likely invest where they or their competitors in the same industry have invested before; 2) that countries which have reputedly similar cultures are a preferred target of investment; and 3) that previous firm-level experience in a country – no matter if licensing or joint venture – leads to an increasing likelihood of wholly owned investment for later entries.

The above studies suggest, therefore, that the choice of entry mode is influenced by cultural differences and firm experience. However, because the statistical studies by Dubin [1975] and Davidson [1980] did not test these relationships while controlling for other variables, the explanation for country patterns could be considered to be derived from two spurious relationships. The first is the relationship between the historically greater involvement of particular countries internationally and the influence of firm experience on entry choice. The second is the relationship between differences in industrial composition among countries, differences in the intensity of marketing and research expenditures across industries, and the influence of the desire of firms to control the international extension of marketing- or research-intensive assets.

In the three studies that investigated the determinants of entry mode while statistically controlling for other variables, experience has not, however, been proven to be instrumental in choice of entry mode. Analyzing entry by acquisition versus greenfield for American, British, German and Japanese firms, Wilson [1980] reported that experience did not significantly influence the decision to invest in foreign countries by a greenfield establishment over an acquisition.[12] The decision to acquire was found, instead, to co-vary positively with diversification and negatively with the proportion of recently established subsidiaries to total establishments and with whether the target country was an LDC.

Caves and Mehra [1986] analyzed 138 decisions of non-American firms to enter the United States by greenfield versus acquisition through a qualitative choice model with industry- and firm-level variables as the independent variables, while controlling for joint ventures. Their data was drawn from a listing of reported announcements for the years of 1974 to 1980. Their results disconfirmed the hypothesis that previous investments in a country influenced a foreign firm's decision to enter by greenfield over acquisition into the United States. Rather, they found that size of the foreign firm, diversity of its product range, and its degree of multinationality positively and significantly influenced the decision to acquire. In addition, industries producing durable goods were more likely to be characterized by entry through acquisition because, argue Caves and Mehra, the adaptation of durable goods to local conditions requires skills better captured through acquisition than through greenfield investment.

Joint ventures were found to be negatively related to the choice of acquisitions, thus supporting the premise of this paper that acquisitions and joint ventures are substitute modes of entry. No control was made for country-level variables.

In a recent study, Gatignon and Anderson [1987] reanalyzed 1267 entry decisions from the Harvard Multinational Database for the years 1960 to 1974, also using a quantal choice model. As described earlier, their analysis of entry as a three-way decision between wholly owned and various levels of joint venture control was not able to discriminate well between the chosen degree of joint venture ownership. Their binomial test of wholly owned versus joint venture, however, confirmed the Stopford and Wells [1972] bivariate results. Wholly owned subsidiaries (greenfield and acquisition) were favored over partial ownership, the greater the R&D and advertising intensity of the foreign firm. They also found support that the degree of multinationality had a negative effect on the likelihood to joint venture.[13] Their dummy variables for regions tended to show strong country patterns. Based on the positive relationships between R&D and marketing/advertising intensity to wholly owned entries, they conclude that a transaction cost theory of entry choice is supported.[14]

In summary, the literature to date has found that uncertainty over the foreign market influences managers' decisions on how to invest overseas, that there are clear but unexplained country patterns in the selection of entry modes, and that both firm- and industry-level variables are related to the choice of entry mode. The previous literature has not, however, clearly extrapolated from the research on cultural traits to implications for country patterns in the relative use of different entry modes, nor has it tested the relationship between cultural factors and entry mode choice while controlling for other factors.

This paper tests explicitly the influence of country cultural characteristics, including attitudes toward uncertainty, upon the choice of the mode of entry into the United States. Though country-level economic variables are currently discounted as explaining why firms invest overseas, cultural differences among countries play a role, this article contends, in explaining how this investment is channeled.

DESCRIPTION OF ENTRY MODE PATTERNS

Because data comparing entry activities of foreign firms in the United States are not easily available, it is worthwhile to report the patterns found in our sample before turning to statistical tests of the above hypotheses. Whereas aggregated data on foreign acquisitions are routinely available from Department of Commerce publications, similar data for joint ventures are generally lacking. In part, this imbalance can be explained by the significance of acquisitions as a mode of entry for foreign firms into the United States. For the years between 1976 and 1983, acquisitions were responsible for over 50% of the foreign direct investment in the United States, rising as high as 79% of the total value in 1981.[15]

On the other hand, data on joint ventures as a mode of entry into the United States is not aggregated and published by the Department of Commerce. While it is thus impossible to have a value estimate of joint ventures, it is possible, based on the sources listed in the appendix, to describe the frequency of the mode of entry across industries and countries. This data is available for acquisitions, greenfield, and joint ventures, as well as other investments not included in this study.

Table 1 provides a breakdown of joint ventures, acquisition, and greenfield by industry for the years 1981 to 1985. There is a clear difference in industry patterns among the modes of entry. Joint ventures are relatively more frequent in pharmaceuticals/chemicals and electric and nonelectric machinery. Acquisitions occur primarily in natural resources, financial services, and miscellaneous manufacturing industries. Chemical and electrical machinery are especially attractive industries for greenfield investments. At a higher level of aggregation, acquisitions tend to be relatively more common than other modes of entry in nonmanufacturing sectors of the economy.

Table 1. Distribution of Modes of Entry by Industrial Sector

	Joint Ventures	Acquisitions	Greenfield	Total N
Resource	18	35	2	55
Paper	3	26	5	34
Chemical	2	15	3	20
Petroleum	25	35	17	77
Rubber	3	3	2	8
Primary Metal	2	20	6	28
Metal Fabrication	2	8	4	14
Machinery	4	7	0	11
Electrical Equipment	24	14	13	51
Transportation	25	21	13	59
Instrumentation	10	3	10	23
Other	3	10	0	13
Manufacturing Communication	1	4	2	7
Wholesale	8	17	3	28
Financial Services	4	30	0	34
Other Services	12	25	5	42
Total	147	274	85	506

The country pattern is given in Table 2. Again, there are strong differences among the modes of entry. For Japan, 46 of its 114 entries are joint ventures.[16] Whereas Japanese acquisitions are not common, Japanese firms have a high proportion of the wholly owned greenfield investments. Scandinavia and, especially France, also lean towards joint ventures. United Kingdom represents the other extreme; 111 of its 141 entries are acquisitions, with the remainder evenly divided between joint ventures and greenfield.

The trends in our sample show clear differences in country propensities regarding the selection of the mode of entry. It is unclear, however, whether these patterns are robust when the relationship is controlled for firm- and industry-level factors. It could well be that the country pattern is generated by differences in the sectoral characteristics of foreign direct investment across the countries of origin. The next section gives a formal statistical test to determine the factors influencing the choice of entry.

SELECTION OF VARIABLES

The hypotheses to be treated posit that the choice of entry is significantly influenced by the cultural characteristics of the home country of the investing firm. Because of the confounding effects of the relationship of firm- and industry-level variables with country identification, it is not possible to test for country effects without controlling for other influences. Consequently, the statistical analysis will investigate the following specification:

Entry Choice $= f$ (cultural characteristics; firm variables, industry variables)

Table 2. Acquisitions, Joint Ventures and Greenfield Entry by Country of Corporate Headquarters

	Joint Ventures	Acquisitions	Greenfield	Total N
United Kingdom	15	111	15	141
Japan	46	35	33	114
Scandinavia	9	5	4	18
Switzerland	4	20	3	27
Germany	6	10	8	24
France	23	6	4	33
Italy	4	3	1	8
Netherlands	6	24	7	37
Belgium	5	10	2	17
Malaysia	1	1	0	2
S. Africa	1	0	2	1
Canada	13	28	3	45
Other	14	20	5	25
Total	147	274	85	506

In previous studies, a number of firm and industry variables have been tested and shown to be significant in explaining the mode of entry choice. These studies indicate several proxies. Because, as discussed below, acquisitions form the baseline case, we discuss the relationship of these proxies to the dependent variable in the context of choosing a joint venture or greenfield relative to acquisition. As our interest is in controlling for specification error, we merely summarize the conventional arguments of the existing literature on the expected relationships between the control variables and the choice variables.

Firm-level variables

Diversification [diversified]

Dubin [1975], Wilson [1980], and Caves and Mehra [1986] have found that firms following diversification strategies are more likely to enter a foreign country by acquisition over greenfield. The presumable explanation for this pattern is that diversified firms are competing on superior management and/or production efficiencies in mature industries, and, therefore, are not concerned with a de novo transfer of a product innovation or brand level. Analogously, diversified firms should be more likely to engage in acquisitions relative to joint ventures.

Country experience [experience]

The effect of previous entry on subsequent entry mode in the same country has not been shown in large-sample multivariate studies to be significant.[17] Nevertheless, theoretically, we can expect that the propensity to joint venture relative to acquisition should decline as a foreign firm learns more about the local environment. It can also be expected as a firm picks up experience, it is more likely to increase its use of acquisitions relative to joint venturing with local partners.

Multinational experience [multinational]

Contrary to their expectation on the sign of the coefficient, Caves and Mehra [1986] found that multinationality (i.e., the number of countries in which a firm has subsidiaries) is significantly correlated with the choice of acquisition over greenfield.[18] One interpretation of this finding is that a firm with greater international experience is able to bear the risk of an acquisition and to integrate subsidiaries of diverse managerial nationality. Along these lines, the greater the multinationality, the greater a firm's ability to acquire; the lesser the multinationality, the more likely a firm will share the risks and management responsibility through a joint venture. Multinationality should, thus, favor the ability to acquire.

Asset size [U.S. asset size and non-U.S. asset size]

It stands to reason that the larger the investing firm, the greater its ability to acquire. Despite the logic, the empirical evidence is mixed. Dubin [1975] found that smaller firms tended to acquire relatively more frequently than large firms, though he did not control for other factors. In his cross-sectional tests, Wilson [1980] confirmed Dubin's findings. However, these studies drew upon entry data of the largest corporations of the United States and other European countries. Caves and Mehra [1986] study did not restrict their attention to entries of the larger corporations. Their results showed that the size of the entering firm is positively and significantly related to entry by acquisition over greenfield. Because acquisitions require generally more financial and managerial resources than joint ventures, size of the foreign firm's assets should be positively correlated with the tendency to acquire. Conversely, acquisitions are discouraged, the larger the assets of the American partner, target firm, or investment size.

Industry-level variables

Industry variables [R&D and advertising]

One explanation for the country pattern is that countries differ in their industrial structures and that choice of entry modes will be influenced by the characteristics of the industry. Because of a substantial literature confirming their importance, industry R&D expenditures to sales and industry media and advertising expenditures to sales were chosen as control variables in the statistical investigations.[19] Data on both variables are taken from the Federal Trade Commission's Line of Business study for 1975.[20]

Conventionally, the relationship of these variables to entry choice is said to discourage joint ventures in order to preserve proprietary assets and to discourage unrelated acquisitions. The previous empirical studies have assumed, however, foreign entry was usually for the purpose of market access or low cost manufacturing. Clearly, foreign entry into the United States may be motivated in order to source technology or purchase brand labels.

The more diverse motives of investing in the American economy make it more difficult to sign the structural variables. For example, firms from R&D-intensive industries might joint venture if they possess the requisite technologies but lack the marketing depth. Or they may tend to acquire if they are investing for technology sourcing. Similarly, firms from marketing-intensive industries might engage in a joint venture if they possess the brand label but lack other resources along the value-added chain. Or they may acquire if they are investing for market penetration and lack label recognition. Stopford and Wells [1972] found that American firms pursuing an advertising-intensive strategy tend to full ownership of their overseas subsidiaries. Their data is drawn, however, from a time when American firms were investing overseas with clear strategic advantages. For our study, it is equally likely that foreign firms are investing in the United States for technology and brand label acquisition as for the exploitation of their proprietary assets. No prediction is made, therefore, on the signs of the coefficients for *R&D* and *Advertising*.[21]

Sectoral dummies [manufacturing and services]

Two sectoral dummies are used in order to control for other exogenous effects not captured by the *R&D* and *Marketing* variables. These dummies are required because there are clear patterns in the modes of entry across services, extractive, and manufacturing industries and we wish to control for sectoral effects not captured by the structural variables. (See Table 1.) Because Japanese firms are active in joint ventures and manufacturing, there would be a bias towards overstating the Japanese contribution in the total number of manufacturing entries and in joint ventures. To avoid a bias, sectoral effects are controlled by using dummies for whether the entry is in manufacturing or in services.

Country-level variables

As noted earlier, previous studies have pinpointed uncertainty as a significant influence upon the investment decision. Whereas uncertainty has been multiply interpreted, one interpretation concerns the ability of the foreign firm to manage the local operations of its subsidiary. The perceived ability to manage may be influenced by two considerations, one concerns the absolute cultural attitudes towards uncertainty avoidance, the second concerning the relative cultural distance between the country of the investing firm and the country of entry. Both considerations are proxied in the specification of the regression equations through the use of variables entitled uncertainty avoidance and cultural distance.

The measures for uncertainty avoidance and cultural distance are derived from the work of Hofstede [1980]. Hofstede found that differences in national cultures vary substantially along four dimensions. These dimensions were labeled uncertainty avoidance, individuality, tolerance of power distance, and masculinity-femininity. Hofstede created ordinal scales for countries for each of these dimensions based on a standardized factor analysis of questionnaires administered between 1968 and 1972 to 88,000 national employees in more than 40 overseas subsidiaries of a major American corporation. Bias for differences in occupational positions among subsidiaries was controlled. As the study consisted of two questionnaires separated by a four-year interval, it was possible to test for the reliability in scores over time; only questions showing a greater than .5 correlation in scores were used to derive the scales.

The indices of Hofstede can be criticized for a number of reasons, especially regarding the internal validity of the dimensions and the method of constructing the scales.[22] Whereas the criticism has a sound basis, Hofstede's study has some appealing attributes, namely, the size of the sample, the codification of cultural traits along a numerical index, and its emphasis on attitudes in the workplace. Our use of the indices are, furthermore, conservative, for if they are poor constructs, they are less likely to be found significant and with the a priori predicted sign.

Based on these scales, the statistical analysis used two cultural variables to test the two hypotheses.

Cultural distance [cultural distance]

We hypothesize that the more culturally distant the country of the investing firm from the United States, the more likely the choice to set up a joint venture. Using Hofstede's indices, a composite index was formed based on the deviation along each of the four cultural dimensions (i.e., power distance, uncertainty avoidance, masculinity/femininity, and individualism) of each country from the United States ranking. The deviations were corrected for differences in the variances of each dimension and then arithmetically averaged. Algebraically, we built the following index:

$$CD_j = \sum_{i=1}^{4} \{(I_{ij} - I_{iu})^2 / V_i\} / 4,$$

where I_{ij} stands for the index for the ith cultural dimension and jth country, V_i is the variance of the index of the ith dimension, u indicates the United States, and CD_j is cultural difference of the jth country from the United States. Though the scaling method imposes weights based on index variance, any resultant measurement error cannot be expected to be correlated theoretically with the other independent variables and should reduce the significance of the statistical relationships.

Uncertainty avoidance [uncertainty avoidance]

Uncertainty avoidance should not be understood as referring to the individual's willingness to bear risk or as the risk profile of a firm regarding its product strategy. Rather, the elements making up the dimension are organizational and managerial in character. The construction is fortunate for our purposes, as we wish to isolate the influence of cultural attitudes towards uncertainty over organizational functions, such as employment relations. The more uncertainty avoiding a culture tends to be, the less attractive is the acquisition mode due to the organizational risks of integrating foreign management into the parent organization.

The above discussion is summarized in Table 3.

MODEL SPECIFICATION

The decision to enter by acquisition, joint venture, or greenfield is modeled as a qualitative choice problem. A multinomial logit model is specified to estimate the effect of the explanatory factors on the probability that each of the three alternatives would be chosen. The multinomial logit allows the explanatory variables to affect differential odds of choosing one alternative relative to another. Thus, the coefficient vector is specific to the alternative, not to the firm making the choice [Judge et al. 1985, pp. 770–72]. Consequently, the specification of the probabilities is:

$$P_{ij} = \exp(x_{ij}B_j) / \sum_{j=1}^{j=3} \exp(x_{ij}B_j),$$

Table 3. Summary of predicted signs

Variable	Joint venture	Greenfield
Diversified	−	−
Experience	−	−
Multinational	−	−
U.S. Asset Size	+	+
Non-U.S. Asset Size	−	−
R&D	NP*	NP
Advertising	NP	NP
Manufacturing	NP	NP
Services	NP	NP
Cultural Distance	+	+
Uncertainty Avoidance	+	+

*NP − No Prediction

where P_{ij} is the probability that the ith firm will choose alternative j, x_{ij} is a vector of variables representing the variables characterizing the ith firm and the jth governance mode and B_j is the vector of coefficients to the independent variables. However, since the probabilities are constrained to sum to one, the system of equations are over-identified. The parameters can be estimated by setting the Bs of one of the alternatives to 0. In our model, it stands to reason to use acquisitions as the baseline case by which to compare the estimated parameters of the other alternatives (joint venture or greenfield).

Under this condition, the specification is reduced to:

$$P_{ij} = \exp(x_{ij}B_j)/1 + \sum_{e=2}^{3} \exp(x_{ij}B_j),$$

with the baseline alternative specified as

$$P_{i1} = 1/1 + \sum_{e=2}^{3} \exp(x_{ij}B_j).$$

The parameters (Bs) are estimated by maximizing a log likelihood function using the Newton-Raphson iteration procedure.[23]

Unfortunately, values for *R&D* and *Advertising* are only available for manufacturing. Since missing values eliminate the entire case from the sample, we follow a technique suggested by Johnston (1972, pp. 238–41).[24] We treat the manufacturing, service, and extractive as three equations with explanatory variables which are not identical. For the nonmanufacturing sectors, *R&D* and *Advertising* are recorded as 0. If we assume the disturbance terms are not correlated, we can run a single multinomial estimation. The dummy variables will pick up the sectoral differences.

RESULTS

The results are provided in Table 4. The estimated coefficients should be interpreted as representing the marginal utility of choosing a joint venture or wholly owned greenfield relative to an acquisition. A positive coefficient signifies that the greater the value of the independent variable, the more likely the alternative (i.e., joint venture or acquisition, as the case may be) will be chosen; the converse is true for a negative sign. *T*-test statistics are given in parentheses.

The estimated parameters for the equation using cultural distance show strong support for the first hypothesis. The effect of *Cultural Distance* is to increase the probability of choosing a joint venture over an acquisition and is significant at the .001 level. Its effect is, however, only significant at the .1 level for greenfield. (We are using a conservative two-tail test, though arguably we could apply, following Caves and Mehra, a one-tail test to the coefficients for which we have predicted signs.) The results for *Uncertainty Avoidance* are more impressive, with the coefficients correctly signed and significant at .001 and .05 for joint venture and greenfield, respectively.

The asset size variables generally are correctly signed. The effect of *U.S. Asset Size* on choosing a joint venture is significant at .001. Clearly, the larger the size of the American partner, the more likely to joint venture than acquire. The effect of *U.S. Asset Size* on choosing greenfield is negative and significant in both the uncertainty avoidance and cultural distance runs at the .1 and .05 level, respectively. It is likely, however, that this result stems from the measurement of asset size for greenfield in terms of the investment and for acquisition or joint venture in terms of the asset size of the target or partner.

The effect of the *Non-U.S. Asset Size* is insignificant for the case of joint venture in the cultural distance estimation, but correctly signed, though still insignificant, for the uncertainty avoidance estimation. Interestingly, larger size of the foreign firm encourages greenfield over acquisition at the .01 level in the cultural distance run and .05 in the uncertainty avoidance run; this result confirms the finding of Dubin.

Experience and *Multinationality* are correctly signed (with the exception of the coefficient to *Multinationality* for joint venture in the *Uncertainty Avoidance* estimation). However, the *t*-tests are not significant. Similar to earlier studies, therefore, experience effects as measured by prior entries are not shown to be robust under large-sample multiple regression estimates. Unlike some other studies (e.g., Caves and Mehra [1986], and Gatignon and Anderson [1987]), our measure for multinational experience is not found to be significant.

We also do not find diversified firms more likely to enter by acquisition. To the contrary, the variable *Diversified* is positively signed, showing that diversified firms tend to enter by joint venture or greenfield. The results are not significant and it would be premature at this time to speculate on the causes.

The industry sectoral variables are of some interest. Of the dummy variables, only *Manufacturing* is significant in both equations, indicating a preference for greenfield investment over acquisition in the manufacturing sector. As shown later, this effect is almost entirely due to Japanese investments.

The most interesting of the industry-level variables is the positive effect of *R&D* on joint venture and greenfield entry, though only significant in the former case (at .1 for the cultural distance estimation and .05 for uncertainty avoidance). Elsewhere, we have shown that joint ventures appear to be particularly encouraged in growing and R&D-intensive industries [Kogut and Singh 1987]. This result is counter to previous findings and some transaction

Table 4. Parameter estimates for multinomial logit model of entry choice

	Constant	Diversified	Experience	Multi-national	U.S. asset size	Non-U.S. asset size	R&D	Advertising	Manufac-turing	Services	Cultural distance	Uncertainty avoidance
Hypothesis 1												
Acquisition	0	0	0	0	0	0	0	0	0	0	0	—
Joint Venture	-10.3	.12	$-.68$	0.009	2.64	.13	.181	$-.24$	1.06	$-.07$	1.35	—
	$(-4.08)^a$	(.58)	$(-.85)$	(.42)	$(4.94)^a$	(.23)	$(1.90)^c$	$(-.73)$	(.95)	$(-.04)$	$(4.7)^a$	
Greenfield	-8.6	.19	-0.63	$-.009$	$-.75$	1.3	.096	$-.16$	3.59	-7.80	.40	—
	$(-4.13)^a$	(1.08)	$(-.96)$	$(-.58)$	$(-1.93)^c$	$(2.78)^b$	(1.37)	$(-.95)$	$(3.15)^a$	$(-.16)$	$(-1.84)^c$	
Hypothesis 2												
Acquisition	0	0	0	0	0	0	0	0	0	0	—	0
Joint Venture	-10.6	.28	$-.78$	.001	2.42	$-.51$	.21	.24	.85	.28	—	.73
	$(-4.62)^a$	(1.33)	(-1.03)	(.04)	$(4.99)^a$	$(-.97)$	$(2.35)^b$	(.91)	(.87)	(.19)		$(4.4)^a$
Greenfield	-9.11	.23	$-.68$	$-.003$	$-.73$	1.09	.09	$-.16$	3.66	-8.6	—	.03
	$(-4.37)^a$	(1.33)	(-1.05)	$(-.23)$	$(-1.86)^c$	$(2.15)^b$	(1.35)	$(-.96)$	$(3.2)^a$	$(-.11)$		$(2.23)^b$

(*t*-statistics in parentheses)
N = 228   [a] $p<.10$ [b] $p<.5$ [c] $p<.01$

cost arguments. A possible interpretation is that non-U.S. firms enter the United States to tap into American technology by joint ventures. At a minimum, given the positive sign to *R&D* for both joint ventures and greenfield (though not significant for the latter), acquisitions appear to be discouraged in high R&D-intensive industries.

Advertising is negatively related to joint ventures and greenfield investments. Though the results are not significant, they are consistent with Caves and Mehra's [1986] argument that acquisitions are favored for the purpose of brand label or product adaptation. This relationship is expected to be more pronounced for mature industries, which we will explore more fully in further work.

CONTROLLING FOR JAPANESE ENTRIES

It could be argued that the cultural results are driven by outliers, namely, that Japan scores highly distant in culture from the United States and scores high on uncertainty avoidance. At the same time, Japanese firms tend toward greenfield and joint venture entries. Thus, the results could be interpreted as a primarily Japanese effect.

From one point of view, Japan as an outlier is consistent with our argument and this result should be expected to hold for entries from other countries that are culturally different from the United States but whose firms have yet to establish a strong foreign investment position. Nevertheless, the effects of cultural distance and uncertainty avoidance should be expected to hold for the sample in the absence of Japanese entries. To show this, we reestimate the earlier equations on a subsample of the data, having removed the Japanese cases. These results are given in Table 5.

The effects of culture are indeed weaker but still correctly signed and significant in two cases. *Cultural Distance* is significant at .05 for joint ventures and just shy of .15 for greenfield. (Again, it is important to note that under a one-tail test, it is significant at .1.) The *Uncertainty Avoidance* effect is negligible in the case of joint ventures but significant at .05 for greenfield.

The other effects remain largely the same as before, except for changes in significance. Interestingly, *Multinationality* is positively signed, showing that acquisitions are discouraged for the more multinational of corporations. On the other hand, *Experience* increases in significance in the runs, and is significant in three of the runs at .1 using a one-tail test. The positive effect of *R&D* for joint ventures remains significant at the .05 level in both runs. The manufacturing dummy coefficient is highly insignificant. Clearly, then, the earlier sectoral effect is driven by the sectoral preference of Japanese firms.

In summary, the statistical estimations provide strong support that cultural distance and national attitudes towards uncertainty avoidance influence the choice of entry mode. It should be underlined that these relationships are robust despite the controls added for industry- and firm-level effects. The weaker results for the subsample when the Japanese entries are removed are partly a result of the reduced sample size (the cases drop from 228 to 173) and partly a result of the outlier effect of Japan.[25] It is impressive, therefore, that cultural effects appear to be still persistent despite the reduction in sample size and the diminishment in variance of the cultural variables.

Table 5. Parameter estimates for multinomial logit model of entry choice excluding Japanese entries

	Constant	Diversified	Experience	Multi-national	U.S. asset size	Non-U.S. asset size	R&D	Advertising	Manufac-turing	Services	Cultural distance	Uncertainty avoidance
Hypothesis 1												
Acquisition	0	0	0	0	0	0	0	0	0	0	0	—
Joint Venture	−21.0	.13	−1.29	−0.01	3.44	−.42	.32	−.31	11.	1.45	1.23	—
	(−.25)	(.41)	(−1.20)	(−.31)	(3.92)[a]	(−.63)	(2.11)[b]	(−.70)	(.14)	(.009)	(2.15)[b]	—
Greenfield	−18.4	.18	−0.18	.006	−.79	1.36	−.02	−.18	13.8	−.009	.59	—
	(−0.19)	(.88)	(−.14)	(.35)	(−1.81)[c]	(2.41)[b]	(−.17)	(−.97)	(.15)	(.000)	(1.48)	—
Hypothesis 2												
Acquisition	0	0	0	0	0	0	0	0	0	0	—	0
Joint Venture	−20.0	.13	−1.66	.001	3.34	−0.43	−.28	−.23	11.1	−0.05	—	.02
	(−.23)	(.42)	(−1.46)	(.03)	(3.9)[a]	(−.68)	(2.24)[b]	(−.58)	(.13)	(−.00)	—	(0.28)
Greenfield	−19.5	.26	−0.50	.01	−.83	1.13	−.02	−.18	13.9	.20	—	.04
	(−.21)	(1.24)	(.41)	(.52)	(−1.89)[c]	(1.94)[c]	(−.23)	(−1.01)	(.15)	(.001)	—	(1.96)[b]

(t-statistics in parentheses) [a]p<.01 [b]p<0.5 [c]p<.01

CONCLUSIONS

The above results offer the first large-sample multiple regression test of the prevailing view that entry mode selection is influenced by cultural factors. The results have a secondary implication in terms of validating the usefulness of Hofstede's measures of cultural dimensions. Unquestionably, a scale measuring the cultural characteristics at the firm level would be preferable. Yet, the collection of such data appears formidable at this time. It is, therefore, all the more remarkable that the strength of the results were found, despite using measures of national cultural attitudes which were developed for other purposes. The results should be interpreted with care. The variable of uncertainty avoidance is defined in the context of organizational and managerial preferences; it is not a measure of cultural attitudes towards risk in a larger sense. Furthermore, the results may only have validity within a particular historical time. Since foreign direct investment has been concentrated historically between the United States and Europe, which are relatively culturally similar, there are confounding effects of cultural distance and experience. As Japan and other Asian countries continue to increase their overseas investments in the West, cultural distance may be increasingly offset by growing experience at the firm level. Though we have tried to control for such effects, it could well be that our proxy variables were insufficient.

A final consideration which deserves further exploration is a more refined analysis of entry decisions in the context of oligopolistic gaming. Competitive dynamics, such as the rush to invest, are likely to influence the entry choice. In addition, the relationship among the variables may change depending on the functional purpose of the entry. Both refinements are the subject of current work.

The results have a wider implication outside of country patterns and the choice of entry. The above study suggests that when economic choice is compared across countries, cultural characteristics are likely to have profound implications. Whereas theories of internalization and the firm may be culturally robust, their empirical application in a comparative setting appears to warrant the consideration of cultural differences on the costs and risks which managers attach to different modes of transacting.

Whether these results are interpreted as contradicting an internalization theory of entry choice is largely a question of the definition of transaction costs. To some, transaction costs are broadly defined to include communication and control costs, even if these costs are derived from cultural factors. In our view, it is theoretically and empirically interesting to distinguish between transaction costs that are independent of a firm's country of origin and those that are determined by cultural factors. The multinational corporation is the heir, to use Philip Curtin's [1984] expression, of the historical cross-cultural broker in world trade. But no matter how superior the current multinational corporation may be in replacing the skills of traders by the international extension of organizational boundaries, the management of these firms are likely to be influenced by the dominant country culture. The results of this paper suggest that further investigation into the cultural determinants of managerial decision-making is soundly warranted.

APPENDIX: DATA SOURCES

Data on joint ventures, acquisitions, and greenfield are not compiled systematically by the United States government and must, therefore, be gleaned from a number of publicly-available sources. Data on acquisitions were taken from two sources: the Department of Commerce's publication *Foreign Direct Investment in the United States* for the years 1981 to 1985 and *Mergerstat Review*, W.T. Grimm & Company, Chicago, 1984, for the years 1981, 1982 and 1983. Acquisitions valued less than $10 million were excluded. In addition to the Commerce publication cited above, sources used for joint ventures were: *Mergers and Acquisitions* and the *Yearbook on Corporate Mergers, Joint Ventures, and Corporate Policy*. For the statistical investigation, data for joint ventures were taken for the years 1981 to 1985. Data on greenfield investments were found in *Foreign Direct Investment in the United States*, again for the years 1981 to 1985.

NOTES

1. For a review. see Ajami and Ricks [1981]; Arpan, Flowers and Ricks [1981]; McClain [1983]; and Hood and Young [1980].

2. An exploratory investigation of strategic motives for the choice of entry is provided in Kogut and Singh [1987].

3. For an extensive argument along these lines, see Robbins [1987].

4. A joint venture is both legally and conceptually different from a minority equity participation investment, where a firm invests directly into a second company but does not share control with a third party.

5. We would like to thank Jean-François Hennart for this observation on the Anderson-Gatignon paper, which came to our attention subsequent to submitting this article for review.

6. Caves (1982, chap. 3) argues similarly in his discussion on the joint determination of exporting and foreign direct investment.

7. The main findings are reported in Hornell, Vahlne and Wiedersheim-Paul [1973]. A brief English description is given in Johanson and Vahlne [1977].

8. The numerous anecdotes on the motivations of Japanese firms to invest in greenfield sites in rural areas are consistent with this argument.

9. It is important to note that our hypothesis is stated at the county level to represent average tendencies. We cannot make statements to the particular firm without more detailed knowledge of the correspondence of the national to corporate culture.

10. Cultural distance is, in most respects, similar to the 'psychic distance' used by the Uppsala school.

11. A common confusion is to treat uncertainty avoidance as equivalent to risk attitudes in general. We, in agreement with Hofstede [1980], use uncertainty avoidance in the original sense of Cyert and March to refer to the way uncertainty is organizationally resolved as separate from the issue of whether an organization or firm chooses or avoids risky environments for a given return.

12. Wilson's data also came from the Multinational Data Base on 187 U.S. multinationals for the period up to 1967, plus from the activities of 202 foreign-based multinationals through 1971.

13. They called this variable an experience effect, but in order to be consistent with our description of similar variables in other studies, we have relabeled it as a measure of multinationality in accordance with Caves and Mehra.

14. Another interpretation is that the results confirm that firms maintain in-house what Dunning [1977] calls 'ownership advantages'.

15. R. David Belli, 'U.S. Business Enterprises Acquired or Established by Foreign Direct Investors in 1983,' *Survey of Current Business*, Department of Commerce, 1984.

16. Though high, it is lower than the 73% reported by Tsurumi [1976] for Japanese overseas manufacturing subsidiaries in 1971. However, Tsurumi included subsidiaries in which Japanese firms had less than a 25% share. If we take out these subsidiaries (which are better considered as minority investments), then the percentage is 60%. Caves reports Tsurumi's estimate as 82%, but we have been unable to locate the source of the figure [Caves 1982, pp. 89–90].

17. Caves and Mehra [1985] proxied experience by whether the firm had made a previous investment in the United States. Wilson [1980] used the proportion of subsidiaries established before an arbitrarily chosen breakpoint.

18. On the other hand, Steuber et al. [1973] found that the percentage of equity share in a United Kingdom subsidiary by a foreign firm increased with the multinationality of the parent.

19. For a summary of studies on R&D and advertising, see Scherer [1980, chaps. 14 and 15]. For a summary of research on the relation of R&D and advertising to foreign entry choice, see Caves [1982, chap. 1].

20. The line of business data are drawn from confidential government surveys of businesses. Though somewhat dated, the published summary statistics for R&D have been found to be reasonably stable over time. For evidence, see Scherer [1982]. We have made a parallel assumption for *Advertising* expenditures.

21. This argument is consistent with Caves and Mehra [1986].

22. Hofstede [1980] points out, however, that the external validity is reasonable high when tested against other variables which should be correlated with cultural differences.

23. We would like to thank Hubert Gatignon for sharing his program and his advice with us.

24. We are indebted to Tom Pugel for this suggestion.

25. Attempts to avoid the loss in sample size by using a country dummy for Japan with the full sample floundered due to the collinearity between the Japan dummy and cultural measures (.81 for *Cultural Distance* and .86 for *Uncertainty Avoidance*).

ACKNOWLEDGEMENTS

Of the many helpful contributions, the authors would like to acknowledge Erin Anderson, Ned Bowman, Mark Casson, Richard Caves, Wujin Chu, Hubert Gatignon, Jean François Hennart, Jake Jacoby, Tom Pugel, Steve Young, and the anonymous referees. The authors thank Dileep Hurry, Ommer Khaw, Eirene Chen, and Craig Stevens for their research assistance. Funding for the project was provided by the Reginald H. Jones Center of the Wharton School under a grant from AT&T.

REFERENCES

Abbegglen, J.C. and Stalk, G. (1984). The role of foreign companies in Japanese acquisitions. *The Journal of Business Strategy*, **4**, 3–10.

Ajami, R.A. and Ricks, D.A. (1981). Motives of non-American firms investing in the U.S. *Journal of International Business Studies*, **13** (Winter), 25–34.

Arpan, J.S., Flowers, E.B. and Ricks, D.A. (1981). Foreign direct investment in the United States. *Journal of International Business Studies*, **12** (Spring/Summer), 137–54.

Bendix, R. 1956. *Work and authority in industry: Ideologies of management in the course of industrialization.* Berkeley: University of California.

Brooke, M.Z. and Remmers, H.L. eds. (1972). *The multinational company in Europe: Some key problems.* London: Longman.

Caves, R.E. (1982). *Multinational enterprise and economic analysis.* Cambridge, U.K.: Cambridge University Press.

—— and Mehra, S. (1986). Entry of foreign multinationals into U.S. manufacturing industries. In M. Porter, ed., *Competition in global industries.* Boston: Harvard Business School.

Curtin, P. (1984). *Cross-cultural trade in world history.* London: Cambridge University Press.

Davidson, W.H. (1980). The location of foreign direct investment activity: Country characteristics and experience effects. *Journal of International Business Studies*, **12** (Fall), 9–22.

Dubin, M. (1975). *Foreign acquisitions and the spread of the multinational firm.* D.B.A. thesis, Graduate School of Business Administration, Harvard University.

Dunning, J. (1977). Trade, location of economic activity and the MNE: A search for an eclectic theory. In B. Ohlin, ed., *The international allocation of economic activity.* London: Holmes and Meier.

Franko, L.G. (1976). *The European multinationals.* Stanford, CT: Greylock Publishers.

Gatignon, H. and Anderson, E. (1987). The multinational corporation's degree of control over foreign subsidiaries: An empirical test of a transaction cost explanation. Report Number 87–103, Marketing Science Institute, Cambridge, Massachusetts.

Hofstede, G. (1980). *Culture's consequences: International differences in work-related values.* Beverly Hills: Sage Publications.

Hood, N. and Young, S. (1980). Recent patterns of foreign direct investment by British multinational enterprises in the United States. *National Westminster Bank Quarterly Review*: 21–32.

Hornell, E., Vahlne, J.E. and Wiedersheim-Paul, F. (1973). *Export och utlandsetableringar.* Uppsala: Almqvist and Wiksell.

Hymer, S. (1960). *The international operations of national firms: A study of direct foreign investment.* Ph.D. thesis, Department of Economics, Massachusetts Institute of Technology.

Jemison, D.B. and Sitkin, S.B. (1986). Corporate acquisitions: A process perspective. *Academy of Management Review,* **11**, 145–63.

Johanson. J. and Vahlne J.E. (1977). The internationalization process of the firm – A model of knowledge development and increasing foreign market commitments. *Journal of International Business Studies,* **8** (Spring/Summer), 22–32.

Johnston, J. (1972). *Econometric methods.* New York: McGraw-Hill.

Judge, G., Griffiths, W., Hill, R., Luetkephl, H. and Lee, T. (1985). *The theory and practice of econometrics.* New York: John Wiley.

Kogut, B. (1987). Joint ventures: Theoretical and empirical perspectives. *Strategic Management Journal,* forthcoming.

——. and Singh, H. (1987). Entering the United States by joint venture: Industry structure and competitive rivalry. In F. Contractor and P. Lorange, eds., *Cooperative Strategies in International Business.* Lexington, MA: Lexington Press.

Lincoln, J.R., Hanada, M. and Olson, J. (1981). Cultural orientations and individual reactions to organizations: A study of employees of Japanese-owned firms. *Administrative Science Quarterly,* **25**, 93–115.

McClain, David. (1983). Foreign direct investment in the United States: Old currents, 'new waves,' and the theory of direct investment. In C.P. Kindleberger and D. Audretsch, eds., *The Multinational Corporation in the (1980)s.* Cambridge, MA: MIT Press.

Pate, J.L. (1969). Joint venture activity. (1960–1968). *Economic Review,* Cleveland: Federal Reserve Board.

Pugel, T.A. (1981). Technology, transfer and the neoclassical theory of international trade. In R.G. Hawkins and A.J. Prasad, eds., *Technology Transfer and Economic Development.* Greenwich, CT: JAI Press.

Puxty, A.G. (1979). Some evidence concerning cultural differentials in ownership policies of overseas subsidiaries. *Management International Review,* **19**, 39–50.

Robbins, J. (1987). Organizational economics: Notes on the use of transaction cost theory in the study of organizations. *Administrative Science Quarterly,* **32**, 68–86.

Robinson, R.D. (1961). Management attitudes toward joint and mixed ventures abroad. *Western Business Review.*

Sales, A.L. and Mirvis, P.H. (1984). When cultures collide: Issues in acquisition. In *Managing organizational transitions.* Homewood, IL: Irwin.

Scherer, F.M. (1980). *Industrial market structure and economic performance.* Chicago: Rand McNally College Publishing Company.

——. (1982). Inter-industry technology flows and productivity growth. *Review of Economies and Statistics,* **64** (November), 627–34.

Steuber, M.D. et al. (1973). *The impact of foreign direct investment on the United Kingdom.* London: Department of Trade and Industry.

Stopford, J. and Wells, L. (1972). *Managing the multinational enterprise: Organization of the firm and ownership of the subsidiaries.* New York: Basic Books.

Stopford, J.M. and Haberich, K.O. (1978). Ownership and control of foreign operations. In M. Ghertman and J. Leontiades, eds., *European Research in International Business,* pp. 141–67. Amsterdam: North Holland.

Wilson, B. (1980). The propensity of multinational companies to expand through acquisitions. *Journal of International Business Studies,* **12** (Spring/Summer), 59–65.

24

The business of international business is culture

Geert Hofstede

CULTURE DEFINED

Management is getting things done through (other) people. This is true the world over. In order to achieve this, one has to know the 'things' to be done, and one has to know the people who have to do them. Understanding people means understanding their background, from which present and future behavior can be predicted. Their background has provided them with a certain culture. The word 'culture' is used here in the sense of 'the collective programming of the mind which distinguishes the members of one category of people from another'. The 'category of people' can be a nation, region, or ethnic group (national etc. culture), women versus men (gender culture), old versus young (age group and generation culture), a social class, a profession or occupation (occupational culture), a type of business, a work organization or part of it (organizational culture), or even a family.

NATIONAL CULTURE DIFFERENCES

In three different research projects, one among subsidiaries of a multinational corporation (IBM) in 64 countries and the other two among students in 10 and 23 countries, respectively, altogether five dimensions of national culture differences were identified (Hofstede, 1980, 1983, 1986, 1991; Hofstede and Bond, 1984, 1988; The Chinese Culture Connection, 1987):

(1) Power distance

This is the extent to which the less powerful members of organizations and institutions (like the family) accept and expect that power is distributed unequally. This represents inequality (more versus less), but defined from below, not from above. It suggests that society's level of inequality is endorsed by the followers as much as by the leaders. Power and inequality, of course, are extremely fundamental facts of any society and anybody with some international experience will be aware that 'all societies are unequal, but some are more unequal than others'.

Table 1 lists some of the differences in the family, the school, and the work situation between small and large power distance cultures. The statements refer to extremes; actual

Reprinted with permission from *International Business Review*, 1994, **3**(1), 1–14.

Table 1. Distances according to power distance

Small power distance societies	Large power distance societies
In the family:	
Children encouraged to have a will of their own	Children educated towards obedience to parents
Parents treated as equals	Parents treated as superiors
At school:	
Student-centered education (initiative)	Teacher-centered education (order)
Learning represents impersonal 'truth'	Learning represents personal 'wisdom' from teacher (guru)
At work place:	
Hierarchy means an inequality of roles, established for convenience	Hierarchy means existential inequality
Subordinates expect to be consulted	Subordinates expect to be told what to do
Ideal boss is resourceful democrat	Ideal boss is benevolent autocrat (good father)

situations may be found anywhere in between the extremes. People's behavior in the work situation is strongly affected by their previous experiences in the family and in the school: the expectations and fears about the boss are projections of the experiences with the father – or mother – and the teachers. In order to understand superiors, colleagues and subordinates in another country we have to know something about families and schools in that country.

(2) Individualism versus collectivism

Individualism on the one side versus its opposite, collectivism, is the degree to which individuals are integrated into groups. On the individualist side, we find societies in which the ties between individuals are loose: everyone is expected to look after him/herself and his/her immediate family. On the collectivist side, we find societies in which people from birth onwards are integrated into strong, cohesive in-groups, often extended families (with uncles, aunts and grandparents) which continue protecting them in exchange for unquestioning loyalty. The word 'collectivism' in this sense has no political meaning: it refers to the group, not to the state. Again, the issue addressed by this dimension is an extremely fundamental one, regarding all societies in the world.

Table 2 lists some of the differences between collectivist and individualist cultures; most real cultures will be somewhat in between these extremes. The words 'particularism' and 'universalism' in Table 2 are common sociological categories (Parsons and Shils, 1951, 1977). Particularism is a way of thinking in which the standards for the way a person should be treated depend on the group or category to which this person belongs. Universalism is a way of thinking in which the standards for the way a person should be treated are the same for everybody.

(3) Masculinity versus femininity

Masculinity versus its opposite, femininity, refers to the distribution of roles between the sexes which is another fundamental issue for any society to which a range of solutions are found.

Table 2. Differences according to collectivism/individualism

Collectivist societies	Individualist societies
In the family:	
Education towards 'we' consciousness	Education towards 'I' consciousness
Opinions pre-determined by group	Private opinion expected
Obligations to family or in-group:	Obligations to self:
– harmony	– self-interest
– respect	– self-actualization
– shame	– guilt
At school:	
Learning is for the young only	Permanent education
Learning how to do	Learn how to learn
At the work place:	
Value standards differ for in-group and out-groups: particularism	Same value standards apply to all: universalism
Other people are seen as members of their group	Other people seen as potential resources
Relationship prevails over task	Task prevails over relationship
Moral order of employer–employee relationship	Calculative model of employer–employee relationship

The IBM studies revealed that: (a) women's values differ less among societies than men's values; (b) men's values from one country to another contain a dimension from very assertive and competitive and maximally different from women's values on the one side, to modest and caring and similar to women's values on the other. The assertive pole has been called 'masculine' and the modest, caring pole 'feminine'. The women in feminine countries have the same modest, caring values as the men; in the masculine countries they are somewhat assertive and competitive, but not as much as the men, so that these countries show a gap between men's values and women's values.

Table 3 lists some of the differences in the family, the school, and the work place, between the most feminine versus the most masculine cultures, in analogy to Tables 1 and 2.

(4) Uncertainty avoidance

Uncertainty avoidance as a fourth dimension was found in the IBM studies and in one of the two student studies. It deals with a society's tolerance for uncertainty and ambiguity: it ultimately refers to man's search for truth. It indicates to what extent a culture programs its members to feel either uncomfortable or comfortable in unstructured situations. Unstructured situations are novel, unknown, surprising and different from usual. Uncertainty avoiding cultures try to minimize the possibility of such situations by strict laws and rules, safety and security measures, and on the philosophical and religious level by the belief in absolute truth; 'there can only be one truth and we have it'. People in uncertainty avoiding countries are also more emotional, and motivated by inner nervous energy. The opposite type, uncertainty accepting cultures, are more tolerant of opinions different from what they are used to: they try to have as few rules as possible, and on the philosophical and religious

Table 3. Differences according to femininity/masculinity

Feminine societies	Masculine societies
In the family:	
Stress on relationships	Stress on achievement
Solidarity	Competition
Resolution of conflicts by compromise and negotiation	Resolution of conflicts by fighting them out
At school:	
Average student is norm	Best students are norm
System rewards students' social adaptation	System rewards students' academic performance
Student's failure at school is relatively minor accident	Student's failure at school is disaster – may lead to suicide
At the work place:	
Assertiveness ridiculed	Assertiveness appreciated
Undersell yourself	Oversell yourself
Stress on life quality	Stress on careers
Intuition	Decisiveness

level they are relativist and allow many currents to flow side by side. People within these cultures are more phlegmatic and contemplative, and not expected by their environment to express emotions.

Table 4 lists some of the differences in the family, the school, and the workplace, between weak and strong uncertainty avoidance cultures.

(5) Long term versus short term orientation

This fifth dimension was found in a study among students in 23 countries around the world, using a questionnaire designed by Chinese scholars (The Chinese Culture Connection, 1987). It can be said to deal with Virtue regardless of Truth. Values associated with long term orientation are thrift and perseverance: values associated with short term orientation are respect for tradition, fulfilling social obligations, and protecting one's 'face', Both the positively and the negatively rated values of this dimension remind us of the teachings of Confucius (King and Bond, 1985). It was originally called 'Confucian dynamism'; however, the dimension also applies to countries without a Confucian heritage.

There has been insufficient research as yet on the implications of differences along this dimension to allow the composition of a table of differences in the family, the school and the work place similar to those for the other four dimensions (Tables 1–4).

Scores on the first four dimensions were obtained for 50 countries and three regions on the basis of the IBM study, and on the fifth dimension for 23 countries on the basis of the student data collected by Bond et al. All scores have been transformed to a scale from approximately 0 for the lowest scoring country to approximately 100 for the highest. Table 5 shows the scores for twelve countries. For the full list the reader is referred to Hofstede (1991).

Power distance scores tend to be high for Latin, Asian and African countries and smaller for Germanic countries. Individualism prevails in developed and Western countries, while

Table 4. Differences according to uncertainty avoidance

Weak uncertainty avoidance societies	Strong uncertainty avoidance societies
In the family:	
What is different, is ridiculous or curious	What is different, is dangerous
Ease, indolence, low stress	Higher anxiety and stress
Aggression and emotions not shown	Showing of aggression and emotions accepted
At school:	
Students comfortable with:	Students comfortable with:
– Unstructured learning situations	– Structured learning situations
– Vague objectives	– Precise objectives
– Broad assignments	– Detailed assignments
– No time tables	– Strict time tables
Teachers may say 'I don't know'	Teachers should have all the answers
At the work place:	
Dislike of rules – written or unwritten	Emotional need for rules – written or unwritten
Less formalization and standardization	More formalization and standardization

collectivism prevails in less developed and Eastern countries; Japan takes a middle position on this dimension. Masculinity is high in Japan, in some European countries like Germany, Austria and Switzerland, and moderately high in Anglo countries; it is low in Nordic countries and in The Netherlands and moderately low in some Latin and Asian countries like France, Spain and Thailand. Uncertainty avoidance scores are higher in Latin countries, in Japan, and in German speaking countries, lower in Anglo, Nordic, and Chinese culture countries. A long term orientation is mostly found in East Asian countries, in particular in China, Hong Kong, Taiwan, Japan, and South Korea.

The grouping of country scores points to some of the roots of cultural differences. These should be sought in the common history of similarly scoring countries. All Latin countries, for example, score relatively high on both power distance and uncertainty avoidance. Latin countries (those today speaking a Romance language, i.e. Spanish, Portuguese, French or Italian) have inherited at least part of their civilization from the Roman empire. The Roman empire in its days was characterized by the existence of a central authority in Rome, and a system of law applicable to citizens anywhere. This established in its citizens' minds the value complex which we still recognize today: centralization fostered large power distance and a stress on laws fostered strong uncertainty avoidance. The Chinese empire also knew centralization, but it lacked a fixed system of laws: it was governed by men rather than by laws. In the present-day countries once under Chinese rule, the mindset fostered by the empire is reflected in large power distance but medium to weak uncertainty avoidance. The Germanic part of Europe, including Great Britain, never succeeded in establishing an enduring common central authority and countries which inherited its civilizations show smaller power distance. Assumptions about historical roots of cultural differences always remain speculative but in the given examples they are quite plausible. In other cases they remain hidden in the course of history (Hofstede, 1980, pp. 127, 179, 235, 294).

The country scores on the five dimensions are statistically correlated with a multitude of other data about the countries. For example, power distance is correlated with the use of

Table 5. Scores of 12 countries on five dimensions of national cultures

Country	Power distance		Individualism		Masculinity		Uncertainty avoidance		Long term orientation	
	Index	Rank	Index	Rank	Index	Rank	Index	Rank	Index	Rank
Brazil	69	14	38	26–27	49	27	76	21–22	65	6
France	68	15–16	71	10–11	43	35–36	86	10–15	no data	
Germany	35	42–44	67	15	66	9–10	65	29	31	14–15
Great Britain	35	42–44	89	3	66	9–10	35	47–48	25	18–19
Hong Kong	68	15–16	25	37	57	18–19	29	49–50	96	2
India	77	10–11	48	21	56	20–21	40	45	61	7
Japan	54	33	46	22–23	95	1	92	7	80	4
The Netherlands	38	40	80	4–5	14	51	53	35	44	10
Sweden	31	47–48	71	10–11	5	53	29	49–50	33	12
Thailand	64	21–23	20	39–41	34	44	64	30	56	8
USA	40	38	91	1	62	15	46	43	29	17
Venezuela	81	5–6	12	50	73	3	76	21–22	no data	

Ranks: 1 = highest, 53 = lowest (for long term orientation, 23 = lowest)

violence in domestic politics and with income inequality in a country. Individualism is correlated with national wealth (per capita gross national product) and with mobility between social classes from one generation to the next. Masculinity is correlated negatively with the share of gross national product that governments of wealthy countries spend on development assistance to the Third World. Uncertainty avoidance is associated with Roman Catholicism and with the legal obligation in developed countries for citizens to carry identity cards. Long term orientation is correlated with national economic growth during the past 25 years, showing that what led to the economic success of the East Asian economies in this period is their populations' cultural stress on the future-oriented values of thrift and perseverance.

THE CULTURAL LIMITS OF MANAGEMENT THEORIES

The culture of a country affects its parents and its children, teachers and students, labour union leaders and members, politicians and citizens, journalists and readers, managers and subordinates. Therefore management practices in a country are culturally dependent, and what works in one country does not necessarily work in another. However not only the managers are human and children of their culture; the management teachers, the people who wrote and still write theories and create management concepts, are also human and constrained by the cultural environment in which they grew up and which they know. Such theories and concepts cannot be applied in another country without further proof; if applicable at all, it is often only after considerable adaptation. Four examples follow.

(1) Performance appraisal systems

These are recommended in the Western management literature. They assume that employees' performance will be unproved if they receive direct feedback about what their superior thinks of them, which may well be the case in individualist cultures. However, in collectivist countries such direct feedback destroys the harmony which is expected to govern interpersonal relationships. It may cause irreparable damage to the employee's 'face' and ruin his or her loyalty to the organization. In such cultures, including all East Asian and Third World countries, feedback should rather be given indirectly, for example through the withdrawing of a favor, or via an intermediary person trusted by both superior and employee.

(2) Management by objectives

Management by Objectives (MBO) is a management concept developed in the USA. Under a system of MBO, subordinates have to negotiate about their objectives with their superiors. The system therefore assumes a cultural environment in which issues can be settled by negotiation rather than rules, which means a medium to low power distance and a not too high uncertainty avoidance. In the German environment it had to be adapted to the more structured culture of a stronger uncertainty avoidance; it became 'Führung durch Zielvereinbarung' which is much more formal than the US model (Ferguson, 1973).

(3) Strategic management

This is a concept also developed in the USA. It assumes a weak uncertainty avoidance environment, in which deviant strategic ideas are encouraged. Although it is taught in countries with a stronger uncertainty avoidance, like Germany or France, its recommendations are rarely followed there, because in these cultures it is seen as the top managers' role to remain involved in daily operations (Horovitz, 1980).

(4) Humanization of work

This is a general term for a number of approaches in different countries trying to make work more interesting and rewarding for the people who do it. In the USA, which is a masculine and individualist society, the prevailing form of humanization of work has been 'job enrichment': giving individual tasks more intrinsic content. In Sweden which is feminine and less individualist, the prevailing form has been the development of semi-autonomous work groups. in which members exchange tasks and help each other (Gohl, 1977). In Germany and German-speaking Switzerland the introduction of flexible working hours has been a very popular way of adapting the job to the worker. Flexible working hours have never become as popular in other countries; their popularity in German-speaking countries can be understood by the combination of a small power distance (acceptance of responsibility by the worker) with a relatively large uncertainty avoidance (internalization of rules).

EASTERN VERSUS WESTERN CATEGORIES OF THINKING

A study of students' values in 23 countries using a questionnaire designed by Chinese scholars (the Chinese Value Survey, CVS) produced partly similar, but partly different results from the two other studies (among 64 IBM subsidiaries and among students in 10 countries) which used questionnaires designed by Western (European and American, respectively) minds. The CVS study did not identify a dimension like uncertainty avoidance, which deals with the search for truth. It seems that to the Chinese minds who designed the questions the search for truth is not an essential issue, so the questions necessary to identify this dimension were not included in their questionnaire.

One of the basic differences between Eastern thinking (represented by, for example Confucianism, Buddhism, and Hinduism) and Western thinking (dominant in the Judaeo–Christian–Muslim intellectual tradition) is that in the East, a qualification does not exclude its opposite, which is an essential element of Western logic (Kapp, 1983). Thus in the East the search for truth is irrelevant, because there is no need for a single and absolute truth and the assumption that a person can possess an objective truth is absent. Instead, the Eastern instrument includes the questions necessary to detect the dimension of long versus short term orientation expressing a concern for virtue: for proper ways of living (like, practising perseverance and thrift, or respecting tradition and social obligations) which is less obvious in the West where virtue tends to be derived from truth.

These findings show that not only practices, values and theories, but even the categories available to build theories from are products of culture. This has far-reaching consequences for management training in a multicultural organization. Not only our tools, but even the categories in which we think, may be unfit for the other environment.

ORGANIZATIONAL CULTURES

The use of the term 'culture' in the management literature is not limited to the national level: attributing a distinct culture to a company or organization has become extremely popular. However. organizational cultures are a phenomenon of a different order from national cultures, if only because membership of an organization is usually partial and voluntary, while the 'membership' of a nation is permanent and involuntary. Our field research to be described below showed that national cultures differ mostly at the level of basic values while organizational cultures differ mostly at the level of the more superficial practices: symbols, heroes and rituals.

In the popular management literature, organization cultures have often been presented as a matter of values (e.g. Peters and Waterman, 1982). The confusion arises because this literature does not distinguish between the values of the founders and leaders and those of the ordinary employees. Founders and leaders create the symbols, the heroes and the rituals that constitute the daily practices of the organization's members. However, members have to adapt their personal values to the organization's needs to a limited extent only. A work organization as a rule is not a 'total institution' like a prison or a mental hospital. Precisely because organizational cultures are composed of practices rather than values they are somewhat manageable: they can be managed by changing the practices. The values of employees cannot be changed by an employer because they were acquired when the employees were children. However, sometimes an employer can activate latent values which employees were not allowed to show earlier: like a desire for initiative and creativity, by allowing practices which before were forbidden.

DIMENSIONS OF ORGANIZATIONAL CULTURES

A research project similar to the IBM studies but focusing on organizational rather than national cultures was carried out by the Institute for Research on Intercultural Cooperation (IRIC) in The Netherlands. Data were collected in twenty work organizations or parts of organizations in The Netherlands and Denmark. The units studied varied from a toy manufacturing company to two municipal police corps. As mentioned above the study found large differences among units in practices (symbols, heroes, rituals) but only modest differences in values, beyond those due to such basic facts as nationality, education, gender and age group.

Six independent dimensions can be used to describe most of the variety in organizational practices These six dimensions can be used as a framework to describe organizational cultures, but their research base in 20 units from two countries is too narrow to consider them as universally valid. For describing organizational cultures in other countries and in other types of organizations, additional dimensions may be necessary or some of the six may be less useful (see also Pümpin, 1984). The dimensions of organizational cultures found are:

(1) Process-oriented versus results-oriented cultures

The former are dominated by technical and bureaucratic routines, the latter by a common concern for outcomes. This dimension was associated with the culture's degree of homogeneity: in results-oriented units, everybody perceived their practices in about the same way; in process-oriented units, there were vast differences in perception among different levels and parts of the unit. The degree of homogeneity of a culture is a measure of its 'strength': the study confirmed that strong cultures are more results-oriented than weak ones, and vice versa (Peters and Waterman, 1982).

(2) Job-oriented versus employee-oriented cultures

The former assume responsibility for the employees' job performance only, and nothing more: employee-oriented cultures assume a broad responsibility for their members' well-being. At the level of individual managers, the distinction between job orientation and employee orientation has been popularized by Blake and Mouton's Managerial Grid (1964). The IRIC study shows that job versus employee orientation is part of a culture and not (only) a choice for an individual manager. A unit's position on this dimension seems to be largely the result of historical factors, like the philosophy of its founder(s) and the presence or absence in its recent history of economic crises with collective layoffs.

(3) Professional versus parochial cultures

In the former, the usually highly educated members identify primarily with their profession; in the latter, the members derive their identity from the organization for which they work. Sociology has long known this dimension as local versus cosmopolitan, the contrast between an internal and an external frame of reference, first suggested by Tönnies (1887).

(4) Open system versus closed system cultures

This dimension refers to the common style of internal and external communication, and to the ease with which outsiders and newcomers are admitted. This dimension is the only one of the six for which there is a systematic difference between Danish and Dutch units. It seems that organizational openness is a societal characteristic of Denmark, much more so than of The Netherlands. This shows that organizational cultures also reflect national culture differences.

(5) Tightly versus loosely controlled cultures

This dimension deals with the degree of formality and punctuality within the organization; it is partly a function of the unit's technology: banks and pharmaceutical companies can be expected to show tight control, research laboratories and advertizing agencies loose control; but even with the same technology, units still differ on this dimension.

(6) Pragmatic versus normative cultures

The last dimension describes the prevailing way (flexible or rigid) of dealing with the environment, in particular with customers. Units selling services are likely to be found towards the pragmatic (flexible) side, units involved in the application of legal roles towards the normative (rigid) side. This dimension measures the degree of 'customer orientation', which is a highly popular topic in the management literature.

MANAGING ORGANIZATIONAL CULTURES

In spite of their relatively superficial nature organizational cultures are hard to change because they have developed into collective habits. Changing them is a top management task which cannot be delegated. Some kind of culture assessment by an independent party is usually necessary which includes the identification of different subcultures which may need quite different approaches. The top management's major strategic choice is either to accept and optimally use the existing culture or to try to change it. If an attempt at change is made it should be preceded by a cost–benefit analysis. A particular concern is whether the manpower necessary for a culture change is available.

Turning around an organizational culture demands visible leadership which appeals to the employees' feelings as much as to their intellect. The leader or leaders should assure themselves of sufficient support from key persons at different levels in the organization. Subsequently, they can change the practices by adapting the organization's structure – its functions, departments, locations, and tasks – matching tasks with employee talents. After the structure, the controls may have to be changed based on a decision on which aspects of the work have to be co-ordinated how and by whom at what level. At the same time it is usually necessary to change certain personnel policies related to recruitment, training and promotion. Finally, turning around a culture is not a one hour process. It takes sustained attention from top management, persistence for several years, and usually a second culture assessment to see whether the intended changes have, indeed, been attained.

MANAGING CULTURE DIFFERENCES IN MULTINATIONALS

Many multinational corporations do not only operate in different countries but also in different lines of business or at least in different product/market divisions. Different business lines and/or divisions often have different organizational cultures. Strong cross-national organizational cultures within a business line or division, by offering common practices, can bridge national differences in values among organization members. Common practices, not common values, keep multinationals together.

Structure should follow culture: the purpose of an organization structure is the co-ordination of activities. For the design of the structure of a multinational, multibusiness corporation, three questions have to be answered for each business unit (a business unit represents one business line in one country). The three questions are: (a) which of the unit's in- and outputs should be co-ordinated from elsewhere in the corporation? (b) where and at what level should the co-ordination take place? and (c) how tight or loose should the co-ordination be? In every case there is a basic choice between co-ordination along geographical lines and along business lines. The decisive factor is whether business know-how or national cultural know-how is more crucial for the success of the operation.

Matrix structures are a possible solution but they are costly, often meaning a doubling of the management ranks, and their actual functioning may raise more problems than they resolve. A single structural principle (geographic or business) is unlikely to fit for an entire corporation. Joint ventures further complicate the structuring problem. The optimal solution is nearly always a patchwork structure that in some cases follows business and in others geographical lines. This may lack beauty, but it follows the needs of markets and business unit cultures. Variety within the environment in which a corporation operates should be matched with appropriate internal variety. Optimal solutions will also change over time, so that the periodic reshufflings which any large organization undergoes, should be seen as functional.

Like all organizations, multinationals are held together by people. The best structure at a given moment depends primarily on the availability of suitable people. Two roles are particularly crucial: (a) country business unit managers who form the link between the culture of the business unit and the corporate culture which is usually heavily affected by the nationality of origin of the corporation, and (b) 'corporate diplomats', i.e. home country or other nationals who are impregnated with the corporate culture, multilingual, from various occupational backgrounds, and experienced in living and functioning in various foreign cultures. They are essential to make multinational structures work, as liaison persons in the various head offices or as temporary managers for new ventures.

The availability of suitable people at the right moment is the main task of multinational personnel management. This means timely recruiting of future managerial talent from different nationalities, and career moves through planted transfers where these people will absorb the corporate culture. Multinational personnel departments have to find their way between uniformity and diversity in personnel policies. Too much uniformity is unwarranted because people's mental programmes are not uniform. It leads to corporate-wide policies being imposed on subsidiaries where they will not work – or only receive lip service from obedient but puzzled locals. On the other side, the assumption that everybody is different and that people in subsidiaries therefore always should know best and be allowed to go their own ways, is unwarranted too. In this case an opportunity is lost to build a corporate culture with unique features which keep the organization together and provide it with a distinctive and competitive psychological advantage.

Increasing integration of organizations across national borders demands that managers have an insight in the extent to which familiar aspects of organizational life like organization structures, leadership styles, motivation patterns, and training and development models are culturally relative and need to be reconsidered when borders are crossed. It also calls for self-insight on the part of the managers involved, who have to be able to compare their ways of thinking, feeling and acting to those of others, without immediately passing judgment. This ability to see the relativity of one's own cultural framework does not come naturally to most managers, who often got to their present position precisely because they held strong convictions. Intercultural management skills can be improved by specific training; this should focus on working rather than on living in other countries. The stress in such courses is on recognizing one's own cultural programmes and where these may differ from those of people in other countries.

REFERENCES

Blake, R.R. and Mouton, J.S. (1964). *The Managerial Grid*. Gulf Publishing, Houston.

Ferguson, I.R.G. (1973). *Management By Objectives in Deutschland*. Herder and Herder, Frankfurt/Main.

Gohl, J. (Ed.) (1977). *Probleme der Humanisierungsdebatte*. Goldmann, München.

Hofstede, G. (1980). *Culture's Consequences: International Differences in Work-Related Values*. Sage Publications, Beverly Hills.

Hofstede, G. (1983). Dimensions of National Culture in Fifty Countries and Three Regions, in Deregowski, J.B., Dziurawiec, S. and Annis, R.C. (Eds), *Expiscations in Cross-Cultural Psychology*, pp. 335–355. Swets & Zeitlinger, Lisse, The Netherlands.

Hofstede, G. (1986). Cultural Differences in Teaching and Learning. *International Journal of Intercultural Relations*, Vol. 10, pp. 301–320.

Hofstede, G. (1991). *Cultures and Organizations: Software of the Mind*. McGraw-Hill, London.

Hofstede, G. and Bond, M.H. (1984) .Hofstede's Culture Dimensions: an Independent Validation Using Rokeach's Value Survey. *Journal of Cross-Cultural Psychology*, Vol. 15, pp. 417–433.

Hofstede, G. and Bond, M.H. (1988). The Confucius Connection: From Cultural Roots to Economic Growth. *Organizational Dynamics*, Vol. 16, No. 4, pp. 4–21.

Hofstede, G., Neuijen, B., Ohayv, D.D. and Sanders, G. (1990). Measuring Organizational Cultures. *Administrative Science Quarterly*, Vol. 35, pp. 286–316.

Horovitz, J.H. (1980). *Top Management Control in Europe*. Macmillan, London.

Kapp, R.A. (Ed.) (1983). *Communicating with China*. Intercultural Press, Chicago.

King, A.Y.C. and Bond, M.H. (1985). The Confucian Paradigm of Man: a Sociological View, in Tseng, W. and Wu, D. (Eds), *Chinese Culture and Mental Health*, pp. 29–45. Columbia University Press, New York.

Parsons, T. and Shils, E.A. (1951). *Toward a General Theory of Action*. Harvard University Press, Cambridge, Massachusetts.

Peters, T.J. and Waterman, R.H. (1982). *In Search of Excellence: Lessons from America's Best-Run Companies*. Harper & Row, New York.

Pümpin, C. (1984). Unternehmenskultur, Unternehmensstrategie und Unternehmenserfolg. *GDI Impuls*, Vol. 2, pp. 19–30.

The Chinese Culture Connection (1987). Chinese Values and the Search for Culture-free Dimensions of Culture. *Journal of Cross-Cultural Psychology*, Vol. 18, pp. 143–164.

Tönnies, F. [1963 (1887)], *Community and Society*. Harper & Row, New York.

25

The psychic distance paradox

Shawna O'Grady and Henry W. Lane

INTRODUCTION

It has been argued in the international business literature that companies begin the internationalization process in countries that are psychically close before venturing to more distant countries (Johanson and Vahlne, 1992). If this description is accurate, then Canadian companies would be expected to begin in the United States which is not only the closest but also, in many ways, the most similar country to Canada. Indeed, evidence from the retail industry indicates that firms have followed this pattern.

The literature on the internationalization process describes the sequence of market entry that firms follow when internationalizing. This sequence reflects a gradual, learning through experience process. What is not explicit in the literature is why firms follow this pattern. Researchers have suggested that entering countries that are psychically close reduces the level of uncertainty firms face in the new market (Johanson and Vahlne, 1992); and that psychically close countries are easier for companies to learn about (Kogut and Singh, 1988). Such explanations seem logical and implicitly support the conclusion that beginning in psychically close countries should improve a company's chances of success in these markets. Although the literature is not prescriptive, an unstated conclusion can be drawn from it linking sequence of entry to performance. There is an implicit assumption that psychically close countries are more similar, and that similarity is easier for firms to manage than dissimilarity, thereby making it more likely that they will succeed in similar markets.

Although sequence of entry is an important consideration, we believe that one limitation of this literature is that it does not address how the perceived psychic distance between countries affects the decisionmakers' choice of entry or the organization's ultimate performance in the new market. This research presents evidence demonstrating that starting the internationalization process by entering a country psychically close to home may result in poor performance and, possibly, failure. We refer to this as the psychic distance paradox. Instead of psychically close countries being easy to enter and to do business in, we argue that perceived similarity can cause decisionmakers to fail because they do not prepare for the differences. The failure lies in the managerial decisionmaking aspect of the internationalization process, to which international business researchers have not paid enough attention (Johanson and Vahlne, 1992). In addition, even in psychically close countries such as Canada and the United States, there may be significant differences that can

Reprinted with permission from *Journal of International Business Studies*, 1996, Second quarter, 309–333.

affect the ability of managers to conduct business. What appears on the surface to be psychically close may, in reality, be more distant that expected.

This research was exploratory in nature and focused on the performance of Canadian retail companies that entered the United States. With the American retail market worth more than $1.5 trillion, there is a very powerful incentive for Canadian retailers to understand how to compete in this market. Consistent with internationalization theory, domestically successful companies entered a country that is not only the closest physically, but probably the most similar country to Canada. However, of the thirty-two Canadian retail companies that entered the United States market, almost 80% failed and only seven (22%) were continuing to function successfully (Evans, Land and O'Grady, 1992). The high failure rate suggests that there may be a paradox, or inherent contradiction, within internationalization theory and the psychic distance concept, and that executives cannot always rely upon measures of psychic distance when making their internationalization decisions.

The purpose of this chapter is to use the experience of Canadian retailers entering the United States to analyze the psychic distance concept in greater detail and to suggest some possible qualifications that could improve its use in research and practice. First, a summary of the psychic distance concept is presented, as well as the evidence in the literature positioning Canada and the United States as being culturally close. Next, the results from both clinical and questionnaire data show areas in which cultural and business differences manifested themselves, as well as empirical evidence of these cultural differences. Then, the paradox inherent in the psychic distance concept is explored, which explains how the perception of a country as having a small psychic distance from one's own can lead decisionmakers to a number of faulty assumptions, creating an inability to learn about that country. Some recommendations are provided to help companies learn in these situations. Finally, we explore the psychic distance concept in greater depth, and propose some qualifications to it. The results of this study suggest that the psychic distance concept is more complex than is generally recognized in the literature and should be explored more fully.

BACKGROUND

The psychic distance concept and the internationalization process

Although the term 'psychic distance' has been used in prior research (Beckermann, 1956; Linnemann, 1966), early studies of Nordic multinationals generally are taken as the starting point in discussions and research on the concept of psychic distance (Johanson and Vahlne, 1977; Johanson and Wiedersheim-Paul, 1975; Hornell, Vahlne & Wiedersheim-Paul, 1973) and the internationalization process (Andersen, 1993).[1] The Swedish researchers postulated that, when establishing international operations, firms need accurate market knowledge, which comes from direct experience in the foreign market and an understanding of its internal relationships, rather than more objective, factual, general market information that is easily transmitted and learned without the need of experience in interpreting it (Johanson and Vahlne, 1977). Psychic distance was an important variable in understanding the dynamics of the internationalization process. It was defined initially as 'factors preventing or disturbing the flow of information between potential or actual suppliers and customers' (Nordström and Vahlne, 1992). The concept was intended to increase the understanding of the location pattern of Swedish exports and foreign subsidiaries, and to complement existing explanations that relied on economic concepts and physical distance. Hornell et al. (1973), *cited in* Nordström and Vahlne (1992), showed that psychic distance had substantial value in explaining the patterns.

The definition of psychic distance varies greatly within the literature, depending upon the way in which the concept is operationalized. For example, Vahlne and Wiedersheim-Paul (1973), *cited in* Nordström and Vahlne (1992), operationalized psychic distance using the following indicators:

- level of economic development in the importing countries;
- difference in the level of economic development between Sweden and the host countries;
- level of education in the importing countries;
- difference in the level of education between Sweden and the host countries;
- difference in 'business language';
- difference in culture and local language;
- existence of previous trading channels between Sweden and the host countries.

These indicators were measured using publicly available statistics and data from the Swedish Export Board. Later studies (Kogut and Singh 1988; Benito and Gripsrud 1992) relied primarily on Hofstede's (1980) research and measures of culture to quantify the cultural distance between countries. Thus, cultural distance was used as a synonym and proxy for psychic distance.

Nordström and Vahlne (1992) developed a cultural distance index that used adjusted Hofstede data. However, they (1992:10) suggested that cultural distance and psychic distance captured 'different but overlapping phenomena,' and that psychic distance included a component of business difficulty, as well as cultural distance. Psychic distance, in their view, is comprised of 'cultural (such as those dimensions defined by Hofstede), structural (such as legal and administrative systems) and language differences' (p.10). Based on this expanded definition of the concept, they created a psychic distance index in which the rankings varied in some respects from those based on the adjusted Hofstede data. Our research supports an expanded definition of psychic distance and suggests including other business factors such as industry structure and the competitive environment, as well as cultural differences.

Psychic distance: United States – Canada

On Nordström and Vahlne's cultural distance index, Canada ranked fifth (index score = 17.7) in distance from Sweden, and the United States ranked seventh (index score = 25.9). The overall range of the index scores was from 1.2 (Norway) to 78.1 (Japan). On their psychic distance index, the United States ranked ninth in distance from Sweden (25.3) and Canada tenth (27.1). This index ranged from 0.5 (Norway) to 79.2 (Chile). It is no surprise that Canada and the United States are so close to each other in both rankings given their proximity and apparent cultural similarities. From their review of eight comparative studies of attitudes and values conducted through the 1960s and 1970s, Ronen and Shenkar (1985) found that Canada and the United States were consistently in the same Anglo cluster. In addition, they were very close to each other in Hofstede's (1980) original research. It is reasonable to assume a substantial degree of cultural similarity between the two countries.

However, a limitation of the current indices used is that they measure cultural or psychic distance at a very high level of aggregation that may hide important variations. Measuring distance at the national level may overlook regional differences that exist within countries;

cultural and structural differences that may exist by industry; and individual differences and experiences. For example, a firm that hires managers with significant experience in a target market that is distant from the culture of the firm's home country would have a much smaller psychic distance from that market than measurements at national levels of aggregation would indicate. One contribution of this research is that it investigates the concept of psychic distance at industry and firm levels.

Implications for the internationalization process

Psychic distance has been viewed as the degree to which a firm is uncertain about a foreign market (Kogut and Singh 1988), and the internationalization process as a *learning process*. Recently, Nordström and Vahlne (1992:3) updated the original definition of psychic distance as 'factors preventing or disturbing firms learning about and understanding a foreign environment'. This re-definition emphasizes and affirms the view of internationalization as a dynamic, learning process, whereby managers must not simply accumulate information, but must learn to interpret it correctly in order to generate an understanding of the market and adapt to it. An inability to learn about important differences hinders adaptation and affects performance outcomes.

As Benito and Gripsrud (1992:464) explain it, 'firms are assumed to successively enter markets at an increasing "cultural distance" from the home country. . . Thus, firms are predicted to start their internationalization by moving into those markets they can most easily understand, entering more distant markets only at a later stage.' This view is confirmed by a wide range of Nordic studies, such as Nordström and Vahlne (1992:4) who state that the 'typical internationalization process tends to be a step-wise entry into gradually more distant markets'; and by Johanson and Vahlne (1992:5) who suggest that the reason firms begin in those markets is because 'there they see opportunities, and there the perceived market uncertainty is low.' Johanson and Wiedersheim-Paul (1975) found that the growth of four large Swedish multinationals was distinguished by a series of small, cumulative steps over time. The entry mode also followed an incremental pattern, with an agency operation preceding a sales subsidiary in 75% of the cases. This 'Uppsala model of internationalization' (Andersen 1993) describes the pattern of entry of firms that have survived in the market.[2]

Van Den Bulcke (1986) found that in a study of forty-one Belgian direct investments abroad, none was without earlier operations while 61% of subsidiaries had been preceded by exports-sales subsidiaries, again supporting the notion of moving sequentially to entry modes requiring more resources and greater company commitment. In addition, Luostarinen's (1979; *cited in* Luostarinen and Welch 1990) research revealed that Finnish companies tended to start their internationalization activities in those countries that were physically and culturally close and that had a short business distance to Finland. Later, these companies advanced stepwise to other countries with greater and greater business distance.

This model of the internationalization process has a practical, common-sense appeal to it. However, although its face validity is very high, the empirical support for it seems to be mixed. There is some support for the concept that national culture and cultural distance have an influence on entry mode selection. Two studies have linked certain national cultures with specific entry mode patterns (Johanson and Vahlne 1977; Puxty 1979), but neither study systematically showed how perceived cultural differences influenced entry choices.

Kogut and Singh (1988) provided the first large-sample study showing that entry mode choice varied depending upon the cultural distance between countries. They found that the greater the cultural distance between the country of the investing firm and the country of entry, the more likely it was that the firm would choose a joint venture to reduce its uncertainty in those markets. Gatignon and Anderson (1988) state that sociocultural distance (the difference between the home and host cultures) causes uncertainty for firms, which makes them shy away from foreign ownership involvement. In their large sample study, they strived to discover if the sociocultural distance between countries affected the amount of control corporations had over their foreign subsidiaries. Their findings indicated that country risk was the most important variable affecting control, and that the sociocultural distance variable (which was based on Ronen and Shenkar's (1985) cultural clusters) did not have a large effect. Significantly, as multinational companies gained experience abroad, they tended to opt for wholly owned subsidiaries, as predicted.

The internationalization literature primarily addresses the *choice of entry mode* for a market and the *sequence of entry* into successive markets. Although mode and sequence are important considerations, we believe a shortcoming of this literature is that it uses an absolute measure of distance, using national averages, and does not deal with how the perceived psychic distance between countries affects the decisionmakers' entry choice or the organization's ultimate performance in the new market. More attention needs to be paid to the perception of similarity and difference, as well as to the decisionmaking process regarding entry and, ultimately, to performance outcomes.

This research presents evidence that demonstrates that starting the internationalization process by entering a country psychically close to home may result in failure. We refer to this as the psychic distance paradox. The similarity perceived to exist when entering psychically close countries does not necessarily reduce the level of uncertainty faced, nor make it easier to learn about the country, due to a failure in the managerial decisionmaking process. Whereas the implicit assumption of the model is that similarity is easier, our results show that similarity may hide unexpected and unforeseen barriers to successful entry and performance.

RESEARCH DESIGN

We designed our study to answer two research questions. First, why did domestically successful Canadian retailers perform poorly in the U.S., a country that is culturally closer to Canada than any country in the world? Second, what cultural and business differences exist between the two countries? Phase 1 involved a literature review and clinical study in which the experiences of ten Canadian retailers that expanded into the United States were documented and analyzed. The strategic decisionmaking process was also analyzed in each of the ten companies studied. In Phase 2, survey research was used to compare the values and attitudes of Chief Executive Officers of Canadian and American retail companies. Each of these phases will be discussed briefly in the following section.

Phase 1: qualitative research

Literature review

First, in order to determine how culturally similar or different Canada and the United States are, the literature comparing the two cultures was analyzed. Culture is defined as the shared attitudes and values of the members of a country. Thus, culture refers to common, deeply rooted attitudes and values, which exist largely irrespective of individual differences. There is a large general literature on attitudes and values that primarily focuses at the individual level of analysis. This shows that culture influences a person's attitudes and values which have an effect on his/her behavior.

Much less is known specifically about societal attitudes and values or the differences in national culture between the United States and Canada. In fact, there are very few empirical studies available comparing the cultural characteristics of the United States and Canada (Hofstede 1980; Rokeach 1973). Although not empirically based, a number of authors (i.e., Lipset (1963, 1989)) have written extensively comparing the two countries. However most of the published work on Canada-US differences is based on observation and historical analyses. This literature, which focuses on comparing only these two countries, suggests that there are a number of cultural differences. Table 1 outlines the key cultural dimensions found in this literature.[3]

The impact of attitudes and values on executive behavior has received attention from practitioners (Harmon and Jacobs 1985; Peters and Waterman 1982) and academics alike (Hambrick 1987; Posner and Munson 1979; England 1978; Rokeach 1973). Several have pointed out the impact of the top executive team's attitudes and values on their strategic choices (Chaganti and Sambharya 1987; Dess 1987; O'Reilly and Flatt 1986) by creating belief structures that influence their interpretation of information and outcome preferences (Walsh and Fahey 1986; Schwenk 1984).

The cross-cultural literature indicates that the culture in which people are raised can affect ways of thinking and behaving. Although it does not hinder the ability to manage within one's own country where business practices generally are similar, it can affect the ability to manage in other countries/cultures. Business people seldom reflect on and articulate their values, although they feel uncomfortable when these values are violated. Also, they are often not aware of the assumptions that underlie and guide their actions. These assumptions can also lead to cross-cultural misinterpretations, such as subconscious cultural 'blinders,' a lack of cultural self-awareness, projected similarity, and parochialism (Adler 1991). As a result of different mental programming, people from various cultures often see situations differently and have different approaches and solutions to problems. Each tends to believe that his or her way makes the most sense and is best. Frequently, managers from one country enter another country and assume that they can implement practices in the same way as at home.

A major contribution of the cross-cultural literature is the recognition that, to manage effectively cross-culturally, one must understand the culture of the people with whom they plan to do business and correspondingly, deal with the implications of these differences for managing in that culture. However, one must be aware that one's own culture can act as a barrier to accurately understand the environment that one is facing. This may be even more crucial when differences are not obvious or noticed as is the case between Canada and the United States.

The case studies

A list of Canadian retailers that had entered the United States market was developed manually using the Canadian Key Business Directory, the Canadian Trade Index and the Directory of Retail Chains in Canada. Major news sources were also used to identify Canadian companies operating in the United States. A population of thirty two Canadian retailers was identified from which a sample could be drawn.

In identifying potential research sites, the following criteria were developed. First, a company had to be profitable in Canada to be considered as a possible site for more in-depth

Table 1. Canada-U.S. cultural differences – a summary of the literature

---

U.S. > C = the U.S. is believed to have a stronger orientation, or a higher score on this factor than Canada; if U.S. < C, the opposite is true.

Achievement Orientation (U.S. > C)
  Lipset (1963, 1989), Rokeach (1973), Thorne and Meyer (1987)

Level of Aggressiveness (U.S. > C)
  Lipset (1963, 1989), Rokeach (1973)

Level of Optimism (U.S. > C)
  Lipset (1963), Berton (1982), Thorne and Meyer (1987)

Action Orientation (Belief in the Timeliness of Action) (U.S. > C)
  Newman (1972)

Belief in Hard Work (U.S. > C)
  Newman (1972)

Attitudes toward Authority (government)
Negative attitudes toward government, questioning of authority (U.S.)/positive attitudes toward government, deference to authority (C)
  Berton (1982), Lipset (1963, 1989)

Belief in Competitiveness (U.S. > C)
  Godfrey (1986), Newman (1972)

Risk Propensity
Positive attitudes toward risk (U.S.)/hunger for security (C)
  Lipset (1963, 1989), Berton (1982), Godfrey (1986)

Masculinity dimension (U.S. > C)
  Hofstede (1980), Rokeach (1973)

Uncertainty Avoidance Dimension (U.S. < C)
  Hofstede (1980), Rokeach (1973)

Individualism/Collectivism Dimension (U.S. more individualistic than C)
  Hofstede (1980), Lipset (1963), Rokeach (1973), Godfrey (1986)

Power distance dimension (U.S. < C)
  Hofstede (1980), Lipset (1963, 1989), Rokeach (1973)

Commitment to Winning (U.S. > C)
  Thorne and Meyer (1987), Lipset (1963, 1989)

Mastery over One's Environment (U.S. > C)
  Newman (1972)

Cautiousness (U.S. < C)
  Lipset (1963, 1989), Berton (1982)

Attitudes toward equality
(U.S. more egalitarian)
  Lipset (1963, 1989)

(C more egalitarian)
  Rokeach (1973)

---

study. This criterion was used so that the results could not be attributed to poor management skills in Canada. Second, companies had to have been operating in the United States for a period of at least two years, unless they had withdrawn from the market and could be analyzed as failures. The two-year criterion was deemed necessary to assess performance and to avoid contaminating the results due to start-up.

Companies meeting the above criteria were contacted and ten companies agreed to in-depth case studies of their experiences in the United States. Eight of the ten companies were unsuccessful. The data were collected via semi-structured interviews with CEOs, as well as with other members of the top executive teams, including vice presidents of finance, merchandising, marketing, operations, administration and real estate. A total of twenty-eight executives were interviewed and the average duration of each interview was two hours. Interviews were conducted by two interviewers, recorded and content-analyzed. Themes were identified along with the number of individuals who referred to these themes. The inter-rater reliability was .95. In addition, secondary source data, such as company minutes, annual reports and newspaper clippings, were used to supplement the interview data.

The decisionmaking process was measured by asking executives to trace the history of the strategic decision to enter the United States market from pre-entry to post-entry. Included were questions about 'whether' and, if so, 'how' cultural and other differences between the United States and Canada were taken into account in the strategic decisionmaking process. Executives were asked about their pre-entry, entry and post-entry perceptions of American culture and whether their perceptions were incorporated into decisions made. The company's decisions related to the U.S. venture were also recorded. The interviews were content-analyzed individually, across teams within companies, and across companies, to identify factors contributing to successful and unsuccessful performance. Success was operationalized by aggregating the following measures: sales and profits in the U.S. over the period of operations; growth in sales and profits over the period of operations; market share over the period; and the ability to meet the expectations of the parent company. Company performance fell into three categories: unprofitable withdrawals; holding in the U.S. (not profitable, but may have increased sales, gained market share, or met the expectations of the parent); and profitably operating in the U.S. Companies in the latter two categories were considered successes. Unprofitable withdrawals were considered failures (there were no profitable withdrawals in our sample of ten).

Results

There were two important findings from Phase 1. First, the executives agreed that there were several cultural differences between Canada and the United States and that these differences affected their ability to compete effectively in the United States. The second and related finding was that, although cultural differences were perceived by the executives to be important, they alone were not responsible for the varying performance levels of the Canadian companies. Rather, it was the recognition of those differences, prior to entry, that differentiated performance. Each of these findings will be elaborated on now.

There was a very high level of agreement among the executives regarding the cultural differences between the United States and Canada in the retail industry. The following characteristics were found to be more descriptive of Americans than Canadians: Winning Attitude; Competitiveness; Sense of Mastery; Action Oriented; Belief in Hard Work; Aggressiveness; Risk Taking; and Individualistic. These perceived differences were incorporated into the questionnaire measuring cultural differences in Phase 2 of the study.

The Canadian executives also concurred that the cultural differences were noticeable in the behaviors and business practices of Americans. Indeed, there were five major areas of the retail business in which cultural differences manifested themselves. These five areas can be grouped into those relating to the market (consumer differences; regional differences) and the competitive environment (level of competition; employee and management attitudes, values and behaviors; and relationships). Some of the more important differences are described briefly below.

MARKET

1. *Consumers/Customers.* American consumers demanded to be treated with importance when they shopped. They demanded service. In the United States, consumers would shop where the bargains were. In Canada, they were more likely to shop automatically at a national chain.

2. *Regional Differences.* Relative to Canada, executives generally found much larger regional differences in buying behavior in the United States. There were especially large East/West differences in the United States. Canada was seen to be more homogeneous politically, economically and socially and to have a more commonly accepted value system. Therefore, doing business in the United States was found to be much more difficult given this heterogeneity. Doing business in the United States required knowledge of each individual region, because the differences between them could be very large.

COMPETITIVE ENVIRONMENT

1. *Relationships.* The executives interviewed commented on the difficulty of gaining access to suppliers and the necessity of building rapport and long term relationships in the United States.

2. *Employee and Management Attitudes, Values and Behaviors.* American employees were described as possessing a greater desire for independence than Canadian employees, and to be much less interested in unions. American employees were found to be very hard working and much more conscientious about productivity. American employees' strong orientation toward work created an expectation that they would be rewarded based on merit. Since they worked more independently, the types of reward systems were different in the United States' retail industry.

American managers were also found to be different from Canadian managers in two major ways. First, the level of professionalism and experience in the retail industry were found to be higher in the United States. Second, the executives found that American executives were expected to live up to higher performance standards. For example, not meeting goals was more likely to lead to termination in the United States than in Canada.

3. *Competition.* Americans were found to be much more competitive than Canadians. Frequently the executives voiced comments typically used to describe battle, such as 'It was all out war' or 'Their arsenal was impressive'. Not expecting this difference in the level of competitiveness, Canadian companies found themselves at a significant disadvantage.

The clinical studies highlighted that one of the most important factors in the decisionmaking process for Canadian companies was the accuracy of the top management team's perceptions of the United States market prior to entry. This aspect of their pre-entry orientation was the base from which all decisions regarding entry into the United States market were made. The executives from the companies that failed in the United States perceived there to be no difference between the two markets prior to entry, and based decisions such as product mix in the stores, store location and entry mode on this inaccurate perception. As a result, they found themselves unprepared for the level of competition and cultural differences they discovered upon entry, which affected their ability to operate successfully in their chosen markets. Although they conducted various forms of market research, their lack of experience in the U.S. market hindered their ability to interpret it. Unfortunately, even after they recognized the obvious differences in the two cultures, they continued to assume that they could operate in the United States as they had in Canada. Mental models appropriate for the Canadian market led top management teams to make decisions as they would at home with generally disastrous outcomes. Consequently, they did not adjust to, nor learn about, the United States market and were forced to withdraw from it.

On the other hand, the companies that were successful in the United States recognized that there were differences prior to entry and incorporated this accurate knowledge into their entry decisions. Executives either had direct experience in the U.S. market, or they hired American management who did, ensuring that decisions made fit with the market.

The above analysis illustrates the psychic distance paradox. First, Canadian executives who erroneously assumed the United States was similar to Canada believed that their strategies were correct and that organizations in the two countries could be managed in the same way. Second, instead of this perceived similarity increasing the ease with which they learned about the market, and reducing the amount of uncertainty faced, it hindered their understanding by masking important differences, and led to decisions that were ineffective.

In addition, we discovered that executives with direct experience in the United States made better decisions because they understood the 'true' distance between the Canadian and American markets. This is consistent with the findings of Johanson and Vahlne (1977). Some of these executives were Americans working in Canada who had experience in the target markets; some were Canadians with experience in the United States; and others were Americans living in the United States who had the requisite experience. This raises the possibility of a further paradox within the psychic distance concept. If a company's management team has direct experience (perhaps through living or working there) in a market that normally would be considered as 'distant' on the indices, the psychic distance to that market might be less than the distance to a 'close' market in which they had no direct experience. Therefore the paradox that a close market can be distant, and that a seemingly distant market can be close, ought to be recognized.

The ability to learn in a new market is an important skill. Many companies encountered unexpected differences in the United States, yet they did not change their modus operandi or their initial perceptions about the market to reflect the reality of what they were experiencing and they continued to make decisions based on the faulty assumptions. Companies with executives who challenged their initial perceptions and adjusted them were able to alter their decisions to fit with the situation. The ability, or inability, to learn during the entry process affected the company's subsequent performance. The differentiating factor was what organizational learning theorists refer to as double loop learning (Argyris and Schon 1978) or an ability to modify underlying beliefs and assumptions rather than simply changing behavior.

The implication of these findings is that executives or researchers should not assume that cultural or psychic distance measured at a national level of aggregation reflects the true distance between a company in one country and a market in another. The results from Phase 2, which now follow, show how inaccurate such an assumption can be.

The interviews confirmed that greater than expected cultural and business differences existed between consumers and retailers in the two countries, and that these influenced the ability of Canadian retailers to enter and adapt successfully to the United States. Although rich and informative, these findings were qualitative and perceptual in nature. They also came from a small, but important, sample. The question still remained whether the differences experienced were representative of the executives in the retail industry in the two countries.

Phase 2: survey research

In Phase 2, survey research was utilized to determine whether or not the cultural differences that the Canadian retailers experienced in the United States could be generalized beyond the responses from the interviews. A questionnaire was designed using 125 items measuring sixteen cultural differences that had been suggested in the literature and the interviews. These attitude/value orientations were operationalized using well-established instruments, such as Hofstede's questionnaire, and Jackson's Personality Research Form (PRF) and Personality Index (JPI).

Sample

The top 400 retail companies in each country were the populations of interest. The list was obtained from the Dun and Bradstreet Canadian Dun's Market Identifier database. The Chief Executive Officer's names were found in the Dun & Bradstreet Key Business Directory (Canadian) and the Million Dollar Directory (United States). However, not all of the companies could be found in the directories, leaving the list of potential respondents somewhat smaller than the original master list.

The questionnaire was mailed to the Chief Executive Officers of the top 369 companies, in Canada, and the top 338 companies in the United States. The implementation of the questionnaire followed the Total Design Method (TDM) suggested by Dillman (1978). The response rates in Canada and the United States were 55% and 37% respectively. The number of usable questionnaires was 180 in Canada and 91 in the United States.

Analysis and results

The first step involved scale reliability analysis using Cronbach's *alpha*, which is presented in Table 2. The reliabilities for Jackson's PRF (achievement and aggression) and JPI (risk-taking and tolerance) measures and Lodahl and Kejner's job involvement measure were considered acceptable (given that these measures were both well-established, with proven reliability and validity (for the established properties of these scales see Jackson (1976, 1984; Cook et al. 1981)). However, there were no previously established reliabilities for Blood's Protestant Work Ethic Scale (Cook et al. 1981). Therefore, the items from this scale were factor-analyzed to determine which items naturally grouped together and could be identified as factors on which the executives could be compared. A principal components analysis was used with varimax rotation. From this analysis, the Protestant Work Ethic Scale items produced a two-factor solution (using an eigenvalue of 1), with one of the factors being labeled Pro-Protestant Work Ethic and the other Non-Protestant Work Ethic, consistent with Blood's findings.

Table 2. Scale reliability analysis

Scales	Reliability coefficient
Jackson's PRF and JPI*:	
Achievement	.61
Aggression	.75
Tolerance	.63
Risk-taking	.84
Lodahl and Kejner's:	
Job involvement	.79
Blood's:	
Protestant work ethic	.63

*Spearman-Brown formula used.

The results comparing the Canadian and American Chief Executive Officers are presented in Table 3. The literature suggests that Americans are more achievement-oriented, aggressive and risk-taking than Canadians. The results supported significant differences for two of Jackson's scales – achievement and risk-taking ($p<.001$). The difference between the means on the aggression scale was not significant. However, the items measuring aggression tended to focus on physical aggression as well as expressing anger or disapproval. Many people use the word aggressive to mean competitive, which is quite different than what was measured. It also should be noted that many of the achievement items are more concerned with competitiveness than are the aggression items.

The other Jackson scale measured tolerance. This was included to determine whether any difference existed between Canadian and American executives in their tolerance for different people, points of view, culture, and so on. The results indicated that the American executives were significantly more tolerant than the Canadian executives ($p<.02$). This could be interpreted as one of the reasons Canadian retail companies failed in the United States – they could not adjust their Canadian pre-entry orientation to what was required to compete in the United States. When presented with a culturally different people and market, Canadians had difficulty accepting these differences. Jackson's items suggest that a person with a high score on tolerance accepts different attitudes and customs (Jackson 1976).

On Hofstede's four cultural dimensions, the results indicated that the two groups of executives were significantly different on each. Three of these were consistent with Hofstede's 1980 study of forty cultures. As in Hofstede's study, the American sample had a higher mean score on items measuring Individualism and Masculinity, and a lower score on items measuring Uncertainty Avoidance ($p<.005$). However, the results for the items measuring the Power Distance dimension were not consistent with Hofstede's findings. Whereas Hofstede found that Canada had a slightly lower Power Distance score than the United States, the reverse was true ($p<.005$) in this study. Thus, it appears that the Canadian respondents are more willing to accept power being distributed unequally in institutions and organizations than the American respondents. Although this finding contradicts Hofstede's findings, it is consistent with a number of others (Lipset 1963, 1989; Rokeach 1973) who have compared

Table 3. Mean differences between Canadians and Americans

	Country	N	Mean	Standard Deviation	Probability
Jackson's PRF Scales:					
Achievement Orientation	C	180	6.32	1.45	.001
	U.S.	91	6.96	1.17	
Aggression	C	180	4.64	1.76	.782
	U.S.	91	4.70	1.89	
Jackson's JPI Scales:					
Risk-Taking	C	180	5.50	2.05	.001
	U.S.	91	6.52	1.79	
Tolerance	C	180	4.71	1.63	.017
	U.S.	91	5.21	1.62	
Lodahl & Kejner's					
Job Involvement	C	180	3.65	.52	.013
	U.S.	91	3.82	.50	
Hofstede's Scales:					
Uncertainty Avoidance	C	180	2.85	.45	.001
	U.S.	91	2.54	.58	
Power Distance	C	180	2.66	.48	.005
	U.S.	91	2.53	.40	
Individualism	C	180	3.16	.42	.001
	U.S.	91	3.76	.55	
Masculinity	C	180	3.22	.46	.001
	U.S.	91	3.43	.52	
Blood's Protestant Work Ethic:					
Factor 1: Pro-Protestant	C	158	−.21	.98	.000
Work Ethic	U.S.	79	.03	1.01	
Factor 2: Non-Protestant	C	158	−.09	1.06	.039
Work Ethic	U.S.	79	.17	.86	

the two cultures. The consistent view has been that Americans are more egalitarian than Canadians. The present results provide support for this position.

Several of the Canadian executives interviewed stated that American executives work harder (meaning they had higher productivity levels, were held to higher performance standards, provided better service, and spent more time at work) than their Canadian counterparts. The questionnaire results were consistent with this, indicating that the American respondents were significantly more job involved than the Canadian executives ($p<.013$). In addition, the results indicated that the American executives had a significantly higher score than the Canadian executives on the Pro-Protestant Ethnic factor ($p<.001$).

DISCUSSION

The psychic distance paradox: familiarity may breed carelessness

The phenomenon we have referred to as the psychic distance paradox seemed to be created by common, but unexplored, assumptions or underlying beliefs about the United States held by decisionmakers in the Canadian retail companies. These mental maps or preconceived ideas of the United States, and what it would be like to do business there, created barriers to learning about this new market. They are described briefly in this section.

Similarity

Canadian executives made the erroneous assumption that 'the United States is just like Canada, only larger.' Learning begins with the ability to see differences, and this projected similarity interfered with executives' ability to learn about the markets, the regions, the consumers, and the competition. It was often believed that Americans were just like Canadians, sharing a similar language, culture, values, tastes, and business practices. Notably, it was precisely the fact that these two countries probably are more similar than any other two that masked some fundamental differences in values and attitudes. Consumers were different; they were more competitive and they reacted differently than in Canada (even the small consumers); the indirect competition was often missed. The attitudes and values of CEOs from Canadian and American retail companies differed significantly also.

Proximity

The proximity of the United States to Canada contributed to the belief that because it was close it must be easier to do business there than in countries that were further away geographically. The view was that the United States was simply the southern extension of Canada, or that it was just like Canada's backyard. Given the assumption of similarity and a belief in Canada that 'ties run north and south,' regions of the United States that were contiguous to Canadian regions, in some cases, were organized as part of those Canadian districts. This assumption also may have been at work in the comment expressed by one of the executives, 'If we can sell to a market 3000 miles west, there's no reason we can't sell to a market 90 miles south.' The United States is a very complex and competitive country. Doing business there successfully is not easy, regardless of the geographic or psychic proximity to one's own country.

Success

This common myth was the belief that because the retail concept worked in Canada, and because the companies were important and well known in Canada, the retail concepts could easily be transferred to the United States, and the important relationships easily established there. This could be stated as 'success in Canada is a predictor of success in the United States' and this belief was evident in a number of the cases. Some executives believed that their retail concept was so powerful that it could overcome any competition, even with disadvantages such as secondary locations.

Many Canadian retailers believed that they could extrapolate from their own past history, culture and experiences in Canada when entering the United States. Instead, the environment they faced was very different, and their experiences from the past were no longer providing useful guidelines. The old rules no longer applied, and what was required to learn the new rule was an attitude of inquisitiveness and sensitivity that many did not develop soon enough. Believing too strongly that success in Canada predicted success in the United States was very costly.

Size and certainty

This was a modern Canadian variation of the old themes, 'The streets are paved with gold in the United States' or 'You can make more money by mistake in the United States than you can on purpose in Canada.' This myth simultaneously conveys a sense of enormous wealth in the United States and the ease, or certainty, of obtaining one's share of those riches. After all, the belief was, it was there for the taking. The size and assumed accessibility of this market were like a soporific, a drug that induces sleep. In the case of Canadian businesses they induced a sense of satisfaction, leading to carelessness, and often, failure. Realizing that the United States retail market is larger than the Canadian market led to dreams of 'if we could just get one percent, we could make it,' and the subsequent assumption that this probably would not be very difficult to do.

There is most likely another assumption related to the one about size that creates problems – the myth of 'the American market.' In reality, as we saw throughout the research, there is no such thing as *the* American market. Rather, there are many regional markets each with their own distinct characteristics, and a series of retail industry systems that must be entered.

LEARNING TO OVERCOME BARRIERS POSED BY PSYCHIC DISTANCE

The psychic distance concept calls attention to important cultural and business differences between countries that can create obstacles to successful market entry and adaptation. These obstacles can be overcome through learning. Nordström and Vahlne (1992) call this process bridging the gap of psychic distance. It is evident from our research that assumptions held by Canadian retailers about doing business in the United States market contributed to their performance problems there. In order to overcome these barriers, it is important to follow an appropriate 'process' in making decisions regarding entering a new market – the United States or any other country – as executives go about completing the activities set forth on their strategic agenda. Some suggestions include the following:

- Treat even psychically close markets as foreign markets. Executives should not assume that the Canadian and American markets are the same, or that companies within each can be managed in the same way. When decisionmakers start with the assumption that they are the same, they are more likely to take the appropriate steps toward entering the new market.
- Test assumptions and perceptions prior to entry. The success of a decisionmaking process relies on the accuracy of information and the knowledge of those making the decisions. The most important part of a company's pre-entry orientation is the perceptions and assumptions of the executive team, because they act as a base from which all of the decisions regarding the venture are made. If the pre-entry aspect of the decisionmaking process is faulty, the remainder of the process is unlikely to be effective. The

decisionmakers' initial perceptions and assumptions also affect their ability to learn from experience in a new market and to respond to this information. Strong beliefs about the similarity of the two markets or the power of a retail concept contributed to the difficulty of adjusting when faced with conflicting information. There comes a time when it is necessary to revise one's basic assumptions and perceptions, rather than continue to alter operating decisions in a way that only supports the initial position.

- Correct interpretation is key. An important observation of the study was that gathering information about a market does not necessarily lead to knowledge of that market unless it is interpreted correctly. A number of the companies conducted market analyses and still failed. The failure of the companies in our study underscores the difference between objective market information and the tacit knowledge or know-how that is critical to success. It seemed that the only ways that Canadian companies were assured of gathering the right information, and accurately interpreting it, were by having executives in Canada who had already learned from previous experience in the United States, or by having qualified American managers as part of the team. The nationality of the executives was not the key, but their having had direct experience in the market was critical. The real indicators of psychic distance are to be found much closer to the ground than researchers have been looking.

- Develop the ability to learn. A final recommendation is that those making the decisions for foreign markets must develop the ability to learn about the other countries. Learning has to do with increasing one's knowledge and understanding. Learning is more likely to occur under conditions where error is tolerated, assumptions are testable, and key aspects of information are not missing. Thus, it is vital to identify and check the assumptions of decisionmakers prior to entry, because their assumptions often seriously limited the effectiveness of their entry decisions. Since assumptions are often subjective and hard to identify, it is a good idea to use an objective person from outside the decision-making process to help decisionmakers to identify them. It appears that to gain the capacity necessary to compete even in 'close' markets, companies should hire management talent experienced in the target market. These people should have an understanding of the targeted consumers, the competition, the competitive intensity of the supplier situation, and regional differences, among other factors.

Only through careful attention to management decision processes can the potential negative consequences of the psychic distance paradox be avoided.

PROPOSED QUALIFICATIONS TO THE PSYCHIC DISTANCE CONCEPT

To improve our understanding of the psychic distance concept and its use in international business research, qualifications or refinements are suggested below.

Refinement of the concept

This study supports the idea that psychic distance is a larger, more encompassing, concept than simply cultural difference. Business factors, such as legal and competitive environments, need to be included when conceptualizing distance in the internationalization process. Further work is necessary that should determine which are the most important factors to consider. For example, American companies entering Canada had a number of advantages over their Canadian counterparts. They had greater financial and managerial resources to apply to their internationalization efforts, and greater sophistication (the retail industry in the United States is estimated to be approximately ten years ahead of Canada's). American retailers are noted for being excellent niche and regional marketers. They have benefited from their large home market by having had greater experience in dealing with its diversity and complexity. This experience may have helped them accurately assess the differences between the United States and Canada. These are the types of issues that need to be included in a concept of 'business difficulty,' such as that proposed by Johanson and Vahlne (1992).

There may also be an issue of directionality or symmetry. Large numbers of Canadian retailers have failed in the United States, but we have found that American retailers have been very successful in Canada. Of the twenty-three American retailers we identified as having entered Canada, all twenty-three were successful. However, the psychic distance from Canada to the United States should be the same as from the United States to Canada. Or should it be? This situation suggests that an asymmetry may exist in the psychic distance concept, at least when performance is taken into consideration. This raises another potential paradox that the 'distance' between the same two countries could be different depending upon the direction one travels.

To learn more about the issue of directionality, future research efforts would be particularly useful in two areas. First, considering Canada's small size in terms of economics and population compared to the United States, it would be interesting to learn whether companies from other small countries have difficulty when entering larger countries. Agren (1990) found that Swedish MNCs were consistently disappointed in the performance of their U.S. affiliates and concluded that Swedish managers have greatly underestimated the difficulty of managing in the United States. Similarly, European MNCs are often unprepared for the intensity of competition in the U.S. (Rosenzweig 1994).

Conversely, perhaps the United States represents a special case, and it is simply a difficult market for everyone. Or perhaps the retail industry has characteristics that make it unique. Arguably, internationalization theory and the psychic distance concept should be able to account for special cases. Further work needs to be done to determine if there are special cases and to map these anomalies.

Measurement

Researchers need to exercise care in the way that they quantify psychic distance. Although several studies show that Canada and the United States are very similar, company experiences within an industry point out significant differences that must be recognized These differences relate directly to what Nordström and Vahlne referred to as business difficulties. The cultural component of the concept generally utilizes national boundaries when there may be substantial variations in regional cultures or industry cultures (i.e. retail). Moreover, as this study has illustrated, true distance to a market must take into account the perceptions, understanding and experience of a company's management team.

Clarify links to performance

We believe that there is an assumption underlying the use of the psychic distance concept that needs to be clarified. The assumption is that similarities are easier to learn about and manage than dissimilarities. A prescription for managers would be that companies should find it easier to begin their internationalization process in countries that are psychically close or similar to their own. Although this is intuitively appealing it has not, until now, been tested using company performance data. However, there is no evidence that pursuing this strategy will lead to better performance than if a company entered a more distant country. Indeed our findings suggest that perceived similarity can lead to carelessness and failure. We think it would be useful to compare the performance of companies pursuing different inter-nationalization sequences in order to make research into the internationalization process more normative.

In particular, it would be useful to analyze the performance of companies from other countries trying to enter 'psychically close countries to learn whether they also have difficulty performing. Consistent with the literature on the internationalization process, Akoorie and Enderwick (1992) found that New Zealand companies attempt to minimize 'psychic distance' in their overseas operations. Therefore, Australia is the country chosen most for their internationalization efforts. However, moving beyond the internationalization decision, to studying the actual performance of New Zealand companies in Australia would fill an important gap in the literature. Similarly, research could be extended to studying the performance of Austrian firms in Germany, Belgian firms in France or firms from Finland and Norway in Sweden. Such studies would be very valuable for testing how widespread the psychic distance paradox is, if at all.

Limitations of the study

The survey responses came primarily from central Canada, where the greatest number of top retail companies are located, and the case studies were of companies in central and western Canada. English/French cultural differences were not examined, nor were differences across respondents from various states – often due to the low number of respondents in each region. By using a cross-sectional research design that focuses on two countries and one industry, we cannot generalize our findings to other industries or other combinations of countries without further research. Comparing two similar countries directly may serve to illuminate the differences that exist more so than when the two are examined in the context of many other countries that are very different. However, comparing them in the context of these other countries may diminish the important and significant differences that we found.

CONCLUSION

The intent of this article is to contribute to the development of internationalization theory and the concept of psychic distance, to improve our understanding of the internationalization process as not only a descriptive, but a prescriptive tool. We have proposed some modifications to the conceptualization and measurement of psychic distance and have suggested that industry could be a moderating variable in the internationalization process.

The study of Canadian retailers has allowed us to identify and explore what we believe to be an implicit assumption in internationalization theory, namely, that following a sequence of entry starting with psychically close countries is related to improved performance in these markets. The paradox was that what appeared to be similar and familiar turned out to be very different than expected. Although the Canadian companies began their internationalization process by entering the United States as the theory would suggest, it is when we look beyond sequence of entry to performance that the paradox lies. Instead of similar cultures being easy to enter and to do business in, we argue that it may be very difficult to enter these markets because decisionmakers may not be prepared for differences.

We found a significant difference in values and attitudes between two countries that on the surface do not appear to have such a gap. Our findings indicate that important cultural and business differences exist that can influence the success of internationalization attempts. They also point to the need for further research to examine the ability of companies to identify accurately, and bridge the gap created by, psychic distance.

NOTES

1. Psychic distance is defined in this paper as a firm's degree of uncertainty about a foreign market resulting from cultural differences and other business difficulties that present barriers to learning about the market and operating there.
2. See Johanson and Vahlne (1992), Benito and Gripsrud (1992), and Andersen (1993) for a discussion of this topic and for a more detailed set of references.
3. Cultural groupings are often larger or smaller than a country. However, in this study, country is used as the level of analysis exclusively to highlight the differences between the United States and Canada.

ACKNOWLEDGEMENTS

The authors would like to thank four anonymous reviewers for their insightful comments. The National Centre for Management Research and Development at the University of Western Ontario provided financial assistance.

REFERENCES

Adler, N. (1991 second edition). *International dimensions of organizational behavior.* Boston, Mass.: Kent Publishing.

Agren, L. (1990). Swedish direct investment in the U.S. Institute of International Business, Stockholm School of Economics.

Akoorie, M. and Enderwick, P. (1992). The international operations of New Zealand companies. *Asia Pacific Journal of Management,* **9**(1): 51–69.

Andersen, O. (1993). On the internationalization process of firms: A critical analysis. *Journal of International Business Studies,* **24**(2): 209–31.

Argyris, C. and Schon, D. (1978). *Organizational learning: A theory of action perspective.* Reading, Mass.: Addison-Wesley.

Beckermann, W. (1956). Distance and the pattern of intra-European trade. *Review of Economics and Statistics,* **28**, 31–40.

Benito, G. and Gripsrud, G. (1992). The expansion of foreign direct investment: Discrete rational location choices or a cultural learning process? *Journal of International Business Studies,* **23**(3): 461–76.

Berton, P. (1982). *Why we act like Canadians.* Toronto: McClelland and Stewart.

Chaganti, R. and Sambharya, R. (1987). Strategic orientation and characteristics of upper management. *Strategic Management Journal,* **8**, 393–401.

Cook, J.D., Hepworth, S.J., Wall, T.D. and Warr, P.B. (1981). *The experience of work: A compendium and review of 249 measures and their use.* London: Academic Press.

Dess, G. (1987). Consensus on strategy formulation and organizational performance: Competitors in a fragmented industry. *Strategic Management Journal,* **8**, 259–77.

Dillman, D.A. (1978). *Mail and telephone surveys. The total design method.* New York: John Wiley.

England, G.W. (1978). Managers and their value systems: A five-country comparative study. *Columbia Journal of World Business,* **13**, 35–44.

Evans, W., Lane, H. and O'Grady, S. (1992). *Border crossings: Doing business in the United States.* Scarborough, Ont.: Prentice Hall Canada.

Gatignon, H. and Anderson, E. (1988). The multinational corporation's degree of control over foreign subsidiaries: An empirical test of a transaction cost explanation. *Journal of Law, Economics and Organization,* **4**(2): 305–36.

Godfrey, J. (1986). The nation in search of a decent cliche. *Financial Post,* Winter: 89–91.

Hambrick, D.C. (1987). The top management team: Key to strategic success. *California Management Review,* Fall: 88–108.

Harmon, F. and Jacobs, G. (1985). *The vital differences: Unleashing the power of sustained corporate success.* New York: AMACOM.

Hofstede, G. (1980). *Culture's consequences: International differences in work-related values.* Beverly Hills. Calif.: Sage Publications.

Hornell, E., Vahlne, J.-E. and Wiedersheim-Paul, F. (1973). *Export och utlandsetableringar* (Export and foreign establishments). Stockholm: Almquist and Wiksell.

Jackson, D. (1976). *Jackson personality inventory.* New York: Research Psychologists Press.

——. (1984). *Personality research form manual.* London, Ont.: Research Psychologists Press.

Johanson, J. and Wiedersheim-Paul, F. (1975). The internationalization of the firm – Four Swedish cases. *Journal of Management Studies,* **12**, 305–22.

Johanson, J. and Vahlne, J.-E. (1977). The internationalization process of the firm – A model of knowledge development and increasing foreign market commitments. *Journal of International Business Studies,* **8**, 22–32.

——. (1992). Management of internationalization. RP 92/2. Institute of International Business. Stockholm School of Economics.

Kogut, B, and Singh, H. (1988). The effect of national culture on the choice of entry mode. *Journal of International Business Studies,* **19**(3): 411–32.

Kogut, B. and Zander, U. (1993. Knowledge of the firm and the evolutionary theory of the multinational corporation. *Journal of International Business Studies,* **24**(4): 625–45.

Linnemann, H. (1966). *An econometric study of international trade flows.* Amsterdam: North-Holland.

Lipset, S.M. (1963). *The first new nation.* New York: Basic Books.

——. 1989. *Continental divide: The values and institutions of the United States and Canada.* Canadian-American Committee, sponsored by C.D. Howe Institute (Toronto) and the National Planning Association (Washington).

Luostarinen, R. and Welch, L. (1990). *International business operations.* Finland: Kyrusi Oy.

Newman, W. (1972). Cultural assumptions underlying U.S. management concepts in J.L. Massie and J. Luytjes. *Management in an international context,* 327–52. New York: Harper and Row.

Nordström, K.A. and Vahlne, J.-E. (1992). Is the globe shrinking? Psychic distance and the establishment of Swedish sales subsidiaries during the last 100 years. Paper presented at the International Trade and Finance Association's Annual Conference, April 22–25. Laredo, Texas.

O'Reilly, C.A., III and Flatt, S. (1986). Executive team demography, organizational innovation, and firm performance. Manuscript. Berkeley: University of California.

Peters, T.J. and Waterman, R.H. Jr. (1982). *In search of excellence.* New York: Harper and Row.

Posner, B. and Munson, J.M. (1979). The importance of values in understanding organizational behavior. *Human Resource Management,* **18**, 9–14.

Puxty, A.G. (1979). Some evidence concerning cultural differentials in ownership policies of overseas subsidiaries. *Management International Review,* **19**, 39–50.

Rokeach, M. (1973). *The nature of human values.* New York: The Free Press.

Ronen, S. and Shenkar, O. (1985). Clustering countries on attitudinal dimensions: A review and synthesis. *Academy of Management Review,* **10**(3): 435–54.

Rosenzweig, P. (1994). The new American challenge: Foreign multinationals in the United States. *California Management Review,* Spring: 107–23.

Schwenk, C.R. (1984). Cognitive simplification processes in strategic decision making. *Strategic Management Journal,* **5**, 111–28.

Thorne, P. and Meyer, B. (1987). The care and feeding of your American management. *International Management*, October: 112–14.

Van Den Bulcke, D. (1986). Role and structure of Belgian multinationals. In K. Macharzina and W.H. Staehle, editors, *European approaches to international management*. New York: De Gruyter.

Walsh, J.P. and Fahey, L. (1986). The role of negotiated belief structures in strategy making. *Journal of Management*, **12**, 325–38.

Index